**Philip Kotler**

*Northwestern University*

second edition
# MARKETING
# FOR
# NONPROFIT
# ORGANIZATIONS

PRENTICE-HALL, INC.
*Englewood Cliffs, New Jersey 07632*

*Library of Congress Cataloging in Publication Data*

KOTLER, PHILIP.
  Marketing for nonprofit organizations.

  Includes bibliographical references and
indexes.
  1. Marketing.  2. Corporations, Nonprofit.
3. Marketing—Case studies.  I. Title.
HF5415.K6312  1982        658.8        81–19952
ISBN  0-13-556142-6                     AACR2

© 1982, 1975 by Prentice-Hall, Inc., Englewood Cliffs, New Jersey 07632

Editorial/production supervision and interior design by Maureen Wilson
Cover design by Barbara Shelley, 20/20 Services
Manufacturing buyer: Ed O'Dougherty

Printed in the United States of America

10 9 8 7

ISBN 0-13-556142-6

Prentice-Hall International, Inc., *London*
Prentice-Hall of Australia Pty. Limited, *Sydney*
Prentice-Hall of Canada, Ltd., *Toronto*
Prentice-Hall of India Private Limited, *New Delhi*
Prentice-Hall of Japan, Inc., *Tokyo*
Prentice-Hall of Southeast Asia Pte. Ltd., *Singapore*
Whitehall Books Limited, *Wellington, New Zealand*

This book is dedicated to my parents,
MAURICE and BETTY KOTLER,
who provided my first introduction
to a not-for-profit organization

# Contents

# 4

### The Entrepreneurial Organization:
### Launching New Services
*112*

---

# II
# ORGANIZING
# MARKETING

# 5

### Marketing Organization
*131*

# 6

### Marketing Information
### and Research
*150*

# 7

### Marketing Planning
### and Control
*170*

---

# III
# ANALYZING
# MARKETING
# OPPORTUNITIES

# 8

### Market Measurement
### and Forecasting
*195*

# 9
## Market Segmentation and Targeting
*213*

# 10
## Consumer Analysis
*234*

---

# IV
## PLANNING THE MARKETING MIX

# 11
## Marketing Programming and Budgeting
*263*

# 12
## Product Decisions
*287*

# 13
## Price Decisions
*303*

# 14
## Distribution Decisions
*319*

# 15
## Sales Force Decisions
*331*

# 16

### Advertising and
### Sales Promotion Decisions
*352*

# 17

### Public Relations Decisions
*377*

---

# V

## ATTRACTING
## RESOURCES

# 18

### Recruitment Marketing:
### Attracting People
*399*

# 19

### Donor Marketing:
### Attracting Funds
*422*

# 20

### Voter Marketing:
### Attracting Votes
*448*

---

# VI

## ADAPTING
## MARKETING

# 21

### Marketing of Services,
### Persons, and Places
*475*

# 22
## Marketing of Ideas and Causes:
## Social Marketing

# Preface

In the last ten years, marketing has become a "hot topic" among managers in public and private nonprofit organizations. They are attending marketing seminars, reading marketing books and articles, and discussing marketing topics with others in the search for understanding. They want to know how marketing can help their organizations face increasingly difficult marketplace problems. They want to understand how marketing relates to promotion, advertising, personal selling, public relations, fundraising, planning, and other organizational functions.

Nonprofit organizations face a host of problems that would be analyzed as straightforward marketing problems if found in the profit sector. Museums and symphonies have a difficult time attracting sufficient funds to carry on their cultural activities. Blood banks find it hard to attract enough donors. Churches are having difficulties attracting and maintaining active members. Many colleges face serious problems in attracting a sufficient number of qualified students. Police departments are hampered by a poor image in many communities. Family planners face formidable problems in selling the idea of "zero population growth." Safety councils seek more effective ways to persuade motorists to wear their safety belts. National parks such as Yellowstone are plagued with overdemand and are seeking ways to discourage or "demarket" the parks. There is hardly a public or private nonprofit organization that is not faced with some problems stemming from its relations to its markets.

But what is marketing? As used in this book, *marketing is the effective management by an organization of its exchange relations with its various markets and publics.* All organizations operate in an environment of one or more markets and publics. A university operates in a student market, faculty market, donor market, and public opinion market. A political party operates in a voter market, contributor market, and interest group market. Each market is made up of significant subgroups called market segments with particular needs, perceptions, and preferences. The organization has goals with respect to each significant market or market segment. Marketing is the organization's undertaking of analysis, planning, implementation, and control to achieve its exchange objectives with its target markets.

Through decades of working in business markets, marketers have formulated a conceptual system that yields systematic insight into the structure and dynamics of market exchanges. Concepts such as market segmentation, market positioning, marketing mix, channels of distribution, and logistical systems, among others, serve to organize the analysis of any marketing problem. The application of these concepts to the problems of nonprofit organizations has already proven its value in a relatively short period of time.

At the same time, the transposition of a conceptual system from one domain (the profit sector) to another (the nonprofit sector) poses a number of challenges that call for creative translation. The concepts of product, price, promotion, and distribution, which are employed by profit-sector marketers, have to be redefined for maximum relevance to all organizations. The concepts of markets and exchange processes must be generalized. The concept of profit maximization must be translated into benefit-cost maximization so that marketing models can be applied fruitfully in the nonprofit sector.

The purpose of this book is to broaden and apply the conceptual system of marketing to the marketing problems of nonprofit organizations. Most marketing texts deal primarily with marketing institutions and practices found in the private-for-profit sector. This makes it difficult for nonprofit organization managers —public administrators, educators, museum directors, hospital administrators, family planners, religious leaders, foundation directors, social activists, urban planners, and others—to gain a direct and comprehensive idea of marketing that is relevant to their types of organizations. This book hopes to provide the needed introduction to marketing for these administrators.

The book is divided into six parts. Part I (Understanding Marketing) explains the nature, role, and relevance of marketing to nonprofit organizations. Part II (Organizing Marketing) shows how marketing can be organized in nonprofit organizations to carry out marketing analysis, planning, and control. Part III (Analyzing Marketing Opportunities) describes the major concepts and tools available to the organization to help it understand its markets and potential strategies. Part IV (Planning the Marketing Mix) discusses the four major instruments—product, price, place, and promotion—that constitute the organization's strategic and tactical means for relating to its markets. Part V (Attracting Resources) deals with attracting three major marketing resources—people, funds, and votes. Finally, Part VI (Adapting Marketing) examines how marketing principles and techniques can be adapted to the marketing of anything—services, persons, places, and ideas.

The reader familiar with the first edition of *Marketing for Nonprofit Organizations* will recognize that the second edition is greatly expanded in size and scope. The following new chapters have been added to the book: The Adaptive Organization (Chapter 3), Marketing Programming and Budgeting (Chapter 11), Public Relations Decisions (Chapter 17), Recruitment Marketing (Chapter 18), Donor Marketing (Chapter 19), and Voter Marketing (Chapter 20). All the other chapters are revised and updated, with expanded sections on consumer satisfaction measurement, marketing organization, marketing research and information, consumer analysis, sales force decisions, marketing of services, idea marketing, and place marketing. Each chapter begins with an appropriate story that sets the theme of the chapter. Many chapters include boxed exhibits of interesting developments and anecdotes concerning nonprofit organization marketing. The second edition treats in depth a greater range of nonprofit sectors including education, health, religion, recreation, social services, performing arts, museums and zoos, libraries, public transportation, charitable organizations, government agencies and services, and trade and professional associations.

The first edition of this book was the result of a happy association with extremely creative and valued colleagues and students in the marketing department of the J. L. Kellogg Graduate School of Management at Northwestern University. The second edition benefited from dialogues with current members of the marketing department: Bobby J. Calder, Richard M. Clewett, Jehoshua Eliashberg, Lakshmanan Krishnamurthi, Stephen A. LaTour, Sidney J. Levy, Trudy Kehret, Api Ruzdic, Louis W. Stern, Brian Sternthal, Alice M. Tybout, and Andris A. Zoltners. Excellent manuscript reviews of the second edition were provided by Professor Paul Bloom (University of Maryland); Professor Roberta N. Clarke (Boston University); and Professor Karen F. A. Fox (University of Santa Clara), who also developed the excellent discussion questions at the end of each chapter. The meticulous secretarial assistance of Marion Davis and Phyllis T. Van Hooser made this manuscript a reality. Finally, my wife Nancy and our three daughters—Amy, Melissa, and Jessica—supported me with their patience and love. To all these persons, I extend my deep-felt gratitude.

# UNDERSTANDING MARKETING

# Marketing's Role in Nonprofit Organizations

While hospital marketing has been coming of age in Massachusetts for a number of years, not many people would admit it publicly. In the past six months, however, a half dozen administrators have named directors of marketing, while other executive officers will admit "off the record" that marketing is now woven into the fabric of their planning and community relations programs. Much of the hush-hush attitude toward marketing has been caused by the hucksterism image it conjures up to physicians and trustees but, claim adherents to the marketing concept, that is due to misunderstanding. "Marketing is not sales, it's not creating a demand that is not needed," says *Diane James,* for six months Director of Marketing at *Malden Hospital.* "It's a way of efficiently tying together information systems, planning, community outreach programs, and public relations." At Burbank Hospital, *Robert Shafner,* corporate planner, defines marketing as "seeing what the public perceives as its needs, having the hospital identify what services it is capable of offering, and then developing those services." Some, however, view marketing in more blunt terms. "Hospitals are scared and marketing is their response to what once was a captive market," said one director. "It's hospitals finally openly admitting that they are competing with each other," claimed another. Among the few facilities that have openly announced marketing programs are: University Hospital (Boston), Malden Hospital, Deaconess Hospital (Boston), and Union Hospital (Lynn). Other institutions will admit that large marketing research proposals are before their boards, that they have performed utilization review studies to identify the most "efficient" physicians, that they are reaching out to industry to sell occupational health programs, and that they are putting large ads in newspapers or placing public service announcements on TV to announce the development of a new service—most of which is geared to expand services. But, as one source said, "demarketing," or cutting back unneeded services, is just as important in a comprehensive marketing program because the ultimate goal is improved efficiency.

SOURCE: Quoted from *Monday Report,* published by the Massachusetts Hospital Research & Educational Association, October 8, 1979.

As time passes, hospitals and other *nonprofit organizations*[1] are increasingly recognizing that they face marketing problems. Shrinkages in clients, members, funds, and other resources remind them of their dependence on the marketplace. Consider the following examples:

The nation's 7,000 hospitals are currently filling only 60 percent of their beds, down from the utilization rate of 80 percent in the early seventies. Fewer patients are being admitted and their length of hospital stay is falling. Departments such as maternity and pediatrics are especially hard hit because of the falling birth rate. Meanwhile, hospital costs are soaring as a result of rising minimum wages and energy costs. Some hospitals are charging a daily room rate of over $300 to meet their costs. Some experts have predicted the closing of 1,000 to 1,500 hospitals in the next ten years.

As many as 55 percent of all adult Catholics under 30 years of age attended mass in a typical week in 1966. By 1975, the attendance rate fell to 39 percent. Other studies show strong discontent among American Catholics and a declining number of people who believe or practice the Church's teachings. The growing alienation is attributed to the Church's doctrinal rigidity and the increasing popularity of other organizations competing for people's time, interest, and loyalty.

Many performing art groups cannot attract large enough audiences. The average attendance at one major university's fine arts program is less than 50 percent.[2] Even groups which have seasonal sellouts, such as the Lyric Opera Company of Chicago, face huge operating deficits at the end of the year.

Many organizations that flourished in earlier years—the YMCA, Salvation Army, Girl Scouts, and Women's Christian Temperance Union—presently are examining the new marketplace and seeking to reformulate their mission in an effort to reverse membership declines.

Many public agencies face tough marketing problems. The U.S. Post Office continues to lose customers to private carriers and runs up large deficits each year. The U.S. Treasury Department launched two new currencies—the $2 bill and the Susan B. Anthony quarter—and both were marketing failures. The U.S. Department of Energy is having a hard time convincing people to lower their thermostats in winter and to adopt other forms of energy conservation behavior.

More than 170 private colleges have closed their doors since 1965 in the face of declining enrollment, dwindling endowments, and sharply rising costs. Some experts predict a further closing of anywhere between 10 and 30 percent of the nation's 3,000 colleges in the next decade as the number of college age students shrinks about 20 to 30 percent from today's level.[3]

Thus we can see that a great variety of nonprofit organizations are facing marketing problems. These organizations are confronting changing client attitudes and societal needs, increasing public and private competition, and diminishing financial resources. Board members, public authorities, and citizens' groups are putting tough questions to administrators of nonprofit organizations about their organization's mission, opportunities, and strategies. One result is that these administrators are forced to take a hard look at marketing to see what this discipline might offer to keep their organizations viable and relevant.

At the same time, many administrators are approaching marketing with caution. Although university presidents, hospital directors, government officials, museum directors, and religious leaders have readily accepted such business functions as finance, accounting, planning, and public relations, they have been more skeptical about marketing. Marketing has the image of being primarily a function for profit-making enterprises. Nonprofit organization administrators worry that marketing is manipulative and expensive, and that their boards and constituencies will feel uncomfortable. These administrators approach marketing with the attitude of "show me." The burden of proof of the relevance of marketing to nonprofit organizations falls to the marketer.

In this chapter, we will address the following questions that nonprofit organization administrators ask about marketing:

1. What is marketing?
2. Why do nonprofit organizations get interested in marketing?
3. What are the distinctive characteristics of nonprofit organization marketing?
4. What are the major marketing problems that nonprofit organizations face?
5. How are nonprofit organizations using marketing today?
6. What are the major criticisms of marketing?
7. What are the major benefits associated with marketing?
8. What is the essence of a marketing orientation?
9. What are the characteristics of an effective marketing organization?

## WHAT IS MARKETING?

What does the term "marketing" mean? This question was recently put to 300 educational administrators whose colleges were in trouble because of declining enrollments, spiraling costs, and rising tuition.[4] Sixty-one percent said that they saw marketing as a combination of *selling, advertising,* and *public relations.* Another 28 percent said that it was only one of these three activities. Only a small percent suggested that marketing had something to do with *needs assessment, marketing research, product development, pricing,* and *distribution.* Most people think of marketing as synonymous with selling and promotion.

*I hear you are building a farm stand and want to sell produce? There is an educational day coming up that will give you lots of answers a. Exchange Monopoly?*

**6**                            UNDERSTANDING MARKETING

No wonder. Americans are bombarded with television commercials, "junk mail," newspaper ads, sales calls, and mass retailing. Someone is always trying to sell something. Therefore, it may come as a surprise to most administrators that the most important part of marketing is not selling! Selling is only the tip of the marketing "iceberg." It is only one of several functions that marketers perform, and often not the most important one. In fact, if the appropriate products and services are offered, and pricing, distributing, and promoting them is done effectively, these goods and services will sell very easily. The amount of promotion and hard selling will not have to be intense. Peter Drucker, one of the leading management theorists, summarized marketing this way: "The aim of marketing is to make selling superfluous."[5]

Marketing is not a peripheral activity of modern organizations but one that grows out of the essential quest of modern organizations to effectively serve some area of human need. To survive and succeed, organizations must know their markets, attract sufficient resources, convert these resources into appropriate products, services, and ideas, and effectively distribute them to various consuming publics. These tasks are carried on in a framework of voluntary action by all the parties. The organization does not employ force to attract resources, convert them, or distribute them. Nor does it beg for resources or distribute them wantonly. The modern organization relies mainly on offering and exchanging values with different parties to elicit their cooperation. In short, modern organizations rely on *exchange mechanisms* rather than *threat systems,* on the one hand, or *love systems,* on the other, to achieve their goals.[6]

*Exchange* is the central concept underlying marketing. It calls for the offering of value to another party in exchange for value. Through exchanges, various social units—individuals, small groups, organizations, whole nations— attain the inputs they need. By offering something attractive, they acquire what they need in return. Since both parties agree to the exchange voluntarily, both see themselves as better off after the exchange.

A professional marketer is someone who is skilled at *understanding, planning, and managing exchanges.* The marketer knows how to research and understand the needs of the other party; to design a valued offering to meet these needs; to communicate the offer effectively; and to present it at the right time and place. Here is our definition of marketing:

> **Marketing** is the analysis, planning, implementation, and control of carefully formulated programs designed to bring about voluntary exchanges of values with target markets for the purpose of achieving organizational objectives. It relies heavily on designing the organization's offering in terms of the target markets' needs and desires, and on using effective pricing, communication, and distribution to inform, motivate, and service the markets.

Several things should be noted about this definition of marketing.

First, marketing is defined as a managerial process involving analysis, planning, implementation, and control. Marketing can also be looked at as a social process in which the material needs of a society are identified, expanded, and served by a set of institutions.[7] However, we will not use the social process view of marketing in this book. That view is appropriate for those interested in social values and public policy, but less relevant to managers and administrators facing very practical marketing problems.

Second, marketing manifests itself in carefully formulated programs, not just random actions to achieve desired responses. If a charitable organization simply asks a group of volunteers to go out and collect money, this is not a program and is likely to produce disappointing revenue. The volunteers are without direction as to whom to call on, what to say about the organization, and how much to ask for. Their effort is more like selling than marketing. Marketing takes place before any selling takes place and manifests itself in carefully formulated plans and programs.

Third, marketing seeks to bring about voluntary exchanges of values. Marketers seek a response from another party, but it is not a response to be obtained by any means or at any price. Marketing is the philosophical alternative to force. The marketer seeks to formulate a bundle of benefits for the target market of sufficient attractiveness to produce a voluntary exchange.

Fourth, marketing means the selection of target markets rather than a quixotic attempt to serve every market and be all things to all men. Marketers routinely distinguish among possible market segments and decide which ones to serve, on the basis of market potential, mission, or some other basis. A symphony orchestra in need of funds does not send letters to all citizens. Rather, it buys mailing lists containing the names of people who, because of education, income, and other characteristics, are more likely to support the local symphony orchestra.

Fifth, the purpose of marketing is to help organizations ensure survival and continued health through serving their markets more effectively. In the business sector, the major objective is profit-making, while in the nonbusiness sector, other objectives prevail: a park district wants to expand the recreational services and opportunities available to the community; the National Safety Council wants to bring down the death and accident rate in the nation; and the city health department wants to improve the level and distribution of health services. Effective marketing planning requires that an organization be very specific about its objectives.

Sixth, marketing relies on designing the organization's offering in terms of the target market's needs and desires rather than in terms of the seller's personal tastes. Marketing is a democratic rather than an elitist technology. It holds that efforts are likely to fail that try to impose on a market a product, service, or idea that is not matched to the market's needs or wants. In the commercial world, companies that design products they feel are good for the market without consulting the market beforehand often find they have few customers. In the noncommercial sector, the same thing holds true. Local governments that design playgrounds or toll roads without studying public attitudes often find the subsequent level of public usage disappointing. Effective marketing is user-oriented, not seller-oriented.

Seventh, marketing utilizes and blends a set of tools called the *marketing mix*—product design, pricing, communication, and distribution. Too often the public equates marketing with only one of its tools, such as advertising. But marketing is oriented toward producing results, and this requires a broad conception of all the factors influencing buying behavior. A church, for example, may do no advertising and yet attract a large following because of other elements appealing to the public's needs.

## WHY DO NONPROFIT ORGANIZATIONS GET INTERESTED IN MARKETING?

Different industries and organizations develop their initial interest in marketing at different times. Organizations that enjoy a sellers' market, one marked by an abundance of customers, tend to ignore or avoid marketing. Thus, colleges in the 1960s had their pick of students and were oblivious to marketing. Ironically, they carried on marketing activities without being conscious of it. The private college ran an admissions office whose staff visited prime local high schools and sought to convince the best students to come to that college. The college's development office assiduously cultivated well-heeled alumni in the never-ending search for the large gift. The college's public relations people busied themselves visiting editors and community organizations in the effort to market favorable news and impressions about the college. The dean of students ran various extracurricular programs to increase student satisfaction with the college. These and other administrators had the responsibility of sensing, serving, and satisfying different markets, although they were rarely conscious that their work was marketing.

Organizations typically become aware of marketing when their market undergoes a change. When buyers, members, funds, or other resources needed by the organization get scarce or harder to attract, the organization gets concerned. If their "sales" decline or become volatile, or new competitors appear, or new buyer needs emerge, these organizations become receptive to possible solutions such as marketing. This began to happen to many nonprofit organizations in the 1970s. This, combined with the growing literature on nonprofit organization marketing, thrust marketing into the center stage.[8]

## WHAT ARE THE DISTINCTIVE CHARACTERISTICS OF NONPROFIT ORGANIZATION MARKETING?

Marketing in the nonprofit sector does not involve new marketing principles so much as new and challenging settings for the application of these principles. Weinberg and Lovelock have identified four major characteristics of the nonprofit organization that call for special attention in seeking to apply marketing principles.[9] They are:

1. *Multiple publics.* Nonprofit organizations normally have at least two major publics to work with from a marketing point of view: their clients and their funders. The former pose the problem of *resource allocation* and the latter, the problem of *resource attraction.* Besides these two publics, many other publics surround the nonprofit organization and call for marketing programs. Thus a college can direct marketing programs toward prospective students, current students, parents of students, alumni, faculty, staff, local business firms, and local government agencies. It turns out that business organizations also deal with a multitude of publics but their tendency is to think about marketing only in connection with one of these publics, namely their customers.

2. *Multiple objectives.* Nonprofit organizations tend to pursue several important objectives simultaneously rather than only one, such as profits. As a result, it is more difficult to formulate strategies that will satisfy all the objectives. Management must do its best to state the relative importance of the several objectives so that a choice can be made among alternative strategies. Business organizations also have multiple objectives but these tend to be dominated by the drive for profits.

3. *Services rather than physical goods.* Most nonprofit organizations are engaged in the production of services rather than goods. Services have the characteristics of being intangible, inseparable, variable, and perishable. Thus, a college offers an intangible service called education; its delivery is inseparable from the deliverers (professors); its quality is variable with respect to who delivers it; and it is perishable in that empty classroom seats mean a loss of the associated revenue since a service cannot be stored. Service marketers must keep these characteristics in mind when developing marketing strategies and plans.[10]

4. *Public scrutiny.* Nonprofit organizations are usually subject to close public scrutiny because they provide needed public services, are subsidized, are tax-exempt, and in many cases are mandated into existence. They experience political pressures from various publics and are expected to operate in the public interest. This means that their marketing activities are likely to come under public scrutiny. For example, when the U.S. Department of Energy proposed to spend $50 million to advertise to the public on ways to conserve energy, many members of Congress objected to the expenditure of public funds in advertising.

We shall say more about the characteristics of nonprofit organization marketing throughout the book.

## WHAT ARE THE MAJOR MARKETING PROBLEMS THAT NONPROFIT ORGANIZATIONS FACE?

Each nonprofit organization needs to identify the specific marketing problems that it faces. The organization might be surprised at the number of marketing problems it discovers. Recently, a large hospital in Chicago undertook a *marketing problem inventory* and identified the following problems:

1. Its overall number of patient admissions was falling.
2. Certain medical departments—such as psychiatry and maternity—were grossly underutilized.
3. The hospital had a particularly low rate of admissions in the summertime because its "product mix" was stronger in serving illnesses and accidents likely to arise in the winter season.

4. The neighborhood was changing from a predominantly white middle-class neighborhood to one of poor blacks and Latinos, whose medical needs and financial resources were radically different.

5. The hospital had a poor image among the newer residents in the community as being elitist and indifferent to their problems.

6. Two newer hospitals in the suburbs had attracted away several doctors and patients who formerly used this hospital.

7. Physician morale was at a low level as a result of complaints from their patients about poor nursing care and poor food, as well as a lack of physician amenities such as generous office space and secretarial help.

8. Nurses' morale was also low as a result of low pay, poor schedules of working hours, and sharp words from the physicians. The hospital needed additional nurses but had trouble recruiting them.

9. Patients reported during exit interviews that they thought the nursing care and food were poor and that their rooms were overly hot and depressing looking.

10. The development office was finding it increasingly hard to attract large contributors to help meet the hospital's expenses.

11. The volunteers' office was finding it increasingly hard to attract additional women volunteers, as more women entered the labor force.

Not all hospitals have the same problems, and other institutions—colleges, social service agencies, churches, and so on—will have to identify their particular marketing problems. What makes these marketing problems is that the institution is failing to achieve a desired relationship with one or more of its markets or publics. Somehow, there is a gap between the target group's needs and the organization's offering.

Marketing arises when an organization forms an idea of a *desired level of transactions* that it wants with a target market. At any point in time, the *actual demand level* may be below, equal to, or above the *desired demand level. Marketing management's task is to influence the level, timing, and character of demand in a way that will help the organization achieve its objectives.*

Demand may be in any one of eight states and each presents a different marketing challenge.[11]

1. *Negative demand.* A market is said to be in a state of negative demand if a major part of the market dislikes the product and in fact may even pay a price to avoid it. People have a negative demand for vaccinations, dental work, vasectomies, and gall bladder operations. Employers feel a negative demand for ex-convicts and alcoholic employees. The marketing task is to analyze why the market dislikes the product, and whether a marketing program can change the market's beliefs and attitudes through product redesign, lower prices, and more positive promotion.

2. *No demand.* Target consumers may be uninterested or indifferent to the product. Thus farmers may not be interested in a new farming method and college students may not be interested in taking foreign language courses. The marketing task is to find ways to connect the benefits of the product with the person's natural needs and interests.

3. *Latent demand.* A substantial number of consumers may share a strong desire for something that cannot be satisfied by any existing product or service. Thus there is a strong latent demand for nonharmful cigarettes, safer neighborhoods, and more

fuel-efficient cars. The marketing task is to measure the size of the potential market and develop effective goods and services that would satisfy the demand.

4. *Falling demand.* Every organization, sooner or later, faces falling demand for one or more of its products. Churches have seen their membership decline, and private colleges have seen their applications fall. The marketer must analyze the causes of market decline and determine whether demand can be restimulated through finding new target markets, changing the product's features, or developing more effective communications. The marketing task is to reverse the declining demand through creative remarketing of the product.

5. *Irregular demand.* Many organizations face demand which varies on a seasonal, daily, or even hourly basis, causing problems of idle capacity or overworked capacity. In mass transit, much of the equipment is idle during the off-peak hours and insufficient during the peak travel hours. Museums are undervisited during weekdays and overcrowded during weekends. Hospital operating rooms are overbooked early in the week and underbooked toward the end of the week. The marketing task is to find ways to alter the time pattern of demand through flexible pricing, promotion, and other incentives.

6. *Full demand.* Organizations face full demand when they are pleased with the amount of business they have. The marketing task is to maintain demand at its current level in the face of the ever-present possibility of changing consumer preferences and more vigorous competition. The organization must keep up its quality and continually measure consumer satisfaction to make sure that it is doing a good job.

7. *Overfull demand.* Some organizations face a demand level which is higher than they can or want to handle. Thus the Golden Gate Bridge carries a greater amount of traffic than is safe; Yellowstone National Park is terribly overcrowded in the summertime; and the Picasso exhibit at the Museum of Modern Art attracted such crowds that visitors had to wait two hours in line to be admitted. The marketing task, called *demarketing,* requires finding ways to reduce the demand temporarily or permanently. General demarketing seeks to discourage overall demand and consists of such steps as raising prices and reducing promotion and service. Selective demarketing consists of trying to reduce the demand coming from those parts of the market which are less profitable or less in need of the service. Demarketing does not aim to destroy demand but only reduce its level.[12]

8. *Unwholesome demand.* Products which are considered unwholesome will attract organized efforts to discourage their consumption. Unselling campaigns have been conducted against cigarettes, alcohol, hard drugs, handguns, X-rated movies, and large families. The marketing task is to get people who like something to give it up. Anti-product marketers use such tools as fear communications, price hikes, and reduced availability to discourage consumption.

Organizational marketers will confront all or most of these demand problems as they work on various marketing problems facing the organizations.

---

## HOW ARE NONPROFIT ORGANIZATIONS USING MARKETING TODAY?

Nonprofit organizations vary greatly in their awareness and use of modern marketing ideas. (See Exhibit 1–1 for a classification of nonprofit institutions.) Some nonprofit institutions, particularly colleges, hospitals, and libraries, are beginning to apply marketing ideas actively. Other nonprofit institutions, such as service agencies and churches, are just becoming aware of marketing. Still other institutions, particularly government agencies, have generally not shown any awareness or interest in marketing. Exceptions, of course, exist. Among government agencies, the U.S. Post Office, Amtrak, and many public transportation companies have established formal marketing functions. Whether an institutional sector or a particular organization goes strongly into marketing depends on the depth of its marketing problems, management's attitudes toward marketing, and other factors.

## EXHIBIT 1–1. A world of organizations

Our society abounds in organizations and most of the work of this society is done through organizations. Few people can satisfy their needs completely through their own exertions. Organizations represent an efficient way to collectively solve problems facing individuals and society.

Organizations can be classified according to whether they are privately or publicly owned, and whether they are operated for profit or some other objective. These distinctions give rise to the four types of organizations shown below:

FOUR TYPES OF ORGANIZATIONS

|  | PRIVATE | PUBLIC |
|---|---|---|
| PROFIT | I<br>Private corporations<br>Partnerships<br>Sole proprietorships | II<br>State-owned airlines<br>State-owned telephone co. |
| NONPROFIT | IV<br>Private museums<br>Private charities<br>Private universities<br>Private associations<br>Private hospitals | III<br>Government agencies<br>Public schools<br>Public hospitals |

Quadrant I consists of private profit-seeking organizations. They carry out the bulk of the economic work in the United States and make up the *first sector.* We shall not discuss the marketing problems of first-sector organizations in this book.

The organizations in quadrants II and III are public organizations, and make up the *second sector.* We consider them nonprofit organizations and will address their problems in this book. Public organizations can be classified into the four types shown below:

**EXHIBIT 1–1. A world of organizations (continued)**

| Type | Function | Examples |
|---|---|---|
| 1. Business-type government agency | Produces goods and services for sale | Postal service, toll roads, nationalized industries |
| 2. Service-type government agency | Produces and disseminates services at no direct charge to the users | Public schools, public libraries, police and fire departments, park districts, public hospitals, highway commissions, government tourist bureaus |
| 3. Transfer-type government agency | Effects unilateral transfers of money | Social security administration, city and state welfare departments, internal revenue service |
| 4. Intervention-type government agency | Exists to regulate the freedom of some group for the sake of promoting the public interest | Penitentiaries, courts, Federal Trade Commission, Federal Food and Drug Commission |

Quadrant IV consists of the private nonprofit organizations. Not being either business or government organizations, they make up the *third sector.* They tend to carry out a social purpose, are more experimental and change oriented, and depend on donations of money and volunteer time. Third-sector organizations fall into the following groups:

1. Religious organizations
   A. churches
   B. church associations
   C. evangelical movements
2. Social organizations
   A. service clubs
   B. fraternal organizations
3. Cultural organizations
   A. museums
   B. symphonies
   C. opera companies
   D. art leagues
   E. zoos

**EXHIBIT 1–1. A world of organizations (continued)**

4. Knowledge organizations
   A. private grade schools
   B. private universities
   C. research organizations
5. Protective organizations
   A. trade associations
   B. trade unions
6. Political organizations
   A. political parties
   B. lobbyist groups
7. Philanthropic organizations
   A. private welfare organizations
   B. private foundations
   C. charity hospitals
   D. nursing homes
8. Social cause organizations
   A. peace groups
   B. family planning groups
   C. environmental groups
   D. racial rights groups
   E. consumerist groups
   F. women's rights groups
   G. anti-vice groups

Efforts have recently been made to form an organization to advance the interest of the third sector (also called the independent sector). John W. Gardner, who earlier organized Common Cause, sees nonprofit organizations as having their own common cause. According to Gardner, "From Yale University to United Way organizations, they're beginning to feel that they do inhabit a common world and that that world is threatened. Some of them have been searching for a meeting-ground." (Quote from "A 'Common Cause' for Non-Profits," *Chronicle of Higher Education,* February 13, 1979, p. 16.) The sponsors of the new organization are the Coalition of National Voluntary Organizations and the National Council on Philanthropy.

Second- and third-sector organizations are numerous and touch our lives more frequently than most people realize. We wake up to the news on a *public broadcasting system.* We leave our house and wait for the *public bus.* Our ride takes us past the *public school,* the *police station,* and the *nonprofit hospital.* We enter our office and open our mail, which includes an inquiry from the *U.S. income tax department.* Our mail also includes a solicitation for funds from our *college,* as well as a notice about a unique exhibition at the *art museum.* During lunch, we saunter over to the *public library* to read some of the magazines. At the end of the day, we walk over to the local *YMCA* where we run around the track. After supper, we go to our *church* to carry out some planning for new membership. Our day has literally been filled with a succession of encounters with nonprofit organizations.

Even within a nonprofit sector that has generally become interested in marketing, specific institutions will exhibit responses that range from open hostility or indifference toward marketing all the way to great enthusiasm. Here we will illustrate the range of responses to marketing in two major institutional sectors, colleges and hospitals.

## COLLEGE RESPONSES TO MARKETING

Colleges, particularly private colleges, are facing an increasingly grim market picture. (1) The annual number of high school graduates will decline between 20 and 30 percent between 1980 and 1990. (2) The proportion of high school students electing to go to college might decline. (3) A higher proportion of college-bound students are electing to attend community colleges instead of four-year colleges. (4) The absolute and relative future level of tuition will deter college-going in general and hurt private colleges in particular. (5) College operating costs are rising more rapidly than college revenue from tuition and fundraising.

What are college administrators doing about this? Their responses fall into three groups. The first group is doing little or nothing. Either enrollment has not slipped, or if it has, the administrators believe the decline is temporary or reversible through normal means. Many of these administrators believe that marketing methods would be "unprofessional," and some believe that it would lower the quality of higher education.

A second group has responded by increasing the budget of the admissions office, which serves as the college's sales department. The admissions office hires more recruiters, issues fancier catalogs, and places discreet ads in certain media. Some admissions offices have experimented with far-out methods to increase their application and enrollment rate:

- The admissions office at North Kentucky State University planned to release 103 balloons filled with scholarship offers in a park in Cleveland and changed its mind at the last minute.
- The admissions staff of one college passed out promotional frisbees to high school students vacationing on the beaches of Fort Lauderdale during the annual Easter break.
- St. Joseph's College in Renssalaer, Indiana, achieved a 40 percent increase in freshmen admissions through advertising in *Seventeen* and on several Chicago and Indianapolis rock radio stations. The admissions office also planned to introduce tuition rebates for students who recruited new students ($100 finders' fee) but this was canceled.
- Bard College offers same-day admission for students who walk into their office and qualify.
- Worcester Polytech offers negotiable admission in which credit is negotiated for previous study or work experience to shorten the degree period.
- The University of Richmond spent $13,000 to create a 12-minute film to be shown to high school students and other interested publics.
- Drake University advertised on a billboard near O'Hare Airport in Chicago that "Drake is only 40 minutes from Chicago" (if one flies).

Promotional competition has not yet led to premiums given to students for enrollment (free radio, typewriter) or offers of "satisfaction guaranteed or your money back," but these may come.

In equating marketing with intensified promotion by the admissions office, these colleges may create new problems for themselves. Aggressive promotion tends to engender strong negative reactions among the college's publics, especially faculty and alumni. Also, promotion may turn off as many prospective students and families as it turns on. Aggressive promotion can attract the wrong students to the college—students who drop out when they discover they do not have the ability to do the work or that the college is not what it was advertised to be. Finally, this kind of marketing creates the illusion that the college has undertaken sufficient response to declining enrollment, an illusion which slows down the needed work on "product improvement" which is the basis of all good marketing.

A genuine marketing response has been undertaken by a small but growing number of colleges. Their approach is best described as *strategic market planning*. In this approach, marketing is recognized as much more than mere promotion and, indeed, the issue of promotion cannot be settled in principle until more fundamental issues are resolved. These institutions analyze their environment, markets, and competition; assess their existing strengths and weaknesses; and develop a clear sense of mission, market targets, and market positioning. By doing this homework, they hope to develop the capability of competing successfully for the students in their target market.

### Hospital Responses to Marketing

We saw earlier that hospitals are beginning to treat marketing as a "hot" topic. A few years ago, health professionals scorned the idea of marketing, imagining that it would lead to ads such as "This week's special—brain surgery—only $595." Hospital administrators argued that patients didn't choose hospitals, their doctors did; so marketing, to be effective, would have to be directed toward doctors. Many hospitals still refuse to consider marketing and, in the words of one administrator, "would rather use prayer than marketing."

Nevertheless, several hospitals have taken their first tentative steps toward marketing. A few rushed into marketing with more enthusiasm than understanding, believing it to consist of clever promotional gimmicks. For example:

- Sunrise Hospital in Las Vegas ran a large advertisement featuring the picture of a ship with the caption, "Introducing the Sunrise Cruise, Win a Once-in-a-Lifetime Cruise Simply by Entering Sunrise Hospital on Any Friday or Saturday: Recuperative Mediterranean Cruise for Two."
- St. Luke's Hospital in Phoenix introduced nightly bingo games for all patients (except cardiac cases), producing immense patient interest as well as a net annual profit of $60,000.

- A Philadelphia hospital, in competing for maternity patients, let the public know that the parents of a newborn child would enjoy a candlelight dinner with steak and champagne on the eve before the mother and child's departure from the hospital.
- A number of hospitals, in their competition to attract and retain physicians, have added "ego services," such as saunas, chauffeurs, and even private tennis courts.

Fortunately, some hospitals are now beginning to apply marketing to a broader set of problems. Where should the hospital locate a new branch or ambulatory care unit? How can the hospital estimate whether a new proposed service will draw enough patients? How can the hospital attract more consumers to preventive care services, such as annual medical checkups and cancer screening tests? How can a hospital successfully compete in the recruitment of highly trained specialists who are in short supply? What marketing programs can attract nurses, build community goodwill, attract more contributions?

An increasing number of hospital administrators are now attending marketing seminars to learn more about marketing research and new service development. The Evanston Hospital, of Evanston, Illinois, a major 500-bed facility, appointed the world's first hospital vice president of marketing. Other hospitals have Board of Trustees marketing committees or administrative positions with responsibility for marketing. And many health care organizations are hiring market researchers to provide needed marketing information. Recently, Mac-Stravic published an entire book devoted to hospital marketing,[13] and many articles are now appearing on health care marketing.[14]

---

## WHAT ARE THE MAJOR CRITICISMS AGAINST MARKETING?

Modern marketing carries negative connotations in the minds of many people that trace back to ancient times. Plato, Aristotle, Aquinas, and other early philosophers thought of merchants as unproductive and acquisitive. Merchants were seen as taking advantage of helpless customers through buying "cheap" and selling "dear." In modern times, marketers are accused of getting people to buy what they do not want. Customers are seen as victims of high-pressure and sometimes deceptive selling.[15]

Until recently, several professions—medicine, law, accounting—banned their licensed members from engaging in any explicit marketing activities in the pursuit of clients. Their codes of professional ethics proscribed direct client solicitation, advertising, and sharp price cutting. In this way, the practitioners could feel that they were above "selling" their services. They were simply available to those who needed their services. Recently, the Supreme Court held that these bans in the canons of professional ethics had the effect of reducing competition through depriving firms of the right to inform potential clients about their services and depriving potential clients of useful information about the firms. As a result, advertising and certain other marketing practices have now been allowed in several professions.

Many nonprofit organizations come close to the professions in their negative attitude toward marketing. Administrators of nonprofit organizations feel that they must proceed cautiously with marketing activity lest their publics challenge them. Three types of criticisms are anticipated.

### 1. MARKETING WASTES THE PUBLIC'S MONEY

A frequent criticism of marketing activities is that they are too expensive. For example, in 1971 the U.S. Army spent $10.7 million on advertising in a thirteen-week period in an effort to increase army enlistments, and this upset many people. Similarly, the U.S. Postal System increased its cost of operations by establishing a marketing department within the postal service and giving it a large budget.[16] Many people carefully watch the marketing expenses of charitable organizations to make sure that they do not get out of line with the amount of money being raised.

Organizations, of course, should not add costs that do not produce an adequate return. Nonprofit organizations owe their publics an explanation of the benefits they are seeking to achieve through their marketing expenditures. They should not overspend and they should not underspend. At this stage, nonprofit organizations are more prone to underspend than to overspend on marketing. If the U.S. Army needs a certain number of recruits, $10 million spent on national television is probably the most efficient way to proceed. The issue should not be the absolute cost but the relative attraction cost per 1,000 new recruits. If the U.S. Postal System needs to develop new and viable mail services for its users, its expenditure on marketing research, planning, testing, and promotion is proper if this expenditure is expected to yield a reasonable return.

### 2. MARKETING ACTIVITY IS INTRUSIVE

A second objection to marketing is that it often intrudes itself into people's personal lives. Marketing researchers go into homes and ask people about their likes and dislikes, their beliefs, their attitudes, their incomes, and other personal matters. For example, a health clinic sent out researchers to study the fears of married men about vasectomies (male sterilization) in order to formulate a more effective information campaign on behalf of vasectomies. There is a widespread concern that if various government agencies started doing a lot of marketing research, the information might eventually be used against individual citizens or in mass propaganda. Citizens also dislike the fact that their tax money is being spent to do the research.

Ironically, marketing research is primarily carried on to learn the needs and wants of people and their attitude toward the organization's current products so that the organization can deliver greater satisfaction to its target publics. At the same time, organizations must show a sensitivity to the public's feelings for privacy.[17]

### 3. MARKETING IS MANIPULATIVE

A third criticism is that organizations will use marketing to manipulate the target market. Many smokers resent the antismoking ads put out by the American Cancer Society as trying to manipulate them through fear appeals. Some congressmen were upset with the report that the Interior Department planned to spend more money on a high-powered campaign to tout itself and "its photogenic boss."[18] Image ads by police departments are seen by some citizens as manipulative.

Administrators should be sensitive to the possible charge of manipulation when they implement a marketing program. In the majority of cases, the nonprofit organization is seeking some public good for which there is widespread consensus and it is using proper means. In other cases, the charge of manipulation may be justified and such efforts, unless they are checked, will bring a "black eye" to the organization and to marketing.

## WHAT ARE THE MAJOR BENEFITS ASSOCIATED WITH MARKETING?

The basic reason nonprofit organizations should be interested in formal marketing principles is that they will enable these organizations to achieve their objectives more effectively. Organizations in a free society depend upon voluntary exchanges to accomplish their objectives. Resources must be attracted, employees must be motivated, customers must be found. The designing of proper incentives is a key step in stimulating these exchanges. Marketing is the applied science most concerned with managing exchanges effectively and efficiently.

Marketing is designed to produce three principal benefits for the organization and its publics.

### 1. IMPROVED SATISFACTION OF THE TARGET MARKET

A substantial number of nonprofit organizations operate in a noncompetitive environment or in an environment where the demand for the service exceeds the supply. These organizations lack the motivation to satisfy their markets and may deliver unsatisfactory services which consumers accept because there are no alternatives. On the other hand, organizations that operate in highly competitive environments often lack the marketing skills to develop satisfactory services for their clientele. The result is bad word-of-mouth and client turnover which ultimately hurts these organizations. Marketing, in stressing the importance of measuring and satisfying consumer needs, tends to produce an improved level of client service and satisfaction.

## 2. Improved Attraction of Marketing Resources

Organizations, in striving to satisfy a set of consumers, must attract various resources, including members, volunteers, employees, funds, and public support. Marketing provides a disciplined approach to improving the attraction of these needed resources.

## 3. Improved Efficiency in Marketing Activities

Marketing places a great emphasis on the rational management and coordination of product development, pricing, communication, and distribution. Many nonprofit organizations make these decisions with insufficient knowledge, resulting in either more cost for the given impact or less impact for the given cost. Because the funds of nonprofit organizations are often inadequate and undependable, the administrator must achieve the maximum efficiency and effectiveness in marketing activities.

Besides the broad benefits of greater satisfaction and increased efficiency, various specific benefits can usually be identified for specific institutions planning to adopt a marketing orientation. Recently, the author addressed a conference of hospital administrators and claimed that hospital marketing would seed a revolution in hospital management in the next ten years. Specifically:

1. Hospitals will be much more sensitive and knowledgeable about community health needs.
2. Hospitals will abandon the attempt to be all things to all people and will seek differentiated niches in the market. Each hospital serving a community will focus on providing those services which are most needed and/or which are competitively viable.
3. Hospitals will be quicker to drop services and programs in which they have no competitive advantage or distinctiveness to offer.
4. Hospitals will be more capable in developing and launching successful new services.
5. Hospitals will create more effective systems of distributing and delivering their services.
6. Hospitals will develop more creative pricing approaches.
7. Hospitals will create more patient, doctor, and nurse satisfaction.

---

## WHAT IS THE ESSENCE OF A MARKETING ORIENTATION?

Many people think that organizations that have added a *marketing function* necessarily have become *market oriented*. This could not be further from the truth. Thus, the U.S. Postal System established a marketing department some years ago with a staff of product managers, advertising experts, and marketing researchers. Yet the U.S. Postal System still falls short of practicing a marketing orientation. What, then, is a marketing orientation?

The best way to understand a marketing orientation is to contrast it to three other orientations that organizations can have. They are described below.

### PRODUCTION ORIENTATION

Many organizations focus their attention on running a smooth production process, even if human needs must be bent to meet the requirements of the production process. For example, the personnel in many U.S. employment offices act as though they are processing objects instead of people. Job seekers come in, sit for long stretches, are asked routine questions, and are offered jobs if any are available. One does not have the impression that the personnel in the employment office exist to serve the job-seeking clientele but, rather, that the job seekers exist to meet the needs of the "system." As another example, consider the bus driver who speeds past dozens of waiting commuters so that he can make his timetable. We define a production orientation as follows:

> A **production orientation** holds that the major task of an organization is to pursue efficiency in production and distribution.

### PRODUCT ORIENTATION

Many organizations can be found which are in love with their product. They believe strongly in its value even if their publics are having second thoughts. They would strongly resist modifying it even if this would increase its appeal to others. Thus, colleges continue to require their students to study a foreign language even though few ever learn the language and most students report the whole experience as a waste of time and money. And museums will feature certain works of art year after year even though they attract the attention or interest of virtually no one. And many churches present the same dull Sunday morning sermons year after year as a matter of tradition, ignoring the changing interests of church-goers and the steadily declining attendance. We define a product orientation as follows:

> A **product orientation** holds that the major task of an organization is to put out products which it thinks would be good for the public.

### SALES ORIENTATION

Some organizations believe they can substantially increase the size of their market by increasing their selling effort. Rather than change their products to make them more attractive, these organizations will increase the budget for advertising, personal selling, sales promotion, and other demand-stimulating activities. Thus the college president reacts to a decline in enrollment by increasing the budget of the admissions office to permit hiring more recruiters, sending out more direct mail, and improving the looks of the college's brochures. These sales-oriented steps will undoubtedly work to produce more customers in the short run. But their use in no way implies that the college has moved into a marketing orientation that would generate higher sales in the long run. A sales orientation is defined as follows:

> A **sales orientation** holds that the main task of the organization is to stimulate the interest in potential consumers in the organization's existing products and services.

### MARKETING ORIENTATION

We can now clarify the meaning of a marketing orientation against the background of these other orientations. Some organizations have discovered the value of focusing their attention not on production, products, or sales, but on meeting their customers' changing needs and wants. They recognize that production, products, and sales are all means of producing satisfaction in target markets. Without satisfied customers, these organizations would soon find themselves "customerless" and tailspin into oblivion.

"Customer-centeredness" is attained in an organization through hard work. The organization must systematically study customers' needs, wants, perceptions, preferences, and satisfaction—using surveys, focus groups, and other means. The organization must act on this information to improve its products constantly to meet its customers' needs better. The employees must be well selected and trained to feel that they are working for the customer (rather than the boss). A customer orientation will express itself in the friendliness with which the organization's telephone operators answer the phone and the helpfulness of various employees in solving customer problems. The employees in a marketing-oriented organization will work as a team to meet the needs of the specific target markets that are to be served.

It is clear that different organizations within the same industry will vary in the degree to which they truly work for the customer. Consider a service industry such as the airlines. Recently, a British guidebook publisher decided to rate the quality of fourteen different airlines as an aid to air travelers.[19] The staff boarded forty-three transatlantic flights armed with tape recorders and evaluated each trip on such factors as check-in service, baggage delivery, food, cleanliness, friendliness, and response to special stress situations such as asking for aspirin, and so on. The scores were combined in a weighted index with a maximum score of 100, and the results showed a great variation, with Delta topping the list at 77 and the worst airline scoring only 36. Airlines and other service institutions can show considerable differences in the degree to which their operations reflect a sensitive and caring attitude toward their customers. We define a marketing orientation as follows:

A **marketing orientation** holds that the main task of the organization is to determine the needs and wants of target markets and to satisfy them through the design, communication, pricing, and delivery of appropriate and competitively viable products and services.

SOCIETAL MARKETING ORIENTATION

A marketing-oriented organization faces two problems in committing itself to satisfy customers' needs and wants. First, customers may have wants that are not proper to satisfy, either because they go against society's interests (such as buying handguns) or against the consumers' long-run interests (such as cigarette smoking). Second, customers may have needs which they do not recognize (such as a need for a quality education) that a nonprofit organization may want to press on the consumer for his/her good, even though it may be costly to do. A growing number of marketers see their responsibility to take four factors into account in their marketing decision making: consumer needs, consumer wants, consumer interests, and society's interests. This orientation can be called a societal marketing orientation:

A **societal marketing orientation** holds that the main task of the organization is to determine the needs, wants, and interests of target markets and to adapt the organization to delivering satisfactions that preserve or enhance the consumer's and society's well-being.

---

## WHAT ARE THE CHARACTERISTICS OF AN EFFECTIVE MARKETING ORGANIZATION?

A marketing orientation contributes greatly to an organization's effectiveness. The organization's effectiveness is reflected in the degree to which it exhibits five major attributes of a marketing orientation. They are:

1. *Customer philosophy.* Does management acknowledge the primacy of the marketplace and of customer needs and wants in shaping the organization's plans and operations?
2. *Integrated marketing organization.* Is the organization staffed to carry out marketing analysis, planning, implementation and control?
3. *Adequate marketing information.* Does management receive the kind and quality of information needed to conduct effective marketing?
4. *Strategic orientation.* Does management generate innovative strategies and plans for achieving its long-run objectives?
5. *Operational efficiency.* Are marketing activities selected and handled in a cost-effective manner?

Each of these attributes can be measured. Table 1–1 presents a *marketing effectiveness rating instrument* based on the five attributes. This instrument is

## Table 1–1

MARKETING EFFECTIVENESS RATING INSTRUMENT

---

### *Customer Philosophy*

---

**A. Does management recognize the importance of designing the organization to serve the needs and wants of chosen markets?**

Score

0    ☐ Management primarily thinks in terms of offering current and new services to whoever will buy them.

1    ☐ Management thinks in terms of serving a wide range of markets and needs with equal effectiveness.

2    ☐ Management thinks in terms of serving the needs and wants of well-defined markets according to their importance.

**B. Does management develop different offerings and marketing plans for different segments of the market?**

0    ☐ No.

1    ☐ Somewhat.

2    ☐ To a good extent.

**C. Does management take a broad view of its publics (members, donors, general public, competitors, etc.) in planning and running the organization?**

0    ☐ No. Management concentrates on selling and servicing current members.

1    ☐ Somewhat. Management takes a broad view of its publics, although the bulk of its efforts goes to selling and servicing current members.

2    ☐ Yes. Management takes a broad view of its publics and continuously reviews new opportunities to serve them.

---

### *Integrated Marketing Organization*

---

**D. Is there high-level integration and control of the major functions affecting various publics?**

0    ☐ No. Various marketing functions are not integrated at the top and there is some unproductive conflict.

1    ☐ Somewhat. There is formal integration and control of major marketing functions but less than satisfactory coordination and cooperation.

2    ☐ Yes. The major marketing functions are effectively integrated.

**E. Do marketing managers work well with management in other parts of the organization?**

0    ☐ No.

1    ☐ Somewhat.

2    ☐ Yes.

**F. How well organized is the new service development process?**

0    ☐ The system is ill defined and poorly handled.

**Table 1–1**

MARKETING EFFECTIVENESS RATING INSTRUMENT (continued)

| | |
|---|---|
| 1 | ☐ The system formally exists but lacks sophistication. |
| 2 | ☐ The system is well structured and effective. |

*Adequate Marketing Information*

**G. When were the latest marketing research studies of customers, buying influences, channels, and competitors conducted?**

| | |
|---|---|
| 0 | ☐ Several years ago. |
| 1 | ☐ A few years ago. |
| 2 | ☐ Recently. |

**H. How well does management know the needs and market size of different market segments?**

| | |
|---|---|
| 0 | ☐ Not at all. |
| 1 | ☐ Somewhat. |
| 2 | ☐ Very well. |

**I. What effort is expended to measure the cost effectiveness of different marketing expenditures?**

| | |
|---|---|
| 0 | ☐ Little or no effort. |
| 1 | ☐ Some effort. |
| 2 | ☐ Substantial effort. |

*Strategic Orientation*

**J. What is the extent of formal marketing planning?**

| | |
|---|---|
| 0 | ☐ Management does little or no formal marketing planning. |
| 1 | ☐ Management develops an annual marketing plan. |
| 2 | ☐ Management develops a detailed annual marketing plan and a careful long-range plan that is updated annually. |

**K. What is the quality of the current marketing strategy?**

| | |
|---|---|
| 0 | ☐ The current strategy is not clear. |
| 1 | ☐ The current strategy is clear and represents a continuation of traditional strategy. |
| 2 | ☐ The current strategy is clear, innovative, data-based, and well reasoned. |

**L. What is the extent of contingency thinking and planning?**

| | |
|---|---|
| 0 | ☐ Management does little or no contingency thinking. |
| 1 | ☐ Management does some contingency thinking although little formal contingency planning. |
| 2 | ☐ Management formally identifies the most important contingencies and develops contingency plans. |

## Table 1–1

MARKETING EFFECTIVENESS RATING INSTRUMENT (continued)

---

*Operational Efficiency*

---

**M. How well is the marketing thinking at the top communicated and implemented down the line?**

0   ☐ Poorly.

1   ☐ Fairly.

2   ☐ Successfully.

**N. Is management doing an effective job with the marketing resources?**

0   ☐ No. The marketing resources are inadequate for the job to be done.

1   ☐ Somewhat. The marketing resources are adequate but they are not employed optimally.

2   ☐ Yes. The marketing resources are adequate and are deployed efficiently.

**O. Does management show a good capacity to react quickly and effectively to on-the-spot developments?**

0   ☐ No. Market information is not very current and management reaction time is slow.

1   ☐ Somewhat. Management receives fairly up-to-date market information; management reaction time varies.

2   ☐ Yes. Management has installed systems yielding highly current information and fast reaction time.

---

*Total Score*

---

The instrument is used in the following way. The appropriate answer is checked for each question. The scores are added—the total will be between 0 and 30. The following scale shows the level of marketing effectiveness:

| | |
|---|---|
| 0–5 = None | 16–20 = Good |
| 6–10 = Poor | 21–25 = Very good |
| 11–15 = Fair | 26–30 = Superior |

filled out by one or more managers and the scores are observed. The instrument has been tested in a number of organizations, and very few managers score their organization in the superior range of 26 to 30 points. Most nonprofit organizations score in the poor-to-fair range, indicating that there is much room for marketing improvement. The breakdown of the total score into the five attribute scores indicates which attributes of effective marketing action need the most attention.[20]

Organizations that move toward a marketing orientation take on three characteristics vital to their survival and effectiveness. They become more *responsive, adaptive,* and *entrepreneurial.* The next three chapters will define and illustrate these three characteristics of the marketing-effective organization.

# SUMMARY

Marketing is a subject of growing interest to nonprofit organizations, both public and private. Hospitals, colleges, religious organizations, performing arts groups, social service organizations, and other nonprofit organizations have been experiencing increasing problems in the marketplace—declining customers, dwindling contributions, volatile demand. Marketing appears to be the management function that offers these organizations hope. Administrators of nonprofit organizations are asking a lot of questions about marketing.

What is marketing? Marketing is more than the use of certain tools such as personal selling, advertising, and publicity to create or maintain demand. Marketing is the skill of knowing how to plan and manage the organization's exchange relations with its various publics. Our definition is: marketing is the analysis, planning, implementation, and control of carefully formulated programs designed to bring about voluntary exchanges of values with target markets for the purpose of achieving organizational objectives. Marketing involves the organization in studying the target market's needs, designing appropriate products and services, and using effective pricing, communication, and distribution to inform, motivate, and service the market.

Four major characteristics of nonprofit organizations call for special attention in applying marketing principles. Nonprofit organizations tend to have multiple publics and multiple objectives, thus making marketing decisions more difficult. Most nonprofit organizations produce services rather than goods and this is challenging, since services are intangible, inseparable, variable, and perishable. Nonprofit organizations are also subject to high public scrutiny and must be able to justify their expenditures on marketing.

Marketing's broad objective is to influence the level, timing, and character of demand in a way that would help the organization achieve its objectives. Marketers have to cope with eight possible states of demand: negative demand, no demand, latent demand, falling demand, irregular demand, full demand, overfull demand, and unwholesome demand.

Marketing has its critics as well as its defenders. Its critics charge that marketing is a waste of money, that it is intrusive, and that it is manipulative. Its defenders say that marketing increases the satisfaction of the target markets by understanding their needs better, and that it improves the efficiency of serving markets by developing viable products, and pricing, communicating, and delivering them effectively.

Marketing is not just a management function: it is total organization orientation. Organizations may be production oriented, product oriented, sales oriented, marketing oriented, or societal marketing oriented. Those which are marketing oriented have five characteristics: a customer philosophy, integrated marketing organization, adequate marketing information, strategic orientation, and operational efficiency. These characteristics create an organization that is highly responsive, adaptive, and entrepreneurial in a rapidly changing environment.

## QUESTIONS

**1.** Why are many nonprofit organizations now turning to marketing? In what ways might an earlier adoption of marketing´ have helped them now?

**2.** What are the basic similarities and differences between profit-making organizations and nonprofit organizations?

**3.** Why has marketing frequently been rejected by nonprofit managers? How would you respond to their criticisms?

**4.** The executive director of a health care institution claimed that he did not need marketing since "we are all professionals here, and we know what the public needs." How would you respond?

**5.** Select a nonprofit organization with which you are familiar. Which orientation seems to guide its interchanges with its markets—production, product, sales, or marketing? Explain.

**6.** Select a service (other than education, the example in the text) provided by a nonprofit organization and explain how the four characteristics of services apply to it.

## NOTES

**1.** The term "nonprofit organization" will be used to cover organizations whose main purpose is other than making a profit. Some writers have proposed the term "nonbusiness organization" and we will use it synonymously. Nonprofit organizations are of two types: *public* and *private.* We will use the term nonprofit organizations to cover both types of organizations.

**2.** See the case "University Arts Program" in Christopher H. Lovelock and Charles B. Weinberg, eds., *Cases in Public and Nonprofit Marketing* (Palo Alto, Calif.: Scientific Press, 1977), pp. 19–30.

**3.** See Humphrey Doermann, "The Future Market for College Education," in *A Role for Marketing in College Admissions* (New York: College Entrance Examination Board, 1976), pp. 1–53.

**4.** Patrick E. Murphy and Richard A. McGarrity, "Marketing Universities: A Survey of Student Recruiting Activities," *College and University,* Spring 1978, pp. 249–61.

**5.** Peter F. Drucker, *Management: Tasks, Responsibilities, Practices* (New York: Harper & Row, 1973), pp. 64–65.

**6.** Kenneth Boulding, *A Primer on Social Dynamics* (New York: Free Press, 1970).

**7.** For a comparison of the managerial and social process definition of marketing, see Daniel J. Sweeney, "Marketing: Management Technology or Social Process?", *Journal of Marketing,* October 1972, pp. 3–10.

**8.** The argument for nonprofit organization marketing was first presented in Philip Kotler and Sidney J. Levy, "Broadening the Concept of Marketing," *Journal of Marketing,* January 1969, pp. 10–15. An attack on this thesis then appeared in David J. Luck, "Broadening the Concept of Marketing—Too Far," *Journal of Marketing,* pp. 53–54, followed by a rejoinder by Kotler and Levy, "A New Form of Marketing Myopia: Rejoinder to Professor Luck," in the same issue. As a further step in the recognition of nonprofit organization marketing, the *Journal of Marketing* published a collection of articles in the July 1971 issue dealing with fundraising, health service marketing, family planning, and so on. Another widely read article is Ben Shapiro, "Marketing for Nonprofit Organizations," *Harvard Business Review,* September–October 1973, pp. 123–32. The first textbook to appear on the subject is Philip Kotler, *Marketing for Nonprofit Organizations* (Englewood Cliffs, N.J.: Prentice-Hall, 1975). The following two books of readings have appeared: Ralph M. Gaedeke, *Marketing in Private and Public Nonprofit Organizations: Perspectives and Illustrations* (Santa Monica, Calif.: Goodyear, 1977); and Christopher H. Lovelock and Charles B. Weinberg, eds., *Readings in Public and Nonprofit Marketing* (Palo Alto, Calif.: Scientific Press, 1978). The major collection of cases is found in Lovelock and Weinberg, *Cases in Public and Nonprofit Marketing.* A general marketing textbook giving equal attention to business and nonbusiness marketing is found in William G. Nickels, *Marketing Principles* (Englewood Cliffs, N.J.: Prentice-Hall, 1978). An extensive bibliography is published by Michael L. Rothschild, *An Incomplete Bibliography of Works Relating to Marketing for Public Sector and Nonprofit Organizations,* 3rd ed. (Madison. Wisc.: Bureau of Business Research and Services, University of Wisconsin, 1981). For an excellent review article, see Lovelock and Weinberg, "Public and Nonprofit Marketing Comes of Age," in Gerald Zaltman and Thomas V. Bonoma, eds., *Review of Marketing 1978* (Chicago: American Marketing Association, 1978).

**9.** See Lovelock and Weinberg, "Public and Nonprofit Marketing Comes of Age," pp. 416–20.

**10.** For further discussion, see Chapter 21.

**11.** See Philip Kotler, "The Major Tasks of Marketing Management," *Journal of Marketing,* October 1973, pp. 42–49.

**12.** See Philip Kotler and Sidney J. Levy, "Demarketing, Yes, Demarketing," *Harvard Business Review,* November–December 1971, pp. 74–80.

**13.** Robin E. MacStravic, *Marketing Health Care* (Germantown, Md.: Aspen Systems, 1977).

**14.** See Richard D. O'Halleron et al., "Marketing Your Hospital," *Hospital Progress,* December 1976; Stephen L. Tucker, "Introducing Marketing as a Planning and Management Tool," *Hospital and Health Services Administration,* Winter 1977; Douglas J. Seaver, "Hospital Revises Role, Reaches Out to Cultivate and Capture Markets," *Journal of the American Hospital Association,* June 1, 1977, pp. 59–63; and Jeff C. Goldsmith, "The Health Care Market: Can Hospitals Survive?", *Harvard Business Review,* September–October 1980, pp. 100–12.

**15.** The major critics in this connection are Vance Packard, *The Hidden Persuaders* (New York: Pocket Books, 1957); and John Kenneth Galbraith, *The Affluent Society* (Boston: Houghton Mifflin, 1958).

**16.** See the case "U.S. Postal Service," in Lovelock and Weinberg, *Cases in Public and Nonprofit Marketing,* pp. 153–62.

**17.** The American Marketing Association has published a Code of Ethics for Marketing Research. A good discussion of ethical perspectives and problems in marketing research is found in C. Merle Crawford, "Attitudes of Marketing Executives Toward Ethics in Marketing Research," *Journal of Marketing,* April 1970, pp. 46–52.

**18.** Jack Anderson, " 'Blow Your Horn Louder,' Interior Department Told," *Chicago Daily News,* September 28, 1971, p. 13.

**19.** "A Guidebook to the Airlines," *Newsweek,* November 26, 1979, p. 88.

**20.** For further discussion of this instrument, see Philip Kotler, "From Sales Obsession to Marketing Effectiveness," *Harvard Business Review,* November–December 1977, pp. 67–75.

# The Responsive Organization: Meeting Consumer Needs

# It's about time somebody exposed Northminster for what it really is.

You may be shocked at what's been going on in the church these days.

Oh, you're probably familiar with what the church is. It's that grey stone and stained glass building on the corner. It's crowded on Sunday mornings. And it's that place you haven't been for awhile because you've been busy. Busy growing up. Busy getting married. Busy having children.

Well, we've been busy too.

**A shocking list of activities.**
We're far more involved with your family, with Evanston and with the world than you might imagine.

For example, if you have children in this area in the Boy Scouts, Cubs, Campfire Girls or Brownies, there's a good possibility that they're already meeting here.

And if you have children 7th grade through high school, maybe they should be meeting here.

Bragging is not our style. But there's a lot going on. And if you'll spend the few minutes it takes to complete this page, you may discover that your family will enjoy sharing ours.

**Families seen laughing out loud.**
To recapture some of the warmth and friendship of having relatives close by, we join together for brunches, pot lucks, picnics and nights at the YMCA.

For the family there are campouts at Stronghold, Wisconsin, weekends at Saugatuck, Michigan and father daughter/son dinners.

It's not fundamental religion, just fundamental.

**TV turned off, tube goes blank.**
Some evenings and weekends we get together for intellectual explorations. There're parenting workshops for parents of teens, a role playing workshop for developing interpersonal relationships, a theater group just for the fun of it, CPR training, an aldermanic forum for the neighborhood, and experts from other fields to stimulate ideas and conversation.

**Neighborhood not the same.**
A portion of our time and effort and income go into help for the community.

We support neighborhood houses, the Presbyterian home, Lake View Academy and Evanston Open Pantry. We've had special days for the blood drive and Evanston Hospital.

And we operate Helpline— an emergency hotline and help service. (One of its benefits is finding transportation for the elderly.)

**Not satisfied to stay home.**
Part of our income goes to help people elsewhere.

Northminster supports the Coptic Evangelical Organization in Egypt. We provide a service center for young people on the northside of Chicago, and send funds to the Ludhiana (India) Christian Medical College.

Along the way we send help to the Cambodian Relief fund, the Asian Immigration service center and the hunger fund.

About 22% of our yearly income is distributed as gifts of support. That's around $60,000.

**Scandalous activities.**
Not all of the time we spend together is serious.

There are bridge nights, bowling leagues, film festivals, square dancing and even a cheese tasting party. They're simple diversions with old friends and new ones.

**Children seen, heard.**
It's never been easy to be a teenager, and this generation is no exception.

But even pre-teens need more support than ever before, to avoid drugs, alcohol and still have the contact of a supportive group.

We've developed a program for them called *Sidedoor*. It compliments our very successful *Tuxis* group of high school age people.

*Sidedoor* is open to any 7th or 8th grader in the community. It's a 6 day a week open door program with activities, like ice skating, bowling, hiking, rap sessions, films, or simply dinner with friends.

For younger children there's the Christian Day School and in the summer a Vacation Church School.

**Other activities investigated.**
For young adults we're planning singles nights at the church.

For older adults there are Dinners for Eight, a loosely organized plan for entertaining at home. It was called Gourmet Dinners until someone pointed out that ordering pizza couldn't really be classed as gourmet.

There's a new adult activity group being formed for daytime meetings to coincide with Day School hours.

After Sunday services during the summer there are casual coffee and lemonade get-togethers on the church lawn.

And there's a traditional Northminster Sunday Picnic started by a parade to a nearby park.

There are ice cream socials, dinners with other churches, a rummage sale, and a book and bake sale.

One Sunday the young people of the church take over and conduct the service.

**Northminster not a country club.**
A large part of what the church has to offer isn't as easy to put into a category and list as what we've shown above.

But it's important.

It's the quiet peace the church can provide.

It's the strength and vigor it can impart.

It's the opportunity to ask and explore the questions you have no answers to.

And, it's the chance to work out answers with the support of others in the real world.

**What are you doing Sunday?**
We would like you to come and share in our acitivites. The fun and the prayer, the outward and inward activities we share.

Sunday services for Easter will be 8:30 and 10:00 AM.

Northminster is on Central Park Avenue just south of Central Street in northwest Evanston.

Come and join us.

Dr. Robert A. Chesnut
Pastor

**NORTHMINSTER PRESBYTERIAN CHURCH**

2515 Central Park
Evanston, IL 60201
869-9210

SOURCE: An ad appearing in the *Evanston Review,* April 3, 1980, p. 77.

.he Northminster Presbyterian Church of Evanston, Illinois, is an exa.
of a highly responsive organization. We define a responsive organization as
lows:

> A **responsive organization** is one that makes every effort to sense,
> serve, and satisfy the needs and wants of its clients and publics within
> the constraints of its budget.

The result is that the people who come in contact with these organizations report
high personal satisfaction. "This is the best church I ever belonged to." "My
college was terrific—the professors really taught well and cared about the students." "I think this hospital is fine—the nurses are cheerful, the food good, and
the room clean." These consumers become the best advertisement for that institution. Their goodwill and favorable word-of-mouth reaches other ears and makes
it easy for the organization to attract and serve more people. The organization
is effective because it is responsive.

Responsive organizations stand out from their competitors in the consumer
mind. Recently a major bank interested in improving its service level sought to
identify and interview those companies that had an outstanding reputation for
service. The candidates included Delta Airlines, Marriott Hotels, Disney, Inc.,
and McDonald's. Each of these service organizations managed to imbue their
employees with a spirit of service to the customers. For example, employees at
Disney go out of their way to answer visitors' questions, pick up litter, smile, and
be friendly. Disney, Inc., continuously interviews visitors to find out what they
thought of the park, food, rides, employee attitudes, and so on. Based on these
responses, they constantly try to improve their guests' experiences at the park.

Unfortunately, most organizations are not highly responsive. They fall into
one of three groups. The first group would like to be more responsive but lack
the resources or power over employees. The organization's budget may be insufficient to hire, train, and motivate good employees, and to monitor their performance. Or management may lack the power to require employees to give good
service, as when the employees are unionized or under civil service and cannot
be disciplined or fired for being insensitive to customers. One inner-city high
school principal complained that his problem was not poor students but poor
teachers, many of whom were "burned out" in the classroom and uncooperative
but who could not be removed. Lacking funds and/or power over employees
keeps these organizations from improving their responsiveness.

A second group of organizations are unresponsive simply because they
prefer to concentrate on other things than customer satisfaction. Thus, many
museums are more interested in collecting antiquarian material than in making
this material relevant or interesting to museum-goers. The U.S. Employment
Service may be more interested in the number of people they process per hour
than in how much help each one really receives. When these organizations are
mandated to exist or are without competition, they usually behave bureaucratically toward their clients.

Finally, there are always a few organizations which intentionally act unre-
sponsively to the publics they are supposed to serve. A local newspaper recently
exposed a public aid food stamp office that chose to be inaccessible in order to
minimize the public's use of its service:

> There is no sign on the building indicating that the food stamp office is inside
> . . . there also was no sign anywhere in the building directing applicants to the
> basement, no sign on the door leading to the stairs, and no sign on the door to the
> office itself. The only indication that a food stamp office is located in the building
> is a small, handwritten sign on the door at the top of the stairs. Adding to the
> inconvenience, the food stamp office was closed from March 10 to April 8.[1]

We are going to assume that most organizations want to be more, rather
than less, responsive to their clienteles and publics. The concept of a responsive
organization makes the following assumptions:

1. Each organization has a *mission.*
2. To perform its mission, the organization needs to attract resources through
*exchange.*
3. The organization will undertake exchanges with a large number of *publics.*
4. The publics will respond to the organization in terms of their *image* of the
organization.
5. The organization can take concrete steps to improve the *satisfaction* it creates
for various publics.

Each of the italicized concepts serves as an important tool for understanding and
improving organizational responsiveness.

## MISSION

Every organization starts with a mission. In fact, an organization can be
defined as a *human collectivity that is structured to perform a specific mission
through the use of largely rational means.* Its specific mission is usually clear at
the beginning. Thus, the original mission of the Northminster Presbyterian
Church was to deepen religious faith among believers through offering religious
training and worship. Over time, this church added further services to meet other
needs of its members, until it is no longer easy to distinguish between the church's
core mission and its peripheral missions. Is the church basically a religious center,
a social center, or a mental health center? The church's growing responsiveness
to other needs is changing its character and its membership composition.

Each organization that wants to be responsive must answer two questions:
*responsive to whom and to what?* An organization cannot serve everyone and every
need. If it tried to serve everyone, it would serve no one very well. From time
to time, each organization must reexamine its mission.

Years ago, Peter Drucker pointed out that organizations need to answer the following questions: *What is our business? Who is the customer? What is value to the customer? What will our business be? What should our business be?*[2] Although the first question "What is our business?" is simple sounding, it is really the most profound question an organization can ask. A church should not define its business by listing the particular services it offers. It should identify the underlying need that it is trying to serve. The church might decide that it is in the "feeling good" business, that is, helping people feel better about themselves and the world. Or it might decide that it is in the "hope" business, that is, helping people feel that they will eventually experience joy and fulfillment, either in this life or in the next. Ultimately, a church has to decide what its mission is so as not to lose sight and confuse it with a lot of intermediate goals and services that it might provide.

Clarifying the organization's mission is a soul-searching and time-consuming process. Different members will have different views of what the organization is about and should be about. One organization held numerous meetings over a two-year period before membership consensus developed on the real mission of the organization.

A helpful approach to defining mission is to establish the organization's scope along three dimensions. The first is *consumer groups,* namely, *who* is to be served and satisfied. The second is *consumer needs,* namely, *what* is to be satisfied. The third is *technologies,* namely, *how* consumer needs are to be satisfied.[3] For example, consider a church that serves mainly senior citizens who only want a simple worship service every Sunday. This church's mission scope is represented by the small cube in Figure 2–1A. Now consider the mission of Northminster Presbyterian Church, which is approximately that shown in Figure 2–1B. This church serves almost all age groups and meets at least four strong needs and provides services through the chapel, meeting rooms, classes, and outings.

**FIGURE 2–1**

The Mission Scope of Two Churches

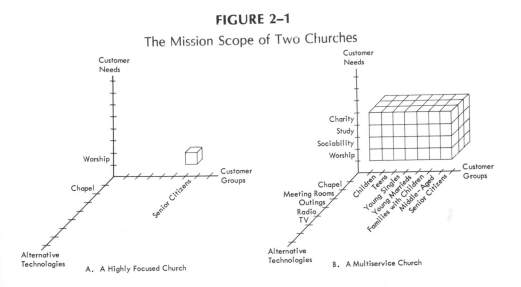

A. A Highly Focused Church    B. A Multiservice Church

Still other churches will have a different mission scope. A campus church will serve primarily students of a particular religious faith and meet a wide variety of needs (for belief, sociability, counseling, and so on) within the four walls of a religious house. On the other hand, Robert Schuller's church, Garden Grove Community Church (Garden Grove, Calif.) meets a wide variety of needs of 7,000 members and serves them through such modern technologies as radio, television, and cassettes, in addition to its $16 million "Crystal Cathedral."[4]

An organization should strive for a mission that is *feasible, motivating,* and *distinctive.* In terms of being feasible, the organization should avoid a "mission impossible." Pastor Robert Schuller wants his church to grow from 7,000 members to 25,000 members and may discover this to be infeasible. His followers must believe in the feasibility of this goal if they are to lend their support. An institution should always reach high, but not so high as to produce incredulity in its publics.

The mission should also be motivating. Those working for the organization should feel they are worthwhile members of a worthwhile organization. A church whose mission includes "helping the poor" is likely to inspire more support than one whose mission is "meeting the social, cultural, and athletic needs of its current members." The mission should be something that enriches people's lives.

A mission works better when it is distinctive. If all churches resembled each other, there would be little basis for pride in one's particular church. People take pride in belonging to an institution that "does it differently" or "does it better." By cultivating a distinctive mission and personality, an organization stands out more and attracts a more loyal group of members.

---

## EXCHANGE

To carry on its mission, the organization needs resources. It must be able to attract and maintain members, money, materials, staff, facilities, and equipment. If these resources became unavailable, the organization would cease to exist. Every organization is *resource-dependent.*

### METHODS OF OBTAINING NEEDED RESOURCES

How can an organization obtain needed resources? There are four possible ways:

1. The organization can attempt to develop the resources through *self-production.* The members of the organization would build their own facilities and find their own materials.
2. The organization can attempt to use *force* to obtain the resources. The organization can threaten the resource owners or resort to theft.
3. The organization can *beg* for the needed resources and play on the sympathy of resource owners. This tactic tends to decline in effectiveness after a while.

4. The organization can offer something of value to resource owners in *exchange* for the needed resources. As long as an organization continues to produce value in the minds of resource owners, it is likely to attract the needed resources and survive.

The discipline of marketing is based on the last solution to the problem of resource dependency, that is, exchange. In mc.iern society, most organizations acquire their resources through engaging in mutually beneficial exchanges with others. Organizations offer satisfactions (goods, services, or benefits) to markets and receive needed resources (goods, services, money, time, energy) in return.

## CONDITIONS UNDERLYING EXCHANGE

Formally speaking, exchange assumes four conditions:

1. *There are at least two parties.* In the simplest exchange situation, there are two parties. If one party is more actively seeking an exchange than the other, we call the first party a *marketer* and the second party a *prospect.* A marketer is someone seeking a resource from someone else and willing to offer something of value in exchange. The marketer can be a seller or a buyer.[5] When both parties are actively seeking an exchange, they are both called *marketers,* and the situation is one of *bilateral marketing.*
2. *Each can offer something that the other perceives to be of value.* If one of the parties has nothing that is valued by the other party, exchange will not take place. Each party should consider what things might be of value to the other party. Three categories of things tend to have value. The first is *physical goods.* A good is any tangible object—food, clothing, furniture, and so on—that is capable of satisfying a human want. The second is *services.* A service is any act that another person might perform that is capable of satisfying a human want. Services are usually character- ized by an expenditure of time, energy, and/or skill. The third category is *money.* Money is a generalized store of value that can be used to obtain goods or services.
3. *Each is capable of communication and delivery.* For exchange to take place, the two parties must be capable of communicating with each other. They must be able to describe what is being offered, and when, where, and how it will be exchanged. Each party must state or imply certain warranties about the expected performance of the exchanged objects. In addition to communicating, each party must be capable of finding means to deliver the things of value to each other.
4. *Each is free to accept or reject the offer.* Exchange assumes that both parties are engaging in voluntary behavior. There is no coercion. For this reason, every trade is normally assumed to leave both parties better off. Presumably each ended up with more value than he or she started with, since they entered the exchange freely.

Exchange is best understood as a process rather than as an event. Two parties can be said to be engaged in exchange if they are anywhere in the process of moving toward an exchange of things of value. The exchange process, when successful, is marked by an event called a *transaction. Transactions are the basic unit of exchange.* A transaction takes place at a time and place and with specified amounts and conditions. Thus, when a minister agrees to accept a new church position, a transaction takes place. Every organization engages in countless numbers of transactions with other parties—clients, employees, suppliers, distributors. Transactions themselves are a subset of a larger number of events called *interactions* which make up the exchange process. Transactions are those interactions that involve the formal trading of values.

### SOME FAMILIAR EXCHANGE SITUATIONS

Whenever two social units are engaged in exchange, it is useful to develop a diagram or map showing what is actually or potentially being exchanged between the two parties. Figure 2–2 presents five familiar exchange situations.

### FIGURE 2–2
Familiar Examples of Exchange

A. Commercial Transaction

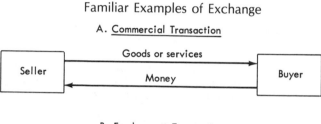

B. Employment Transaction

C. Civic Transaction

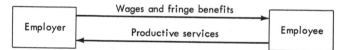

D. Religious Transaction

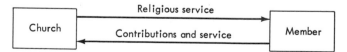

E. Charity Transaction

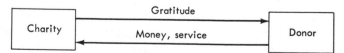

The first (Figure 2–2A) describes the classic commercial transaction. There are two parties designated respectively as *buyer* and *seller*. The seller offers things of value to the buyer in the form of goods and/or services. The buyer offers money in exchange. It is important to note that the designations "buyer" and "seller" are somewhat arbitrary, for we might also say that the party with money is offering to "sell" his money for goods. In fact, if both parties were exchanging goods, a condition known as *barter*, we could not easily distinguish the buyer from the seller. In this case, both could be called *traders*. In any event, two parties partake in a commercial transaction because each expects to be better off after the exchange. The buyer expects more satisfaction from the goods than from other uses to which money can be put; and the seller has obtained a desired profit through the sale.

Another basic economic exchange is that between the employer and the employee (Figure 2–2B). The employee offers productive services (made up of time, energy, and skill) to the employer; in exchange, the employee receives wage and fringe benefits. There is also an overlay of psychological exchanges (not shown) in this relationship, such as fear, respect, loyalty, and so on.

A third type of exchange occurs between a local police department and the local citizens (Figure 2–2C). The local police department offers the citizens protective services; in exchange, the citizens provide taxes and cooperation. There is a question of how voluntary this transaction is, but we shall assume for the present that a social contract is voluntarily entered into between the police and the citizens.

A fourth exchange occurs between a church and its members (Figure 2–2D). The church offers its members religious services and experiences; in exchange, the members offer the church contributions and support.

A fifth exchange occurs between a charity and donors (Figure 2–2E). The charity offers the donor a sense of good conscience or well-being in return for the donor's time, money, or other donations.

## ANALYZING EXCHANGE FLOWS

The preceding diagrams show only the basic resources being exchanged by the two parties. A marketer interested in actualizing a potential transaction needs to make a more complete analysis of what the other party wants and what might be offered in return. We will illustrate this in the case of an employment transaction.

Suppose a hospital in a small town needs to attract a staff physician to replace one who has just retired. The hospital chief-of-staff makes some inquiries among physicians, medical school professors, and local medical society executives, and collects the names of a dozen prospects. Their resumés are screened by a hospital committee which establishes criteria of what it wants in a prospective physician. These wants can be represented in the following abstract way,

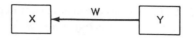

which says that X wants W from Y. In the concrete case, this is expanded to read:

*Wants*

1. competence
2. high admitting rate
3. cooperativeness
4. cost consciousness

That is, the hospital is looking for a physician who is competent, can bring a lot of patients to the hospital, is cooperative in committee work, and conscious of costs to patients and the hospital. The hospital will usually attach different weights to these wants.

Suppose the hospital search committee finds one physician who is highly attractive on these criteria. He has a private practice in a large city and is rumored to be looking for a small town practice. The chief-of-staff contacts the physician to gather information on this physician's wants. He establishes that the physician's wants are as follows:

*Wants*

1. competent colleagues and staff
2. improved income
3. good facilities and equipment
4. good living area

That is, the physician is seeking competent colleagues and staff, an improved income, good facilities and equipment, and a good part of the country to live in. It would be helpful to know the respective weights that the physician puts on these wants.

The hospital has to consider whether it can really make a good "case" to attract this physician. If the hospital is located in an unattractive area and its facilities are poor, there is little or no *exchange potential.* The hospital would have to offer the physician a substantially higher income to compensate for its deficiencies. On the other hand, the hospital's potential resources may match well the physician's needs and thus create a basis for a transaction.

In the latter case, the hospital will invite the physician for an interview. The staff will show its enthusiasm and the strong points about the hospital. If they like the visiting physician, the chief-of-staff will make an offer:

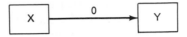

That is, X offers O to Y. In more concrete terms, the offer might be:

*Offer*

1. $60,000 salary
2. four-week vacation
3. secretarial service
4. one new piece of equipment worth $20,000

The physician might like the offer but suggest certain additions or modifications:

*Counteroffer*

1. $65,000 salary
2. five-week vacation
3. secretarial service
4. two new pieces of equipment worth $30,000

In turn, the chief-of-staff might make another counteroffer. This process of trying to find mutually agreeable terms is called *negotiation.* Negotiation either ends in mutually acceptable terms of exchange or a decision not to transact.

We have examined the exchange process as if it involved only two parties. But additional parties might be involved before an agreement can be struck. The chief-of-staff needs the board of trustees' approval on the offer terms. The physician needs his wife's approval and willingness to relocate to the small town. Thus, the buyer and seller might not act as two persons but as two organizations with each involving some participants.

   We can illustrate a multiparty exchange process by introducing the physician's wife and her wishes into the picture. This is shown in Figure 2–3. The wife wants the hospital to help her find a job in her profession, hopes to find friendly physicians and wives at the hospital, hopes for a good income and home, and a good area for raising children. She wants her husband to be happy and to have enough time to give to the family. At the same time, the hospital hopes the wife will support her husband's work and participate in community affairs. Finally, the husband wants his wife to be supportive and happy in the new situation. Clearly, the hospital, as marketer, must take these various needs into consideration in formulating an offer to attract the physician.

   When marketers are anxious to consummate a transaction, they may be tempted to exaggerate the actual benefits of the product being offered. Thus, the chief-of-staff might be tempted to overstate the competence of the staff or understate the amount of expected committee work. He may succeed in attracting the physician but the physician will be turned into an unhappy customer. The physician will be dissatisfied because of the difference between his *expectations* and the hospital's *performance.* As an unhappy customer, he can be expected either to complain a lot, talk badly about the hospital to others, or quit, leaving the hospital

**FIGURE 2–3**

Three-Party Exchange Map Showing Want Vectors

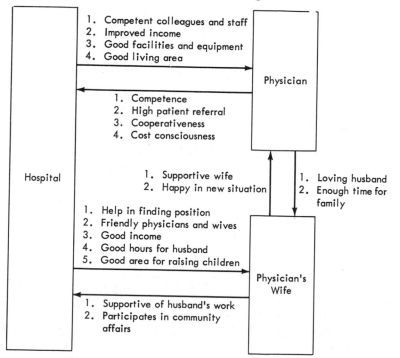

with the task of finding another physician. The best transactions are those that deliver the expected values to the respective parties.

## A MODEL OF THE DETERMINANTS OF EXCHANGE

Bagozzi has formulated a comprehensive model of the major determinants affecting exchange. The model is summarized in Figure 2–4. We will apply it to the hospital's problem of attracting the new physician to its staff.

First, we consider the two primary social actors involved in the exchange, namely, the chief-of-staff (source) and the prospective physician (receiver). The chief-of-staff and the prospective physician will engage in actions, communications, and information to influence each other. The chief-of-staff's influence will be a function of several personal qualities, namely, attraction, similarity to the physician, expertise, prestige, trustworthiness, and status. The prospective physician's perception of these qualities will be influenced by his self-confidence, self-esteem, sex, race, religion, social class, intelligence, and personality. The physician's ultimate decision will additionally be influenced by situational variables, such as the availability of alternative sources of satisfaction (other hospitals and career opportunities), the opinion of other parties (wife, children, friends, and other colleagues), physical and psychological variables (time pressure for making a decision, number of issues that have to be considered, pleasantness of the surroundings, type of communication setting), and legal or normative variables (his contract with his present hospital and any normative concerns that might be triggered off by the thought of leaving his community).

The physician will also be influenced by his picture of the contrasting outcomes associated with his staying versus leaving his present hospital. Three kinds of outcomes can be envisioned. First, his money income will be influenced by the outcome. Second, he will experience different social rewards in the form of approval, praise, and status. Third, he might also experience some social punishment such as disapproval or blame.

Thus, a large number of factors will influence the exchange process involving a hospital and a prospective physician. The direction of influence of most of these factors is pretty clear, although their relative importance varies with each situation. This model is presented not as an elegant predictive theory of how an exchange situation will be resolved, but as a comprehensive view of the factors that the marketer will want to analyze in preparing a marketing plan.

## THEORIES PREDICTING EXCHANGE OUTCOMES

At the same time, there are some simple theories predicting how exchange situations will be resolved. Three of these theories will be briefly reviewed: economic theory, equity theory, and power theory.

**Economic theory.**     Economists have spent the most time studying the conditions under which a transaction takes place. The basic concept in their analysis

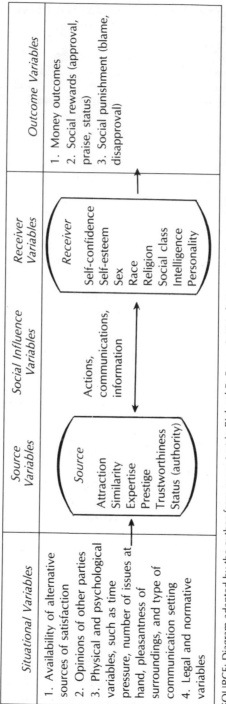

**FIGURE 2–4**

A Model of the Determinants of Exchange

| Situational Variables | Source Variables | Social Influence Variables | Receiver Variables | Outcome Variables |
|---|---|---|---|---|
| 1. Availability of alternative sources of satisfaction<br><br>2. Opinions of other parties<br><br>3. Physical and psychological variables, such as time pressure, number of issues at hand, pleasantness of surroundings, and type of communication setting<br><br>4. Legal and normative variables | *Source*<br><br>Attraction<br>Similarity<br>Expertise<br>Prestige<br>Trustworthiness<br>Status (authority) | Actions, communications, information | *Receiver*<br><br>Self-confidence<br>Self-esteem<br>Sex<br>Race<br>Religion<br>Social class<br>Intelligence<br>Personality | 1. Money outcomes<br>2. Social rewards (approval, praise, status)<br>3. Social punishment (blame, disapproval) |

SOURCE: Diagram adapted by the author from prose text in Richard P. Bagozzi, "Marketing as Exchange: A Theory of Transactions in the Marketplace," *American Behavioral Scientist,* March–April 1978, pp. 535–56.

is that of *self-interest*. Individuals and organizations, when faced with two or more choices, will always favor the choice that will maximize their long-run self-interest. Put another way, people and organizations are *utility maximizers*. This interpretation of human behavior is rooted in a psychological theory that people basically respond to pleasure and pain in their activities and are able to calculate and sum the pleasure and pain consequences of different decisions.

Whether a transaction will be consummated between two social actors depends on the expected benefit-cost consequences for each actor. Economic theory holds that each actor will form an estimate of the expected personal net gain of engaging in the transaction. The expected personal net gain *(G)* is the difference between the total benefits *(B)* and the total cost *(C)* as seen by the actor. In the case of actor *i,* the personal expected net gain is represented by:[6]

$$G_i = B_i - C_i$$

Whether the physician and hospital will consummate the transaction can now be predicted by this theory. There are three possible outcomes.

1. If both actors expect that their net gain will be negative, then no transaction will take place, for both actors will be worse off.
2. If both actors expect that the net gain will be positive, the transaction is likely to take place, because both will be better off. The only qualification here is that one or both actors might visualize still another transaction which will make him (them) even better off.
3. Finally, if one actor will be better off and the other worse off, a transaction will not take place unless the "better off" actor finds a way to compensate the "worse off" actor so that both will be better off. The "better off" actor can decide to accept a lower gain, just enough to leave the "worse off" actor with a slight positive gain.

We have examined the conditions under which two actors are likely to consummate a transaction. Economic theory would also like to predict the terms of exchange, but here it is less successful, at least in the case of a two-party transaction. Thus, in the case of the physician considering joining the new hospital, he may be willing to affiliate as long as the salary is at least $62,000 and his other conditions are met. The hospital might be willing to offer him as much as $67,000 as long as he is willing to meet its conditions. In other words, the physician expects a positive net gain at any salary greater than $62,000 and the hospital expects a positive net gain at any salary less than $67,000. Economists can predict that the physician will join the hospital and that the final salary figure will be somewhere between $62,000 and $67,000. However, they are not able to predict the specific figure. They see this as an issue that will be settled on other grounds, such as equity or power considerations.

**Equity theory.**     One way for two parties to reach a "transaction price" within a negotiating range is to bring in considerations of equity. The two parties may be motivated to seek a price that they jointly consider to be "fair." For example, the chief-of-staff may propose that the physician's salary should have an equitable relation to the salary of another physician already on the staff. The other physician has the same background and skills, but has been in practice for one year longer than the prospective physician. He is earning $66,000. The chief-of-staff says that salaries usually rise $2,000 a year. He therefore offers the prospective physician $64,000, which is $2,000 less (or one year of salary less) than the earnings of the other physician, and bases this on equity considerations.

In general, equity theory holds that the two parties will seek to arrive at a "price" that appeals to their sense of fairness. Suppose the hospital is interviewing two candidates, $Y$ and $Z$, for the position. In considering the salary to offer each, the chief-of-staff may be guided by his picture of the relative value each would contribute to the hospital. Equity theory would lead him to offer salaries that would satisfy the following relationship:

$$\frac{\text{Salary } Y}{\text{Salary } Z} = \frac{\text{Value of } Y}{\text{Value of } Z}$$

Thus, if candidate $Y$ is considered to offer twice as much value to the hospital as candidate $Z$, the hospital can offer $Y$ twice as much salary and feel that this is equitable. Of course, people might have other views of what constitutes equity.[7]

**Power theory.** Power theory takes a different view about how the two parties will arrive at a mutually agreed upon transaction price within a negotiating range. It sees each as driven to obtain the maximum possible gain, and as willing to exploit the power possessed to achieve it. If the prospective physician has more bargaining power than the hospital, the final price will be closer to the hospital's maximum of $67,000. If the hospital has more bargaining power, the final price will be closer to the physician's minimum of $62,000.

This leaves the question of what determines the amount of power each party has in the situation. $X$'s power relative to $Y$ is a function of (1) how much $X$ needs some resource that $Y$ has, and (2) how available is this resource from some alternative party.[8] In concrete terms, we can say that physician $Y$ possesses considerable power if (1) hospital $X$ badly needs to add a physician to its staff, and (2) there are few other qualified physicians who are available. In this case, the physician is in a seller's market and possesses considerable power to command the salary he wants.

In general, a transaction will take place when both parties gain. The transaction price will fall in a range between the minimum price that the seller will accept and the maximum price that the buyer will offer. Where the price settles will depend on equity and power considerations.

The reason that we examined exchange theory in detail is because it is central to being a responsive organization. To be responsive requires analyzing the other party's needs and wants and determining how far the organization can go toward satisfying them. An organization that is oblivious to or indifferent to the needs of the other party cannot, by definition, be responsive.

## PUBLICS

In every organization's life there are several publics, and the organization has to manage responsive relations with most or all of them. We define a public in the following way:

A **public** is a distinct group of people and/or organizations that has an actual or a potential interest and/or impact on an organization.

It is fairly easy to identify the key publics that surround a particular organization. Consider a university. Figure 2–5 shows sixteen major publics with which a university deals. The publics include groups within the university and outside the university.

Not all publics are equally active or important to an organization. Publics come about because the organization's activities and policies can draw support or criticism from outside groups. A *welcome public* is a public that likes the organization and whose support the organization welcomes. A *sought public* is a public whose support the organization wants but which is currently indifferent or negative toward that organization. An *unwelcome public* is a public that is negatively disposed toward the organization and that is trying to impose constraints, pressures, or controls on the organization.

Publics can also be classified by their functional relation to the organization. Figure 2–6 presents such a classification. An organization is viewed as a resource-conversion machine in which certain *input publics* supply resources that are converted by *internal publics* into useful goods and services that are carried by *intermediary publics* to designated *consuming publics*. Here we will look at the various publics more closely.

### INPUT PUBLICS

Input publics mainly supply original resources and constraints to the organization, and as such consist of donors, suppliers, and regulatory publics.

**Donors.**      Donors are those publics who make gifts of money and other assets to the organization. Thus a university's donors consist of alumni, friends of the university, foundations, corporations, and government organizations. Each university runs a development office consisting of a staff of professional fundraisers. This staff develops a philosophy of fundraising and specific proposals that might excite possible donors. It tries to match its financial needs with the appropriate donor groups. It tries to build value in the eyes of its donors so that they can feel pride and other satisfactions from their association with the institution.

**FIGURE 2–5**

The University and Its Publics

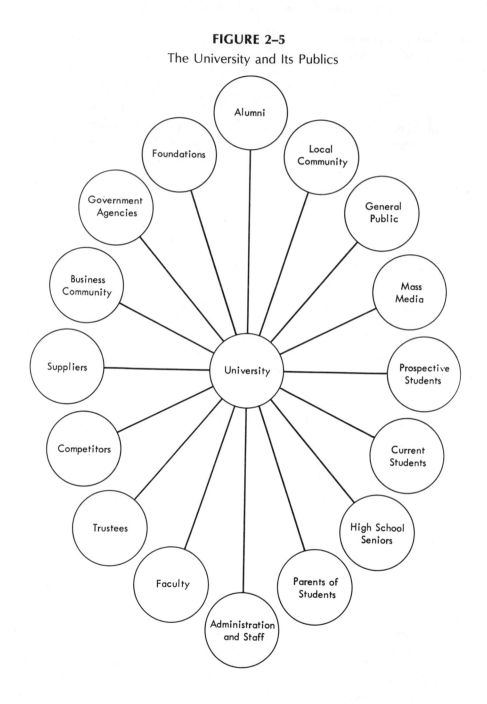

FIGURE 2–6

The Main Publics of an Organization

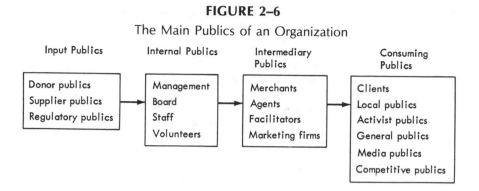

| Input Publics | Internal Publics | Intermediary Publics | Consuming Publics |
|---|---|---|---|
| Donor publics<br>Supplier publics<br>Regulatory publics | Management<br>Board<br>Staff<br>Volunteers | Merchants<br>Agents<br>Facilitators<br>Marketing firms | Clients<br>Local publics<br>Activist publics<br>General publics<br>Media publics<br>Competitive publics |

**Suppliers.**    Suppliers are those organizations that sell needed goods and services to the focal organization. Nonprofit organizations often try to obtain price concessions or even free donations of goods and services but don't often succeed. In recent times, supply shortages and the rapidly rising cost of supplies have made skillful supply planning and purchasing more important than ever.

**Regulatory organizations.**    The third input public consists of regulatory organizations that impose rules of conduct. The regulatory publics of a university include federal, state, and local government agencies, trade unions, and various academic accreditation associations. The focal organization must keep in close contact with these regulatory organizations and be ready to argue against regulations that will harm their ability to create value for their clients.

INTERNAL PUBLICS

The various inputs are managed by the organization's internal publics to accomplish the organization's mission. The internal publics consist of up to four groups: *management,* a *board of directors, staff,* and *volunteers.* (Public agencies are an exception and normally lack a board of directors and volunteers.)

**Management.**    Every organization has a management group that is responsible for running the organization. The top officer is called the president or chief administrator. Reporting to the president are high-level managers who are organized by functions, products, markets, and/or geographical areas. Thus, reporting to a college president are deans taking care of functions (e.g., business manager), products (e.g., dean of engineering school), and markets (e.g., dean of students).

**Board of directors.**    The president and the management team may be responsible to a board of directors (also called a board of trustees or overseers). The board's job is to oversee the organization and to make sure that it is operating efficiently to reach its objectives. Among the board's more important responsibilities are the following:

1. The board selects or approves the chief officer of the organization.
2. The board participates in setting or approving long-range strategy for the organization.
3. The board develops or approves policies for the conduct of organizational affairs.
4. The board develops or approves compensation levels and salaries of higher management.
5. The board participates in fundraising.
6. The board considers major issues that have come before the organization.
7. The board adds members who are influential and can provide further contacts with other influentials.
8. The board legitimizes the organization in the eyes of others.
9. The board provides specialized skills and advice, as would come from lawyers and businessmen.

Clearly the board is an important part of the organization, and in some organizations the most important part. Because of this, board members must be carefully selected. Most organizations seek "high-prestige" members, some seek "ordinary citizen" members, and others go after a mixture. A new small private college in Kentucky, for example, asked a wealthy and influential civic leader to head its new board. This person in turn attracted other prestigious individuals. The board then added members with certain skills, such as a lawyer, accountant, banker, and politician. Finally, one of the most prominent professors at the school was added to the board.

Board selection is very challenging. There is often a tradeoff between getting prestigious members on the board (who may miss a number of meetings and not be able to do much work) and working members on the board. Too many boards are window dressing and private clubs that do not get involved in what is really happening. Some managements want it this way, so that the board does not interfere with their plans and schemes.

Other managements want a more active board than the one they have. The board is too conservative and not willing to change with the times. Or it is not willing to work hard. Here management may have to take some drastic steps, such as asking certain members to drop out or setting up attendance rules and dropping those members who miss a certain number of meetings. The main way to create a working board is to hold frequent meetings, establish attendance rules, form working committees that must deliver reports, and, in general, establish the idea that work is expected.

Some boards are so involved in the organization that they are a major force in driving the organization to its best performance. They make demands on management to produce plans and results. They are a "whip" to the management group. Other boards are a drag on the organization. They are too conservative, and do not change with the times. They remember the organization as working a certain way and do not let it change with the times. Here is where management groups must market change to the board, get them "out of the dark ages." And this may require a marketing plan.[9]

**Staff.**    The staff consists of the various employees who work on a paid basis. This would include middle management, secretaries, workmen, telephone operators, and so on. The staff would also include the skilled practitioners who deliver the organization's services to its consumers, such as the hospital's nurses, the college's professors, the police department's police officers, and the social agency's social workers.

Management faces the normal problems of building an effective staff: defining job positions and responsibilities, recruiting qualified people, training them, motivating them, compensating them, and evaluating them. We discussed earlier all the "marketing" work that one hospital took to recruit one physician, and now this example has to be multiplied by the number of new people an organization hires each year. Employee training is another critical task with significant marketing implications. Those employees who come in contact with consumers must be trained in a "customer service" orientation. A college whose professors are cold or indifferent to the students is much more likely to have falling enrollment than a college with student-oriented professors.

Motivating the staff takes careful planning. The staff wants several things from the organization: adequate salaries, fair treatment, respect and recognition, and the feeling of working for a worthwhile enterprise. Management must create these benefits if it expects to get in return solid work, high morale, and continuous support. Employees are a "market" to which management must creatively communicate and relate.

**Volunteers.**    Many nonprofit organizations—churches, charities, hospitals— use volunteers as an important part of their operations. The volunteers perform work which usually requires less skill, and this helps to keep down the costs of running the organization. On the other hand, volunteers are less controllable and often less productive. They may not show up for meetings, resist doing certain tasks, and tend to be slow in getting their work done on time. Some organizations claim to be able to accomplish more by increasing the size of the paid staff and reducing the number of volunteers.

At the same time, a better answer might be for the organization to improve its skill in managing and motivating the volunteers. Volunteers are sensitive to small slights, like not receiving recognition for a job well done, or being pushed hard. They feel that they are giving their time free and want to be appreciated and respected.

The competent volunteer staff manager will be skilled in attracting good and reliable volunteers and in motivating and rewarding them. A marketing approach means understanding the volunteers' needs and meeting them in a way which draws their support and hard work. The volunteer staff manager is likely to sponsor social functions for volunteers, confer awards for many years of service, and arrange a number of other benefits that will recognize their contributions.[10]

### INTERMEDIARY PUBLICS

The focal organization enlists other organizations, called marketing intermediaries, to assist in promoting and distributing its goods and services to the final consumers. For example, a college may decide to offer off-campus educational services to consumers who cannot avail themselves of courses offered on campus. The college may work with four different marketing intermediaries to distribute and promote its educational services and products. They are described below.

**Merchants.**    Merchants are organizations—such as wholesalers and retailers —that buy, take title to, and resell merchandise. Suppose the college makes an arrangement with a local bookstore to carry and sell certain textbooks, where the bookstore cannot return the unsold books. The bookstore is performing a merchant role in the distribution system used by the college.

**Agents.**    Agent middlemen are organizations—such as manufacturer's representatives, agents, and brokers—that are hired by producers to find and/or sell to buyers without ever taking possession of the merchandise. Suppose the college signs a contract with a person who agrees to recruit new students for the college. This person is acting as an agent for the college. The college would have to negotiate the terms on which the agent would be remunerated for services.

**Facilitators.**    Facilitators are organizations—such as transportation companies, real estate firms, and media firms—that assist in the distribution of products, services, and messages, but do not take title to or negotiate purchases. Thus, the college will use the telephone company and the post office to send messages and materials to prospective students. These facilitators are paid a normal rate for their transportation, communication, and storage services.

**Marketing firms.**    Marketing firms are organizations—such as advertising agencies, marketing research firms, and marketing consulting firms—that assist in identifying and promoting the focal organization's products and services to the right markets. The college will hire the services of these marketing firms to investigate, develop, and promote new educational services. The focal organization has to select these firms wisely and negotiate terms which are mutually rewarding.

### CONSUMING PUBLICS

Various groups consume the output of an organization. They are described below.

**Clients.**    Customers represent an organization's primary public, its *raison d'être.* Drucker insists that the only valid definition of a business is to create a customer.[11] He would hold that hospitals exist to serve patients, colleges to serve students, opera companies to serve opera lovers, and social agencies to serve the needy.

Various names are used interchangeably to describe customers, such as consumers, clients, buyers, and constituents. The appropriate term is elusive in some cases. Consider a state penitentiary. The prisoners are clearly the penitentiary's consumers. A psychiatrist in the prison will have certain prisoners as clients. The prisoners are not buyers in the sense of paying money for the service; instead, the citizens are the buyers and they are buying protection from criminal elements through their taxes. The citizens are also the prison's constituents in that the prison exists to serve their interests. We might conclude that the citizens are the prison's primary customers.

What this illustrates is that an organization can have a multiple set of customers, and one of its jobs is to distinguish these customer groups and their relative importance. Consider this issue in relation to a state college. Who is the state college's primary customer? Is it the *students* because they consume the product? Is it the students' *parents,* who expect the college to transmit knowledge and ambition to their sons and daughters? Is it *employers,* who expect the college to produce people with marketable skills? Is it *taxpayers,* who expect the college to produce educated individuals? Or is it the college's *alumni,* who expect their alma mater to do notable things to give them pride?

Clearly, a college must take the interest of all of these "customer" groups into account in formulating its services and policies. At times, the college will aim to increase its service to one group more than to another. If the students complain about poor lectures and unavailable professors, then the administration will have to focus its energy on improving service to the students. This may require putting pressure on the professors to be more responsive to students. At other times, professors may complain that their teaching load is too heavy to get any research done, and the administration may seek additional money from alumni to finance lighter teaching loads. Most of the time the administration is busy balancing and reconciling the interests of diverse customer groups rather than favoring one group all the time at the expense of the other groups.

**Local publics.**    Every organization is physically located in one or more areas and comes in contact with local publics such as neighborhood residents and community organizations. These groups may take an active or passive interest in the activities of the organization. Thus, the residents surrounding a hospital usually get concerned about ambulance sirens, parking congestion, and other things that go with living near a hospital.

Organizations usually appoint a community relations officer whose job is to keep close to the community, attend meetings, answer questions, and make contributions to worthwhile causes. Responsive organizations do not wait for local issues to erupt. They make investments in their community to help it run well and to acquire a bank of goodwill.

**Activist publics.**     Organizations are increasingly being petitioned by consumer groups, environmental groups, minority organizations, and other public interest groups for certain concessions or support. Hospitals, for example, have had to deal with demands by environmental groups to install more pollution control equipment and engage in better waste handling methods.

Organizations would be foolish to attack or ignore demands of activist publics. Responsive organizations can do two things. First, they can train their management to include social criteria in their decision making to strike a better balance between the needs of the clients, citizens, and the organization itself. Second, they can assign a staff person to stay in touch with these groups and to communicate more effectively the organization's goals, activities, and intentions.

**General public.**     An organization is also concerned with the attitude of the general public toward its activities and policies. The general public does not act in an organized way toward the organization, as activist groups do. But the members of the general public carry around images of the organization which affect their patronage and legislative support. The organization needs to monitor how it is seen by the public, and to take concrete steps to improve its public image where it is weak.

**Media publics.**     Media publics include media companies that carry news, features, and editorial opinion: specifically, newspapers, magazines, and radio and television stations. Organizations are acutely sensitive to the role played by the press in affecting their capacity to achieve their marketing objectives. Organizations normally would like more and better press coverage than they get. Getting more and better coverage calls for understanding what the press is really interested in. The effective press relations manager knows most of the editors in the major media and systematically cultivates a mutually beneficial relation with them. The manager offers interesting news items, informational material, and quick access to top management. In return, the media editors are likely to give the organization more and better coverage.

**Competitive publics.**     In carrying out its task of producing and delivering services to a target market, the nonprofit organization will typically face competition. Many nonprofit organizations deny the existence of competition, feeling that this is more characteristic of business firms. Thus, hospitals until recently did not like to think of other hospitals as competitors, and the YMCA does not like to think of other social agencies as competitors. They would rather think of all their sister organizations as providing needed services and not competing. Yet the reality of competition is driven home when one hospital starts attracting many doctors and patients from another hospital, or a local YMCA starts losing members to local racquetball clubs and gymnasiums.

An organization must be sensitive to the competitive environment in which it operates. The competitive environment does not consist only of similar organizations or services but also of more basic things. An organization can face up to four major types of competitors in trying to serve its target market. They are:

1. *Desire competitors:* other immediate desires that the consumer might want to satisfy.
2. *Generic competitors:* other basic ways in which the consumer can satisfy a particular desire.
3. *Service form competitors:* other service forms that can satisfy the consumer's particular desire.
4. *Enterprise competitors:* other enterprises offering the same service form that can satisfy the consumer's particular desire.

We will illustrate these four types of competitors in relation to a small ivy-league college. Consider a high school senior deciding what to do after graduation. Suppose her decision process follows the path shown in Figure 2–7. The student realizes that she has several competing desires *(desire competitors):* getting an education, getting a job, traveling to Europe, and so on. Suppose she favors getting an education. She then considers the best way to do this *(generic competitors):* read books, hire a tutor, go to college, and so on. She decides in favor of going to college. Then she considers what type of college *(service form competitors):* private college, state college, or community college. She favors a private college. This leads her to consider which private colleges to apply to *(enterprise competitors):* Harvard, Stanford, Princeton, and so on. Thus, this private college faces at least four types of competitors in attempting to attract this student.

## FIGURE 2–7

### Types of Competitors Facing a Private College

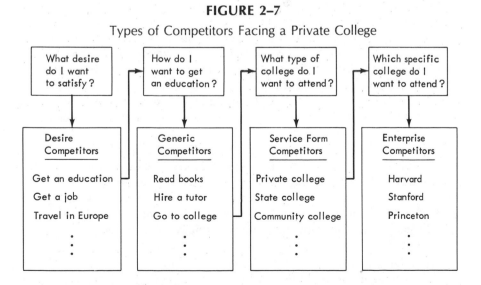

Having demonstrated that every organization is surrounded by a multitude of publics, we can now pose the question: What is the relation between a public and a market? The term "market" has a different origin than the term "public" and yet has several affinities with it.

From the point of view of an organization, a market is *a potential arena for the trading of resources.* For an organization to operate, it must acquire resources through trading other resources. In each case, it must offer something to the market to receive in return the resources it seeks. For this reason, we define a market as follows:

A **market** is a distinct group of people and/or organizations that have resources which they want to exchange, or might conceivably be willing to exchange, for distinct benefits.

We can now see the affinities between a market and a public. A *public* is any group that has an actual or potential interest or impact on an organization. If the organization wishes to attract certain resources from that public through offering a set of benefits in exchange, then the organization is taking a *marketing viewpoint* toward that public. Once the organization starts thinking in terms of trading values with that public, it is viewing the public as a market. It is engaged in trying to determine the best marketing approach to that public.

---

## IMAGE

Responsive organizations have a strong interest in how their publics see the organization and its products and services. For it is the organization's image, not necessarily its reality, that people respond to. Publics holding a negative image of an organization will avoid or disparage the organization, while those holding a positive image will be drawn to it. The same organization will be viewed as responsive by some groups and unresponsive by other groups. Therefore, the organization has a vital interest in learning about its "images" in the marketplace and making sure that these images facilitate rather than impede the delivery of satisfaction.

An organization does not acquire a favorable image simply through public relations planning. Its image is a function of its *deeds* and its *communications.* Good deeds without good words, or good words without good deeds, are not enough. A strong favorable image comes about when the organization creates real satisfaction for its clients and lets others know about this.

Managers want to know the following things about image:

1. What is an image?
2. How can it be measured?

3. What determines the image?
4. How can an image be changed?
5. What is the relation between the person's image of an object and his/her behavior toward the object?

## DEFINITION OF IMAGE

The term "image" came into popular use in the 1950s. It is currently used in a variety of contexts: organization image, corporate image, national image, brand image, public image, self-image, and so on. Its wide use has tended to blur its meanings. Our definition of image is:

An **image** is the sum of beliefs, ideas, and impressions that a person has of an object.

This definition enables us to distinguish an image from similar sounding concepts such as *beliefs, attitudes,* and *stereotypes.*

An image is more than a simple belief. The belief that the American Medical Association (AMA) is more interested in serving doctors than serving society would be only one element in a large image that might be held about the AMA. An image is a whole set of beliefs about an object.

On the other hand, people's images of an object do not necessarily reveal their attitudes toward that object. Two persons may hold the same image of the AMA and yet have different attitudes toward it. An attitude is a disposition toward an object that includes cognitive, affective, and behavioral components.

How does an image differ from a stereotype? A stereotype suggests a widely held image that is highly distorted and simplistic and that carries a favorable or unfavorable attitude toward the object. An image, on the other hand, is a more personal perception of an object that can vary greatly from person to person.

## IMAGE MEASUREMENT

Many methods have been proposed for measuring images. We will describe a two-step approach: first, measuring how familiar and favorable the organization's image is, and second, measuring the organization's image along major relevant dimensions.

**Familiarity–favorability measurement.**     The first step is to establish, for each public being studied, how familiar they are with the organization and how favorable they feel toward it. To establish familiarity, respondents are asked to check one of the following:

| Never heard of | Heard of | Know a little bit | Know a fair amount | Know very well |
|---|---|---|---|---|

The results indicate the public's awareness of the organization. If most of the respondents place the organization in the first two or three categories, then the organization has an awareness problem.

Those respondents who have some familiarity with the organization are then asked to describe how favorable they feel toward it by checking one of the following:

| Very unfavorable | Somewhat unfavorable | Indifferent | Somewhat favorable | Very favorable |
|---|---|---|---|---|

If most of the respondents check the first two or three categories, then the organization has a serious image problem.

To illustrate these scales, suppose the residents of an area are asked to rate four local hospitals, A, B, C, and D. Their responses are averaged and the results displayed in Figure 2–8. Hospital A has the strongest image: Most people know it and like it. Hospital B is less familiar to most people but those who know it like it. Hospital C is negatively viewed by the people who know it but fortunately not too many people know it. Hospital D is in the weakest position: It is seen as a poor hospital and everyone knows it.

Clearly, each hospital faces a different task. Hospital A must work at maintaining its good reputation and high community awareness. Hospital B must bring itself to the attention of more people since those who know it find it to be a good hospital. Hospital C needs to find out why people dislike the hospital and take steps to mend its ways, while keeping a low profile. Hospital D would be

**FIGURE 2–8**

Familiarity–Favorability Analysis

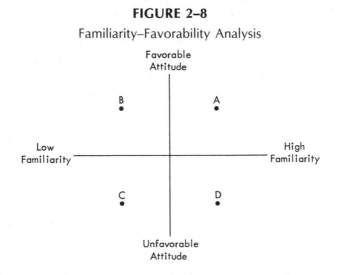

well advised to lower its profile (avoid news), mend its ways, and when it is a better hospital, it can start seeking public attention again.

**Semantic differential.**    Each hospital needs to go further and research the content of its image. One of the most popular tools for this is the semantic differential.[12] It involves the following steps:

1. *Developing a set of relevant dimensions.* The researcher first asks people to identify the dimensions they would use in thinking about the object. People could be asked: "What things do you think of when you consider a hospital?" If someone suggests "quality of medical care," this would be turned into a bipolar adjective scale —say, "inferior medical care" at one end and "superior medical care" at the other. This could be rendered as a five- or seven-point scale. A set of additional relevant dimensions for a hospital are shown in Figure 2–9.

2. *Reducing the set of relevant dimensions.* The number of dimensions should be kept small so as to avoid respondent fatigue in having to rate *n* organizations on *m* scales. Osgood and his coworkers feel that there are essentially three types of scales:
- evaluation scales (good–bad qualities)
- potency scales (strong–weak qualities)
- activity scales (active–passive qualities)

Using these scales as a guide, or performing a factor analysis, the researcher can remove redundant scales that fail to add much information.

3. *Administering the instrument to a sample of respondents.* The respondents are asked to rate one organization at a time. The bipolar adjectives should be arranged so as not to load all of the poor adjectives on one side.

4. *Averaging the results.* Figure 2–9 shows the results of averaging the respondents' pictures of hospitals A, B, and C. Each hospital's image is represented by a vertical "line of means" that summarizes how the average respondent sees that institution. Thus Hospital A is seen as a large, modern, friendly, and superior hospital. Hospital C, on the other hand, is seen as a small, dated, impersonal, and inferior hospital.

5. *Checking on the image variance.* Since each image profile is a line of means, it does not reveal how variable the image actually is. If there were 100 respondents, did they all see Hospital B, for example, exactly as shown, or was there considerable

## FIGURE 2–9
### Images of Three Hospitals (Semantic Differential)

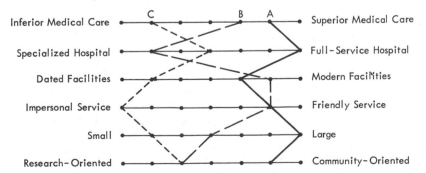

variation? In the first case, we would say that the image is highly *specific*, and in the second case that the image is highly *diffused*. An institution may or may not want a very specific image. Some organizations prefer a diffused image so that different groups can project their needs into this organization. The organization will want to analyze whether a variable image is really the result of different subgroups rating the organization with each subgroup having a highly specific image.

The semantic differential is a flexible image-measuring tool that can provide the following useful information.

1. *The organization can discover how a particular public views the organization and its major competitors.* It can learn its image strengths and weaknesses along with those of the competitors and take remedial steps that are warranted.

2. *The organization can discover how different publics and market segments view the organization.* One can imagine that the image profiles in Figure 2–9 represent the images of one organization held by three different publics. The organization would then consider taking steps to improve its image among those publics who view the organization most unfavorably.

3. *The organization can monitor changes in its image over time.* By repeating the image study periodically, the organization can detect any significant image slippage or improvement. Image slippage signals that the organization is doing something wrong. Image improvement, on the other hand, verifies that the organization is performing better as a result of some steps it has taken.

IMAGE CAUSATION

What determines the image that a person holds of an object? A theory of image determinants would help the organization understand the factors that have caused its present image, and understand how to produce a change.

There are two opposite theories of image formation. One holds that image is largely *object-determined*—that is, persons are simply perceiving the reality of the object. If a hospital is located next to a lake and surrounded by beautiful trees, then it is going to strike people as a beautiful hospital. A few individuals might describe it as ugly but this would be dismissed as the peculiarity of certain individuals or their lack of real experience with the object. The object-determined view of images assumes that (1) people tend to have first-hand experience with objects; (2) people get reliable sensory data from the object; and (3) people tend to process the sensory data in a similar way in spite of having different backgrounds and personalities. These assumptions in turn imply that organizations cannot easily create false images of themselves.

The other school holds that images are largely *person-determined*. Those holding this view argue that (1) people have different degrees of contact with the object; (2) people placed in front of the object will selectively perceive different aspects of the object; (3) people have individual ways of processing sensory data leading to selective distortion. For these reasons, it is held that people are likely to hold quite different images of the object. That is, there is a weak relation between the image and the actual object.

The truth lies somewhere in between—that is, an image is influenced both by the objective characteristics of the object and the subjective characteristics of the perceiver. We might expect people to hold rather similar images of a given object mainly under the following conditions: when the object is simple rather than complex; when it is frequently and directly experienced; and when it is fairly stable in its real characteristics over time. Conversely, people may hold quite different images of an object if it is complex, infrequently experienced, and changing through time. People have quite different images of a particular hospital because it is complex, infrequently experienced in direct contact, and changes through time.

## IMAGE MODIFICATION

The leaders of an organization are often surprised and disturbed by the measured image. Thus the chief administrator of Hospital C (see Figure 2–9) might be upset that the public sees the hospital as dated, impersonal, and of low quality. Management's immediate reaction is to disbelieve the results by complaining that the sample is too small or unrepresentative. But if the results can be defended as reliable, management must consider what it ought to do about this image problem.

The first step is for management to develop a picture of the *desired image* that they want to have in the general public's mind, in contrast to the *current image*. Suppose the management of Hospital C wants an image closer to that of Hospital A. Hospital C would like the public to have a more favorable view of the quality of its medical care, facilities, friendliness, and so on. It is not aiming for perfection because the hospital recognizes its limitations. The desired image must be feasible in terms of the organization's present reality and resources.

The second step is for management to decide which image gaps it wants to work on initially. Is it more desirable to improve the hospital's image of friendliness (through staff training programs, etc.) or the look of its facilities (through renovation)? Each image dimension should be separately reviewed in terms of the following questions:

1. What contribution to the organization's overall favorable image would be made by closing that particular image gap to the extent shown?
2. What strategy (combination of real changes and communication changes) would be used to close the particular image gap?
3. What would be the cost of closing that image gap?
4. How long would it take to close that image gap?

For example, management might decide that it would be more impactful, swifter, and less costly to improve the hospital's image of friendliness than to improve the physical facilities of the hospital. An overall image modification plan would involve planning the sequence of steps through which the organization would go to transform its current image into its desired image.

An organization seeking to change its image must have great patience. Images tend to be "sticky" and last long after the reality of the organization has changed. Thus, the quality of medical care might have deteriorated at a major hospital and yet it continues to be highly regarded in the public mind. Image persistence is explained by the fact that once people have a certain image of an object, they tend to be selective perceivers of further data. Their perceptions are oriented toward seeing what they expect to see. It will take highly disconfirming stimuli to raise doubts and open them to new information. Thus an image enjoys a life of its own for a while, especially when people are not likely to have new first-hand experiences with the changed object.

### The Relation Between Image and Behavior

The reason why organizations are interested in image measurement and modification is because of the great influence they feel an image has on the behavior of people. They assume that there is a close relationship between the public's image of the organization and their behavior toward it. The organization feels that it can obtain better public response by acquiring a better image.

Unfortunately, the connection between image and behavior is not as close as many organizations believe. Images are only one component of attitudes. Two people may view a hospital as large and have opposite attitudes toward a large hospital. Furthermore, the connection between attitudes and behavior is also tenuous. A person might prefer a large hospital to a small one, and yet end up in the small one because it is closer to home or the doctor recommended it.

Nevertheless, one should not dismiss image measurement and planning simply because images are hard to change and their effects on behavior are unclear. Quite the contrary. Measuring an object's image is a very useful step in understanding what is happening to the object and to point to some possible desirable changes in its image. Furthermore, though the connection between image and behavior is not strong, it does exist. The connection should neither be overrated nor underrated. The organization should attempt to make an investment in developing the best image it can for the advantages this might bring.

## SATISFACTION

A responsive organization is one that makes every effort to sense, serve, and satisfy the needs and wants of its focal clients and publics. Each organization must determine how responsive it wants to be and the appropriate systems for measuring and improving its satisfaction creating ability.

### Levels of Organizational Responsiveness

Organizations fall into four levels of organizational responsiveness. They are shown in Table 2–1 and described in the following paragraphs.

## Table 2–1

### FOUR LEVELS OF CONSUMER-RESPONSIVE ORGANIZATIONS

|  | Unresponsive | Casually Responsive | Highly Responsive | Fully Responsive |
|---|---|---|---|---|
| Complaint system | No | Yes | Yes | Yes |
| Surveys of satisfaction | No | Yes | Yes | Yes |
| Surveys of needs and preferences | No | No | Yes | Yes |
| Customer-oriented personnel | No | No | Yes | Yes |
| Empowered customers | No | No | No | Yes |

**The unresponsive organization.** An unresponsive organization is at one extreme. Its main characteristics are:

1. It does not encourage inquiries, complaints, suggestions, or opinions from its customers.
2. It does not measure current customer satisfaction or needs.
3. It does not train its staff to be customer-minded.

The unresponsive organization is typically characterized by a bureaucratic mentality. Bureaucracy is the tendency of organizations to routinize their operations, replace personal judgment with impersonal policies, specialize the job of every employee, create a rigid hierarchy of command, and convert the organization into an efficient machine.[13] Bureaucrats are not concerned with innovation, with problems outside their specific authority, with qualifying human factors. They will serve people as long as their problems fall within the limits of their jurisdiction. People's problems are defined in terms of how the bureaucratic organization is set up rather than having the organization set up to respond to people's problems. Questions of structure dominate questions of substance; means dominate ends.

This kind of organization either assumes that it knows what its publics need or that their needs do not matter. It sees no reason to consult with its consumers. Many hospitals were bureaucratically operated in the 1960s when they had far more patient demand than beds. Consider the following:

> Why is it necessary to awaken a patient a couple of hours before breakfast to wash his face? . . . Why does it sometimes take many minutes for a nurse to answer the patient's light? . . . We've all seen nurses standing in the hallway talking and ignoring call lights. . . . Too many hospitals are drab.[14]

Whether the physician, the house staff member or the nurse, the waiter, X-ray or emergency room, or the admitting clerk who is rude, the maid who bumps the bed while cleaning, the parking lot attendant who is less than helpful when the lot is full, the cafeteria that turns away visitors, the pharmacy that has limited hours for outpatients—all of this suggests that hospitals operate for their own convenience and not that of the patient, his family and friends.[15]

Such an unresponsive organization brings about a host of undesirable consequences. The products and services are usually poor or irrelevant. Citizens or customers become frustrated and dissatisfied. Their dissatisfaction leads to rebellion, withdrawal, or apathy, and may ultimately doom the organization.

**The casually responsive organization.**     The casually responsive organization differs from the unresponsive organization in two ways:

1. It encourages customers to submit inquiries, complaints, suggestions, and opinions.
2. It makes periodic studies of consumer satisfaction.

When American universities began to experience a decline in student applications in the early seventies, they began to pay more attention to their students and publics. College administrators who formerly were largely oriented toward problems of hiring faculty, scheduling classes, and running efficient administrative services—the earmarks of the bureaucratic mentality—now began to listen more to the students. They left their doors open, made occasional surprise appearances in the student lounge, encouraged suggestions from students, and created faculty–student committees. These steps moved the university into being casually responsive.

The result is to create a better feeling in the organization's customers. It is the first step in building a partnership between the served and the serving. Whether or not the increased customer satisfaction continues depends on whether the organization merely makes a show of listening or actually undertakes to do something about what it hears. It may merely offer a semblance of openness and interest without intending to use the results in any way. It sooner or later becomes apparent to the consumers that this is a public relations ploy. It can lead to greater strain because of rising consumer expectations than when the organization was completely unresponsive. If their voices fall on deaf ears, they resent the organization and may try to force it into greater responsiveness.

**The highly responsive organization.**     A highly responsive organization differs from a casually responsive organization in two additional ways:

1. It not only surveys current consumer satisfaction but also researches unmet consumer needs and preferences to discover ways to improve its service.
2. It selects and trains its people to be customer-minded.

Many nonprofit organizations fall short of being highly responsive. Universities rarely take formal surveys of their students' real needs and desires, nor do they incentivize and train their faculty to be student-minded. Recently a small liberal arts college recognized this failing, and it developed the following philosophy to guide its professors:

The students are:
- the most important people on the campus; without them there would be no need for the institution
- not cold enrollment statistics, but flesh-and-blood human beings with feelings and emotions like our own
- not dependent on us; rather, we are dependent on them
- not an interruption of our work, but the purpose of it; we are not doing them a favor by serving them—they are doing us a favor by giving us the opportunity to do so

If this could be successfully implemented, the college would have moved a long way into being highly responsive.

**The fully responsive organization.**        The highly responsive organization is free to accept or reject complaints and suggestions from its consumers, based on what it thinks is important and what it is willing to do. The public proposes and the organization disposes. A fully responsive organization overcomes the "we–they" distinction by accepting its customers as voting members. Its characteristics are:

1. It encourages the consumers to participate actively in the affairs of the organization.
2. It responds to the wishes of the organization's consumers as expressed through the ballot box or their representatives.

Among examples of fully responsive organizations, at least in principle, are local town democracies, churches, trade unions, and democratic nation-states. The organization is seen as existing for and serving the interests of the citizen-members. There is no question of the organization going off on its own course to pursue goals that are not in the interest of its members. The organization shows an extreme interest in measuring the will of the members and responding to their wishes and needs.

When these principles are fulfilled, the expectation is that the citizen-members will be highly involved, enthusiastic, and satisfied. Recently, a Canadian university was searching for ways to build a more active alumni association. Just sending out newsletters about the school did not build up alumni pride or interest. It developed the idea of conferring membership status on its alumni, with certain privileges and voting rights on certain issues. Suddenly, the alumni became alive with interest in the school. This gesture proved very meaningful to the alumni, who had hitherto felt that the university was simply using them for their money.

Since responsive organizations aim to create satisfaction, it is necessary to define the term "satisfaction." Our definition is:

**Satisfaction** is a state felt by a person who has experienced a *performance* (or outcome) that has fulfilled his or her *expectations.*

Thus, satisfaction is a function of the relative levels of expectation and perceived performance. A person will experience one of three states of satisfaction. If the performance exceeds the person's expectations, the person is *highly satisfied.* If the performance matches the expectations, the person is *satisfied.* If the performance falls short of the expectations, the person is *dissatisfied.*

In the last case, the amount of dissatisfaction depends upon the consumer's method of handling the gap between expectations and performance. Some consumers try to *minimize* the felt dissonance by seeing more performance than there really is or thinking that they set their expectations too high. Other consumers will exaggerate the perceived performance gap because of their disappointment.[16] They are more prone to reduce or end their contacts with the organization.

Thus to understand satisfaction, we must understand how people form their expectations. Expectations are formed on the basis of people's past experience with the same or similar situations, the statements made by friends and other associates, and the statements made by the supplying organization. Thus, the supplying organization influences satisfaction not only through its performance but also through the expectations it creates. If it overclaims, it is likely to create subsequent dissatisfaction; and if it underclaims, it might create high satisfaction. The safest course for the organization is to plan to deliver a certain level of performance and communicate this level to its consumers.

### MEASURING SATISFACTION

Consumer satisfaction, in spite of its central importance, is difficult to measure. Organizations use various methods to make an inference about how much consumer satisfaction they are creating. The major methods are described below.

**Sales-related methods.** Many organizations feel that the extent of consumer satisfaction created by their activities is revealed by such objective measures as their *sales growth, market share,* and/or *repeat purchase ratio.* If these measures are rising, management draws the conclusion that the organization is satisfying its customers. Thus, if the Lyric Opera Company sells all of its seats and next year has a 100 percent subscription renewal rate, it must be satisfying its patrons. If a college manages to attract more students each year in a declining market, it must be satisfying its students.

These indirect measures are important but hardly sufficient. In situations of no competition or excess demand, these measures may be high and yet not reflect actual satisfaction, because consumers have no alternatives. In other situations, sales can remain strong for a while even after satisfaction has started to decline because dissatisfied patrons might transact with an organization a little longer out of inertia.

**Complaint and suggestion systems.**     A responsive organization will make it easy for its clients to complain if they are disappointed in some way with the service they have received. Management will want complaints to surface up on the theory that clients who are not given an opportunity to complain might reduce their business with the organization, bad-mouth it, or abandon it completely. Not collecting complaints represents a loss of valuable information which the organization could have used to improve its service.

How can complaints be facilitated? The organization can set up systems that make it easy for dissatisfied customers (or satisfied customers) to express their feelings to the organization. Several devices can be used in this connection. For example, a hospital could place *suggestion boxes* in the corridors. It could supply exiting patients with a *comment card* which can be easily checked off (see Figure 2–10). It can establish a *patient advocate or ombudsman system* to hear patient grievances and seek remedies.[17] It can establish a *nurse grievance committee* to review nurse complaints.

An organization should try to identify the major categories of complaints. Thus a hospital might count the number of complaints about food, nursing care, and room cleanliness and focus its corrective actions on those categories showing a high frequency, high seriousness, and high remediability.

A good complaint management system will provide much valuable information for improving the organization's performance. At the same time, a complaint system tends to understate the amount of real dissatisfaction felt by customers. The reasons are:

1. Many people who are disappointed may choose not to complain, either feeling too angry or feeling that complaining would do no good. One study found that only 34 percent of a group of dissatisfied people said they would complain.
2. Some people overcomplain (the chronic complainers) and this introduces a bias into the data.

Some critics have argued that complaint systems do more harm than good. By giving people an opportunity—indeed, an incentive—to complain, people are more likely to feel dissatisfied. Instead of ignoring their disappointment, they are asked to spell it out, and they are also led to expect redress. If the latter is not forthcoming, they will be more dissatisfied. Although this might happen, it is our view that the value of the information gathered by soliciting complaints far exceeds the cost of possibly overstimulating dissatisfaction.

FIGURE 2–10

A Hospital Comment Card

**You are a VERY IMPORTANT PERSON!**

**Will you let us know how we did?**

We strive to provide the best possible hospital care to the patients who come to us. Please take a couple of minutes to complete this questionnaire, there is space on the back for additional comments, which will help us improve our service and continue Memorial's tradition of excellent patient care.

When completed drop it in the mail. It is addressed and the postage is paid.

Thank you for your valuable assistance.

*Robert M. Magnuson*
Robert M. Magnuson
*President*

Your room number _____

From _____ To _____

Male _____ Female _____

Your name, if you wish _____

**A. Your admission:**  Yes  No

Were you courteously received and processed by the admitting office?  __ __

Were you admitted to the hospital from the Emergency Department?  __ __

**B. Your room:**

Was it ready for you?  __ __

Was it attractive?  __ __

Was it kept clean during your stay?  __ __

Cat. No. 193540

Yes  No

Was the proper temperature maintained?  __ __

Were lighting and ventilation facilities adequate?  __ __

Was your room quiet enough for you to sleep and rest?  __ __

**C. Your meals:**

Was the food well-prepared and appetizing, considering your diet?  __ __

Were you satisfied with the portions?  __ __

Did hot food arrive hot at your bedside?  __ __

Was your food served attractively?  __ __

Overall, were you pleased with the food service during your stay?  __ __

**D. Nursing service:**

In your opinion were the nurses skilled in the performance of their duties?  __ __

Were they attentive to your needs and did they explain reasons for medications, treatments, and diagnostic procedures?  __ __

Was your call for assistance answered with reasonable promptness?  __ __

**E. Were you satisfied with the services given by:**

X-ray technicians?  __ __

Laboratory technicians?  __ __

Yes  No

Housekeeping personnel?  __ __

Nursing assistants, orderlies and other nursing personnel?  __ __

Volunteers?  __ __

Telephone operators?  __ __

Admitting clerks?  __ __

Other personnel?  __ __

**F. Were you informed about tests and treatments ordered by your physician?**  __ __

**G. Was your schedule arranged so that you could get enough rest?**  __ __

**H. Personal:**

Were your visitors courteously received?  __ __

Were visiting hours satisfactory?  __ __

Were services such as delivery of mail, flowers and packages satisfactory?  __ __

**I. Business office:**

Was the cashier courteous and helpful?  __ __

**J. Overall, are you satisfied with your care at Memorial Hospital?**  __ __

**K. Overall, are you satisfied with the information given you about your health, your treatments, and follow-up care?**  __ __

**L. Would you recommend our Hospital to family members, friends and neighbors?**  __ __

**Consumer panels.**     Some organizations set up a consumer panel to keep informed of consumer satisfaction. A consumer panel consists of a small group of customers who have been selected to make up a panel that will be sampled from time to time about its feelings toward the organization or any of its services. Thus, a hospital may set up a doctor panel that would be sampled periodically for its reactions or suggestions. A university may set up a student panel that would be sampled periodically for its reactions to current services.

Consumer panel members may volunteer or they may be paid for their time. Some provision is usually made to rotate membership on the panel to get fresh views from new people. The panel is typically a source of valuable information to the organization. At the same time, the information may not be completely trustworthy. The panel's representativeness can be called into question. People who do not like to be members of panels are not represented. Those who join the panel may be more loyal to the organization and thus less likely to see its faults.

**Consumer satisfaction surveys.**     Many organizations supplement the preceding devices with direct periodic surveys of consumer satisfaction. They send questionnaires or make telephone calls to a random sample of past users to find out how much they like the service and what they might dislike about the service. In this way, they avoid the possible biases of complaints systems, on the one hand, and consumer panels, on the other.

Consumer satisfaction can be measured in a number of ways, three of which will be described here. We will illustrate them in a university setting.

DIRECTLY REPORTED SATISFACTION.     A university can distribute a questionnaire to a representative sample of students, asking them to state their felt satisfaction with the university as a whole and with specific components. The questionnaire would be distributed on a periodic basis either in person, in the mail, or through a telephone survey.

The questionnaire would contain questions of the following form:

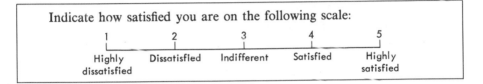

Here five intervals are used, although some scales use only three intervals and others as many as eleven. The numbers assigned to the intervals are arbitrary, except that each succeeding number is higher than the previous one. There is no implication that these are unit distances. When the results are in, a histogram can be prepared showing the percentage of students who fall into each group. Of course, students within any group—such as the highly dissatisfied group— may have really quite different intensities of dissatisfaction ranging from mild feelings of disappointment with the university to intense feelings of anger. Unfortunately, there is no way to make interpersonal comparisons of utility and we can only rely on the self-reported feelings of the respondents.

If the histogram is highly skewed to the left, then the university is in deep trouble. If the histogram is bell-shaped, then it has the usual number of dissatisfied, indifferent, and satisfied students. If the histogram is highly skewed to the right, the university can be very satisfied that it is a responsive organization meeting its goal of delivering high satisfaction to the majority of its consumers. It is necessary to repeat this survey at regular intervals to spot any significant changes in the distribution. Furthermore, the respondents should check similar scales for the significant components of the university, such as its academic program, extracurricular program, housing, and the like. It would help to know how the various components of satisfaction relate to overall satisfaction.

DERIVED DISSATISFACTION.     The second method of satisfaction measurement is based on the premise that a person's satisfaction is influenced by the perceived state of the object and his expectation. He is asked two questions about each component of the university; for example:

```
The quality of the academic program:
a. How much is there now?
(min)    1    2    3    4    5    6    7    (max)
b. How much should there be?
(min)    1    2    3    4    5    6    7    (max)
```

Suppose he circles 2 for part a and 5 for part b. We can then derive a "need deficiency" score by subtracting the answer for part a from part b, here 3. The greater the need deficiency score, the greater his degree of dissatisfaction (or the smaller his degree of satisfaction).

This method provides more useful information than the previous method. By averaging the scores of all the respondents to part a, the researcher learns the average perceived level of that attribute of the object. The dispersion around the average shows how much agreement there is. If all students see the academic program of the university at approximately 2 on a 7-point scale, this means the program is pretty bad. If students hold widely differing perceptions of the program's actual quality, this will require further analysis of why the perceptions differ so much and what individual or group factors it might be related to.

It is also useful to average the scores of all the respondents to part b. This will reveal the average student's view of how much quality is expected in the academic program. The measure of dispersion will show how much spread there is in student opinion about the desirable level of quality.

By finding the need deficiency score for each component of the university's product, the administration will have a good diagnostic tool to understand current student moods and to make necessary changes. By repeating this survey at regular intervals, the university can detect new need deficiencies as they arise and take timely steps to remedy them.

IMPORTANCE/PERFORMANCE RATINGS.   Another satisfaction-measuring device is to ask consumers to rate several services provided by the organization in terms of (1) the importance of each service, and (2) how well the organization performs each service. Figure 2–11A shows how fourteen services of a college were rated by students. The importance of a service was rated on a four-point scale of "extremely important," "important," "slightly important," and "not important." The college's performance was rated on a four-point scale of "excellent," "good," "fair," and "poor." For example, the first service, "academic program," received a mean importance rating of 3.83 and a mean performance rating of 2.63, indicating that students felt it was highly important, although not being performed that well. The ratings of all fourteen services are displayed in Figure 2–11B. The figure is divided into four sections. Quadrant A shows impor-

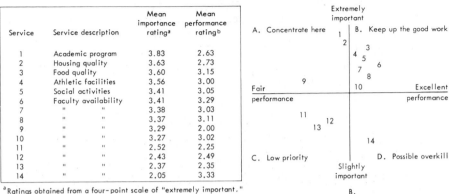

## FIGURE 2–11

### Importance and Performance Ratings for Several College Services

| Service | Service description | Mean importance rating[a] | Mean performance rating[b] |
|---|---|---|---|
| 1 | Academic program | 3.83 | 2.63 |
| 2 | Housing quality | 3.63 | 2.73 |
| 3 | Food quality | 3.60 | 3.15 |
| 4 | Athletic facilities | 3.56 | 3.00 |
| 5 | Social activities | 3.41 | 3.05 |
| 6 | Faculty availability | 3.41 | 3.29 |
| 7 | " " | 3.38 | 3.03 |
| 8 | " " | 3.37 | 3.11 |
| 9 | " " | 3.29 | 2.00 |
| 10 | " " | 3.27 | 3.02 |
| 11 | " " | 2.52 | 2.25 |
| 12 | " " | 2.43 | 2.49 |
| 13 | " " | 2.37 | 2.35 |
| 14 | " " | 2.05 | 3.33 |

[a] Ratings obtained from a four-point scale of "extremely important," "important," "slightly important," and "not important."

[b] Ratings obtained from a four-point scale of "excellent," "good," "fair," and "poor." A "no basis for judgment" category was also provided.

A.

B.

tant services that are not being offered at the desired performance levels. The college should concentrate on improving these services. Quadrant B shows important services that the college is performing well; its job is to maintain the high performance. Quadrant C shows minor services that are being delivered in a mediocre way, but which do not need any attention since they are not very important. Quadrant D shows a minor service that is being performed in an excellent manner, a case of possible "overkill." This rating of services according to their perceived importance and performance provides the college with guidelines as to where it should concentrate its efforts.

### RELATION BETWEEN CONSUMER SATISFACTION AND OTHER GOALS OF THE ORGANIZATION

Many people believe that the marketing concept calls upon an organization to *maximize* the satisfaction of its consumers. This, however, is not realistic and it would be better to interpret the marketing concept as saying that the organization should strive to create a high level of satisfaction in its consumers, though not necessarily the maximum level. The reasons for this are explained below.

First, consumer satisfaction can always be increased by accepting additional cost. Thus a university might hire better faculty and build better facilities and charge lower tuition to increase the satisfaction of its students. But obviously a university faces a cost constraint in trying to maximize the satisfaction of a particular public.

Second, the organization has to satisfy many publics. Increasing the satisfaction of one public might reduce the satisfaction available to another public. The organization owes each of its publics some specific level of satisfaction. Ultimately, the organization must operate on the philosophy that it is trying to satisfy the needs of different groups at levels that are acceptable to these groups within the constraint of its total resources. This is why the organization must systematically measure the levels of satisfaction expected by its different constituent publics and the current amounts they are, in fact, receiving.

The organization hopes to derive a number of benefits as a result of creating high satisfaction in its publics. First, the members of the organization will work with a better sense of purpose and pride. Second, the organization creates loyal publics and this reduces the costs of market turnover. Third, the loyal publics say good things to others about the organization and this attracts new consumers without requiring as much direct effort on the part of the organization.

---

## SUMMARY

A responsive organization is one that makes every effort to sense, serve, and satisfy the needs and wants of its clients and publics within the constraints of its budget. The concept of a responsive organization rests on the concepts of mission, exchange, publics, image, and satisfaction.

Every organization starts with a mission that answers: What is our business? Who is the customer? What is value to the customer? What will our business be? What should our business be? A helpful approach to defining mission is to identify which customer groups will be served, which of their needs will be addressed, and which technologies will be used to satisfy these needs. A mission works best when it is feasible, motivating, and distinctive.

To carry out its mission, an organization needs resources. An organization can attract resources through self-production, force, begging, or exchange. Marketing is based on the last solution and assumes that there are at least two parties; each can offer something of value to the other; each is capable of communication and delivery; and each is free to accept or reject the offer. Exchanges take place when both parties expect to be better off after a transaction. The terms of the transaction will be influenced by economic, equity, and power considerations.

Organizations carry on exchanges with several publics. A public is a distinct group of people and/or organizations that has an actual or potential interest and/or impact on an organization. Publics can be classified as input publics (donors, suppliers, regulatory publics), internal publics (management, board, staff, volunteers), intermediary publics (merchants, agents, facilitators, marketing firms), and consuming publics (clients, local publics, activist publics, general public, media publics, and competitive publics). When the organization seeks some response from a public, we call it a market. A market is a distinct group of people and/or organizations that has resources which they want to exchange, or might conceivably be willing to exchange, for distinct benefits.

Responsive organizations are interested in their image because it is their image that people respond to. An organization's image is the sum of beliefs, ideas, and impressions that a person or group has of an object. Images can be measured by scaling techniques. Organizations can try to modify undesirable aspects of their image through changing their behavior and their communications.

The acid test of an organization's responsiveness is the satisfaction it creates. Organizations range from those which are unresponsive and casually responsive to those which are highly responsive and fully responsive. The more responsive organizations make use of complaint systems, surveys of satisfaction, surveys of needs and preferences, customer-oriented personnel, and empowered customers. Responsive organizations create more satisfaction for their publics. Satisfaction is a state felt by a person or group that has experienced organizational performance that has matched expectations.

---

## QUESTIONS

**1.** The environmental protection agency of an industrial state has as its mission "to clean up the environment for the citizens of our state." Evaluate the scope, feasibility, and distinctiveness of this mission.

**2.** A public hospital offers free prenatal courses on nutrition, exercise, infant care, and the birth process to expectant parents. How do the four conditions underlying exchange apply in this instance?

**3.** Develop a diagram similar to Figure 2–5 showing the publics of a hospital.

**4.** A group of supporters of the Equal Rights Amendment is seeking to get the legislature of a southern state to ratify the amendment. Identify the publics and markets this group must deal with and suggest what they might be able to offer to their markets in exchange for ratification.

**5.** The Cancer Information Office of the National Institutes of Health wants to promote the practice of breast self-examination for the early detection of breast cancer. Recommend several intermediaries for furthering this goal and give support for your recommendations.

**6.** The state consumer protection office in a major city is swamped with telephone calls from irate consumers who have been gypped or swindled in rather small transactions. The office feels that it can utilize its scarce resources best by prosecuting cases of larger magnitude that affect numerous consumers. What should the office do about the phone calls?

---

## NOTES

**1.** Bill Grady, "This Food Stamp Office Is Hiding," *Chicago Tribune,* May 22, 1980.

**2.** See Peter F. Drucker, *Management: Tasks, Responsibilities, Practices* (New York: Harper & Row, 1973), Chapter 7.

**3.** See Derek F. Abell, *Defining the Business: The Starting Point of Strategic Planning* (Englewood Cliffs, N.J.: Prentice-Hall, 1980), Chapter 2, esp. p. 17.

**4.** See C. Peter Wagner, *Your Church Can Grow* (Glendale, Calif.: G/L Publications, 1976), pp. 52–53. See also "Religion Inc.: 'Possibility Thinking' and Shrewd Marketing Pay Off for a Preacher," *Wall Street Journal,* August 26, 1976, p. 1.

**5.** See Philip Kotler and Sidney J. Levy, "Buying Is Marketing, Too," *Journal of Marketing,* January 1973, pp. 54–59.

**6.** Alternatively, the actor may judge the potential gain as the rate $B_i/C_i$ —in other words, as a rate of return on investment.

**7.** For additional reading, see John W. Huppertz, Sidney J. Arenson, and Richard H. Evans, "An Application of Equity Theory to Buyer–Seller Exchange Situations," *Journal of Marketing Research,* May 1978, pp. 250–60.

**8.** See Richard M. Emerson, "Power-Dependence Relations," *American Sociological Review,* February 1962, pp. 32–33.

**9.** For an interesting discussion of hospital boards, see Alfred R. Stern, "Instilling Activism in Trustees," *Harvard Business Review,* January–February 1980, pp. 24ff.

**10.** See David L. Sills, *The Volunteers—Means and Ends in a National Organization* (Glencoe, Ill.: Free Press, 1957). Also note that the National Center for Voluntary Action, 1785 Massachusetts Avenue, N.W., Washington, D.C. 20036, researches, runs seminars, and disseminates up-to-date techniques for managing volunteers.

**11.** Drucker, *Management,* p. 61.

**12.** C. E. Osgood, G. J. Suci, and P. H. Tannenbaum, *The Measurement of Meaning* (Urbana: University of Illinois Press, 1957). Other image-measuring tools exist, such as *object-sorting* (see W. A. Scott, "A Structure of Natural Cognitions," *Journal of Personality and Social Psychology,* Vol. 12, No. 4, 1969, pp. 261–78), *multidimensional scaling* (see Paul E. Green and Vithala R. Rao, *Applied Multidimensional Scaling,* New York: Holt, Rinehart and Winston, Inc., 1972), and *item lists* (see John W. Riley, Jr., ed., *The Corporation and Its Public,* New York: John Wiley & Sons, Inc., 1963, pp. 51–62).

**13.** See Anthony Downs, *Inside Bureaucracy* (Boston: Little, Brown, 1967).

**14.** Quoted from a speech given by Frank Sinclair at a public relations conference of hospital administrators.

**15.** Bernard J. Lachner, "Marketing—An Emerging Management Challenge," *Health Care Management Review,* Fall 1977, p. 27.

**16.** See Ralph E. Anderson, "Consumer Dissatisfaction: The Effect of Discomfirmed Expectancy on Perceived Product Performance," *Journal of Marketing Research,* February 1973, pp. 38–44.

**17.** See "Medical Ombudsmen: More Hospitals Move to Improve Service Through 'Advocates' Who Help Patients," *Wall Street Journal,* Friday, August 27, 1976.

# The
# Adaptive Organization:
# Developing
# Strategic Plans

The third largest charitable organization in the United States is the National Foundation. It accounts for 10 percent of the annual donations collected by national health agencies, exceeded only by the American Cancer Society (20 percent) and the American Heart Association (12 percent). Until 1958 its full name was the National Foundation for Infantile Paralysis. President Franklin D. Roosevelt founded the organization in 1938 to raise money to support research, education, and patient care in connection with the dreaded disease of infantile paralysis. President Roosevelt, himself a victim of polio, called for a "March of Dimes" to support the cause. The public responded generously, and their funds eventually produced a solution in the form of the Salk vaccine introduced in 1955 and, shortly thereafter, the oral Sabin vaccine. Within a short time, the disease was virtually eliminated and so, too, was the need for the National Foundation for Infantile Paralysis.

When an organization loses its mission, it is on the road to extinction. The National Foundation for Infantile Paralysis, however, decided not to give up, believing that it could contribute value to the society by using its vast army of volunteers to raise money for some other cause. The National Foundation for Infantile Paralysis identified a number of health causes that needed financial support and chose one—birth defects—that was consistent with its reputation for serving children who are victims of ill health. In 1958 it changed its name to the National Foundation and became the major charitable organization supporting research, education, and patient care for the victims of birth defects. The National Foundation realized that its essential strength was fundraising and it simply had to identify a new market for its services.

An organization, such as the National Foundation, may be highly responsive to its clients and yet fall into trouble. In a dynamic society, there is continuous change in demographic, economic, technological, political, and social forces. New client needs and wants appear, new competition emerges, social values change, new laws are passed, and radically different technostructures appear. The organization that sticks to its historical business may find itself serving a declining market. Organizational survival is not just a matter of being *efficient*—the National Foundation was efficient—but of being *adaptive*, that is, managing to do the appropriate things in the changing environment.

This chapter examines the characteristics of an adaptive organization. We define an adaptive organization as follows:

> An **adaptive organization** is one that operates systems for monitoring and interpreting important environmental changes and shows a readiness to revise its mission, objectives, strategies, organization, and systems to be maximally aligned with its opportunities.

Organizations vary considerably in their adaptiveness to change. Some of the main factors influencing the organization's adaptability are:

1. *Organization size.* Large organizations tend to be less adaptive than small organizations. Changing the direction of a battleship is much harder than changing the direction of a rowboat. The large organization has developed complex procedures for managing large groups of people, funds, equipment, and so on, and a substantial amount of work has to be done to produce a change in direction for the organization.

2. *Organization funds.* Organizations with smaller financial resources are slower to adapt than organizations with larger financial resources. Changing an organization costs money. Money is needed to carry out research on the contemplated change, to retrain management and employees, to hire new specialists that the organization needs, to build new internal systems for planning and control, and to inform the organization's publics about the new developments.

3. *Organization leadership.* Organizations run by the original founders tend to be less adaptive than organizations run by professional managers. The original founders have a vested interest in preserving the form of the organization which they designed because it was successful in the past and they understand it. Professional managers are more interested in making the organization work than in preserving its form.

4. *Organization constraints.* Organizations which are more subject to legal, political, and union constraints are less adaptive in the face of needed change. Highly regulated nonprofit and public organizations are going to be slower to change.

These factors indicate why organizations vary in their capacity to change. In this chapter, we will examine more deeply the need for adaptability and the tools for guiding change. Specifically, we will look at (1) the theory of the adaptive organization, (2) the nature of environmental change, (3) organizational responses to change, (4) organization life cycles, (5) strategic planning, and (6) marketing strategy.

## THE THEORY OF THE ADAPTIVE ORGANIZATION

In the ideal case, an organization finds itself operating in a hospitable environment. It has chosen appropriate objectives and has developed a strategy for achieving its objectives. It has developed a management structure that can effectively carry out the strategy. And it has constructed workable systems of information, planning, and control that yield the data and plans needed to stay on track. The ideal case can be illustrated as follows:

In most cases, this ideal alignment is not realized. The main problem is that these various components alter at different rates, resulting in a lack of fit. The most rapidly changing component is normally the environment. Such contemporary forces as rapid inflation, changing demographics, increased competition, increased government regulation, changing social behavior and values, and new technologies have led social commentators to call this "an age of discontinuity"[1] and "future shock."[2] Clearly, the environment's rate of change is faster than the ability of any organization to keep up with it. The result is that most organizations are less than optimally adapted to their environmental opportunities. Here is a typical situation:

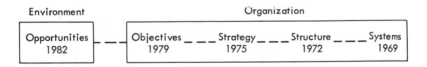

The particular organization is operating in a 1982 environment but with objectives that were chosen in 1979 and which are no longer appropriate. The organization's basic strategy has not changed since 1975. The management structure itself has not been modernized since 1972. Finally, the organization is using systems of information, planning, and control that were designed in 1969. We can go further and predict that the organization's strategy, structure, and systems are dictating what opportunities it sees and pursues, rather than the organization studying its total opportunities and adapting its objectives, strategy, structure, and systems to work in the new environment.

The chief hope for avoiding organization obsolescence is for an organization to look five or ten years into the future and ask where the environment is going, what the appropriate objectives would be in the emerging environment, what strategy would work, what organization structure is needed, and what systems would be required. It should start making the appropriate changes now. This is the logic underlying the new tool known as *strategic planning* which we shall examine later in this chapter. Before that, we want to look at two prior considerations, namely, the phenomenon of *environmental change* and the concept of *organization life cycles.*

---

## ENVIRONMENTAL CHANGE

Although an organization may be currently well matched to its environment, the ever present possibility of *environmental change* poses a potential threat to the organization's continued survival. The character of an organization's environment is as much or more of a determinant of its survival as the quality of its leadership.[3] Organizational environments range from the stable to the turbulent. We can distinguish four types of environments:[4]

1. *Stable and unchanging.* An organization might be lucky enough to find itself operating in a stable and unchanging environment. In this case, it can focus its attention on making the optimally efficient adaptation to this environment. Tactical planning is much more important than strategic planning in this type of environment. For example, telephone companies until recently operated in a stable environment and could safely invest great amounts of resources in this business in the interest of achieving maximally efficient telephone service.

2. *Stable with minor fluctuations.* Many organizations operate in an environment characterized by seasonal and/or cyclical fluctuations within a fairly stable framework. Thus, the U.S. Employment Service can follow a given set of procedures in handling the unemployed, only having to adjust its scale of operation with the level of unemployment.

3. *Slowly changing in a predictable fashion.* Other organizations recognize that their environments are slowly being transformed into something new and predictable. Thus, today's colleges can see a future environment of continuously rising costs and a shrinking pool of 18- to 22-year-olds. With this awareness, they can begin to make the necessary adjustments of their objectives, strategy, structure, and systems so they can continue to carry on meaningful work in the future.

4. *Rapidly changing in an unpredictable fashion.* Some organizations operate in highly turbulent and unpredictable environments. Thus, hospitals in recent years have experienced a succession of shocks and surprises: Medicare, new government constraints on hospital expansion, new forms of competition, rapidly changing medical technology, consumerism, and so on. Some hospitals have had to close while others have had to find creative ways to adjust to their new environment in order to survive. Strategic planning is much more important than tactical planning in this environment. It is more important for the organization to be *effective*—that is, to do the right things—than to be *efficient*—that is, to do them right.

Clearly, each successive environment listed above becomes increasingly difficult to operate in. What is worse, environments are tending to grow more turbulent over time. An organization that stubbornly or blindly maintains its form while its environment drastically changes is courting disaster. It faces the same fate as dinosaurs, which could not adapt to the new conditions of their new environment. The size of an organization, just like the size of a dinosaur, makes no difference to its chances of survival, and may even be a liability. The only thing that counts is whether the organization can adapt to the conditions and opportunities in the new environment.

## ORGANIZATIONAL RESPONSES TO CHANGE

Most organizations, when threatened, do not sit still. They attempt to respond, even though their response is not always appropriate or timely. In principle, an organization can respond to a challenge in four ways:

1. *Denial.* The organization can ignore or deny that a real change is occurring. Thus, many small private colleges still refuse to recognize the shrinking pool of students and how it will hurt them. They believe that they will survive difficult times and are not developing new strategies for the coming decade.
2. *Opposition.* The organization can try to fight, restrain, or reverse the unfavorable development. Thus, hospitals use their trade association to lobby against legislation that will dictate how much they can charge for their services and what services they can offer the public.
3. *Modification.* The organization can try to modify its own characteristics so that it is more attractive or efficient in the new environment. Thus, the Girl Scouts have shifted their programs toward developing the "new woman" rather than the "future mother."
4. *Relocation.* The organization can try to stay the same but shift its services to a more compatible environment. In recent years, the YMCA has increased its units in the suburbs and abandoned some of its units in the less hospitable inner city.

Pfeffer and Salancik have looked at the adaptation problem in terms of how an organization can lessen its *resource dependency.*[5] They have identified three specific modes by which organizations can improve their survival chances in a turbulent environment, namely, (1) gaining control of key resources, (2) establishing interorganizational alliances, and (3) altering the legal and social environment. We shall consider them here.

### GAINING CONTROL OF KEY RESOURCES

Organizations can strengthen their positions by gaining more control over critical resources. As an example, consider a *health maintenance organization* (HMO), which is a prepaid plan of health care services provided by a group of physicians. Suppose an HMO wishes to improve its resource position. One possibility is *vertical integration,* namely, trying to gain control over sources of supply *(backward integration)* or means of distribution *(forward integration).* For example, a large HMO might decide to operate its own school to train paramedics (backward integration). Or it might decide to buy a small hospital so that it is always assured of enough beds (forward integration).

Another strategy for dependency reduction is *horizontal integration.* The HMO might seek to acquire or merge with another HMO in order to increase its resources and clients.

Finally, the HMO might consider *diversification,* that is, entering additional businesses not related to its present business. For example, an HMO with a highly developed computerized management information system (MIS) might undertake to start a business to help other HMOs improve their MIS systems.

Making sound decisions on vertical integration, horizontal integration, and diversification all require substantial marketing information and analysis. Marketing can help answer such questions as: What are the opportunities and risks in the present business area? Which competitors would be the best for takeover; which other businesses would be attractive to enter? Thus, marketing offers a disciplined way to ask and answer critical questions regarding the organization's best dependency reduction strategies.

### ESTABLISHING INTERORGANIZATIONAL ALLIANCES

Another way in which an organization can adapt to a changing environment is by forming alliances with other organizations having similar interests and bringing their joint power to bear on the situation. Consider again the HMO. To increase its influence, the HMO can form a *trade association* or *professional association* with other HMOs in the same city. The association can take the form of a *coordinating council, advisory board,* or *cartel.* Another device is an *interlocking directorate* in which key persons are on the boards of directors of two or more HMOs. All of these interorganizational linkages increase the ability of the particular organization to survive.

Forging useful alliances calls for identifying organizations worth linking up with, and then "marketing" to them the advantages of an alliance. Thus, if the HMO wants to form an association of HMOs, it must apply marketing principles toward figuring out how to attract the other HMOs.

### ALTERING THE LEGAL AND SOCIAL ENVIRONMENT

Although the environment is largely beyond the organization's control—something to which organizations normally must adapt—organizations can exercise some influence on their environments. They can adjust their environment as well as adapt to it. They can attempt to influence or alter actual and potential legislation, regulatory procedures, and social sanctions in their favor. Thus, HMOs can send representatives to Congress to lobby against a proposed new bill regulating HMOs, or to lobby for a new bill that will finance HMOs. HMOs can also appoint influential people in the community to their boards in order to gain more allies in whatever causes they are pursuing. They can bring suits against hospitals that refuse cooperation to which they feel entitled. Organizations can take a number of steps to change or control the character of the environment in which they operate.

Marketing skills play an important role in these efforts, especially in the case of lobbying. Lobbying is essentially the marketing of a cause to the target audience known as legislators. Effective lobbyists get to know their market (legislators), build a reputation for providing dependable information, and act in a way to service their market. The effective lobbyist avoids going after the "single sale" and, instead, concentrates on building long-term goodwill and trust (see Chapter 20).

## ORGANIZATION LIFE CYCLES

An adaptive organization, through making timely and appropriate changes, increases its chances for survival. This does not mean, however, that it will enjoy continuous stability or growth. Organizations tend to pass through life cycle stages. Adaptability may help to prolong these phases or produce new life cycles. Figure 3–1 shows the four stages in the life cycle of a typical organization. The organization is founded at some point and grows slowly *(introduction stage)*. This is followed by a more rapid period of growth if the organization is successful *(growth stage)*. The growth eventually slows down and the organization enters maturity *(maturity stage)*. This is followed by a period of decline as long as the organization fails to find a new mission *(decline stage)*. This life cycle model has been used not only to describe organizations, but also the history of product categories, product forms, and brands.

The organization life cycle can be refined for each institutional sector through observing a large number of cases. Dr. John Shope, a church planning consultant, described the "theoretical life cycle of a church" as falling into eight stages:

Stage 1—The church is organized.
Stage 2—The nucleus of the church organization survives and grows slowly.
Stage 3—The growth rate increases due to the confidence of potential members being translated into church participation and membership.
Stage 4—The membership plateau. Membership in the church stabilizes and

## FIGURE 3–1
Typical S-Shaped Life Cycle Curve

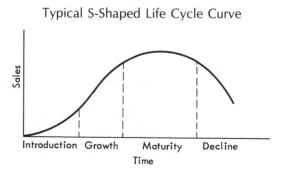

contentment and routine become obvious in the membership and church programs.
Stage 5—Initial decline—membership of the church declines, little is done to reverse
trend.
Stage 6—Rapid decline—membership decline accelerates, members find logical
excuses to join other churches.
Stage 7—Nothing but a small nucleus of members remain, the church is a financial
burden to those who stay.
Stage 8—Dissolution—the congregation disbands and the church dissolves.

This institutional life cycle, for example, describes accurately the history of
Second Presbyterian Church of Evanston, Illinois.[6]

> The Second Presbyterian Church of Evanston is a magnificent edifice built in
> 1926 in the then-affluent southeast Evanston at a time when South Evanston was
> synonymous with wealth and gracious living. After a slow start, membership started
> to grow rapidly and the eventually 1,300 adult voices gave life to the sanctuary.
> Eventually the character of South Evanston began to change. The monied Evanston
> social classes were dying or leaving for southern climes, to be replaced by less
> affluent, younger people who either were not interested in joining a Presbyterian
> church or were likely to move a bit farther north where two other Presbyterian
> churches were closer. In the mid-1960s, the church's Reverend David H. Pottie was
> attacked by minority groups as anti-Semitic and bigoted, and sidewalk demonstra-
> tions by human rights groups took place. Pottie resigned in 1967, and the church
> dropped almost 500 members in the next year. Shortages of funds led to the cutting
> of youth programs and as a result, young families never came for a second visit.
> Finally in 1977, the church was down to a membership of 200, with regular Sunday
> attendance of only 60 to 80 persons in a sanctuary built for 1,300. The church finally
> closed its doors in 1978, a victim of a changing neighborhood and social environ-
> ment.

When viewing these institutional life cycles, one must be cautious and
recognize possible exceptions. For example, the Second Presbyterian Church of
Evanston might still be flourishing today had it welcomed the new people coming
into the neighborhood, provided the right programs, had a dynamic minister, and
so on. In fact, some institutions enjoy a second life cycle as a result of the coming
of a new leader or other key development. There is nothing inevitable about
maturity leading in to decline. One of the major contributions of marketing
analysis is to identify new opportunities for an organization to return to a period
of healthy growth or extended maturity.

The growth stage of the organization's life cycle is particularly important to understand. Carman and Langeard have observed that the growth
stage of a service organization tends to consist of the five substages shown in
Figure 3–2.[7] The organization starts by successfully introducing a new service
to a single market segment. Thus a church starts by attracting a certain type
of member to its core service, namely, Sunday morning worship. Its strategy
for growth is to attract as many more similar members as possible. Over

## FIGURE 3–2

### Substages of the Growth Stage

| One core service one market segment | Growth through increasing peripheral service bundle | Growth through new geographic markets and/or new sociodemographic market segments | Growth through major innovative redesign of existing service | Growth through developing new core service for existing market segments |

time, the church adds peripheral services that will appeal to current and potential members, such as religious schooling, dances, bingo games, and so on. At some point, this church may decide to open a second church, in another geographic area to serve similar type members, or to start attracting new sociodemographic groups, such as black or hispanic members. Later, the church may undertake to redesign its physical plant and services to bring them more into line with the new groups it is servicing. Finally, the church may start some new core businesses, such as operating nursing homes or day care centers. The model does not say that all churches or institutions go through this particular sequence of growth stages, but describes a growth pattern that some organizations have exhibited.

---

## STRATEGIC PLANNING

Organizations that want to be adaptive are increasingly turning to strategic planning as the major systematic theory for adapting to change.[8] We define strategic planning as follows:

**Strategic planning** is the managerial process of developing and maintaining a strategic fit between the organization's goals and resources and its changing marketing opportunities.

Management has to pay attention to *market evolution* and *strategic fit*. All markets undergo evolutionary development marked by changing customer needs, technologies, competitors, channels, and laws. The organization should be looking out of a *strategic window* watching these changes and assessing the requirements for continued success in each market.[9] There is only a limited period when the fit between the requirements of a particular market and the organization's competencies is at an optimum. At these times the strategic window is open, and the organization should be investing in this market. In some subsequent period the organization will find that the evolutionary path of this market is such that it can no longer be effective and efficient in serving this market. It should then consider disinvesting and shifting its resources to areas of growing opportunity.

The major steps that an organization must take to remain strong in a changing environment are shown in Figure 3–3. First, the organization must carry out a careful analysis of its *environment,* both today's environment and tomorrow's probable environment, to ascertain its major opportunities and challenges. Then it must review its major *resources* as indicating what it can feasibly hope to do. The environment and resource analysis lead the organization to formulate new and appropriate *goals* to pursue in the coming planning period. Goal formulation is followed by *strategy formulation* in which the management chooses the most cost-effective strategy for reaching its goals. Its strategy will undoubtedly point to certain changes that must be made in the *organization's structure.* Finally, attention is turned to improving the organization's *systems* of information, planning, and control to permit carrying out the strategy effectively. When all of these components are aligned, they spell performance.

Strategic planning should be carried out at each major level in the organization. Consider, for example, a major university. First, the president and vice presidents should carry out strategic planning as it affects the university as a whole. Then each dean of a school (liberal arts school, business school, music school, and so on) should carry out strategic planning as it affects the future of that school. Then the chairman of each department within each school can carry out strategic planning for that department. If the university operates branches in different locations, each branch should carry out strategic planning. In general, strategic planning should begin at the *corporate* level, then move to *divisional levels,* then to *product market levels,* and finally to *geographical areas.*

We will now examine and illustrate each step of the strategic planning process shown in Figure 3–3, using colleges as the major example.

### ENVIRONMENTAL ANALYSIS

The first step in strategic planning is to analyze the environment in which the organization operates, trying to identify the leading trends and their implications for the organization. If the organization is going to adapt, it must figure out what to adapt to. An internal committee and/or external consultant should be charged with the task of studying the changing environment.

### FIGURE 3–3

Strategic Market Planning Process

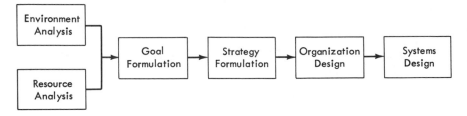

**Major components of the organization's environment.**     The environment in which an organization operates is complex and constantly changing. The environment consists of five components:

1. *Internal environment,* consisting of the internal publics of the organization, specifically, the *board of directors, management, staff,* and *volunteers.* The task is to examine their needs, wants, and interests. For example, a move on the part of a college faculty toward unionization will warrant a quick and thoughtful response by management because unionization can change the economics and decision latitude of the organization and its ability to serve its core market.

2. *Market environment,* consisting of the groups and other organizations that the focal organization directly works with to accomplish its mission. The main groups in the market environment are the *clients, marketing intermediaries, suppliers,* and *supporters.* The focal organization must monitor trends and changes in the needs, perceptions, preferences, and satisfactions of these key groups.

3. *Public environment,* consisting of other groups and organizations that take an interest in the activities of the focal organization. The public environment consists of *local publics, activist publics,* the *general public, media publics,* and *regulatory agencies* whose actions can affect the welfare of the focal organization.

4. *Competitive environment,* consisting of groups and organizations that compete for attention and loyalty from the audiences of the focal organization. The competitive environment includes *desire competitors, generic competitors, form competitors,* and *enterprise competitors.*

5. *Macroenvironment,* consisting of large-scale fundamental forces that shape opportunities and pose threats to the focal organization. The main macroenvironmental forces that have to be watched are the *demographic, economic, technological, political,* and *social* forces. These forces largely represent "uncontrollables" in the organization's situation to which it has to adapt.

**Method of analyzing environmental components.**     Management should research each major environment component following a three-step procedure. The procedure consists of (1) listing the major factors and subfactors making up the environment component, (2) describing the major trends in each factor, (3) describing the implications of these trends for the organization, and (4) converting these implications into specific opportunities and threats. For example, one component of the macroenvironment is the demographic component, which can be broken into five factors, namely, the birthrate, life expectancy, marital status, median age at first marriage, and population density. The trends in each factor can be identified along with their implications for the organization. Thus, the trend toward increasing life expectancy has several implications for colleges, hospitals, and other organizations. The final step is to turn these implications into concrete threats and opportunities that the organization must consider.

THREAT ANALYSIS.     Every organization must attempt to identify the major threats it faces. We define threat as follows:

An **environmental threat** is a challenge posed by an unfavorable trend or specific disturbance in the environment which would lead, in the absence of purposeful marketing action, to the stagnation, decline, or demise of an organization or one of its products.

Not all threats warrant the same attention or concern. Managers should assess each threat according to two dimensions: (1) its *potential severity* (measured by the amount of money the organization would lose if the threat materialized), and (2) its *probability of occurrence.* Suppose the president of a private college identified the following four threats:

1. The college next year might suffer an enrollment decline of 20 percent in its liberal arts program.
2. The college's cost of operation—heating, lighting, salaries, and so on—might rise 15 percent next year.
3. The college might lose the support of a major donor who has given the college $100,000 in each of the last five years.
4. The college might lose its tax-exempt status in connection with a restaurant that it operates on the campus.

These threats have to be evaluated according to their potential severity and probability of occurrence. Suppose the results are those shown in Figure 3–4A. The most serious threats are those shown in the upper left cell, and they require the administration to come up with contingency plans. The least serious threats are shown in the lower right cell and the administration can safely ignore them. The other two cells contain threats of medium seriousness and the administration should at least monitor them, although contingency plans are not necessary. By identifying and classifying threats, the administration knows which environmental developments to plan for, monitor, or ignore.

OPPORTUNITY ANALYSIS.   Opportunity analysis is as important as threat analysis, and probably more important. By managing its threats successfully, an organization stays intact but it doesn't grow. But by managing its opportunities successfully, the organization can make great strides forward. Here we are con-

## FIGURE 3–4

Threat and Opportunity Matrices

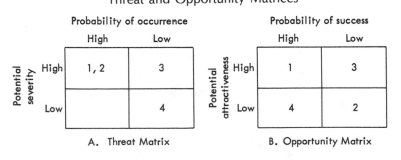

A. Threat Matrix          B. Opportunity Matrix

cerned with marketing opportunities. We define marketing opportunity as follows:

> A **marketing opportunity** is an attractive arena of relevant marketing action in which a particular organization is likely to enjoy superior competitive advantages.

Every level of management in an organization should make an effort to identify several opportunities facing the organization. Suppose the president of the private college perceives the following opportunities:

1. The college could start an undergraduate business school to capitalize on the growing demand for business education.
2. The college could start a nursing program to meet the growing need for trained nurses.
3. The college could open a branch campus in a nearby city.
4. The college could start an evening noncredit program featuring skill and leisure courses.

Not all opportunities are equally attractive. An opportunity can be assessed in terms of two basic dimensions: (1) its *potential attractiveness* (measured by the amount of revenue or other results that an organization might value), and (2) its *success probability* (measured by the ability of the organization to develop the opportunity). The results of assessing the preceding opportunities is shown in the opportunity matrix of Figure 3–4B. Opening a business school seems to be the best opportunity for the college since it will produce a good revenue stream *and* the college has a high probability of running a successful business school. Opportunities in the upper left cell deserve specific plans to be designed. On the other hand, the nursing program falls in the lower right cell, which means it should be rejected since it could be costly to develop and is not likely to be successful. Opportunities in the other two cells are worth monitoring, although specific planning is not warranted.

All the levels of management in an organization should be required to develop each year their own list and evaluation of the major opportunities and threats facing their unit. In this way, they will become habituated to thinking in future terms and in opportunity terms. Furthermore, their superiors can review these lists and raise questions and be alerted to problems. The activity of identifying threats and opportunities can result in four different findings on the organization's situation. The organization might be lucky and find that it faces many strong opportunities and few threats (an ideal situation). It might find that it faces strong opportunities and strong threats (a speculative situation). It might find that it faces only strong threats (a threatening situation). Or it might find that it faces neither significant threats nor opportunities (a mature situation).

Following the environmental analysis, management should undertake an analysis of its resources and capabilities. The purpose is to identify the major resources that the organization has (its *strengths*) and lacks (its *weaknesses*). The premise is that an organization should pursue goals, opportunities, and strategies which are suggested by, or congruent with, its strengths and avoid those where its resources are too weak.

Figure 3–5 shows a form that the organization can use, with appropriate changes, to develop a *resource audit.* The major resources listed are people, money, facilities, systems, and market assets. Management indicates whether its position with respect to each resource constitutes a strength (high, medium, low), is neutral, or constitutes a weakness (low, medium, high). Suppose the checks reflect the college's evaluation of its resources. The college believes that it has very adequate and skilled personnel who, unfortunately, are not very enthusiastic, loyal, or service-minded. As for money, the college has enough for its operations but most funds are committed, and therefore the college does not have the flexibility to take on many new projects. The college's facilities are adequate, flexible, and well located. Its management systems for information, planning, and control are quite weak. Finally, it is in a strong position with respect to customers, donors, contacts, and general reputation.

In considering opportunities, the organization should generally avoid those for which necessary resources are weak or inadequate. If the college is considering a nursing program but its science faculty is weak, it should probably drop the idea, because a good science faculty is critical to a successful nursing program. But a weakness is not fatal to a project if the organization can see a way to acquire the resources it needs. If the college has the funds to hire or build a good science faculty, it might consider going ahead with the nursing program.

As a clue to its best opportunities, the organization should pay attention to its distinctive competences. *Distinctive competences* are those *resources and abilities that the organization is especially strong in.* If the private college happens to have a strong foreign language program, it might want to consider such opportunities as starting an international studies program or an evening noncredit language program. Organizations will find it easiest to work from their strengths rather than trying to build up a more balanced set of strengths. At the same time, a distinctive competence may not be enough if the organization's major competitors possess the same distinctive competence. The organization should pay attention to those strengths in which it possesses a *differential advantage*—that is, it can outperform competitors on that dimension. For example, Georgetown University not only has a distinctive competence in international studies, but its location in Washington, D.C., gives it a differential advantage in pursuing preeminence in international studies.

In evaluating its strengths and weaknesses, the organization must not rely on its own perceptions, but must go out and do an *image study* of how it is

# FIGURE 3–5

## Organization Resource Analysis

| Resource | Strength | | | | Weakness | | |
|---|---|---|---|---|---|---|---|
| | H | M | L | N | L | M | H |
| **People** | | | | | | | |
| 1. Adequate? | ✓ | | | | | | |
| 2. Skilled? | ✓ | | | | | | |
| 3. Enthusiastic? | | | | | | ✓ | |
| 4. Loyal? | | | | | | | ✓ |
| 5. Service-minded? | | | | | | ✓ | |
| **Money** | | | | | | | |
| 1. Adequate? | | | ✓ | | | | |
| 2. Flexible? | | | | | ✓ | | |
| **Facilities** | | | | | | | |
| 1. Adequate? | ✓ | | | | | | |
| 2. Flexible? | ✓ | | | | | | |
| 3. Location quality? | ✓ | | | | | | |
| **Systems** | | | | | | | |
| 1. Information system quality? | | | | | ✓ | | |
| 2. Planning system quality? | | | | | | ✓ | |
| 3. Control system quality? | | | | | | ✓ | |
| **Market assets** | | | | | | | |
| 1. Customer base? | | ✓ | | | | | |
| 2. Donor base? | | ✓ | | | | | |
| 3. Contact base? | ✓ | | | | | | |
| 4. General reputation? | | ✓ | | | | | |

Note:  H = high; M = medium; L = low; N = neutral.
Checks ✓ are illustrative.

perceived by its key publics. For example, the college's administration may think that the college has a fine reputation in the hard sciences, but an image study might reveal that high school counselors see the college's main strength as the humanities. A college should study how different key publics—students, parents, business firms, and so on—see its strengths and weaknesses. The findings might indicate certain strengths and weaknesses that the college is not aware of, and other strengths and weaknesses that it exaggerated.

## GOAL FORMULATION

The environment and resource analyses are designed to provide the necessary background and stimulus to management thinking about its basic goals as an organization. Every organization at its inception is clear about its goals. However, as it grows and accomplishes many things, and the environment changes and presents new challenges, management must review and reassess its goals. In some organizations, a review will convince management that its current goal structure is clear, relevant, and effective. Other organizations will find their goals clear but of diminishing appropriateness to the new environment and resource situation. Still other organizations will discover that their goals are no longer even clear and that the organization is drifting.

The purpose of developing a clear set of organizational goals is to keep the organization from drifting into an uncertain future. Management must assess the future environment and decide what it wants to accomplish in the coming planning period. The organization needs to have a clear picture of what kind of organization it wants to look like at the end of the decade. Goals enable the organization to determine what it should be doing, develop effective plans, set objectives for individuals' performances, and evaluate results. Without goals, anything the organization does or achieves can be considered acceptable; there is no standard for planning or control.

The issue of organizational goals breaks into two distinct steps, namely, (1) determining what the current goals are, and (2) determining what the goals should be. Even the image of the current goals will differ from person to person and group to group in the organization. The president of a college may see the primary goal as upgrading the quality of the student body, the vice president of admissions may see the primary goal as increasing the size of the student body, and the vice president of finance may see the primary goal as increasing the number of nonscholarship students in relation to scholarship students. The faculty as a whole may pursue the goal of a reduced teaching load to permit more time for research, whereas the administration may adopt the goal of an increased teaching load to reduce the cost of education. To discover the current goals requires interviewing several individuals and groups as to what they think the institution's goals and their own goals are, and trying to make sense out of the resulting data. The data will show that the organization is really a coalition of several groups, each giving and seeking different things from the organization.

Determining what the goals of the organization should be is even a harder task. In principle, the president and/or the board of a college can unilaterally set new goals for the college for the next decade. Increasingly, however, top management has found it useful to involve other publics in the process of goal formulation for the organization, such as employees, members, and other constituencies. Their ideas on proper goals may not only be valuable, but are more likely to be embraced and supported because of their involvement in the goal formulation process.

Goal formulation involves the organization in determining an appropriate mission, objectives, and goals for the current or expected environment. The three terms are distinguished below:

- *Mission:* the basic purpose of an organization, that is, what it is trying to accomplish.
- *Objective:* a major variable which the organization will emphasize, such as market share, profitability, reputation.
- *Goal:* an objective of the organization that is made specific with respect to magnitude, time, and who is responsible.

We shall examine these concepts in the following paragraphs.

**Mission.**    An organization's mission is usually clear in the beginning. Over time, however, its mission may become unclear as the organization grows and develops new products and markets. Or the mission may remain clear but some managers may have lost their interest in the mission. Or the mission may remain clear but may lose its appropriateness to new conditions in the environment.

For these reasons, an organization should reexamine its mission from time to time. Consider Beloit College, a small private college in southern Wisconsin. Clearly, Beloit is in the *educational business.* But so are Harvard, Vassar, Indiana University, Oakton Community College, and Oral Roberts University. Beloit has to define a particular concept or brand of education that meets the needs of some group. Beloit was in the *liberal arts business,* but in the late 1960s a pure liberal arts education was losing its attractiveness to students. So the college introduced the Beloit Plan, which put it into the *experiential education business*—namely, its students would spend some time out of the classroom to learn about the world. This did not succeed in attracting enough students, and more recently Beloit moved to the *applied liberal arts education business* with an emphasis on career preparation through the liberal arts. Some colleges have responded differently, by moving into the *college fun and games business,* believing that today's students want a good time and a prolongation of their adolescence.

Each mission implies a particular type of customer and calls for a particular way of rendering value to the customer. If Beloit wants to be in the liberal arts business, its main appeal will be to students who enjoy the life of the mind. Beloit would invest in intellectually stimulating professors, a large library, good bookstores on the campus, small classes, intellectual events on campus, and so on. This would put Beloit in direct competition with such colleges as the University of Chicago, St. John's, Oberlin, and Swarthmore. Beloit must believe that the intellectual market is large enough and that it has the resources and potential reputation to compete effectively for a reasonable share of those students seeking intellectual training.

On the other hand, if Beloit chooses to be in the applied liberal arts business, it would promote itself to those students who place high value on career preparation. Beloit would select careers to specialize in—law, medicine, business, engineering—and build educational programs to include solid classroom work plus field experience and visiting practitioners. Beloit would build a major network of contacts with businesses and the professions so that it could draw on these resources to hire students. Thus, developing a clear definition of its mission will lead Beloit—or any institution—to emphasize certain things and deemphasize others. Defining its mission is critically important, because it affects everything else.

A growing number of organizations have taken to writing formal *mission statements* to gain the needed clarity. A well-worked-out mission statement provides everyone in the organization with a shared sense of purpose, direction, significance, and achievement. The mission statement acts as an "invisible hand" which guides widely scattered employees to work independently and yet collectively toward the realization of the organization's goals.

Unfortunately, it is not easy to write a meaningful mission statement. An executive committee will have to hold many meetings and survey many people before it can prepare a meaningful mission statement. The time is not wasted because, in the process, management will discover a lot about the institution and its best opportunities. The mission statement should serve the organization for many years. The mission is not something to change every few years in response to environmental changes or new unrelated opportunities. On the other hand, sometimes an organization has to reconsider its mission if it no longer works or it does not define an optimal course for the organization.

**Objectives.**     The mission of an institution suggests more about where that institution "is coming from" than where "it is going to." It describes what the institution is about rather than the specific objectives and goals it will pursue in the coming period. Each institution has to develop major objectives and goals for the coming period separate from but consistent with its mission statement.

For every type of institution, there is always a potential set of relevant objectives, and the institution's task is to make a choice among them. For example, the objectives of interest to a college are: *increased national reputation, improved classroom teaching, higher enrollment, higher quality students, increased efficiency, larger endowment, improved student social life, improved physical plant, lower operating deficit,* and so on. A college cannot successfully pursue all of these objectives simultaneously because of a limited budget and because some of them are incompatible, such as increased cost efficiency and improved classroom teaching. In any given year, therefore, institutions will choose to emphasize certain objectives and either ignore others or treat them as constraints. For example, if Beloit's enrollment continues to fall, Beloit will make increased enrollment a paramount objective subject to not letting student quality fall below a certain level. Thus, an institution's major objectives can vary from year to year depending on the administration's perception of the major problems that the institution must address at that time.

**Goals.**     The chosen objectives must be restated in an operational and measurable form called *goals.* The objective "increased enrollment" must be turned into a goal, such as "a 15 percent enrollment increase in next year's Fall class." A goal statement permits the institution to think about the planning, programming, and control aspects of pursuing that objective. Such questions arise as: Is a 15 percent enrollment increase feasible? What strategy would be used? What resources would it take? What activities would have to be carried out? Who would be responsible and accountable? All of these critical questions must be answered when deciding whether to adopt a proposed goal.

Typically, the institution will be evaluating a large set of potential goals at the same time and examining their consistency. The institution may discover that it cannot simultaneously achieve "a 15 percent enrollment increase," "a 10 percent increase in student quality," and a "12 percent tuition increase" at the same time. In this case, the executive committee may make adjustments in the target levels or target dates, or drop certain goals altogether in order to arrive at a meaningful and achievable set of goals. Once the set of goals are agreed upon in the goal formulation stage, the organization is ready to move on to the detailed work of strategy formulation.[10]

## STRATEGY FORMULATION

Strategy formulation calls for the organization to develop a strategy for achieving its goals. The college may discover that it cannot find a feasible strategy to deliver this enrollment increase. If so, it will have to revise its goals. Goals and strategies interact closely and planners may have to move back and forth in determining a final set of goals and strategies.

In seeking feasible strategies, the organization should proceed in two stages. First, it should develop a *product portfolio strategy,* that is, decide what to do with each of its current major products. Second, it should develop a *product/market expansion strategy,* that is, decide what new products and markets to add.

**Product portfolio strategy.**     Most organizations are multiproduct organizations. They usually start with one product (program, service, etc.) and over time add other products. Thus a major university will operate, in addition to a school of liberal arts, such schools as a law school, music school, engineering school, and so on. It may add an evening program and later a weekend program. Similarly, a hospital will consist of several inpatient departments as well as an ambulatory care facility and possibly a health maintenance organization. As another illustration, the YMCA operates a large number of businesses: hotels, schools, camps, recreational facilities, and so on. In fact, the YMCA has been called the "General Electric of social services."

An organization's programs will vary in their importance and contribution to the organization's mission. Some programs are large, others small; some grow-ing, some declining; some of high quality, others of low quality. The various programs will be in different stages of their *life cycle* (or *periodic cycle*) and warrant different strategies, funding, and attention.

Most organizations find it easier to add new programs to their product mix than to remove failing programs. Existing programs have built-in advocates who argue for equal or proportionate resources from the administration. Thus, the foreign languages faculty at a college will resist efforts to scale down their size even though foreign language enrollment continues to decline. In periods of economic prosperity, the institution may have enough money to satisfy everyone. All programs tend to get some increase in funds. The top administration does not want to make enemies and settles for an inefficient allocation of resources. How-ever, in periods of economic slowdown or decline, the administration is forced to make hard choices because there is not enough money to make everyone happy. Part of adaptation is to eliminate weak programs which would otherwise act as a drag on the institution.

An increasing number of organizations are being forced to make hard-nosed evaluations of the programs in their portfolio. The term "portfolio" comes from the image of an investment portfolio. An investor reviews his investments from time to time and eliminates some, scales down others, scales up still others, and adds new ones. By analogy, an organization should critically review its product portfolio at periodic intervals and make hard decisions about the future of its various products.

The first step in portfolio analysis is to identify the key businesses, pro-grams, or products of the organization. For example, a college might choose to view its portfolio as consisting of its academic departments such as history, economics, philosophy, psychology, geography, and so on. This is an appropriate level of analysis if each department has its own leadership, adopts distinct goals, faces competition inside and outside, needs a strategy, and has a separate budget.

The task of the administration is to determine which departments should be given increased support *(build),* maintained at the present level *(hold),* phased down *(harvest),* and terminated *(divest).* The principle is that the institution's resources should be allocated in accordance with the "attractiveness" of each program rather than equally to all programs. The task is to identify appropriate criteria for evaluating the attractiveness of various programs. And, here, different schemes have been proposed. We shall examine three of them.

BOSTON CONSULTING GROUP PORTFOLIO APPROACH.    One of the earliest and most popular portfolio evaluation approaches was developed by the Boston Consulting Group (BCG), a management consulting group. Its scheme called for rating all of the organization's products along two dimensions, namely, *market growth* and *market share* (see Figure 3–6). Market growth is the annual rate of growth of the relevant market in which the product is sold. Market share is the

FIGURE 3–6

Boston Consulting Group Portfolio Approach

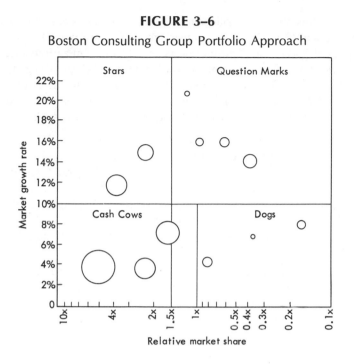

organization's sales as a ratio to the leading firm's sales.[11] By dividing market growth into high growth and low growth, and market share into high share and low share, four types of products (businesses, programs) emerge:

1. An organization's *stars* are those products for which the organization enjoys a high share in fast-growing markets. The organization will pour increasing resources into its stars in order to keep up with the market's growth and maintain its share leadership.

2. An organization's *cash cows* are those products for which the organization enjoys a high share in slow-growth markets. Cash cows typically yield strong cash flows to an organization which pay the bill for those other products that lose money. Without cash cows, an organization would need continuous subsidy.

3. An organization's *question marks* are those products for which the organization has only a small share in a fast-growing market. The organization faces the decision of whether to increase its investment in its question mark products, hoping to make them stars, or to reduce or terminate its investment, on the grounds that the funds could find better use elsewhere in the business.

4. An organization's *dogs* are those products that have a small market share in slow-growth or declining markets. Dogs usually make little money or lose money for the organization. Organizations often consider shrinking or dropping dogs unless they are necessary to offer for other reasons.

Applying this scheme, a college might find that its business school is a star, its engineering school a cash cow, its music school a question mark, and its school of education a dog. The BCG evaluation is useful for organizations interested in tracing the cash implications of their product portfolios. High sales generate cash and high growth consumes cash. Nonprofit organizations, to the extent that they are not seeking rapid growth or high market share, are less interested in these criteria for evaluating current products, and seek a different set of criteria.

GENERAL ELECTRIC APPROACH.    General Electric (GE) has formulated another approach to portfolio evaluation that has more applicability to nonprofit organizations. They call it the *strategic business planning grid* (see Figure 3–7). It uses two basic dimensions, *market attractiveness* and *organizational strength*. The best programs to offer are those which serve attractive markets and for which the organization has high organizational strength.

Market attractiveness is a composite index made up of such factors as

- *Market size.* Large markets are more attractive than small markets.
- *Market growth rate.* High-growth markets are more attractive than low-growth markets.
- *Profit margin.* High-profit-margin programs are more attractive than low-profit-margin programs.
- *Competitive intensity.* Markets with many strong competitors are less attractive than markets with a few weak competitors.
- *Cyclicality.* Highly cyclical markets are less attractive than cyclically stable markets.
- *Seasonality.* Highly seasonal markets are less attractive than nonseasonal markets.
- *Scale economies.* Programs where unit costs fall with large volume production and marketing are more attractive than constant cost programs.
- *Learning curve.* Programs where unit costs fall as management accumulates experience in production and distribution are more attractive than programs where management has reached the limit of its learning.

Organizational strength is a composite index made up of such factors as

- *Program quality.* The higher the program quality relative to competitors, the greater its organizational strength.
- *Efficiency level.* The more efficient the organization is at producing the program relative to competitors, the greater its organizational strength.
- *Market knowledge.* The deeper the organization's knowledge of customers in that market and their needs and wants, the greater its organizational strength.
- *Marketing effectiveness.* The greater the organization's marketing effectiveness, the greater its organizational strength.

The factors making up each dimension are scaled and weighted so that each current program achieves a number indicating its market attractiveness and organizational strength and therefore can be plotted in the grid.

## FIGURE 3-7

### General Electric Portfolio Approach
### (Called the Strategic Business Planning Grid)

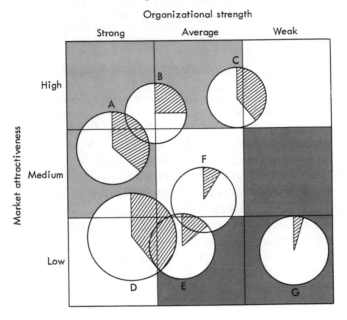

The grid is divided into three zones—green, yellow, and red. The green zone consists of the three cells at the upper left, indicating those programs that are located in attractive markets and for which there is organizational strength. The implication is that the organization should "invest and grow" these programs. The yellow zone consists of the diagonal cells stretching from the lower left to the upper right, indicating programs that are medium in overall attractiveness. The organization usually spends enough to maintain these products, rather than expanding or contracting them. The red zone consist of the three cells on the lower right, indicating those programs that are low in overall attractiveness. Here the organization gives serious consideration to harvesting or divesting.

As an example, consider program G shown in Figure 3-7. The graph indicates that program G is in an unattractive market and the organization does not have strong strengths to bring to it. It is a fairly large volume product (indicated by the size of the circle) and the organization has only a small market share (indicated by the shaded wedge). The organization will want to consider phasing this product down or out.

ACADEMIC PORTFOLIO APPROACH. Nonprofit organizations may want to build their own portfolio evaluation models, using the preceding ones as suggestive. The task calls for identifying appropriate criteria for judging the programs offered by that type of institution. As an example, consider a college administration trying to determine how much support to give to each academic department. One college developed the following criteria:

- *Centrality.* The degree to which an academic program is central to the mission of the college.
- *Quality.* The quality and reputation of the academic department relative to those in other colleges.
- *Market viability.* The degree to which the market for the academic program is sufficient in size and growth.

The three criteria can be combined in the grid shown in Figure 3–8. Each criterion is divided into high, medium, and low. (Market viability is represented by MV and its level is represented by H, M, or L, for high, medium, or low, respectively.) According to Figure 3–8, the administration rates the psychology department high in centrality, quality, and market viability. Because the psychology department is one of the stars, the administration may want to increase its budget further. On the other hand, classical languages' rating fell in the lower right. The administration feels that classical languages are not central to its purpose, that the faculty is poor, and that the market viability is low insofar as few students enroll in the course. The administration will give serious thought to reducing or dropping classical languages.

## FIGURE 3–8

### Academic Portfolio Model

Centrality

|  |  | High | Medium | Low |
|---|---|---|---|---|
| Quality | High | Psychology (MV–H)<br>Decision:<br>•Build size<br>•Build quality |  | Home Economics (MV–H)<br>Decision:<br>•Build size<br>•Build quality |
|  | Medium |  | Geography (MV–M)<br>Decision:<br>•Hold size<br>•Hold quality |  |
|  | Low | Philosophy (MV–L)<br>Decision:<br>•Reduce size<br>•Build quality |  | Classical Languages (MV–L)<br>Decision:<br>•Reduce size or terminate |

A major benefit of this analysis is to help the college identify the real stars so that they can be built further and its real dogs so that they can be scaled down or terminated. Final decisions will require additional information and discussion. In the case of classical languages, for example, the faculty may be tenured and therefore cannot be terminated. Or the department may be given one year to try to increase enrollment through "marketing" its program to students. Or the classical language faculty may be asked to teach some basic English courses to make up for its lighter teaching loads in classics. The academic portfolio evaluation model simply signals opportunities, problems, and possible solutions, and each case has to be thought through on its merits.[12]

**Product/market expansion strategy.** As a result of examining its current portfolio of products, an organization might discover that it does not have enough stars or cash cows and that it must become more aggressive in searching for new products and markets. For example, the YMCA is finding that some of its former strong cash cows—adult recreation, for example—are turning into weak cash cows or dogs, posing the problem of how the YMCA is going to subsidize its other programs which lose money. In other words, the YMCA needs new cash-generating programs to help support its cash-draining programs.

Needed is a systematic approach to opportunity identification. A useful device for doing this is known as the product/market opportunity matrix (see Figure 3–9).[13] Originally a 2-by-2 matrix proposed by Ansoff, here it is expanded into a 3-by-3 matrix. Markets are listed at the left and products along the top.

Each cell in Figure 3–9 has a name. Potential opportunities—in this case, for a college—are listed in small letters. The administration should first consider cell 1, called *market penetration*. This cell raises the question of whether the college can maintain or expand its enrollment by deepening its penetration into its existing markets with its existing products. If further market penetration does not look hopeful, then it will have to look for ideas in another cell.

Cell 2 raises the question of whether the college should consider expanding into new geographical markets with its existing products. The college could open a branch in another part of the city, or in a new city, or start a new campus in another country. Southern Methodist of Dallas is offering courses in its M.B.A. program in Houston. Similarly, Notre Dame now grants an M.B.A. in London, and Antioch operates campuses in several countries.

The administration then moves to cell 3 and considers possibly offering its existing products to new individual and institutional markets. Colleges are increasingly recruiting nontraditional student groups, such as senior citizens, homemakers, and ethnic minorities. For instance, Iowa State University has instituted "Eldercollege," which is a program for retired and older adults meeting once a week for two months. In addition, colleges are trying to interest business firms, social agencies, and other organizations in buying educational and training programs to be delivered in-house by the faculty.

Next, the administration can consider whether it should modify some of its

## FIGURE 3-9

### Product/Market Opportunity Matrix

Products

| | Existing | Modified | New |
|---|---|---|---|
| **Existing** | 1. Market Penetration | 4. Product Modification<br>• short courses<br>• evening program<br>• weekend program<br>• new delivery system | 7. Product Innovation<br>• new courses<br>• new departments<br>• new schools |
| **Geographical** | 2. Geographical Expansion<br>• new areas of city<br>• new cities<br>• foreign | 5. Modification for Dispersed Markets<br>• programs offered on military bases or at U.S.-based firms abroad | 8. Geographical Innovation |
| **New** | 3. New Markets<br>A. Individual<br>  • senior citizens<br>  • homemakers<br>  • ethnic minorities<br>B. Institutional<br>  • business firms<br>  • social agencies | 6. Modification for New Markets<br>A. Individual<br>  • senior citizens<br>  • homemakers<br>  • ethnic minorities<br>B. Institutional<br>  • business<br>  • government | 9. Total Innovation<br>• new courses<br>• new departments<br>• new schools |

Markets

current products to attract more of the existing market (cell 4). Standard courses can be shortened, or offered in the evening or on weekends. For example, Alverno College, a private women's school in Milwaukee, instituted a weekend college and drew large numbers of housewives and employed women. Some colleges are beginning to offer courses in the late late evening or early early morning, having discovered a number of working people for whom these hours would be more convenient.

Cell 5 is named *modification for dispersed markets.* The University of Maryland, for example, offers modified programs for members of the armed forces both domestically and abroad.

*Modification for new markets* (cell 6) may be a more realistic growth approach for colleges and universities. To penetrate the senior citizen market, for example, may require a modification of standard courses. Specifically, the time period might need to be shorter and less reading might be required, with more comfortable seats and probably books with larger print.

*Product innovation* (cell 7) involves developing new courses, departments, or schools for existing markets. For example, a business school might develop a new program in managing nonprofit organizations to offer to its students.

*Geographical innovation* (cell 8) involves finding new ways to serve new geographical areas. For instance, Illinois Bell has developed an electronic blackboard that allows a professor to write on a blackboard in one location and have it transmitted over telephone lines to a distant city. With the advent of home computers, interactive television, and other new media technologies, it will be possible to offer courses to a national audience.

The final category, *total innovation,* refers to offering new products for new markets. The "university without walls" college where learning takes place away from a campus is an example.

The product/market opportunity matrix helps the administration imagine new opportunities in a systematic way. These opportunities are evaluated and the better ones pursued. The results of the product/market analysis and the previous portfolio analysis allow the organization to formulate its strategic plans.

## ORGANIZATION DESIGN

The purpose of strategy formulation is to develop strategies that will help the organization achieve its goals in the new environment. The existing organization must be capable of carrying out these strategies. It must have the *structure, people,* and *culture* to implement the strategy successfully. For example, if a college plans to open new branch campuses, it should have a staff that is skilled in locating real estate, negotiating land purchase, and developing facilities. If the college plans to build a reputation in the hard sciences, it will need a faculty that is strong in the hard sciences. Clearly, an organization's chosen strategies require appropriate organizational skills to succeed. Most organization theorists believe that "structure should follow strategy."[14]

At the same time, organizational structures are hard to change. Vested interests build up over time in any organization. If a college administration wants to start an undergraduate business school, the liberal arts faculty may oppose it. They will rail about not diluting general education. But behind this is their fear that students will transfer from majoring in their areas to majoring in business. The president will have to develop a plan to market the organizational change. If the president fails, then the organization is stuck with the old situation in spite of the new environment. Only strategies compatible with the existing organization would be accepted. In this case, "strategy follows structure," and the institution has limited its adaptiveness in order to satisfy internal constituents.

Under dynamic strategic planning, not only is it necessary to transform the organizational structure in the direction required by the strategic plan, but it may also be necessary to retrain or change some of the people who occupy sensitive positions in the organization. Thus, if a private college decides to change its fundraising strategy from reliance on wealthy donors to reliance on foundations, the vice president of development who is used to "old-boy-network" fundraising may need retraining in "foundation grantsmanship" or may be replaced with a foundation-oriented development vice president.

In adopting a new strategic posture, the college may also have to develop a plan for changing the "culture" of the organization. Every organization has a culture, that is, its people share a certain way of looking at things. Colleges have an "academic culture," one that prizes academic freedom, highmindedness, abstract theorizing, and so on. The academic culture is an outspoken critic of the "business culture" (profit is a worthwhile end) and the "marketing culture" (institutions have to please their publics). College presidents who try to get their faculties to improve their teaching, spend more time with students, develop new courses for nontraditional markets, and so on encounter tremendous resistance. The faculty thinks, "Our job is to teach. The administration's job is to get students." With the growing shortage of students, the challenge facing the president is to develop a market-oriented faculty, where everyone sees its job as sensing, serving, and satisfying its customers. Changing the culture of an organization is a mammoth task, but one that may be essential if the organization is to survive in the new environment. More will be said about organization design in Chapter 5.

### SYSTEMS DESIGN

The final step in strategic planning is to install the systems that the organization needs to develop and carry out the strategies that will achieve its goals in the new environment. The three principal systems are the marketing information system, marketing planning system, and marketing control system.

**Marketing information system.**    The job of effectively running an organization calls for continuous information about customers, marketing intermediaries, suppliers, competitors, publics, and the larger macroenvironment forces (demography, economy, politics, technology, and culture). This information can be obtained through sales analysis, marketing intelligence, and marketing research. The information, if it is to be useful, must be accurate, timely, and comprehensive. The design of a modern marketing information system to support the organization's drive toward its goals is discussed in Chapter 6.

**Marketing planning system.**    Information, to be effectively used, should be incorporated in a modern planning system. An increasing number of organizations are operating formal planning systems in which long-term and annual goals, strategies, marketing programs, and budgets are developed each year. The planning discipline calls for a planning staff, planning resources, and a planning culture if it is to be successful. A planning discipline is essential if the organization hopes to achieve optimal results in the marketplace. The nature and design of an effective marketing planning system is discussed in the first part of Chapter 7.

**Marketing control system.**    Plans are only useful if they are going to be implemented and monitored. The purpose of a marketing control system is to measure the ongoing results of a plan against the plan's goals and to take corrective action before it is too late. The corrective action may be to change the goals, plans, or implementation in the light of the new circumstances. The components of a marketing control system are described in the second part of Chapter 7.

## MARKETING STRATEGY

In this last section, we will examine the concept of marketing strategy and its relation to strategic planning. Strategic planning indicates the particular product markets that represent the organization's best opportunities. For each product market, the organization must develop a marketing strategy for succeeding in that product market. Marketing strategy represents the organization's adaptive strategy to that product market. We define a marketing strategy as follows:

> **Marketing strategy** is the selection of a *target market(s),* the choice of a *competitive position,* and the development of an effective *marketing mix* to reach and serve the chosen customers.

We shall examine the three basic components of marketing strategy in terms of the following example:

> Desert University [name disguised], located in the Southwest, operates a liberal arts college and several professional schools. One of these, the journalism school, enjoys a good local reputation. Although it has attracted a large number of students in the past, the number of applicants has fallen in recent years because of the growing difficulty of finding journalism jobs for graduates and the low pay. The dean of the journalism school allowed enrollment to decline rather than lower the school's admission standards. The university president, however, is upset with the enrollment decline. The president wants the journalism school to remain at its present size and quality and wants the dean to develop a marketing strategy for the 1980s that will adapt the school to its best opportunities.

### TARGET MARKET STRATEGY

The first step in preparing a marketing strategy is to understand the market thoroughly. We define a market as follows:

> A **market** is the set of all people who have an actual or potential interest in a product or service and the ability to pay.

Thus, the journalism student market is the set of all people who have an actual or potential interest in studying journalism and the ability and qualifications to buy this education. At the outset, it becomes clear that the national market must be quite large and that Desert University would only need a small share of it to fill its classes. But the administration realizes that not every person in this market would know about Desert University, find it attractive, or be able to attend. Nor would Desert University find every person attractive. When looked at closely, every market is heterogeneous, that is, it is made up of quite different types of consumers, or *market segments.* Therefore, the administration would benefit from constructing some market segmentation scheme that would reveal the major groups making up the market. Then it could decide whether to try to serve all of these segments *(mass marketing)* or concentrate on a few of the more promising ones *(target marketing).*

There are many ways to segment a market.[15] A market could be segmented by age, sex, income, geography, life style, and many other variables. The market analyst tries different approaches until a useful one is found. Suppose the administration settles on the *product/market segmentation* scheme shown in Figure 3–10. Three customer markets for journalism are shown: college-age learners, adult learners, and practicing journalists. And three product types are shown: broadcast journalism (radio and TV), print journalism (newspapers and magazines), and public relations (a program found in most schools of journalism). Suppose the journalism school at Desert University at present caters to all nine market segments, but is not doing a distinguished job in any. At the same time, competitors are beginning to concentrate on certain market segments and doing a first-class job: the University of Texas in training college-age students for broadcast journalism, Northwestern University in training college-age students for print journalism, and so on. The dean is wondering whether to pursue target marketing, and if so, what pattern of target marketing to choose.

The dean will recognize that there are five basic patterns of market coverage possible with a product/market segmentation scheme. They are shown in Figure 3–11 and are described below:

1. *Product/market concentration* consists of an organization concentrating on only one market segment, here teaching print journalism to adult learners.
2. *Product specialization* consists of the organization deciding to produce only one product (here print journalism) for all three markets.
3. *Market specialization* consists of the organization deciding to serve only one market segment (adult learners) with all the journalism products.

**FIGURE 3–10**

Segmentation of the Journalism Product Market

| Products \ Markets | College-age Learner | Adult Learner | Practicing Journalist |
|---|---|---|---|
| Broadcast Journalism | | | |
| Print Journalism | | | |
| Public Relations | | | |

# FIGURE 3-11

## Five Patterns of Market Coverage

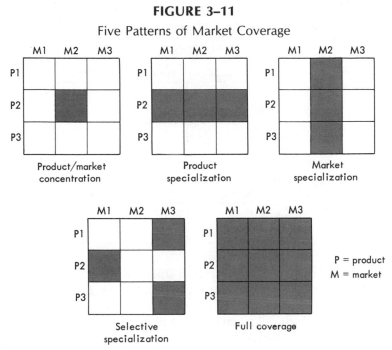

SOURCE: Adapted from Derek F. Abell, *Defining the Business: The Starting Point of Strategic Planning* (Englewood Cliffs, N.J.: Prentice-Hall, 1980), Chapter 8.

4. *Selective specialization* consists of the organization working in several product markets that have no relation to each other except that each constitutes an individually attractive opportunity.

5. *Full coverage* consists of an organization making the full range of products to serve all the market segments.

After researching these alternatives, the dean decides that the most attractive one for the school is product specialization, here print journalism. The journalism school does not have the funds to buy expensive television and radio equipment and sound rooms for student training, and would only be doing a second-rate job compared to the neighboring University of Texas with its $12 million facility for teaching broadcast journalism. And the school's program in public relations is quite weak and cannot be the basis for building a distinguished journalism school. The region lacks a good print journalism school, which happens to be Desert University's strong suit. And it would be best to develop print journalism programs for all three markets, because the number of college-age students is shrinking.

Having decided on product specialization, the administration should now proceed to developing a finer segmentation of the market for print journalism education. Figure 3-12 shows one possible *subsegmentation* of the print journalism market. The columns show different geographical areas from which the

FIGURE 3–12

Subsegmentation of the Print Journalism Market

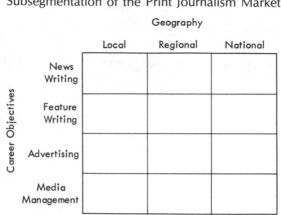

journalism school can try to actively recruit students. The school can concentrate on attracting journalism majors from the local area, using easy admission standards since the market is quite small. Or it can try to compete for students in the Southwest region, which will require a larger recruiting budget and contacts with a larger number of newspapers and magazines for placing students. Or it can try to develop national eminence and attract journalism students from all over the nation. The rows show that journalism majors have different career objectives— some seeking training in news writing, others in feature writing, still others in advertising, and finally some in managing media organizations. Looking at the subsegmentation, the dean may decide to cultivate the regional market and emphasize careers in news writing and feature writing. Although the school will also teach advertising and media management, it will seek to build its reputation as a writer's training school.

### COMPETITIVE POSITIONING STRATEGY

Having selected its target market, the journalism school will now have to develop its competitive position strategy vis-à-vis other journalism schools serving the same target market. Suppose there are three other journalism schools in the Southwest that do a good job of training students in print journalism. If the four schools are similar, then high school students going into journalism would not have much basis for choice among the four. Their respective market shares would be left to chance. The antidote for this is competitive positioning, defined as follows:

> **Competitive positioning** is the art of developing and communicating meaningful differences between one's offer and those of competitors serving the same target market.

The key to competitive positioning is to identify the major attributes used by the target market to evaluate and choose among competitive institutions. Suppose the target market judges journalism schools by their perceived quality (high versus low) and perceived orientation (liberal arts versus vocational). Figure 3–13 shows the perceived competitive positions of the other three journalism schools (A, B, C) and Desert University's journalism school (D). Schools A and B are liberal-arts-oriented journalism schools of low quality, B being somewhat larger and slightly better in quality than A. They are locked in competition for the same students since their differentiation is negligible. School C is seen as a high-quality vocationally oriented journalism school and draws well those students seeking this type of school. Desert University's journalism school is shown as D, because it comes closest to being perceived as a high-quality liberal-arts-oriented school. Fortunately, it has no competition in this preference segment. The only question is whether there are enough students seeking a high-quality liberal-arts-oriented journalism school. If not, then D is not in a viable competitive position and the administration has to think about repositioning the school toward a part of the market in which the demand is larger.

MARKETING MIX STRATEGY

The next step in marketing strategy is to develop a *marketing mix* and a *marketing expenditure level* that supports the school's ability to compete in its target market. By marketing mix, we mean:

## FIGURE 3–13

Competitive Positioning of Four Colleges

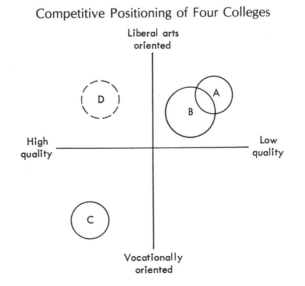

**Marketing mix** is the particular blend of controllable marketing variables that the firm uses to achieve its objective in the target market.

Although many variables make up the marketing mix, they can be classified into a few major groups. McCarthy formulated a popular classification called the "four Ps": *product, price, place,* and *promotion.* [16] The particular marketing variables under each P are shown in Figure 3–14. The figure emphasizes that the marketing mix must be adapted to the target market.

The organization chooses a marketing mix that will support and reinforce its chosen competitive position. Since the journalism school wants to maintain and project a reputation as a high-quality liberal-arts-oriented journalism school, it will hire high-quality faculty, require students to take many liberal arts courses, develop high-quality school catalogs and brochures, send them to potential students seeking this type of school, and so on. In other words, the chosen competitive position dictates the elements of the marketing mix that will be emphasized.

As for the marketing expenditure level, this depends on estimating how much money is needed to accomplish the school's enrollment objectives. If past experience shows that the school has spent about $400 per student recruited, and the school wants to recruit 100 students, it will need a marketing budget of

**FIGURE 3–14**

The Four Ps of the Marketing Mix

$40,000. If the market shrinks or if competitive schools increase their marketing budgets, it may cost, say, $500 per student recruited and the budget would have to be raised to $50,000 to do the job. We shall say more about establishing the marketing budget in Chapter 11.

This illustration shows that strategic planning must be supported by marketing strategy in order for the organization to adapt optimally to its market opportunities.

---

## SUMMARY

The rapidly changing environment requires organizations to be adaptive. Otherwise they are doomed to a life cycle of introduction, growth, maturity, and decline. An adaptive organization operates systems for monitoring and interpreting important environmental changes, and it shows a readiness to revise its mission, objectives, strategies, organization, and systems to be maximally aligned with its opportunities.

Strategic planning is the major tool for adapting to a changing environment, and it consists of several steps. The first step is environmental analysis, in which the organization researches its five environments: internal environment, market environment, public environment, competitive environment, and macroenvironment. Each environment component is subdivided into factors, the major trends are identified for each factor, and then the implied opportunities and threats are identified. The organization prepares plans for its most important opportunities and threats, and monitors the others that might have some eventual significance.

Following the environmental analysis, the organization proceeds to identify its major strengths and weaknesses in personnel, funds, facilities, systems, and market assets. It will favor those opportunities where it has distinctive competences and differential advantages in relation to competitors.

The environmental and resources analyses are followed by goal formulation, in which the organization establishes what it wants to achieve. It formulates its basic mission, its major objectives (qualitative variables to pursue), and its specific goals (quantified objectives with respect to magnitude, time, and who is responsible).

Strategy formulation is the organization's effort to figure out its broad strategy for achieving its goals. First, the organization analyzes its current product portfolio to determine which businesses it should build, maintain, harvest, and terminate. Second, it seeks ideas for new or modified products and markets by using a product/market expansion matrix.

The organization's strategy is likely to call for changes in the organization's structure, people, and culture. Organizational structure should not dictate strategy, but an organization's strategy should shape its structure.

Finally, the organization reviews its systems of information, planning, and control to be sure that they are adequate to carry out the strategy successfully.

The strategic planning process needs marketing inputs. Following the choice of particular product/market targets, the organization proceeds to develop marketing strategies for each product market. Marketing strategy is the selection of a target market segment(s), the choice of a competitive position, and the development of an effective marketing mix to reach and serve the chosen customers. Marketing mix consists of the particular blend of product, price, place, and promotion that the organization uses to achieve its objectives in the target market.

## QUESTIONS

**1.** Private colleges and universities are strongly affected by changes in the environment. Apply the three modes of reducing resource dependency to these institutions.

**2.** Describe the organizational life cycle of homes for unwed mothers, indicating factors influencing changes.

**3.** Prepare an opportunity analysis for a home for unwed mothers.

**4.** Why is it important for an organization to have a mission statement, objectives, *and* goals? What function does each perform?

**5.** Develop a product portfolio similar to Figure 3–8 for the products/services of a nonprofit organization with which you are familiar.

**6.** Develop a product/market opportunity matrix similar to Figure 3–9 for the public library system of a large city.

## NOTES

**1.** Peter Drucker, *Age of Discontinuity* (New York: Harper & Row, 1969).

**2.** Alvin Toffler, *Future Shock* (New York: Bantam, 1970).

**3.** Pfeffer and Salancik argue that environment is more critical than management quality in determining an organization's longevity. See Jeffrey Pfeffer and Gerald R. Salancik, *The External Control of Organizations: A Resource Dependence Perspective* (New York: Harper & Row, 1978).

**4.** Environments have been classified in many ways. Among the dimensions used are the rapidity of change, the environment's simplicity or complexity, and so on. For a well-known classification see F. E. Emery and E. L. Trist, "The Causal Texture of Organizational Environments," *Human Relations,* February 1965, pp. 21–32.

**5.** Pfeffer and Salancik, *The External Control of Organizations,* chapters 6–8.

**6.** Excerpted from Richard Phillips, "Silent 'Church of Good Cheer' Awaits Auctioneer's Gavel," *Chicago Tribune,* Thursday, July 20, 1978, Section 7, pp. 1–2. Copyrighted ©, Chicago Tribune. Used with permission.

**7.** Modified from James M. Carman and Eric Langeard, "Growth Strategies for Service Firms," *Strategic Management Journal,* Vol. 1 (1980), pp. 7–22.

**8.** For an excellent discussion of strategic planning, see Derek F. Abell and John S. Hammond, *Strategic Market Planning* (Englewood Cliffs, N.J.: Prentice-Hall, 1979).

**9.** See Derek F. Abell, "Strategic Windows," *Journal of Marketing,* July 1978, pp. 21–26.

**10.** For an advanced example of goal setting in a university setting, see David

P. Hopkins, Jean-Claude Larreche, and William F. Massy, "Constrained Optimization of a University Administrator's Preference Function," *Management Science,* December 1977, pp. 365–77.

**11.** This definition of market share is called "relative market share." Thus, a relative market share of 10 means that the organization sells 10 times as much as the next largest organization. It should not be confused with absolute market share, which measures the organization's sales as a percentage of the total market size.

**12.** For additional readings on portfolio analysis applied to universities, see Peter Doyle and James E. Lynch, "A Strategic Model for University Planning," *Journal of the Operations Research Society,* July 1979, pp. 603–609; and Gerald D. Newbould, "Product Portfolio Diagnosis for U.S. Universities," *Akron Business and Economic Review,* Spring 1980, pp. 39–45.

**13.** H. Igor Ansoff, "Strategies for Diversification," *Harvard Business Review,* September–October 1957, pp. 113–24.

**14.** See Jay R. Galbraith and Daniel A. Nathanson, *Strategy Implementation: The Role of Structure and Process* (St. Paul, Minn.: West, 1978). The authors elaborate on the thesis first proposed in Alfred D. Chandler, *Strategy and Structure* (Cambridge, Mass.: MIT Press, 1962).

**15.** See Chapter 9.

**16.** E. Jerome McCarthy, *Basic Marketing: A Managerial Approach,* 6th ed. (Homewood, Ill.: Irwin, 1978), p. 39 (1st ed., 1960).

# The
# Entrepreneurial Organization:
# Launching
# New Services

New York University (NYU) is the nation's largest private university, with 35,000 students, located in New York City. It operates several undergraduate colleges and professional schools, including law, business, science, arts, and education. In the early 1970s, NYU faced a number of formidable problems, including (1) a mounting annual deficit of several million dollars; (2) a declining number of students; (3) a lack of a strong image within New York City; (4) a number of weak educational programs. The deficit grew so worrisome that NYU began to consider which programs to close down, such as its School of Social Work, which involved a high cost per student to operate. It ultimately dropped its School of Engineering and also sold its University Heights campus to the city of New York for $62 million.

Then new leadership came to NYU and worked hard to turn this battle-scarred institution into a high-quality, innovative institution of national stature. One major move was to raise entrance requirements in many of its schools, which resulted in fewer but better students. Another move was to add new buildings, including a $25 million library. It carried out marketing research which indicated that NYU did not have a strong image and was often confused with the City University of New York. NYU hired the marketing firm of Barton-Gillette to revise its various brochures and also to improve NYU's advertising and public relations. Soon people were hearing more and better things about NYU. NYU was becoming the university to watch in New York City.

NYU began to innovate programs instead of sitting back and teaching the same old programs year after year. Deans and chairmen were appointed who had a more entrepreneurial view of their markets. They were going to "find needs and fill them."

The university's new entrepreneurial spirit is well illustrated by the program it pioneered in 1978 to meet the educational needs of jobless Ph.D.s. NYU's business school noted the large number of Ph.D.s who had majored in history, literature, and other general education subjects who could not find teaching jobs in their field or attract job offers from companies because of their lack of business training. Many of these unemployed Ph.D.s were reduced to driving taxis or waiting on tables. NYU designed a six-week summer program to teach enrolling Ph.D.s the rudiments of business—finance, accounting, economics, marketing, and management—to ease them into the world of business. It also worked on changing the antibusiness attitudes and dress of some of these students, to remove these impediments to their being hired. The NYU course ended with career counseling and visits from corporate recruiters. As a result of this training, most of the Ph.D.s received good job offers. NYU pioneered this innovative program, which has since been imitated by the University of Texas, University of Virginia, Wharton School at the University of Pennsylvania, Harvard University, and University of California at Los Angeles. Clearly, NYU exhibited the characteristics of an entrepreneurial organization.

An entrepreneurial organization goes one step further than a responsive and adaptive organization. It is not only willing but eager to change with the times. It does not simply watch things happen, or wonder what happened; it makes things happen. It has developed a capacity to produce successful changes. We define an entrepreneurial organization as follows:

An **entrepreneurial organization** is one with a high motivation and capability to identify new opportunities and convert them into successful businesses.

Nonprofit organizations typically do not have an entrepreneurial view of themselves. Colleges, hospitals, museums, symphonies, and government agencies tend to operate in the same way year after year. Colleges will add some new courses and drop some old courses but remain the same in their basic operating characteristics. The U.S. employment offices will use the same procedures in handling the unemployed year after year in spite of new technologies for improving the job-seeking and job-matching process. Nonprofit organizations tend to be noninnovative for a number of reasons:

1. Nonprofit organizations have typically not faced or recognized competition and therefore lack a spur to do better.
2. Nonprofits usually lack the budgets to experiment with new products or meth-

ods. Furthermore, their boards and/or legislators often refuse to support innovation.

3. Nonprofit managers are typically not entrepreneurial. Their training consists of a specialty (e.g., social work, art history, etc.) or administration with an emphasis on running existing organizations rather than creating new ones.

4. Nonprofit organizations see their services as necessary and not requiring justification or marketing.

Nevertheless, every nonprofit sector contains a few organizations that can be called "innovators." We saw that New York University is an innovative university that has launched successful new programs. The Metropolitan Museum of Art, under its former director, Thomas Hoving, created new directions for museums, such as developing a major gift store operation, putting together some unprecedented exhibits, initiating art deaccession policies, attracting ethnic minorities to the museum, and so on. The New York Philharmonic Orchestra, under its former director, Leonard Bernstein, launched many innovations, such as children's concerts, televised symphony programs, and so on. The Brookfield Zoo of Chicago pioneered new ways to present animals in open spaces that other zoos later copied. Clearly, certain nonprofit organizations play the role of innovators in their respective industries.

However, a will to innovate is not enough. Many organizations launch new services that fail.

A 300-bed hospital in southern Illinois got the bright idea of establishing an Adult Day Care Program as a solution to its underutilized space. It designed a whole floor to serve senior citizens who required personal care and services in an ambulatory setting during the day, but who would return home each evening. The cost was $16 a day to the patient's family and transportation was to be provided or paid for by the patient's family. About the only research that was done on this concept was to note that a lot of elderly people lived within a three-mile radius. The Adult Day Care Center was opened with a capacity to handle thirty patients. Only two signed up!

There are many reasons why this and similar new programs fail:

1. Top administrator pushes the idea through in spite of the lack of supporting evidence.

2. Poor organizational systems for handling new-product ideas (poor criteria, poor procedures, poor coordination of departments).

3. Poor market-size measurement, forecasting, and market research.

4. Poor marketing planning, such as poor product positioning, poor segmentation, underbudgeting, overpricing.

5. Lack of product distinctiveness or consumer benefits.

6. Poor product design.

7. Unexpectedly high product development costs.

8. Unexpectedly intense competitive response.

9. Poor or inadequate promotion.

An organization that wishes to be entrepreneurial must set up systems that will lead to successful new product launches. There is a proper methodology for new product introduction which, while it does not guarantee success, usually raises the probability of success. Figure 4–1 shows the overall steps involved in new product development. These steps are developed in the following sections.

## FIGURE 4–1
### Major Stages in New-Product Development

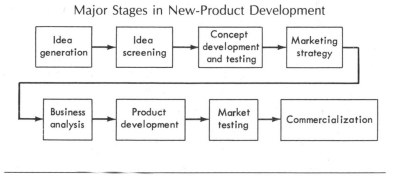

---

## IDEA GENERATION

Organizations differ in their need for new product ideas. Some organizations are pretty busy carrying out their current activities and do not need to find new things to do. A social security office, for example, is mandated to carry out certain procedures and is not interested, or even legally able, to consider undertaking new ventures not related to its main business. Other organizations are in need of one or two big ideas because their main business is taking a turn for the worse. Thus, a drug abuse center may want to add new services such as nonsmoker programs and alcoholic abuse programs if they find fewer drug abusers coming to them for treatment. Still other organizations need several new ideas to keep up with the changing environment. Colleges, for example, need to consider new courses and programs to meet the changing interests of the public. Similarly, the YMCA needs to develop new programs as interest in some of its existing programs fades.

The idea generation stage is therefore relevant to those organizations in need of one or more ideas to maintain or expand their services. In looking for new-product ideas, there are many excellent sources. Clients are a logical starting point in the search for new-product ideas. Their needs and wants can be monitored through direct surveys, projective tests, focused group discussions, and the letters and complaints they send in. Competitors should also be watched for the new activities that they launch which successfully attract clients. The organization's managers and employees are another good source of ideas. Other idea sources are management consultants, advertising agencies, trade associations, and marketing research firms.

Whatever the source of an idea, at least one of four general processes is responsible for producing it—*inspiration, serendipity, client request,* or *formal creativity techniques.* Organizations have little influence on the first two processes, other than maintaining an open atmosphere and encouraging creativity. They should carefully study customer requests for good ideas. Organizations can also train their managers to use certain "creativity techniques." There are dozens of such techniques, three of which are described below.[1]

> 1. *Client problem analysis.* This calls for interviewing clients and asking them to name problems they have with the current service. Thus, a psychological counseling center may learn that patients are afraid of being seen in the waiting office by people who know them. This problem can be solved by developing an extra waiting room and separate exit for the patients.
>
> 2. *Product modification analysis.* This calls for looking at the various attributes of the current service and thinking about ways to modify, magnify, minify, substitute, rearrange, reverse, or combine one or more features.[2] For example, psychological counseling originally called for a one-hour session with a single patient one or a few times a week. Over the years, psychological counseling has spawned such modifications as family therapy, group therapy, and more recently therapy for several hundred people gathered in one room. There has also been modification of the role of the therapist from authority figure, to listener, to facilitator.
>
> 3. *Brainstorming.* This calls for a group of six to ten people to discuss a specific problem, such as "think of new ways to deliver psychological counseling to more people." The participants are encouraged to come up with ideas, the wilder the better. The participants agree not to criticize any ideas until the group runs out of further ideas.[3]

## IDEA SCREENING

The purpose of idea screening is to take a preliminary look at the new product ideas and eliminate those that do not warrant further attention. There is some chance that screening might result in an excellent idea being prematurely dropped (a drop-error). What might be worse, however, is accepting a bad idea for further development (a go-error) as a result of not screening. Each idea that is developed takes substantial management time and money. The purpose of screening is, therefore, to eliminate all but the most promising ideas.

Organizations should require each idea to be written up in a standard form that could be reviewed by a committee. The form should describe the new service, target market, competition, and a rough guess as to market size, price, development time and costs, and probable success.

As an example, De Paul University, in the early seventies, was looking for ideas for new programs to expand its educational services in the greater Chicago area. Among the new program ideas were: (1) a new program of women studies, (2) a new program of black studies, (3) a school of dentistry, (4) a new adult degree program, and (5) a weekend executive master's degree program in business. De Paul did not have the resources to launch more than one of these new programs, and so it needed a way to identify the most attractive program.

A screening procedure for evaluating new product proposals is shown in Figure 4–2. The first task is to determine whether the product idea is attractive

## FIGURE 4–2
### A Product Idea Screening Procedure

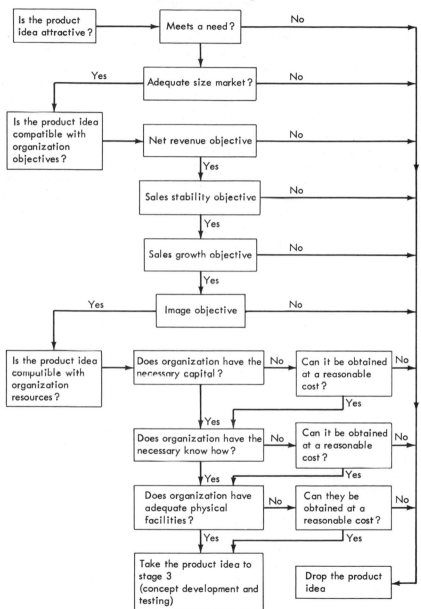

independent of the organization. A new product idea is attractive when it meets a real need and there are a sufficient number of people who would adopt it. Otherwise, the idea should be dropped from consideration. The second task is to determine whether the product is compatible with the company's objectives. Four objectives are mentioned—new revenue, sales stability, sales growth, and image —and others could be added. A strong negative answer to any one of these questions can disqualify the product idea from further consideration. The third task is to determine whether the product idea is compatible with the organization's resources; in the illustration, capital, knowhow, and facilities are used. If any of these resources is lacking, the question is asked whether it is obtainable at a reasonable cost. A strong negative answer to any of these questions will also disqualify the product idea from further consideration. Product ideas that pass all these tests move on to the third stage, that of concept development and testing.

This procedure will eliminate a number of new product ideas as inconsistent with the organization's objectives and/or resources. The remaining new product ideas can then be rated against each other in terms of which would contribute the most to the organization's objectives in relation to the required resources. Various checklists have been developed to facilitate this comparison.[4]

## CONCEPT DEVELOPMENT AND TESTING

Those ideas that survive screening must undergo further development into full product concepts. It is important to distinguish between a product idea, a product concept, and a product image. A *product idea* is an idea for a possible product that the organization can see itself offering to the market. *A product concept* is an elaborated version of the idea expressed in meaningful consumer terms. A *product image* is the particular picture that consumers acquire of an actual or potential product.

### CONCEPT DEVELOPMENT

As a result of screening the various new program ideas, De Paul University decided the best one was a new adult degree program.[5] This is a product idea. De Paul's task was to turn this product idea into an appealing product concept. Every product idea can be turned into several product concepts, not all of them equally attractive. Among the product concepts that might be created around this product idea are:

- Concept 1. An evening program with a liberal arts orientation, mostly required courses, and no credit for past experience.
- Concept 2. An evening program with a career development orientation, much latitude in the courses that could be taken, and credit for past experience.
- Concept 3. An evening program with a general education orientation for people over 50 years of age who want a bachelor's degree.

Clearly, one product idea can give rise to a number of alternative product concepts.

### Concept Testing

Concept testing calls for gathering the reactions of target consumers to each product concept. Each concept should be presented in written form in enough detail to allow the respondent to understand it and express his or her level of interest. Here is an example of concept 2 in more elaborate form:

> An evening program, called the School for New Learning, with a career development orientation and much latitude in the courses that can be taken. The program would be open to persons over 24 years of age; lead to a bachelor's degree; give course credit for past experiences and skills that the individual has acquired; give only pass–fail grades; and involve a "learning contract" between the student and the school.

Target consumers are identified and interviewed about their reaction to this concept. Table 4–1 shows the types of questions that are useful to ask in testing a concept. For example, the last question in Table 4–1 goes after the consumer's *intention-to-buy* and usually reads: "Would you definitely, probably, probably not, definitely not enroll in this program?" Suppose 10 percent of the target consumers said "definitely will enroll" and another 5 percent said "probably will enroll." De Paul would apply this percentage to the corresponding size of the target market to estimate whether the estimated number of enrollees would be sufficient. Even then, the estimate is at best tentative because people often do not carry out their stated intentions. Nevertheless, by testing the alternative concepts with target consumers in this way, De Paul would learn which product concept has the best market potential.

### Table 4–1

MAJOR QUESTIONS IN A CONCEPT TEST FOR
A NEW EDUCATIONAL PROGRAM

1. Is the concept of this adult degree evening program with its various features clear to you?
2. What do you see as reasons why you might enroll in this program?
3. What expectation would you have about the program's quality?
4. Does this program meet a real need of yours?
5. What improvements can you suggest in various features of this program?
6. Who would be involved in your decision about whether to enroll in this program?
7. How do you feel about the tuition cost of this program?
8. What competitive programs come to mind and which appeals to you the most?
9. Would you enroll in this program?

# MARKETING STRATEGY

At this point, the organization should develop a preliminary concept of the marketing strategy that it would use to introduce the new program to the greater Chicago area. This is necessary in order that the full revenue and cost implications of the new program can be evaluated in the next stage of business analysis.

The marketing strategy should be spelled out in a statement consisting of three parts. The first part describes the size, structure, and behavior of .he target market, the intended positioning of the new product in this market, and the enrollment and income goals in the first few years. Thus:

> The target market is adults over 24 living in the greater Chicago area who have never obtained a bachelor's degree but have the skills and motivation to seek one. This program will be differentiated from other programs by offering course credit for relevant past experience, as well as in its career development emphasis. The school will seek a first-year enrollment of 60 students with a net loss not to exceed $100,000. The second year will aim for an enrollment of 100 persons and a net income of at least $20,000.

The second part of the marketing strategy statement outlines the new product's intended price, distribution strategy, and marketing budget for the first year.

> The new program will be offered at the downtown location of De Paul University. All courses will take place once a week in the evening from 6:00 to 9:00 P.M. Tuition will be $500 per course. The first year's promotion budget will be $80,000, $50,000 of which will be spent on advertising materials and media and the remainder on personal contact activities. Another $10,000 will be spent on marketing research to analyze and monitor the market.

The third part of the marketing strategy statement describes the intended long-run sales and profit goals and marketing mix strategy over time:

> The university ultimately hopes to achieve a steady enrollment of 400 students in this degree program. When it is built up to this level, a permanent administration will be appointed. Tuition will be raised each year in line with the rate of inflation. The promotion budget will stay at a steady level of $50,000. Marketing research will be budgeted at $10,000 annually. The target income level for this program is $100,000 a year, and the money will be used to support other programs which are not self-paying.

# BUSINESS ANALYSIS

As soon as a satisfactory product concept and marketing strategy have been developed, the organization is in a position to do a hardheaded analysis of the business attractiveness of the proposal. The organization must estimate the possible revenues and costs of the program for different possible enrollment levels. *Breakeven analysis* is the most frequently used tool in this connection (see Chapter 13, p. 310). Suppose De Paul learns that it needs an enrollment of 260 students to break even. If De Paul manages to attract more than 260 students, this program will produce a net income that could be used to support other programs; otherwise, if there is a student shortfall, De Paul will lose money on this new program.

## PRODUCT DEVELOPMENT

If the organization is satisfied that the product concept is financially viable, it can move toward turning the concept into a concrete form. The person in charge of the concept can begin to develop brochures, schedules, ads, sales call plans, and other things to implement the program. Each of the developed materials should be *consumer tested* before being printed and issued. For example, a sample of prospects in the target audience might be asked to respond to a mockup of the brochure describing the new program. This usually results in some valuable suggestions leading to an improved brochure.

## MARKET TESTING

When the organization is satisfied with the initial materials and schedules, it might set up a market test to see if the concept is really going to be successful. Market testing is the stage where the product and marketing program are introduced into an authentic consumer setting to learn how many consumers are really interested in the program. Thus, De Paul University might decide to mail 10,000 brochures to strong prospects in the Chicago area during the month of April to see whether at least 30 students can be attracted. If more than, say, 30 students sign up, the market test will be regarded as successful and full-scale promotion can be launched.

*Test markets* are the ultimate form of testing a new product and would be used by an organization with two or more sites where it wants to measure the viability of the new program without installing it wholesale throughout the system. Suppose that the State University of New York (SUNY) was considering the same new program. SUNY consists of sixty-four campuses, not just one campus. SUNY could develop the concept and test it at one of the campuses to see how well it works. Or it could test it at two campuses, each campus promoting it in a somewhat different way to test the cost effectiveness of different promotion approaches. If the new program proves successful in one or both test markets, it can then be launched at other campuses where appropriate.

# COMMERCIALIZATION

Commercialization is the decision to launch a new service or program. As a guide, the organization should pay attention to the theory of consumer adoption behavior, which throws light on how consumers react when they learn about new products.

### THE CONSUMER ADOPTION PROCESS

The *consumer adoption process* begins where the organization's *innovation process* leaves off. It deals with the process by which potential customers come to learn about the new product, try it, and eventually adopt or reject it. The organization must understand this process so that it can bring about early market awareness and trial usage.

The earliest approach used by new-product marketers for launching a new product was a *mass market approach.* For example, a hospital might start a first aid course and try to attract everyone to take it. A mass-market approach, however, has two drawbacks: (1) it requires heavy marketing expenditures, and (2) it involves a substantial number of wasted exposures to nonpotential and low-potential buyers. These drawbacks have led to a second approach called *target marketing,* that of directing the product to the groups that are likely to be most interested. This makes sense, provided strong prospects are identifiable. But even within strong prospect groups, persons differ in how much interest they show in new products and in how fast they could be drawn into trying them. Certain persons are early adopters and the new-product marketer ought to direct marketing effort to them. *Early-adopter theory* holds that:

1. Persons within a target market will differ in the amount of time that passes between their exposure to a new product and their trial of the new product.
2. Early adopters are likely to share some traits in common that differentiate them from late adopters.
3. There exist efficient media for reaching early-adopter types.
4. Early-adopter types are likely to be high on opinion leadership and therefore helpful in "advertising" the new product to other potential buyers.

### CONCEPTS IN INNOVATION DIFFUSION AND ADOPTION

The theory of innovation diffusion and adoption provides clues to identifying the best early prospects. The central concept is that of an *innovation,* which refers to any good, service, or idea that is *perceived* by someone as new. The idea may have had a long history, but it is still an innovation to the person who sees it as being new.

Innovations are assimilated into the social system over time. *Diffusion process* is the name given to "the spread of a new idea from its source of invention or creation to its ultimate users or adopters."[6] The *adoption process,* on the other hand, focuses on "the mental process through which an individual passes from first hearing about an innovation to final adoption." *Adoption* itself is a decision by an individual to use an innovation regularly.

The differences among individuals in their response to new ideas is called their *innovativeness.* Specifically, innovativeness is "the degree to which an individual is relatively earlier in adopting new ideas than the other members of his social system." On the basis of their innovativeness, individuals can be classified into different *adopter categories* (see below).

Individuals can also be classified in terms of their influence on others with respect to innovations. *Opinion leaders* are "those individuals from whom others seek information or advice." Individuals or firms who actively seek to change other people's minds are called *change agents.*

### PROPOSITIONS ABOUT THE CONSUMER ADOPTION PROCESS

We are now ready to examine the main generalizations drawn from hundreds of studies of how people accept new ideas.

**Stages in the adoption process.** The first proposition is that *the individual consumer goes through a series of stages of acceptance in the process of adopting a new product.* The stages are classified by Rogers as follows:

1. *Awareness:* the individual becomes cognizant of the innovation but lacks information about it.
2. *Interest:* the individual is stimulated to seek information about the innovation.
3. *Evaluation:* the individual considers whether it would make sense to try the innovation.
4. *Trial:* the individual tries the innovation on a small scale to improve his or her estimate of its utility.
5. *Adoption:* the individual decides to make full and regular use of the innovation.

The value of this model of the adoption process is that it requires the innovator to think carefully about new-product acceptance. Adults hearing about De Paul's program for the first time are not going to sign up immediately. De Paul will have to take concrete steps to maintain their interest, help them evaluate whether the program meets their needs, and make it easy for prospects to attend a session or take one course to sample the new program.

**Individual differences in innovativeness.** The second proposition is that *people differ markedly in their penchant for trying new products.* In each product area, there are apt to be "consumption pioneers" and early adopters. Some women are the first to adopt new clothing fashions or new appliances, such as the microwave oven, some doctors are the first to prescribe new medicines,[7] and some farmers are the first to adopt new farming methods.[8]

Other individuals, however, tend to adopt innovations much later. This has led to a classification of people into the adopter categories shown in Figure 4–3.

## FIGURE 4–3

### Adopter Categorization on the Basis of Relative Time of Adoption of Innovations

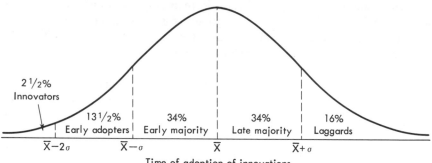

SOURCE: Redrawn from Everett M. Rogers, *Diffusion of Innovations* (New York: Free Press, 1962), p. 162.

The adoption process is represented as following a normal (or near normal) distribution when plotted over time. After a slow start, an increasing number of people adopt the innovation, the number reaches a peak, and then it diminishes as fewer persons remain in the nonadopter category.

Convenient breaks in the distribution are used to establish adopter categories. Thus innovators are defined as the first 2½ percent of the individuals to adopt a new idea; the early adopters are the next 13½ percent who adopt the new idea, and so forth.

Rogers has characterized the five adopter groups in terms of ideational values. The dominant value of innovators is *venturesomeness;* they like to try new ideas, even at some risk, and are cosmopolite in orientation. The dominant value of early adopters is *respect;* they enjoy a position in the community as opinion leaders and adopt new ideas early but with discretion. The dominant value of the early majority is *deliberateness;* these people like to adopt new ideas before the average member of the social system, although they rarely are leaders. The dominant value of the late majority is *skepticism;* they do not adopt an innovation until the weight of majority opinion seems to legitimize its utility. Finally, the dominant value of the laggards is *tradition;* they are suspicious of any changes, mix with other tradition-bound people, and adopt the innovation only because it has now taken on a measure of tradition itself.

The marketing implication of the adopter classification is that an innovating firm should direct its communications to those people who are likely to be early in adopting the innovation; messages reaching late adopters and laggards are wasted. Drawing on several studies, Rogers offered the following hypotheses about early adopters:

The relatively earlier adopters in a social system tend to be younger in age, have higher social status, a more favorable financial position, more specialized operations, and a different type of mental ability from later adopters. Earlier adopters utilize information sources that are more impersonal and cosmopolite than later adopters and that are in closer contact with the origin of new ideas. Earlier adopters utilize a greater number of different information sources than do later adopters. The social relationships of earlier adopters are more cosmopolite than for later adopters, and earlier adopters have more opinion leadership.[9]

Once the characteristics of early adopters are identified, a marketing communications program can be developed for the new product calculated to reach and interest these people. The known media habits of these people can be used to increase the effectiveness of the organization's advertising.

**Role of personal influence.**    The third proposition is that *personal influence plays a very large role in the adoption of new products.* By *personal influence* is meant the effect of product statements made by one person on another's attitude or probability of purchase.[10] The significance of personal influence is greater in some situations and for some individuals than for others. Personal influence seems to be more important in the evaluation stage of the adoption process than in the other stages. It seems to have more influence on the later adopters than on the earlier adopters. And it appears to be more important in risky situations than in safe situations.

**Influence of product characteristics on the rate of adoption.**    The fourth proposition is that *the character of the innovation itself affects the rate of adoption.* Five characteristics seem to have an especially important influence on the adoption rate. The first is the innovation's *relative advantage,* or the degree to which it appears superior to previous ideas. The greater the perceived relative advantage, whether in terms of higher quality, lower cost, and so on, the more quickly the innovation will be adopted.

The second characteristic is the innovation's *compatibility,* or the degree to which it is consistent with the values and experiences of the individuals in the social system.

Third is the innovation's *complexity,* or the degree to which it is relatively difficult to understand or use. The more complex innovations are likely to take a longer time to diffuse, other things being equal.

Fourth is the innovation's *divisibility,* or the degree to which it may be tried on a limited basis. The evidence of many studies indicates that divisibility helps to increase the rate of adoption.

The fifth characteristic is the innovation's *communicability,* or the degree to which the results are observable or describable to others. Innovations that lend themselves to better demonstration or description of advantage will diffuse faster in the social system.

Other characteristics have also been found to influence the rate of adoption, such as initial cost, continuing cost, risk and uncertainty, scientific credibility, and social approval. The new-product marketer has to research the role of all these factors and give the key ones maximum attention in developing the new-product and marketing program.

---

## SUMMARY

Organizations are more viable when they are entrepreneurial. An entrepreneurial organization is one with a high motivation and capability to identify new opportunities and convert them into successful businesses. An organization that wants to be entrepreneurial must set up systems that will lead to successful new ventures. Each stage in the new-product development process must be carefully conducted.

The first stage, idea generation, involves a search for new-product and service ideas through talking to various parties and applying idea-generating techniques. The second stage, idea screening, seeks to eliminate those ideas that are unattractive or which cannot be carried out by the organization. The third stage, concept development and testing, involves the effort to develop the idea into a sound concept and estimate the number of target consumers who might be interested. The fourth stage, marketing strategy, involves developing a tentative plan for marketing the product. The fifth stage, business analysis, uses all the estimates of demand and cost to determine whether the product idea should be pursued any further. If the answer is yes, the sixth stage, product development, calls for developing a prototype of the product or service so that it can be tested in tangible form. The seventh stage, market testing, involves presenting the product to sample customers to improve the estimates of demand. The eighth stage, commercialization, involves the decision to actually launch the product. Commercialization strategy benefits greatly when based on the theory of innovation diffusion and consumer adoption processes.

---

## QUESTIONS

**1.** A hospital plans to introduce a low-cost health risk screening program to the community. To test the attractiveness of the program, it plans to provide it at no cost to the first hundred people who sign up and agree to fill out an evaluation of the service. Comment on the proposed approach to testing.

**2.** At the idea screening stage, it is possible to make two types of errors: a drop-error or a go-error. What are the risks involved in each type of error and how can errors be minimized?

**3.** The board of directors of a local YMCA sets aside an hour during each of its quarterly meetings to generate ideas for new programs. Comment on this approach to developing new programs.

**4.** A small private college has attractive dormitories which go unused during vacation periods. Fortunately, the college is in a pleasant semirural area which is likely to attract people who seek a low-cost way to get away from big-city smog and pressures. What information would a breakeven analysis provide to the college's administration for making the decision whether to proceed?

**5.** A public library is considering the attractiveness and feasibility of lending children's toys and games in the same way that it now provides books and records. What steps should the library administration take in making a decision on whether to proceed?

## NOTES

**1.** For a useful discussion of creativity techniques, see Sidney J. Parnes and Harold F. Harding, eds., *Source Book for Creative Thinking* (New York: Scribner's, 1962).

**2.** See Alex F. Osborn, *Applied Imagination,* 3rd ed. (New York: Scribner's, 1963), pp. 286–87.

**3.** *Ibid.,* p. 156.

**4.** See Barry M. Richman, "A Rating Scale for Product Innovation," *Business Horizons,* Summer 1962, pp. 37–44; and John T. O'Meara, Jr., "Selecting Profitable Products," *Harvard Business Review,* January–February 1961, pp. 83–89.

**5.** "De Paul's New Study Plan," *Chicago Tribune,* January 6, 1974.

**6.** The following discussion leans heavily on Everett M. Rogers, *Diffusion of Innovations* (New York: Free Press, 1962).

**7.** See James Coleman, Elihu Katz, and Herbert Menzel, "The Diffusion of an Innovation Among Physicians," *Sociometry,* December 1957, pp. 253–70.

**8.** See J. Bohlen and G. Beal, *How Farm People Accept New Ideas,* Special Report No. 15 (Ames: Iowa State College Agricultural Extension Service, November 1955).

**9.** Rogers, *Diffusion of Innovations,* p. 192.

**10.** See Elihu Katz and Paul F. Lazarsfeld, *Personal Influence* (New York: Free Press, 1955), p. 234.

# ORGANIZING
# MARKETING

# Marketing Organization

The YMCA of Metropolitan Chicago is a federation of 49 autonomous local operating units in the greater Chicago area. Serving approximately 480,000 people, the YMCA budget totals $50 million annually. Employing 3,900 full- and part-time employees, the Y is involved in eight different businesses: health and physical education (32%); guidance and counseling (3%); neighborhood and community services (9%); outdoor and environmental education (10%); education and training (18%); residence and related services (11%); social recreation/cultural arts (7%); and human relations (10%). The Chicago Y may be the world's largest private social service organization, the "General Electric" of social services.

The Metropolitan Offices of the YMCA (Metro Y) plans for the Chicago area and provides assistance to the various operating units through a central management staff working through nine district directors. In recent years, the Y has experienced increasing financial problems. Many of the local units are suffering membership declines. Part of this is due to members turning to other sources for physical fitness, such as jogging, tennis, and racquetball. Some members are "trading up" by taking out memberships in Nautilus Clubs, the Chicago Health Club, and other for-profit organizations offering better facilities. Teens are coming less frequently, partly because of changing teen values.

Each Y has combated these declines by developing new programs and increasing its advertising budget. But these steps have slowed down, not reversed, the decline. The Metro Y was increasingly being asked to help.

Unfortunately, the Metro Y was without a professional marketing executive. It had some board members who are marketing executives, and also occasionally bought marketing research and advertising services from outside suppliers. The Metro Y recently sponsored a marketing conference for 150 local Y executives, and this succeeded in intensifying the demand for professional marketing assistance.

One solution would be for each local Y to hire a marketing director. But most units are too weak financially to afford this. Another solution is for Metro Y to hire a marketing director, who could begin to implement a marketing function on an organization-wide basis.

Metro Y decided on the second approach and faced a number of decisions. Should it go after a marketing VP or a marketing director? With the help of a grant from the Chicago Community Trust, it developed a job description for a marketing director. The director's responsibilities would include:

- the evaluation of the Y's current position in the marketplace
- the analysis of the Y's membership, program offerings, and competition
- the development of a marketing plan for the entire Y organization
- participation in specific marketing project assignments, as needed

The next decision is how to recruit a marketing director. Should a marketer be recruited from a consumer packaged goods company such as Procter and Gamble, or IBM, or a bank, and so on? Or should the Y find a social worker who has a marketing background? What should the Y pay? What should be the relationship between marketing and related corporate functions such as planning, public relations, and fundraising?

In announcing the job position, the Y received 150 applications. The applications were examined against several criteria, such as the applicant's experience, training, age, and salary requirements. Metro Y finally selected one candidate, who accepted the position. Now the real work was to begin. The new marketing director had to figure out a plan for the coming year to create value for the Chicago Metro Y through the application of marketing concepts and techniques.[1]

The YMCA story illustrates how one nonprofit organization recognized a need for marketing and took steps to install a trained marketing capacity into the organization. A growing number of colleges, hospitals, and other nonprofit institutions have taken similar steps. Most nonprofit organizations, however, have still not organized a marketing function. Although they have introduced other standard business functions—accounting, finance, personnel, planning, information systems, public relations—they are reluctant to install a marketing function. There are a number of reasons for this:

- Some organizations think that formal marketing is inappropriate. Thus, the faculty of a college might be contemptuous of the notion that education has to be marketed.
- Some organizations think that marketing is everyone's job. They fear that appointing a marketing director will lead employees to think that marketing is something done by a marketing director rather than everyone in the organization, and they will sit around expecting the marketing director to miraculously solve their problems.
- Some organizations feel that they are getting all the marketing they need from their directors of public relations, planning, and development. They identify marketing with these functions.
- Some organizations feel that they would be better off hiring marketing expertise as needed—from marketing consultants, advertising agencies, and marketing research firms—instead of hiring a full-time marketing director.
- Some organizations feel that a director of marketing would not contribute enough to pay for his or her salary. They believe that they can buy more important things with the same money.
- Some organizations are too small or too poor to afford a marketing director.

Thus, nonprofit organizations resist installing a marketing function for a number of reasons. This chapter will examine the following issues:

1. Does an organization need a formal marketing function in order to be effective in its marketing?
2. If an organization decides to establish a formal marketing office, what should be its level and job description, and where and how should the marketer be recruited?
3. What can this person do to accomplish useful results in the first year?
4. How can the marketing function be expanded over time?
5. What steps can be taken to make the whole organization more market oriented?

---

## ASSESSING THE NEED FOR MARKETING

The issue of whether an organization should install a formal marketing function is not the issue of whether it should do marketing. All organizations do marketing whether or not they organize it in a formal way. Colleges, for example, search for prospects (students), develop products (courses), price them (tuition and fees), distribute them (announce time and place), and promote them (college catalogs). Similarly, hospitals, social agencies, museums, and other nonprofit organizations also carry on marketing. When this dawns on a nonprofit organization, the response is much like that of Molière's character in *Le Bourgeois Gentilhomme* who utters, "Good heavens! For more than forty years I have been speaking prose without knowing it."

Some organizations feel that they are not only doing marketing but that they already have formal staff positions responsible for marketing. Therefore, they don't need to add another staff position called "marketing." A college president may feel that the admissions director, the public relations director, the planning vice president, and the development vice president are the institution's professional marketers. This may or may not be correct, however. Many admissions directors are sales oriented rather than marketing oriented. They are good at "pounding the pavement" for prospective students, but not skilled in marketing research and marketing strategy which would make this selling job easier. Most public relations directors are skilled in journalism and communication, but are not trained in analyzing, researching, and planning for markets. Planning vice presidents may concentrate on developing the physical plant and on financial problems, without having much marketing knowledge or aptitude. Development vice presidents are often sales oriented and fail to put their fundraising efforts on a modern marketing management basis. Though these officers should be professional marketers handling their respective markets, they typically are not.

The president may acknowledge this but feel that there are several ways to get marketing resources without going through the expense of establishing a formal marketing position. In fact, the nonprofit organization that cannot afford or chooses not to install formal marketing can get some marketing resources in the following ways:

1. Appoint a marketing executive to the board of directors, hoping to get help or advice from this marketing executive as needed. Also invite voluntary help from other marketing executives in the community.
2. Invite help from the marketing faculty of a business school, such as using a marketing research class to research a problem facing the organization.
3. Hire a marketing consulting firm, marketing research firm, or advertising agency to do specific projects when needed.
4. Send key staff to marketing seminars and workshops to learn marketing.

Although these makeshift ways of acquiring marketing services will not do the full job of creating a market-oriented organization, they will normally produce good value in the short term. But certain cautions must be exercised. In drawing on the voluntary services of marketing executives in the community, it should be realized that they will be offering advice without the benefit of research data or much time to analyze the problem. Furthermore, they will be heavily influenced by their own industry background. A P&G soap marketing executive will put heavy emphasis on advertising spending because this is what works in the soap industry; and an IBM marketing executive will put heavy emphasis on personal selling because this is what works in the computer industry. Every marketing executive has biases as to what works best and the nonprofit organization must maintain a critical attitude.

If the nonprofit organization decides to get marketing help by hiring marketing firms as needed, it must be able to discriminate between good, average, and poor firms. For example, a poor advertising agency will try to solve a membership decline by creating an instant advertising campaign. An average ad agency will ask management questions to help clarify the nature of the membership decline and then create an advertising campaign. A good ad agency will ask about the organization's overall mission, goals, and plans and do some research with members and ex-members before developing an advertising campaign. Naturally, the nonprofit organization will get the most value from a market-oriented advertising agency.

As a step toward considering whether a formal marketing function should be installed, the organization should appoint a *marketing committee* charged with three objectives:

1. identifying marketing problems and opportunities facing the organization
2. assessing the felt need of different department heads for professional marketing assistance
3. recommending whether the organization should establish a formal marketing position

The marketing committee should include representatives from a cross-section of the organization's departments that might have a stake in marketing. Thus, a university's marketing committee should include the vice president of faculty, some deans and department chairpersons, admissions director, public relations director, development vice president, planning vice president, a board member, and possibly a student representative. The marketing committee might also include an outside marketing executive or paid marketing consultant to provide professional guidance. This committee should gather information from various groups (deans, chairpersons, students) as to how they see the environment (its opportunities and threats), the organization's strengths and weaknesses, the organization's strategy, the organization's marketing problems and possible solutions, and so on. Many surprising, if not shocking, things will be discovered in this process.

The committee should digest the information and prepare a report for the president. The report should first present major findings about marketing problems and needs at the institution. Second, it should present recommendations as to courses of action. The recommendations can be divided into short-term actions (which can be implemented early and normally at low cost) and long-term actions (which take more time to implement and involve a higher cost).

This report of marketing findings and recommendations is called a *marketing audit* (see Chapter 7, pp. 185–90). Although it is an inside audit done by a committee of nonprofessionals, it is likely to be highly useful. The organization always has the option of hiring a marketing consulting firm to do a full-scale marketing audit, which will cost more and be likely to yield even greater value because of the marketing auditor's independence, objectivity, and experience in doing marketing auditing in a large number of industries.

---

## ESTABLISHING MARKETING

At some point, the nonprofit organization may wish to install a formal marketing function. The organization may find the makeshift use of outside marketing resources to be too costly or unreliable, or it may find that its marketing needs are extensive enough to hire a full-time person. The organization should recognize that establishing a marketing function is undertaken at some risk if the rest of the organization is resistant and/or if the new appointee is not given sufficient authority to carry out his/her responsibilities. However, if the organization decides to move forward, it must decide on (1) the level at which to hire, (2) the job description, and (3) the recruiting strategy.

The major issue concerning level is whether to hire a *director of marketing services* or a *vice president of marketing.* The former person is hired at a middle management level and basically acts as a resource person or internal marketing consultant to various other managers in the organization who need marketing services. This director can help define marketing problems, arrange for marketing research, and hire advertising agency services as needed. This person may be located in the planning department under the vice president of planning or in public relations or development, though these functions might overspecialize the use to which marketing is put. Some hospitals and colleges have preferred to call the person "assistant to the president" reporting directly to the president.

Alternatively, the organization might hire a vice president of marketing. This is an upper-level management position which gives more scope, authority, and influence to marketing. A vice president of marketing not only coordinates and supplies services to others in the organization but also participates in the setting of policy and direction for the institution. This person has a better chance to help create a marketing orientation in the organization. The vice president of marketing would be responsible for planning and managing relations with several publics of the institution; in fact, this person would conceivably manage client relations, donor relations, public relations, and government relations. The person's title might be "vice president of institutional relations" or "vice president of external affairs" to avoid unnecessary semantic opposition to the term "marketing." A vice president of marketing would cost the institution more but might ultimately contribute more to the institution.

Which position should it be initially? Some organizations prefer to appoint a director of marketing on the idea that the position costs less, its value can be tested, and, if the director proves effective, he or she can be promoted to vice president of marketing. Other organizations feel that a director of marketing services can only accomplish minor things because he or she would not have the ear of the president and would not participate in strategy formulation. The author favors establishing a vice president of marketing initially because marketing's job is to transform the thinking of top management into a marketing mode.

Suppose, however, that the organization decides initially to hire a director of marketing services. Needed is a job description that outlines the functions, responsibilities, and major liaison relations associated with the job. A sample job description for a university director of marketing services is shown in Table 5–1.

Before searching for a qualified person to fill the job, the organization will want to define further the desirable age of the person, years and type of marketing experience, salary range, and planned budget for the job. The organization may decide that it wants a person with substantial marketing training and experience

## Table 5–1

### JOB DESCRIPTION:
### A UNIVERSITY DIRECTOR OF MARKETING SERVICES

*Position title:* Director of Marketing Services

*Reports to:* Vice President, University Relations

*Scope:* University-wide

*Position concept:* The Director of Marketing Services is responsible for providing marketing guidance and services to university officers, school deans, department chairmen, and other agents of the university.

*Functions:* The Director of Marketing Services will:

1. contribute a marketing perspective to the deliberations of the top administration in its planning of the university's future
2. prepare data that might be needed by any officer of the university on a particular market's size, segments, trends, and behavioral dynamics
3. conduct studies of the needs, perceptions, preferences, and satisfactions of particular markets
4. assist in the planning, promotion, and launching of new programs
5. assist in the development of communication and promotion campaigns and materials
6. analyze and advise on pricing questions
7. appraise the workability of new academic proposals from a marketing point of view
8. advise on new student recruitment
9. advise on current student satisfaction
10. advise on university fundraising

*Responsibilities:* The Director of Marketing Services will:

1. contact individual officers and small groups at the university to explain services and to solicit problems
2. prioritize the various requests for services according to their long-run impact, cost saving potential, time requirements, ease of accomplishment, cost, and urgency
3. select projects of high priority and set accomplishment goals for the year
4. prepare a budget request to support the anticipated work
5. prepare an annual report on the main accomplishments of the office

*Major liaisons:* The Director of Marketing Services will:

1. relate most closely with the President's Office, Admissions Office, Development Office, Planning Office, and Public Relations Department
2. relate secondarily with the deans of various schools and chairpersons of various departments

---

in industry in preference to a person who has worked in its field—whether education, health, the arts—who has only weak training in marketing. The organization would find it easier to educate a person about the field than to train the person as a marketer.

The search will use the normal recruitment channels—job ads in the *Wall Street Journal* or *Marketing News* (published by the American Marketing Association); phone calls to business school professors for leads; use of an executive search firm; and so on. This should produce a large number of leads, leaving the organization to prune the list and interview a few of the most promising candidates and make a choice among them.

## DEVELOPING MARKETING PROJECTS

The new marketing director will want to demonstrate that marketing thinking can contribute value to the organization. Many members of the organization will be critical of marketing, arguing that it is inappropriate or a waste of money, or that the money could be spent better elsewhere. Others will be puzzled about what marketing is or does. Only a few will see it as a strong opportunity for the organization.

In the face of this skepticism, the new director must carefully choose initial projects which, if successfully executed, demonstrate the value of marketing. The marketing director can imagine these projects, but it would be better if he or she meets key groups and conducts a needs assessment to get ideas on important marketing needs. For example, a new marketing director at a college should meet with some deans and department heads, individually or in groups, describe the work that can be done (marketing analyses, new program assessment, communication planning, and so on), and ask about any projects they might be interested in seeing done. This approach will build goodwill and understanding with various people in the organization and lead to many project ideas, often more than can be handled by a single marketing director operating with a small budget. The director should not promise to do work on any project until he or she reviews the possible projects and chooses the best ones. The best early projects to undertake would have four characteristics:

1. a high impact on making money or saving money for the institution
2. a relatively small cost to carry out
3. a short period of time for completion
4. a high visibility potential if successful

Presumably, some projects will stand up better than others under these criteria. The main thing is to avoid major projects that will take a long time, cost a lot of money, and not yield definitive results. The organization will not have the patience to support costly, drawn-out marketing projects, at least not until the marketing function is well established and respected.

## EXPANDING THE MARKETING FUNCTION

If the marketing director does a good job, which is recognized by others in the organization, more resources will become available.[2] The marketing executive may want to hire one or more assistants to specialize in marketing research, advertising, new services evaluation, and other marketing functions. It pays to hire a full-time expert in any specialized marketing function that the organization needs to cover on a continuous basis.

Large-scale public organizations, such as the U.S. Postal Service or Amtrak, because of their "business" character, will not think initially in terms of hiring a single marketing executive, but in terms of creating a whole marketing department. They will see the need for marketing professionals from the beginning and develop a budget to establish a whole department. For example, consider the marketing organization that the U.S. Postal Service (USPS) established:[3]

> Marketing activities within the USPS are centered in the Customer Department, which is headed by a former Procter and Gamble executive. The department is divided into eight divisions: special events division; planning and management division; office of stamps; office of international postal affairs; office of advertising; office of product management; office of customer marketing; and office of consumer advocate. Each division, in turn, has subdivisions. For example, the office of product management has six subdivisions: letter mail, parcel mail, retail products, special services, electronic mail, and market research. Many of the division heads are ex–marketing executives from private industry.

Although most nonprofit organizations will never need such elaborate marketing departments, it is useful to list the variety of job positions found in a full-scale marketing department. A description of these job positions is presented in Table 5–2.

Of particular interest is the question of whether a nonprofit organization should establish a product management system, a market management system, neither, or both. Normally, the first step in expanding a marketing department is to add some functional specialists, such as a marketing researcher and/or advertising manager. The question of product and market managers arises later. Consider this question in connection with the YMCA. The Y has many "products"—physical fitness programs, arts and crafts programs, educational programs, and so on. A product management system would call for appointing a person to head each major program. Thus, a physical fitness director would study people's needs and interests in physical fitness and would develop plans for expanding the offerings and attracting more users, as well as for pricing the programs. This person would advise various local Y units on how to make their physical fitness programs stronger.

The Y also serves a variety of markets divided by sex (male, female) and age (teens, young adults, adults, senior citizens). A market management system would call for appointing a person to head each major market. Thus, the market manager for teens would study their needs and develop programs that satisfy their needs. This person would consult local Ys that are having trouble attracting teens and propose new programs that might be offered.

Clearly, the Y would be more effective by operating both a product and market management system. This is called a *matrix organization.* However, the

## Table 5–2
### GENERIC MARKETING POSITIONS

MARKETING MANAGER

1. Other names: vice president of marketing, marketing director, chief marketing officer, marketing administrator.
2. The marketing manager heads the organization's marketing activities. Tasks include providing a marketing point of view to the top administration; helping to formulate marketing plans of the organization; staffing, directing, and coordinating marketing activities; and proposing new products and services to meet emerging market needs.

PRODUCT MANAGER

1. Other names: program manager, brand manager.
2. A product manager is responsible for managing a particular product or program of the organization. Tasks include proposing product objectives and goals, creating product strategies and plans, seeing that they are implemented, monitoring the results, and taking corrective actions.

MARKETING RESEARCH MANAGER

1. Other names: marketing research director.
2. The marketing research manager has responsibility for developing and supervising research on the organization's markets and publics, and on the effectiveness of various marketing tools.

COMMUNICATIONS MANAGER

1. Other names: advertising manager, advertising and sales promotion director.
2. The communications manager provides expertise in the area of mass and selective communication and promotion. Person is knowledgeable about the development of messages, media, and publicity.

SALES MANAGER

1. Other names: vice president of sales.
2. The sales manager has responsibility for recruiting, training, assigning, directing, motivating, compensating, and evaluating sales personnel and agents of the organization, and coordinating the work of sales personnel with the other marketing functions.

NEW-PRODUCTS MANAGER

1. Other names: new-products director.
2. The new-products manager has responsibility for conceiving new products and services; screening and evaluating new product ideas; developing prototypes and testing them; and advising and helping to carry out the innovation's introduction in the marketplace.

DISTRIBUTION MANAGER

1. Other names: channel manager; physical distribution manager; logistics manager.
2. The distribution manager has responsibility for planning and managing the distribution systems that make the organization's products and services available and accessible to the potential users.

**Table 5–2**

GENERIC MARKETING POSITIONS (continued)

PRICING MANAGER

1. Other names: pricing executive.
2. The pricing manager is responsible for advising and/or setting prices on the organization's services and programs.

CUSTOMER RELATIONS MANAGER

1. Other names: customer service manager, account manager.
2. The customer relations manager has responsibility for managing customer services and handling customer complaints.

GOVERNMENT RELATIONS MANAGER

1. Other names: legislative representative; lobbyist.
2. The government relations manager provides the organization with intelligence on relevant developments in government and manages the organization's program of representation and presentation to government.

PUBLIC RELATIONS MANAGER

1. Other names: public affairs officer.
2. The public relations manager has responsibility for communicating and improving the organization's image with various publics.

TERRITORY MANAGER

1. Other names: regional manager, district manager.
2. The territory manager has responsibility for managing the organization's products, services, and programs in a specific territory.

Y would have to consider the costs of these systems against the benefits. A good way to proceed is to install a few product and market managers on a trial basis to see what the system produces and costs.

## CREATING A MARKET-ORIENTED ORGANIZATION

An organization can have a marketing officer or marketing department and still not be run in a market-oriented way. The marketing manager has a limited influence on how others in the organization will think and behave toward customers and other publics. The marketing officer in a college, for example, cannot order professors to show a stronger interest in students. A marketing vice president in a hospital cannot require nurses to smile and act promptly to meet patient needs. The marketing manager, instead, will have to work patiently to build up a market-oriented organization. It is not possible for a non-market-oriented organization to be transformed into a fully responsive market-oriented organization overnight. Installing the marketing concept calls for major commitments and changes in the organization. As noted by Edward S. McKay, a long-time marketing consultant:

It may require drastic and upsetting changes in organization. It usually demands new approaches to planning. It may set in motion a series of appraisals that will disclose surprising weaknesses in performance, distressing needs for modification of operating practices, and unexpected gaps, conflicts, or obsolescence in basic policies. Without doubt, it will call for reorientation of business philosophy and for the reversal of some long-established attitudes. These changes will not be easy to implement. Objectives, obstacles, resistance, and deep-rooted habits will have to be overcome. Frequently, even difficult and painful restaffing programs are necessary before any real progress can be made in implementing the concept.[4]

Any attempt to reorient an organization requires a plan. The plan must be based on sound principles for producing organizational change. Achieving a marketing orientation calls for several measures, the sum of which will hopefully produce a market-oriented organization within three to five years. These measures are described below.

### TOP MANAGEMENT SUPPORT

An organization is not likely to develop a strong marketing orientation until its chief executive officer (CEO) believes in it, understands it, wants it, and wins the support of other high-level executives for building this function. The CEO is the organization's highest "marketing executive," and has to create the climate for marketing by talking about it and agitating for it. The CEO of a university, for example, must remind the faculty, bursar, housing director, and others of the importance of serving the students. By setting the tone that the organization must be service-minded and responsive, the CEO prepares the groundwork for introducing further changes later (see Exhibit 5–1).

### EFFECTIVE ORGANIZATION DESIGN

The CEO cannot do the whole marketing job. Eventually, a marketing manager must be added to the organization, either a marketing director or a marketing vice president. As we saw earlier, a marketing director essentially operates as a *resource manager* who takes responsibility for building and coordinating marketing resources and activities. A marketing vice president operates as a high-level *strategy and policy manager,* capable of influencing other top managers to take a market-oriented view of the organization's customers and publics. The cost of failing to establish an adequate marketing function is described below:

> An illustration of the failure to position the marketing function properly within the organization is that of a large city hospital which made the mistake of assigning the organization's marketing to a mid-level supervisor already overloaded with administrative tasks. Not only was the supervisor unable to spend adequate time analyzing the hospital's major markets and competitive stance, but also the supervisor found that he was unable to obtain support for the few (quite reasonable) marketing actions he recommended. Because no one in top management had initi-

**EXHIBIT 5–1.** Memo from a college president on the need for a customer orientation

> As surely as there are "Fifty Ways to Leave Your Lover," as the popular song says, there are fifty ways and fifty reasons for a student to end his love affair with his college. Short-term campaigns to accommodate students meet the urgency of the moment, but do not build long-term goodwill. Some research indicates that students leave colleges not for big reasons, but for accumulations of little reasons that erode their justifications of college choice.
>
> The problem is how to inculcate responsiveness, or "marketing consciousness," within the entire collegiate community, making everyone connected with the institution aware that (1) no one *has* to attend your college; (2) no one has to *remain* at your college; and (3) everyone wants to be treated with respect, and to be appreciated. In modern society, no service- or people-oriented establishment can prosper without a sense of responsiveness, a may-I-help-you approach on the part of all.
>
> An educational institution has a responsibility to set a high example in valuing humankind. A surly clerk in the registrar's office, a defensive custodian, an irritable residence director, an abrasive secretary can easily undo in moments the goodwill created by the warm friendship of a professor or the congeniality of a dean. How may we heighten the marketing consciousness of the whole institution? How do we assure the student consumer that he is entitled to as much courtesy and kindness at his or her school as at the bank, airlines, clothing shop, grocery, and so on?
>
> At the heart of a consumerist approach in any *service* industry is an adaptation of an old rule: Perform your service as if you were on the *receiving* point rather than the delivery point of the transaction. If teachers would teach as they would like to be taught, custodians cleaned as they would like their houses cleaned, questions were answered as we would want our own questions answered, the world would be happier, and the college would be a better place. In truth, marketing consciousness will have to be promoted (perhaps "marketed") within the college community.
>
> 1. The president, as chief executive, will have to strike the official posture with an initial memo or position paper in which he makes it clear that: (a) students and all publics are due the utmost courtesy, consideration, and thoughtfulness; (b) temper tantrums, "telling people off," deviousness have no part in the academic setting; (c) this is not just a passive policy, but everyone should be constantly asking, How can I be of help? The clientele is the key to institutional good fortune, personal prosperity, and a clear conscience toward consumers and the society.
>
> 2. Since most institutions now use some sort of evaluative process, included among performance standards for personnel judgments could be the matter of marketing consciousness. How does the individual reflect the institution's commitment to a consumeristic approach? That

standard then feeds into salary decisions just as do job skill, productivity, professional growth, and so on.

3. Short seminars and workshops for different classes of employees can point up the priority the college gives to marketing consciousness. The airlines and telephone companies have been very good at instilling this approach—I have never been treated with anything but the utmost courtesy and kindness by telephone operators and airline personnel. It would be worthwhile to assemble the custodians to say: Be responsive to student needs and requests; be looking for helpful things you can accomplish that may not be in your job description; see to it that leaky faucets get fixed, light bulbs replaced, trash bins emptied, spills cleaned. Offer short courses to secretaries and clerks in telephone manners and good reception techniques. Chances are there are resource persons on every campus who could provide such instruction.

4. Put a statement in the catalog declaring the college's intent. You may want to note that constraints of purpose, law, finances, propriety will not permit the institution to say "yes" to everything. But it is institutional intent to be responsive, consumeristic, courteous, and conscientious in all matters.

5. Place statements in the faculty handbook and in personnel policy manuals concerning the college's commitment to a high level of marketing consciousness.

6. Place squawk boxes in a few prominent places so that anyone who feels he's been dealt less than the minimum of human kindness may report the incident. A follow-up by the worker's supervisor will impress the point that the institution is serious about its commitment.

7. Encourage supervisory personnel to make a special effort to reward and compliment those who consistently go the extra mile, and who exhibit a heightened concern for the welfare of the clientele. Let the president write thank yous for exceptional courtesy and responsiveness. Word will spread.

8. If the institution publishes an internal newsletter, each issue could highlight a particular example of consumer concern: a faculty member's visit to the hospital bedside of a student recovering from an accident; a student providing a spontaneous campus tour in response to the request of a "walk-on" visiting alumnus; a secretary's detailed explanation of a complicated Bureau of Immigration form for the benefit of a befuddled international student.

Human kindness ought to be in generous supply among the humane personnel of the learning community. Such will also prove to reduce attrition and to be good for the institution.

SOURCE: Written by Thomas E. Corts, president, Wingate College of Wingate, North Carolina, and included with his permission.

ated the analysis from which the recommendation came and no top level manager was responsible for the marketing function, no one with the power to implement the recommended marketing actions would support them. The result was a frustrated supervisor who spent a good deal of his overallocated time on a nonproductive task and a hospital which missed out on two substantial market opportunities.[5]

### IN-COMPANY MARKETING TRAINING

An early task of the new marketing executive is to develop a series of workshops to introduce marketing to various groups in the organization. These groups are likely to have incorrect ideas about marketing and little understanding of its potential benefits.

The first workshop should be presented to top corporate and divisional management. Their understanding and support is absolutely essential if marketing is to work in the organization. The workshop may take place at the organization's headquarters or at a retreat; it may consist of a highly professional presentation of concepts, cases, and marketing planning exercises. From there, further presentations can be made to the operations people, financial people, and others to enlist their understanding. These presentations should cover such topics as market opportunity identification, market segmentation, market targeting and positioning, marketing planning and control, pricing, selling, and marketing communication.

### BETTER EMPLOYEE HIRING PRACTICES

Training can only go so far in inculcating the right attitudes in employees. If a college faculty has grown accustomed to concentrating on research instead of good teaching, it will be hard to change their attitudes. The college can gradually rectify the imbalance by hiring faculty who are more teaching and student oriented. The first principle in developing a caring faculty is to hire caring people. Some people are more naturally service-minded than others, and this can be a criterion for hiring. Delta Airlines does most of its stewardess recruiting from the deep South where there is a tradition of hospitality; and it avoids hiring in large northern cities because people from these cities tend to be less hospitable. Delta operates on the principle that it is easier to hire friendly people than to train unfriendly people to be friendly.

New employees should go through a training program that emphasizes the importance of creating customer satisfaction. They can be taught how to handle complaining and even abusive customers without getting riled up. Skills in listening and customer problem solving would be part of the training (see Exhibit 5–2).

### REWARDING MARKET-ORIENTED EMPLOYEES

One way for top management to convince everyone in the organization of the importance of customer-oriented attitudes is to reward those who demonstrate these attitudes. The organization can make a point of citing employees who

**EXHIBIT 5–2.** Walt Disney Enterprises—a highly responsive organization

Service organizations—colleges, hospitals, social agencies, and others—are increasingly recognizing that their marketing mix consists not of four Ps but five—product, price, place, promotion, and people. And people may be the most important P! The organization's employees come in continuous contact with consumers and create good or bad impressions about the organization, as the case may be. Service organizations are eager to figure out how to produce a genuine customer orientation and service-mindedness in their employees.

Not many organizations have really figured out how to "turn on" their inside people (employees) to serve their outside people (customers). Consider the following things that the Disney organization does to market "positive customer attitudes" to its employees:

1. The personnel staff at Disney makes a special effort to welcome new job applicants and make a good impression on them. The initial impression is very important. Those who are hired are given clearly written instructions on what to expect—where to report, what to wear, and how long each training phase will take.

2. On the first day, new employees report to Disney University for an all-day orientation session. They sit four to a table, receive name tags, and enjoy coffee, juice, and pastry. The four new employees at each table are asked to get acquainted and then introduce each other. As a result, each new employee immediately knows three other people and feels part of a group.

3. During the next eight hours, the employees are introduced to the Disney philosophy and operations through the most modern audio-visual presentations. The new employees learn that they are in the entertainment business. They are "cast members" whose job it is to be enthusiastic, knowledgeable, and professional in serving Disney's "guests." Each division in the organization is described, and how these divisions relate to each other to produce the "show." They are then treated to a free lunch, and in the afternoon, the new employees are given a tour of the park and also shown the private recreational area set aside for the employees' exclusive use, consisting of a lake, recreation hall, picnic areas, boating and fishing, and a large library.

4. The next day, the new employees report to their assigned jobs, such as security hosts (policemen), transportation hosts (drivers), custodial hosts (street cleaners), or food and beverage hosts (restaurant workers). They will receive a few days of additional training before they go "on stage." When they really know their function, they receive their "theme costume" for that function and are ready to go on stage.

5. The new employees receive additional training on how to answer the scores of questions guests frequently ask about the park. When they don't have the answer, they can dial a special number where a cadre of switchboard operators armed with thick factbooks stand ready to answer any question.

6. The employees regularly receive an eight-page 8½ × 11 newspaper

**EXHIBIT 5–2.** Walt Disney Enterprises—a highly responsive organization (continued)

> called *Eyes and Ears* that features all sorts of activities, employment opportunities, special benefits, educational offerings, and so on. Each issue contains a generous number of employee pictures, all of them smiling.
>
> 7. Each Disney manager spends a week each year in "cross-utilization," namely, giving up the desk and heading for the front line, such as taking tickets, selling popcorn, or loading or unloading rides. In this way, management stays in touch with the daily challenges of running the park and problems of maintaining quality service to satisfy the millions of people who visit the theme park yearly. All the managers and employees wear name badges and address each other on a first-name basis, regardless of rank.
>
> 8. All exiting employees receive a questionnaire to indicate how they felt about working for Disney, particularly any dissatisfactions they might have had. In this way, Disney's management can measure how good a job they are doing in producing employee satisfaction and ultimately customer satisfaction.
>
> No wonder the Disney people have had such huge success in satisfying their "guests." Their exchange with employees makes the latter feel important and personally responsible for the "show." The employees' sense of "owning this organization," of being worthwhile members of a worthwhile organization, results in their satisfaction spilling over to the millions of visitors with whom they come in contact.

SOURCE: This is a summary of the major points found in N. W. Pope, "Mickey Mouse Marketing," *American Banker,* July 25, 1979; and "More Mickey Mouse Marketing," *American Banker,* September 12, 1979.

have done an outstanding job of serving customers. Many colleges have "best teacher" awards based on student voting. Some hospitals carry a picture in their employees' magazine showing the "nurse-of-the-month" and describing how this person handled a difficult situation. By calling attention to examples of commendable customer-oriented performance, it is hoped that other employees will be motivated to emulate this behavior.

### PLANNING SYSTEM IMPROVEMENT

One of the most effective ways to build a demand for stronger marketing is through improving the organization's planning system. Suppose the nonprofit organization has neither strong marketing nor strong planning. The organization might first design and install a business planning system. To make this system work, strong marketing data and analysis will be necessary. The planners will see that business plans must begin with an analysis of the market. This will require strengthening the organization's marketing function. Top management will see that business planning is largely an empty gesture without good marketing data and analysis.

---

## SUMMARY

All organizations carry on marketing activities whether or not they acknowledge this. The issue is whether they should utilize marketing more formally. Organizations can draw on marketing resources in a number of ways, such as appointing a marketing executive to the board of directors, inviting help from marketing professors, hiring marketing firms (advertising agencies and marketing research firms), and sending their staff to marketing workshops. When the organization feels ready to establish a formal marketing function, it can hire a marketing services director, whose job is to supply marketing assistance and services to others in the organization. Or it could hire a vice president of marketing whose job is to participate with top management in strategy and policy formulation. A careful search should be made for the right person, who understands both marketing and the institutional area. This person should choose initial marketing projects that promise to have a high impact on the organization for a relatively small cost in a reasonably short period of time. If marketing's contribution is strong, its size will expand over time to cover different marketing functions, products, markets, and territories. The presence of a marketing department, however, does not mean that the organization as a whole is market oriented, since this department may have limited influence. To create a truly market-oriented organization requires several things: top management support, effective organization design, in-company marketing training, better employee hiring practices, rewarding market-oriented employees, and improving the planning system.

---

## QUESTIONS

**1.** The central administration of a suburban high school district has jurisdiction over eight very large high schools (over 2,000 students each). It also runs a large adult education program. At the present time, the administration has no marketing specialist, although it does have two people who take care of public relations and advertising. What type of marketing organization would be best for this school district?

**2.** The Boy Scouts of America is having trouble recruiting new scouts, volunteers, and funds, particularly in urban areas. What type of marketing organization should it have to help it overcome these problems?

**3.** One local affiliate of the American Lung Association serves two large counties with a combined population of over one million. Yet the permanent paid staff consists of an executive director, a program director, and a secretary. What steps can this organization take toward implementing marketing?

**4.** Develop a diagram of a matrix organization framework for a metropolitan Planned Parenthood chapter. Would you recommend a product management system, a market management system, or a matrix organization? Why?

5. What do you believe are key conditions for creating a market-oriented organization? Rank these in order of importance and explain your ranking.

---

## NOTES

1. For another example and analysis, see Jacqueline Janders, "Marketing: One YMCA Attacks Its Problems," *Perspective Magazine,* May 1975, pp. 23–26.
2. Sometimes, unfortunately, the reverse happens. At one college, the director of marketing helped improve recruitment effectiveness substantially. At this point the president terminated the position, feeling that all the value had been obtained. Needless to say, other marketing problems emerged down the road, and the president realized that he had been hasty. Marketing is not a "fair weather" function, but one that has a continuous job to perform in an organization.
3. See "United States Postal Service," in Christopher H. Lovelock and Charles B. Weinberg, eds., *Cases in Public and Nonprofit Marketing* (Palo Alto, Calif.: Scientific Press, 1977), pp. 153–62.
4. Edward S. McKay, *The Marketing Mystique* (New York: American Management Association, 1972), p. 22.
5. Roberta N. Clarke, "Marketing Health Care: Problems in Implementation," *HCM Review,* Winter 1978, p. 24.

# Marketing Information and Research

Johnson Hospital (real name disguised) is a 300-bed, private, nonprofit institution located on Chicago's South Side. Its primary patient area is an inner-city minority residential neighborhood largely composed of family housing. The immediate vicinity, stimulated in large part by efforts initiated by the hospital, is in the process of economic renewal. Johnson's main competitors in the provision of hospital care are South Shore, Roseland, and South Chicago County hospitals.

Johnson Hospital is a modern facility; much of it is new. The recently opened emergency room is the most modern in the area, and is equipped to handle a far greater patient load than its predecessor. Johnson's new emergency room is being underutilized. Worse, its patient volume has fallen by approximately 2,000 visits compared to the past year. In addition, 40 percent of the current patient volume is made up of indigents who "fall through the cracks" of the welfare system, thus burdening the hospital with a nonreimbursable cost of service. This has pushed the emergency room into the red and flows down into the hospital's books as 6 percent of total revenue, all lost.

The goal here is to increase the use of the emergency room by paying customers. The target population is working people, hopefully with third-party payment insurance, and people on public aid (currently at 32 percent, they are the largest group to use the emergency room) whose expenses would be picked up by some welfare agency.

The hospital's administration does not know how to proceed. The administration feels that it needs to know certain things before it can develop a marketing plan. To this end, the administration invited a well-known marketing research firm to propose a research study that would help the administration in its deliberations. The marketing research firm identified the following critical issues:

- What percent of the people in Johnson's primary service area currently use or would consider using an emergency room as a private physician substitute?
- If they are currently using an emergency room in this way, which one is it and why do they go there?
- If they are not currently using an emergency room this way, why not? What would encourage them to do so?
- What do people find most important when they are seeking emergency care?
- How do they rate local emergency rooms on the issues most important to them? How does Johnson stack up?
- What market needs are currently not being filled and how can Johnson fill them?
- What social services can be approached to seek additional patients for Jackson Park, and how?

To answer these questions, the marketing research firm would carry out four steps: (1) in-depth analysis of hospital data, (2) interviews with selected members of the professional and administrative staff at Johnson Hospital, (3) survey research on selected target populations, and (4) analysis, recommendations, and presentation. The cost of carrying out this work would be $20,000. The hospital now has to decide whether to (1) authorize this research, (2) ask for a lower-cost study that will yield some but not all of the indicated information, or (3) drop the idea of marketing research and simply try out a number of things that might increase the drawing power of the Johnson Hospital emergency room.

SOURCE: Based on a report by Alan Minoff, Vice President of Management Analysis Center, 1980; with permission.

Managers need timely, accurate, and adequate market information as a basis for making sound marketing decisions. We shall use the term marketing information system (MIS) to describe the organization's system for gathering, analyzing, storing, and disseminating relevant marketing information. More formally:

A **marketing information system** is a continuing and interacting structure of people, equipment, and procedures designed to gather, sort, analyze, evaluate and distribute pertinent, timely, and accurate information for use by marketing decision makers to improve their marketing planning, execution, and control.[1]

The role and major subsystems of an MIS are illustrated in Figure 6–1. At the left is shown the marketing environment that marketing managers must monitor—specifically target markets, marketing channels, competitors, publics, and macroenvironmental forces. Developments and trends in the marketing environment are picked up in the company through one of four subsystems making up the marketing information system—namely, the internal reports system, the marketing intelligence system, the marketing research system, and the analytical marketing system. The information then flows to the appropriate marketing managers to help them in their marketing planning, execution, and control. The resulting decisions and communications then flow back to the marketing environment.

We will now expand on the four major subsystems of the organization's MIS.

## INTERNAL RECORDS SYSTEM

The oldest and most basic information system used by managers is the internal records system. Every organization accumulates information in the regular course of its operations.

A hospital will keep records on its patients, including their names, addresses, ages, illnesses, lengths of stay, supplies and room charges, attending physicians, complaints, and so on. From these patient records, the hospital can develop statistics on the number of daily admissions, average length of patient stay, average patient charge, frequency distribution of different illnesses, and other useful statistics. The hospital will also have records on their physicians, nurses, costs, billings, assets, and liabilities, all of which is indispensable information for making management decisions.

A museum will keep several record systems. Its contributor file will list the names, addresses, past contributions, and other data of its contributors. Its campaign progress file will show the amount raised to date from each major source, such as individuals, foundations, corporations, and government grants. Its cost file will show how much money has been spent on direct mail, newspaper advertising, brochures, salaries, consultant fees, and so on.

Every internal records system can be improved in its speed, comprehensiveness, and accuracy. Periodically, an organization should survey its managers for possible improvements in the internal records system. The goal is not to design the most elegant system, but one that is cost-effective in meeting the manager's information needs. A cross-section of managers should be queried as to their information needs. Table 6–1 shows the major questions that can be put to them.

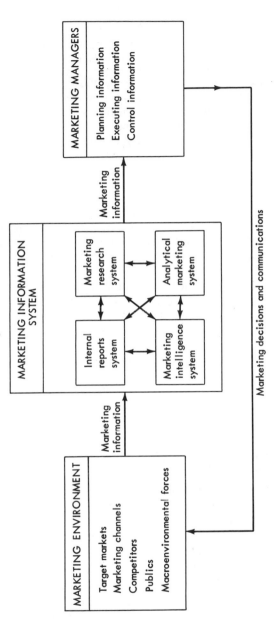

**FIGURE 6-1**

The Marketing Information System

**Table 6–1**

1. What types of decisions are you regularly called upon to make?
2. What types of information do you need to make these decisions?
3. What types of information do you regularly get?
4. What types of special studies do you periodically request?
5. What types of information would you like to get that you are not now getting?
6. What information would you want daily? weekly? monthly? yearly?
7. What magazines and reports would you like to see routed to you on a regular basis?
8. What specific topics would you like to be kept informed of?
9. What types of data analysis programs would you like to see made available?
10. What do you think would be the four most helpful improvements that could be made in the present marketing information system?

Once their opinions are gathered, the information system designers can design an internal records system that reconciles (1) what managers think they need, (2) what managers really need, and (3) what is economically feasible.

## MARKETING INTELLIGENCE SYSTEM

Whereas the internal reports system supplies executives with *results data,* the marketing intelligence system supplies executives with *happenings data.* Our definition is:

The **marketing intelligence system** is the set of sources and procedures by which marketing executives obtain their everyday information about developments in the external marketing environment.

Managers carry on marketing intelligence mostly on their own by reading newspapers and trade publications and talking to various people inside and outside the organization. In this way, they are able to spot important developments. At the same time, their casual approach to gathering marketing intelligence can also result in missing or learning too late of some other important developments, such as a fundraising opportunity with an important donor, or a new law that might hurt the organization's nonprofit status.

An organization can take some concrete steps to improve the quality of marketing intelligence available to its managers. First, the organization must "sell" its managers and staff on the importance of gathering marketing intelligence and passing it on to others in the organization. Its intelligence responsibilities can be facilitated by designing information forms that are easy to fill out and circulate. Managers should know the kind of information that would be useful to other managers.

Second, the organization should encourage outside parties with whom they deal—advertising agencies, professional associations, lawyers, accountants—to pass on any useful bits of information. For example, a museum's lawyer may hear about a wealthy donor who is revising his will, and this information can be useful to the development office of the museum.

Third, the organization could hire people to carry on specialized intelligence gathering activity. Many organizations hire "mystery shoppers" to canvass their own organization and competitors' organizations. A mystery shopper might visit the admissions offices of several colleges and report back on the quality of their "customer handling." In one case, the "bogus student" reported receiving widely different receptions, some of which were absolute "turnoffs" and others which were highly effective. Mystery shopping is also an important means for learning whether the organization's own staff is really practicing a customer orientation in its dealings with the public.

Fourth, the organization can establish an office that is specifically responsible for gathering and disseminating marketing intelligence. The staff would perform a number of services. It would scan major publications, abstract the relevant news, and disseminate the news to appropriate managers. It would install suggestion and complaint systems so that clients and others would have an opportunity to express their attitudes toward the organization. It would develop a master index so that all the past and current information could be easily retrieved. The staff would assist managers in evaluating the reliability of different pieces of information. These and other services would greatly enhance the quality of the information available to marketing managers.

---

## MARKETING RESEARCH SYSTEM

From time to time, managers need to commission specific marketing research studies in order to have adequate information to make pending decisions. Administrators of nonprofit organizations are increasingly finding that they need marketing research, such as when a hospital wants to know whether people in its service area have a positive attitude toward the hospital, or when a college wants to determine what kind of image it has among high school counselors, or when a political organization wants to find out what voters think of its candidate and the other candidates. Many studies could prove worthwhile to an organization but, in the face of a limited budget, the organization must have knowhow to choose marketing research projects carefully, design them efficiently, and implement the results effectively.

First, we define marketing research:

> **Marketing research** is the systematic design, collection, analysis, and reporting of data and findings relevant to a specific marketing situation or problem facing an organization.

The key idea is that management initiates or commissions a study to develop information on a subject by a certain date. There are numerous types of studies that qualify as marketing research projects. Table 6–2 lists 33 different marketing research activities and the percentage of American companies carrying on each. The ten most common activities are determination of market characteristics, measurement of market potentials, market-share analysis, sales analysis, studies of business trends, competitive product studies, short-range forecasting, new-product acceptance and potential, long-range forecasting, and pricing studies.

Who does these studies for an organization? Large organizations often have their own marketing research directors or departments. In fact, over 73 percent of all large business firms have formal marketing research departments, ranging in size from one or a few professional researchers to as many as two dozen researchers.[2] The marketing research department selects problems, design studies, and even carries out some of them, although often they contract with outside marketing research companies for help. As much as one-half of a marketing research department's budget may be spent buying the services of outside marketing research companies. In the case of smaller organizations, they are not likely to employ a marketing research director and will typically buy outside marketing research when needed. *Bradford's Directory* lists over 350 outside marketing research companies. They fall into three major categories.[3]

1. *Syndicated service research firms.* These firms specialize in gathering continuous consumer and trade information which they sell in the form of standardized product reports on a fee-subscription basis to all clients. Marketing management can purchase syndicated reports on television audiences from Nielsen or the American Research Bureau (ARB); on radio audiences from ARB; on magazine audiences from Simmons or Target Group Index (TGI); and so on. The largest of these firms, A. C. Nielsen Company, had estimated billings of $211 million in 1975.

2. *Custom marketing research firms.* These firms can be hired to carry out one-of-a-kind research projects to provide data needed by a particular client. They participate with the client in designing the study and the report becomes the client's property. One of the leading custom marketing research firms is Market Facts, with annual billings of approximately $15 million.

3. *Specialty-line marketing research firms.* These firms provide specialized services to other marketing research firms and company marketing research departments. The best example is the field service firm which sells field interviewing services to other firms.

Marketing researchers have been steadily expanding and improving their techniques. Many techniques were developed outside of marketing by researchers in economics, statistics, sociology, social psychology, and psychology. They were adopted by marketing researchers who recognized opportunities for their use.

## Table 6–2

### MAJOR MARKETING RESEARCH ACTIVITIES

| Type of Research | Percent Doing |
|---|---|
| Advertising research: | |
|   Motivation research | 48 |
|   Copy research | 49 |
|   Media research | 61 |
|   Studies of ad effectiveness | 67 |
| Business economics and corporate research: | |
|   Short-range forecasting (up to 1 year) | 85 |
|   Long-range forecasting (over 1 year) | 82 |
|   Studies of business trends | 86 |
|   Pricing studies | 81 |
|   Plant and warehouse location studies | 71 |
|   Product mix studies | 51 |
|   Acquisition studies | 69 |
|   Export and international studies | 51 |
|   MIS (management information system) | 72 |
|   Operations research | 60 |
|   Internal company employees | 65 |
| Corporate responsibility research: | |
|   Consumers "right to know" studies | 26 |
|   Ecological impact studies | 33 |
|   Studies of legal constraints on advertising and promotion | 51 |
|   Social values and policies studies | 40 |
| Product research: | |
|   New-product acceptance and potential | 84 |
|   Competitive-product studies | 85 |
|   Testing of existing products | 75 |
|   Packaging research—design or physical characteristics | 60 |
| Sales and market research: | |
|   Measurement of market potentials | 93 |
|   Market-share analysis | 92 |
|   Determination of market characteristics | 93 |
|   Sales analysis | 89 |
|   Establishment of sales quotas, territories | 75 |
|   Distribution channels studies | 69 |
|   Test markets, store audits | 54 |
|   Consumer-panel operations | 50 |
|   Sales compensation studies | 60 |
|   Promotional studies of premiums, coupons, sampling, deals, etc. | 52 |

SOURCE: Dik Warren Twedt, ed., *1978 Survey of Marketing Research* (Chicago: American Marketing Association, 1978), p. 41 (based on 798 companies).

Some of them—such as questionnaire construction and area sampling—came along naturally and were quickly accepted. Others—such as motivation research and mathematical methods—came in uneasily, with prolonged and heated debates among practitioners over their practical usefulness. But they, too, eventually received acceptance by marketing researchers.

The challenge facing managers who need marketing research is to know enough about its potentialities and limitations so that they can get the right information at a reasonable cost and use it intelligently. If they know nothing about marketing research, they might allow the wrong information to be collected, or collected too expensively, or interpreted incorrectly. One protection against this is to work with only highly experienced and credible marketing researchers and agencies because it is in their interests to do a good job and produce information that leads to correct decisions. An equally important protection is that managers should know enough about marketing research procedures to assist in its planning and in the interpretation of results.

Figure 6–2 describes the five basic steps in good marketing research. We will illustrate these steps in connection with the following situation:

> Camp Star (name disguised) is an overnight summer camp in Wisconsin operated by the Jewish Federation of Chicago. The camp has experienced an enrollment decline in the last few years resulting in operating at about 70 percent of capacity. The camp director is not sure whether the decline is due to a general decline in overnight camping in the nation as a whole (a shrinkage in market size) or is specific to Camp Star (a shrinkage of market share). Not knowing the causes, the camp director is not sure about what marketing actions, if any, can halt the enrollment decline. He recognizes the need to do some marketing research although his budget will not permit doing a large-scale study. He decided to hire Social Marketing Consultants, a small marketing research firm that was recommended to him. Arthur and Dini Sterngold, proprietors of the firm, agreed to design and implement a low-cost study that would yield useful findings and recommendations.

### RESEARCH OBJECTIVES AND PROBLEM DEFINITION

The first step in research is to define carefully the research objectives. The objective may be to learn about a market, or to find a practical idea for increasing the demand for a product or service, or to measure the impact of a marketing tool. The research objectives make it easier to arrive at a useful definition of the problem. If the problem is stated vaguely, if the wrong problem is defined, or if

## FIGURE 6–2

### The Marketing Research Process

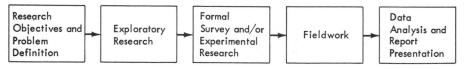

the uses of the research are not made clear, then the research results may be useless or even misleading to the manager.

The marketing researchers working on the Camp Star case defined the overall research objective as that of discovering the main factors that affect parents' decisions to send their children to an overnight summer camp, and, on the basis of these factors, recommending specific marketing actions available to Camp Star to increase its enrollment. To accomplish this objective, the researchers identified the following main elements as influencing "camp choice behavior":

1. the decision-making process people go through in selecting an overnight camp
2. people's images of overnight camps in general, and of Camp Star in particular
3. the alternative activities people consider in making summer plans
4. people's motives for selecting overnight camps
5. what people look for in an overnight camp
6. important consumer characteristics and divisions among groups of consumers (market segmentation)
7. the role and effectiveness of different promotional material

### EXPLORATORY RESEARCH

This step calls for carrying out preliminary research to learn more about the market before any formal research survey is undertaken. The major procedures at this stage include collecting secondary data, doing observational research, and carrying out informal interviewing with individuals and groups.

**Secondary data research.**    In seeking information, a researcher should initially gather and review secondary data if any exists. *Secondary data* are relevant data that already exist somewhere, having been collected for another purpose. Secondary data are normally quicker and less expensive to obtain and will give the researcher a start on the problem. Afterward, the researcher can gather *primary data,* namely, original data to meet the problem at hand.

In looking for secondary data, the Camp Star researchers can consult the following major sources of secondary data:[4]

1. *Internal records.* The researchers should check Camp Star files for past figures on enrollment, dropouts, complaints, competitive advertising, and other data that might be relevant.
2. *Government.* The federal government publishes more marketing data than any other source in the country. Many organizations depend on data found in the *Census of Population, Census of Housing, Census of Business, Census of Manufacturers, Census of Agriculture, Census of Minerals,* and *Census of Governments,* as well as on special research reports issued at all levels of government. The Camp Star's researchers can use local census data to determine what is happening to the number of children ages 8–11 who are normal prospects for overnight camps.
3. *Trade, professional, and business associations.* Camp Star is a member of the American Camp Association, which provides information on camp enrollment and capacity by state, year, and type of camp. The researchers can ascertain whether

Camp Star's enrollment decline is in line with a normal decline in its area or is exceptional.

4. *Competitors and other private organizations.* The researchers could see whether any useful secondary data can be obtained directly from other camps in the area.

5. *Marketing firms.* Marketing research firms, advertising agencies, and media firms may possess some useful past studies of the overnight camp market.

6. *Universities, research organizations, and foundations.* These organizations may have conducted studies of the camping industry.

7. *Published sources.* Researchers should examine published material in libraries on the subject of camping. Among the marketing journals, marketers like to consult the *Journal of Marketing, Journal of Marketing Research,* and *Journal of Consumer Research.* Useful general business magazines include *Business Week, Fortune, Forbes, Harvard Business Review,* and *Sales & Marketing Management.* Newspapers such as the *Wall Street Journal* and *The New York Times* are very useful.

These secondary data are likely to provide useful ideas and findings. The researchers must be careful in making inferences, however, because the secondary data were collected for a variety of purposes and under a variety of conditions that might limit their usefulness. Marketing researchers should check these data for relevance, impartiality, validity, and reliability. The researchers are also likely to find that the secondary data leave many questions unanswered for which they will have to turn to collect primary data, either through observation or interviewing.

**Observational research.**     One major way to collect primary data is to carry out personal observation in various situations. The researchers could visit the camp during the season and observe the campers' reactions to the food, facilities, and various activities. Off-season, the researchers could observe how the camp staff handles telephone inquiries and personal visits from prospects. The researchers could also examine the camp's brochures and mailings for possible deficiencies. The purpose of the observational method is to discover factors that affect enrollment, the importance of which can be measured later.

**Qualitative interviewing.**     In addition to gathering data through observation, the researchers need to conduct some interviewing during the exploratory stage of a marketing research project. The purpose of the interviewing is to collect further ideas on the factors that play a role in the marketing problem being investigated. In the exploratory stage, the interviewing should be qualitatively rather than quantitatively oriented. Qualitative interviewing is largely open-ended. People are asked leading questions as a means of stimulating them to share their thoughts and feelings regarding overnight camps or other relevant topics. The distinct uses of qualitative research are to (1) probe deeply into consumers' underlying needs, perceptions, preferences, and satisfaction, (2) gain greater familiarity and understanding of marketing problems whose causes are not known, and (3) develop ideas that can be further investigated through quantitative research. On the other hand, quantitative research seeks to generate statistically reliable estimates of particular market or consumer characteristics. Quantitative research entails sampling a much larger number of people than qualitative research, and it assumes that one knows in advance what specific questions to ask.

Qualitative research is not only a desirable first step, it is sometimes the only step permitted by the budget of many nonprofit organizations. For the Camp Star project, the researchers decided to interview new prospects for the camp as well as people associated with Camp Star in the past. The new prospects included parents and their children. The Camp Star group included past campers, counselors, and parents of returnees and nonreturnees. In addition, the researchers interviewed staff members about their attitudes toward the camp. Two methods would be used: individual interviewing and group interviewing.

*Individual interviewing* consists of interviewing one person at a time either in person, over the telephone, or through the mails. The Camp Star researchers gathered about 50 individual interviews, half in person and half over the phone.

*Group interviewing* consists of inviting from six to ten persons to gather for a few hours with a trained interviewer to discuss a product, service, organization, or other marketing entity. The interviewer needs good qualifications, such as objectivity, knowledge of the subject matter and industry to be discussed, and some understanding of group dynamics and consumer behavior; otherwise the results can be worthless or misleading when led by the wrong people. The participants are normally paid a small sum for attending. The meeting is typically held in pleasant surroundings (a home, for example) and refreshments are served to increase the informality. The group interviewer starts with a broad question, such as "How would you like to see your children spend their summer vacation?" Questions would then move to the subject of summer camps, then to overnight camps, and then to Camp Star versus other camps. The interviewer encourages free and easy discussion among the participants, hoping that the group dynamic will bring out real feelings and thoughts. At the same time, the interviewer "focuses" the discussion, and hence the name *focus group interviewing*. The comments are recorded through note taking or tape recording and subsequently studied to understand the consumers' buying process. The Camp Star researchers conducted two focus group discussions, one with parents and another with children, and learned a great deal from this form of interviewing. Focus group interviewing is becoming one of the major marketing research tools for gaining insight into consumer thoughts and feelings.[5]

## FORMAL RESEARCH

After defining the problem and doing exploratory research, the researchers may wish to carry out more formal research to measure magnitudes or test hypotheses.

Suppose the Camp Star researchers found that some of the past campers reported dissatisfaction with their camping experience at Camp Star. The researchers, however, were not sure how extensive the dissatisfaction was and the relative important of different factors. In addition, they learned that some camp prospects had little or no knowledge of Camp Star and, among those who did, several had a negative image of this camp. The researchers, however, were not sure of how extensive this was. The camp director agreed that it would be desirable to quantify these factors.

At this point, the marketing researcher can design a formal survey or a marketing experiment. Each is described below.

**Survey research.**     Many managers take an overly simplistic view of survey work. They think that it consists of writing a few obvious questions and finding an adequate number of people in the target market to answer them. The fact is that amateur research is liable to many errors that can waste anywhere from $3,000 to $50,000 of the organization's funds. Designing a reliable survey is the job of a professional marketing researcher. Here we will describe the main things that users of marketing research should know about developing the research instrument, the sampling plan, and the fieldwork.

**Research instrument.**     The main survey research instrument is the questionnaire. The construction of good questionnaires calls for considerable skill. Every questionnaire should be pretested on a pilot sample of persons before being used on a large scale. A professional marketing researcher can usually spot several errors in a casually prepared questionnaire (see Exhibit 6–1).

A common type of error occurs in the *types of questions asked:* the inclusion of questions that cannot be answered, or would not be answered, or need not be answered, and the omission of other questions that should be answered. Each question should be checked to determine whether it is necessary in terms of the research objectives. Questions should be dropped that are just interesting (except for one or two to start the interview) because they lengthen the time required and try the respondent's patience.

The *form of questions* can make a substantial difference to the response. An *open-end question* is one in which the respondent is free to answer in his or her own words. For example, "What is your opinion of Camp Star?" A *closed-end question* is one in which the possible answers are supplied. A closed-end question can take several forms:

> *Dichotomous question:* "Have you heard of Camp Star?" yes( ), no( ).
> *Multiple choice question:* "Camp Star is a camp in Wisconsin run by (a) the YMCA, (b) the Jewish Federation, (c) the Black Panthers, (d) some other group."
> *Semantic differential question:* "Camp Star is (a) a very large camp, (b) a large camp, (c) neither large nor small, (d) a small camp, (e) a very small camp."
> *Likert scale question:* "Camp Star plans to turn itself into a music camp. How do you feel about this? (a) strongly approve, (b) approve, (c) undecided, (d) disapprove, (e) strongly disapprove."

The *choice of words* also calls for considerable care. The researcher should strive for simple, direct, unambiguous, and unbiased wording. Other "dos" and "don'ts" arise in connection with the *sequencing of questions* in the question-

**EXHIBIT 6–1.** A "questionable" questionnaire

> Suppose the following questionnaire was prepared by a summer camp director to be used in interviewing parents of prospective campers. How do you feel about each question?
>
> 1. What is your income to the nearest hundred dollars?
>
> | People don't necessarily know their income to the nearest hundred dollars nor do they want to reveal their income that closely. Furthermore, a questionnaire should never open with such a personal question. |
>
> 2. Are you a strong or weak supporter of overnight summer camping for your children?
>
> | What do "strong" and "weak" mean? |
>
> 3. Do your children behave themselves well in a summer camp? Yes ( ) No ( )
>
> | "Behave" is a relative term. Besides, will people want to answer this? Furthermore, is "yes" and "no" the best way to allow a response to the question? Why is the question being asked in the first place? |
>
> 4. How many camps mailed literature to you last April? This April?
>
> | Who can remember this? |
>
> 5. What are the most salient and determinant attributes in your evaluation of summer camps?
>
> | What is "salience" and "determinant attributes"? Don't use big words on me. |
>
> 6. Do you think it is right to deprive your child of the opportunity to grow into a mature person through the experience of summer camping?
>
> | Loaded question. How can one answer "yes," given the bias? |

naire. The lead questions should create interest, if possible. Open questions are usually better here. Difficult questions or personal questions should be introduced toward the end of the interview, in order not to create an emotional reaction that may affect subsequent answers or cause the respondent to break off the interview. The questions should be asked in as logical an order as possible in order to avoid confusing the respondent. Classificatory data on the respondent are usually asked for last, because they tend to be less interesting and are on the personal side.

SAMPLING PLAN. The other element of research design is a sampling plan, and it calls for four decisions.

1. *Sampling unit.* This answers the question: *Who is to be surveyed?* The proper sampling unit is not always obvious from the nature of the information sought. In the Camp Star survey of camping decision behavior, should the sampling unit be

the father, mother, child, or all three? Who is the usual instigator, influencer, decider, user, and/or purchaser?

2. *Sample size.* This answers the question: *How many people should be surveyed?* Large samples obviously give more reliable results than small samples. However, it is not necessary to sample the entire target market or even a substantial part of it to achieve satisfactory precision. Samples amounting to often less than a fraction of 1 percent of a population can often provide good reliability, given a creditable sampling procedure.

3. *Sampling procedure.* This answers the question: *How should the respondents be chosen?* To draw valid and reliable inferences about the target market, a random probability sample of the population should be drawn. Random sampling allows the calculation of confidence limits for sampling error. But random sampling is almost always more costly than nonrandom sampling. Some marketing researchers feel that the extra expenditure for probability sampling could be put to better use. Specifically, more of the money of a fixed research budget could be spent in designing better questionnaires and hiring better interviewers to reduce response and nonsampling errors, which can be just as fatal as sampling errors. This is a real issue, one that the marketing researcher and marketing manager must carefully weigh.

4. *Means of contact.* This answers the question: *How should the subjects be contacted?* The choices are telephone, mail, or personal interviews. *Telephone interviewing* stands out as the best method for gathering information quickly. It also permits the interviewer to clarify questions if they are not understood. The two main drawbacks of telephone interviewing are that only people with telephones can be interviewed, and only short, not too personal, interviews can be carried out. The *mail questionnaire* may be the best way to reach persons who would not give personal interviews or who might be biased by interviewers. On the other hand, mail questionnaires require simple and clearly worded questions, and the return rate is usually low and/or slow. *Personal interviewing* is the most versatile of the three methods. The personal interviewer can ask more questions and can supplement the interview with personal observations. Personal interviewing is the most expensive method and requires more technical and administrative planning and supervision.

**Experimental research.**      We talked about formal research in its most common form, that of designing a survey. An increasing number of marketing researchers are eager to go beyond measuring the perceptions, preferences, and intentions of a target market and seeking to measure actual cause-and-effect relationships. For example, the Camp Star researchers might like to know the answers to such questions as:

- Would an expensive four-color Camp Star brochure sent to prospective campers produce at least twice as many inquiries as the normal one-color plain brochure?
- Would Camp Star attract more parent interest if it emphasized the educational or the recreational aspects of summer camping?
- What would be the impact on next summer's enrollment of a 20 percent increase in the price?

Each of these questions could be answered by the survey method by asking people to state their reactions. However, they may not give their true opinions or carry them out. Experimental research is more rigorous. Situations are created where the actual behavior of the target market can be observed and its causes identified.

Let us apply the experimental method to the first question. The Camp Star director would have to design an expensive four-color brochure as well as a traditional one. The researcher would select a subsample—say, 100 families—from the mailing list. Half of these families would receive the expensive brochure and half would receive the traditional one. As inquiries came in, the director would check whether that family received either the first or second brochure. The inquiry rate would be calculated for the two groups of families to see whether the more expensive brochure stimulated at least twice as many inquiries to cover its higher cost. If it did, and the camp director could think of no other factor that could explain the difference in the inquiry rates, he would now want to mail only the expensive brochure to the rest of the families on the mailing list.

The experimental method is being increasingly recognized in marketing circles as the most rigorous and conclusive one to use if the proper controls can be exercised and the cost afforded. The method requires selecting matched groups of subjects, giving them different treatments, controlling extraneous variables from making a difference, and checking on whether observed differences are statistically significant. To the extent that the design and execution of the experiment eliminates alternative hypotheses that might explain the same results, the research and marketing manager can have confidence in the conclusions.[6]

### FIELDWORK

The fieldwork phase of survey or experimental research follows after the research design has been finished and pretested. Some organizations will carry out the interviewing using volunteers. Other organizations will hire professional interviewers. Marketing research firms work hard to select and train interviewers who can be trusted, are personable, and are able to do their work in a reasonably short time. The fieldwork phase could be the most expensive and the most liable to error. Four major problems have to be dealt with in this phase:

1. *Not present.* When randomly selected respondents are not reached on the first call, the interviewer must either call them back later or substitute another respondent. Otherwise, nonresponse bias may be introduced.
2. *Refusal to cooperate.* After reaching the subjects, the interviewer must interest them in cooperating. Otherwise, nonresponse bias may be introduced.
3. *Respondent bias.* The interviewer must encourage accurate and thoughtful answers.
4. *Interviewer bias.* Interviewers are capable of introducing a variety of biases into the interviewing process, through the mere fact of their age, sex, manner, or intonation. In addition, there is the problem of conscious interviewer bias or dishonesty.

The final step in the marketing research process is to develop meaningful information and findings to present to the manager. The researcher will tabulate the data and develop one-way and two-way frequency distributions. Averages and measures of dispersion will be computed for the major variables. The researcher might attempt to apply some advanced statistical techniques and decision models in the hope of discovering additional findings.

The researcher's purpose is not to overwhelm management with numbers and fancy statistical procedures. The researcher's purpose is to present major findings that will help the manager make better marketing decisions.

## ANALYTICAL MARKETING SYSTEM

The marketing information system contains a fourth subsystem called the analytical marketing system. The analytical marketing system consists of a set of advanced techniques for analyzing marketing data and marketing problems. These systems are able to produce more findings and conclusions than can be gained by only commonsense manipulation of the data. Large organizations tend to make extensive use of analytical marketing systems. In smaller organizations, managers resist these approaches as too technical or expensive.

An analytical marketing system consists of two sets of tools known as the statistical bank and the model bank (see Figure 6–3). The *statistical bank* is a collection of advanced statistical procedures for learning more about the relationships within a set of data and their statistical reliability. They allow management to go beyond the frequency distributions, means, and standard deviations in the data.

Managers often want answers to such questions as:

- What are the most important variables affecting my sales volume and how important is each one?
- If I raise my price 10 percent and increase my advertising expenditures by 20 percent, what will happen to sales?
- What are the most discriminating predictors of persons who are likely to buy my service versus my competitor's service?
- What are the best variables for segmenting my market, and how many segments should be created?

The statistical techniques are somewhat technical, and the reader is advised to consult other sources for understanding and using them.[7]

The *model bank* is a collection of models that will help marketers make better marketing decisions. Each model consists of a set of interrelated variables that represent some real system, process, or outcome. These models can help answer "what if?" and "which is best?" questions. In the last twenty years,

**FIGURE 6–3**

Analytical Marketing System

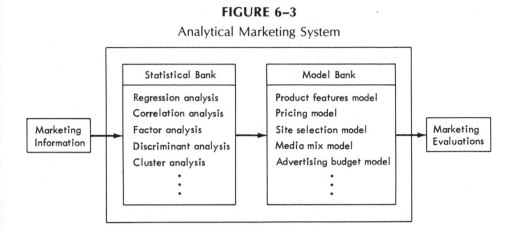

marketing scientists have developed a great number of models to help marketing executives do a better job of pricing, designing sales territories and sales call plans, selecting sites for outlets, developing optimal advertising media mixes, developing optimal size advertising budgets, and forecasting new product sales.[8]

This concludes our review of the nature of a marketing information system and its main subsystems—internal reports, marketing intelligence, marketing research, and analytical marketing.

## SUMMARY

To carry out effective marketing, the organization needs timely, accurate, and adequate information. Four systems make up the organization's marketing information system.

The first, the internal records system, consists of all the information that the organization gathers in the regular course of its operations. It includes sales and cost information by product, customer, territory, and so on. Many useful questions can be answered by analyzing the information in the internal records system.

The second, the marketing intelligence system, describes the set of sources and procedures by which executives obtain their everyday information about developments in the marketplace. An organization can improve the quality of its marketing intelligence by motivating its managers to scan the environment and report useful information to others, and hiring intelligence specialists to find and disseminate important information.

The third, the marketing research system, consists of the systematic design, collection, analysis, and reporting of data and findings relevant to a specific marketing situation or problem facing an organization. The marketing research process consists of five steps: developing the research objectives and problem definition; exploratory research; formal survey and/or experimental research; fieldwork; and data analysis and report presentation.

The fourth, the analytical marketing system, consists of two sets of advanced tools for analyzing marketing data and marketing problems. One set of tools is the statistical bank, which is a collection of statistical procedures for analyzing the relationships within a set of data and their statistical reliability. The other is the model bank, which is a collection of mathematical models that will help marketers make better marketing decisions.

## QUESTIONS

**1.** What is the difference between primary and secondary data? What are the advantages of reviewing available secondary data before collecting other data?

**2.** The principal of a Catholic high school would like to have information to help understand what current and prospective students and parents consider in selecting a Catholic education. What kinds of exploratory and formal research would you recommend to her, and why?

**3.** Many organizations have extensive internal records. How can these records be made useful for marketing planning and decision making?

**4.** Describe a marketing intelligence system which would be useful to a community college offering vocationally oriented evening programs for adults.

**5.** Common Cause, a national grass-roots lobbying organization, has its headquarters in Washington, D.C. Propose one or more ways in which Common Cause can determine the concerns of its members across the United States.

## NOTES

**1.** The definition is adapted from Samuel V. Smith, Richard H. Brien, and James E. Stafford, "Marketing Information Systems: An Introductory Overview," in their *Readings in Marketing Information Systems* (Boston: Houghton Mifflin, 1968), p. 7.

**2.** See Dik Warren Twedt, ed., *1978 Survey of Marketing Research* (Chicago: American Marketing Association, 1978).

**3.** Ernest S. Bradford, *Bradford's Directory of Marketing Research Agencies and Management Consultants in the United States and the World,* 15th ed. (Middlebury, Vt.: Bradford, 1973–74).

**4.** For an excellent annotated reference to major secondary sources of business and marketing data, see Thomas C. Kinnear and James R. Taylor, *Marketing Research: An Applied Approach* (New York: McGraw-Hill, 1979), pp. 128–31, 138–71.

**5.** See Keith K. Cox, et al., "Applications of Focus Group Interviews in Marketing," *Journal of Marketing,* January 1976, pp. 77–80; and Bobby J. Calder, "Focus Groups and the Nature of Qualitative Marketing Research," *Journal of Marketing Research,* August 1977, pp. 353–64.

**6.** For more reading on experimental research, see Seymour Banks, *Experimentation in Marketing* (New York: McGraw-Hill, 1965).

**7.** See David A. Acker, ed., *Multivariate Analysis in Marketing: Theory and Applications* (Belmont, Calif.: Wadsworth, 1971).

**8.** Various models are described in Philip Kotler, *Marketing Decision Making— A Model Building Approach* (New York: Holt, Rinehart & Winston, 1971).

# Marketing Planning and Control

Pick–Staiger Concert Hall, a $4 million facility located on Northwestern University's main campus in Evanston, Illinois, opened its doors in October 1975. The concert hall seats 1,000 people and is designed with excellent acoustics. The concert hall's manager, Thomas Willis, selects visiting artists, administers his own budget, and reports directly to the dean of the Music School at Northwestern University. Thomas Willis' staff consists of 58 employees, most of whom are students at the university. By working in rotating fashion as ushers, box office personnel, publicity agents, stage managers, and administrative assistants, the staff gains experience in managing over 400 events in a 33-week season.

During its first season, the concert hall featured faculty and student recitals and miscellaneous visiting artists. Variety was the only controlling principle: Jazz and PDQ Bach were offered, along with a famous operatic baritone, a little known pianist, and an equally little known cellist. Understandably, the concert office found it hard to market this heterogeneous package. Willis was hired to improve the quality of the Performing Art Series and to make it the core of the concert hall's revenue programming. Three mini–Performing Arts Series were also developed: a "Guitar" series, a "Mostly Baroque" series, and a "Contemporary Sound" series. These mini-series were intended to tap special interest markets and also to attract patrons who were unwilling to subscribe to a longer series. The response to these series was encouraging.

Each season's "product mix of performances" is selected by Willis on the basis of recommendations by others and his own instincts. No marketing research is conducted into the interests and preferences of the general audience living around the university, faculty and staff, and students. Pricing is established on the low side without testing the strength of market demand. The annual promotion budget is set at $12,000 and spent on posters, radio advertising, direct mail, and so on, without any measurement of the cost effectiveness of these expenditures. Only 15 percent of the promotional budget is spent on the subscription campaign. The remainder is spent promoting single concerts.

The lack of systematic marketing planning and control is partly responsible for the following less-than-satisfactory results:

1. The Performing Arts Series at present has only 510 subscribers (51 percent of capacity), which means that much annual effort must go into attracting another 49 percent of individual ticket buyers to fill the hall.

2. The most recent subscription renewal rate was 42 percent, and only 11 percent of current subscribers have subscribed for three consecutive seasons. Although Pick–Staiger may have large numbers of "occasional" or "frequent users," it has so far failed to gain a loyal, committed audience of subscribers.

3. "General Admission" sales account for 25 percent of attenders. This market pays more per ticket and needs to be expanded. Students account for about 20 percent of subscribers to the various series. There is a potential to develop much more student attendance.

4. Ticket sales for the latest season generated revenues of $70,000, which cover only 84 percent of the artists' fees, not to mention other costs. This deficit is too great to be sustained indefinitely by grants and donations.

To solve these and other problems, Willis invited an MBA major in marketing, Jeanne Lockridge Mueller, to perform a marketing audit of the Pick–Staiger Concert Hall. A marketing audit is a control tool designed to evaluate and improve the marketing performance of an organization. Ms. Mueller conducted her research and produced a marketing audit containing a number of useful recommendations, including the following:

1. The concert manager needs to establish a larger professional staff. Many good projects are begun—preliminary efforts at group sales, senior citizen solicitation, students' questionnaires, "exit" interviews of nonrenewing subscribers—only to be forgotten as soon as the student interns move on or the season is ready to begin.

2. A marketing planning system should be installed which produces each year a long-range plan and an annual plan, with clearly stated objectives, strategies, actions, and budgets, and responsibility for each part of the plan assigned to specific people.

3. Marketing communications need to be strengthened. There is virtually no "glitz" to concert office literature. Pick–Staiger Concert Hall does not even have its own letterhead, using School of Music stationery. There is no continuity of design or logo to set Pick–Staiger's

publications apart from the tide of promotional materials that inundate potential subscribers. The Performing Arts Series brochures are not particularly informative about the contents of the various performances. New posters are designed each year with no logo continuity. Faculty receive only plain form letters through campus mail, listing the artists and ticket prices with no descriptive information.

4. The potential audience in and around the university is huge and only minimally tapped. The concert office should launch an aggressive subscription campaign aimed at the general public, and later at the faculty and student body. The concert manager should consider raising the prices on General Admission tickets and possibly on the more expensive category of faculty/staff tickets, and then offering a genuine discount if patrons became subscribers. Subscriptions savings at present (between 2 and 12 percent) are too marginal to incentivize subscription, and frequent attenders know that they can usually get seating without subscribing in advance.

Thomas Willis received Ms. Mueller's marketing audit and began to think freshly about her proposals for improving marketing planning and control at Pick–Staiger.

SOURCE: Based on material found in Jeanne Lockridge Mueller's unpublished class paper, "Pick–Staiger Concert Hall: A Marketing Audit," May 29, 1980.

Most nonprofit organizations operate very rudimentary systems of planning and control. What they often call a planning and control system turns out to be a budgeting system, designed to make sure that payrolls are met and expenses don't get out of hand. The chief executive officer may have a plan in mind, and so might the department heads, but these plans are not put into writing, scrutinized, and approved. Most of the staff is busy doing things and seems too overworked to have the time to prepare formal plans.

When budget time rolls around, each manager proposes next year's needed budget for his or her department. Thus, universities receive budget requests from their deans, museums from their curators, and hospitals from their executive directors. These managers make exaggerated requests in the knowledge that these requests might be cut down and the department would still get what they would have proposed in the first place. These managers are not required to outline departmental goals and strategies. The assumption is that they will pursue the same goals they have always pursued ("excellence in teaching," "a high standard of care") and simply need more money to meet the department's needs.

When chief executives of nonprofit organizations are advised to establish formal planning and control systems, they often object and say that these systems are inappropriate to their type of organization. A university president gave the author five reasons why he did not believe in formal planning systems:

1. The department heads (deans and chairpersons) do not have the time to write formal plans, nor does the top administration have the time to read them.
2. Most department heads would not be able to plan even if they were asked. They head their departments because they are scholars or leaders in their field, not because they are managers. They might refuse to plan, or plan poorly, and this would be tolerated as long as they were performing well in other respects.
3. The department heads would not use their plans. The plans would be window dressing and filed away. The plans might even be obsolete the day they were written, with so much change occurring in the academic world.
4. The administration has plans which are best kept secret from the department heads, because some department heads would feel threatened by them. The department heads should not be encouraged to come up with unrealistic ideas of what they want that the president would have to reject.
5. Installing a formal planning system and making it work would cost too much in money and time.

Without denying some validity to these arguments, this chapter will argue that formal planning and control systems are beneficial on the whole and needed for the improvement of organizational performance. The fact that many business firms use modern planning/control systems and that an increasing number of nonprofit organizations are introducing these systems indicates some apparent satisfaction with the results of these systems. Melville C. Branch has perceptively summarized the main benefits of a formal planning system:

1. Encourages systematic thinking-ahead by management
2. Leads to a better coordination of company efforts
3. Leads to the development of performance standards for control
4. Causes the company to sharpen its guiding objectives and policies
5. Results in better preparedness for sudden developments
6. Brings about a more vivid sense in the participating executives of their interacting responsibilities[1]

The relationship between marketing planning and control is shown in Figure 7–1 and constitutes a three-step process. The first step calls upon the organization to plan its marketing effort, specifically to identify attractive target markets, develop effective marketing strategies, and develop detailed action programs. The second step involves executing the action programs in the marketing plan, both geographically and over time. The third step calls for marketing control activity to make sure that the objectives are being achieved. Marketing control requires measuring results, analyzing the causes of poor results, and taking corrective actions. The corrective actions consist of adjustments in the plan, its execution, or both.

We will first deal with marketing planning and then with marketing control.

## FIGURE 7-1

### The Marketing Planning and Control System

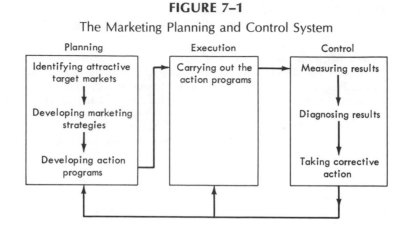

## MARKETING PLANNING

When an organization *establishes* a marketing planning system it faces three questions: (1) How sophisticated should the planning system be? (2) What procedures should be used to carry on the planning process? (3) What should the contents of a marketing plan be? These issues are now taken up.

### DEGREES OF SOPHISTICATION IN MARKETING PLANNING

Most organizations start with little or no formal planning and over the years upgrade their planning systems. In fact, planning systems tend to evolve through the following stages.

**Unplanned stage.**    When organizations are first established, their organizers are so busy soliciting funds, attracting clients, and seeking facilities that they have little time for formal planning. Management is totally engrossed in making the day-to-day decisions required for survival. There is no planning staff and hardly any time to plan.

**Budgeting system stage.**    Management eventually recognizes the desirability of installing a budgeting system to improve the management of the organization's cash flow. Management estimates the expected income and costs for the coming year. Each department manager prepares a department budget. These budgets are financially oriented, not strategically oriented. Budgets are not the same as plans.

**Project planning stage.**    Many organizations find that they need to develop plans for specific projects. Thus, a university needs to plan new buildings and usually establishes a planning office to carry out this work. Yet the university's planning department is not concerned with strategic or annual planning.

**Annual planning stage.**     Management eventually recognizes the need to develop an annual planning system based on *management by objectives.* [2] It has three options.

The first is *top-down planning,* so called because top management sets *goals* and *plans* for all the lower levels of management. This model is taken from military organizations where the generals prepare the plans and the troops carry them out. In nonprofit organizations this goes along with a Theory X view of employees, that they dislike work and responsibility and prefer to be directed.[3] Top-down planning is most prevalent in government agencies where each level establishes the plans for the next lower level.

The second system is *bottom-up planning,* so called because the various units of the organization prepare their own goals and plans based on the best they think they can do, and they send them to upper management for approval. This style is based on Theory Y thinking about human nature, that employees like work and responsibility and are more creative and committed if they participate in the planning and running of the organization. Bottom-up planning is most often found in collegial organizations and smaller organizations.

Most companies use a third system known as *goals down–plans up planning.* Here top management takes a broad look at the organization's opportunities and requirements and sets organizational goals for the year. The various units of the organization are responsible for developing plans designed to help the organization reach these goals. These plans, when approved by top management, become the official annual plan.

**Long-range planning stage.**     In this stage, the organization refines the planning system in a number of directions to improve its overall effectiveness. The major change is the addition of *long-range planning.* Management realizes that annual plans make sense only in the context of a long-range plan. In fact, the long-range plan should come first and the annual plan should be a detailed version of the first year of the long-range plan. The long-range plan, however, is reworked each year (called *rolling planning*) because the environment changes rapidly and requires an annual review of the long-run planning assumptions.

A further development is that the various plans begin to take on a more *strategic character.* When an organization first turns to long-range planning, it usually assumes that the future will largely be an extension of the present and that past strategies, organizational forms, and procedures will remain appropriate. Eventually, management begins to recognize that the environment is full of probabilities, not certainties, and broader strategic thinking is required. The planning format is redesigned to stimulate managers to contemplate and evaluate alternative strategies that will leave the organization as well off as possible.

As the company gains experience with planning, an effort is made to *standardize the plan formats* so that higher management can make more meaningful comparisons among similar units. It is important that the plans written for comparable units, such as divisions, departments, and programs, follow the same or a similar format to permit intelligent comparison by higher management.

As the planning culture takes hold in the organization, further improvements are introduced. Managers receive more training in the use of *financial analysis* and are required to justify their recommendations not only in terms of enrollment, attendance, contributions, and so on, but also in terms of financial measures such as cost-benefit or cost effectiveness of an activity. *Computer programs* might be developed to help managers examine the impact of alternative marketing plans and environments on "sales" and "profit." The managers might also be asked to develop *contingency plans* showing how they would respond to specific major threats and opportunities that might arise. These and other developments mark the emergence of a true strategic planning culture in the organization.

### Designing the Marketing Planning Process

A planning system doesn't just happen. An appropriate system must be designed that will be acceptable to the managers and compatible with the level of information and skill at their disposal. Often the initial system will be designed simplistically so that managers get accustomed to writing plans. As experience is gained, changes and improvements will be made in the planning system to increase its effectiveness. Eventually, the managers will accept planning not as a chore to meet their boss' needs but as a tool to increase their own effectiveness.

Someone has to be responsible for developing the initial planning system. The following three-step procedure is recommended. First, top management appoints a committee to study whether a formal planning system is needed, and if so, what kind of system, and when and how it should be established. The second step is to hire an outside consultant who has broad experience in designing management planning systems for other organizations. The outside consultant can provide valuable perspectives on planning as well as specific procedures and forms. The third step involves the hiring of a director of planning. The planning director would take responsibility for designing the final system.

The planning director's job is not to write the plans but to educate and assist the managers in writing their plans. A maxim of planning is that planning should be done by those who must carry out the plans. By involving the line managers in planning their operations, they are (1) stimulated to think out their business objectives and strategies, and (2) motivated to achieve their goals.

One major task of the planning director is to develop a calendar for the planning process. The normal calendar steps are:

1. Develop a set of relevant environmental facts and trends to distribute to the managers in preparation for their planning.
2. Work with top management to develop a set of overall corporate objectives for the coming year to pass on to the managers in preparation for their planning.

3. Work with individual managers to complete their marketing plans by a certain date.
4. Work with top management to review, approve, or modify the various plans.
5. Develop a consolidated official plan for the organization for the coming period.

This calendar sequence underscores the critical role of marketing planning in the overall management planning process. Individual managers start the process by setting marketing goals (for attendance, enrollment, contributions, etc.) for their programs for the coming period, along with proposed strategies and marketing budgets. Once top management approves these marketing goals and strategies, decisions can be made on how much personnel to hire, how much supplies to order, and how much money to borrow. Thus, a commitment to a set of marketing goals precedes decisions on personnel, production, and financial requirements.

### THE FORMAT OF A MARKETING PLAN

Another major task of the planning director is to design the appropriate standard format that managers should follow in preparing their marketing plans. The topics and their sequence can make a difference in the quality of planning results. A marketing plan should contain the following major sections: *executive summary, situation analysis, objectives and goals, marketing strategy, action programs, budgets and controls.* These sections will be discussed in the context of the following situation:

> The concert manager of the Pick–Staiger Concert Hall at Northwestern University asks each manager to develop a plan for his or her area of responsibility. One of them is Janet Smith, who is responsible for building up general audience attendance at the Performing Arts Series.

**Executive summary.** The planning document should open with a summary of the main goals and recommendations presented in the plan. Here is an abbreviated example:

> The 1981 marketing plan for community audience development seeks to attract 2,000 new first-time "nonuniversity" attenders to the Performing Arts Series at Pick–Staiger. Assuming an average attendance of one performance per new attender, and an average ticket price of $7, this step, if successful, will add $14,000 to concert hall revenue. To accomplish this, the plan calls for a marketing expenditure of $10,000. Of this, $2,000 will be spent on marketing research to measure present levels of community awareness and interest in the Performing Arts Series, and $5,000 will be spent in buying appropriate mailing lists and producing a new "hard-selling" brochure about the series. Finally, $3,000 will be spent on radio and newspaper ads to stimulate interest in the series.

The purpose of the executive summary is to permit higher management to preview the major thrust of each plan and read further in search of the information that is critical in evaluating the plan. To facilitate this, a table of contents should follow the executive summary.

**Situation analysis.**     The first major in-depth section of the plan is the *situation analysis*, in which the manager describes the major features of the situation facing his or her operation. The situation analysis consists of four subsections—background, normal forecast, opportunities and threats, and strengths and weaknesses.

BACKGROUND.   This section starts with a summary of key performance indices for the last few years. An example (hypothetical) is shown in Table 7–1 for the Pick–Staiger Concert Hall.

Row 1 shows that the concert hall has increased the number of performances in the Performing Arts Series from 20 to 40 a year over a three-year period. Row 2 shows the annual capacity, that is, the maximum number of tickets that could have been sold. Row 3 shows that a growing audience has been attracted, and Row 4 shows that audience as a percent of capacity has been growing. Row 5 shows that the average ticket price has been rising from $5 to $7 over the three-year period. Row 6 shows that total revenue has risen substantially over the three-year period. Rows 7, 8, 9, and 10 show how performers' cost, marketing cost, and administrative cost have risen over the same period. Finally, Row 11 indicates that the concert hall's loss has increased over the period in spite of higher attendance and ticket prices.

Clearly, the concert hall is making progress in a sales sense, but not in a financial sense. These data should be followed by a description of major develop-

## Table 7–1

### BACKGROUND DATA

|  | 1978 | 1979 | 1980 |
|---|---|---|---|
| 1. Number of performances | 20 | 30 | 40 |
| 2. Annual capacity[1] | 20,000 | 30,000 | 40,000 |
| 3. Audience | 5,000 | 9,000 | 10,000 |
| 4. Audience as % of capacity | 25% | 30% | 40% |
| 5. Average ticket price[2] | $5 | $6 | $7 |
| 6. Total revenue | $25,000 | $54,000 | $70,000 |
| 7. Performers' cost | $35,000 | $60,000 | $83,000 |
| 8. Marketing cost | $6,000 | $8,000 | $12,000 |
| 9. Administrative cost | $20,000 | $24,000 | $30,000 |
| 10. Total cost | $61,000 | $92,000 | $125,000 |
| 11. Net operating loss | $36,000 | $38,000 | $55,000 |

[1]One thousand seats are available for each performance, and this is multiplied by the number of performances to find annual capacity.
[2]Average ticket price is found by dividing total ticket revenue by the number of tickets distributed, whether they were sold at full price, discounted price, or free.

ments occurring in the marketplace, such as changes in audience size and interests, trends in ticket prices, new competition, and other factors that would throw light on the marketplace and provide guidance in the development of an effective strategy.

NORMAL FORECAST.    The background information should be followed by a forecast of audience size under "normal conditions," that is, assuming no major changes in the *marketing environment* or *marketing strategies.* This forecast could be obtained in a number of ways. The assumption could be made that audience size would stay constant, or grow at the most recent rate of growth, or even decline. The basis of the forecast could be statistical curve fitting, surveying a sample of people who attended last year, and so on.

The forecast would have to be revised if quite different environmental conditions are expected or strategies are planned. If the forecast does not satisfy higher management, the planner would have to consider new strategies, hopefully finding one that promises a higher level of audience growth.

OPPORTUNITIES AND THREATS.    The normal forecast should be followed by a section in which the manager identifies the main opportunities and threats facing the business unit. Usually, the manager is aware of a number of these but should be required to put them down on paper. Higher management can review this list and raise questions about threats and opportunities that are listed or missing. In the following year, management can see how many opportunities were acted on and what threats really occurred.

Table 7–2A shows the opportunities and threats listed by a manager at the concert hall. The opportunities and threats describe *outside* factors facing the organization. They are written so as to suggest some actions that might be warranted. The manager may be asked to rate the opportunities and threats for their potential impact and probability as an indicator of which deserve the most planning attention.

STRENGTHS AND WEAKNESSES.    The manager should next list the main internal strengths and weaknesses of the organization (see Table 7–2B). The list of strengths has implications for strategy formulation, while the list of weaknesses has implications for investments to correct weaknesses. Higher management can raise critical questions about the strengths and weaknesses identified by each manager.

**Objectives and goals.**    The situation analysis describes where the organization stands and where it might go. Now management must propose where that organization should go. Specific objectives and goals have to be set. Top management typically promulgates overall goals for the coming period for the organization as a whole. The top management of the Pick–Staiger Concert Hall might state that they want to achieve (1) a 15 percent growth in audience size, and (2) an operating loss not to exceed $40,000.

Each manager develops goals for his or her department within the context

## Table 7–2

AN EXAMPLE OF OPPORTUNITIES, THREATS, STRENGTHS, AND WEAKNESSES

---

### A. Opportunities and Threats Facing the Concert Hall

**OPPORTUNITIES**

1. There is a large potential audience in the nearby suburb of Winnetka that is unaware of Pick–Staiger Concert Hall who could be attracted to the Performing Arts Series.
2. Many of Chicago's large corporations would buy blocks of tickets if they could be effectively reached.
3. If Ticketron would handle these tickets, city-wide distribution would be guaranteed.

**THREATS**

1. The expected downswing in the economy may reduce the subscription renewal rate.
2. The increasing parking problem is producing a lot of unhappy patrons.
3. Top performing groups are planning to raise their fees by an average of 20 percent, resulting in higher costs to the concert hall.

### B. Strengths and Weaknesses of the Concert Hall

**STRENGTHS**

1. The audience has been highly satisfied with most of the past performers.
2. The acoustics of the concert hall are among the best in the Midwest.
3. The concert hall has an air of ambiance and excitement.

**WEAKNESSES**

1. The staff, though enthusiastic, is not well trained in handling the various tasks that have to be done.
2. The access roads to the university are slow and discourage people from coming at greater distances.
3. The ticket office is open only from 1:00 to 5:00 P.M. and some sales are lost as a result.

---

of these overall goals. Thus the general audience manager, reviewing top management's goals, decided on the following specific goals: (1) to attract 2,000 new first-time attenders at an average ticket price of $7, and (2) to spend $10,000 to accomplish this. Other goals would also be listed here.

**Marketing strategy.**    The manager next outlines a marketing strategy for attaining the objectives. The marketing strategy describes the "game plan" by which the manager hopes to "win." We define marketing strategy as follows:

> **Marketing strategy** is the fundamental marketing logic by which an organizational unit intends to achieve its marketing objectives. Marketing strategy consists of a coordinated set of decisions on (1) target markets, (2) marketing mix, and (3) marketing expenditure level.

TARGET MARKETS.   Management should introduce criteria to identify the most attractive markets, defined in terms of age, education, income, geographic and other variables. Various markets should be rated on these criteria and the markets selected with the greatest probable response to a unit of marketing effort. Thus management might conclude that the suburbs of Skokie, Wilmette, and Winnetka are likely to deliver a larger audience increase than Highland Park, Glenview, and Deerfield.

MARKETING MIX.   The organization should develop a *strategic marketing mix* which answers such basic questions as whether to emphasize subscriptions or single-performance tickets, or whether to rely on word-of-mouth or mass media. It should then develop a *tactical marketing mix.* For the Winnetka market, the manager may decide on local newspaper advertising and a telephone campaign. For the Skokie market, the manager may decide to mail free tickets for one performance to every resident of Skokie.

MARKETING EXPENDITURE LEVEL.   Marketing strategy also calls for deciding on the marketing expenditure level. Organizations typically establish their marketing budget at some percentage of the sales revenue. For example, the concert manager might be willing to spend 20 percent of sales revenue on marketing. Clearly the more spent on marketing, the larger the audience will be. What an organization needs to know is the point where increased sales no longer bring increased profits and, in fact, cut into profits. Most nonprofit organizations do not allocate nearly enough to marketing. While for-profit organizations may spend 15–25 percent of sales on all forms of marketing, many nonprofit organizations allocate less than 1 percent to it.

**Action program.**   The marketing strategy needs to be turned into a specific set of actions for accomplishing the marketing goals. Each strategy element should be elaborated into appropriate actions. For example, the strategy element, "decrease the personal cost of attending performance to off-campus people," could lead to the following actions: "increase the parking space available to off-campus attenders," "improve traffic management for incoming and outgoing traffic," and "arrange for a bus to bring people to the campus." The actions which appear most cost-effective should then be assigned to specific individuals with specified completion times.

The overall action plan can take the form of a table, with the twelve months (or 52 weeks) of the year serving as columns and various marketing activities serving as rows. Dates can be entered when various activities or expenditures will be started, reviewed, and completed. This action plan can be changed during the year as new problems and opportunities arise.

**Budgets.**   The goals, strategies, and planned actions allow the manager to build a budget, which is essentially a projected profit-and-loss statement. On the revenue side, it shows the forecasted unit sales and the expected net realized price. On the expense side, it shows the costs of production, marketing, and administration. The difference is the projected profit or loss. Management reviews the budget and either approves or modifies it. Once approved, the budget is the basis for marketing operations, financial planning, and personnel recruitment.

**Controls.**      The last section of the plan describes the controls that will be applied to monitor the plan's progress. Normally, the goals and budgets are spelled out for each month or quarter. This means that higher management can review the results each period and spot those managers who are not attaining their goals. These managers will be asked to indicate what actions they will take to improve the results.

This completes the description of the contents of a marketing plan. We now turn to the problem of marketing control.

---

## MARKETING CONTROL

The purpose of marketing control is to maximize the probability that the organization will achieve its short-run and long-run objectives in the marketplace. Many surprises are likely to occur during the plan's execution that will call for new responses or adjustments. Marketing control systems are an intrinsic part of the marketing planning process.

Marketing control is far from being a single process. Three types of marketing control can be distinguished. *Annual plan control* refers to the steps taken during the year to monitor and correct performance deviations from the plan. *Profitability control* consists of efforts to determine the actual profit or loss of different products, services, territories, market segments, and distribution channels. *Strategic control* consists of a systematic evaluation of the organization's marketing performance in relation to its market opportunities. We describe each form of marketing control in the following sections.

### ANNUAL PLAN CONTROL

The purpose of annual plan control is to make sure during the course of the year that the organization is achieving the marketing objectives that it established in its annual plan. This calls for the four steps shown in Figure 7–2. First, the various managers set well-defined goals for each month, quarter, or other period during the plan year. Second, steps are taken to monitor the ongoing results and developments during the year. Third, the managers seek to diagnose the causes of any serious deviations in performance. Fourth, the managers choose *corrective actions* that will hopefully close the gap between goals and performance.

This system is called *management by objectives.* Top management starts the process by developing the "sales," "profit," and other aggregate goals for the planning period. These goals are broken down into subgoals for lower levels of management. During the period, managers receive reports that allow them to

## FIGURE 7–2

### The Control Process

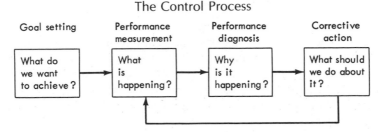

| Goal setting | Performance measurement | Performance diagnosis | Corrective action |
|---|---|---|---|
| What do we want to achieve? | What is happening? | Why is it happening? | What should we do about it? |

follow whether their subordinates are reaching their goals and, if not, to take the necessary corrective actions.

What are the control tools used by management to check on the progress of their subordinates in reaching their goals? The four main ones are sales analysis, market-share analysis, marketing expense-to-sales analysis, and market attitude tracking.

**Sales analysis.** *Sales analysis* is the effort to measure and evaluate the actual sales being achieved in relation to the sales goals set for different managers. Thus, the management of a concert hall would compare actual to expected sales of tickets by season, audience type, specific performance, and so on, to understand audience behavior and preferences. If too few students are attending the concert series, if certain areas of the city are underrepresented, or if a certain type of music is not well attended, the reasons should be sought out. Management should avoid jumping to conclusions without some research. Too few students attending the Performing Arts Series could be due to any number of causes: (1) high ticket prices, (2) low interest in this season's performers, (3) heavy competing social events on the same nights, (4) increased academic pressure for grades, and so on. The proper corrective actions would vary with each cause.

**Market share.** Organizations should periodically review whether they are gaining or losing ground relative to their competition. For example, zoo attendance continues to rise for many zoos, and yet zoos are declining in their share of the recreational dollar. They are losing ground relative to theme parks such as Disneyworld and Great America. The Chicago Lung Association continues to raise more money each year but is slipping in its share of the total medical charity dollar, and also in relation to specific competitors such as the American Heart Association and the American Cancer Association. Market share is a much better indicator of marketing effectiveness than total sales. It must, however, be used cautiously. The organization must correctly identify its real competitors. Beloit College, for example, should not measure its enrollment performance against the large state universities or the elite private universities. Instead, it should measure its enrollment performance against the other colleges to which Beloit applicants also apply. A "perfect competitor" would be another college that students applying to Beloit see as equally desirable.

**Marketing expense-to-sales analysis.** Annual plan control also requires checking on various marketing expenses as a ratio to sales to make sure that the organization is not overspending to achieve its sales goals. The ratios to watch are total *marketing expense-to-sales, sales force expense-to-sales, advertising-to-sales, sales promotion-to-sales, marketing research-to-sales,* and *sales administration-to-sales.* The organization should continuously check whether these ratios are appropriate, and whether shifting from one marketing tool to another could bring down its total cost of sales. Management has to keep an eye on other performance ratios that say something about the efficiency of marketing effort. An experienced fundraising director, for example, periodically checks the following ratios: revenue per fundraiser, number of prospects contacted per fundraiser per day, number of minutes per contact, revenue per contact hour, percentage of closure per contact, percentage of potential contributors covered, and number of lost contributors.

**Market attitude tracking.** Organizations should periodically check on customer attitudes toward the organization. If market attitudes start eroding, they can lead to later declines in sales. Knowing this early can lead to preventative actions. Market attitudes can be measured through well-established control systems such as complaint and suggestion boxes, customer panels, and customer satisfaction surveys.

PROFITABILITY CONTROL

Besides annual plan control, organizations need to carry on periodic research to determine the actual profit or loss on their various products, territories, customer groups, and distribution channels. Consider hospitals. Hospitals today are under great pressure for cost containment. An increasing number are driven to examine the costs of their various departments and activities. They are discovering a great deal of variation in the financial results of different services. For example, hernia operations generally yield a profit to the hospital while inpatient psychiatric services represent a loss to the hospital, at least under the present pricing and reimbursement programs. Hospitals need some cash-generating services to pay for the cash-losing services, and some hospitals have been dropping those services whose losses are too great.

Marketing profitability analysis requires a procedure for identifying all revenues generated by a particular unit or service and all costs associated with it. Sometimes this is fairly easy to do. Thus, a hospital can evaluate the cost of running a satellite branch because costs like rent, salaries, and utilities can be assigned to it. It is more difficult to isolate the revenues and costs of, say, an obstetrics department because it may generate additional business in the future, and also the assignment of overhead charges is somewhat arbitrary.

Marketing profitability analysis provides information on the relative profitability of different products, services, programs, territories, and other marketing entities. It does not imply that the best course of action is to drop the unprofitable marketing entities, nor does it actually measure the likely profit improvement if these marginal marketing entities are dropped. Thought has to be given to possible ways of improving the revenue or reducing the costs, if possible, of the unit.

### STRATEGIC CONTROL

From time to time, organizations need to take a critical look at their overall marketing performance. Marketing is one of the major areas where rapid obsolescence of objectives, policies, strategies, and programs is a constant possibility.

A major tool in this connection is the marketing audit. Organizations are increasingly turning to marketing audits to assess their marketing opportunities and operations. A marketing audit is defined as follows:[4]

> A **marketing audit** is a *comprehensive, systematic, independent,* and *periodic* examination of an organization's marketing environment, objectives, strategies, and activities with a view of determining problem areas and opportunities and recommending a plan of action to improve the organization's marketing performance.

The four characteristics of a marketing audit are expanded below:

1. *Comprehensive.* The marketing audit covers all of the major marketing issues facing an organization, and not only one or a few marketing troublespots. The latter would be called a functional audit if it covered only the sales force, or pricing, or some other marketing activity.
2. *Systematic.* The marketing audit involves an orderly sequence of diagnostic steps covering the organization's marketing environment, internal marketing system, and specific marketing activities. The diagnosis is followed by a corrective action plan involving both short-run and long-run proposals to improve the organization's overall marketing effectiveness.
3. *Independent.* The marketing audit is normally conducted by an inside or outside party who has sufficient independence from the marketing department to attain top management's confidence and the needed objectivity.
4. *Periodic.* The marketing audit should normally be carried out periodically instead of only when there is a crisis. It promises benefits for the organization that is seemingly successful, as well as the one that is in deep trouble.

A marketing audit is carried out by an auditor who gathers information that is critical to evaluating the organization's marketing performance. The auditor collects secondary data and also interviews managers, customers, dealers, salespeople, and others who might throw light on the organization's marketing performance. The auditor cannot rely only on internal management opinion, and must seek the opinions and evaluations of outsiders regarding the organization. Often the findings are a surprise, and sometimes a shock, to management.

Table 7–3 is a guide to the kinds of questions that the marketing auditor

## Table 7–3

### MARKETING AUDIT GUIDE

---

*Part I. Marketing Environment Audit*

*Macroenvironment*

#### A. DEMOGRAPHIC

1. What major demographic developments and trends pose opportunities or threats for this organization?
2. What actions has the organization taken in response to these developments?

#### B. ECONOMIC

1. What major developments and trends in income, prices, savings, and credit have an impact on the organization?
2. What actions has the organization taken in response to these developments and trends?

#### C. ECOLOGICAL

1. What is the outlook for the cost and availability of natural resources and energy needed by the organization?
2. What concerns have been expressed about the organization's role in conservation and what steps has the organization taken?

#### D. TECHNOLOGICAL

1. What major changes are occurring in relevant product, service, and process technology? What is the organization's position in these technologies?
2. What major generic substitutes might replace this product or service?

#### E. POLITICAL

1. What new legislation could affect this organization? What federal, state, and local agency actions should be watched?
2. What actions has the organization taken in response to these developments?

#### F. CULTURAL

1. What changes are occurring in consumer life styles and values that might affect this organization?
2. What actions has the organization taken in response to these developments?

*Task Environment*

#### A. MARKETS

1. What is happening to market size, growth, and geographical distribution?
2. What are the major market segments? What are their expected rates of growth? Which are high-opportunity and low-opportunity segments?

#### B. CUSTOMERS

1. How do current customers and prospects rate the organization and its competitors, particularly with respect to reputation, product quality, service, sales force, and price?
2. How do different classes of customers make their buying decisions?
3. What are the evolving needs and satisfactions being sought by consumers in this market?

## Table 7–3

MARKETING AUDIT GUIDE (continued)

### C. COMPETITORS

1. Who are the major competitors? What are the objectives and strategy of each major competitor? What are their strengths and weaknesses? What are the sizes and trends in market shares?
2. What trends can be foreseen in future competition and substitutes for this product?

### D. DISTRIBUTION AND DEALERS

1. What are the main distribution channels bringing products to customers?
2. What are the efficiency levels and growth potentials of the different distribution channels?

### E. SUPPLIERS

1. What is the outlook for the availability of different key resources used in production?
2. What trends are occurring among suppliers in their pattern of selling?

### F. FACILITATORS AND MARKETING FIRMS

1. What is the outlook for the cost and availability of transportation services?
2. What is the outlook for the cost and availability of warehousing facilities?
3. What is the outlook for the cost and availability of financial resources?
4. How effectively is the advertising agency performing?

### G. PUBLICS

1. What publics (financial, media, government, citizen, local, general, and internal) represent particular opportunities or problems for the company?
2. What steps has the company taken to deal effectively with its key publics?

*Part II. Marketing Objectives and Strategy Audit*

### A. ORGANIZATION'S OBJECTIVES

1. Is the mission of the organization clearly stated in market-oriented terms? Is the mission feasible in terms of the organization's opportunities and resources?
2. Are the organization's various objectives clearly stated so that they lead logically to the marketing objectives?
3. Are the marketing objectives appropriate, given the organization's competitive position, resources, and opportunities?

### B. MARKETING STRATEGY

1. What is the core marketing strategy for achieving the objectives? Is it a sound marketing strategy?
2. Are enough resources (or too much resources) budgeted to accomplish the marketing objectives?
3. Are the marketing resources allocated optimally to prime market segments, territories, and products of the organization?
4. Are the marketing resources allocated optimally to the major elements of the marketing mix, i.e., product quality, service, sales force, advertising, promotion, and distribution?

## Table 7–3

MARKETING AUDIT GUIDE (continued)

*Part III. Marketing Organization Audit*

### A. FORMAL STRUCTURE

1. Is there a high-level marketing officer with adequate authority and responsibility over those organizational activities that affect the customer's satisfaction?
2. Are the marketing responsibilities optimally structured along functional, product, end user, and territorial lines?

### B. FUNCTIONAL EFFICIENCY

1. Are there good communication and working relations between marketing and sales?
2. Is the product management system working effectively? Are the product managers able to plan profits or only sales volume?
3. Are there any groups in marketing that need more training, motivation, supervision, or evaluation?

### C. INTERFACE EFFICIENCY

1. Are there any problems between marketing and operations that need attention?
2. What about marketing and R&D?
3. What about marketing and financial management?
4. What about marketing and purchasing?

*Part IV. Marketing Systems Audit*

### A. MARKETING INFORMATION SYSTEM

1. Is the marketing intelligence system producing accurate, sufficient, and timely information about developments in the marketplace?
2. Is marketing research being adequately used by managers?

### B. MARKETING PLANNING SYSTEM

1. Is the marketing planning system well conceived and effective?
2. Is sales forecasting and market potential measurement soundly carried out?
3. Are sales quotas set on a proper basis?

### C. MARKETING CONTROL SYSTEM

1. Are the control procedures (monthly, quarterly, etc.) adequate to ensure that the annual plan objectives are being achieved?
2. Is provision made to analyze periodically the profitability of different products, markets, territories, and channels of distribution?
3. Is provision made to examine and validate periodically various marketing costs?

### D. NEW PRODUCT DEVELOPMENT SYSTEM

1. Is the organization well organized to gather, generate, and screen new-product ideas?
2. Does the organization do adequate concept research and business analysis before investing heavily in a new idea?
3. Does the organization carry out adequate product and market testing before launching a new product?

**Table 7–3**

MARKETING AUDIT GUIDE (continued)

*Part V. Marketing Productivity Audit*

A. PROFITABILITY ANALYSIS

1. What is the profitability of the organization's different products, customer markets, territories, and channels of distribution?
2. Should the organization enter, expand, contract, or withdraw from any market segments, and what would be the short- and long-run profit consequences?

B. COST-EFFECTIVENESS ANALYSIS

1. Do any marketing activities seem to have excessive costs? Are these costs valid? Can cost-reducing steps be taken?

*Part VI. Marketing Function Audits*

A. PRODUCTS

1. What are the product line objectives? Are these objectives sound? Is the current product line meeting these objectives?
2. Are there particular products that should be phased out?
3. Are there new products that are worth adding?
4. Are any products able to benefit from quality, feature, or style improvements?

B. PRICE

1. What are the pricing objectives, policies, strategies, and procedures? To what extent are prices set on sound cost, demand, and competitive criteria?
2. Do the customers see the organization's prices as being in line or out of line with the perceived value of its offer?
3. Does the organization use promotional pricing effectively?

C. DISTRIBUTION

1. What are the distribution objectives and strategies?
2. Is there adequate market coverage and service?
3. Should the organization consider changing its degree of reliance on distributors, sales reps, and direct selling?

D. ADVERTISING, SALES PROMOTION, AND PUBLIC RELATIONS

1. What are the organization's advertising objectives? Are they sound?
2. Is the right amount being spent on advertising? How is the budget determined?
3. Are the ad themes and copy effective? What do customers and the public think about the advertising?
4. Are the advertising media well chosen?
5. Is sales promotion used effectively?
6. Is there a well-conceived public relations program?

E. SALES FORCE

1. What are the organization's sales force objectives?
2. Is the sales force large enough to accomplish the organization's objectives?
3. Is the sales force organized along the proper principle(s) of specialization (territory, market, product)?

## Table 7–3

### MARKETING AUDIT GUIDE (continued)

4. Does the sales force show high morale, ability, and effort? Are they sufficiently trained and incentivized?
5. Are the procedures adequate for setting quotas and evaluating performances?
6. How is the organization's sales force perceived in relation to competitors' sales forces?

will raise. Not all the questions are important in every situation. The instrument will be modified depending on whether the organization is a museum, college, social service agency, government agency, and so on.[5] However, the sequence of topics should be maintained.

The purpose of the audit is to judge whether the organization is performing optimally from a marketing point of view. The auditor will produce some short-run and long-run recommendations of actions that the organization could take to improve its performance. Management has to weigh carefully these recommendations and implement those which it feels would contribute to improved marketing performance. The marketing audit is not a marketing plan, but an independent appraisal by a competent consultant of the main problems and opportunities facing the organization, and what it can do about them.

## SUMMARY

The marketing planning and control system guides the organization's operations in the marketplace. Organizations can be found operating planning systems of various degrees of sophistication from simple budgeting systems, to annual planning systems, to long-range planning systems. The planning process starts with marketing forecasting and planning, followed by the development of a detailed business plan. The marketing plan contains the following sections: executive summary, situation analysis, objective and goals, marketing strategy, action program, budgets, and controls. The marketing strategy section of the plan defines the target markets, marketing mix, and marketing expenditure level that will be used to achieve the marketing objectives.

Marketing control is an intrinsic part of marketing planning. Organizations exercise at least three types of marketing control. Annual plan control consists of monitoring the current marketing performance to be sure that the annual sales and profit goals are being achieved. The main tools are sales analysis, market-share analysis, marketing expense-to-sales analysis, and market attitude tracking. If underperformance is detected, the organization can implement a variety of corrective measures. Profitability control consists of determining the actual profitability of different marketing entities, such as the organization's products, territories, market segments, and distribution channels. Marketing profitability analysis reveals the weaker marketing entities, although it does not indicate whether the weaker units should be bolstered or phased out. Strategic control consists of making sure that the organization's marketing objectives, strategies, and systems are optimally adapted to the current and forecasted marketing environment. It uses the tool known as the marketing audit, which is a comprehensive, systematic, independent, and periodic examination of the organization's marketing environment, objectives, strategies, and activities. The purpose of the marketing audit is to determine marketing problem areas and recommend corrective short-run and long-run actions to improve the organization's overall marketing effectiveness.

## QUESTIONS

**1.** In what ways is marketing control an intrinsic part of marketing planning?

**2.** St. Mary's High School draws its students from a number of Catholic elementary schools and from public schools. Describe how the administration might apply each of the following four control tools—sales analysis, market-share analysis, market expense-to-sales analysis, and market attitude tracking.

**3.** What are the forces which encourage organizations to move from annual planning to long-range planning?

**4.** What is the purpose of preparing a situation analysis before setting objectives and goals in a marketing plan?

**5.** Explain the importance of specified goals and objectives to the control process.

## NOTES

**1.** Melville C. Branch, *The Corporate Planning Process* (New York: American Management Association, 1962), pp. 48–49.

**2.** See D. D. McConkey, *MBO for Nonprofit Organizations* (New York: AMACOM, 1975).

**3.** See Douglas McGregor, *The Human Side of Enterprise* (New York: McGraw-Hill, 1960).

**4.** For details see Philip Kotler, William Gregor, and William Rodgers, "The Marketing Audit Comes of Age," *Sloan Management Review,* Winter 1977, pp. 25–43.

**5.** For a marketing audit guide for social service organizations, see Douglas B. Herron, "Developing a Marketing Audit for Social Service Organizations," in Christopher H. Lovelock and Charles B. Weinberg, eds., *Readings in Public and Nonprofit Marketing* (Palo Alto, Calif.: Scientific Press, 1978), pp. 269–71. For arts organizations, see Tom Horwitz, *Arts Administration* (Chicago: Chicago Review Press, 1978), pp. 81–85. For hospitals, see Eric N. Berkowitz and William A. Flexner, "The Marketing Audit: A Tool for Health Service Organizations," *HCM Review,* Fall 1978, pp. 55–56.

# ANALYZING
# MARKETING
# OPPORTUNITIES

# Market Measurement and Forecasting

8

Grant Hospital is a 500-bed community hospital located a few miles north of downtown Chicago in an area of varied ethnic groups. One of its major services is its Alcoholism Program designed to help employed alcoholics. The program, which was launched in 1968, has a 45-person staff who manage three distinct programs: (1) *inpatient treatment* consisting of a 21-bed, 21-day hospital-based program; (2) *outpatient treatment* offering counseling to about 170 patients per week; and (3) *training and consultation* directed to professionals and employers.

The program's director recently became interested in adding a new service to treat the teenage alcoholic, a segment that Grant Hospital was not presently serving. The National Institute on Alcohol Abuse and Alcoholism estimates that 3.3 million teenagers—almost one in five—are "problem drinkers" who lose control at least once a year. Teenage alcoholism appears to have increased in recent years as a result of many states lowering the legal drinking age in the early seventies. The Insurance Institute of Highway Safety links the lowering of legal drinking ages to increases in teenage auto accidents and juvenile crime such as rowdyism and vandalism. For example, the under-20 group, although only 8.6 percent of the driving population in 1978, accounted for 18 percent of all traffic accident fatalities, and 25 percent were alcohol-related. Teenage drinking has become such a problem that 6 states recently reversed themselves and raised the drinking age, and 12 others are planning to follow suit.

The director would like to launch an inpatient program to treat male teenage alcoholics that would involve 15 beds and a 21-day stay. The viability of this program will depend upon Grant Hospital being able to attract about 255 patients each year to this program (15 patients for 17 program cycles during the year). The director proceeded to make some rough calculations of the market size. The relevant area of Chicago was estimated to have about 100,000 alcoholics. About 10 percent, or 10,000, were estimated to be teenagers. Four-fifths of all alcoholics are male, and therefore she estimated that 8,000 male teenager alcoholics would be in the relevant area of Chicago. She estimated that only about half of them, or 4,000, would accept formal treatment. Of these, about 20 percent, or 800, would be willing to enter an inpatient program as opposed to an outpatient program. Since three other Chicago hospitals also ran male inpatient teenage alcoholism programs, the director figured that Grant Hospital could attract about one out of four of these teenagers, or 250. If these estimates were correct, Grant Hospital could attract roughly the number of alcoholic teenagers it needed to run at 100 percent capacity. Since it could afford to run even at 80 percent capacity, the director felt that the market was probably large enough to enter and serve. Still, the director had some misgivings and decided that the next step would be to refine these estimates to have a better measure of how many male teenage alcoholics might be attracted to the inpatient program.

We are now ready to turn attention to the marketplace and seek ways to understand and measure it. The market is the organization's source of opportunities. The job of analyzing the marketplace breaks into three major tasks:

1. *Market measurement and forecasting:* determining the current and future size of the available market for an organization's products and services.
2. *Market segmentation:* determining the main groups making up a market with a view of choosing the best target groups to serve.
3. *Consumer analysis:* determining the characteristics of consumers, specifically their needs, perceptions, preferences, and behavior, with a view toward adapting the offer to these consumer characteristics.

All of these steps make up *market analysis.* This chapter will deal with market measurement and forecasting. Chapter 9 will deal with market segmentation analysis, and Chapter 10 will deal with consumer analysis.

Market measurement and forecasting consists in the organization researching three questions:

1. Who is the market? *(market definition)*
2. How large is the current market? *(current market size measurement)*
3. What is the likely future size of the market? *(market forecasting)*

These questions are examined in the following sections.

## DEFINING THE MARKET

Every organization faces the task of defining who is in its market. It knows that not everyone is a potential customer of its market offer. Not everyone is in the market for a college education, or day care center services, or cancer treatment, or a job with the police department. Organizations must distinguish between their customers and noncustomers.

To define the market, the organization must carefully define its market offer. Take the case of a small private college. We can talk about the market for the college's bachelor's degree, or for its sociology program, or for its specific course on The Sociology of Religion. The market definition and size would vary in each case. Even the market for the course on The Sociology of Religion would be affected by the cost of the course and the place and time it is offered. The more specifically we can define the product, the more carefully we can determine the market's boundaries and size.

We define a market as follows:

> A **market** is the set of actual and potential consumers of a market offer.

Two comments are in order. The term "consumers" is shorthand for a number of other possible terms, such as buyers, clients, adopters, users, responders. Furthermore, the consumers can be individuals, families, groups, or organizations. The term "market offer" is also shorthand for a tangible good, service, program, idea, or anything that might be put out to a group of responders.

Those in the market for something have three characteristics: *interest, income,* and *access.* To illustrate this, consider the following situation:

> The chairman of a French department at a small college is concerned with the declining number of students signing up for French. One faculty member has already been dismissed, and another will be dismissed if the market for studying French continues to shrink. The French department chairman is thinking of offering an evening noncredit course on French culture to adults in the community. He is interested in estimating whether enough adults in the community would be in the "market" for this course.

The first thing to estimate is the number of adults in the community with a potential interest in a course on French culture. There are a number of ways to do this. The chairman could contact other colleges offering this course and find out their enrollment levels. A more direct approach would be to phone a random sample of adults in the community and ask about their level of interest in a French culture course. The question could be asked: "If a noncredit French culture course is offered in the evening at our college, would you definitely take it, probably take it, or not be interested in taking it?" Suppose 4 out of 100 say they would definitely take the course, 6 say they might take it, and 90 say they would not take it. At the most, it appears that 10 percent have an interest in this course.[1] This percentage can be multiplied by the adult population in the community to estimate the potential market for this course. We define the potential market as follows:

> The **potential market** is the set of consumers who profess some level of interest in a defined market offer.

Now consumer interest is not enough to define a market. If a price is attached to the offer, potential consumers must have adequate *income* to afford the purchase. They must be *able to buy* besides being *willing to buy*. Furthermore, the higher the price, the fewer the number of people who will stay in the market. The size of a market is a function not only of the interest level but also of the income level.[2]

Market size is further cut down by personal *access* barriers that might prevent response to the offer. Interested consumers may not be able to take the French course at the place at the time it is offered. Access factors will make the market smaller. The market that remains is called the available market. We define the available market as follows:

> The **available market** is the set of consumers who have interest, income, and access to a particular market offer.

In the case of some market offers, the organization will establish some restrictions regarding with whom they will transact. Although a college sells football tickets to everyone in the community wishing to attend a game, it may not be willing to accept everyone who wants to take a course in French culture. The college may choose to accept only adults who are (1) 24 years or older and (2) have a high school diploma. These adults constitute the qualified available market:

> The **qualified available market** is the set of consumers who have interest, income, access, and qualifications for the particular market offer.

Now the college has the choice of going after the whole qualified available market or to concentrate its efforts on certain segments. In the latter case, we need the concept of the served market. We define the served market as follows:

> The **served market** is the part of the qualified available market that the organization puts effort into attracting and serving.

Suppose the college prefers to attract primarily middle- and upper-class adults to its evening classes and, as a result, promotes the French culture course primarily in certain sections of the city. This is an example of where the served market is somewhat smaller than the qualified available market.

Once the course is advertised, it will attract an actual number of adult learners that will represent some fraction of the served market. The number who enroll is called the penetrated market. We define the penetrated market as follows:

> The **penetrated market** is the set of consumers that are actually consuming the product.

Figure 8–1 brings all the preceding concepts together. The bar on the left illustrates the ratio of the potential market—all interested persons—to the total population, here 10 percent. The figure on the right illustrates several breakdowns of the potential market. The available market—those who have interest, income, and access—are 40 percent of the potential consumers. The qualified available market—those who would meet the college's admissions requirements—are 20 percent of the potential market, or 50 percent of the available market. The college is actively trying to attract half of these, or 10 percent of the potential market. Finally, the college is shown as actually enrolling 5 percent of the potential market in the course.

These definitions of a market are a useful tool for marketing planning. If the organization is not satisfied with the size of its penetrated market, it can consider a number of actions. First, it could try to attract a larger percentage of people from its served market. If it finds, however, that the nonenrolling part of the served market has chosen to study French culture at a competing college, this

**FIGURE 8–1**

Levels of Market Definition

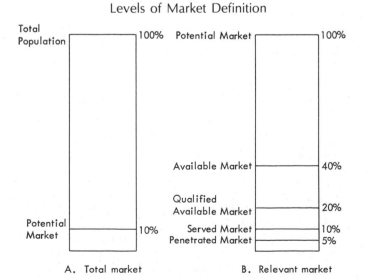

college might try to widen its served market by promoting the course in other parts of the city. Beyond this, the college could relax the qualifications for admission, thus expanding the qualified available market. The next step would be to consider expanding the available market by lowering the tuition, improving the location and time of the course offering, and doing other things to reduce cost and access. Ultimately, the college could try to expand the potential market by launching a campaign to convert noninterested consumers into interested consumers.

---

## MEASURING CURRENT MARKET DEMAND

We are now ready to examine practical methods of estimating current market demand for a market offer. There are four types of estimates that an organization will want to make: *total market demand, area market demand, total industry sales,* and *organization market share.*

### ESTIMATING TOTAL MARKET DEMAND

Total market demand is defined as follows:

**Total market demand** for a product is the total volume that would be bought by a defined consumer group in a defined geographical area in a defined time period in a defined marketing environment under a defined marketing program.

The most important thing to realize about total market demand is that it is not a fixed number but a function of the specified conditions. One of these conditions, for example, is the marketing program (product features, price, promotional expenditure level, etc.), and another is the state of the economy. The dependence of total market demand on these conditions is illustrated in Figure 8–2. The horizontal axis shows different possible levels of marketing expenditure by the organization in a given time period. On the vertical axis is shown the resulting demand level. The curve represents the estimated level of market demand associated with different marketing expenditure levels by the organization. We see that some base sales (called the *market minimum*) would take place without any demand-stimulating expenditures by the organization. Positive marketing expenditures would yield higher levels of demand, first at an increasing rate, then at a decreasing rate. Marketing expenditures higher than a certain level would not stimulate much further demand, thus suggesting an upper limit to market demand called the *market potential.*

The distance between the market minimum and the market potential shows the overall *marketing sensitivity of demand.* We can think of two extreme types of markets, the *expansible* and the *nonexpansible.* An expansible market, such as a market for a new sport such as racquetball, is quite affected in its total size

## FIGURE 8–2

### Market Demand

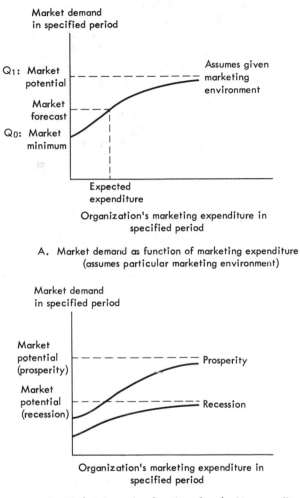

A. Market demand as function of marketing expenditure
(assumes particular marketing environment)

B. Market demand as function of marketing expenditure
(two different environments assumed)

by the level of marketing expenditures. In terms of Figure 8–2A the distance between $Q_0$ and $Q_1$ is relatively large. A nonexpansible market, such as the market for opera, is not much affected by the level of marketing expenditures; the distance between $Q_0$ and $Q_1$ is relatively small. The organization selling in a nonexpansible market can take the market's size (the level of *primary demand*) for granted and concentrate its marketing resources on getting a desired market share (the level of *selective demand*).

Only one of the many possible levels of marketing expenditure will actually

**201**

be chosen by the organization. The market demand corresponding to this expenditure level is called the *market forecast.* The market forecast shows the expected level of market demand for the expected level of organizational marketing expenditure in the given environment.

If a different environment is assumed, the market demand function would have to be freshly estimated. For example, the market for theatregoing is higher during prosperity than recession because market demand is income-elastic. The dependence of market demand on the environment is illustrated in Figure 8–2B.

The main point is that the marketer should carefully define the situation for which market demand is being estimated. The marketer can use a method known as the *chain ratio method* to form the estimate. The chain ratio method involves multiplying a base number by a succession of percentages that lead to the defined consumer set. Here is an example:

> The U.S. Navy seeks to attract 112,000 new male recruits each year from American high schools. The question is whether this is a high or low target in relation to the market potential. The market potential has been estimated by the chain ratio method as follows:

| | |
|---|---:|
| Total number of male high school graduating students | 10,000,000 |
| Percentage who are militarily qualified (no physical, emotional, or mental handicaps) | × .50 |
| Percentage of those qualified who are potentially interested in military service | × .15 |
| Percentage of those qualified and interested in military service who consider the navy the preferred service | × .30 |

This chain of numbers shows the market potential to be 225,000 recruits. Since this exceeds the target number of recruits sought, the U.S. Navy should not have much trouble meeting its target, if it does a reasonable job of marketing the navy. But many of the potential recruits are lost somehow. They are not contacted; their parents talk them out of military service; they hear negative things from friends; they form a bad impression at the recruiting office. The result is that the navy barely manages to recruit the target number it seeks.

Often, the marketer has to estimate the total revenue that might be realized through a market offer. This is accomplished by multiplying the number of consumers by the price of the product. Suppose, however, that consumers can buy more than one unit, as is the case of adult learners who can take from one to four courses during a semester. The total potential revenue would be estimated using the following formula:

$$R = NQP \tag{8-1}$$

where:

$R$ = total potential revenue
$N$ = number of buyers in the specific product market who might buy under the given assumptions
$Q$ = quantity purchased by an average buyer
$P$ = price of an average unit

Thus if there are 1,000 potential adult learners in a community who might sign up for courses, and the average adult enrolls in two courses a semester, and the average tuition is $30 a course, the total potential revenue would be $60,000 (= 1,000 × 2 × $30).

### ESTIMATING AREA MARKET DEMAND

The market demand for a product or service will vary geographically. Given this fact, the organization will have to decide on the geographical areas deserving the most attention. These will normally be the areas having the highest market demand although some areas may have to be served for reasons other than maximizing demand.

There are a number of ways to estimate the relative attractiveness of different geographical areas. We will illustrate these ways in connection with the following situation:

> The Organic Theatre of Chicago attracts most of its season ticket subscribers from Chicago and nearby suburbs. The management feels that additional theatregoers can be attracted from more distant suburbs such as Oak Park, Hinsdale, Arlington Heights, and Highland Park. However, the theatre cannot mount a campaign to promote subscriptions in all of these suburbs and wants to identify the suburbs with the highest potential.

Four methods of estimating area market potential will be described in the following paragraphs.

**Area analysis of current sales.**    A common approach is to study the areas that current subscribers are coming from. One can prepare a dot map showing the number of consumers in different areas. Suppose the management finds that 6 percent of its audience comes from Oak Park and 2 percent from Hinsdale. The management will conclude that Oak Park is a better "market" than Hinsdale, in that it might have more people who like theatre. The further implication is that Oak Park might deserve three times the marketing effort as Hinsdale.

Although this is a common way to estimate area market potential, it can be misleading. Current area sales reflect not only differences in market potential but also differences in market cultivation. Maybe the Organic Theatre mailed more promotional literature to Oak Park residents than to Hinsdale residents. In the extreme, suppose the Organic Theatre had run a direct mail campaign in Oak

Park and no campaign in Hinsdale. One might then conclude that Hinsdale might have substantially more potential since 2 percent of the audience came from Hinsdale without the benefit of any promotion. Furthermore, even if we believe that Oak Park had three times as much market potential as Hinsdale, it does not follow that Oak Park deserves three times the effort. It may deserve four times the effort, two times the effort, or the same effort. We would have to estimate the marginal response to additional promotional effort that would occur in each community.

**Single-factor index.**     Here management tries to discover a single measurable factor that would reflect the market potential of different communities. Suppose management believes the best single indicator of the propensity to attend theatre is the "number of college-educated people in the community." Using this criterion, if Oak Park has 6,000 college-educated residents and Hinsdale has 4,000, we could argue that Oak Park deserves more marketing effort—indeed, something like 50 percent more than Hinsdale.

**Multiple factor index.**     Often, management feels that it cannot put its whole confidence in a single factor. Instead, two or more factors may seem to indicate the level of market potential in a community. The problem is to form an index that combines these factors. Suppose the Organic Theatre management believes that two factors are highly associated with demand: (1) "the number of college-educated people," and (2) "the number of people earning over $20,000." Suppose statistics are not available on the combined variable. Figure 8–3 shows how a multiple factor index can be formed.

The rows list the communities in greater Chicago that are accessible to the theatre. The first two columns list the two factors. The third and fourth columns convert these two factors into percentages expressing each community's share of the total of each column. Thus, Oak Park has 6 percent of the total college-educated people in the greater Chicago area and 4 percent of the high earners.

## FIGURE 8–3

### Multiple Factor Index

| | *(1)* | *(2)* | *(3)* | *(4)* | *(5)* |
|---|---|---|---|---|---|
| | *Number of College Educated* | *Number Earning More Than $20,000* | *Percent of Total College Educated* | *Percent Earning More Than $20,000* | *Multiple Factor Index* |
| Oak Park | 6,000 | 8,000 | 6 | 4 | 5 |
| Hinsdale | 4,000 | 4,000 | 4 | 2 | 3 |
| • | • | • | • | • | • |
| • | • | • | • | • | • |
| • | • | • | • | • | • |
| | 100,000 | 100,000 | | | |

We can take a simple average of the two percentage figures for each community and call this the multiple factor index number. Thus, Oak Park can be said to have about 5 percent of the total market potential, whereas Hinsdale has 3 percent. These numbers can be used to guide the percentage of the promotional budget to spend in each community.

The multiple factor index can be refined in a number of ways. First, management may want to use more than two factors, and this would require additional columns. Second, management may want to assign unequal weights to the factors instead of taking a simple average. Third, some of the factors may not be expressible in percentage terms, and it may be necessary to convert all the row numbers into standard scales (say, 1- to 10-point scales) which are then weighed. The general approach outlined here is the one used to develop the "index of consumer buying power" that is used by business to determine the market potential of different geographical areas for basic products.[3]

**Distance-adjusted index.**     One more factor should be taken into account in developing the market potentials of different communities. Studies show that market potential drops with distance from the site of the offer, because people view travel as a cost and would prefer to patronize outlets nearer their residence. In fact, some early studies indicated that market attractiveness falls off with the square of the distance of the buyer from the seller. Market potential is considered positively correlated with the size of the target population and inversely correlated with the squared distance of the target population from the seller.[4]

There is a simpler way to make an adjustment for distance. Management could decide, arbitrarily, to reduce the multiple factor index by 1 percentage point for every 8 miles of distance between the community and the theatre. Oak Park happens to be 8 miles from the theatre and Hinsdale is 16 miles away. Instead of Oak Park's multiple factor index standing at 5, it would be reduced to 4; and Hinsdale's index, instead of standing at 3, would stand at 1. Thus, Oak Park is seen to have five times the potential for the sale of theatre tickets over Hinsdale, and not just 1⅔ the potential.

### ESTIMATING TOTAL INDUSTRY SALES

Besides measuring potential demand, an organization will want to know the actual total sales taking place in its market. This requires identifying the other organizations serving the same market. This is not as simple as it sounds because of the many definitions of a market. Grant Hospital, for example, would have to identify other alcoholic treatment centers in the greater Chicago area where some of its potential consumers might have gone. Should this include Highland Park Hospital, which is a long distance away but might have some alcoholism patients? The organization must carefully define its real competition as the first step in developing an estimate of total sales and its share of sales.

Then the organization has to estimate the sales of each competitor. How is this information to be obtained? The easiest way is to contact each competitor and offer to exchange sales information. In this way, each organization can measure its performance against every other organization and against the total sales for the industry. However, this solution is not always available. Trading sales information is illegal in some industries. In other cases, particular competitors are not willing to divulge this information. In the latter case, the organization can still compare its sales to the sales of the cooperating organizations and find this useful.

Another solution calls for the trade association to collect the data and publish the sales of each organization and/or the total sales. In this way, each organization can evaluate its performance against specific competitors or the industry as a whole.

If this solution is not available, the organization will have to estimate the sales of one or more competitors through indirect methods. For example, Grant Hospital might infer the number of inpatient alcoholism treatments at a particular competitive hospital by knowing the number of beds, the size of the staff, or other clues. In the industrial world, a company may estimate the sales of another company by finding out how many shifts the factory is operating or how much raw material it is ordering from suppliers.

### ESTIMATING ORGANIZATION MARKET SHARE

The organization's own sales do not tell the whole story of how well it is doing. Suppose the organization's sales are increasing at 5 percent a year and its competitors' sales are increasing at 10 percent. This organization is actually losing its relative standing in the industry. Organizations will therefore want to compare their sales with those of competitors.

Organizations can estimate at least three market share figures. Ideally, the organization should know its: (1) share of the total market, (2) share of the served market, and (3) share relative to the leading competitor or leading three competitors. Each of these measures yields useful information about the organization's market performance and potential.

## FORECASTING FUTURE MARKET DEMAND

Having looked at ways to estimate current demand, we are now ready to examine the problem of forecasting future demand. Very few products or services lend themselves to easy forecasting. The few cases generally involve a product whose absolute level or trend is fairly constant and whose competition is nonexistent or stable. In the vast majority of markets, total market demand and specific organization demand are not stable from year to year and good forecasting becomes a key factor in effective performance. Poor forecasting can lead to excess personnel and supplies or, on the other hand, to insufficient personnel and supplies. The more unstable the demand, the more critical is forecast accuracy and the more elaborate is forecasting procedure.

In approaching forecasting, one should list all the factors that might affect future demand and predict each factor's likely future level and effect on demand. The factors affecting demand might be classified into three categories: (1) *noncontrollable macroenvironmental factors* such as the state of the economy, new technologies, and legal developments; (2) *competitive factors* such as competitors' prices, new products, and promotional expenditures; and (3) *organizational factors* such as the organization's prices, new products, and promotional expenditures.

In view of the many factors that might be involved, organizations have turned to various approximation methods to forecast future demand. Five major methods are discussed below. They arise out of three information bases for building a forecast. A forecast can be based on *what people say, what people do,* or *what people have done.* The first basis—what people say—involves systematic determination of the opinions of buyers or of those close to them, such as salespersons or outside experts. It encompasses two methods: (1) buyer intentions surveys, and (2) middleman estimates. Building a forecast on what people do involves another method: (3) market testing. The final basis—what people have done—involves using statistical tools to analyze records of past buying behavior, using either (4) time-series analysis, or (5) statistical demand analysis. Each of these methods is described and illustrated below.

## BUYER INTENTIONS SURVEYS

One way to form an estimate of future demand is to ask a sample of target buyers to state their buying intentions for the forthcoming period. Suppose a college is trying to estimate the number of majors to expect next year in each of its disciplines. The purpose is to schedule enough courses and faculty to service the level of demand for the various majors. A small number of sophomores can be asked to indicate their intended major next year. If 20 percent say that they intend to make economics their major, the college can multiply this against the size of the sophomore class and infer the number of actual students who plan to major in economics.

The reliability of buyer intentions forecasts depends on (1) buyers having clear intentions, (2) buyers being likely to carry out their intentions, and (3) buyers being willing to describe their intentions to interviewers. To the extent that these assumptions are weak, then the results must be used with caution. Suppose a theatre at mid-season asked its subscribers about their intention to renew their subscription for the following year. The problem is that the current subscribers may not have thought about renewal and they may want to finish the series before forming their intention. Buyer intention data in this case would be weak.

Buyer intentions could be asked in a number of ways. A "yes-or-no" form of the question would be: "Do you intend to buy a season ticket next year?" This requires the respondent to make a definite choice. Some researchers prefer the following form of the question: "Will you (a) definitely buy, (b) probably buy, (c) probably not buy, or (d) definitely not buy a season ticket next year?" These researchers feel that the "definitely buys" would be fairly dependable as a minimum estimate and some fraction of the "probably buys" could be added to arrive at a forecast. More recently, some researchers have recommended using a *full purchase probability scale:*

Do you intend to buy a season theatre ticket for next year?

| .00 | .10 | .20 | .30 | .40 | .50 | .60 | .70 | .80 | .90 | 1.00 |
|---|---|---|---|---|---|---|---|---|---|---|
| No chance | Very slight possibility | Slight possibility | Some possibility | Fair possibility | Fairly good possibility | Good possibility | Probably | Very probably | Almost | Certain |

The researcher uses various fractions of the positive responders to form an estimate. The researcher can improve the system over time by checking the forecasts against the actuals and seeing what weights would have improved the forecast.

## MIDDLEMAN ESTIMATES

Another way of developing a forecast is to ask people who are close to the buyers what those buyers are likely to do. For example, the college that is trying to anticipate enrollments to different majors might ask each department chairperson to estimate these enrollments. The chairpersons will examine past data and what they have recently heard and prepare a forecast. Some chairpersons will overestimate (the optimists) and some will underestimate (the pessimists). If individual chairpersons are fairly consistent overestimators or underestimators, their forecasts can be adjusted by the administration for their known bias before using the forecasts for planning purposes.

When business firms use this method, they ask for estimates from their sales force, distributors, and dealers, since all of these are presumably closer to the customers and can render an opinion about likely demand. Nonprofit organizations can also find similar "experts." Thus a national fundraising organization can ask its regional chairpersons to make estimates, and they in turn can ask their individual fundraisers for estimates. Asking people who come in contact with the buyers for their estimates is called "grassroots forecasting." In using the method, the grassroots forecasters should be given a set of basic assumptions about the coming year, such as the state of the economy, the organization's tentative marketing plans, and so on. This is preferable to allowing each expert to make personal assumptions about major demand influences that will operate next year.

Grassroots forecasting has two major advantages. Since people involved in the marketing process submit them, these people will have more confidence in the derived sales quotas they get back and they will have more incentive to achieve them. Also, grassroots forecasting results in estimates broken down by product, territory, customer, and estimator, which makes the setting of individual quotas easier.

## MARKET TESTS

In cases where buyers do not plan their purchases carefully or are very erratic in carrying out their intentions or where experts are not very good guessers, a more direct market test of likely behavior is desirable. A direct market test is especially desirable in forecasting the sales of a new product or the likely sales of an established product in a new channel of distribution or territory. Where a short-run forecast of likely buyer response is desired, a small-scale market test is usually an ideal answer.

## TIME-SERIES ANALYSIS

As an alternative to costly surveys or market tests, many organizations prepare their forecasts on the basis of a statistical analysis of past data. The underlying logic is that past time series reflect causal relations that can be uncovered through statistical analysis. The findings can be used to predict future sales.

A time series of past sales of a product can be analyzed into four major components.

The first component, *trend (T)*, reflects the basic level and rate of change in the size of the market. It is found by fitting a straight or curved line through the time-series data. The past trend can be extrapolated to estimate next year's trend level.

A second component, *cycle (C)*, might also be observed in a time series. Many sales are affected by periodic swings in general economic activity. If the stage of the business cycle can be predicted for the next period, this would be used to adjust the trend value up or down.

A third component, *season (S)*, would capture any consistent pattern of sales movements within the year. The term "season" is used to describe any recurrent hourly, daily, weekly, monthly, or quarterly sales pattern. The seasonal component may be related to weather factors, holidays, and so on. The researcher would adjust the estimate for, say, a particular month by the known seasonal level for that month.

The fourth component, *erratic events (E)*, includes strikes, blizzards, fads, riots, fires, war scares, price wars, and other disturbances. This erratic component has the effect of obscuring the more systematic components. It represents everything that remains unanalyzed in the time series and cannot be predicted in the future. It shows the average size of the error that is likely to characterize time-series forecasting.

Here is an example of how time-series forecasting works:

A county historical museum had 12,000 visitors this year. It wants to predict next year's December attendance in order to schedule enough guards. The long-term trend shows a 5 percent attendance growth rate per year. This implies attendance next year of 12,600 (= 12,000 × 1.05). However, a business recession is expected next year, and this generally depresses attendance to 90 percent of the expected trend level. This means attendance next year will more likely be 11,340 (= 12,600 × .90). If attendance is the same each month, this would mean monthly attendance of 945 (= 11.340 ÷ 12). However, December is an above-average month, with a seasonal index standing at 1.30. Therefore, December attendance may be as high as 12,285 (= 945 × 1.3). No erratic events, such as public transportation strikes or new competitive exhibits, are expected. Therefore, the best estimate of next December's attendance is 12,285.

## STATISTICAL DEMAND ANALYSIS

Numerous real factors affect the sales of any product. *Statistical demand analysis* is a set of statistical procedures designed to discover the most important real factors affecting sales and their relative influence. The factors most commonly analyzed are prices, income, population, and promotion.

Statistical demand analysis consists of expressing sales *(Q)* as a dependent variable and trying to explain sales variation as a result of variation in a number of independent demand variables $X_1, X_2, \ldots, X_n$; that is,

$$Q = f(X_1, X_2, \ldots, X_n) \tag{8–2}$$

This says that the level of sales, $Q$, is a function of the levels of the independent factors $X_1, X_2, \ldots, X_n$. Using a technique called multiple regression analysis, various equation forms can be statistically fitted to the data in the search for the best predicting factors and equations.[5]

Here is an example:

A central library wanted to forecast book circulation next year at each of its ten branch libraries. The following equation was fitted to past data:

$$Q = 5000 - 300 X_1 + 1000 X_2 \tag{8–3}$$

where

$X_1$ = average education level in the branch's neighborhood
$X_2$ = age of the branch library

For example, the Lincoln branch library would be 10 years old next year and was located in a neighborhood whose residents averaged 12 years of formal education. Using (8–3), we would predict that book circulation would be:

$$Q = 5000 - 300(10) + 1000(12) = 14,000$$

If this equation predicts book circulation satisfactorily for the various branches, then the central library can assume that it has identified two key factors influencing book circulation. It may want to explore the exact influence of these factors, as well as other factors that might be added to improve the equation's forecasting accuracy.

Marketing researchers are constantly improving the available tools for producing reliable market size estimates and sales forecasts. The great demand by marketers for market measures and forecasts on which to base their marketing decisions is being matched on the supply side by an encouraging increase in data and tools to aid marketers in their marketing planning, execution, and control.

---

## SUMMARY

In order to carry out their responsibilities for marketing planning, execution, and control, marketing managers need measures of current and future market size. We defined a market as the set of actual and potential consumers of a market offer. Being in the market means having interest, income, and access to the market offer. The marketer's task is to distinguish various levels of the market that is being investigated, such as the potential market, available market, qualified available market, served market, and penetrated market.

The next step is to estimate the size of current demand. Total current demand can be estimated through the chain ratio method, which involves multiplying a base number by a succession of appropriate percentages to arrive at the defined market. Area market demand can be estimated in four ways: area analysis of current sales, single factor index, multiple factor indices, or distance-adjusted indices. Actual industry sales requires identifying the relevant competitors and using some method of estimating the sales of each. Finally, the organization should compare its sales to industry sales to find whether its market share is improving or declining.

For estimating future demand, the organization can use one or any combination of five forecasting methods: buyer intentions surveys, middleman estimates, market tests, time-series analysis, or statistical demand analysis. These methods vary in their appropriateness with the purpose of the forecast, the type of product, and the availability and reliability of data.

---

## QUESTIONS

**1.** What is the definition of a "market"? What is meant by "being in the market"?

**2.** South Valley Christian School has an enrollment of 240 students. The principal knows from census data that approximately 80,000 children between 5 and 13 years of age live within a ten-mile radius of the school. Advise the principal on how these two figures are relevant to the task of defining the school's market.

**3.** The Chicago Art Institute frequently features heavily attended major traveling exhibits, which may require special ticketing arrangements and the hiring of additional guards. What marketing forecasting approach(es) might be useful in anticipating attendance levels?

**4.** Why might it be important to determine the total market demand, even when the organization intends to serve only a small number of people?

**5.** A university's School of Business is considering establishing a part-time Executive M.B.A. Program for selected managers working for local companies. Before making the decision to go ahead, the dean wants to be sure of adequate enrollment to demonstrate the program's potential while covering costs. What contribution might buyer intentions surveys make to this decision?

**6.** A county mass transit agency wants to project bus ridership for the next five years as a basis for planning hiring, purchases of new equipment, and routes. List examples of noncontrollable macroenvironmental factors, competitive factors, and organizational factors which might influence bus ridership.

---

## NOTES

**1.** Some analysts use all of the "definites" and some arbitrary fraction of the "probablys" to estimate the demand level. Thus, they may say that the demand is made up of four "definites" and half of the six "probablys," namely seven people, or 7 percent of the population.

**2.** However, it must be added that for many nonprofit organization markets, income is not a defining variable, because the consumer is not expected to pay for the service. Thus, in such cases as the Girl Scouts, U.S. Army, cigarette smokers, and so on, the target consumer's income is not a factor in the size of the market.

**3.** See "Putting the Four to Work," *Sales Management,* October 28, 1974, pp. 13ff.

**4.** See George Schwartz, *Development of Marketing Theory* (Cincinnati: Southwestern, 1963), pp. 9–36.

**5.** See William F. Massy's "Statistical Analysis of Relations Between Variables," in David A. Aaker, ed., *Multivariate Analysis in Marketing: Theory and Applications* (Belmont, Calif., Wadsworth, 1971), pp. 5–35.

# Market Segmentation and Targeting

The American Red Cross is a multiservice nonprofit organization running such varied programs as blood collection, natural disaster relief, international assistance, first aid, armed forces services, and home nursing. Each program has its own management group that is responsible for developing short- and long-run goals, plans, and budgets.

In the field of blood collection, the American Red Cross is the nation's top recruiter and supplier. In 1979, the American Red Cross recruited almost 4 million donors through its 1,900 Red Cross chapters as well as cooperating community blood banks. Other blood collection agencies include hospitals and various commercial blood donor services.

The total amount of blood collected in the nation often falls short of the need level at certain times of the year and in certain locations in the country. At these times, blood collecting agencies have to wage major publicity campaigns to inform people of the blood emergency. Two broad groups respond: those who give blood for some tangible reward and those who give for altruistic reasons. Contrary to a prevalent myth, which claims that most blood is freely given by volunteers, nearly 50 percent of the blood transfused in the United States comes from "industrial" donors—people who sell their blood for cash (usually for between $5 and $15, depending on location and blood type). Commercial blood banks sell this blood at heavy markup to hospitals, which transfuse it into the patient, who is charged for the cost of the blood plus administering fees. Some of the paid donors are indigents, addicts, winos, and others whose blood, in spite of lab screening, is eleven times more likely to cause hepatitis than the blood coming from healthier sources.

Some years ago, Titmuss, in his *The Gift Relation* (Pantheon, 1971) classified blood donors into a finer segmentation of eight groups instead of two:

Type A: *The paid, walk-in donor.*

Type B: *The "professional" donor:* differentiated from Type A only in being a more regular donor, due either to having a rare blood type, or being on retainer for a pharmaceutical company which draws large quantities of his plasma by a process called plasmapheresis.

Type C: *Paid-induced:* This donor accepts the blood fee, or possibly a fee paid by a group (often a union) to which he belongs—but claims that the money is not his primary motivation. Often group pressures are at work here, and the fee is considered a just return for time and effort expended, not for the blood itself.

Type D: *Responsibility fee:* A person who responds to the request of a family member or friend to replace blood which that friend used in an operation. Note that the appeal is not to save the friend's *life,* but only to save him *money,* since the operation was in the past.

Type E: *Family credit:* A person who finds the blood assurance programs offered by a blood bank attractive: by paying a "premium" of a pint of blood, he is assured of not being charged a responsibility fee for any blood which he or his family may require.

Type F: *Captive voluntary:* Usually a person in prison or the military, upon whom stronger sanctions and benefits can be laid than general social pressure.

Type G: *Fringe benefit:* A person who responds to certain benefits offered either by the bank or his employer—football tickets, free meals, days off work, and so on.

Type H: *Voluntary community donor:* The person for whom tangible benefits such as assurance programs have little appeal; hence his motives fall under the general category of altruism. In order to prove their altruism, some have been known to refuse assurance programs. Most donors accept the programs, but they are not the donors' prime motivation.

The American Red Cross, which usually uses several methods to attract donors, including hospital sites, college campus sites, industrial sites, and bloodmobiles, is at the point of wanting to move toward more market segmentation in order to approach the different groups of donors with appropriate appeals and collection systems. It would particularly like to improve its attraction of voluntary community donors (type H). Assuming that there are a large number of altruistic people in the country who have never given blood, the Red Cross wonders what the best way is to attract them.

The answer appears to lie in a subsegmentation of these potential donors into five stages, according to their readiness to give. The stages are described below, along with the appropriate marketing strategy.

1. *Unaware stage.* People are potentially receptive to altruistic appeals, but unaware of either the blood bank system or the need for blood. The appropriate strategy is a general awareness campaign stressing altruism and the need for blood.

2. *Aware stage.* People are aware of blood banks and of blood needs but ignorant of the satisfaction felt and have some fear about personal pain or discomfort. The appropriate strategy is articles in the media describing the blood-giving experience and stressing the lack of pain.

3. *Interested stage.* People are aware of the benefits of giving but these are outweighed by the perceived costs in terms of pain, time, and distance. The appropriate strategy is to increase the perceived benefits and lower the perceived costs.

4. *Desirous stage.* People are desirous of giving blood but await opportunity or initiative. The appropriate strategy is to provide opportunity through bloodmobiling and telephone and direct mail solicitation.

5. *Action stage.* People have given blood for the first time and need reminders to give again. The appropriate strategy is to satisfy the first-time donor through providing a friendly staff and keeping waiting time to a minimum. Monthly newsletters should be sent to past givers plus a postcard reminder after a reasonable time interval.

The American Red Cross believes that a refined segmentation of blood donors by the benefits they seek and their stage of readiness to give can lead to more precise marketing programs that will increase the number of donors and the frequency of donation.

An organization that decides to operate in the blood donor market, or any other market, soon recognizes that it cannot reach and appeal to all consumers. The consumers may be too numerous, widely scattered, and varied in their needs and preferences. Different competitors will be in the best position to go after particular segments of the market. Each organization, instead of trying to reach everyone, should identify the most attractive parts of the market that it could effectively serve.

This philosophy has not always been practiced by organizations. Organizations have gone through three stages in their thinking about how to operate in a market.

- *Mass marketing.* Mass marketing is a style of marketing where the organization mass-produces and mass-distributes one market offer and attempts to attract every eligible person to its use. Thus, the Philadelphia Transit Authority could conceivably offer only one form of transportation—buses—and try to attract all commuters to use this form. The argument for mass marketing is that it would result in the lowest costs and prices, and therefore create the largest potential market. The mass marketer pays little or no attention to differences in consumer preferences.

- *Product differentiated marketing.* Product differentiation is a style of marketing where the organization prepares two or more market offers for the market as a whole. The market offers may exhibit different features, styles, quality, and so on. Thus, the Philadelphia Transit Authority could create a bus system and subway system and leave it to commuters to make the choice. The offers are not designed for different groups so much as to offer alternatives to everyone in the market.
- *Target marketing.* Target marketing is a style of marketing where the organization distinguishes between different segments making up the market, chooses one or more of these segments to focus on, and develops market offers and marketing mixes tailored to meet the needs of each target market. For example, the Philadelphia Transit Authority could develop a commuter train system designed to meet the needs of affluent commuters for a clean train and comfortable ride, albeit at a high price.

Organizations can be found today practicing each style of marketing. However, there is a strong movement away from mass marketing and product differentiated marketing toward target marketing. At least three benefits can be identified for target marketing.

1. *Organizations are in a better position to spot market opportunities.* They are able to notice market segments whose needs are not being fully met by current product offers.
2. *Sellers can make finer adjustments of their product to match the desires of the market.* They are able to interview members of the target market and get a good picture of their specific needs and desires.
3. *Sellers can make finer adjustments of their prices, distribution channels, and promotional mix.* Instead of trying to draw in all potential buyers with a "shotgun" approach, sellers can create separate marketing programs aimed at each target market (called a "rifle" approach).

In order to practice target marketing, the company has to go through two major steps. They are shown in Figure 9–1. The first is *market segmentation,* the

## FIGURE 9–1

### Steps in Market Segmentation and Target Marketing

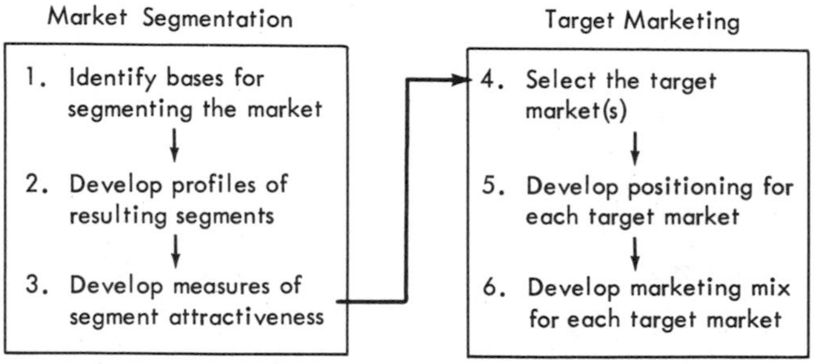

| Market Segmentation | Target Marketing |
|---|---|
| 1. Identify bases for segmenting the market | 4. Select the target market(s) |
| 2. Develop profiles of resulting segments | 5. Develop positioning for each target market |
| 3. Develop measures of segment attractiveness | 6. Develop marketing mix for each target market |

act of dividing a market into distinct and meaningful groups of consumers who might merit separate products and/or marketing mixes. Market segmentation requires identifying the different bases for segmenting the market, developing profiles of the resulting market segments, and developing measures of each segment's attractiveness. The second step is *target marketing,* the act of selecting one or more of the market segments and developing a positioning and marketing mix strategy for each. This chapter will describe the major concepts and tools for market segmentation and targeting.

---

## MARKET SEGMENTATION

Markets consist of buyers, and buyers are likely to differ in one or more respects. They may differ in their desires, resources, geographical locations, buying attitudes, buying practices, and so on. Any of these variables can be used to segment a market. We will first illustrate the general approach to segmenting a market.

### THE GENERAL APPROACH TO SEGMENTING A MARKET

Figure 9–2A shows a market consisting of six buyers before it is segmented. The maximum number of segments that a market can contain is the total number of buyers making up that market. Each buyer is potentially a separate market, because of unique needs and desires. Ideally, a seller might study each buyer in

### FIGURE 9–2
Different Approaches to Segmentation of a Market

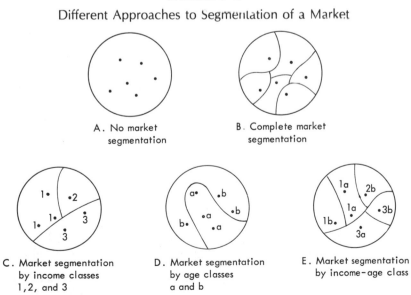

A. No market
segmentation

B. Complete market
segmentation

C. Market segmentation
by income classes
1, 2, and 3

D. Market segmentation
by age classes
a and b

E. Market segmentation
by income-age class

order to tailor the best marketing program to that buyer's needs. Where there are only a few buyers, this may be feasible. For example, a therapist tailors a different treatment to each patient, depending on what each patient needs. This ultimate degree of market segmentation is illustrated in Figure 9–2B.

Most sellers will not find it worthwhile to "customize" their product to satisfy each buyer's specific requirements. Instead, the seller identifies broad classes of buyers who differ in their product requirements and/or marketing responses. For example, the seller may discover that income groups differ in their product requirements and marketing responses. In Figure 9–2C a number (1, 2, or 3) is used to identify each buyer's income class. Lines are drawn around buyers in the same income class. Segmentation by income class results in three segments, the most numerous one being income class 1 in the illustration.

On the other hand, the seller may find pronounced differences in buyer behavior between younger and older buyers. In Figure 9–2D the same individuals are shown, except a letter (a or b) is used to indicate the buyer's age class. Segmentation of the market by age class results in two segments, both equally numerous.

It may turn out that income and age both count heavily in differentiating the buyer's behavior toward the product. The seller may find it desirable to partition the market according to those joint characteristics. In terms of the illustration, the market can be broken into the following six segments: 1a, 1b, 2a, 2b, 3a, and 3b. Figure 9–2E shows that segment 1a contains two buyers, segment 2a contains no buyers (a null segment), and each of the other segments contains one buyer. In general, as the market is segmented on the basis of a larger set of joint characteristics, the seller achieves finer precision, but at the price of multiplying the number of segments and reducing the population in each segment. If the seller segmented the market, using all conceivable characteristics, the market would again look like Figure 9–2B, where each buyer would be a separate segment.

In the preceding illustration, the market was segmented by income and age. This resulted in different *demographic segments.* Suppose, instead, buyers are asked how much they want of each of two product attributes (say, *academic rigor* and *social life,* in the case of a college). This results in identifying different *preference segments* in the market. Three different patterns can emerge.

> 1. *Homogeneous preferences.* Figure 9–3A reveals a market where all the students have roughly the same preference. The market shows no *natural segments,* at least as far as the two attributes are concerned. We would predict that colleges would highly resemble each other because they all have to please the same kind of student.
> 2. *Diffused preferences.* At the other extreme, student preferences may be scattered fairly evenly throughout the space with no concentration (Figure 9–3B). We would predict that different types of colleges would appear to satisfy different parts of the market.
> 3. *Clustered preferences.* An intermediate possibility is the appearance of distinct preference clusters called *natural market segments* (Figure 9–3C). We would predict

FIGURE 9–3

Basic Market Preference Patterns

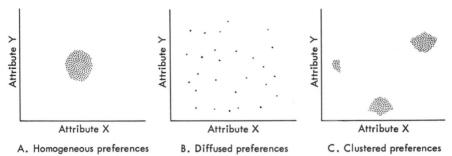

| A. Homogeneous preferences | B. Diffused preferences | C. Clustered preferences |

that colleges would cluster into three basic groups catering to the three types of students.

Thus, we find that segmentation procedures could indicate the existence of natural market segments, or could be used to construct artificial market segments, or could reveal the lack of any market segments. We now turn to specific variables that can be used in segmenting consumer markets.

BASES FOR SEGMENTING MARKETS

There is no one, or right, way to segment a market. A market can be segmented in a number of ways by introducing different variables and seeing which reveal the most in the way of market opportunities. Sometimes the marketer simply has to try out the various segmentation variables, singly and in combination, before hitting on an insightful way to view the market structure. Here we will review the major geographical, demographic, psychographic, and behavioristic variables used in segmenting consumer markets. They are shown in Table 9–1.

**Geographical segmentation.** In geographical segmentation, the market is divided into different geographical entities, such as nations, states, regions, counties, cities, or neighborhoods, based on the notion that consumer needs or responses vary geographically. The organization either decides to operate in one or a few parts of the country as a specialist in meeting their needs or to operate broadly but paying attention to variations in geographical needs and preferences. For example, the State University of New York (SUNY) operates 64 college campuses, each with programs adapted partly to the interests of the local inhabitants. This is in contrast to running 64 college campuses that are all doing the same thing.

**Demographic segmentation.** In demographic segmentation, the market is divided into different groups on the basis of demographic variables such as age, sex,

## Table 9–1

### MAJOR SEGMENTATION VARIABLES FOR CONSUMER MARKETS

| Variable | Typical breakdowns |
|---|---|
| **Geographical** | |
| Region | Pacific, Mountain, West North Central, West South Central, East North Central, East South Central, South Atlantic, Middle Atlantic, New England |
| County size | A, B, C, D |
| City of SMSA size | Under 5,000, 5,000–20,000, 20,000–50,000, 50,000–100,000, 100,000–250,000, 250,000–500,000, 500,000–1,000,000, 1,000,000–4,000,000, over 4,000,000 |
| Density | Urban, suburban, rural |
| Climate | Northern, southern |
| **Demographic** | |
| Age | Under 6, 6–11, 12–19, 20–34, 35–49, 50–64, 65 + |
| Sex | Male, female |
| Family size | 1–2, 3–4, 5+ |
| Family life cycle | Young, single; young, married, no children; young, married, youngest child under 6; young, married, youngest child 6 or over; older, married, with children; older, married, no children under 18; older, single; other |
| Income | Under $2,500, $2,500–$5,000, $5,000–$7,500, $7,500–$10,000, $10,000–$15,000, $15,000–$20,000, $20,000–$30,000, $30,000–$50,000; over $50,000 |
| Occupation | Professional and technical; managers, officials, and proprietors; clerical, sales; craftsmen, foremen; operatives; farmers; retired; students; housewives; unemployed |
| Education | Grade school or less, some high school, graduated high school, some college, graduated college |
| Religion | Catholic, Protestant, Jewish, other |
| Race | White, black, oriental |
| Nationality | American, British, French, German, Scandinavian, Italian, Latin American, Middle Eastern, Japanese |
| **Psychographic** | |
| Social class | Lower lowers, upper lowers, lower middles, upper middles, lower uppers, upper uppers |
| Life style | Straights, swingers, longhairs |
| Personality | Compulsive, gregarious, authoritarian, ambitious |
| **Behavioristic** | |
| Purchase occasion | Regular occasion, special occasion |
| Benefits sought | Quality, service, economy |
| User status | Nonuser, ex-user, potential user, first-time user, regular user |
| Usage rate | Light user, medium user, heavy user |
| Loyalty status | None, medium, strong, absolute |
| Readiness stage | Unaware, aware, informed, interested, desirous, intending buy |
| Attitude toward product | Enthusiastic, positive, indifferent, negative, hostile |

family size, family life style, income, occupation, education, religion, race, and nationality. Demographic variables have long been the most popular bases for distinguishing consumer groups. One reason is that consumer wants, preferences, and usage rates are often highly associated with demographic variables. Another is that demographic variables are easier to measure than most other types of variables. Even when the target market is described in nondemographic terms (say, a personality type), the link back to demographic characteristics is necessary in order to know the size of the target market and how to reach it efficiently.

Here we will illustrate how certain demographic variables have been applied creatively to market segmentation.

AGE AND LIFE CYCLE STAGE.    Consumer wants and capacities change with age. Thus churches have developed different programs for children, youth, singles, married adults, and senior citizens. The churches try to "customize" the religious and social experiences to the interests of these different groups. Some churches are even subsegmenting the senior citizens into those between 55 and 70 ("the young old") and 70 and up ("the old old"). The young old still feel vigorous and want challenge and variety in their lives; and the old old want to settle into a comfortable and routine existence.

SEX.    Sex segmentation appears in many nonprofit sectors, such as male and female colleges, service and social clubs, prisons, and military services. Within a single sex, further segmentation can be applied. The continuing education department of a large university segments the female adult learners into "at homes" and "working outside the homes." The "at-homes" are subdivided into homemakers and displaced homemakers. Homemakers are attracted to courses for self-enrichment and improved homemaking skills, while displaced homemakers are more interested in career preparation. The "working outside the home" segment breaks into two subsegments, clerical–technical businesswomen and management businesswomen. Each segment has a different set of motivations for attending college, and different educational programs are appropriate for each. Furthermore, each segment faces certain problems in attending college. By addressing the specific problems of each segment, the college is in a better position to attract more women to its campus.

INCOME.    Income segmentation is another long-standing practice in the nonprofit sector. In the medical field, the standard health insurance policy pays for semi-private rooms. However, most hospitals offer patients the option of a private room at an additional cost in order to cater to the preferences of higher income groups. Some hospitals have designed entire wings and even whole buildings to serve more affluent patients. Hospitals that establish outreach ambulatory centers vary the decor and service to match the different income groups.

MULTIVARIABLE SEGMENTATION.    Very often an organization will segment a market by combining two or more variables. The Charles Home for the Blind (name disguised) has accepted in the past all blind people who needed residential care, psychological counseling, or vocational training. However, it will not be able to serve all blind people in the coming years because of limited facilities and funds, and because other institutions are serving certain groups well. Management is trying to figure out which groups to serve. To aid in this decision, they segmented blind people into 20 groups through the use of four segmentation variables (see Figure 9–4). Management felt that the needs and required treatments of these segments differed, and undertook to study which blind groups suffered the most neglect, with the intention of concentrating on these groups.[1]

**Psychographic segmentation.**    People within the same demographic group can exhibit very different psychographic profiles. The fact that demographics do not necessarily reveal anything about attitudes and living styles has led to psychographic segmentation. In psychographic segmentation, buyers are divided into groups on the basis of their social class, life style, or personality characteristics.

SOCIAL CLASS.    Social classes are relatively homogeneous and enduring divisions in a society which is hierarchically ordered and whose members share similar values, interests, and behavior. Social scientists have distinguished six social classes: (1) upper uppers (less than 1%); (2) lower uppers (about 2%); (3) upper middles (12%); (4) lower middles (30%); (5) upper lowers (35%); and (6) lower lowers (20%), using variables such as income, occupation, education, and type of residence.[2] Social classes show distinct consumption preferences in the nonprofit area. For example, a recent study of museum-goers attending the King Tut exhibit in New Orleans showed that attendance came heavily from the upper and middle classes, in spite of the mass marketing of this extraordinary exhibit.[3] Operas, plays, the ballet, symphonies, and lectures also attract the upper classes

## FIGURE 9–4

### Segmentation of the Blind Market

| | | Single Handicapped | | Multiple Handicapped | |
|---|---|---|---|---|---|
| | | Partially sighted | Totally blind | Partially sighted | Totally blind |
| Congenital | Elderly | | | | |
| | Working-age adult | | | | |
| | Child | | | | |
| Adventitious | Elderly | | | | |
| | Working-age adult | | | | |
| | Child | | | | |

SOURCE: Adapted from teaching note, *The Richardson Center for the Blind,* prepared by Roberta N. Clarke under the supervision of Benson P. Shapiro.

most heavily. Cultural institutions that wish to overcome their elitist image and attract lower-class audiences to appreciate their art form will have to develop separate marketing programs and strategies.

LIFE STYLE.   Different consumer life styles are found within and even between social classes. Researchers have found that they can identify life styles by interviewing people about their *activities, interests,* and *opinions* and clustering similar groups. The advertising agency of Needham, Harper & Steers has identified ten major consumer life styles—five for men and five for women—and the percentage of the population in each life style group.[4]

---

### Ten Life Style Groups

| | |
|---|---|
| Ben, the self-made businessman (17%) | Cathy, the contented housewife (18%) |
| Scott, the successful professional (21%) | Candice, the chic suburbanite (20%) |
| Dale, the devoted family man (17%) | Eleanor, the elegant socialite (17%) |
| Fred, the frustrated factory worker (19%) | Mildred, the militant mother (20%) |
| Herman, the retiring homebody (26%) | Thelma, the old-fashioned traditionalist (25%) |

---

Each life style group is characterized by specific activities, interests, and opinions, as well as product preferences and media preferences. A community college, for example, might want to attract more professional people to its campus for evening courses. It would try to imagine Scott's life style and the kinds of educational needs he might have. The college might develop a special brochure to attract professionals, using various cues that professionals would respond to.

Some researchers prefer more product-specific life style studies. Ruth Ziff has studied life styles related to drug purchase that would be of interest to hospitals and physicians. She identified the following four drug life styles (percentage of each shown in parenthesis):

- *Realists* (35%) are not health fatalists, or excessively concerned with protection or germs. They view remedies positively, want something that is convenient and works, and do not feel the need of a doctor-recommended medicine.
- *Authority seekers* (31%) are doctor-and-prescription oriented, are neither fatalists nor stoics concerning health, but they prefer the stamp of authority on what they do take.
- *Skeptics* (23%) have a low health concern, are least likely to resort to medication, and are highly skeptical of cold remedies.
- *Hypochondriacs* (11%) have high health concern, regard themselves as prone to any bug going around, and tend to take medication at the first symptom. They do not look for strength in what they take, but need some mild authority reassurance.[5]

PERSONALITY.   Marketers have also used personality variables to segment markets. They try to endow their products with *brand personalities* (brand image, brand concept) designed to appeal to corresponding *consumer personalities* (self-images, self-concepts). The U.S. Marine Corps tries to attract "he-man" personalities to join its service. Its posters and other communications portray tough-looking men who are proud to be part of the Marine Corps.

**Behavioristic segmentation.** In behavioristic segmentation, buyers are divided into groups on the basis of their knowledge, attitude, use, or response to an actual product or its attributes. Many marketers believe that behavioristic variables are the best starting point for constructing meaningful market segments.

PURCHASE OCCASION. Buyers can be distinguished according to occasions when they purchase a product. For example, commuters using public transportation include those who are traveling to work, those who are shopping, those who are going for entertainment, and those who are visiting friends. Some public transit companies have launched campaigns to encourage the shopping segment to travel in off-peak hours and have even considered charging lower fares as an incentive.

BENEFITS SOUGHT. Buyers can be segmented according to the particular benefit(s) that they are seeking through the consumption of the product. Some consumers look for one dominant benefit from the product and others seek a particular *benefit bundle*. [6] Many markets are made up of three core benefit segments: *quality buyers, service buyers,* and *economy buyers.* Quality buyers seek out the best reputed product and are not concerned with the cost. A quality seeker in the college market would consider only the elite universities, and a quality seeker in the hospital market would consider only the best hospitals and surgeons. Service buyers look for the best value for the money and expect the service to match the price. A service-seeker would choose a college that provides a good education and social life for the money, regardless of its reputation. Economy buyers are primarily interested in minimizing their cost and favor the least expensive market offer. An economy-seeker would go to a community college to keep college costs to a minimum. Benefit segmentation, it should be added, works best when people's preferences are correlated with demographic and media characteristics, making it easier to reach them efficiently.

In addition to general benefits, each product should be evaluated for the specific benefits that different buyers might seek. Goodnow found that adults attending the College of DuPage, a large community college in Illinois, fell into five benefit segments: (1) social improvement learners, (2) career learners, (3) leisure learners, (4) submissive learners, and (5) ambivalent learners. [7] She recommended a separate marketing strategy directed at each benefit segment, based on the segment's characteristics. Thus, the leisure learners could be best attracted to noncredit physical education and creative arts programs which meet informally in small groups for three hours on weekday evenings. This segment could be effectively reached by sending an *Extension Bulletin,* appealing to their desire for a "night out." Certain programs might be promoted to this group through women's clubs and the suburban newspaper. A separate marketing strategy can be worked out for each of the other segments, based on the benefit sought and associated characteristics.

USER STATUS. Many markets can be segmented into nonusers, ex-users, potential users, first-time users, and regular users of a product. This segmentation variable is helpful to antidrug agencies in planning their education programs and campaigns. Much of their effort is directed at identifying potential users of hard drugs and discouraging them through information and persuasive campaigns. They also sponsor rehabilitation programs to help regular users who want to quit their habit. They utilize ex-users in various programs to add credibility to their effort.

USAGE RATE. Many markets can be segmented into light-, medium-, and heavy-user groups of the product (called volume segmentation). Heavy users may constitute only a small percentage of the numerical size of the market but a major percentage of the unit volume consumed. Marketers make a great effort to determine the demographic characteristics and media habits of the heavy users and aim their marketing programs at them. An antismoking campaign, for example, might be aimed at the heaviest smokers, a safe driving campaign may be aimed at those having the most accidents, and a family planning campaign may be aimed at those likely to have the most children. Unfortunately, the heaviest users are the most resistant to change. Fertile families are the most resistant to birth control messages and unsafe drivers are the most resistant to safe driving messages. The agencies must consider whether to use their limited budget to go after a few heavy users who are highly resistant or many light users who are less resistant.

Semenik and Young segmented the audience attending opera into three attendance level segments—subscribers, frequent attenders, and infrequent attenders—and found significant differences.[8] Subscribers tended to be long-time patrons, attended as husband and wife, and considered themselves to be opera fans. Frequent attenders had similar characteristics but were younger and lower in income, and often attended with a friend rather than a spouse. Infrequent attenders did not consider themselves as opera fans but attended because of a featured star or well-known opera. The identification of segment characteristics enables the development of separate market strategies designed to maximize attendance and loyalty.

LOYALTY STATUS. Loyalty status describes the strength of a consumer's preference for a particular entity. The amount of loyalty can range from zero to absolute. We find consumers who are deeply loyal to a brand (Budweiser beer, Crest toothpaste, Cadillac automobiles); an organization (Harvard University, the Republican Party); a place (New England, Southern California); a person (Ralph Nader); and so on. Being loyal means preferring the particular object in spite of increased incentives to switch to something else.

An organization should research its present customers and analyze their degree of loyalty. Four groups can be distinguished: (1) *hard-core loyals,* who are exclusively devoted to the organization; (2) *soft-core loyals,* who are devoted to two or three organizations; (3) *shifting loyals,* who are gradually moving from favoring this organization to favoring another organization; and (4) *switchers,* who show no loyalty to any organization. If most of the organization's customers are hard-core loyals, or even soft-core loyals, the organization is basically healthy. It might study its loyals to find out the basic satisfactions they derive from affiliation, and then attempt to attract others who are seeking the same satisfactions.

STAGES OF BUYER READINESS.   At any point of time, people are in various stages of readiness toward buying the product. Some members of the potential market are *unaware* of the product; some are *aware;* some are *informed;* some are *interested;* some are *desirous;* and some *intend to buy.* The distribution of people over stages of readiness makes a big difference in designing the marketing program. Suppose a health agency wants to attract women to take an annual Pap test to detect cervical cancer. At the beginning, most of the potential market is unaware of the concept (see Figure 9–5A). The marketing effort should go into high-reach advertising and publicity using a simple message. If successful, more of the market will be aware of the Pap test but needing more knowledge (see Figure 9–5B). After knowledge is built up, the advertising should be changed to dramatize the benefits of taking an annual examination and the risks of not taking it, so as to move more people into a stage of desire (see Figure 9–5C). Facilities should also be readied for handling the large number of women who may be motivated to take the examination. In general, the marketing program must be adjusted to the changing distribution of buyer readiness.

### FIGURE 9–5

Stages of Market Readiness

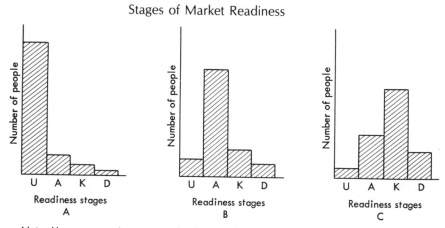

Note: U = unaware; A = aware only; K = knowledgeable; D = desirous.

**Attitude.**      Markets can be segmented according to consumer attitudes toward adopting the product. For example, a chapter of the Sigma Chi fraternity in an eastern college was interested in knowing more about college freshmen's attitudes toward fraternities. Chapter members interviewed incoming freshmen and found that 10 percent were *enthusiasts,* 20 percent *positives,* 30 percent *indifferents,* 25 percent *negatives,* and 15 percent *hostiles.* Each segment had a distinct consumer profile. For example, enthusiasts generally came from higher income, better educated families living in suburban homes, while hostiles generally came from lower income, lower educated families living in cities. The fraternity got a better picture of its natural market and in addition saw some opportunities for trying to convert indifferent people toward more positive feelings about fraternities.

### BASES FOR SEGMENTING ORGANIZATIONAL MARKETS

Public and nonprofit organizations not only market to individual consumers but also have many occasions to market to organizations. A small art museum wants to identify appropriate foundations to solicit for financial support. A state hospital association wants to motivate its local chapters to improve their member services. A local hospital wants to convince adjacent hospitals to use its blood bank services. In all these cases, the organization is seeking to get other organizations to "buy" something. We will discuss how organizations "buy" things in the next chapter. Here we want to examine how a market of organizations can be segmented.

We will use the example of a small art museum trying to identify appropriate foundations for support. Here are some of the major ways to segment organizations as applied to foundations:

1. *Organization size.* Foundations can be divided into large, medium, and small foundations. The small museum could decide that its best chances for a grant lay with small foundations rather than with large or medium-sized ones.

2. *Geographical location.* Foundations can be divided as to whether they are in the same city as the museum, in the same state, or far away. The small museum would decide to focus on the local foundations because they would have stronger contacts with these foundations.

3. *Interest profile.* Foundations have different interest profiles. The museum could identify those foundations that have given the most support to the arts.

4. *Resource level.* Foundations differ in the amount of resources they have and are willing to devote to particular programs. The museum would only want to approach foundations that can give the size grant it seeks.

5. *Buying criteria.* Foundations differ in the qualities they look for in grant applications. Some foundations emphasize applicants' neediness, others the quality of their management, and still others the amount of social benefit that would be produced. The museum should focus on those foundations whose buying criteria match the museum's strengths.

6. *Buying process.* Foundations differ in how much documentation they require and the length of their review process. The museum may want to work only with foundations that require little documentation and announce awards early.

Clearly, there are many ways to segment a market. Not all resulting segments are meaningful from a marketing point of view. To be maximally useful, market segments should exhibit the following characteristics:

- The first is *measurability,* the degree to which the size, purchasing power, and profile of the resulting segments can be readily measured. Certain segments are hard to measure. An illustration would be the size of the segment of white upper-income teenage female drug addicts, since this segment is engaged in secretive behavior.
- The second is *accessibility,* the degree to which the resulting segments can be effectively reached and served. Thus, it would be hard for a drug treatment center to develop efficient media to locate and communicate with white female drug addicts.
- The third is *substantiality,* the degree to which the resulting segments are large enough to be worth pursuing. The drug treatment center is likely to decide that white affluent female drug addicts are too few in number to be worth the development of a special marketing program.

---

## TARGET MARKETING

Market segmentation reveals the market segment opportunities facing the organization. At this point, the organization has to decide between three broad market selection strategies. They are shown in Figure 9–6.

1. *Undifferentiated marketing.* The organization can decide to go after the whole market with one offer and marketing mix, trying to attract as many consumers as possible (this is another name for mass marketing).
2. *Differentiated marketing.* The organization can decide to go after several market segments, developing an effective offer and marketing mix for each.
3. *Concentrated marketing.* The organization can decide to go after one market segment and develop the ideal offer and marketing mix.

Here we will describe the logic and merits of each of these strategies.

### UNDIFFERENTIATED MARKETING

In undifferentiated marketing,[9] the organization chooses not to recognize the different market segments making up the market. It treats the market as an aggregate, focusing on what is common in the needs of consumers rather than on what is different. It tries to design a product and a marketing program that appeal to the broadest number of buyers. It would be exemplified by a church that runs only one religious service for everyone, a politician who gives the same speech to everyone, and a family planning organization that tries to promote the same birth control method for everyone.

Undifferentiated marketing is typically defended on the grounds of cost economies. It is "the marketing counterpart to standardization and mass produc-

## FIGURE 9–6

### Three Alternative Market Selection Strategies

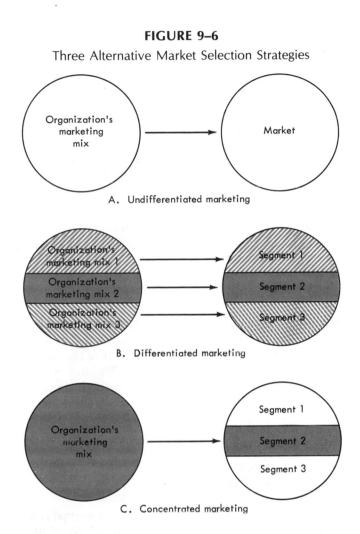

A. Undifferentiated marketing

B. Differentiated marketing

C. Concentrated marketing

tion in manufacturing."[10] Product costs, research costs, media costs, and training costs are all kept low through promoting only one product. The lower cost, however, is accompanied by reduced consumer satisfaction through failure of the organization to meet individually varying needs. Competitors have an incentive to reach and serve the neglected segments, and become strongly entrenched in these segments.

### Differentiated Marketing

Under differentiated marketing, an organization decides to operate in two or more segments of the market but designs separate product and/or marketing programs for each. By offering product and marketing variations, it hopes to attain higher sales and a deeper position within each market segment. It hopes

229

that a deep position in several segments will strengthen the customers' overall identification of the organization with the product field. Furthermore, it hopes for greater loyalty and repeat purchasing, because the organization's offerings have been bent to the customer's desire rather than the other way around.

The net effect of differentiated marketing is to create more total sales for the organization than undifferentiated marketing. However, it also tends to create higher costs of doing business. The organization has to spend more in product management, marketing research, communication materials, advertising, and sales training. Since differentiated marketing leads to higher sales and higher costs, nothing can be said in advance about the optimality of this strategy. Some organizations push differentiated marketing too far in that they run more segmented programs than are economically feasible; some should be pruned. The majority of public and nonprofit organizations, however, probably err in not pushing differentiated marketing far enough in the light of the varying needs of their consumers.

### Concentrated Marketing

Concentrated marketing occurs when an organization decides to divide the market into meaningful segments and devote its major marketing effort to one segment. Instead of spreading itself thin in many parts of the market, it concentrates on serving a particular market segment well. Through concentrated marketing the organization usually achieves a strong following and standing in a particular market segment. It enjoys greater knowledge of the market segment's needs and behavior and it also achieves operating economies through specialization in production, distribution, and promotion. This type of marketing is done, for example, by a private museum that decides to concentrate only on African art; or an environmental group that concentrates only on the problem of noise pollution; or a private foundation that awards grants only to transportation researchers.

Concentrated marketing does involve higher than normal risk, in that the market may suddenly decline or disappear. The National Foundation for Infantile Paralysis almost folded when the Salk vaccine was developed. Fortunately, the national foundation was able to turn its huge fundraising apparatus over to another medical cause.

### Choosing Among Market Selection Strategies

The actual choice of a marketing strategy depends on specific factors facing the organization. If the organization has *limited resources,* it will probably choose concentrated marketing because it does not have enough resources to relate to the whole market and/or to tailor special services for each segment. If the market is fairly *homogeneous* in its needs and desires, the organization will probably choose undifferentiated marketing because little would be gained by differentiated offerings. If the organization aspires to be a leader in several segments of the market, it will choose differentiated marketing. If *competitors* have already established dominance in all but a few segments of the market, the organization might try to concentrate its marketing in one of the remaining segments. Many organizations start out with a strategy of undifferentiated or concentrated marketing and if they are successful, evolve into a strategy of differentiated marketing.

If the organization elects to use a concentrated or differentiated marketing strategy, it has to evaluate carefully the best segment(s) to serve. The best way to do this is to apply the General Electric strategic business planning grid discussed in Chapter 3 (pp. 96–97). Each segment should be rated on its market attractiveness and the organization's strengths. The organization should focus on those market segments which have intrinsic attractiveness and which it has a differential advantage in serving.

---

## SUMMARY

Organizations can take three different approaches to a market. Mass marketing is the decision to mass-produce and mass-distribute one product and attempt to attract everyone to its purchase. Product differentiation is the decision to produce two or more products differentiated in terms of style, features, quality, sizes, and so on, so as to offer variety to the market and distinguish the organization's products from those of competitors. Target marketing is the decision to distinguish the different groups that make up a market and to develop appropriate products and marketing mixes for each target market. Organizations today are moving away from mass marketing and product differentiation toward target marketing, because the latter is more helpful in spotting market opportunities and developing more attractive products and marketing mixes.

The key step in target marketing is market segmentation, which is the act of dividing a market into distinct and meaningful groups of buyers who might merit separate products and/or marketing mixes. Market segmentation is a creative act. The investigator tries different variables to see which reveal the best segmentation opportunities. For consumer marketing, the major segmentation variables are broadly classified as geographical, demographic, psychographic, and behavioristic. Organizational markets can be segmented by such variables as organization size, geographical location, interest profile, resource level, buying criteria, and buying process. The effectiveness of the segmentation exercise depends upon arriving at segments that are measurable, accessible, and substantial.

The organization then has to choose a market selection strategy, either ignoring segment differences (undifferentiated marketing), developing differentiated products and marketing programs for several segments (differentiated marketing), or going after only one or a few segments (concentrated marketing). No particular strategy is superior in all circumstances. Much depends on organizational resources, product homogeneity, product stage in the life cycle, market homogeneity, and competitive marketing strategies. The organization should focus on those segments that are intrinsically attractive and that can be served with a differential advantage.

## QUESTIONS

**1.** The American Cancer Society is interested in developing programs to reduce cigarette smoking. How would you recommend that the society segment the smoking market? Would you recommend that it use an *undifferentiated, differentiated,* or *concentrated* marketing approach?

**2.** Do a benefit segmentation analysis of the market for the services of a YMCA/YWCA.

**3.** Most medical schools in the United States depend on donations to supply the human cadavers needed for students' medical education. Do a segmentation analysis of potential donors that would serve as a basis for an information campaign. Which segment(s) would you recommend targeting in the campaign?

**4.** The National Council for the Social Studies is an organization of elementary school teachers with an interest in social studies, high school social studies teachers (who teach history, economics, government, sociology, and related subjects), and college professors who are involved in training social studies teachers. The council has a monthly journal, a monthly newspaper, an annual convention, and regional, state, and local conferences. The council would like to increase its membership. Propose a multivariable segmentation approach that would be useful in designing a campaign for new members.

**5.** A public health agency is considering conducting a program to train volunteers to counsel callers seeking information on venereal disease from a "VD hotline," still in the planning stages. The agency is unsure whether they will be able to locate and successfully recruit suitable volunteers. Apply the requirements for effective segmentation to their problem.

**6.** The Church of Jesus Christ of Latter Day Saints (Mormons) has been using segmentation to provide specific church experiences for each segment. For example, the ward (individual church meeting place) near Stanford University is for unmarried young adults, particularly students. Married couples and their children belong to a ward in Menlo Park, several miles away, even though they may live next door to the Stanford ward meetinghouse. What market selection strategy is the church using? What advantages and disadvantages might this strategy present?

## NOTES

**1.** For an interesting case, see "The Richardson Center for the Blind," in Christopher H. Lovelock and Charles B. Weinberg, eds., *Cases in Public and Nonprofit Marketing* (Palo Alto, Calif.: Scientific Press, 1977), pp. 61–72. This case was prepared by Roberta N. Clarke.

**2.** See James F. Engel, Roger D. Blackwell, and David T. Kollat, *Consumer Behavior,* 3rd ed. (New York: Holt, Rinehart & Winston, 1978), pp. 127–28.

**3.** See John E. Robbins and Stephanie S. Robbins, "Segmentation for 'Fine Arts' Marketing: Is King Tut Classless as Well as Ageless?", in Neil Beckwith, et al., eds., *1979 Educators' Conference Proceedings* (Chicago: American Marketing Association, 1979), pp. 479–84.

**4.** See Peter W. Bernstein, "Psychographics Is Still an Issue on Madison Avenue," *Fortune,* January 1978, pp. 78–84.

**5.** Ruth Ziff, "Psychographics for Market Segmentation," *Journal of Advertising Research,* April 1971, pp. 3–9. The female life style classification unfortunately fails to recognize the working or professional woman.

**6.** See Paul E. Green, Yoram Wind, and Arun K. Jain, "Benefit Bundle Analysis," *Journal of Advertising Research,* April 1972, pp. 31–36.

**7.** See Wilma Elizabeth Goodnow, "Benefit Segmentation: A Technique for Developing Program and Promotional Strategies for Adults in a Community College," unpublished Ph.D. dissertation, Northern Illinois University, DeKalb, Ill., May 1980.

**8.** Richard J. Semenik and Clifford E. Young, "Market Segmentation in Arts Organizations," in Beckwith, et al., *1979 Educators' Conference Proceedings,* pp. 474–78.

**9.** See Wendell R. Smith, "Product Differentiation and Market Segmentation as Alternative Marketing Strategies," *Journal of Marketing,* July 1956, pp. 3–8; and Alan A. Roberts, "Applying the Strategy of Market Segmentation," *Business Horizons,* Fall 1961, pp. 65–72.

**10.** Smith, "Product Differentiation," p. 4.

# Consumer Analysis

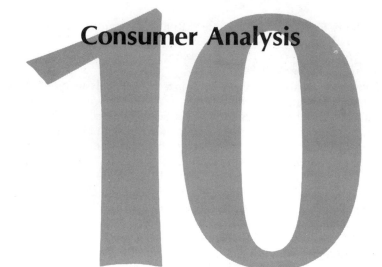

The San Francisco Zoo, like many of the nation's 132 nonprofit zoos, is struggling to keep alive in the face of rapidly mounting costs and stable or declining budgets. Besides the rising costs of food and energy, zoos are faced with the need to improve the housing of their animals, their animal medical services, and so on. Investigators of the Humane Society have accused the San Francisco Zoo to be among the country's worst-run municipal zoos and have urged the zoo to improve its facilities and services. In the meantime, the San Francisco City Council is struggling with how to allocate scarce funds to parks, museums, poverty programs, and other urban programs, besides the zoo.

The administration at the San Francisco Zoo recognizes the importance of demonstrating the benefits that the zoo provides to the citizens of San Francisco. Yet the zoo has not conducted any formal study of its visitors and their characteristics and satisfactions. The zoo's public relations director believes that the time is right to conduct a marketing research study of the zoo's visitors and nonvisitors. She met with the zoo director and they drew up several questions as relates to the zoo's "customers."

1. How many visitors are attracted to the San Francisco Zoo each year? What areas do they come from? (city, suburbs, out-of-town)

2. How many are rare attenders, moderate attenders, and frequent attenders? What kinds of people make up each group?

3. Why do visitors come to the zoo? What events trigger their decision to come?

4. Whom do they come with to the zoo?

5. How much time do visitors spend at the zoo?

6. What animals do they enjoy seeing the most?

7. How do visitors move through the zoo?

8. What do the visitors see as the most satisfying aspects of the zoo and the least satisfying?

9. How would visitors react to an admission price of $1 per adult and 50 cents per child under 12?

10. Who are the nonvisitors to the zoo? What are their reasons for nonattendance?

The public relations director feels that the information would be useful to the zoo director in improving zoo operations and in preparing a "case" for the benefits that the zoo is creating for San Francisco citizens. She decided to contact a marketing research firm to learn how much this study would cost. The marketing research firm estimated that questionnaire design, data collection, and report preparation would cost about $10,000. Since the zoo was short of funds, the zoo director toyed with the idea of designing and conducting a homegrown consumer research study using volunteer interviewers, where the total cost might be $2,000. She talked to the zoo director to find out whether he was willing to spend $10,000, or even $2,000, to know more about the zoo's visitors? Would this knowledge be worth the cost?

Organizations vary in the amount of systematic information they gather about their target consumers. In the health field, federally funded health organizations (such as the regional HSAs) do a fairly good to very good job of collecting information. Health care providers (hospitals, neighborhood health centers, medical group practices) do a poor to fair (with an occasional excellent) job of gathering information on consumer groups. But almost all of this information is demographic. Rarely does one see usage information, attitudes, or perception data.[1]

Organizations must go beyond measuring total market size and market segment characteristics into trying to understand how individual consumers see, think, feel, and act. This is the meaning of a consumer orientation, that is, being consumer-minded. Knowing the consumer is the basis for effective product development, pricing, distribution, and promotion.

When we say "consumer," we mean the person or organization that is the target of marketing effort. We will deal with *individual buyers* in the first part of the chapter and *organizational buyers* in the second part. In both cases, we will seek to understand the buying process through which the consumer goes. We see the buying process as consisting of the five stages shown in Figure 10–1. The stages answer the following questions:

1. What needs and wants give rise to the interest in buying or consuming the product? (need arousal)
2. What does the consumer do to gather information relevant to the felt need? (information gathering)
3. How does the consumer evaluate the decision alternatives? (decision evaluation)
4. How does the consumer carry out the purchase? (decision execution)
5. How does the consumer's postpurchase experience with the product affect his or her subsequent attitude and behavior toward the product? (postdecision assessment)

## FIGURE 10-1

Five-Stage Model of the Consumer Buying Process

This model emphasizes that the buying process starts long before the actual purchase and has consequences long after the purchase. It encourages the marketer to focus on the buying process rather than on the purchase decision.[2]

## INDIVIDUAL BUYER BEHAVIOR

We will now examine the buying behavior of individuals and families seeking to satisfy their own wants. We want to understand how consumers make choices among health, educational, recreational, social, and other services they may need or want. We will choose one "buying" situation—that of students selecting a college—and examine it carefully. Private colleges are particularly anxious to understand this process because of the shrinking pool of high school graduates. We shall refer from time to time to a hypothetical high school senior named Bob Jones who is beginning to think about the college choice process.

### NEED AROUSAL

The first task is to understand how consumers develop their initial interest in the product class and what needs and wants become involved in their decision making. Need arousal breaks down into three issues:

1. What factors initially trigger an interest in a product class? (triggering factors)
2. What deeper needs and values come into play when the consumer considers the product class? (basic needs)
3. What specific wants usually become activated by these needs? (specific wants)

**Triggering factors.**     A person's interest in a product class can be stimulated by *internal or external cues.* An internal cue consists of the person beginning to feel a need for, or readiness to do, something. The cue might take the form of a physiological stimulus, such as hunger or thirst, or a psychological stimulus, such as boredom or anxiety. An external cue consists of something from the outside coming to the person's attention and stimulating interest in the product class. The external cue can be *personal* (a friend, coworker, or salesperson) or *nonpersonal* (a magazine article, store display, or ad). Furthermore, the external cues can be either *marketer controlled* (such as ads and salespeople) or *nonmarketer controlled* (such as friends and natural settings).

An important marketing task is to survey consumers to learn the major types of triggering cues that stimulate their interest in the particular product class. They can be asked: "Recall what set your interest in motion in this object or activity." In the case of college decision making, the following cues tend to stimulate student thinking about college.

1.  Students begin to face the end of high school and wonder what they want to do with their lives.
2.  High school counselors send forms to students on which they are to indicate their future plans.
3.  Other students start talking about *their* college plans.
4.  College brochures arrive in the mail and the student starts reading them.

The triggering cues under marketer control can be beamed to the target market to stimulate interest in the product category.

**Basic needs.** The triggering cues have the capacity to arouse a set of needs in the person. They do not create the needs but only activate existing needs. The marketer task is to understand which basic needs of the individual might be served by the product class.

One of the most useful typologies of basic needs is Maslow's *hierarchy of needs* shown in Figure 10–2.[3] Maslow held that people act to satisfy the lower needs first before satisfying their higher needs. For example, a starving man first devotes his energy to finding food. If this basic need is satisfied, he can spend more time on his safety needs, such as eating the right foods and breathing good air. When he feels safe, he can take the time to deepen his social affiliations and friendships. Still later, he can develop pursuits that will meet his need for self-esteem and the esteem of others. Once this is satisfied, he is free to actualize his potential in other ways. As each lower level need is satisfied, it ceases to be a motivator and a higher need starts defining the person's motivational orientation.

We can ask what basic needs are stimulated by the aroused interest in college. Some high school seniors will become concerned about whether they can afford college and meet their basic needs for food and adequate housing. Others will wonder about how safe they will be away from home. Still others will be concerned with whether they can find people they like and who like them. And others will be concerned with self-esteem or self-actualization. A college will not be able to give attention to all of these needs. Thus, we find colleges that primarily

## FIGURE 10–2
### Maslow's Hierarchy of Needs

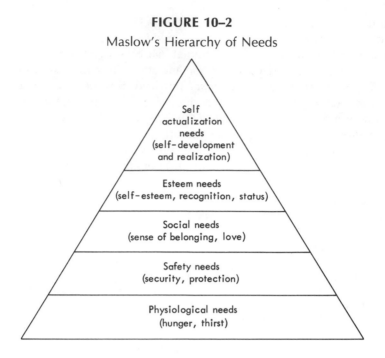

cater to the need for belonging (small schools with small classes, a caring faculty, and a good social life), others to the students' need for esteem (many "name" colleges), and still others to the need for self-actualization (many "arty" schools).

Students often want to satisfy several needs by the same decision, some of which are in conflict. Thus, a student may have a high need for both achieving and belonging. This can create mental conflict, which can be resolved either by treating one need as more important or by fluctuating between the two needs at different times. Here is where the person's *values* come into play, namely, the principles the person employs to choose among competing ends. Marketers should study people's value systems as well as need systems to understand their behavior.

**Specific wants.**    People who develop an interest in a specific product class are usually able to identify specific wants that they would like the product class to satisfy. Wants are product-specific, whereas basic needs are not product-specific. These wants can be discovered, in the case of a college, by asking students what *product attributes* they look for in a college. The ones that are most frequently mentioned by students are: (1) academic reputation, (2) cost, (3) location of campus (urban, rural), (4) distance from home, (5) size of campus, (6) social life, (7) physical look of campus, (8) housing and living, and (9) job placement.[4] Students vary in what they want with respect to each product attribute and the relative importance of each product attribute. We can imagine Bob Jones, for example, saying that he wants a high academic quality college with at least a medium social life, located in the South, with an Ivy League look, good housing, medium tuition, and good job placement. He might add that the first three wants are the most important in his thinking.

No college can satisfy every student's *hierarchy of wants,* and therefore must shape itself to meet the want hierarchy of some segment(s) of the college-bound population. The college should review from time to time whether student want patterns are shifting in a way that would favor or disfavor the college's "brand" of education. For example, a college with a weak social program would be increasingly threatened by a shifting preference of college-bound students toward colleges with an active social life.

Exhibit 10–1 shows the major methods for measuring consumer needs and wants.

### INFORMATION GATHERING

Consumers facing a buying decision will go into varying degrees of information gathering, depending on the product class and their own level of need for information. The marketer is interested in the following two questions at this stage:

1. How much information are consumers likely to gather before making a decision in this product class? (information neediness)
2. What information sources will consumers use, and what will be their relative influence? (information sources)

**Information neediness.**    Buyers vary greatly in their information gathering, from those who jump right into a decision (as with impulse purchases) to those who spend months gathering information before deciding (as with major expenditure decisions). We can distinguish between two broad levels of information gathering. The milder level is called *heightened attention.* Thus, Bob Jones may simply become more attentive to information about colleges, by noticing news about colleges and listening to friends discuss colleges. On the other hand, he may undertake an active *information search,* where he looks for books on the subject, phones friends, and writes for catalogs. How much he undertakes depends upon the strength of his drive, the amount of information he initially has, the ease of obtaining additional information, the value he places on additional information, and the satisfaction he gets from the search.

Normally, the amount of consumer information gathering increases as the consumer moves to more complex and important buying decisions. John A. Howard has distinguished three buying situations, each calling for a different level of information gathering.[5]

**EXHIBIT 10–1.** How can consumer needs and wants be measured?

There are three methods for learning the needs of an individual. The individual might be asked to describe his needs directly (the direct method); he might be asked to respond to vague material on which he will end up projecting his needs (the projective method); or he might be exposed to a real or prototyped object to help him clarify his needs (the prototype method).

Most marketing researchers use direct questioning to assess consumer needs. They may conduct an interview with a single individual or lead a focused group discussion. They may use open-end questions, such as "What courses would you like to see added to the college curriculum?" or "What recreational facilities would you like to see added on the campus?" Closed-end questions may also be included, such as "Rank the following activities in terms of your level of interest," or "Rate each of the following services on a scale from one to ten."

The direct questioning method assumes consumers are aware of their own needs and wants and willing to share the information with interviewers. But there are many issues on which they may not know or want to share their true feelings. For example, college students may ask for more study time when what they really want is less work. Or they may want younger teachers and what they may really believe is that younger teachers will be less demanding.

Thus, the needs that are verbalized may mask the real needs operating in the individual. Various projective techniques have been proposed to probe more deeply into the real needs of consumers. The four main projective techniques are:

1. *Word association.* Here the person is asked to name the word that first comes to mind when each of a set of words is mentioned. The interviewer might say "college" and the person might respond with "boring." By mentioning key words, the interviewer hopes to infer the pattern of needs and wants that people connect with a particular object.

2. *Sentence completion.* The person is presented with a set of incomplete sentences and asked to finish them. One sentence might read: "The basic reason most people go to college is —————." Since the question is about other people's behavior, the person more freely projects his own feeling.

3. *Picture completion.* The person is shown a vague picture and asked to make up a story about what he sees (called the Thematic Apperception Test or TAT). Or he may be shown a cartoon involving two people talking to each other, with one of their remarks deleted. The person is asked to fill in the words and this suggests something about his attitudes toward the object.

4. *Role playing.* Here one or more respondents are asked to act out a given role in a situation that is described in the briefest terms. For example, one person may be asked to play the role of a successful

**EXHIBIT 10–1.** How can consumer needs and wants be measured? (continued)

> business alumnus of a major university and the other the university president asking for a larger contribution. Through role playing, the respondents project their needs and personalities into the amorphous situation which provides useful clues on fundraising.
>
> A third method of probing consumer needs is to present a prototype of a possible product and let the subject experience and respond to it. Instead of asking a group of college students what they want in the way of a new gymnasium, they can be shown alternative blueprints and asked to comment on what they like and dislike about each.

1. *Routinized response behavior.* The simplest type of buying behavior occurs in the purchase of low-cost, frequently purchased items. For example, persons buying aspirins have very few decisions to make because they are well acquainted with the product class, know the major brands, and have a fairly clear brand preference. They do not always buy the same brand because the choice can be influenced by special deals or a wish for variety. But, in general, buyers' operations are routinized, and they are not likely to give much thought, search, or time to the purchase. The goods in this class are often called *low involvement goods*.

The marketer has two tasks in this situation. With respect to current customers, the marketer needs to provide continuous reinforcement by maintaining the brand's quality, stock level, and value. With respect to noncustomers, the marketer must break through their normal preferences by arranging cues that call attention to the new brand and its value. These cues can consist of new features or benefits, point-of-purchase displays, price specials, and premiums.

2. *Limited problem solving.* Buying is more complex when buyers confront an unfamiliar brand in a familiar product class that requires information before making a purchase choice. For example, persons wishing to go to the theatre may ask questions about various plays before choosing. This is described as limited problem solving because buyers are fully aware of the product class (plays) and the qualities they want (involvement, suspense, etc.) but are not familiar with all the plays being performed.

The alert marketer recognizes that consumers in this situation are trying to reduce risk through information gathering. The marketer must design a communication program that will attract attention and describe the product in an appealing way to the target market.

3. *Extensive problem solving.* Buying reaches its greatest complexity when buyers face an unfamiliar product class and do not know the criteria to use. For example, a high school senior who wants to go to college needs to define the qualities to look for in a college as well as to learn about specific colleges and how close they come to delivering these qualities.

The marketer of products in this class must understand the information gathering and evaluation activities of prospective buyers. The marketer's task is to facilitate the buyer's learning of the attributes of the product class, their relative importance, and the high standing of the particular brand on the more important attributes.

**Information sources.**     Of key interest to the marketer are the major information sources that the consumer will turn to and the relative influence each will have. Earlier, we classified consumer information sources into four groups: (1) *personal nonmarketer controlled* (family, friends, acquaintances); (2) *personal marketer controlled* (sales representatives); (3) *nonpersonal nonmarketer controlled* (mass media, natural settings); and (4) *nonpersonal marketer controlled* (ads, catalogs). A consumer will normally be exposed to all of these sources. The marketer's task is to interview consumers and ask what sources of information they sought or received in the course of the buying process. On this basis, a picture can be drawn of the most frequent sources. Ihlanfeldt has studied this for the college choice decision and identified the major sources shown in Figure 10–3.[6]

The key issue is the relative influence of these information sources on the consumer. This is found by asking consumers to describe the type and amount of influence that different persons had in their decision making. Normally, we can identify up to five *buyer roles:*

1. *Initiator.* The initiator is the person who first suggests or thinks of the idea of buying the particular product or service.

2. *Influencer.* An influencer is a person whose views or advice carry some influence on the final decision.

3. *Decider.* The decider is a person who ultimately determines any part or the whole of the buying decision: whether to buy, what to buy, how to buy, when to buy, or where to buy.

4. *Buyer.* The buyer is the person who makes the actual purchase.

5. *User.* The user is the person(s) who consumes or uses the product or service.

## FIGURE 10–3

Information Sources Influencing the College-Bound Student

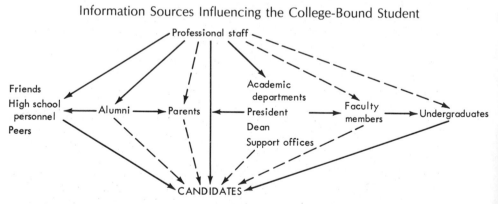

Note:  Solid lines imply direct influence in the college-choice process;
       dashed lines indirect influence

SOURCE: William Ihlanfeldt, *Achieving Optimal Enrollments and Tuition Revenues* (San Francisco: Jossey-Bass, 1980), p. 129.

For example, Bob Jones might report that his uncle initiated his interest in college by asking a year ago where Bob planned to go to college. His friends provided considerable information and influence about the types of colleges to consider. His parents acted both as influences and as buyers, since they were paying for his education. Bob Jones, however, made the final decision and was the user of the product.

Bob Jones not only receives different information from each source, but also places different value on the information from each source. He consciously or unconsciously gives weight to the *source's credibility* in deciding how to use the information. An information source is more credible when the source is *trustworthy, expert,* and *likeable.* [7] Thus, Bob would give more credence to the information provided by an older brother in college than to a college recruiter who is obviously biased. In addition, Bob would have a higher *motivation to comply* with his brother's advice than with a college recruiter's advice.

All said, marketers find it worthwhile to study the consumers' information sources whenever (1) a substantial percentage of consumers engage in active search, and (2) consumers show some stable patterns of using the respective information sources. Identifying the information sources and their respective influence calls for interviewing consumers and asking them how they happened to hear about the product, what sources of information they turned to, what type of information came from each source, what credence they put in each source, and what influence each source of information had on the final decision. Marketers can use the findings to plan effective marketing communications and stimulate favorable word-of-mouth.

### DECISION EVALUATION

Through the process of gathering information, the consumer arrives at an increasingly clear picture of the major available choices. He eliminates certain alternatives and moves toward making a choice among the few remaining alternatives.

This process of *choice narrowing* can be illustrated for Bob Jones as he faced the problem of what he should do after high school. Bob Jones considered a number of alternatives to college, including working, joining the army, traveling, and loafing. He decided that going to college made the most sense. Should it be a community college, a state university, or a private college? Examining his needs and values, he decided to attend a private college.

We can now examine how Bob narrowed his choice to a specific set of colleges. Figure 10–4 shows a succession of sets involved in this consumer's decision process. The *total set* represents all private colleges that exist whether or not the consumer knows them; this list runs into the thousands. The total set can be divided into the consumer's *awareness set* (those colleges he has heard of) and the *unawareness set.* Of those he is aware of, he will want to consider only a limited number; they constitute his *consideration set,* and the others are rele-

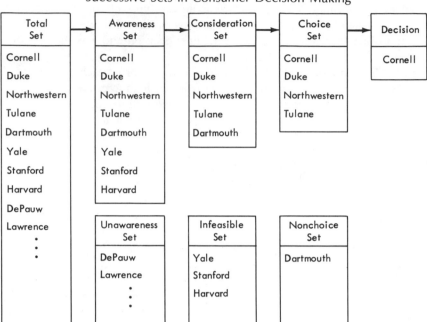

**FIGURE 10–4**

Successive Sets in Consumer Decision Making

| Total Set | Awareness Set | Consideration Set | Choice Set | Decision |
|---|---|---|---|---|
| Cornell | Cornell | Cornell | Cornell | Cornell |
| Duke | Duke | Duke | Duke | |
| Northwestern | Northwestern | Northwestern | Northwestern | |
| Tulane | Tulane | Tulane | Tulane | |
| Dartmouth | Dartmouth | Dartmouth | | |
| Yale | Yale | | | |
| Stanford | Stanford | | | |
| Harvard | Harvard | | | |
| DePauw | | | | |
| Lawrence | | | | |

| | Unawareness Set | Infeasible Set | Nonchoice Set |
|---|---|---|---|
| | DePauw | Yale | Dartmouth |
| | Lawrence | Stanford | |
| | | Harvard | |

gated to an *infeasible set.* As he gathers additional information, a few colleges remain strong and they constitute his *choice set,* the others being relegated to a *nonchoice set.* Let us assume that the student sends applications to the four colleges in his choice set and receives acceptances by all four. In the final step, he carefully evaluates the colleges in the choice set (we shall examine this process shortly) and then makes a final choice, in this case Cornell University.

The implication of this choice-narrowing process is that a product competes with a large number of other products for the consumer's interest. If a product is not in the *evoked set,* the set of alternatives that the buyer considers at the relevant stage of the decision process, then that product will not be purchased. One marketing task, then, is to get the product into the evoked set of the target buyers. Another marketing task is to identify the major competitors. We saw how colleges compete not only with each other but also with alternatives to college, such as going to work or military service. If high school seniors start favoring some of these generic alternatives, then all colleges will suffer. Therefore, colleges must constantly try to prove their value to high school students, either in terms of raising their ultimate incomes or their appreciation and enjoyment of life. In addition, each college must watch the trends in the interform competition. If the high tuitions of private colleges drive more students into community colleges and state universities, private colleges will suffer. Finally, each college must undertake research to determine its closest brand competitors and monitor its strengths and weaknesses. Its close competitors can be identified by noting the other colleges that students applying to this college have also applied to, and surveying those who were accepted and went elsewhere, where they went, and why.

Now we turn to the question: "How does the consumer make a choice among the final objects in the choice set?" The simple answer is that he forms a set of preferences by some process and chooses his first preference. Three standard methods of measuring consumer preferences are described in Exhibit 10–2. Here we shall want to explore the process by which the consumer forms his preferences.

**EXHIBIT 10–2.** How can consumer preferences be measured?

Suppose a specific individual is asked to consider a set of three objects —A, B, and C. They might be three political candidates for an office, three alternative advertisements for a charity drive, or three different medical plans offered by a health maintenance organization. There are three methods—simple rank ordering, paired comparison, and monadic rating—for measuring an individual's preference.

The simplest method is to ask the individual to rank the three objects in order of preference. The individual might respond with $A > B > C$. This method does not reveal how intensely the individual feels about each object. He may not like any one of them very much. Nor does this indicate how much he prefers one object to another. The method is also difficult to use when the set of objects is large.

A second method is to present a set of objects to the individual, two at a time, asking which is preferred in each pair. Thus, the individual could be presented with the pairs AB, AC, and BC and say that he prefers A to B, A to C, and B to C. Then we could conclude that $A > B > C$. Many researchers use paired comparisons because of two major advantages. First, people find it easy to state their preference between two objects at a time. The second advantage is that the paired comparison method allows the individual to concentrate intensely on the two objects, noting their differences and similarities.

The third method is to ask the individual to rate his liking of each product on a scale. Suppose the following seven-point scale is used:

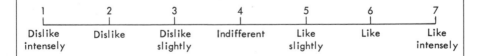

| 1 | 2 | 3 | 4 | 5 | 6 | 7 |
| --- | --- | --- | --- | --- | --- | --- |
| Dislike intensely | Dislike | Dislike slightly | Indifferent | Like slightly | Like | Like intensely |

Suppose the individual returns the following ratings: $A = 6$, $B = 5$, and $C = 3$. This yields more information than the previous preference rating methods. We can readily derive the individuals' preference order (i.e., $A > B > C$) and even know the qualitative levels of his preference for each and the rough distance between preferences. This method is also easier for respondents to use than the previous methods, especially when there is a large set of objects to evaluate.

We shall return to Bob Jones trying to make a choice among four colleges to be identified as A, B, C, and D. We will assume that he has provided the information shown in Figure 10–5. Six basic concepts are necessary to analyze the consumer evaluation process.

The first concept is the notion of a *choice set,* which we already described as consisting of colleges A, B, C, and D.

The second concept is that of *product attributes.* We assume that each consumer sees a given product as consisting of one or more attributes. These attributes are determined for each product class by asking consumers to name the factors they consider when thinking about the product. In Bob Jones's case, he named four attributes: academic quality, social life, location, and cost.

Third, the consumer is assumed to have a set of *brand perceptions* about where each brand stands on each attribute. The set of perceptions about a particular brand is known as the *brand image.* Each row of Figure 10–5 represents Bob's brand image of the corresponding college. A number from 1 to 10 is assigned to represent how much of each attribute Bob sees the college as possessing.

Fourth, the consumer is assumed to have a *utility function* for each attribute. The utility function describes the consumer's varying level of satisfaction with varying levels of an attribute. For example, Bob Jones believes that his satisfaction will rise with higher levels of academic quality and social life; he would most prefer a college in the East and least in the West; and his satisfaction falls as the cost rises. If we combine the attribute levels where Bob's utilities are highest, they make up Bob's ideal college. This college would be the preferred college if it were affordable.

Fifth, the consumer is likely to attach different *importance weights* to the various attributes. The consumer's importance weights can be elicited in at least

## FIGURE 10–5

### A High School Student's Beliefs about Four Colleges

Attribute

| College | Academic Quality | Social Life | Location | Cost |
|---------|------------------|-------------|----------|------|
| A | 10 | 8 | 6 | 4 |
| B | 8 | 9 | 8 | 3 |
| C | 6 | 8 | 7 | 5 |
| D | 4 | 3 | 10 | 8 |

Note: Ten represents the highest desirable score on that attribute. In the case of tuition, a high number means a low tuition, which makes the college more desirable.

three ways: (1) the consumer can be asked to rank the attributes in order of their importance (ranking method); (2) the consumer can be asked to distribute 100 points to the set of attributes to indicate their relative importance (constant sum method); (3) the consumer can be asked to rate the importance of each attribute on a scale going from zero to one (rating method).

Sixth, the consumer arrives at attitudes (judgments, preferences) toward the brand alternatives through some *evaluation procedure.* Unfortunately, there is not one decision evaluation process used by all consumers, or even by one consumer in all buying situations. Consumers apply different evaluation procedures to make a choice among multiattribute objects.[8] The major ones are described below:

1. *Conjunctive model.* Here the consumer sets minimum attribute levels that he will consider and drops from consideration those products that fall short on any attribute. Jones might decide that he will only consider colleges with an academic quality greater than 7 *and* a social life greater than 8. Only college B will satisfy him in this case.

2. *Disjunctive model.* Here the consumer will consider products that meet at least one minimum attribute level. Jones might decide that he will only consider colleges with an academic quality greater than 7 *or* a social life greater than 8. Here colleges A or B will remain in the choice set.

3. *Lexicographic model.* Here the consumer will rank the attributes in order of importance. He will compare all the products on the first ranked attribute and choose the superior one. If two products are tied, he repeats the process with the second attribute. Jones might decide that academic quality is the most important attribute. In this case, he will choose college A.

4. *Expectancy-value model.*[9] Here the consumer assigns importance weights to the attributes and chooses the product that maximizes the expectancy value. Suppose Jones assigned the following importance weights to the four respective attributes: .4, .3, .2, and .1. That is, Jones assigns 40 percent of the importance to the college's academic quality, 30 percent to its social life, 20 percent to its location, and 10 percent to its tuition cost. To find the expectancy value for each college, these weights are multiplied by the perceptions about that college. This would lead to the following expectancy values:

$$\text{College A} = .4(10) + .3(8) + .2(6) + .1(4) = 8.0$$
$$\text{College B} = .4(8) + .3(9) + .2(8) + .1(3) = 7.8$$
$$\text{College C} = .4(6) + .3(8) + .2(7) + .1(5) = 6.7$$
$$\text{College D} = .4(4) + .3(3) + .2(10) + .1(8) = 5.3$$

We would predict that Jones will favor college A.

5. *Ideal product model.* Here the consumer decides on the ideal level of each attribute. Suppose Jones would prefer a college with the levels of 9, 9, 10, and 4 on the respective attributes. The further a college is from these levels, the more it would be disliked by Jones, assuming Jones assigns the same importance weights as shown earlier. We multiply the weighted distances of each college from the ideal levels and take the sum. The lower the number, the more ideal the college. The results are shown below (the vertical bars mean that we are interested only in the absolute distance and not in the relative distance):

$$\text{College A} = .4|10\text{–}9| + .3|8\text{–}9| + .2|6\text{–}10| + .1|4\text{–}4| = 1.5$$
$$\text{College B} = .4|8\text{–}9| + .3|9\text{–}9| + .2|8\text{–}10| + .1|3\text{–}4| = .9$$
$$\text{College C} = .4|6\text{–}9| + .3|8\text{–}9| + .2|7\text{–}10| + .1|5\text{–}4| = 2.2$$
$$\text{College D} = .4|4\text{–}9| + .3|3\text{–}9| + .2|10\text{–}10| + .1|8\text{–}4| = 4.2$$

We would predict that Jones will favor college B because it is the smallest weighted distance from his ideal college.

6. *Determinance model.* Here the consumer ignores attributes that may be important but pretty much at the same level for all products. Suppose the four colleges all have excellent athletic programs. In spite of the fact that Bob Jones may attach high importance to the athletic program, it will have no determinance on his college choice since all colleges in his set are equal on this attribute. Determinant attributes are those which are both important and highly variable in the product class.[10]

Marketers can gain useful insights by interviewing a sample of buyers to find out how most of them form their evaluations in that product class. Suppose the marketer discovers that most of the buyers form their preferences by comparing actual products to their ideal product. Suppose college A, which would be the second choice to people like Bob Jones (according to the ideal product model), wants to strengthen its chances of attracting this consumer segment. It can consider at least six alternative strategies:[11]

1. *Modifying the product.* The college could alter its attributes to bring it closer to this segment's ideal college. For example, college A could improve the social life so it gets a higher rating. This is called *real repositioning.*

2. *Altering perceptions of the product.* The college could try to alter students' perceptions of where it actually stands on key attributes. Thus, Bob Jones may believe that the tuition is higher than it actually is, and marketing communications can be used to correct this. This is called *psychological repositioning.*

3. *Altering perceptions of the competitors' brands.* The college could try to alter students' perceptions of where a leading competitor stands on different attributes. This is called *competitive repositioning.*

4. *Altering the attribute importance weights.* The college could try to persuade students to attach more importance to those attributes that the college happens to excel in. For example, college A can attempt to persuade students that academic quality is the most important aspect of any college.

5. *Calling attention to neglected attributes.* The college could try to convince students to pay attention to an attribute that they are normally unaware of or indifferent to. If college A is located near a skiing area, it might tout skiing as a fringe benefit of attending college.

6. *Shifting the ideal product.* The college could try to persuade students to change their ideal levels for one or more attributes. College A might try to convince students that a location in a cold climate is ideal, since they can get more studying done.

The college will need to carefully evaluate these alternative strategies according to their feasibility and cost. The difficulty of implementing each strategy, such as repositioning the college or shifting the importance weights, should not be minimized.

## DECISION EXECUTION

The evaluation stage leads the consumer to form a ranked set of preferences among the alternative products in the choice set. Normally, the consumer will move toward the purchase of the most preferred product. He or she will form a purchase intention. However, at least three factors can intervene between a purchase intention and its being converted into a purchase decision.[12]

The first is the *attitude of others.* Suppose Bob Jones prefers college B but his father prefers college A. As a result, Bob's *purchase probability* for college A will be somewhat reduced. The extent to which the attitude of another buying participant will reduce one's preferred alternative depends upon two things: (1) the intensity of the other person's negative attitude toward the consumer's preferred alternative, and (2) the consumer's motivation to comply with the other person's wishes. The more intense the other person's negativism, and the closer the other person is to the consumer, the more the consumer will revise downward his or her purchase intention.[13]

Purchase intention is also influenced by *anticipated situational factors.* The consumer forms a purchase intention on the basis of such factors as expected family income, expected total cost of the product, and expected benefits of the product.

When the consumer is about to act, *unanticipated situational factors* may erupt to prevent carrying out the purchase intention. Bob Jones may learn that he cannot get a college loan to attend college A. He may not like the looks of the campus when he visits it. He may be turned off by some of the students or professors he meets. Marketers believe that unanticipated factors in the *critical contact situation* can have a great influence on the final decision.

Thus, preferences and even purchase intentions are not completely reliable predictors of actual buying behavior. They give direction to purchase behavior but fail to include a number of additional factors that may intervene.

The decision of an individual to modify, postpone, or avoid a purchase decision is heavily influenced by *perceived risk.* Marketers have devoted a lot of effort to understand buying behavior as *risk taking.*[14] Consumers cannot be certain about the performance and psychosocial consequences of their purchase decision. This produces anxiety. The amount of perceived risk varies with the amount of money at stake, the amount of attribute uncertainty, and the amount of consumer self-confidence. A consumer develops certain routines for reducing risk, such as decision avoidance, information gathering from friends, and preference for national brand names and warranties. The marketer must understand the factors that provoke a feeling of risk in the consumer and attempt to provide information and support that will help reduce this risk.

After purchasing and using the product, the consumer will experience some level of satisfaction or dissatisfaction. Based on this, the consumer will engage in postpurchase actions that will have implications for the marketer. Here we want to look at the marketing implications of postpurchase satisfaction and postpurchase actions.

**Postpurchase satisfaction.** What determines whether the consumer is highly satisfied, somewhat satisfied, somewhat unsatisfied, or highly unsatisfied with a purchase? There are two major theories about this.

One theory, called *expectations–performance theory,* holds that a consumer's satisfaction is a function of the consumer's product *expectations* and the product's *perceived performance.* [15] If the product matches expectations, the consumer is satisfied; if it exceeds them, he or she is highly satisfied; if it falls short, he or she is dissatisfied.

Consumers form their expectations on the basis of messages and claims sent out by the seller and other communication sources. If the seller makes exaggerated claims for the product, consumers who buy the product will experience *disconfirmed expectations* which lead to dissatisfaction. Thus, if college A fails to perform as Bob Jones was led to expect, Bob will revise downward his attitude toward college A and may drop out, transfer, or bad-mouth the college. On the other hand, if the college meets his expectations, he will tend to be a satisfied student.

The consumer's satisfaction or dissatisfaction will be greater, the larger the gap between expectations and performance. Here the consumer's coping style also comes in. Some consumers will tend to magnify the gap when the product is not perfect, and they will be highly dissatisfied. Other consumers will tend to minimize the gap and feel less dissatisfied. [16]

This theory suggests that the seller should make product claims that faithfully represent the product's likely performance so that buyers experience satisfaction. Some sellers might even understate performance levels so that consumers would experience higher-than-expected satisfaction with the product.

The other theory of postpurchase satisfaction is called *cognitive dissonance theory.* It holds that almost every purchase is likely to lead to some postpurchase discomfort, and the issues are how much discomfort and what will the consumer do about it. As stated by Festinger:

> When a person chooses between two or more alternatives, discomfort or dissonance will almost inevitably arise because of the person's knowledge that while the decision he has made has certain advantages, it also has some disadvantages. Dissonance arises after almost every decision, and further, the individual will invariably take steps to reduce this dissonance. [17]

Under this theory, we can expect Bob Jones to feel some postpurchase dissonance about his college choice. Problems with professors, other students, housing, or athletics are likely to stir doubts in his mind as to whether he made the right choice. He will undertake certain actions to reduce this dissonance.

**Postpurchase actions.** The consumer's satisfaction or dissatisfaction with the purchase choice will feed back on subsequent behavior. If the consumer is satisfied, then he or she will exhibit a higher probability of purchasing the product on the next occasion. The satisfied consumer will also tend to say good things about the product to others. According to marketers: "Our best advertisement is a satisfied customer."

A dissatisfied consumer will respond differently. The dissonant consumer will seek ways to reduce the dissonance because of a drive in the human organism "to establish internal harmony, consistency, or congruity among his opinions, knowledge, and values."[18] Dissonant consumers will resort to one of two courses of action. They may try to reduce the dissonance by *abandoning or returning* the product, or they may try to reduce the dissonance by seeking information that might *confirm* its high value (or avoiding information that might disconfirm its high value). In the case of Bob Jones, he might withdraw from the college or, alternatively, he might seek information that would lead him to feel better about the college.

Organizations can take positive steps to help buyers feel good about their choices. A college can send a warm congratulatory letter to recently admitted candidates. It can invite their suggestions and complaints after they have spent a few months on the campus. It can develop effective communications describing the college's philosophy and aspirations to reinforce the students' reasons for coming. Postpurchase communications to buyers have been shown to reduce the amount of consumer postpurchase dissatisfaction.[19]

We have now completed the exposition of the consumer buying process and its five stages of need arousal, information gathering, decision evaluation, decision execution, and postdecision assessment. We deliberately chose an example involving extensive problem solving—the college selection decision—in which the consumer normally passes carefully through each stage. But we should note that even in this buying situation some consumers will pass through the process much faster than others, and even skip certain stages. We can imagine the high school senior who immediately thinks of one college he would like to attend, sends in his application, receives acceptance, and matriculates. He engages in hardly any information gathering or decision evaluation. And when we examine other buying situations of a less demanding character—such as buying aspirin or going to a zoo—the buying process may be greatly contracted. Michael L. Ray has even suggested that the stages in the buying model are reversed in some situations.[20] The consumer may end up buying something on impulse, develop feelings afterward, and then seek more information. For example, a consumer may suddenly decide to buy a swimming membership in the YMCA, then develop feelings of satisfaction, and then seek more information about other programs. The model of the buying process that we have presented is a way of featuring various important aspects of buying rather than an assertion that all consumers in all buying situations move smoothly and deliberately through each of the stages in the order shown. The purpose of the model is to help marketers raise and answer key questions about the behavior of consumers. Doing this will provide clues to the marketers as to how they can better attract, serve, and satisfy a given group of consumers.

In this exposition, we have focused on the similarities among consumers as they go through the buying process rather than on their differences. Each consumer will be uniquely influenced by *cultural factors* (subculture and social class), *social factors* (reference groups, family roles and statuses), *personal factors* (age and life cycle, occupation, economic circumstance, life style, personality, and self-concept), and *psychological factors* (motivation, perception, learning, beliefs and attitudes).[21] Many of these factors have been discussed in the preceding chapter on market segmentation. We should simply be aware that each consumer comes under unique influences in making buying decisions.

## ORGANIZATION BUYER BEHAVIOR

Nonprofit organizations not only market to individuals but also to organizations. Here are some examples:

- A performing arts group needs a foundation grant to support a new experimental theatre. It must know how to identify likely foundations and their "buying criteria" for choosing among the various proposals they receive.
- A large hospital is trying to convince nearby hospitals to share services—such as laundry and lab work—to bring down costs. The hospital is also trying to convince the local health systems agency to approve its application to open a new burn unit to serve the area.
- A national association needs a strategy to convince its local chapters to increase membership dues so that more money would be available to lobby for legislative reforms.
- Mississippi's Industrial Development Department needs a plan to attract companies to locate new plants in Mississippi. Meanwhile, Mississippi's Department of Tourism is trying to convince major hotel chains to locate new hotels in Mississippi's major cities.

Thus, nonprofit organizations get involved in selling goods, services, and ideas to other organizations. They need to understand the buying organizations' needs, resources, policies, and buying procedures. They need to take into account several considerations not normally found in consumer marketing:

1. Organizations buy goods, services, and ideas for such purposes as making profits, reducing costs, serving their internal clienteles' needs, and meeting social and legal obligations.

2. More persons tend to participate in organizational buying decisions than in consumer buying decisions. The decision participants usually have varying organizational responsibilities and apply varying criteria to the purchase decision.

3. The buyers operate under formal policies, constraints, and requirements established by their organizations.

4. Selling to organizations tends to involve more personal contact and negotiation than consumer marketing.

We are now ready to examine how organization buyers move through the buying process. As an illustration, we will assume that the San Francisco Zoo hopes to attract a large corporation to make a major grant toward building a new lion house.

## NEED AROUSAL

The first step calls for the marketer identifying corporate prospects and trying to gain their attention and interest in the proposal. Thus, the San Francisco Zoo would approach corporations that have made generous civic gifts in the past. "Qualifying the prospect" can save the marketer a lot of time.

The marketer's next step is to try to understand the basic needs and wants of target organizations. This is fairly straightforward in the case of corporations, whose main objectives are to make money, save money, and be a good corporate citizen. The San Francisco Zoo cannot help corporations make or save money but it can appeal to the corporation's wish to be a good corporate citizen. Most corporations welcome favorable publicity about their "good deeds": In this way, they build a fund of goodwill which they can draw upon when adverse events take place. The zoo can meet this need by offering to name the new lion house after the corporation or arrange for other publicity showing the corporation's generosity.

The selling organization needs to analyze the mission, goals, plans, and criteria of each prospect organization so that it can develop appropriate appeals. When the San Francisco Zoo seeks a higher annual budget from the San Francisco City Council, it must respect the fact that money is tight and the council expects the zoo's needs to be convincingly presented. The zoo will state its case in a way that meets the issues uppermost in the minds of the city council.

## INFORMATION GATHERING

The buying organization will normally need time to consider the proposition and gather information. The amount of needed information will depend on the type of buying situation and on the buying organization's familiarity with the seller. Robinson, et al., distinguished among three types of buying situations called *buyclasses*. [22] They are:

1. *Straight rebuy.* Here the buying organization is buying something similar to what it bought before. For example, the San Francisco City Council gives a new budget every year to the zoo and in the absence of major new factors, it might approve a budget pretty much like last year's budget. This is analogous to "routinized response behavior" in the individual consumer buying situation. In a straight rebuy, the buyer will not need much information because he knows the proposition and the seller from previous dealings with him.

2. *Modified rebuy.* The modified rebuy describes a situation where the buyer is considering modifying something it has purchased in the past. The task calls for "limited problem solving" and hence more information than in the case of a straight rebuy. Thus, the San Francisco City Council will want specific information to evaluate whether the zoo's lion house needs to be remodeled and what alternatives are available.

3. *New task.* The new task faces an organizational buyer when he is presented with a new offer of an unfamiliar kind from an unfamiliar seller. An example would be a Japanese corporation being asked to build a new lion house at the San Francisco Zoo to improve Japanese–American relations. The Japanese corporation will face "extensive problem solving" and need to gather considerable information prior to making any decision.

Another issue deals with the likely sources of information to which the organizational buyer will turn. One source is the seller, and the seller can be more effective by supplying relevant and credible information to the buying organization. The seller should also anticipate other information sources that the organization buyer is likely to tap in developing its marketing plans.

### DECISION EVALUATION

Each buying organization will have certain well-established ways of evaluating different types of "purchases." Straight rebuy decisions may be in the hands of a single officer who makes the decision in a fairly routine way. Modified rebuys may be in the hands of a small middle-management committee with the members coming from different business functions. New tasks may be in the hands of a high-level management committee, again with members representing different expertise.

The seller must attempt to identify the people in the buying organization who are likely to get involved in the buying process. Webster and Wind call the decision-making unit of a buying organization the *buying center,* and define it as "all those individuals and groups who participate in the purchasing decision-making process, who share some common goals and the risks arising from the decisions." [23] The buying center includes all members of the organization who play any of five roles in the buying process: [24]

1. *Users.* Users are the members of the organization who will use the product or service. In many cases, the users initiate the buying project and play an important role in defining the buying specifications.

2. *Influencers.* Influencers are those members of the organization who directly or indirectly influence the buying decision. They often help develop specifications and also provide information for evaluating alternatives. Expert personnel are particularly important as influencers.

3. *Buyers.* Buyers are organizational members with formal authority for selecting among competitive suppliers and negotiating terms. Buyers may help shape product specifications, but they play their major role in selecting vendors and negotiating within the buying constraints.

4. *Deciders.* Deciders are organizational members who have either formal or informal power to select or approve the final suppliers. In the routine buying of standard items, the buyers are often the deciders. In more complex buying, the officers of the buying organization are often the deciders.

5. *Gatekeepers.* Gatekeepers are members of the organization who control the flow of information to others. For example, the foundation director can prevent sellers from seeing and influencing others in the organization.

The seller's task is to identify the members of the buying center and try to figure out (1) in what decisions they exercise influence, (2) what their relative degree of influence is, and (3) what evaluation criteria each decision participant uses. This knowledge can help the seller know the *key buying influences* who must be reached personally (through multilevel in-depth selling) or through nonpersonal communications.

Organization buyers are subject to many influences when they meet to make their buying decisions. Some of the process is highly rational in that the buyers rate proposals on such attributes as (1) seller credibility, (2) seller efficiency, (3) impact of the proposal on profits, costs, and other dimensions, (4) amount of goodwill created, and so on. To the extent that the process is a rational one, the seller will want to make the strongest case in rational terms.

Sellers also recognize the role of personal motives in the organization buying process, such as buyers who respond to personal favors (self-aggrandizement), to attention (ego enhancement), or to personal risk containment (risk avoiders). A study of buyers in ten large organizations concluded:

> Corporate decision-makers remain human after they enter the office. They respond to "image"; they buy from companies to which they feel "close"; they favor suppliers who show them respect and personal consideration, and who do extra things "for them"; they "over-react" to real or imagined slights, tending to reject companies which fail to respond or delay in submitting requested bids.[25]

This suggests that sellers should also take into account the human and social factors in the buying situations and address more emotional and interpersonal appeals.

## DECISION EXECUTION

After the buying organization has decided to favor the offer, it must put the finishing touches on it. The buyer and seller would have to negotiate the exact terms and timing of various steps. Thus, the corporation that agrees to make a gift to the San Francisco Zoo would need to decide on the exact amount, how to pay it, when to pay it, and what compliance conditions to establish. Any of these steps can involve further negotiation. The seller should anticipate these issues of detail and be prepared to work them through smoothly.

Organization buyers have also been known to cancel or withdraw at the last minute, given new conditions or information. The buyer may have heard something negative about the seller or might have encountered a cash flow problem. The practical implication is that the seller's work is not finished after receiving news of a favorable decision. The alert seller will want to keep in touch with the buyer to make sure that the agreement is enacted smoothly and that no snags develop.

## POSTDECISION ASSESSMENT

The buying organization will usually undertake a periodic performance audit to make sure that the seller is performing according to expectations. It is in the seller's interests to negotiate clear performance goals with the buying organization in the decision execution stage. Then the seller knows what is expected, and it can periodically supply the buyer with relevant information on performance. The San Francisco Zoo, for example, can keep a large corporate donor informed of the way the money is spent and the results achieved with the grant. By demonstrating responsible performance, the zoo will be able to go back to the same corporate donor some years later and ask for another grant based on the satisfactory results it has produced.

---

## SUMMARY

At the heart of marketing analysis is understanding the consumer's needs, wants, and buying behavior. We can distinguish between individual and organizational buying behavior.

Individual buyers tend to pass through five stages in connection with a purchase. The first stage is need arousal. Need arousal involves understanding what factors triggered interest in the product category, what basic needs became involved, and what specific wants became activated by these underlying needs. The second stage, information gathering, consists of the prospective buyer needing a certain amount of information and going to certain sources for this information. The third stage, decision evaluation, consists of the buyer evaluating his choices and developing a preference for one of them. The fourth stage, decision execution, describes additional factors (the attitudes of others, anticipated and unanticipated situational factors) that influence the final choice. The fifth stage, postdecision assessment, involves the buyer in reviewing his purchase, experiencing satisfaction or dissatisfaction, and taking postpurchase action.

Organizations go through the same five stages in buying a good or service. The organization's buying center consists of individuals who participate in the purchasing decision-making process either as users, influencers, buyers, deciders, or gatekeepers. The number and behavior of members of the buying center varies with the complexity, expensiveness, and riskiness of the purchase.

---

## QUESTIONS

**1.** Community Hospital has noted a steady decline in the number of women coming there to have their babies, in part due to a drop in the birthrate. Those women who come to Community Hospital are typically those who have given birth there before. Of the three buying situations described in the text, which best describes the expectant mothers currently selecting Community Hospital? How can the hospital meet the information needs of potential users in the other two buying situations?

**2.** Apply the five buyer roles (a) to the decision of whether to buy season tickets to the San Francisco Opera, (b) to the decision of where to send a child to summer camp.

**3.** The Drug Hotline gives advice to current or potential drug users who have questions about drug effects and treatment. What factors should be considered to ensure that users consider the Hotline credible?

**4.** The Civic Light Opera wanted to attract more young adults to their performances. They found that when asked where they would go for an enjoyable relaxing evening of entertainment, only 3 percent of young adults surveyed mentioned the Civic Light Opera as a possible place to go. Describe the succession of sets an unaware consumer would go through before deciding to attend the Civic Light Opera.

**5.** What are some ways in which the Red Cross and other blood collection agencies could increase the "postpurchase" (after-donation) satisfaction of volunteer blood donors?

**6.** The Chicago Lung Association has developed a program to provide area businesses with low-cost lung function monitoring to detect changes in employees' lung capacity which might be work-related. What considerations from organization buyer behavior should they consider?

---

## NOTES

**1.** For exceptions, see Irwin M. Rosenstock, "Why People Use Health Services," *Milbank Memorial Fund Quarterly,* Vol. 44 (1966), pp. 94–127. See also Richard L. Oliver and Philip K. Berger, "A Path Analysis of Preventive Health

Care Decision Models," *Journal of Consumer Research,* September 1979, pp. 113–22.

2. Several models of the consumer buying process have been developed by marketing scholars. The most prominent models are: John A. Howard and Jagdish N. Sheth, *The Theory of Buyer Behavior* (New York: Wiley, 1969); Francesco M. Nicosia, *Consumer Decision Processes* (Englewood Cliffs, N.J.: Prentice-Hall, 1966); and James F. Engel, Robert D. Blackwell, and David T. Kollat, *Consumer Behavior,* 3rd ed. (New York: Holt, Rinehart & Winston, 1978).

3. Abraham H. Maslow, *Motivation and Personality* (New York: Harper & Row, 1954), pp. 80–106.

4. For studies, see Patrick E. Murphy, "Consumer Buying Roles in College Choice: Parents' and Students' Perceptions," *College and University,* Winter 1981, p. 146.

5. Howard and Sheth, *The Theory of Buyer Behavior,* pp. 27–28.

6. See William Ihlanfeldt, *Achieving Optimal Enrollments and Tuition Revenues* (San Francisco: Jossey-Bass, 1980).

7. Herbert C. Kelman and Carl I. Hovland, " 'Reinstatement' of the Communicator in Delayed Measurement of Opinion Change," *Journal of Abnormal and Social Psychology,* Vol. 48 (1953), pp. 327–35.

8. See Paul E. Green and Yoram Wind, *Multiattribute Decisions in Marketing: A Measurement Approach* (Hinsdale, Ill.: Dryden Press, 1973), Chapter 2.

9. For an excellent review of this model, see William L. Wilkie and Edgar A. Pessemier, "Issues in Marketing's Use of Multi-Attribute Attitude Models," *Journal of Marketing Research,* November 1973, pp. 428–41.

10. See James H. Myers and Mark I. Alpert, "Determinant Buying Attitudes: Meaning and Measurement," *Journal of Marketing,* October 1968, pp. 13–20.

11. See Harper W. Boyd, Jr., Michael L. Ray, and Edward C. Strong, "An Attitudinal Framework for Advertising Strategy," *Journal of Marketing,* April 1972, pp. 27–33.

12. See Jagdish N. Sheth, "An Investigation of Relationships Among Evaluative Beliefs, Affect, Behavioral Intention, and Behavior," in John U. Farley, John A. Howard, and L. Winston Ring, eds., *Consumer Behavior: Theory and Application* (Boston: Allyn & Bacon, 1974), pp. 89–114.

13. See Martin Fishbein, "Attitude and Prediction of Behavior," in Martin Fishbein, ed., *Readings in Attitude Theory and Measurement* (New York: Wiley, 1967), pp. 477–92.

14. See Raymond A. Bauer, "Consumer Behavior as Risk Taking," in Donald F. Cox, ed., *Risk Taking and Information Handling in Consumer Behavior* (Boston: Division of Research, Harvard Business School, 1967); and James W. Taylor, "The Role of Risk in Consumer Behavior," *Journal of Marketing,* April 1974, pp. 54–60.

15. See John E. Swan and Linda Jones Combs, "Product Performance and Consumer Satisfaction: A New Concept," *Journal of Marketing Research,* April 1976, pp. 25–33.

16. See Ralph E. Anderson, "Consumer Dissatisfaction: The Effect of Dis-

confirmed Expectancy on Perceived Product Performance," *Journal of Marketing Research,* February 1973, pp. 38–44.

**17.** Leon Festinger and Dana Bramel, "The Reactions of Humans to Cognitive Dissonance," in Arthur J. Bachrach, ed., *Experimental Foundations of Clinical Psychology* (New York: Basic Books, 1962), pp. 251–62.

**18.** Leon Festinger, *A Theory of Cognitive Dissonance* (Stanford, Calif.: Stanford University Press, 1957), p. 260.

**19.** See James H. Donnelly, Jr., and John M. Ivancevich, "Post-Purchase Reinforcement and Back-Out Behavior," *Journal of Marketing Research,* August 1970, pp. 399–400.

**20.** Michael L. Ray, *Marketing Communication and the Hierarchy-of-Effects* (Cambridge, Mass.: Marketing Science Institute, November 1973).

**21.** For a discussion of these factors, see Philip Kotler, *Marketing Management: Analysis, Planning and Control,* 4th ed. (Englewood Cliffs, N.J.: Prentice-Hall, 1980), pp. 136–50.

**22.** Patrick J. Robinson, Charles W. Faris, and Yoram Wind, *Industrial Buying and Creative Marketing* (Boston: Allyn & Bacon, 1967).

**23.** Frederick E. Webster, Jr., and Yoram Wind, *Organizational Buying Behavior* (Englewood Cliffs, N.J.: Prentice-Hall, 1972), p. 6.

**24.** *Ibid.,* pp. 78–80.

**25.** See Murray Harding, "Who Really Makes the Purchasing Decision?", *Industrial Marketing,* September 1966, p. 76. This point of view is further developed in Ernest Dichter, "Industrial Buying Is Based on Same 'Only Human' Emotional Factors That Motivate Consumer Market's Housewife," *Industrial Marketing,* February 1973, pp. 14–16.

# IV

PLANNING
THE
MARKETING
MIX

# Marketing Programming and Budgeting

The city of Minneapolis, Minnesota, is an attractive modern city that boasts of 153 parks and 22 lakes. One of these parks is Minnehaha Park, renowned for Minnehaha Falls mentioned in Longfellow's "Song of Hiawatha." The various parks have playgrounds, rose gardens, golf courses, and swimming pools. Managing these parks is in the hands of the Minneapolis Parks and Recreation Department.

The superintendent of the Minneapolis Parks and Recreation Department sees public parks as providing a product called *outdoor recreation.* Outdoor recreation yields three primary utilities. The first is *immediate enjoyment*— that is, a sense of pleasure experienced immediately before, during, and after participation in outdoor recreation. The second is *personal long-term benefits,* which consist of physical and mental benefits associated with outdoor exercise and sport. The third is *benefits to the community as a whole,* which consist of the conservation of the natural environment and ecology.

Park administrators operate with severely limited budgets and must make difficult choices among alternative projects such as playgrounds, baseball fields, tennis courts, bicycle paths, and safety patrols. Too often these choices are made on the basis of subjective judgment unaided by any consumer research and responding to political pressures. For example, an organized group of parents demanding a playground will probably get it without any benefit-cost comparison being made to other possible projects.

Fortunately, parks departments throughout the country are beginning to make more use of benefit-cost analysis to analyze competing projects. The superintendent of the Minneapolis Parks and Recreation Department found an opportunity to try out benefit-cost analysis for one of the small parks where two groups of citizens were pressing for two competing recreational projects. The superintendent felt that only one of these projects could be built and decided to use benefit-cost analysis as an aid in making a rational choice.

The two competing proposals were as follows:

1. *A four-court outdoor tennis court.* The total cost would be $30,000 to build and $1,000 a year to maintain. The courts would be usable from the beginning of April to the beginning of October. There were many people living near the park and about 200 persons presently played tennis.

2. *A bicycle path around the perimeter of the park.* This path would cost about $60,000 to construct and $600 a year to maintain. The path would be usable from April to October. There were many bicyclists in the area.

The superintendent turned the problem over to the recreational department director with the request that a quantitative analysis of the benefits and costs be prepared. The director worked on the problem during the week and finally turned in the following analysis to the superintendent:

### Tennis Court

1. The tennis courts would be in constant use for 6 months (180 days) of the year. Each hour, 8 people would be playing (2 players per court times 4 courts). The court would be open for 12 hours a day (8:00 A.M. to 8:00 P.M.), which means 96 players a day (12 × 8). This means 17,280 players per year (96 × 180). Over 20 years, this means 345,600 users.

2. The total cost of the courts over 20 years consists of a $30,000 initial cost and a $20,000 maintenance cost ($1,000 a year). Thus the total out-of-pocket cost would be $50,000.

3. Therefore the cost per hourly user of the tennis court is 15 cents ($50,000/345,600). That is, the cost to society of producing the benefits of playing a single game is 15 cents.

### Bicycle Path

1. The bicycle path would be usable for 6 months (180 days) a year. About 20 riders would be found riding it per hour. The path would be usable for 12 hours a day (8:00 A.M. to 8:00 P.M.), which means about 240 riders a day. This means 43,200 riders per year (240 × 180). Over 20 years, this means 864,000 riders.

2. The total cost of the bicycle path over 20 years consists of a $60,000 initial cost and a $12,000 maintenance cost ($600 × 20), or $72,000 altogether.

3. Therefore the cost per ride is 8 cents ($72,000/864,000). That is, the cost to society of producing the benefits of a bike ride is 8 cents.

The recreation director's report concluded:

> If we make the assumption that the benefit one person gets from riding a bike is the same as another person gets from playing tennis, then the bicycle path is the superior social good. It costs only 8 cents to produce a bike-riding benefit whereas it would cost 15 cents to produce a tennis-game benefit.

We are now ready to consider the technical aspects of choosing and developing cost-effective marketing programs. This chapter will examine the planning and budgeting tools that are available to marketing managers in the nonprofit sector. The remaining chapters in Part IV will examine specific marketing elements—namely, product, price, place, and promotion.

An organization seeking to be cost-effective in its marketing programming will have to face the following four issues:

1. How can the organization choose among competing marketing programs? (Benefit-cost analysis)
2. What marketing/financial objectives should be pursued? (Goal specification)
3. How much should the organization spend on marketing? (Optimal marketing expenditure level)
4. How can the organization determine the optimal marketing mix? (Optimal marketing mix)

## CHOOSING AMONG COMPETING PROGRAMS THROUGH BENEFIT-COST ANALYSIS

A common problem facing nonprofit organizations is that of choosing between alternative programs that all fall within the scope of the organization's objectives. Consider the following situations:

- The American Cancer Society is trying to decide between sponsoring a national cervical cancer detection program or a national breast cancer detection program.
- A public school system is trying to decide between establishing a gifted children program or a retarded children program.
- A police department is trying to decide between a campaign to educate people against pickpockets or adding a few more permanent policemen to the force.
- An art museum is trying to decide between establishing an arts library within the museum or adding a few more major paintings to its collection.
- A university is trying to decide between building some badly needed dormitories or building a badly needed student union.

- A public library is trying to decide between adding a bookmobile to bring books into neighborhoods or using the same funds to permit opening the library on Sundays.

These examples involve organizations facing a choice between two programs. They can choose one of the programs or allocate funds to the two programs in which each may be operated at a smaller scale than planned. In principle, the nonprofit organization can make a calculation similar to the profit organization. It should attempt to measure the benefits and the costs expected from each program. The benefits are all the contributions that the particular program will make to the organization's objectives. The costs are all the deductions that the particular program will take from alternative organization objectives. A particular program is considered worthwhile when its benefits exceed its costs.

### THEORY OF BENEFIT-COST ANALYSIS

Suppose a nonprofit organization is considering a choice between three programs, X, Y, and Z. Each program is estimated to cost about the same—say, 10 (in thousands of dollars). Each program, however, is estimated to yield a different level of benefits. The data on the three programs are shown in Table 11-1A.

All three programs show a positive net benefit $(B - C)$ as well as a benefit cost ratio $(B/C)$ greater than one. On both criteria, the best program is X, the next Y, and the last Z. If the organization has funds of only 10, it should invest in program X. If the organization has funds of 20, it should invest in programs

### Table 11-1

EXAMPLES OF BENEFIT-COST COMPARISONS

| | | A. Equal Costs | | |
|---|---|---|---|---|
| Program | B Benefits | C Costs | B – C Net Benefit | B/C Benefit-Cost Ratio |
| X | 60 | 10 | 50 | 6 |
| Y | 30 | 10 | 20 | 3 |
| Z | 20 | 10 | 10 | 2 |
| | | B. Unequal Costs | | |
| Program | B Benefits | C Costs | B – C Net Benefit | B/C Benefit-Cost Ratio |
| X | 60 | 30 | 30 | 2 |
| Y | 30 | 10 | 20 | 3 |
| Z | 20 | 5 | 15 | 4 |

X and Y. If the organization has funds of 30, it should invest in all three programs, because in all programs the benefits exceed the costs.

Now consider the data in Table 11–1B, where the three programs differ in costs as well as benefits. In this case, the net benefits and the benefit-cost ratios do not show the same rank order. Program X stands highest in net benefit but lowest in benefit-cost ratio. Which criteria should dominate? Generally, the benefit-cost ratio is the more rational criteria because it shows the productivity of the funds. If funds of 5 were available, they should be spent on Z because they will yield four times the benefit per dollar of cost. If funds of 15 are available, they should be spent on Y and Z and this will yield benefits of 50 altogether, which is an average benefit-cost ratio of 3 ⅓ per dollar of cost. Notice that program X, although yielding net benefits of 30, only shows a benefit-cost ratio of 2. The only time program X would be preferred is if the three programs were mutually exclusive, funds of 30 were available, and the objective was to maximize the net benefit.

We will now ask how these benefits and costs are quantified in the first place.

The organization is usually in a position to quantify the dollar costs of a program. If the program leads to some social costs, these are harder to estimate. A city government, for example, typically looks at the cost of building a cross-town expressway in financial terms. But an expressway destroys certain neighborhoods and increases local pollution and noise. These social costs should be included in the total evaluation of costs.

Evaluating benefits poses many tough problems. Identified benefits tend to fall into three groups: They are:

1. *Monetarily quantifiable benefits*—benefits whose total value can be expressed in dollars.
2. *Nonmonetary quantifiable benefits*—benefits whose total value can be expressed in some specific nonmonetary measure, such as "lives saved."
3. *Nonquantifiable benefits*—benefits whose total value cannot be expressed quantitatively, such as amount of happiness created or beauty produced.

Suppose a certain program is estimated to have several benefits, all of which can be measured in dollars. This is the easiest case to handle.

A second possibility occurs when all the benefits can be measured in terms of a common nonmonetary value, such as "lives saved." In this case, we sum up the lives saved as a result of each benefit of the program.

A third possibility occurs when the various benefits do not all share a common value. Some analysts prefer to make a two-stage analysis, the first stage including only the quantifiable benefits and costs. If the benefit-cost ratio exceeds one, the program is considered good, unless there is a conviction that the nonquantifiable costs substantially exceed the nonquantifiable benefits. If the benefit-cost ratio is less than one, the program may nevertheless be good if the nonquantifiable benefits substantially exceed the nonquantifiable costs.

The value of trying to quantify the benefits in dollars or some other common denominator is readily apparent. This has led to a number of ingenious ways to try to capture the dollar value of a benefit. The first approach is to try to find an existing market price for this benefit. If a school dropout prevention program persuades a certain number of students to stay in school, the present value of their increased lifetime earnings can be used as a measure of the value of the program. If a farmer fertilizer-education program increases farm output, the expected market value of the additional crops attributable to the educational program could be used as the monetary value of this benefit. The second approach occurs when there is no existing market price for the type of benefit being created by the program. Here people can be asked how much they would be willing to pay for that benefit. If a tennis court is being considered for a local park, local residents could be asked how much they would pay per hour to use it, or how much additional taxes they would accept. If the National Aeronautical Space Agency is contemplating a ten-year program to send a manned flight to Mars, it might ask people how much they would be willing to pay over a ten-year period to achieve a successful mission.

### PROBLEMS IN BENEFIT-COST ANALYSIS

Some of the problems in putting benefit-cost analysis to practical use should now be apparent. Even if one manages to achieve dollar values for the various benefits and costs, the technique makes certain assumptions that should be stated clearly.

First, the technique assumes that the program, if adopted, would not yield outputs sufficient to change the market prices that were used to estimate the benefits of the program. For example, if school dropout prevention programs are introduced throughout the country, they will increase the skill level of the population and probably result in a fall in the market price of skilled workers. Therefore, the life earnings calculation based on today's earnings of skilled workers overstates the market value of the benefit.

Second, the technique makes no allowance for redistributional benefits caused by the program. For example, a vocational education program and a gifted children program may both improve lifetime incomes to the same extent. But the vocational education program may improve the incomes of the poor and a gifted children program may improve the incomes of the well off. Some analysts believe the technique should give weight to positive redistribution effects.

Third, the technique assumes that economic value should be given the main weight in deciding between programs. Critics resent the notion that everything worthwhile can be measured in dollars or that the growth of GNP is the major goal. They see the value of a school dropout prevention program not so much in increased dollars of earnings but in terms of increased self-esteem and improved social attitudes.

Finally, the technique assumes that the rank ordering of projects is insensitive to the particular measure of benefit used. In a study of the net benefit of investing in different disease control programs, the ailment of arthritis did not seem important when the criterion "lives saved" was used because arthritis does not kill people. On the other hand, arthritis rates as a high-priority research problem when the criterion "dollars saved through avoiding medical treatment" was used.[1] Thus, various programs may rank differently depending on the benefit measure used.

These difficulties are not created by the technique but exist because the world is complex. The technique was never intended to replace judgment, but to systematize and quantify it where possible. Benefit-cost analysis suggests the important factors that should be considered, and the information that is needed. It inputs relevant data into what otherwise would be a wholly subjective act of decision making. It rests on the premise that organized ignorance is preferred to disorganized ignorance in making decisions.

---

## ESTABLISHING THE MARKETING/FINANCIAL OBJECTIVES

A major requirement in the marketing programming process is to clarify the organization's overall objective in the marketplace. This can be facilitated by developing a marketing/financial equation and viewing various objectives in terms of this equation. The purpose of the equation is to show the factors that influence the size of the surplus or deficit incurred by the organization in carrying out alternative marketing activities.

We start with the definition of a *surplus ($)* as being the difference between *total revenue (R)* and *total cost (C);* that is:

$$\$ = R - C \tag{11-1}$$

The total revenue *(R)* is the *average price (P)* charged by the organization times the *quantity sold (Q)*, plus *donations (D):*

$$R = PQ + D \tag{11-2}$$

The total cost *(C)* is made up of *variable cost (V), fixed cost (F),* and *marketing cost (M).* Variable cost *(V)* is the *unit cost (c)* times the *quantity sold (Q),* that is, $V = cQ$. Then, total cost is:

$$C = cQ + F + M \tag{11-3}$$

Substituting (11–2) and (11–3) into (11–1), the equation for surplus is:

$$\$ = PQ + D - cQ - F - M$$

or

$$S = (P - c)Q + D - F - M \tag{11-4}$$

The term $(P - c)$ is called the gross surplus per unit, since it represents the markup of price over cost.

In order to use equation (11–4), we have to ask what influences $Q$, the number of units sold. Clearly, $Q$ is influenced by the price $(P)$ and the marketing expenditures $(M)$; that is:

$$Q = f(P,M) \tag{11-5}$$

This expression says $Q$ is a function of price and marketing expenditure, and is called the *sales response function* (or *demand function*). The vector $(P, M)$ is called the *marketing mix*.

### ALTERNATIVE OBJECTIVES OF NONPROFIT ORGANIZATIONS

We are now ready to contrast seven alternative marketing/financial objectives that might be pursued by nonprofit organizations.

**Surplus maximization.**    Some nonprofit organizations pursue the objective of maximizing their surplus. A performing arts group, for example, might want to accumulate as much cash surplus as possible in order to build a new theatre. This does not mean that it will charge the highest possible ticket price because this would reduce attendance. It would need to know how the quantity of tickets sold is affected by price, as well as how the donations are affected.[2] Nor will the group spend the least on marketing to keep costs low; it knows that more marketing will pull in larger audiences. It will want to know how attendance and donations are affected by the marketing expenditure level. This will enable it to find the price and marketing expenditure level that will maximize the organization's surplus. (See the specific example in Chapter 13, pp. 306–7).

**Revenue maximization.**    An alternative objective is to maximize the total revenue $(PQ + D)$, even though high costs might be incurred. For example, a public transportation company might feel that a high total revenue tells the market that the organization is important and doing a good job. Management might feel that increased revenue will lead to further confidence in the organization.

**Usage maximization.**    Many nonprofit organizations are primarily interested in maximizing the number of users of its services. Thus, art museums and zoological parks are eager to maximize the annual number of visitors, because this is taken as a sign that they are providing worthwhile educational and recreational services to the community. Various city councils look at the institution's attendance growth to determine its budget for next year.

**Usage targeting.**          Organizations with fixed service capacities typically set their price and marketing expenditure to produce a capacity audience, $Q^*$. For example, a symphony orchestra experiencing low attendance might lower its price in order to fill more of the seats in the auditorium. If the potential ticket seekers exceed capacity, the orchestra would set a high price to improve its revenue while filling the auditorium.

**Full cost recovery.**          Many nonprofit organizations are primarily interested in breaking even each year. They would like to provide as much service as they can as long as their sales revenue plus donations just cover their costs. Many universities want to be in this position of spending just short of the amount where they would have to report a deficit. Many public agencies also have this objective, making sure to spend any remaining funds toward the end of the year to avoid showing a surplus that might lead to receiving a lower budget next year.

**Partial cost recovery.**          Other organizations operate with a chronic deficit each year. Examples include the U.S. Post Office, Amtrak, and many local public transportation companies. There is no reasonable price and marketing expenditure level that would bring these organizations close to breakeven. Instead, their aim is to keep the annual deficit from exceeding a certain amount. The public authorities cover the annual deficit with public funds raised through taxes.

**Producer satisfaction maximization.**          Many nonprofit organizations are as eager to satisfy the wants of their own staff as those of the publics they serve. One often hears the criticism that hospitals place the needs of doctors ahead of those of patients, and colleges place the needs of faculty ahead of those of students. One can imagine the members of a symphony orchestra playing primarily music that please them, whether or not this attracts a large audience. This introduces a new variable not shown in the equation, maximization of producer satisfaction. According to Etgar and Ratchford:

> ... the product is created mainly for the satisfaction of producers themselves. ... The organization will modify its product away from the one which gives its own members the most satisfaction only insofar as is necessary to obtain enough revenue from these customer groups to survive financially.[3]

McKnight goes further and argues that most nonprofit organizations and professionals are basically self-serving and oriented toward maximizing their own interests.[4]

### EXAMPLES OF REVENUE FUNCTIONS

The preceding analysis used the simple sales revenue function, $PQ$. This function, when elaborated, reveals a large number of marketing actions that an organization can take to increase its revenue. Three examples are shown below.

**Hospital revenue function.**     A hospital gets its revenue from operating a number of "businesses," including inpatient services, outpatient services, a gift shop, and so on. Each of these requires pricing and marketing expenditure planning. Consider the case of inpatient service. Here the hospital is interested in filling its beds to capacity, that is, it seeks a high occupancy rate. Its revenue function, $PQ$, can be decomposed into the following elements:

$$\text{Inpatient revenue} = \left[\begin{array}{l}\text{average revenue per} \\ \text{patient per day}\end{array} \times \begin{array}{l}\text{annual number} \\ \text{of admissions}\end{array} \times \begin{array}{l}\text{average length of} \\ \text{patient stay in days}\end{array}\right]$$

Hospitals have been recently experiencing declining inpatient revenue because one or more of the three factors has declined. First, as hospitals take on a larger proportion of Medicaid and Medicare patients, their average revenue falls because government reimbursement covers less of the cost. Second, the annual number of admissions has declined in many hospitals because of changing neighborhoods and new forms of competition. Third, the average length of stay has been declining because the government is putting pressure on hospitals to get patients out as fast as possible.

Hospitals can attempt to offset each of these factors by taking positive marketing actions. The average revenue per patient can be increased by raising prices where allowed and seeking a more profitable mix of patients. The annual number of admitted patients can be boosted by attracting more active physicians, improving patient care, and adding high growth specialties. The average length of stay can be boosted by the hospital emphasizing those specialties that produce longer patient stays.

**Trade association revenue function.**     A trade association gets its revenue from three major sources: membership dues, publications, and conferences. The revenue function can be modeled as follows:

$$\text{Revenue} = \left[\begin{array}{l}\text{annual} \\ \text{dues}\end{array}\right]\left[\left(\begin{array}{l}\text{Number of last} \\ \text{year's members}\end{array}\right)\left(\begin{array}{l}\text{Percentage} \\ \text{who renew}\end{array}\right) + \begin{array}{l}\text{Number of} \\ \text{new members}\end{array}\right]$$
$$+ \left[\begin{array}{l}\text{Price per} \\ \text{issue}\end{array}\right]\left[\begin{array}{l}\text{Average number of} \\ \text{copies sold per issue}\end{array}\right]\left[\begin{array}{l}\text{Number of} \\ \text{issues/yr.}\end{array}\right]$$
$$+ \left[\begin{array}{l}\text{Registration} \\ \text{fee}\end{array}\right]\left[\begin{array}{l}\text{Average number of} \\ \text{attendees per conference}\end{array}\right]\left[\begin{array}{l}\text{Annual number} \\ \text{of conferences}\end{array}\right]$$

This elaboration of the revenue function helps pinpoint positive marketing actions that can be taken. First, the trade association can consider raising the annual dues, although it must take into account the impact of a dues increase on the membership renewal rate and number of new members attracted. The trade association can also improve the job it is doing to encourage membership renewal (see Chapter 18, p. 412) and attract new members. Second, the trade association can increase its publication revenue by raising the price per issue and/or increasing the average number of copies sold per issue and/or increasing the number of issues per year. Third, the trade association can increase its conference revenue by raising the registration fee, attracting a larger average number of attendees per conference, and increasing the annual number of conferences. Each of these variables can be influenced by specific marketing actions. The organization, in fact, can build up its marketing plans by examining each revenue component and determining what can be accomplished.

**Church revenue function.**     A church gets revenue from three major sources: donations, facility rental, and sale of complementary services. Specifically, the revenue function looks like this:

$$
\begin{aligned}
\text{Revenue} =\ & \begin{bmatrix} \text{Average} \\ \text{contribution} \\ \text{per visit} \end{bmatrix} \begin{bmatrix} \text{Average number} \\ \text{of visits per} \\ \text{member per year} \end{bmatrix} \begin{bmatrix} \text{Number of} \\ \text{church} \\ \text{members} \end{bmatrix} \\
& + \begin{bmatrix} \text{Average} \\ \text{rental fee} \end{bmatrix} \begin{bmatrix} \text{Average number of rentals} \\ \text{per facility per year} \end{bmatrix} \begin{bmatrix} \text{Number of} \\ \text{facilities for rent} \end{bmatrix} \\
& + \begin{bmatrix} \text{Net revenue from} \\ \text{complementary services} \end{bmatrix} + \begin{bmatrix} \text{Donations due to} \\ \text{impact of services} \end{bmatrix}
\end{aligned}
$$

In its marketing planning, the church will want to consider how to attract more contributions at its weekly worship services. The number of attendees, frequency of attendance, and average contribution is a function of religious service times, inspirational quality of the religious service, parking, child care services, and a number of other factors. Churches are increasingly seeking to improve the quality of their worship services through hiring dynamic ministers, easing the dress code, and having a social hour after the services. Facility revenue is dependent on attracting weddings, receptions, baptisms, socials, and funerals. The number of functions attracted is dependent upon the public awareness of the facility's availability, rental fee, use restrictions, and so on. Complementary services such as bingo, bake sales, and bazaars will yield some revenue after cost and also tend to increase the cash and time donations to the church.

Thus, we see that marketing planning can be aided by elaborating the relevant revenue and cost elements and seeing what each suggests in the way of appropriate marketing actions.

---

## DECIDING ON THE OPTIMAL LEVEL OF MARKETING EXPENDITURES

Many nonprofit organizations that turn to formal marketing raise the question, "What is the proper amount to spend on marketing?" One college president specifically asked: "How many marketing dollars should we budget to increase our enrollment by 10 percent?" Unfortunately, the answer is not simple. We will describe the five major approaches available to organizations to establish their marketing budgets.

### Affordable Method

Many organizations set the marketing budget on the basis of what they think they can afford. Thus, a college president will balance all the competing claims for funds and arrive at an arbitrary amount that can be spent on recruitment, publicity, and fundraising efforts. Setting budgets in this way is tantamount to saying that the relationship between advertising expenditure and sales is unknown and unknowable. As long as the organization can spare some funds for marketing, this will be done as a form of insurance. The basic weakness is that this approach leads to a changing level of marketing expenditure each year, making it difficult to attain long-run results.

### Percentage-of-Sales Method

Many organizations prefer to set their marketing budget as a specified percent of sales (either current or anticipated) of the sales price. Thus, a private college might decide to spend $100 per recruited student to cover the admissions office salaries, advertising, and brochure preparation. If the college aims to recruit 2,000 freshmen, then the admissions office would receive a budget of $200,000.

The main advantage of the percentage-of-sales method is that it leads to a predictable budget each year, once the sales goal is set. It also keeps marketing costs within reasonable control. Nevertheless, the method has little else to recommend it. The method does not provide a logical basis for the choice of a specific percentage, except what has been done in the past, or what competitors are doing. It discourages experimentation with countercyclical advertising. It does not encourage the development of budgets on an opportunity basis.

### Competitive-Based Method

Some organizations set their marketing budgets specifically in relation to competitors' outlays. Thus, a college may decide on its marketing budget by investigating what its main competitor is spending on marketing. The college may decide to spend more, less, or the same. It would spend more if it wants to overtake or surpass the other college. It would spend less if it believes that it can achieve more impact and/or efficiency with the funds. It would spend the same if it believes that the competitor has figured out the proper amount to spend or if it believes that maintaining competitive parity would avoid an aggressive reaction by the competitor.

Knowing what competition is spending on marketing is undoubtedly useful information. However, basing one's spending on this information alone is not warranted. Marketing objectives, resources, and opportunities are likely to differ so much among organizations that their budgets are hardly a guide for other organizations to follow.

### Objective-and-Task Method

The objective-and-task method calls upon marketers to develop their budget by (1) defining their marketing objectives as specifically as possible, (2) determining the tasks that must be performed to achieve these objectives, and (3) estimating the costs of performing these tasks. The sum of these costs is the proposed marketing budget.

As an example, consider the private college that seeks to recruit 2,000 freshmen. The admissions office might estimate, on the basis of past experience, that the college would have to mail 20,000 letters to select high school seniors, which would result in approximately 8,000 inquiries, which would produce 4,000 applications, 3,000 admissions, and finally 2,000 acceptances. Each step requires a specific set of activities, the cost of each of which can be estimated. Table 11–2 shows the hypothetical estimate of costs involved in recruiting 2,000 freshmen. The admissions director built up the marketing budget by defining the objectives, identifying the required tasks, and costing them.

This method of setting the marketing budget is superior to the preceding methods. It requires management to think through its objectives and marketing activities. Its major limitation is the failure to consider alternative marketing objectives and marketing budgets in the search for the optimal course of action. We now turn to a method that is theoretically the soundest method for setting the marketing budget.

### Table 11–2

#### HYPOTHETICAL BUDGET FOR COLLEGE RECRUITING

| 20,000 leads | Purchase of names | $4,000 |
|---|---|---|
|  | Mailing cost | 20,000 |
|  | Office processing | 6,000 |
|  | Staff costs, including travel | 50,000 |
|  | Advertising | 33,000 |
| 8,000 inquiries | Staff cost | 16,000 |
|  | Mailing cost | 24,000 |
| 4,000 applications | Staff cost | 40,000 |
|  | Mailing cost | 2,000 |
| 2,000 acceptances | Staff cost | 4,000 |
|  | Mailing cost | 1,000 |
|  |  | $200,000 |

NOTE: Cost per recruited student = $200,000/2,000 = $100.

## SALES RESPONSE OPTIMIZATION METHOD

Sales response optimization requires that the manager estimate the relation between sales response and alternative levels of the marketing budget. The estimate is captured in the sales response function, which is defined as follows:

A **sales response function** forecasts the likely sales volume during a specified time period associated with different possible levels of a marketing element.

The best known sales response function is the demand function, illustrated in Figure 11–1A. This function shows that sales are higher in any given period, the lower the price. In the illustration, a price of $24 leads to sales of 8,000 units in that period, but a price of $16 would have led to sales of 14,000 units in that period. The illustrated demand curve is curvilinear, although other shapes are possible.

Suppose that the marketing variable is not price but total marketing dollars spent on sales force, advertising, and other marketing activities. In this case, the sales response function is likely to resemble Figure 11–1B. This function states that the more the organization spends in a given period on marketing effort, the higher the sales are likely to be. The particular function is S-shaped although other shapes are possible. The S-shaped function says that low levels of marketing expenditure are not likely to produce much sales. The reason is that too few buyers will be reached, or reached effectively, by the organization's message.

## FIGURE 11–1

### Sales Response Functions

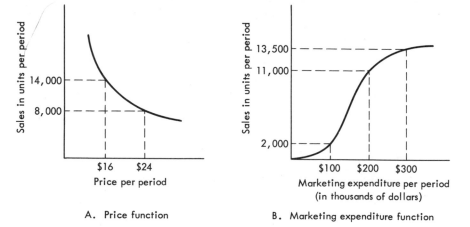

A. Price function

B. Marketing expenditure function

Higher levels of marketing expenditure per period will produce much higher levels of sales. Very high expenditures per period, however, may not add much more sales and would represent "marketing overkill."

The occurrence of eventually diminishing returns to increases in marketing expenditures is plausible for a number of reasons. First, there is an upper limit to the total potential demand for any particular product. The easier sales prospects are sold first; the more recalcitrant sales prospects remain. As the upper limit is approached, it becomes increasingly expensive to stimulate further sales. In the second place, as an organization steps up its marketing effort, its competitors are likely to do the same, with the net result that each organization experiences increasing sales resistance. In the third place, if sales were to increase at an increasing rate throughout, natural monopolies would result. A single organization would tend to take over in each industry because of the greater level of its marketing effort. Yet this is contrary to what we observe in industry.

How can a marketing manager estimate the sales response function? Essentially, three methods are available. The first is the *statistical method,* where the manager gathers data on past sales and levels of marketing mix variables and estimates the sales response functions using statistical estimation procedures.[5] The second is the *experimental method,* which calls for deliberately varying the marketing expenditure levels in matched samples of geographical or other units and noting the resulting sales volume.[6] The third is the *judgmental method,* where experts are asked to estimate the probable sales response.[7]

Once the sales response function is estimated, how is it used to set an optimal marketing budget? We would have to define the organization's objective. Suppose the organization wants to maximize its surplus. Graphically, we must introduce some further curves to find the point of optimal marketing expenditure. The analysis is shown in Figure 11–2. The key function that we start with is the sales response function. It resembles the S-shaped sales response function in the earlier Figure 11–1B except for two differences. First, sales response is expressed in terms of sales dollars instead of sales units, in order that we can find the surplus-maximizing marketing expenditure. Second, the sales response function is shown as starting above zero sales on the argument that some sales might take place even in the absence of marketing expenditures.

To find the optimal marketing expenditure, the marketing manager subtracts all nonmarketing costs from the *sales response function* to derive the *gross surplus curve.* Next, marketing expenditures are drawn in such a way that a dollar on one axis is projected as a dollar on the other axis. This amounts to a 45° line when the axes are scaled in identical dollar intervals. The *marketing expenditures curve* is then subtracted from the *gross surplus curve* to derive the *net surplus curve.* The net surplus curve shows positive net surplus with marketing expenditures between $M_L$ and $M_U$, which could be defined as the rational range of marketing expenditure. The net surplus curve reaches a maximum at $M$. Therefore, the marketing expenditure that would maximize net surplus is $\$M$.

## FIGURE 11-2

### Relationship between Sales Volume, Marketing Expenditures, and Surplus

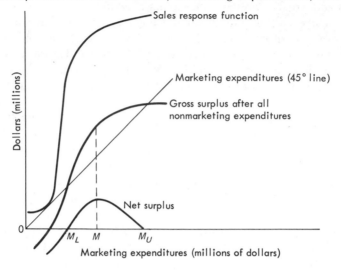

## DEVELOPING A COST-EFFECTIVE MARKETING MIX

The impact on a given marketing budget on demand depends not only on the size of the budget, but also on how the budget is allocated to the various marketing activities. An organization has a lot of options on how to spend a given budget. For example, a college recruitment office can spend the marketing budget on the following items: (1) recruiting staff, (2) direct mail, (3) media advertising, (4) marketing research, (5) publicity, and so on. The key task is to decide, for any given marketing objective, on the most cost-effective marketing mix.

Before looking at how the marketing mix should be established, let us consider how it is established in practice. Most organizations develop rules of thumb to guide the budget's allocation to marketing activities. One college may find that sending out recruiters to select high schools produces the greatest number of applications, and thus decides to commit over 50 percent of its budget to supporting a recruiting staff. Another college may find that direct mail works well in producing inquiries and makes this the largest part of its budget. After a certain division of the funds gets established, management tends to adhere to it year after year. Management only gives thought to a drastic redeployment of its budget if major changes occur in the known effectiveness or cost of different marketing tools. For example, the cost of travel has recently increased so much that college recruiters are reducing the number of high school campuses they visit and increasing the use of mail and telephone recruiting. In principle, each marketing element can substitute for another to some extent. A college can seek more students by lowering tuition, or increasing the number of recruiters, or using more direct mail. The organization must constantly try to assess the relative sales productivity of these different tools. This is another reason why marketing departments should be created, mainly to achieve administrative coordination over all of the interrelated tools of marketing.

### THEORY OF THE OPTIMAL MARKETING MIX

We want to explore how the optimal marketing mix would be determined in principle. Assume a college recruiting office that uses advertising and sales forces as the two major elements of the marketing mix. Clearly, there are an infinite number of combinations of spending on these two items. This is shown in Figure 11–3A. If there are no constraints on advertising and sales force expenditure, then every point in the $A–S$ plane shown in Figure 11–3A is a possible marketing mix. An arbitrary line drawn from the origin, called a *constant-mix line,* shows the set of all marketing mixes where the two tools are in a fixed ratio but where the budget varies. Another arbitrary line, called a *constant-budget line,* shows a set of varying mixes that would be affordable with a fixed marketing budget.

Associated with every possible marketing mix is a resulting sales level. Three sales levels are shown in Figure 11–3A. The marketing mix $(A_1S_2)$—calling for a small budget and a rough equality between advertising and sales force—is expected to produce sales of $Q_1$. The marketing mix $(A_2S_1)$ involves the same budget with more expenditure on advertising than on sales force; this is expected to produce slightly higher sales, $Q_2$. The mix $(A_yS_2)$ calls for a larger budget but a relatively equal splitting between advertising and sales force, and with a sales

### FIGURE 11–3

The Sales Function Associated with Two Marketing Mix Elements

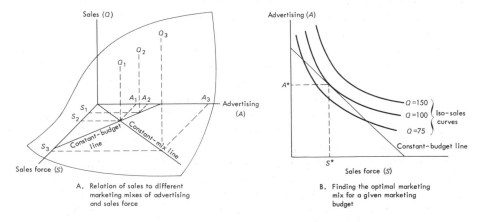

A. Relation of sales to different
   marketing mixes of advertising
   and sales force

B. Finding the optimal marketing
   mix for a given marketing
   budget

estimate of $Q_3$. Given these and many other possible marketing mixes, the mar-keter's job is to find the sales equation that predicts the $Q$s.

For a given marketing budget, the money should be divided among the various marketing tools in a way that gives the same marginal profit on the marginal dollar spent on each tool. A geometrical version of the solution is shown in Figure 11–3B. Here we are looking down at the $A$–$S$ plane shown in Figure 11–3A. A constant-budget line is shown, indicating all the alternative marketing mixes that could be achieved with this budget. The curved lines are called *iso-sales curves*. An iso-sales curve shows the different mixes of advertising and sales force that would produce a given level of sales. It is a projection into the $A$–$S$ plane of the set of points resulting from horizontal slicing of the sales function shown in Figure 11–3A at a given level of sales. Figure 11–3B shows iso-sales curves for three different sales levels: 75, 100, and 150 units. Given the budget line, it is not possible to attain sales of more than 100 units. The optimum marketing mix is shown at the point of tangency between the budget line and the last-touching iso-sales curve above it. Consequently, the marketing mix $(A^*S^*)$, which calls for somewhat more advertising than sales force, is the sales-maximizing (and in this case profit-maximizing) marketing mix.[8]

## PRACTICAL METHOD FOR DETERMINING THE OPTIMAL MARKETING MIX

The preceding theory can be turned into a practical method for evaluating different marketing mixes. Suppose a college admissions director, Ms. Barbara Smith, has to make three decisions regarding the recruitment program: the appli-cation fee *(P)*, the amount to spend on advertising *(A)*, and the amount to spend on sales force *(S)*. Last year, the office charged $16 for an application fee, and spent $10,000 on advertising and another $10,000 on sales force. The office now wants to consider possibly departing from this low price, low sales force strategy, which has drawn around 12,400 inquiries. Barbara Smith is considering raising the application fee to $24, and possibly spending as much as $50,000 on either advertising or sales force or both. She develops a set of alternative marketing mix strategies from among which to make a choice. Suppose Ms. Smith generates the eight strategies shown in the first three columns of Table 11–3 (the first listed strategy is the one used last year). These strategies were formed by assuming a high and low level for each of the three marketing variables.

Her next step is to estimate the likely number of inquiries *(Q)* that would be attained with each alternative mix. These estimates cannot come out of statisti-cal analysis of past data because her office never charged an application fee of $24 or spent more than approximately $20,000 on marketing. She and her associates have to make educated guesses based on their "feel" for the market. The resulting estimates are shown in the next-to-last column of Table 11–3. The whole table represents Barbara Smith's picture of the sales response function $Q = f(P,A,S)$, where the number of inquiries is a function of price, advertising, and sales force.

The optimal marketing mix strategy will depend on the organization's objective. If the college wants to maximize the number of inquiries, the best

## Table 11–3

### MARKETING MIXES AND ESTIMATED NUMBER OF INQUIRIES

| Marketing Mix No. | Price (P) | Advertising (A) | Sales Force (S) | Inquiries (Q) | Surplus ($) |
|---|---|---|---|---|---|
| 1. | $16 | $10,000 | $10,000 | 12,400 | $16,400 |
| 2. | 16 | 10,000 | 50,000 | 18,500 | 13,000 |
| 3. | 16 | 50,000 | 10,000 | 15,100 | −7,400 |
| 4. | 16 | 50,000 | 50,000 | 22,600 | −2,400 |
| 5. | 24 | 10,000 | 10,000 | 5,500 | 19,000 |
| 6. | 24 | 10,000 | 50,000 | 8,200 | 16,800 |
| 7. | 24 | 50,000 | 10,000 | 6,700 | −4,200 |
| 8. | 24 | 50,000 | 50,000 | 10,000 | 2,000 |

strategy is marketing mix #4, consisting of a low application fee of $16, and a high expenditure of $50,000 on advertising and sales force, respectively. But the college should be aware of the cost of this marketing mix strategy. Suppose the admissions office's fixed costs are $38,000 and unit variable costs are $10 for each inquiry handled. Using the earlier surplus equation (11–4), we find:

$$\$ = (P - c)Q + D - F - M$$
$$\$ = (16 - 10)22,600 + 0 - 38,000 - \$100,000 = -\$2,400$$

That is, the admissions office will contract a deficit of $2,400 by using this strategy. The surpluses (deficits) yielded by the other strategies are shown in the last column of Table 11–3.

Suppose the admissions office wanted to avoid a deficit, and in fact wanted to maximize its surplus at the inquiry stage of the recruiting process to help pay for the costs of evaluating applications later. Then the optimal marketing mix strategy would be #5, consisting of a fee of $24 and a low budget of $10,000 spent on advertising and sales force, respectively. Unfortunately, this will produce only 5,500 inquiries, far fewer than the number needed to result in the target level of enrollment. The main point is that Ms. Smith should prepare these sales response estimates in order to determine the strategy that would produce the best balance among the competing objectives of inquiries and cost. For example, marketing mix strategy #2 would produce substantially more inquiries than last year (18,500 instead of 12,400) at a slightly lower surplus ($13,000 instead of $16,400), and thus seems to be more attractive than last year's strategy.

### USING COST-EFFECTIVENESS ANALYSIS FOR MARKETING MIX DETERMINATION

Once a global marketing mix strategy is chosen, there are further marketing mix decisions of a more tactical nature to solve. Suppose the admissions office decided to use global marketing mix #4 because it is anxious to produce the largest possible number of inquiries, even though this will cause a deficit at this stage of the admissions process. In deciding to spend $50,000 on advertising, it must allocate this to competing advertising media, such as direct mail, newspaper ads, and radio ads. As an aid to determining the optimal media mix, the admissions office can apply *cost-effectiveness analysis.* Cost-effectiveness analysis is the general name given to researching the effect of variations in cost on results. Figure 11–4 shows Barbara Smith's estimates of how many inquiries would be produced by using different advertising media at different levels. She sees direct mail producing a linear growth in inquiries. Newspaper advertising is seen to produce a low level of response if used at a low level, increasing returns if used at a medium level, and diminishing returns if used at a high level. Radio is seen to produce a high number of inquiries if used at a low level and rapidly diminishing incremental returns thereafter.

Given the cost-effectiveness functions shown in Figure 11–4, which method is the most cost-effective to produce inquiries? The answer depends on how many inquiries the college is seeking. If the college would be satisfied to attract fewer than $n_1$ inquiries, then radio is the most cost-effective media. If the college is trying to attract between $n_1$ and $n_2$ inquiries, then direct mail is the most cost-effective media. If the college is trying to attract between $n_2$ and $n_3$ inquiries, then newspaper advertising is the most cost-effective single method. If the college is trying to attract more than $n_3$ inquiries, then direct mail is once again the most cost-effective single media.

If these media reach entirely different segments of the market, it would be better to use a combination of media to attract a given number of inquiries. Each media would be used to a level at which all marginal productivities are equal.

## FIGURE 11–4

### Cost-Effectiveness Functions

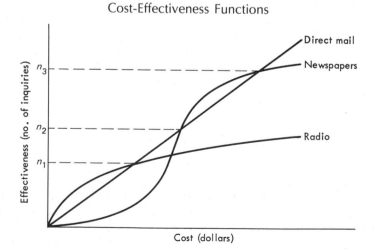

We have examined the appropriate marketing mix in terms of sales response functions. We will now go behind those sales response functions to see what real factors influence the appropriate mix. The appropriate marketing mix is influenced by the following four factors: (1) the type of consumer—individual versus organizational, (2) the communications task to be accomplished, (3) the stage of the product life cycle, and (4) the economic outlook.

**The type of consumer—individual versus organization.** Historically, there has been a considerable difference in the marketing mixes used by organizations selling services to households versus to other organizations. The mix differences are illustrated in Figure 11–5A. Advertising is believed to be the most important tool in marketing to households and personal selling the most important tool in marketing to organizations. Sales promotion is considered of equal, though smaller, importance in both markets. And publicity is considered to have even smaller, but equal, importance in both markets. These proportions, however, are not to be taken as authoritative, and many cases exist where marketers adopted different proportions with good success.

**The communications task.** The optimal marketing mix also depends on the nature of the communications task or objective. Figure 11–5B shows the general findings that have come out of a number of studies.[9] Advertising, sales promotion, and publicity are the most cost-effective tools in building buyer awareness, more than "cold calls" from sales representatives. Advertising is highly cost-effective in producing comprehension, with personal selling coming in second. Buyer conviction is influenced most by personal selling, followed by advertising. Finally,

**FIGURE 11–5**

Communications Mix as a Function of Type of Market
and Buyer Readiness Stage

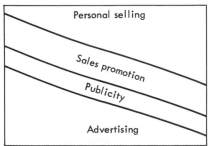

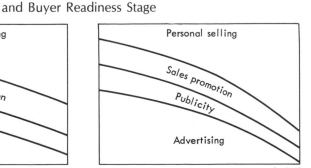

←Household buyers  Organization buyers→     Awareness Comprehension Conviction Ordering

A. Normal marketing mix for
household buyers versus
organization buyers

B. Marketing mix cost
effectiveness at different
buyer readiness stages

placing an order is predominantly a function of the sales call, with an assist from sales promotion.[10]

These findings have important practical implications. First, the organization could effect promotional economies by cutting back on the involvement of salespeople in the early stages of the selling job so that they can concentrate on the vital phase closing the sale. Second, when advertising is relied on to do more of the job, it should take different forms, some addressed to building product awareness and some to producing comprehension.

**The stage of the product life cycle.**    The effectiveness of marketing expenditures varies at different stages of the product life cycle.

Advertising and promotion are important in the introduction stage because the market is not aware of the product, and the cost per exposure is low. Sales promotion in particular stimulates interest and trial of the new product.

In the growth stage, word-of-mouth processes begin to work for the new product and partially replace or supplement the organization's promotion efforts. If the organization wants to build its market share, it should continue to promote vigorously during the growth stage.

The maturity stage is marked by intensified promotional expenditures to meet competition and to advertise new-product uses and features. There is generally an increase in *sales promotion* effort relative to *advertising* effort.

In the decline stage, many organizations reduce their promotion expenditures to improve their profit margins. Publicity is cut down; the sales force gives the product only minimal attention; and advertising is cut down to a reminder level. Sales promotion is probably the most exercised promotion tool at this stage.

**The economic outlook.**    Organizations would do well to revise their marketing mixes with shifts in the economic outlook. During inflation, for example, buyers become highly price conscious. They will be looking for value. The organization can do at least three things to respond: (1) it can increase its sales promotion relative to advertising, since people are looking for deals; (2) it can emphasize value and price in its communications; and (3) it can develop messages that help customers know how and where to buy intelligently.

---

## SUMMARY

This chapter deals with four tasks in developing and choosing cost-effective marketing programs.

The first task is to choose between alternative products or programs. Here cost-benefit analysis is helpful. Programs are preferred which have the highest benefit-cost ratio. To calculate benefits and costs, monetary and quantitative measures are preferred, although ultimately nonquantifiable benefits should be taken into account.

The second task is to choose between alternative marketing objectives. Expressing the situation in terms of a "profit" equation allows evaluating the different objectives. The most common objectives of nonprofit organizations are surplus maximization, revenue maximization, usage maximization, usage targeting, full cost recovery, partial cost recovery, and producer satisfaction maximization.

The third task is to decide on the marketing expenditure level. Organizations decide on their expenditure level using one of five methods: affordable method, percentage-of-sales method, competitive-based method, objective-and-task method, and sales response optimization method.

The fourth task is to develop an optimal marketing mix of product, price, place, and promotion. The optimal marketing mix can be set if the sales response function for each separate marketing mix element is known. The appropriate marketing mix varies with the type of buyer (individuals or organizations), the communication task, the stage of the product life cycle, and the economic outlook.

---

## QUESTIONS

**1.** Describe the factors a church might consider in carrying out a benefit-cost analysis to decide between continuing a church-supported summer Bible school enrolling 300 children at a cost to the church of $30,000 per year or beginning an assistance program for 100 elderly shut-ins in the area for the same cost. Include both quantifiable and nonquantifiable benefits.

**2.** Discuss the problems of applying benefit-cost analysis to the situation in question 1 above.

**3.** A museum administrator is working on a set of objectives. He realizes that there are many alternative attendance objectives the museum might adopt in place of the current one, to maximize the total number of museum visits during the year. List these other attendance objectives.

**4.** Draw a model of the sales revenue function for one of the following: (a) an art museum, (b) an adult education program, (c) a presidential candidate's campaign.

**5.** Describe the strengths and weaknesses of each of the five approaches for establishing the marketing budget for a hospital.

**6.** There are many ways a college can recruit more students. Compare the cost effectiveness of the following strategies: (a) placing ads in newspapers, (b) having admissions personnel visit high schools, (c) improving the quality of the faculty, and (d) raising the percentage of students who receive financial aid.

---

## NOTES

**1.** "Benefit/Cost Analyses for Health Care Systems," *Annals of the American Academy of Political and Social Science,* January 1972, pp. 90–99, esp. p. 94.

**2.** Weinberg has argued in favor of theatres charging a low rather than a high price. His argument is that a low price will lead to a larger audience, and a larger audience will lead to more people who know about the theatre and who will contribute money to its support. See Charles B. Weinberg, "Marketing Mix

Decision Rules for Nonprofit Organizations," in Jagdish Sheth, ed., *Research in Marketing,* Vol. 3 (Chicago: JAI Press, 1980), pp. 191–234.

**3.** Michael Etgar and Brian T. Ratchford, "Marketing Management and Marketing Concept: Their Conflict in Non-Profit Organizations," *1974 Proceedings* (Chicago: American Marketing Association, 1974).

**4.** John McKnight, "Professional Service Business," *Social Policy,* November–December 1977, pp. 110–16.

**5.** As an example of this method, see David B. Montgomery and Alvin J. Silk, "Estimating Dynamic Effects of Market Communications Expenditures," *Management Science,* June 1972, pp. 485–501.

**6.** As an example, see Russell Ackoff and James R. Emshoff, "Advertising Research at Anheuser-Busch," *Sloan Management Review,* Winter 1975, pp. 1–15.

**7.** See Philip Kotler, "A Guide to Gathering Expert Estimates," *Business Horizons,* October 1970, pp. 79–87.

**8.** For additional theory, see Robert Dorfman and Peter O. Steiner, "Optimal Advertising and Optimal Quality," *American Economic Review,* December 1954, pp. 826–36; and Robert Ferber and P. J. Verdoorn, *Research Methods in Economics and Business* (New York: Macmillan, 1962), p. 535.

**9.** "What IBM Found About Ways to Influence Selling," *Business Week,* December 5, 1959, pp. 69–70; and Harold C. Cash and William J. Crissy, "Comparison of Advertising and Selling," in *The Psychology of Selling,* Vol. 12 (Flushing, N.Y.: Personnel Development Associates, 1965).

**10.** Swinyard and Ray have challenged the finding that advertising is more effective when it precedes the sales call. They found that female household residents who were contacted by a Red Cross volunteer followed by some mailings expressed a higher intention to donate blood than a similar group who first received the mailings and then received the sales call. See William R. Swinyard and Michael L. Ray, "Advertising–Selling Interactions: An Attribution Theory Experiment," *Journal of Marketing Research,* November 1977, pp. 509–16.

# Product Decisions

No one can accuse the U.S. Treasury Department of understanding or practicing marketing. Their record is clean and consistent: All three of the new products they introduced in the last decade—the $1 Eisenhower coin, the reissued $2 Jefferson bill, and the $1 Susan Anthony coin—have been dismal flops in the marketplace.

In 1971, the Treasury introduced a heavy, poker-chip-sized Eisenhower dollar. The public found it clumsy to carry around and merchants were not eager to handle it. Today, the 700 million Eisenhower dollars in circulation have been pretty much relegated to the slot machines in Las Vegas and Atlantic City, as well as a gift item for children's birthdays.

In 1976, the Treasury decided to reintroduce the Jefferson $2 bill to save on costs of printing and transporting $1 bills. Treasury officials estimated that if one-half of the 1.6 billion $1 bills in circulation were replaced with $2 bills, the country would save $35 million in printing costs within a five-year period. The Treasury commissioned a Harvard Business School survey to see if the public, banks, and retailers would use the new $2 bill. The survey discovered some negative attitudes, but believed that these could be overcome by a substantial advertising campaign. When the $2 bill was introduced, it met with great resistance from merchants as well as consumers. Merchants felt they needed another drawer in their cash registers or else the $2 bill would be confused with the $20 bills. The Treasury, which had planned to spend $300,000 advertising the $2 bill, dropped the idea because of the expense. A Federal Reserve System official said: "They could have test-marketed the bill in two big cities for a year, found out their problems, and applied the information to marketing bills in the rest of the country." Another official, however, was pessimistic: "I wonder if there is anything to market. There is no real advantage to the $2 bill to the customer.'' The Bureau had planned to print 400 million $2 bills a year but stopped in January 1977 because 200 million of them had accumulated and were not being requested by the banks.

In the same year, the Treasury also launched a new "downsized" $1 coin featuring Susan B. Anthony, the 19th century suffragette leader. The motivation was once again a producer motivation rather than a consumer motivation. Each Anthony dollar costs only 3 cents to make and has an anticipated life expectancy of 15 years, 10 times longer than the 18-month life expectancy of a paper dollar. The savings to the government were calculated at $50 million a year. The U.S. Mint designed an 11-sided coin made of nickel-covered copper, only slightly larger than the American quarter. Some university-based research was conducted among consumers and retailers but the findings and recommendations were essentially ignored. The government minted about 850 million before production was halted. Three years later, about 62 percent remained undistributed because of considerable consumer and retailer resistance. Many Americans found this coin easy to confuse with the American quarter and chose to avoid it. Stella B. Hackel, director of the U.S. Mint, disagrees: "The Anthony dollar is 43% heavier than the quarter and should be easily distinguishable.'' But this is another example of marketing myopia where producers refuse to see things through the eyes of consumers.

Having launched a poor product, the Treasury refuses to give up and wants "marketing" to come to its rescue in finding ways to persuade consumers and retailers to use the coin. They are distributing a 20-page press kit to bankers with ideas such as naming their new branch the Susan B. Anthony branch and to sponsor poetry contests in her name. Another brochure encourages retailers to schedule a Susan B. Anthony sale and shows merchants how to reorganize their cash drawers to accommodate the new coins. Citizen groups are advised to throw "Susan" bingo parties using the coins as prizes. The Treasury is even toying around with the idea of reissuing the coin in a bronze-colored alloy so that users can distinguish it more easily from American quarters.

SOURCES: See Michael B. Amspaugh, "Americans Continue to Ignore the $2 Bill," *Flint Journal,* November 7, 1977, reprinted in Christopher H. Lovelock and Charles B. Weinberg, eds., *Readings in Public and Nonprofit Marketing* (Palo Alto, Calif.: Scientific Press, 1978), pp. 221–23; and "Numismatic Ms.," *Time,* July 9, 1979, p. 54.

The most basic marketing decision organizations make is what products (i.e., goods and services) to offer to the target market. Most organizations offer a product mix. The product mix is periodically modified by product additions and eliminations. Each new product involves risk, as we saw in the U.S. Treasury Department experience, which hopefully could be reduced by better marketing research, product development, and communication. Each product elimination also involves risk in that its product life could conceivably have been extended through better marketing strategy.

Organizations face a large number of decisions in the product area. We shall examine the following three questions:

1. How can the organization assess and improve its overall product mix? *(product mix decisions)*
2. How can the organization assess and improve individual products in its mix? *(product item decisions)*
3. How can the organization improve its handling of its products over their life cycles? *(product life cycle decision)*

## PRODUCT MIX DECISIONS

Most nonprofit organizations are multiproduct firms. Here are some examples:

- The Memorial Hospital of DuPage County, Illinois, has four basic product lines, each with several specific products. They are: (1) *diagnosis and cure products* (outpatient clinics, emergency services, laboratories, and inpatient care); (2) *illness prevention products* (health screenings, counseling); (3) *health education products;* and (4) *restorative products* (rehabilitation center, psychiatric center).
- The Shedd Aquarium of Chicago operates a number of product lines, including exhibits, classes, trips, publications, and a library. Each product line contains specific products. Thus classes are run separately for children, lay adults, and professionals.
- The Faith Evangelical Covenant Church of Wheaton, Illinois, manages four product lines: (1) worship services on Sunday morning and Sunday evening; (2) education programs for children, teens, and adults; (3) counseling programs on marriage and bereavement; and (4) recreational activities such as sports programs and dancing.

For clarity, we will use the following definitions:

**Product mix** is the set of all product lines and items that a particular organization makes available to consumers.

**Product line** is a group of products within a product mix that are closely related, either because they function in a similar manner, are made available to the same consumers, or are marketed through the same types of outlets.

**Product item** is a distinct unit within a product line that is distinguishable by size, appearance, price, or some other attribute.

We can describe an organization's product mix in terms of its *length, width,* and *depth.* These concepts are illustrated in Figure 12–1 for the product mix of a hypothetical zoo. We see that the product mix, in terms of its length, consists

## FIGURE 12-1

Length, Width, and Depth of a Zoo's Product Mix

| | ← Product Mix Length → | | |
|---|---|---|---|
| Product Line Width ↕ | Exhibited Animals | Education | Research |
| | Lions (5) | Classes (20) | Basic research projects (2) |
| | Bears (8) | Field trips (5) | |
| | Monkeys (12) | Public lectures (50) | Applied research projects (8) |
| | Elephants (2) | | |

of three product lines: exhibited animals, education, and research. Each product line has a certain width: Thus the exhibited animals include lions, bears, monkeys, and elephants. Finally, each product item has a certain depth: The zoo contains five lions, for example.

Suppose the zoo is thinking of expanding its product mix. This could be accomplished in any of three ways. The zoo could lengthen its product mix by adding, say, a restaurant operation. Or the zoo could add another animal category, say zebras; this extends the width of its animal line. Or the zoo could add a sixth lion; this deepens its number of lions.

Suppose, on the other hand, that the zoo considered contracting its product mix either to bring down its costs or to attain a more specialized position in the marketplace. The zoo could drop research and even education, concentrating exclusively on exhibiting live animals. It could, alternatively, eliminate certain animal types, such as bears, in a move to be, say, a "safari type" zoo. Or it could decide to carry fewer animals of each type. The "specialization" possibilities are commented on by Kovach:

> A few "zoos" have chosen to adopt a product-line specialization approach (the Arizona–Sonora Desert Museum), a limited product-line strategy (the Santa Barbara Zoo), or special-situation (Seaworld).[1]

In considering the product mix, we should recognize that the various products differ in their relative contribution to the enterprise. Some products constitute the *core* products of that institution and others are *ancillary* products. Thus, live animals are the core product of a zoo and research is an ancillary product. Furthermore, certain animals will play a major role in attracting visitors: They are called *product leaders* or *flagship products*. Most zoo visitors, for example, will want to view gorillas and lions, and feel less drawn to antelopes and wolves. Often, an organization will seek to add a *star product* or *crown jewel* to its mix. The Washington National Zoo's crown jewel is the panda bears that the country received when diplomatic relations were reestablished with China. An organization can showcase its crown jewel as a symbol in its literature and promotion. The high cost of acquiring one crown jewel is often well repaid by the public relations value it produces.

A nonprofit organization should periodically reassess its product mix. Its product mix establishes its position vis-à-vis competitors in the minds of consumers. Its product mix is also the source of its costs. The organization must be constantly alert to products whose costs have begun to exceed their benefits, and whose elimination would release funds for bringing in new, more worthwhile products into its product mix.

## PRODUCT ITEM DECISIONS

We will now turn to the management and marketing of a product item. We define product as follows:

A **product** is anything that can be offered to a market to satisfy a need. It includes physical objects, services, persons, places, organizations, and ideas. Other names for a product would be the *offer, value package,* or *benefit bundle.*

In developing a product to offer to a market, the product planner has to distinguish three levels of the concept of a product: the core, tangible, and augmented levels.

### CORE PRODUCT

At the most fundamental level stands the core product, which answers the questions: What is the consumer really seeking? What need is the product really satisfying? A hospital produces surgery, but the patient is really buying "hope." A university produces knowledge but many students are buying "marketability." A zoo presents animals but visitors are buying "diversion." The marketer's job is to uncover the essential needs hiding under every product so that product benefits, not just product features, can be described. The core product stands at the center of the total product, as illustrated in Figure 12–2.

### TANGIBLE PRODUCT

The core product is always made available to the buyer in some tangible form. Consider a mother in labor in a hospital. The core product that the laboring mother wants is an easy and safe delivery. One tangible product takes the form of a hospital delivery ward where the woman in labor is wheeled in, transferred to an examining table, and anesthetized. A physician and nurses aid her in delivery, and her husband is not allowed into the room. Clearly, this is not the

## FIGURE 12–2

### Three Levels of Product

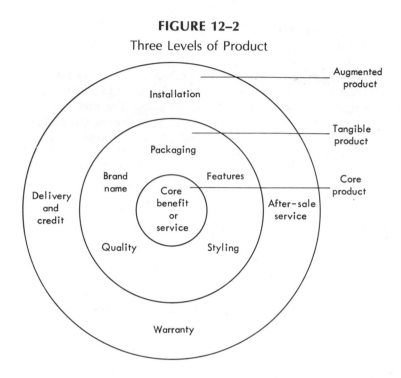

only form that the tangible product can take, as witness the growing popularity of the new form known as the Alternative Birthing Center:

> Mickey Johnson . . . entered what might have been a cheery, yellow-tinted bedroom in suburbia furnished with rocking chairs and an old-fashioned walnut armoire. Well-tended plants hung from the ceiling. There was even a stereo to play Mickey's favorite music. During the long, painful hours of labor, she was free to get up and pace the corridors. Her husband, Bruce, was at her side during the critical moment of delivery. Almost immediately afterward, the doctor handed him the squealing infant, and the awed father was allowed to cut the umbilical cord and give his 7-pound, 8-ounce son his first bath. The baby was not taken away but spent the night with his parents.[2]

A tangible product can be described as having up to five characteristics: First, it has a certain *styling,* as is apparent in the difference between a cold hospital delivery room and a warm "suburban-like" bedroom. Second, it has certain *features,* such as the fact that the mother is free to move around the room, allowed to have her husband with her, and so on. Third, the tangible product has a certain *quality level,* both in its physical materials and the care with which it is run. Fourth, the tangible product has a certain *packaging,* here represented by the larger hospital in which it is contained. Fifth, the tangible product may have a *brand* name; in this case, Illinois Masonic's Alternative Birthing Center. We will examine these five controllable characteristics of a tangible product in more detail.

**Styling.**     Styling means giving a product or service a distinctive look or "feel." Much of the competition in durable goods—such as automobiles, watches, and electronic products—is style competition. Style is also expressed in the design of post offices, hospitals, museums, and other edifices where services are offered. Services can also be styled: Consider the style of the American Ballet Theatre (classical dance) and the Twyla Tharp Company (modern dance).

The style of a product or service can be established before or after the target market is identified. Symphony orchestras tend to choose the style that pleases them, and then they hope to attract a sufficient number of people who like that style. Occasionally, they will take a market-oriented view and design the style for the intended audience, as when the Boston Symphony established the Boston Pops under Arthur Fiedler to play music that would be enjoyed by audiences with less-sophisticated musical tastes.

An organization can discover that its style is no longer appropriate or effective with its target audience. Thus, a college that sticks with a classic liberal arts program may find itself drawing fewer students in relation to colleges emphasizing career preparation. This college may want to consider modifying its style to meet the changing market wants.

**Features.**     Features represent individual components of the tangible product that could be easily added or subtracted without changing the product's style or quality. Consider a health maintenance organization (HMO) that is seeking to expand its membership. There are many feature improvements that it could offer:

1. expanding its hours of operation to include two evenings a week
2. adding dental service as an optional feature for a small additional fee
3. offering a free ten-week smokers' clinic for members wishing to quit smoking

The use of features has many advantages. The organization can go after specific market segments by selecting those features that would appeal to these segments. Features are a tool for achieving product differentiation vis-à-vis competitors. They have the advantage of being easy to add quickly or drop quickly, or they can be made optional at little expense. They are often newsworthy and can be used to get free media publicity.[3]

**Quality.**     Quality represents the perceived level of performance in a product or service. Service products in particular are tremendously variable, depending upon who is providing them and how much control the organization exercises over its service providers. Consider the case of college education. College A is a high-pressure, publish-or-perish institution where professors are judged primarily by their research output and not by their classroom performance. College B, on the other hand, insists on high-quality teaching and drops instructors who do not meet this standard. Whether college A will continue to attract a sufficient number of students depends upon the extent to which students get information about these quality differences and care enough about quality to make it a determinant factor in their choice of a college. A basic issue is how does sales response vary with the level of quality in that particular market. Figure 12–3A shows a plausible relationship between sales and quality level. The curve says that higher perceived quality leads to higher sales. It also says that very high quality may not add much additional sales either because consumers cannot perceive very high quality or do not value it that much.

An organization must not only set an initial standard for quality but must also manage its quality level over time. Assume that college A's teaching quality level today is average. College A has three options (see Figure 12–3B). It can attempt to improve its quality level over time through better selection, training, and rewarding of employees and through improving its facilities. This strategy of quality improvement should lead to improved market interest and response. The second option is to maintain its present level of quality and put its emphasis on other dimensions of the business. The third option is to allow its quality to decline over time. This may be done deliberately when the institution wants to withdraw from the business. Otherwise, it indicates poor management, makes little strategic sense, and leads the organization down the road to extinction.

**Packaging.**    Packaging is the container or wrapper surrounding the specific product or service. We know that good packaging can add value beyond that perceived in the product itself; consider the fancy perfume bottle and its contribution to the "feeling" of the perfume. In the case of a service, packaging is the contribution of the larger context in which the product is found. Thus, a college campus's environment serves as the packaging of the academic product. Sturner

## FIGURE 12–3
### Quality Level Strategies

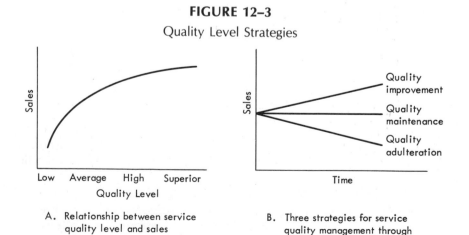

A.  Relationship between service quality level and sales

B.  Three strategies for service quality management through time

recognizes the importance of the campus' environment in contributing to the goals of a college:

> The architecture, topography, and landscaping of a campus should support the educational function of the university. . . . The campus should evoke the feeling of a tone poem, a festival, a composition that washes over the inhabitants. It should combine all the senses—sight, sound, touch, taste, and scent—becoming a street scene, a block party, a family gathering, a tactile encounter, a tribute to the intermeshing of the sights and sounds of human beings.[4]

**Branding.**     The products and services of a seller can be branded, that is, given a name, term, sign, symbol, or design—or some combination—which identifies them as the seller's to differentiate them from competitors' offerings. Branding can add value to the seller's offer and more satisfaction for the buyer. As an example, there are thousands of mental health centers throughout the country. They have found that the term "mental health center" is a turnoff to many people, since it suggests mental illness. The whole industry is looking for another name that would create more positive feelings. The Rush Presbyterian Hospital of Chicago recently renamed its mental health center The Institute for Living, believing that this brand name would work better.

In a similar vein, the social movement known as "birth control" came under sharp attack from certain religious, ethnic, and economic groups that viewed it as a government attempt to dictate who can and cannot have babies. The advocates of "birth control" changed the name to "family planning," since this eliminated the suggestion of outside control and replaced it with the notion that the family makes the decision. This has worked well, but today in some countries the term family planning has fallen into disrepute. For example, family planning has acquired a bad name in India because the government pushed birth control measures too harshly on the population, and a new brand name is needed.

The power of a brand name should never be underestimated. Most political candidates win the election not on their own merits but because they are lucky enough to carry the right brand name—Republican or Democrat—whichever is more popular in the particular voting district. Even the candidate's own name can win the election where the electorate is split over the party brand names. Thus, an unemployed taxi driver named John Adams, who did no political campaigning, won the Republican nomination in New Hampshire's First Congressional District on the strength of his name.[5]

Many services and social movements carry brand names to distinguish them from one another. Thus, the environmental movement has spawned such action groups as FOE (Friends of the Earth), Sierra Club, and Save the Redwoods League. Charitable organizations carry such names as Christmas Seal (lung association), Easter Seal (handicapped people), and March of Dimes (birth defects). Help-the-poor organizations carry such brand names as Salvation Army, Goodwill Industries, and so on. Mass therapy organizations carry such brand names as Scientology, Transcendental Meditation, Silva Mind Control, and Est.

The creation of a brand name to symbolize the organization's product or service can contribute a number of values. An organization feels proprietary toward its brand name, and therefore normally works hard to ensure the quality and consistency of its service. It wants its brand name to create buyer confidence in its service, and lead to consumer brand preference and repeat purchase. Buyers benefit because they can identify the various brands, acquire a stock of information about their respective quality, choose the best brand, and stick with it as long as it satisfies them.

### AUGMENTED PRODUCT

The marketer can offer to the target market additional services and benefits that go beyond the tangible product, thus making up an augmented product. Thus the Illinois Masonic Hospital can, along with the birthing room, offer longer payment terms, a satisfaction guarantee, home visits to the new mother, and so on. Organizations augment their tangible product to meet additional consumer wants and/or to differentiate their product from competition. As more birthing rooms appear in America's hospitals, competition will increase not only between delivery wards and birthing rooms but also among the new birthing rooms themselves. Final outcomes will depend not only on the tangible product characteristics but upon what organizations add to their tangible products in the way of additional benefits. As stated by Levitt:

> The *new competition* is not between what companies produce in their factories, but between *what they add to their factory output in the form of packaging, services, advertising, customer advice, financing, delivery arrangements, warehousing, and other things that people value.* [6]

Thus we see that a product is not a simple thing but a complex offer consisting of a core need-satisfying service, a set of tangible characteristics, and a set of augmented benefits. The organization should deeply examine each of its products and design them in a way that will distinguish them from competitors' offers and carry the intended qualities to the intended target market. The more the product can be taken out of the commodity class and moved toward the branded class, the more control the organization will have over the level, timing, and composition of demand for its product.

## PRODUCT LIFE CYCLE

It is not possible for a product's characteristics and marketing approach to remain optimal for all time. Broad changes in the macroenvironment (population, economy, politics, technology, and culture) as well as specific changes in the market environment (buyers, competitors, dealers, suppliers) will call for major product and marketing adjustments at key points in the product's history. The nature of the appropriate adjustments can be conveyed through the concept of the *product life cycle.*

Many products and services can be viewed as having something analogous to a "biological" life cycle. They received high acceptance at one time and then moved into a period of decline later. One only has to think of buggy whips, the World Federalists, and the Single Tax movement. The life cycle of a typical product exhibits an S-shaped sales curve marked by the following four stages (see Figure 3–1, p. 81, for similar curve):

1. *Introduction* is a period of slow sales growth as the product is introduced in the market.
2. *Growth* is a period of rapid market acceptance.
3. *Maturity* is a period of slowdown in sales growth because the product has achieved acceptance by most of the potential buyers.
4. *Decline* is the period when sales show a strong downward drift.

The product life cycle (PLC) concept can be defined further according to whether it describes a product class (mental health service), a product form (psychoanalysis), or a brand (Menninger Clinic). The PLC concept has a different degree of applicability in each case. *Product classes* have the longest life cycles. The sales of many product classes can be expected to continue in the mature stage for an indefinite duration. Thus, "mental health service" began centuries ago with organized religion and can be expected to persist indefinitely. Product forms, on the other hand, tend to exhibit more standard PLC histories than product classes. Thus, mental health services are dispensed in such forms as psychoanalysis, bioenergetics, group therapy, and so on, some of which are beginning to show signs of maturity. As for brands, they are the most likely to show finite histories. Thus, the Menninger Clinic is a well-known psychoanalytically oriented clinic that had a period of rapid growth and is now mature. It will pass out of existence eventually, as is the fate of most brands and institutions.

It is important to note that not all products exhibit an S-shaped life cycle. Three other common patterns are:

1. *Scalloped pattern.* (Figure 12–4A) In this case, product sales during the mature stage suddenly break into a new life cycle. The product's new life is triggered by product modifications, new uses, new users, changing tastes, or other factors. For example, the market for psychotherapy reached maturity at one point and then the emergence of group therapy gave it a whole new market.
2. *Cyclical pattern.* (Figure 12–4B) The sales of some products show a cyclical pattern. For example, engineering schools go through alternating periods of high enrollment and low enrollment, reflecting changes in demand and supply in the marketplace. The decline stage is not a time to eliminate the product but to maintain as much of it as possible, waiting for the next boom.
3. *Fad pattern.* (Figure 12–4C) Here a new product comes on the market, attracts quick attention, is adopted with great zeal, peaks early, and declines rapidly. The acceptance cycle is short and the product tends to attract only a limited following

## FIGURE 12–4

### Three Anomalous Product Life Cycle Patterns

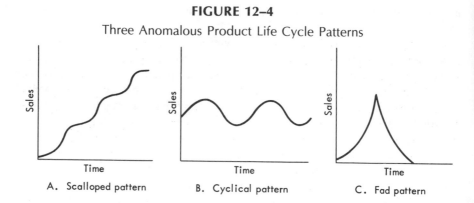

A. Scalloped pattern      B. Cyclical pattern      C. Fad pattern

of people who are looking for excitement or diversion. Some art forms and therapy forms exhibit the pattern of a fad.

We will now return to the S-shaped PLC and examine the characteristics and appropriate marketing strategies at each stage.

### INTRODUCTION STAGE

The introduction stage takes place when the new product is first made available for purchase in the marketplace. The introduction into one or more markets takes time, and sales growth is apt to be slow. Consider how long it took for the "new math" to be accepted in America's public schools, or the fluoride treatment of water to be introduced in America's cities. Today, nutrition experts are trying to find faster ways to get a malnourished population to accept new foods that will contribute to their health.

Buzzell identified four causes for the slow growth during the introduction stage: (1) delays in the expansion of production capacity, (2) technical problems ("working out the bugs"), (3) delays in making the product available to customers through distribution outlets, and (4) customer reluctance to change established behavior patterns.[7] In the case of expensive new products, sales growth is retarded by additional factors, such as the small number of buyers who are attuned to innovations and the high cost of the product.

In the introductory stage, costs are high because of the low adoption and heavy distribution and promotion expenses. Promotional expenditures are at their highest ratio to sales "because of the need for a high level of promotional effort to (1) inform potential consumers of the new and unknown product, (2) induce trial of the product, and (3) secure distribution in retail outlets."[8] There are only a few competitors and they produce basic versions of the product, since the market is not ready for product refinements. The organizations direct their selling effort to those buyers who are the readiest to buy, namely, early adopter types. Management should be guided by the findings in the field of innovation and diffusion theory in designing their introductory marketing plans (see Chapter 4, pp. 122–26).

### GROWTH STAGE

If the new product satisfies the market, sales will start climbing substantially. The early adopters will continue their purchasing and other consumers will follow their lead, especially if there is favorable word-of-mouth. New competitors will enter the market, attracted by the opportunity. They will introduce feature, style, and packaging variations, and this will expand the market. During this stage the organization tries to sustain rapid market growth as long as possible. This is accomplished in several ways:

1. The organization undertakes to improve product quality and add new-product features and models.
2. It vigorously searches out new market segments to enter.
3. It keeps its eyes open for new distribution channels to gain additional product exposure.
4. It shifts its promotion from building product awareness to trying to bring about product conviction and purchase.

### MATURITY STAGE

At some point a product's rate of sales growth will slow down, and the product will enter a stage of relative maturity. This stage normally lasts much longer than the previous stages, and it poses some of the most formidable challenges to marketing management. *Most products are in the maturity stage of the life cycle, and therefore most of marketing management deals with the mature product.*

The beginning of a slowdown in the rate of sales growth has the effect of producing overcapacity in the industry. This overcapacity leads to intensified competition. Competitors engage more frequently in price cutting, and there is a strong increase in promotional budgets. Other organizations increase their research and development budgets to find better versions of the product. Still others resort to modifying their customer mix or product mix. These steps result in higher costs. Some of the weaker competitors start dropping out. The industry eventually consists of a set of well-entrenched competitors whose basic orientation is toward gaining competitive advantage.

### DECLINE STAGE

Most product forms and brands eventually enter a stage of sales decline. The decline may be slow, as in the case of barber shop quartet singing, or rapid, as in the case of politicians who fall out of public favor. Sales may plunge to zero and the product may be withdrawn from the market. Or sales may petrify at a low level and continue for many years at that level. Many universities have witnessed a long-term decline in their schools of education and social work, and have wrestled with what to do with these weakening products.

Sales decline for a number of reasons. Technical advances may give birth to new-product classes, forms, and brands, which become effective substitutes. Changes in fashion or tastes lead to buyer erosion. All of these have the effect of intensifying overcapacity and competition.

As sales decline, some organizations withdraw from the industry in order to invest their resources in more attractive markets. Those remaining in the industry tend to reduce the number of product offerings. They withdraw from smaller market segments and marginal distribution channels. The promotion budget is reduced. The price may also be reduced to halt the decline in demand.

Unless strong retention reasons exist, carrying a weak product is very costly to the organization. The cost of maintaining a weak product is not just the amount of uncovered cost. No financial accounting can adequately convey all the hidden costs. The weak product tends to consume a disproportionate amount of management's time; it often requires frequent price adjustment; it generally involves short production runs in spite of expensive setup times; it requires both advertising and sales force attention that might better be diverted to making the "healthy" products more profitable; its very unfitness can cause customer misgivings and cast a shadow on the organization's image. The biggest cost imposed by carrying weak products may lie in the future. By not being eliminated at the proper time, these products delay the aggressive search for replacement products; they create a lopsided product mix, long on "yesterday's breadwinners" and short on "tomorrow's breadwinners"; they depress current cash and weaken the organization's foothold on the future.

An organization faces a number of tasks and decisions in handling its aging products.

**Identifying the weak products.**      The first task is to establish a system that will identify those products that are in a declining stage. Six steps are involved:

1. A product review committee is appointed with the responsibility for developing a system for periodically reviewing weak products in the organization's mix.

2. This committee meets and develops a set of objectives and procedures for reviewing weak products.

3. The controller's office fills out data for each product showing trends in market size, market share, prices, and costs.

4. This information is run against a computer program that identifies the most dubious products. The criteria include the number of years of sales decline, market-share trends, and cost trends.

5. Products put on the dubious list are then reported to those managers responsible for them. The managers fill out forms showing where they think sales and costs on dubious products will go with no change in the current marketing program and with their recommended changes in the current program.

6. The product review committee examines the product rating form for each dubious product and makes a recommendation to leave it alone, or to modify its marketing strategy, or to drop it.[9]

**Determining marketing strategies.**     In the face of declining sales, some organizations will abandon the market earlier than others. The organizations that remain enjoy a temporary increase in sales as they pick up the customers of the withdrawing organizations. Thus, any particular organization faces the issue of whether it should be the one to stay in the market until the end.

If it decides to stay in the market, the organization faces further strategic choices. The organization could adopt a *continuation strategy*, in which case it continues its past marketing strategy: same market segments, channels, pricing, and promotion. Or it could follow a *concentration strategy*, in which case it concentrates its resources in the strongest markets, while phasing out its efforts elsewhere. Finally, it could follow a *harvesting strategy*, in which case it sharply reduces its expenses to increase its positive cash flow, knowing that this will accelerate the rate of sales decline and the ultimate demise of the product.

**The drop decision.**     When a product has been singled out for elimination, the organization faces some further decisions. First, it has the option of selling or transferring the product to someone else or dropping it completely. Second, it has to decide whether the product should be dropped quickly or slowly. Third, it has to decide on the level of service to maintain to cover existing units.

Recently, various government units have adopted sunset proposals for the review and termination of government programs on a regular cycle. Each federal program would receive a review on a five- or six-year cycle. The reviewing government committee would determine whether the current program had met its objectives, whether it should be continued at the same budget level, or with higher or lower funding.

## SUMMARY

Most nonprofit organizations are multiproduct firms. They make decisions on the product mix, on each product item, and on marketing mix strategies for each product at each stage of its life cycle.

An organization's product mix can be described in terms of its length, width, and depth. Some of the organization's products constitute its core products and others its ancillary products. Organizations like to develop a flagship product or crown jewel product to advertise the organization.

A product itself can be defined as anything that can be offered to a market to satisfy a need. It includes physical objects, services, persons, places, organizations, and ideas. Three levels of the concept of a product can be distinguished. The core product answers the question: What need is the product really meeting? The tangible product is the form in which the product is seen or held: It includes the product's features, styling, quality, brand name, and packaging. The augmented product consists of the tangible product and the additional services and benefits such as installation, after-sale service, delivery, credit, and warranty. As competition increases, organizations augment their product offer to compete.

Products pass through a product life cycle consisting of four stages: introduction, growth, maturity, and decline. The S-shaped life cycle is the most common, but other patterns include a scalloped pattern, cyclical pattern, and fad pattern. Each stage of the life cycle presents new marketing challenges and requires adjustments in the target market and marketing mix.

## QUESTIONS

**1.** Identify the tangible product, the essential product, and the augmented product provided to season ticketholders of a symphony series.

**2.** Apply the five characteristics of the tangible product to a family counseling center.

**3.** How can a high school use branding to attract more students to use the remedial reading center?

**4.** Generate some ideas that a zoo could use to augment the free zoo admission that is now the sole benefit of joining the Zoo Society.

**5.** Describe the evolution of chest X-ray TB screening programs through the four stages of the product life cycle, indicating the key characteristics and marketing tasks at each stage.

**6.** Describe the various marketing strategies available to the manager of a day care center which is experiencing a steady decline in enrollment.

## NOTES

**1.** Carol Kovach, "A Hungry Problem for Zoos: In Search of New Prey," in Subhash C. Jain, ed., *Research Frontiers in Marketing: Dialogues and Directions* (Chicago: Proceedings of the American Marketing Association Educators Conference, Series No. 43), 1978, pp. 350–54.

**2.** "Special Delivery: With Even a Little Labor Music," *Time,* April 24, 1978, p. 60.

**3.** See John B. Stewart, "Functional Features in Product Strategy," *Harvard Business Review,* March–April 1959, pp. 65–78.

**4.** See William F. Sturner, "Environmental Code: Creating a Sense of Place on the College Campus," *Journal of Higher Education,* February 1972, pp. 97–109.

**5.** *Newsweek,* September 27, 1976, p. 36.

**6.** Theodore Levitt, *The Marketing Mode* (New York: McGraw-Hill, 1969), p. 2.

**7.** Robert D. Buzzell, "Competitive Behavior and the Product Life Cycle," in John S. Wright and Jac L. Goldstucker, ed., *New Ideas for Successful Marketing* (Chicago: American Marketing Association, 1966), pp. 46–68, here p. 51.

**8.** *Ibid.,* p. 51.

**9.** This system is spelled out in the author's "Phasing Out Weak Products," *Harvard Business Review,* March–April 1965, pp. 107–18.

# Price Decisions

In the mid-1970s, the British Parliament passed an act requiring its top museums to charge admission for the first time in history. This created a storm of protest. The proponents of the admission price supplied the following arguments: (1) the government could no longer afford all of the annual cost of $44 million to maintain the museums; (2) visitors from abroad were getting something free by not being charged; (3) visitors would better appreciate the institutions if they were charged; (4) museum directors would have the incentive to put on better shows and be more responsive; (5) the money could be used to finance extensions and better collections; and (6) museums on the Continent and in the United States charged admission fees. Those who opposed the admission price countered with the following arguments: (1) the charge would discourage attendance by slum children, students, and the old; (2) the cost of collecting the money—more attendants, gates at the entrance, more paperwork—would reduce much of the benefit; and (3) museums should not be forced to go into the entertainment business to please the public but should concentrate on presenting serious exhibits. Despite these counterarguments, the act was passed, and the British museums began to consider the best form of charging admission. They examined three major pricing approaches:

1. Museums could charge daily admission except for one day of the week. A free day would allow the poor or young to visit the museum. The admission charge could be varied for different visitors, being lower (or waived) for children and students, people over 65, handicapped people, and veterans.
2. Museums could encourage donations from visitors rather than

charge a fixed price. At the Metropolitan Museum in New York, people are encouraged to contribute $2.50, or anything they can. The voluntary nature of the donation allows the poor and young to enter without cost if they choose.

3. The museums could charge a small admission fee and also sponsor a membership plan which provides members with special benefits such as a monthly magazine, an annual report, invitation to exhibit openings, a discount at the gift shop, and a waiver of admission charges. The museum would establish different levels of membership and membership privilege, with dues going from $15 (regular membership) to $100 (special membership) to $500 (life membership).

The various museums considered these and other alternatives, and soon realized that the key issue was what objectives they were seeking to accomplish through the pricing mechanism.

Administrators of many nonprofit organizations have a strong interest in the price question. The U.S. Postal System periodically reviews whether postage rates could be increased to cover rising costs. Universities carefully consider how much they can raise tuition without losing students. Churches must carefully consider whether to raise money through membership fees, tithes, or special fundraising campaigns.

Prices are placed on a great range of goods and services and go by various names:

> Price is all around us. You pay RENT for your apartment, TUITION for your education, and a FEE to your physician or dentist. The airline, railway, taxi, and bus companies charge you a FARE; the local utilities call their price a RATE; and the local bank charges you INTEREST for the money you borrow. The price for driving your car on Florida's Sunshine Parkway is a TOLL, and the company that insures your car charges you a PREMIUM. The guest lecturer charges an HONORARIUM to tell you about a government official who took a BRIBE to help a shady character steal DUES collected by a trade association. Clubs or societies to which you belong may make a special ASSESSMENT to pay unusual expenses. Your regular lawyer may ask for a RETAINER to cover her services. The "price" of an executive is a SALARY; the price of a salesman may be a COMMISSION; and the price of a worker is a WAGE. Finally, although economists would disagree, many of us feel that INCOME TAXES are the price we pay for the privilege of making money![1]

In addition, price includes subsidiary decision elements. *List price* refers to the stated price of the product or service. *Actual price* may be greater or smaller, depending upon the presence of a *premium* or *discount.* Discounts can be extended to special groups such as senior citizens and students. If the buyers finance the purchase, they will be interested in the *credit* terms—that is, the monthly cost and time period of payments. Finally, the actual price might include additional charges representing *delivery, taxes,* and so on. All these elements can be varied as part of pricing strategy.

Although price is used here to describe the actual charge made by an organization, it is not the only cost to the customer. Adam Smith noted long ago: "The real price of everything, what everything really costs to the man who wants to acquire it, is the toil and trouble of acquiring it." In addition to the price, customers might have to face three other costs: *effort costs, psychic costs,* and *waiting costs.* Consider the problem of encouraging more middle-aged men to take a cardiovascular test. A prospect's resistance to doing this can be based on (1) an actual price of $100 for the test, (2) the time, cost, and trouble of traveling a long distance to the test center, (3) the fear of hearing bad news about one's heart condition, and (4) the waiting in the office for the test to begin. The cardiovascular center must recognize that its price of $100 is not the only deterrent, and that finding ways to reduce other consumer costs may lead to more purchases.[2]

In handling the complex issues in pricing, an organization should proceed through three stages. First, it should determine the *pricing objective,* whether it is to maximize profit, usage, fairness, or some other objective. Second, it should determine the *pricing strategy,* whether it should be cost-based, demand-based, or competition-based. Third, it should determine when and whether a *price change* is warranted and how to implement it.

---

## SETTING THE PRICING OBJECTIVES

The first thing an organization must decide in developing a price or pricing policy is the objectives that it wants to achieve. Often the objectives are in conflict, and a choice must be made. Consider the following statement made by a camp director:

> I want to keep my camp tuition fees as low as possible to enable more people to enjoy a Christian camping experience, but I also must keep the price high enough to insure that the camp will not lose money in the long run.[3]

In this case, the camp director is conflicted over the two opposing goals of *audience size maximization* and *cost recovery maximization.*

Four different pricing objectives can be distinguished: surplus maximization, cost recovery, market size maximization, and market disincentivization. Returning to the camp illustration, the camp may aim for surplus maximization on conferences, full cost recovery on weekend retreats, and market size maximization for its summer camp program.

One would think that nonprofit organizations never use the principle of profit or surplus maximization. This is not so. There are many situations in which a nonprofit organization will want to set its price to yield the largest possible surplus. Thus, a charity organization will set the price for attending a major benefit dinner with the objective of maximizing its receipts over its costs. A university whose faculty developed patented inventions will price these inventions to yield the maximum return to the university. A hospital may set up a dental clinic to maximize the profits on that service.

Surplus maximizing pricing requires the organization to estimate two functions—namely, the demand function and the cost function. These two functions are sufficient for deriving the theoretically best price. The demand function describes the expected quantity demanded per period $(Q)$ at various prices $(P)$ that might be charged. (See the earlier discussion in Chapter 11, p. 276.) Suppose the firm is able to determine through demand analysis that its *demand equation* is

$$Q = 1,000 - 4P \tag{13-1}$$

This says that demand is forecasted to be at most 1,000 units; and for every \$1 of price, there will be four fewer units sold. Thus, the number of units purchased at a price of, say, \$150, would be 400 units $[Q = 1,000 - 4(150)]$.

The cost function describes the expected total cost $(C)$ for various quantities per period $(Q)$ that might be produced. Suppose the company derived the following *cost equation* for its product:

$$C = 6,000 + 50Q \tag{13-2}$$

With the preceding demand and cost equations, the organization is in a position to determine the surplus maximization price. Needed are two more equations, both definitional in nature. First, *total revenue (R)* is equal to price times quantity sold:

$$R = PQ \tag{13-3}$$

Second, total surplus $(\$)$ is the difference between total revenue and total cost:

$$\$ = R - C \tag{13-4}$$

With these four equations, the organization is in a position to find the surplus maximizing price. The surplus equation (13–4) can be turned into a pure function of the price charged:

$$\$ = R - C$$
$$\$ = PQ - C$$
$$\$ = PQ - (6{,}000 + 50Q)$$
$$\$ = P(1{,}000 - 4P) - 6{,}000 - 50 \, (1{,}000 - 4P)$$
$$\$ = 1{,}000P - 4P^2 - 6{,}000 - 50{,}000 + 200P$$
$$\$ = -56{,}000 + 1{,}200P - 4P^2 \tag{13-5}$$

Equation (13–5) shows total surplus expressed as a function of the price that will be charged. The surplus maximizing price can be found in one of two ways. The researcher could use trial and error, trying out different prices to determine the shape of the profit function and the location of the maximum price. The surplus function turns out to be a parabola or hat-like figure and surplus reaches its highest point ($34,000) at a price of $150. At this price, the organization sells 400 units that produce a total revenue of $60,000.

This model for finding the surplus maximizing price, in spite of its theoretical elegance, is subject to four practical limitations:

1. The model shows how to find the price that maximizes short-run surplus rather than long-run surplus. There may be a tradeoff between short-run and long-run surplus maximization, as when clients get angry at the high price and eventually switch to other sellers.

2. There are other parties to consider in setting a price. The model only considers the ultimate consumers' response to alternative prices. Other groups that may respond are competitors, suppliers, middlemen, government, and the general public. A high price might lead competitors to raise their price, in which case the demand would be different than suggested by the demand function if it assumed no competitive reaction. Various suppliers—employees, banks, raw material producers—take the price to reflect the organization's ability to pay and they may raise their prices accordingly, in which case the cost function would be different than assumed with no supplier reaction. Middlemen who handle the product may have some strong feelings about the proper price. The government, acting in the interests of the public, might establish a price ceiling, and this may exclude the surplus maximizing price. Finally, the general public might complain about the organization if its price appears to be too high.

3. This pricing model assumes that price can be set independently of the other elements in the marketing mix. But the other elements of the marketing mix will affect demand and must be part of the demand function in searching for the optimal price. Thus, a ballet company can charge a higher price if it advertises extensively and builds up consumer interest.

4. This pricing model assumes that the demand and cost function can be accurately estimated. In the case of a new service, there is no experience upon which to base these estimates. Unless data are available on a similar service, estimates are likely to be highly subjective. Because the demand and cost equations are estimated with an unknown degree of error, the criterion of maximizing surplus may have to be replaced with the criterion of maximizing *expected* surplus. In any situation of risk and uncertainty, the pricing decision maker will want to see how sensitive the theoretically calculated price is to alternative estimates of the demand and cost functions.

## COST RECOVERY

Many nonprofit organizations seek a price that would help them recover a "reasonable" part of their costs. This is the idea behind the pricing of toll roads, postal services, and public mass transit services. Although the organizations could conceivably charge higher prices and increase their revenue (because of their monopolistic position), they do not want to incite an adverse reaction from the public or legislature.

How much cost should the organization try to recover through its pricing? Some organizations—such as universities and public mass transit organizations—aim at recovery of their operating costs. This would not provide money for expansion; they would rely on gifts or bond issues to raise the needed capital. Other organizations aim for *full cost recovery,* because they cannot rely on raising sufficient funds from other sources.

## USAGE MAXIMIZATION

Some nonprofit organizations—public libraries and museums, for example—want to maximize the total number of users of their service. These organizations feel that the users and society profit from their services. In this case, a zero price will attract the greatest number of users. Even here there can be exceptions. Consider the following situation:[4]

> Family planners in India initially believed the distribution of free contraceptives would lead to the greatest level of usage. However, they discovered two flaws in the reasoning. Some potential consumers interpreted the zero price to signify low quality and avoided the free brand. In addition, many retailers would not carry it or display it prominently because it did not yield them profit, with the result that fewer units were ultimately available to consumers.

In most situations, a low price normally stimulates higher usage *and* may produce more revenue in the long run. Weinberg advocates that theatres should set low ticket prices because this attracts a larger audience, many of whom would eventually make donations to the theatres that would more than make up for the lower ticket prices.[5]

## MARKET DISINCENTIVIZATION

Pricing might be undertaken for the objective of discouraging as many people as possible from purchasing a particular product or service. There are many reasons an organization might want to do this. It might consider the product to be bad for people; or it might want to discourage people from overtaxing a facility; or it might be trying to solve a temporary shortage; or it might want to discourage certain classes of buyers.

The purpose of the high government tax on cigarettes and liquor is to discourage the use of these products. But the price is never raised high enough because the government has come to rely on the substantial revenue produced by these taxes. A tax that is truly disincentivizing would yield the government no revenue and possibly create a large black market.

The Golden Gate Authority of San Francisco resorted to disincentive pricing when it learned that the famous bridge structure was overtaxed with traffic. A motorist was charged according to how many passengers were in the car, with the highest fee charged to cars with only the driver. This led to the formation of more driving car pools, although not as many as the authority had hoped.

Public mass transit companies have considered using disincentive pricing to discourage commuting during rush hours. These companies are in a weak financial situation because they have to finance the purchase of enough equipment to cover needs during the rush hours, while the equipment sits idle the rest of the time. The pricing possibilities include raising the fare during rush hours or offering a lower fare at off-hours.

The emergence of shortages of gasoline, natural gas, and electrical energy has increased the interest of organizations in disincentive pricing. The theoretical pricing model described earlier can be used to find the price that would achieve a specified reduction in usage.

---

## CHOOSING A PRICING STRATEGY

After the organization has defined its pricing objective, it can consider the appropriate pricing strategy. Pricing strategies tend to be cost oriented, demand oriented, or competition oriented.

### COST-ORIENTED PRICING

Cost-oriented pricing refers to setting prices largely on the basis of costs, either marginal costs or total costs including overhead. Two examples are markup pricing and cost-plus pricing. They are similar in that the price is determined by adding some fixed percentage to the unit cost. *Markup pricing* is commonly found in the retail trades where the retailer adds predetermined but different markups to various goods. Museum gift shops use markup pricing in pricing their various items. *Cost-plus pricing* is used to describe the pricing of jobs that are nonroutine and difficult to "cost" in advance, such as construction and military weapons development.

Nonprofit organizations vary in where they peg their price in relation to their costs. The American Red Cross charges a price for its blood that covers the "irreducible cost of recruiting, processing, collecting, and distributing the blood to the hospitals." On the other hand, several nonprofit organizations have histori-cally charged less than their costs (called cost-minus pricing). Tuitions at private colleges and ticket prices for symphony orchestras often cover less than 50 percent of the total cost of these services; the remaining costs are covered by donations and interests on endowment funds.

The most popular form of cost-oriented pricing is known as *breakeven analysis.* The purpose of breakeven analysis is to determine, for any proposed price, how many units of an item would have to be sold to cover fully the costs; this is known as the *breakeven volume.* To illustrate, the director of a summer camp wants to set a tuition for an eight-week summer session that would cover the total costs of operating the camp. Suppose the fixed costs of the camp—real estate taxes, interest changes, physical property, insurance, building maintenance, vehicle expense, and so on—are $200,000. This is shown on the breakeven chart in Figure 13–1 as a horizontal line at the level of $200,000. The variable cost for serving each camper—food, handicraft supplies, camper insurance, and so on— is $500 per camper. This is shown as the variable cost line, starting at $200,000 and rising $500 for each camper. Finally, the camp director initially considers charging $1,000 tuition per camper. This is shown as the total revenue line, which begins at $0 and rises $1,000 per camper. The number of campers needed to break even is determined by the intersection of the total revenue and the total costs curves, here 400 campers. If the camp fails to attract at least 400 campers at $1,000 each, it will suffer a loss varying with the number of campers attracted. If the camp attracts more than 400 campers at $1,000 each, it will generate profits. The camp director's task is to estimate whether it will be easy or difficult to attract 400 campers at a tuition of $1,000.

## FIGURE 13–1

### Illustration of Breakeven Analysis

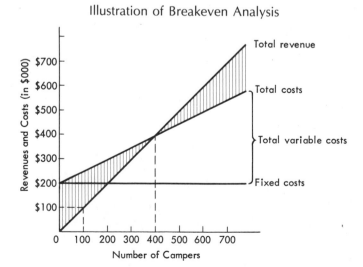

The breakeven volume can be readily calculated for any proposed price by using the following formula:

$$\text{Breakeven volume} = \frac{\text{Fixed cost}}{\text{Price } - \text{ Variable cost}} \tag{13-6}$$

Using the numbers in the previous example, we get:

$$\text{Breakeven volume} = \frac{\$200,000}{\$1,000 - \$500} = 400$$

On the other hand, if the camp director thought of charging $700 tuition, equation (13–6) indicates that he would have to attract 1,000 campers to break even.

Suppose the camp has a capacity to handle 1,000 campers and the camp director would like to attract that number. He can try to estimate a demand curve showing how many campers would be attracted at each price. Figure 13–2 shows the estimated demand curve. Accordingly, the $1,000 tuition would succeed in attracting 400 campers and allow the camp to break even. But the $700 tuition would attract only 800 campers, not 1,000 campers, and result in a loss. The camp director may decide to bear the loss, making it up through fundraising, in order to attract 800 campers. If he wants to attract 1,000 campers a $550 tuition would be required according to Figure 13–2, thus spelling an even larger loss.

Cost-oriented pricing is popular for a number of reasons. First, there is generally less uncertainty about costs than about demand. By basing the price on cost, the seller simplifies the pricing task considerably; there is no need to make frequent adjustments as demand conditions change. Second, when all organizations in the industry use this pricing approach, their prices are similar if their costs and markups are similar. Price competition is therefore minimized, which

**FIGURE 13–2**

Estimated Demand Curve for a Summer Camp

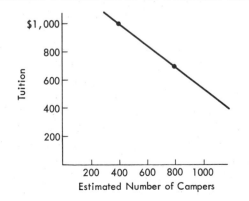

would not be the case if competitors paid attention to demand variations. Third, there is the feeling that cost-markup pricing is socially fairer to buyers and sellers. Sellers do not take advantage of buyers when the demand becomes acute; yet sellers earn a fair return on their investment. Thus the popularity of cost-oriented pricing rests on its administrative simplicity, competitive harmony, and social fairness.

### DEMAND-ORIENTED PRICING

Demand-oriented pricing looks at the condition of demand rather than the level of costs to set the price. Demand-oriented sellers estimate how much value buyers see in the market offer, and they price accordingly. Thus, a fine arts organization might set a ticket price of $20 for an Isaac Stern concert and $10 for a violin concert by a less-well-known performer. The premise is that price should reflect the *perceived value* in the consumer's head. A corollary is that an organization should invest in building up the perceived value of the offer if it wants to charge a higher price. Thus, a private college that builds a reputation for excellence in teaching and research can charge a higher tuition than can an average private college.

A common form of demand-oriented pricing is price discrimination, in which a particular product is sold at two or more prices. Price discrimination takes various forms.

Pricing that discriminates on a *customer basis* is illustrated when a museum charges a lower price to students than to the general public. Pricing that discriminates on a *product-version basis* occurs when the U.S. Postal System charges more for registered mail than for unregistered mail. Pricing that discriminates on a *place basis* occurs when a symphony charges more for front-row seats than back-row seats. Pricing that discriminates on a *time basis* occurs when a telephone company charges less for long-distance calls placed after business hours.

For price discrimination to work, certain conditions must exist.[6] First, the market must be segmentable, and the segments must show different intensities of demand. Second, there should be no chance that the members of the segment paying the lower price could turn around and resell the product to the segment paying the higher price. Third, there should be little chance that competitors will undersell the firm in the segment being charged the higher price. Finally, the cost of segmenting and policing the market should not exceed the extra revenue derived from price discrimination.

### COMPETITION-ORIENTED PRICING

When an organization sets its prices chiefly on the basis of what its competitors are charging, its pricing policy can be described as competition oriented. It may choose to charge (1) the same as competition, (2) a higher price, or (3) a lower price. The distinguishing characteristic is that the organization does *not* seek to maintain a rigid relation between its price and its own costs or demand. Its own costs or demand may change, but the organization maintains its price because competitors maintain their prices. Conversely, the same organization will change its prices when competitors change theirs, even if its own costs or demand have not altered.

The most popular type of competition-oriented pricing is where an organization tries to keep its price at the average level charged by the industry. Called *going-rate* or *imitative pricing*, it is popular for several reasons. Where costs are difficult to measure, it is felt that the going price represents the collective wisdom of the industry concerning the price that would yield a fair return. It is also felt that conforming to a going price would be least disruptive of industry harmony. The difficulty of knowing how buyers and competitors would react to price differentials is still another reason for this pricing.

Going-rate pricing primarily characterizes pricing practice in homogeneous product or service markets. The organization selling a homogeneous product has little choice about the setting of its price. Daring to charge more than the going rate would attract virtually no customers. Deciding to charge less is unnecessary either because the organization can sell its current output at the going price or because it fears that competitors will cut their prices too.

In markets characterized by *product differentiation*, organizations have more latitude in their price decision. Product differences serve to desensitize the buyer to existing price differentials. Organizations such as private universities try to establish themselves in a pricing zone with respect to their competitors, assuming the role of either a high-tuition university, a medium-tuition university, or a low tuition university. Their product and marketing programs are made compatible with this chosen pricing zone or vice versa. They respond to competitive changes in price to maintain their pricing zone.

## CHANGING THE PRICE

Pricing is a challenging decision when the organization is thinking about initiating a price change. The organization may be considering a *price reduction* in order to stimulate demand, to take advantage of lower costs, or to gain on weaker competitors. Or it may be considering a *price increase* in order to take advantage of strong demand or to pass on higher costs. Whether the price is to be moved up or down, the action will affect buyers, competitors, distributors, and suppliers, and can attract the interest of government as well. The success of the move depends critically on how the parties will respond. Yet their responses are among the most difficult things to predict. Thus, a contemplated price change carries great risks. Here we will examine methods of estimating probable customer reactions to price changes.

The traditional analysis of buyers' reactions to price change is based on the assumption that all buyers learn of the price change and take it at face value. The magnitude of their response to the price change is described by the concept of *price elasticity of demand.* This term refers to the ratio of the percentage change in demand (quantity sold per period) caused by a percentage change in price.[7] A price elasticity of − 1 means that sales rise (fall) by the same percentage as price falls (rises). In this case, total revenue is left unaffected. A price elasticity greater than − 1 means that sales rise (fall) by more than price falls (rises) in percentage terms; in this case, total revenue rises. A price elasticity lower than − 1 means that sales rise (fall) by less than price falls (rises) in percentage terms; in this case, total revenue falls.

Price elasticity of demand gives more precision to the question of whether the organization's price is too high or too low. For example, suppose the price elasticity for the Massachusetts Turnpike is − ½. This means that the Massachusetts Turnpike could raise the present toll and increase its total revenue. A 1 percent increase in the toll will lead to only a ½ percent decline in usage. If, on the other hand, the price elasticity of the Massachusetts Turnpike is − 2, it could increase its total revenue by lowering the toll. This is why it is critical to measure price elasticity.

In practice, price elasticity is extremely difficult to measure. There are definitional as well as statistical hurdles. Definitionally, price elasticity is not an absolute characteristic of the demand facing a seller but a conditional one. Price elasticity depends on the magnitude of the contemplated price change. It may be negligible with a small price change and substantial with a large price change. Price elasticity also varies with the original price level. A 5 percent increase over a current price of $1 may exhibit quite a different elasticity than a 5 percent increase over a current price of $2. Finally, long-run price elasticity is apt to be different from short-run elasticity. Buyers may have to stick with the seller immediately after a price increase because choosing a new seller takes time, but they eventually stop purchasing from him. In this case, demand is more elastic in the long run than in the short run. Or the reverse might happen; buyers drop a seller in anger after he increased prices but return to him later. The significance of this distinction between short-run and long-run elasticity is that sellers might not know how wise their price change is for a while.

Major statistical hurdles face the organization wishing to evaluate elasticity. Different techniques have evolved, none completely appropriate or satisfactory in all circumstances. We shall describe four techniques and illustrate them for a public mass transit company that is thinking about lowering its single ride fare from 50 cents to 25 cents to attract more riders.

**Direct attitude survey.**     The transit company can interview a sample of potential riders as to whether they would begin to use mass transit (instead of their automobile) if the fare were lowered from 50 cents to 25 cents. The percentage who said yes could then be applied against the known total number of potential riders to find the number of extra passengers this would mean.

**Statistical analysis of relationship between price and quantity.** This can take the form of either a historical or cross-sectional analysis. A historical analysis consists in observing how ridership has been affected in the past by rate reductions. A cross-sectional analysis consists in observing how ridership varies with the rates charged by transit companies in different cities.

**Market test.** The company can reduce its fare for one month to see how many new riders are attracted.

**Analytic inference.** The company can conjecture how many car riders are likely to find the lower fare to mean a significant saving to them without too much added inconvenience. Persons with lower incomes and longer distances to drive might be more amenable than persons with higher incomes and shorter distances to drive. The estimate would be built up by segments.

These are the major approaches to estimating demand elasticity.[8] They work with different degrees of reliability in different circumstances, and sometimes two or more of them are undertaken to gain increased confidence.

PERCEPTUAL FACTORS IN BUYERS' RESPONSE

In discussing elasticity, we assumed that price changes would be interpreted in a straightforward manner. This is not necessarily true. A *fare reduction* by a transit company might symbolize any number of things to consumers:

- The quality of the service will go down.
- The service has some fault.
- The transit company is in financial trouble and may not survive very long.
- The price will come down even further and it pays to wait.

A *fare increase* might also be given unexpected interpretations.

- The service is going to be improved.
- The service was given away at a cost below its true value.

These perceptual factors might lead consumers to react to a price change in a way opposite to that expected. If riders thought that a lower fare was going to mean poorer service, more crowding, and less safety, then it would not attract more riders. If students thought that a higher tuition suggested more quality and services, then a high tuition might actually increase the number of applicants. To the extent that price is associated with prestige, a higher price might stimulate demand.[9]

Often a nonprofit organization will maintain its list price but introduce "price specials" in order to stimulate increased buying. Promotional pricing can take many forms. Consider a theatre performing arts group that wants to attract a larger audience to its performances. Here are some promotional pricing options:

1. The theatre group can promote a series subscription that represents a saving over buying individual tickets to all of the performances. A popular way to express the savings is "See five plays for the price of four." Newman strongly favors discounts for subscription series on the grounds that the savings are a prime motivator for buying a subscription.[10] But Ryans and Weinberg, in a survey of subscription buyers for ACT in San Francisco, found that subscribers reported that the main reason for buying subscription series was not the savings but to make sure they went to the theatre more often. ACT abandoned the discount in the next season with no palpable impact on subscription sales.[11]

2. The theatre group can offer an "early bird" discount on the series subscription to those subscribing up to two months in advance of the first performance.

3. The theatre group can offer second tickets at half price. Andreasen and Belk found potential theatregoers reacting extremely favorably to this proposal. It tapped into the notion of bringing a date or friend along to the theatre.[12]

4. The theatre group can offer unsold tickets at half price on the day of the performance. The method is used successfully in New York City and results in selling many unused seats. The theatre not only gets the extra seat revenue it would have lost, but also the revenue from the sale of more drinks and candy during intermission.

Price promotions of various kinds have also been used by public transportation companies to attract more people to use mass transit instead of the automobile. Seattle introduced no-fare public transit service, and this led to a dramatic increase in ridership. The city of Denver ran an experiment of free fares for off-peak hours for one year, and ridership rose 45 percent during the period. After the fares were restored, two-thirds of the new riders were retained, and the experiment was considered successful. Other cities have introduced low fares at special times (off-peak hours, weekends), low fares in special locations (downtown, etc.), and low fares for specific groups (shoppers, students, the elderly), and generally found a good response to the promotional pricing of public transportation.[13]

---

## SUMMARY

Price is an important element of the marketing mix. Nonprofit organizations such as the U.S. Postal System, public mass transit companies, universities, hospitals, museums, charity organizations, and others must make difficult pricing decisions that will affect substantially the amount of money they raise.

An organization can be guided by any of four objectives in setting its price: surplus maximization, cost recovery, usage maximization, and market disincentivization. There is an elegant theoretical model for surplus maximizing pricing that utilizes demand and cost functions, but it may be too simple for practical pricing problems because of long-run considerations, other parties than the buyers, other marketing mix elements, and data estimation problems.

Price setting in practice is normally oriented to cost, demand, or competitive considerations. Organizations that are planning to change an existing price should take into account the price elasticity of demand and perceptual factors in buyer's response.

---

## QUESTIONS

**1.** A community organization in a black urban area has convinced several famous black entertainers to donate their performances at a fundraising concert in a city park. Discuss the pricing objective(s) you would recommend.

**2.** On what basis should city governments set the fine for normal parking violations? Analyze the appropriateness of each of the four basic pricing objectives to this situation.

**3.** Can an organization that has enough funds to eliminate the need to charge a price for its products or services charge a price that is too low? Give some examples of organizations that should avoid undercharging.

**4.** A day care center administrator is trying to decide which pricing strategy would be most appropriate—cost oriented, demand oriented, or competition oriented. Advise her on the strengths and weaknesses of each strategy.

**5.** Bus and subway fares, once kept low by massive government subsidies, are rising rapidly as costs rise and subsidies are reduced. What marketing recommendations would you make to mass transit agencies that must raise fares?

**6.** An art gallery is considering doubling its $1 admission fee and wonders what the effect of the price increase will be on attendance. Based on an understanding of the concept of price elasticity of demand, what suggestions would you make?

---

## NOTES

**1.** David J. Schwartz, *Marketing Today: A Basic Approach,* 3rd ed. (New York: Harcourt Brace Jovanovich, 1981), p. 271.

**2.** For an excellent discussion of how marketers can reduce effort cost, see Karen F. A. Fox, "Time As a Component of Price in Social Marketing," a paper presented at the American Marketing Association's Educators' Conference, Chicago, August 1980.

**3.** Quoted from article by Ben F. Doddridge, "Toward the Development of a Practical Approach for a Solution of the Pricing Dilemma," *Christian Camping International,* January–February 1978, pp. 19–22.

**4.** See T. R. L. Black and John Farley, "Retailers in Social Program Strategy: The Case of Family Planning," *Columbia Journal of World Business,* Winter 1977, pp. 33–43.

**5.** Charles Weinberg, "Marketing Mix Decision Rules for Nonprofit Organizations," in Jagdish Sheth, ed., *Research in Marketing,* Vol. 3 (Greenwich, Conn.: JAI Press, 1980), pp. 191–234.

**6.** See George Stigler, *The Theory of Price,* rev. ed. (New York: Macmillan, 1952), pp. 215ff.

**7.** In symbols,

$$Eqp = \frac{(Q_1 - Q_0)/\frac{1}{2}(Q_0 + Q_1)}{(P_1 - P_0)/\frac{1}{2}(P_0 + P_1)}$$

where:

$Eqp$    = elasticity of quantity sold with respect to a change in price
$Q_0, Q_1$ = quantity sold per period before and after price change
$P_0, P_1$ = old and new price

**8.** Still other approaches are outlined in Edgar A. Pessemier, "A New Way to Determine Buying Decisions," *Journal of Marketing* (October 1959), pp. 41–46; and Wayne A. Lee, "Techniques for Pretesting Price Decisions," in *Pricing: The Critical Decision,* Marketing Division Report No. 66 (New York: American Management Association, 1961).

**9.** The psychology of pricing has spawned a large literature. See Kent B. Monroe, "Buyers' Subjective Perceptions of Price," *Journal of Marketing Research* (February 1973), pp. 70–80.

**10.** Danny Newman, *Subscribe Now!* (New York: Publishing Center for Cultural Resources, 1977).

**11.** Adrian B. Ryans and Charles B. Weinberg, "Consumer Dynamics in Nonprofit Organizations," *Journal of Consumer Research,* September 1978, pp. 89–95.

**12.** Alan R. Andreasen and Russell W. Belk, "Broadening the Audience for the Arts," an unpublished paper, September 14, 1978.

**13.** See Christopher Lovelock and Jon Twichell, "Low Fare Transit Plans Gain Nationwide Trials," *Metropolitan,* May–June 1974, pp. 24–27.

# Distribution Decisions

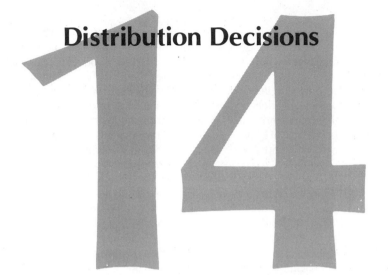

The University of Illinois is a multicampus system of education operated by the State of Illinois. It consists of several campuses, the main one located in Champaign–Urbana, Illinois. The system represents the State of Illinois' commitment to delivering affordable higher education to its citizens. Instead of operating one huge campus in Champaign–Urbana, it delivers quality educational programs in several locations designed to make education more available and accessible throughout the state.

The University of Illinois' administrators recognize the need to continually examine ways to improve the delivery of higher education to the citizens of Illinois. A committee was appointed to research the latest educational delivery systems. Ultimately the committee reported on five key developments to watch.

First, some private colleges are opening *satellite branches* in areas of strong population growth, thus presenting competition to the state system. For example, Roosevelt University, a 7,000-student private college in downtown Chicago, opened up satellite campuses in the Chicago suburbs of Arlington Heights, Waukegan, and Glenview. Each campus consists of a rented facility in which several programs leading to degrees are offered. Antioch College of Yellow Springs, Ohio, has gone further, operating over 30 campuses in the United States and abroad. There is even talk about some colleges eventually developing nation-wide systems of higher education, offering a standardized quality level, much like McDonald's.

Another development is the rapid growth of *telecourses*. A telecourse is a whole course of study available on videotape with accompanying workbooks. For example, Oakton Community College in suburban Chicago offers each semester telecourses in accounting, child psychology, and so on. The student registers at the college, buys a workbook, watches thirty 30-minute videotapes, and when ready, is examined. The videotapes can be viewed either on a local television station at scheduled times or on video cassettes located in select public libraries that have agreed to carry them. Telecourses, which were originally developed for shut-in populations, have attracted a growing number of student consumers, who find it more convenient to learn this way than to attend classes. One entrepreneur is thinking of making telecourses available at Holiday Inns so that traveling businesspeople could pursue their education by watching videotapes in their room at night.

A third development is the *electronic classroom* in which various classes in an area are hooked up electronically so that widely dispersed students can all listen to one instructor presenting a lecture. In the teleconferencing format, a student in any one of these classrooms could present a question to the instructor who would then respond. Ultimately, this educational delivery system might use holography:

> Imagine a "celebrity" biology teacher entering a holography studio at 8:45 A.M. At 9:00, he starts teaching and his three-dimensional image is transmitted simultaneously into 50 college classrooms, some of which may be thousands of miles away. Students in these classrooms see him, in three-dimensional full color, waving his hands, pacing the floor, furrowing his brow. In this manner, one gifted teacher instead of 50 average teachers presents the course, thereby providing better instruction with enormous cost savings . . . there would be phone hookups in each of the 50 classrooms to permit students to raise questions directly with the "holographic" professor.[1]

A fourth development is the emergence of *unusual classroom settings* for the conduct of education. The leading example is the railroad car classrooms operated by Adelphi University on the Long Island Railroad. Since 1971, commuters seeking master's degrees in business administration meet twice a week in special railway cars equipped as a classroom and take 50-minute classes coming to and leaving Manhattan. In this way, they earn six credit hours per semester at $129 per hour, and a degree in two years.

A fifth development is the emergence of unusual *classroom scheduling times.* Evening courses are well established and some colleges are beginning to offer late, late evening courses. One community college, located in a steel mill town, offers courses running from 1:00 A.M. to 3:00 A.M. to correspond to the end of a work shift. Their main problem is attracting instructors rather than students. Another college offers early, early morning courses from 6:00 A.M. to 8:00 A.M. for people to take before going to work. Northwestern University offers a Master of Management degree to qualified middle-managers who are able to attend all-day classes on alternate Fridays and Saturdays for two years. Mundelein College of Chicago operates a weekend college consisting of courses on Friday evening and all day Saturday and Sunday. Some colleges are providing company employees one-hour-long courses at lunchtime in factories and offices.

The committee showed that new opportunities were opening for delivering cost-effective educational services, and the university should not overrely on the traditional classroom. The committee noted with satisfaction that the University of Illinois is pioneering a major educational delivery system breakthrough, namely, the PLATO system, in which students learn by sitting at a computer terminal and working through programmed self-instruction at their own pace.

Every organization has to think through how it will make its products and services *available* and *accessible* to its target consumers. Marketers call this the *place* or *distribution* decision, and it is one of the key decisions in the marketing mix. Nonprofit marketers may use other terms for this decision. Public health practitioners speak about designing *health care delivery systems* such as neighborhood clinics, health maintenance organizations, hospitals, ambulatory care centers, and so on (see Exhibit 14–1). Organized religion can be thought of as operating a religious service distribution system:

> In order to put the church structure in a marketing context, one might view the national organization, the Evangelical Covenant Church of America, as the *manufacturer* or originator of the church's products; the regional offices throughout the country can be viewed as the *wholesaler;* and the individual churches, such as Faith Evangelical Covenant Church in Wheaton, might be viewed as the *retail outlets* for the church's services and products. As a "retailer" of the Evangelical Covenant Church of America's services and products, Faith Covenant Church is the part of the organization which comes face to face with the customer or members of the church and potential members. It is the individual "outlet" which can perform many of the critical functions needed to maintain members of the church and in fact, to increase its membership rolls.[2]

A host of other organizations face the problem of locating a set of facilities to serve optimally a spatially distributed population. This is illustrated in Figure 14–1 and characterized in the following terms:

> Hospitals must be located in geographic space to serve the people with complete medical care, and we must build schools close to the children who have to learn. Fire stations must be located to give rapid access to potential conflagrations, and voting booths must be placed so that people can cast their ballots without expending unreasonable amounts of time, effort, or money to reach the polling stations. Many of our states face the problem of locating branch campuses to serve a burgeoning and increasingly well educated population. In the cities we must create and locate playgrounds for the children. Many overpopulated countries must assign birth control clinics to reach the people with contraceptive and family planning information.[3]

**EXHIBIT 14–1.** The health care delivery system of the United States

Health care delivery systems are institutions that deliver preventative and curative health services to the public. In the past, Americans obtained health care services in two ways: by visiting a private physician or an emergency room of a local hospital. Some consumers sought out their pharmacists for advice on minor problems such as the common cold.

Today's health care services are available through several channels.

1. *Health maintenance organizations.* A growing number of people obtain their medical care through health maintenance organizations. By joining and paying a monthly fee, they can see staff doctors at any time and also get their hospitalization cost covered.

2. *Neighborhood health clinics.* Consumers in poorer neighborhoods often go to neighborhood health clinics for help. The clinic charges no fee or a low fee and has doctors ready to examine sick patients. The clinic is supported by public and/or private money.

3. *Hospital-based ambulatory care units.* Many hospitals have opened clinics in shopping areas or apartment buildings where people pay a fee for service. Since some of these patients will need hospital care, these clinics serve as feeder operations to the hospital.

4. *Group practices.* The vast majority of physicians now belong to private group practices, which give them the opportunity to structure their hours better and gain the advantages of expert colleagues. Patients pay a fee for service every time they visit their physician.

5. *Freestanding specialized service units.* Consumers can directly obtain specific services such as X-ray, blood tests, and minor surgery, in specialized units set up for these purposes. They pay fees which in most cases are reimbursed by their health insurance plans.

## FIGURE 14-1

### Assigning a Set of Facilities to Serve a Given Population

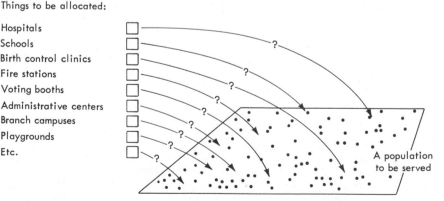

SOURCE: Ronald Abler, John S. Adams, and Peter Gould, *Spatial Organization* (Englewood Cliffs, N.J.: Prentice-Hall, 1971), p. 532.

Distribution channels must be chosen for persons as well as for goods and services. For example, a professional comedian seeking an audience before 1940 had available seven different channels: vaudeville outlets, special events, night-clubs, radio, movies, carnivals and circuses, and theatres. Then in the 1950s television became extremely popular and vaudeville disappeared as a distribution channel. Political candidates also must develop a plan to reach their market, namely, voters. Their scarce time and money must be carefully allocated among such channels as television, radio, billboards, major speaking engagements, coffees and teas, factory visits, and so on.

Channels are normally thought to describe routes for the forward movement of products. Recently, there has been talk about the development of *backward marketing channels.*

> The recycling of solid wastes is a major ecological goal. Although recycling is technologically feasible, reversing the flow of materials in the channel of distribution—marketing trash through a "backward" channel—presents a challenge. Existing backward channels are primitive, and financial incentives are inadequate. The consumer must be motivated to undergo a role change and become a producer—the initiating force in the reverse distribution process.[4]

## DECISION PROBLEMS IN DISTRIBUTION

We are now ready to examine the major decision problems that arise in designing and operating an efficient distribution system.

### THE LEVFL AND QUALITY OF CUSTOMER SERVICE

The first decision the marketer has to make is to determine the level and quality of service to offer to the target market. Each organization can visualize a maximum level of service that could be offered. Here are some examples:

- A public welfare department must distribute thousands of checks a year to people on public relief. The maximum level of service would be to mail a check daily to their homes or even to deliver the checks personally to avoid mail theft.
- A public library would render the maximum amount of service if it stood ready to receive calls for books and to deliver them within a few hours to the person's home.
- A city health department could dispatch doctors to the homes of sick patients upon call.
- A university could send a lecturer to any home or site upon request.

These solutions are oriented toward maximum consumer convenience. They are not practical because consumers would probably not pay for the extra convenience and the supplying organization could not afford the cost. Organizations have to find solutions that offer less consumer convenience in order to keep down the cost of distribution. Libraries and health departments, for example, can bring down their costs by offering their services in only a few locations and leaving the cost of travel to the consumers. They can cut down their costs still further by running a lean organization in which waiting time is borne mainly by customers instead of becoming idle time borne by the staff. If a health clinic had five doctors instead of ten, the doctors would be continuously busy while patients would absorb the cost of waiting. Thus, we see that organizations must begin their distribution planning with a concept of the level and quality of service they will offer.

### THE NUMBER AND LOCATION OF BRANCHES

The organization that decides to retail its service rather than directly deliver it has the further decision of how many retail outlets to operate. The most economical decision is to open a single outlet. By having one large library in a major city, duplication of books, staff, and building costs are avoided. Citizens gain in that they will find an extensive collection of books. They pay the price, however, of having to travel a longer distance. A system consisting of many library branches would attract more users. Most major cities compromise by building a central library and several branch libraries for the convenience of consumers. Some go further and operate bookmobiles, which are mobile libraries that park in different neighborhoods on different days and make books available to consumers.

The cost of running a state university is normally minimized by operating a single campus. Years ago, the University of California was located in Berkeley, California, and the University of Wisconsin was located in Madison, Wisconsin. Gradually these universities opened additional branches, partly to offer more convenience to residents in other parts of the state and partly to keep a single campus from becoming overly large and impersonal. Today the State University of New York (SUNY) operates 64 campuses! Once these universities decided to distribute their product throughout the state, they encountered all the classic distribution problems faced by business firms: how many branch locations to establish, how large should they be, where should they be located, and what specialization should take place at each branch.

### THE DESIGN OF FACILITIES

Nonprofit organizations have to make decisions on the "look" of their facilities, because the look can affect customers' attitudes and behavior. Consider how the "atmosphere" of a hospital can affect patients. Many older hospitals have an institutional look, with long narrow corridors, drab wall colors, and badly worn furniture, all contributing a depressed feeling to patients who are already depressed about their own condition. Newer hospitals are designed with colors, textures, furnishings, and layouts that reinforce positive patient feelings. They have circular or rectangular layouts with the nursing station in the center, permitting nurses to monitor patients better. Single-care units are replacing the tradi-

**EXHIBIT 14–2.** The Boston Museum of Fine Arts opens a satellite museum

Nonprofit organizations such as the U.S. Post Office, public libraries, and state colleges all operate branches. It is quite something new, however, when a major arts museum decides to open a branch. In the mid-seventies, the Boston Museum of Fine Arts was looking for new ways to expose larger audiences to art. The museum was located five miles from downtown Boston. The idea arose that the museum should consider bringing art to where the people are, in addition to bringing people to where the art is. The museum decided to open a branch in the new renovated Faneuil Hall marketplace section of Boston. Faneuil Hall, a three-building historic landmark in downtown Boston, had recently been redeveloped into a retail mall of many boutiques, food stalls, and bistros, and has become one of the great attractions in Boston, with thousands of people promenading the area daily. The museum rented several adjoining rooms on the upper floor of one of the buildings on a short-term lease basis. It opened its doors on June 2, 1979. The opening show was called "Faces of 5,000 Years" and presented some extremely fine and varied materials—paintings, busts, miniature objects— selected from the museum's vast collection. A dramatic sign in the mall called attention to the museum's existence on the upper floor. Tens of thousands of people, many of whom had never gone to the Boston Museum of Fine Arts, or any museum, dropped in to see the exhibits. A box for donations (suggested amount of $1) stood at the door. Questionnaires were placed at the exit for people who wished to make suggestions or record their reactions. The overwhelming number of visitors reported satisfaction. This branch represented a bite-size museum where a person could spend a pleasant half hour enjoying some great art treasures. It offered a qualitatively different experience than the huge museum five miles away with its endless corridors and treasures. The success of this branch led the museum managers to think about other possible sites where art could be brought to the people.

---

tional semiprivate rooms, based on the overwhelming preference for single-care units by both patients and physicians.

One of the most dramatic changeovers in atmosphere has occurred in abortion clinics.[5] When abortions were performed illegally, women would enter a depressing office with a single table on which the abortion would be performed. The sight of the office contributed to the patient's feeling of risk and sense of guilt and shame. Today's abortion clinics resemble normal doctor's offices with a comfortable waiting room and a competent receptionist who shows great understanding in dealing with the patient's needs and fears. The patient feels that she is being professionally supported in this difficult moment in her life.

Marketing planners in the future will use atmospherics as consciously and skillfully as they now use price, advertising, personal selling, public relations, and other tools of marketing. *Atmospherics* describes the conscious designing of space to create or reinforce specific effects on buyers, such as feelings of well-being, or safety, or intimacy, or awe.[6]

An organization that is designing a service facility for the first time faces four major design decisions. Suppose a city wishes to build a public art museum. The four decisions are as follows:

> 1. *What should the building look like on the outside?* The building can look like a Greek temple (as many museums have looked in the past), a villa, a glass skyscraper, or another genre. It can look awe-inspiring, ordinary, or intimate. The decision will be influenced by the type of art collection and the message that the museum wants to convey about art in general.
>
> 2. *What should be the functional and flow characteristics of the building?* The planners have to consider whether the museum should consist of a few large rooms or many small ones. They also have to consider whether the major exhibits and best-known art works should be located near the entrance or at the other end of the building. The rooms and corridors must be designed in a way to handle capacity crowds so that people do not have to wait in long lines and experience congestion.
>
> 3. *What should the museum feel like on the inside?* Every building conveys a feeling, whether intended or unplanned. The planners have to consider whether the museum should feel awesome and somber, or bright and modern, or warm and intimate. Each feeling will have a different effect on the visitors and their overall satisfaction with the museum.
>
> 4. *What materials would best support the desired feeling of the building?* The feeling of a building is conveyed by visual cues (color, brightness, size, shapes), aural cues (volume, pitch), olfactory cues (scent, freshness), and tactile cues (softness, smoothness, temperature). The museum's planners have to choose colors, fabrics, and furnishings that create or reinforce the desired feeling.

The same questions arise for other organizations such as a post office, social service agency, unemployment office, college science building, city police station, and so on. Each facility will have a look that may add or detract from consumer satisfaction and employee performance. The latter point deserves special emphasis. Since the employees work in the facility all day long, the facility should be designed to support them in performing their work with ease and cheerfulness. Granted, many nonprofit organizations are financially weak and cannot afford the facilities that would be desired in principle. But the organization should pay attention to small details of the present facility and take even minor steps to improve the comfort or effectiveness of the facility. Every facility conveys something to the users about the attitudes felt toward them by the service providers.

### The Use and Motivation of Middlemen

In deciding to establish outlets for its services, the organization can operate its own branches ("company branches") or contract for the services of middlemen. A *middleman* is defined as "a business concern that specializes in performing operations or rendering services directly involved in the purchase and/or sale of goods in the process of their flow from producer to consumer."[7] Familiar types of middlemen include wholesalers, retailers, and brokers, among others. But why should an organization relinquish any of the selling or supplying activities to middlemen? The delegation usually means relinquishing some control over how and to whom the products are sold. Because the use of middlemen is very common, there must be certain major advantages. Some of them are described below.

Many organizations lack the financial resources to carry out a full program of direct marketing.

> The government of India adopted family planning as an official cause and set up a department to disseminate birth control information and contraceptives. The department's goal was to make contraceptives available to the smallest, remotest villages of a vast nation.[8] The solution took the form of engaging the distribution services of some of the largest packaged-goods companies in India because of their reach into the remotest corners of India. For example, the government used the intricate distribution system of Lever Brothers of India and saved itself the tremendous cost of building its own pipeline to the final markets. In choosing types of retailers, their objective was to make contraceptives maximally available and accessible to target users. They eventually elected to work with the following retailers: (a) health clinics, (b) barbers, (c) field workers, (d) retail stores, and (e) vending machines. By placing contraceptives in these channels, the Indian government felt that potential users would have no difficulty finding the product.

Even if an organization has the funds to build its own distribution channel to the final markets, it might not be able to do it as cheaply as through using an existing distribution system. The cost of distributing contraceptives through India is low because the middlemen carry many other products which share in the cost of the distribution network. In a one-product distribution system, all the cost would be borne by that product.

Nor should the organization build its own distribution system if it can put its funds to better use. Thus, the number of births averted may be higher if the Indian government spends its funds to advertise family planning nationwide rather than using all its money to set up efficient distribution.

The case for using middlemen would rest on their superior efficiency in the performance of basic marketing tasks and functions. Marketing intermediaries, through their experience, specialization, contacts, and scale offer the producing organization more than it can usually achieve on its own.

The decision to use middlemen involves the organization in a number of further decisions. The first is the problem of choosing the best middlemen from the large number who are available. The Indian government had to decide which of several large packaged-goods companies could do the best job. It might decide to use only one of them *(exclusive distribution),* a few of them *(selective distribution),* or many of them *(intensive distribution).* But it might find that a desired distributor is not willing to accept the assignment. Or the distributor might handle the product only if given exclusive distribution. Or the distributor might handle the product only if it receives better financial terms than are being offered. Thus the first problem is to select and interest good distributors.

The organization must follow this up by carefully establishing the terms and responsibilities of the distributors. This is called the *trade-relations mix* and consists of the price policies, conditions of sale, territorial rights, and specific services to be performed by each party. For example, an increasing number of public welfare agencies have decided not to mail checks directly to welfare recipients (because of mailbox theft) but to deposit these checks in bank accounts set up for the welfare recipients. This distribution solution requires clarifying how much the banks will charge for checking services, what other services they will offer, and what rights the welfare recipients have.

The next requirement is that the organization provide continuous motivation of its middlemen to do their best job. This may require frequent contact, sales training, joint setting of quotas, and bonuses. Without a plan to provide motivation to the middlemen, they may have a tendency to neglect the organization's product in favor of the many other products they handle.

The final need is to evaluate middlemen performance periodically. Those middlemen who do not perform according to their market potential can be singled out for training in an effort to help them improve their performance; otherwise they might have to be dropped. For example, the U.S. Treasury Department uses commercial banks to retail its bonds. If it wished, it could also invite the U.S. Postal System to become an agent for selling U.S. bonds. Periodically, the U.S. Treasury Department may want to evaluate alternative systems and specific middlemen within each system to see how efficient they are at selling U.S. bonds.

### The Use of Facilitating Marketing Intermediaries

The last step in designing a distribution system is for the organization to engage the services of *facilitating intermediaries* where they are required. Facilitating intermediaries differ from middlemen in that they are not involved in direct selling or negotiation but provide ancillary marketing services, such as shipping, warehousing, financing, advertising, marketing research, and so on. In the case of each of these functions, the organization must decide whether to hire from the outside or provide its own service internally. The organization may design its own marketing research survey or hire a marketing research firm. It may design its own advertisements or hire an advertising agency. The organization must take into account the quality, cost, and other aspects of running its own service versus buying it from the outside. Typically, an organization can perform its own service for less but at the sacrifice of some quality.

---

## SUMMARY

Distribution, the third major variable in the marketing mix, is as relevant to nonprofit organizations as it is to profit organizations. An organization's product or service is typically removed in space from the location of the consumer; and it may be removed in time according to when the consumer would like to use it. This creates a storage and/or distribution problem, the costs of which might be borne entirely by the organization, the consumers, or both.

To design an efficient distribution, delivery, or dissemination system, an organization must first decide on the level and quality of service to offer to its target market. Usually, it cannot afford to maximize the customer's convenience by direct delivery so it resorts to creating one or more retail branches. Its second problem is to decide on the number and location of these branches in relation to the locations of the final consumers. Its third problem is to design the facilities in a way that contributes to customers' and employees' satisfaction. Atmospherics describes the conscious designing of space to create or reinforce salutary effects on buyers. Its fourth problem is to decide on how much of the distribution task should be subcontracted to middlemen. The final problem is to decide how much of the services of facilitating intermediaries to contract for and how much to do internally.

## QUESTIONS

**1.** A city school district with three high schools has experienced steady declines in enrollment and anticipates that one high school will be closed to reduce expenditures. What are the likely effects of this action on students? On the district?

**2.** The Chicago Lung Association offers smoking cessation classes. What factors should be considered in deciding where to hold these classes? What middlemen could be used to carry out these classes?

**3.** U.S. Congresspeople often have more than one staff office within their districts in order to have more visibility and closer contact with their constituents who come to these offices for help in dealing with government agencies. Evaluate this distribution strategy.

**4.** The congressional offices described in question 3 also serve as backward marketing channels. Explain how they function in this way. What other backward marketing channels are available to perform the same purposes?

**5.** Describe the distribution systems of the U.S. Postal Service for (a) letter mail, (b) large packages, (c) stamps, and (d) passports. What factors account for the substantial differences?

**6.** A Planned Parenthood clinic would like to attract more of the sexually active teenagers who could use their counseling and other services. What recommendations would you make to them about the appropriate atmospherics to appeal to teenagers?

## NOTES

**1.** See Philip Kotler, "Educational Packagers: A Modest Proposal," *Futurist,* August 1978, pp. 239–42.
**2.** Quoted from an unpublished term paper on the Faith Covenant Church of Wheaton written by Mark F. Pufundt at Northwestern University, 1980.
**3.** Ronald Abler, John S. Adams, and Peter Gould, *Spatial Organization* (Englewood Cliffs, N.J.: Prentice-Hall, 1971), pp. 531–32.

**4.** William G. Zikmund and William Stanton, "Recycling Solid Wastes: A Channels-of-Distribution Problem," *Journal of Marketing,* July 1971, p. 34.

**5.** Donald W. Ball, "An Abortion Clinic Ethnography," in William J. Filstead, ed., *Qualitative Methodology* (Chicago: Markham, 1970).

**6.** For more details, see Philip Kotler, "Atmospherics as a Marketing Tool," *Journal of Retailing,* Winter 1973–74, pp. 48–64.

**7.** *Marketing Definitions: A Glossary of Marketing Terms,* compiled by the Committee on Definitions of the American Marketing Association, Ralph S. Alexander, chairman (Chicago: American Marketing Association, 1960).

**8.** Nicholas J. Demerath, "Organization and Management Needs of a National Family Planning Program: The Case of India," *Journal of Social Issues,* No. 4 (1967), pp. 179–93.

# Sales Force Decisions

It was a fair, of sorts.

Booths were set up throughout the room, and low-key barkers tried to lure people in with slide shows, picture displays, pins, pamphlets, and promises of the good life.

All the people visiting the fair were doctors, or doctors-soon-to-be. And all the barkers and booth-tenders were from little towns. Little towns in Illinois that desperately need doctors.

It was the Illinois State Medical Society's seventh annual job fair Sunday at the Sheraton Oak Brook Hotel, an event that each little town hoped would net them a doctor.

Finding doctors for small towns is not a problem unique to Illinois—nationwide, young doctors are reluctant to set up practices in rural or semi-rural areas.

"It's not that they can't make money in my town," says R. V. Livengood, of Danville, who was looking for a family physician. "We'll guarantee a young doctor a gross income of $70,000 the first year and give him office space rent-free for the first six months.

"But the problem is doctors can go anywhere, and most of them want the mountains or the ocean, or they want to be associated with big hospitals. That's why they're not coming so easily to little towns in the Midwest.

"But you can make a good living in Danville, I tell them. It's a good place to practice good medicine. If they are single, I tell them, why, there's Champaign not too far away with all sorts of good-looking coeds. And if they are married, why, Danville is a great place to live and raise your kids, no problem with traffic or parking, and nobody will shoot you on Saturday night."

"We need two family physicians and a general surgeon," says Gary Deer, administrator for the Illini Community Hospital in Pittsfield, population 4,100. "We've advertised in magazines and got some recruiters looking for us. And I've had a few nibbles here.

"There are so many doctors who want the bright lights and so many little towns looking for doctors, that there aren't enough doctors who want small-town life to go around.

"But I tell them if a family physician moved to Pittsfield today, he'd have a waiting room full tomorrow morning. I'm sure there are a lot of unhappy physicians in Chicago and my job is finding one and bringing him home."

"We really need a nice young doctor; we really do," says Dr. Dorothy Hubler, 63, of Casey, Ill., which has a population of 3,600. "There's a lot of work to be done, and we are really tired. Look at the lines under my eyes. I work 60 hours a week.

"The doctors in Casey are eager for a new one and will help him get set up in practice. We need help."

Dr. Hubler was one of eight enthusiastic citizens of Casey who showed up at the fair sporting "Love Casey" pins.

They are trying to find a doctor to help the three aging doctors at the Casey Medical Center and Nursing Home. With them, they brought photos of their town, of the Casey National Bank, of the grain elevator, of the Methodist Church.

"Our doctors are gaining in years, so we need a young one who can help Dr. Hubler and the two others," says Don Hutton, chairman of the Casey Medical Center and owner of Hutton's Auto Parts.

"We'll fly them down to take a look at our little town. If a young doctor wants to live in a small town and wants to work, really put something into it, then he can make mucho dollars in Casey and live the good life."

"We came through snow, sleet, rain, and ice up here to find a doctor," says town pharmacist Tom Perillo. "That shows you how much we want one. Maybe we'll just have to tie one up and take him back by force."

SOURCE: "Towns Try to Make a Doctor Say 'Ah!'", *Chicago Tribune,* Monday, December 11, 1978, Section 1, p. 14.

In this chapter, we want to look at the *boundary personnel* of an organization, namely, those members of the organization who deal with people outside of the organization. Boundary personnel fall into two groups. The first are *sales personnel,* those whose major job is to sell something to others. Major examples of sales personnel in the nonprofit area are:

- *recruiters* (college recruiters, military recruiters, job recruiters)
- *fundraisers* (development officers, door-to-door callers, telephone solicitors)
- *change agents* (agricultural extension agents, outreach workers, family planners, community organizers)
- *vote-seekers* (politicians, lobbyists)

The second group consists of *service personnel,* those who provide the organization's services to members of the public. The group includes:

- *operators* (bus drivers, librarians, U.S. income tax advisors, ticket takers, museum guards)
- *protective personnel* (policemen, firemen)
- *repair personnel*
- *receptionists*

Although the job of service personnel is service, it is important that they are also trained to be client oriented. If service personnel are cold or rude, they can undermine all the marketing work done to attract customers. If they are friendly and warm, they can increase customer satisfaction and loyalty.

In this chapter we will concentrate on sales personnel and the problems of running an effective sales force. Personal selling is the most effective tool at certain stages of the buying process, particularly in building up preference, conviction, and action on the part of buyers. This is because personal selling has three distinctive qualities in comparison to advertising:[1]

> 1. *Personal confrontation.* Personal selling involves an alive, immediate, and interactive relationship between two or more persons. Each party is able to observe each other's needs and characteristics at close hand and make immediate adjustments.
>
> 2. *Cultivation.* Personal selling permits all kinds of relationships to spring up, ranging from a matter-of-fact selling relationship to a deep personal friendship. In most cases, the sales representative must use art to woo the buyer. The sales representative at times will be tempted to put on pressure to close the sale, but normally will keep the customer's long-run interests at heart.
>
> 3. *Response.* Personal selling makes the buyer feel under some obligation for having listened to the sales talk or using up the sales representative's time. The buyer has a greater need to attend and respond, even if the response is a polite "thank you."

These distinctive qualities come at a cost. Personal selling is the organization's most expensive customer contact tool, costing organizations an average of $60 a sales call in 1978.[2] Even when the sales force consists of volunteers, there is a cost of recruiting, training, and motivating them and their time should be used wisely.

We will examine the major decisions in building and managing an effective sales force as part of the total marketing mix. These steps are shown in Figure 15–1 and examined in the following sections.

## FIGURE 15–1

Major Steps in Sales Force Management

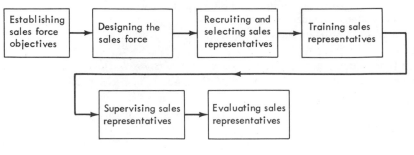

## ESTABLISHING SALES FORCE OBJECTIVES

The sales force is part of the marketing mix and, as such, is capable of achieving certain marketing objectives better than other tools in the marketing mix. Sales representatives can perform as many as six tasks for their organization:

1. *Prospecting.* Sales representatives can find and cultivate new customers.
2. *Communicating.* Sales representatives can communicate useful information about the organization.
3. *Selling.* Sales representatives can be effective in the art of "salesmanship"—approaching, presenting, answering objections, and closing sales.
4. *Servicing.* Sales representatives can provide various services to customers—consulting on their problems, rendering technical assistance, and expediting service times.
5. *Information gathering.* Sales representatives can supply the organization with useful market research and intelligence.
6. *Allocating.* Sales representatives can advise the organization on how to allocate scarce services to customers in times of service shortages.

The organization has to decide on the relative importance of these different tasks and coach their sales representatives accordingly. For example, college recruiters spend most of their time in prospecting, communicating, and selling. Lobbyists, on the other hand, tend to emphasize communicating, servicing, and information gathering. Each organization normally gets its representatives to set specific goals for each of their activities so that their performance against these goals can be measured.

## DESIGNING THE SALES FORCE

Given the objectives, the organization has to make basic decisions on (1) sales force strategy, (2) sales force structure, (3) sales force size, and (4) sales force compensation.

## SALES FORCE STRATEGY

Sales force strategy deals with determining how best to reach prospects and customers, given the marketing objectives. Suppose a college is seeking to increase its grants from the Ford Foundation. It wants to (1) "sell" the Ford Foundation on funding some immediate proposals and (2) build up a stronger relationship with the Ford Foundation for the future. The college can use one or more of five sales force strategies to meet its objectives:

1. *Sales representative to buyer.* Here a college development officer talks to a Ford Foundation officer in person or over the phone.
2. *Sales representative to buyer group.* Here a college development officer makes a sales presentation to a group of Ford Foundation executives.
3. *Sales team to buyer group.* Here a team of people from the college (president, professor, college development officer) makes a sales presentation to a group of Ford Foundation executives.
4. *Conference selling.* Here a college development officer arranges a meeting between people from the college and Ford Foundation executives to discuss mutual problems and opportunities.
5. *Seminar selling.* Here a team of experts from the college present an educational seminar to Ford Foundation executives about recent state-of-the-art developments. The college provides the free seminar to improve relations with the foundation.

We see that the sales representative does not always do the whole selling job. The sales representative may act as the "account manager" who initiates and facilitates interactions between various people in the two organizations. Selling is increasingly becoming a matter of teamwork, requiring the support of other personnel: (1) *Top management* (such as the president) is increasingly getting involved in the sales process, especially when *major sales* are at stake. (2) *Technical people* (such as professors) often work with the sales representatives to supply expert information needed by the customer before, during, or after the purchase. (3) *Service representatives* provide information, clerical work, and other services to the customer.

Once the organization clarifies the type of selling it needs, it has a choice between using (1) paid employees, (2) volunteers, and (3) temporary paid help. All three may be used to advantage. Thus, Stanford University's Office of Development consists of a small employee staff of professional fundraisers who raise money directly; a very large group of alumni who volunteer their services in fundraising drives; and temporary help as needed to make phone calls, stuff envelopes, and so on.

## SALES FORCE STRUCTURE

Part of sales force strategy is how to structure the organization's sales force to achieve maximum market coverage and effectiveness. This is relatively simple if the organization provides only one service to one type of customer who is found in many locations. The answer would be a territorial-structured sales force. If the organization sells many different services to many types of customers, it might have to develop product-structured or customer-structured sales forces. We shall review here these alternative sales force structures.

**Territorial-structured sales force.**    In the simplest sales organization, each sales representative is assigned a territory in which to sell the organization's services. Thus, the U.S. Army operates army recruiting stations in different cities and each station is responsible for planning and attracting enlistments in its area. Likewise, the Easter Seal Society raises money through regional, state, and local organizations, each responsible for fundraising in its respective territory.

A territorially structured sales force has a number of advantages. First, it results in a very clear definition of the sales person's responsibilities. As the only salesperson working the territory, he or she bears the credit or blame for area sales to the extent that personal selling effort makes a difference. This tends to encourage a high level of effort, especially when management is able to gauge fairly accurately the area's sales potential. Second, responsibility for a definite territory increases the sales representative's incentive to cultivate local business and personal ties. These ties tend to improve the quality of the sales representative's selling effectiveness and personal life. Third, travel expenses are likely to be relatively small, since each sales representative's travel takes place within the bounds of a small geographical territory.

Along with this structure goes a hierarchy of sales management positions. Several territories will be supervised by a district sales manager, several districts will be supervised by a regional sales manager, and the several regions will be supervised by a national sales manager or sales vice president. Each higher level sales manager takes on increasing marketing and administrative work in relation to the time available for selling. In fact, sales managers are paid for their management rather than selling skills.

**Product-structured sales force.**    Organizations that produce a large number of products and services often prefer to organize the selling activity by product line. Harvard University, for example, allows each of its major schools—business, law, medicine, and so on—to do its own fundraising and recruitment. Personnel within each school can do a good job of representing it to prospects and customers. Specialization of the sales force by product is warranted where the organization's products are technically complex, highly unrelated, and/or numerous.

The major disadvantage is that of higher travel costs and possible sales redundancy. Thus, instead of Harvard sending one development officer to the Ford Foundation to represent all of the proposals submitted by Harvard, several development officers from Harvard's different schools will converge on the Ford Foundation. Each will come with more knowledge of the relevant proposals at the cost of high sales force expense.

**Customer-structured sales force.**    Organizations often specialize their sales forces according to customer type. For example, Cornell University fundraisers are specialized by donor category: foundations, corporations, government agencies, alumni, and wealthy donors. By working full time to raise money from (say) corporations, the corporate fundraiser gets to know them well and to use his or her time more effectively. Furthermore, the person needed for this job may have higher skill requirements than someone who raises money from alumni. This is better than using a highly skilled person to raise money from all donor sources.

The major disadvantage of customer-structured sales forces arises if the various types of customers are scattered evenly throughout the country. This means an overlapping coverage of territories, which is always more expensive.

**Complex sales force structures.**    When an organization sells a wide variety of products to many types of customers over a broad geographical area, it often combines several principles of sales force structure. Thus, the University of Chicago has a fundraising staff with personnel specialized by territory, type of school, and type of donor. Each fundraiser has a line or dotted-line reporting relation to the development office and various other parts of the university.

### SALES FORCE SIZE

Once the organization clarifies its sales force strategy and structure, it is ready to consider the question of sales force size. Sales representatives are among the most productive and expensive assets in a company. Increasing their number will increase both sales and costs.

Most organizations use the *workload approach* to establish the size of their sales force.[3] The method consists of the following steps:

1. Customers are grouped into segments according to their sales potential.
2. The desirable call levels (number of days on an account per year) are established for each segment.
3. The number of accounts in each segment are multiplied by the corresponding call level to arrive at the total workload in sales calls per year.
4. The average number of call days a sales representative has per year is determined, allowing for other tasks, holidays, and so on.
5. The number of sales representatives needed is determined by dividing the total number of call days required by the average annual number of calls a sales representative can make.

To illustrate, suppose a college recruiting office determines that the recruitment target will require calling on 100 class A high schools, 80 class B high schools, and 40 class C high schools each year. To be effective, a recruiter will have to spend two days at a class A high school, one day at a class B high school, and one half day at a class C high school. Furthermore, each recruiter has only sixty call days available per year. Thus, the high schools will require 300 call days ($100 \times 2 + 80 \times 1 + 40 \times \frac{1}{2}$), and the college will require a staff of five recruiters ($300 \div 60$).

In the case of college fundraising, a similar analysis can be undertaken. Given the campaign sales target and the potential of different donor groups, the college can figure out how many fundraisers it needs. Most colleges tend to hire too few fundraisers rather than too many, in that an additional competent fundraiser can usually add more money to the college's coffers than he or she costs.

### SALES FORCE COMPENSATION

In order to attract the desired number of paid sales representatives, the organization has to develop an attractive compensation plan. Sales representatives would like a plan that provides income regularity, reward for above-average performance, and fair payment for experience and longevity. An ideal compensation plan from management's point of view would emphasize control, economy, and simplicity.

Management must determine the level and components of an effective compensation plan. The *level of compensation* must bear some relation to the "going market price" for the type of sales job and type of organization. Nonprofit organizations tend to pay less than business firms, and this may result in attracting less skilled people and achieving lower results. Yet nonprofits feel that they can attract good people who are motivated by nonmonetary considerations and a belief in the value of their work.

The organization must also determine the *components of compensation*— a fixed amount, a variable amount, expenses, and fringe benefits. The *fixed amount,* which might be salary or a drawing account, is intended to satisfy the sales representatives' need for some stability of income. The *variable amount,* which might be commissions or bonus, is intended to stimulate and reward greater effort. *Expense allowances* are intended to enable the sales representatives to undertake necessary selling costs, such as travel, taking prospects to lunch, and so on. And *fringe benefits,* such as paid vacations, sickness or accident benefits, pensions, and life insurance, are intended to provide security and job satisfaction.

Fixed and variable compensation, taken alone, gives rise to three basic types of sales force compensation plans—straight salary, straight commission, and combination salary and commission. In industry, most plans are combination salary and commission, with 70 percent going to salary. In nonprofit organizations, most salespeople are on straight salary. Army recruiters, for example, who are especially effective tend to be rewarded with badges and recognition rather than extra money.

---

## RECRUITING AND SELECTING SALES REPRESENTATIVES

Having established the strategy, structure, size, and compensation of the sales force, the organization has to manage the steps of recruiting and selecting, training, supervising, and evaluating sales representatives.

## IMPORTANCE OF CAREFUL SELECTION

At the heart of a successful sales force operation is the selection of effective sales representatives. The performance levels of an average and a top sales representative are quite different. A survey of over five hundred companies revealed that 27 percent of the sales force brought in over 52 percent of the sales.[4] Beyond the differences in sales productivity are the great wasted cost in hiring the wrong persons. Of the 16,000 sales representatives who were hired by the surveyed companies, only 68 percent still worked for their company at the end of the year, and only 50 percent were expected to remain through the following year.

The financial loss due to turnover is only part of the total cost. The new sales representative who remains with the organization receives a direct income averaging around half of the direct selling outlay. If he or she receives $14,000 a year, another $14,000 may go into fringe benefits, expenses for travel and entertainment, supervision, office space, supplies, and secretarial assistance. Consequently, the new sales representative should be capable of creating sales on which the amount left after other expenses at least covers the selling expenses of $28,000.

## WHAT MAKES A GOOD SALES REPRESENTATIVE?

Selecting sales representatives would not be such a problem if one knew the characteristics of an ideal salesperson. If ideal salespersons are outgoing, aggressive, and energetic, it would not be too difficult to check for these characteristics in applicants. But a review of the most successful sales representatives in any company is likely to reveal a good number who are introverted, mild-mannered, and far from energetic. The successful group will also include men and women who are tall and short, articulate and inarticulate, well groomed and slovenly.

Nevertheless, the search for the magic combination of traits that spells surefire sales ability continues unabated. The number of lists that have been drawn up is countless. Most of them recite the same qualities. McMurry wrote:

> It is my conviction that the possessor of *effective* sales personality is *a habitual "wooer," an individual who has a compulsive need to win and hold the affection of others.* . . . His wooing, however, is not based on a sincere desire for love because, in my opinion, he is convinced at heart that no one will ever love him. Therefore, his wooing is primarily exploitative . . . his relationships tend to be transient, superficial and evanescent.[5]

McMurry went on to list five additional traits of the super salesperson: a high level of energy, abounding self-confidence, a chronic hunger for money, a well-established habit of industry, and a state of mind that regards each objection, resistance, or obstacle as a challenge.[6]

Mayer and Greenberg offered one of the shortest lists of traits exhibited by effective sales representatives.[7] Their seven years of fieldwork led them to conclude that the effective sales person has at least two basic qualities: (1) *empathy,* the ability to feel as the customer does, and (2) *ego drive,* a strong personal need to make the sale. Using these two traits, they were able to make fairly good predictions of the subsequent performance of applicants for sales positions in three different industries.

It may be true that certain basic traits may make a person effective in any line of selling. From the viewpoint of a particular organization, however, these basic traits are rarely enough. Each selling job is characterized by a unique set of duties and challenges. One only has to think about college recruiting, corporate fundraising, and congressional lobbying to realize the different educational, intellectual, and personality requirements that would be sought in the respective sales representatives.

How can an organization determine the characteristics that its prospective sales representatives should "ideally" possess? The particular duties of the job suggest some of the characteristics to look for in applicants. Is there a lot of paperwork? Does the job call for much travel? Will the salesperson confront a high proportion of refusals? In addition, the traits of the company's most successful sales representatives suggest additional qualities to look for. Some organizations compare the standing of their best versus their poorest sales representatives to see which characteristics differentiate the two groups.

### RECRUITMENT PROCEDURES

After management develops general criteria for its sales personnel, it has the job of attracting a sufficient number of applicants. Recruiting is turned over to the personnel department, which seeks applicants through various means, including soliciting names from current sales representatives, using employment agencies, placing job ads, and contacting college students.

---

## TRAINING SALES REPRESENTATIVES

Not too long ago many organizations sent their new salespeople into the field almost immediately after hiring them. Nowadays a new sales representative can expect to spend from a few days to a few months in training. Training has the following objectives:

1. The sales representative should know the organization's history and mission and identify with it.
2. The sales representative should know the organization's products.
3. The sales representative should know customers' and competitors' characteristics.
4. The sales representative should know how to make effective sales presentations.
5. The sales representative should know the organization's systems and procedures.

One of the major objectives of sales training programs is to train sales personnel in the art of selling. The sales training industry today involves expenditures of hundreds of millions of dollars in training programs, books, cassettes, and other materials. Almost a million copies of books on selling are purchased every year, bearing such provocative titles as *How to Outsell the Born Salesman, How to Sell Anything to Anybody, The Power of Enthusiastic Selling, How Power Selling Brought Me Success in 6 Hours, Where Do You Go From No. 1,* and *1000 Ways a Salesman Can Increase His Sales.* One of the most enduring books is Dale Carnegie's *How to Win Friends and Influence People.*

All of the sales training approaches are designed to convert a salesperson from being a passive *order taker* to a more active *order getter. Order takers* operate on the following assumptions: (1) customers are aware of their own needs, (2) they cannot be influenced or would resent any attempt at influence, and (3) they prefer salespersons who are courteous and self-effacing. An example of an order-taking mentality would be a college fundraiser who phones alumni and asks if they would like to give any money.

In training salespersons to be *order getters,* there are two basic approaches —a sales-oriented approach and a customer-oriented approach. The first one trains the salesperson to be adept in the use of *hard sell techniques,* such as those used in selling encyclopedias or military service. The techniques include overstating the product's merits, criticizing competitive products, using a slick canned presentation, selling yourself, and offering some concession to make the sale on the spot. The assumptions behind this form of selling are that: (1) the customers are not likely to buy except under pressure, (2) they are influenced by a slick presentation and ingratiating manners, and (3) they won't regret the purchase, or if they do, it doesn't matter.

The other approach attempts to train sales personnel in *customer need satisfaction.* Here the salesperson studies the customers' needs and wants and tailors a proposal to meet these needs. An example would be a college fundraiser who senses that a wealthy shoe manufacturer has a strong ego and need for recognition as a supporter of the arts. The fundraiser could propose building and naming a new campus art gallery after this person. The assumptions behind this approach are that: (1) the customers have latent needs that constitute opportunities for the sales representative, (2) they appreciate good suggestions, and (3) they will be responsive to sales representatives who have their long-term interests at heart. Certainly, the need satisfier is a more compatible image for the salesperson under the marketing concept than the hard seller or order taker.

Most sales training programs view the selling process as consisting of a set of steps, each involving certain skills. These steps are shown in Figure 15–2 and discussed below.[8]

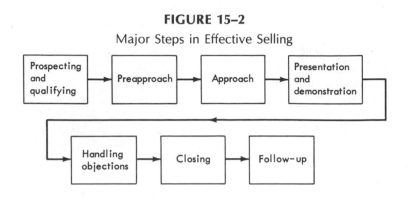

## FIGURE 15–2
### Major Steps in Effective Selling

**Prospecting and qualifying.**    The first step in the sales process is to identify prospects. For example, a hospital fundraiser could obtain the names of wealthy people in the following ways: (1) asking current wealthy donors for the names of other potential donors, (2) asking friendly referral sources, such as lawyers, accountants, and bankers, (3) joining organizations, such as country clubs, where there is a high probability of meeting wealthy people, (4) giving speeches or writing articles of interest to wealthy people that are likely to increase the salesperson's visibility, (5) examining various data sources (newspapers, directories) in search of names, and (6) using the telephone and mail to track down leads.

Sales representatives also need to know how to screen the leads to avoid wasting valuable time on poor leads. Prospects can be qualified by examining their financial ability, giving history, personality, and location. The salesperson may use the phone or mail to qualify the prospects further.

**Preapproach.**    This step involves the salesperson in learning as much as possible about each good prospect. The salesperson can consult reference sources, acquaintances, and others. The salesperson should determine *call objectives,* which may be to make an introduction, or gather information, or make an immediate sale. Another task is to decide on the best *approach,* which might be a personal visit (possibly with a respected intermediary), phone call, or letter. The best *timing* should be thought out because many prospects are especially busy at certain times of the year. Finally, the salesperson should give thought to an *overall strategy* to use in the approach stage.

**Approach.**    This stage involves the salesperson knowing how to meet and greet the prospect to get the relationship off to a good start. It consists of how the salesperson looks, the opening lines, and the follow-up remarks. The salesperson's looks include his or her appearance, manner, and mannerisms. The salesperson is encouraged to wear clothes similar to what the prospect usually wears, such as an open shirt and no ties in Texas; show courtesy and attention to the prospect; and avoid distracting mannerisms such as pacing the floor or staring. The opening line should be positive and pleasant, such as "Mr. Smith, I am Bill Jones from

St. Luke's Hospital. My hospital and I appreciate your willingness to see me. I will be brief and do my best to make this visit worthwhile for you."

**Presentation and demonstration.**     After this introduction, the salesperson can make a brief statement about the organization and the purpose of the call. The salesperson will follow the AIDA formula: get *attention,* hold *interest,* arouse *desire,* and obtain *action.*

There are three contrasting styles of sales presentation. The oldest is the *canned approach,* which is a memorized sales talk covering the main points deemed important by the organization. It is based on stimulus-response thinking, that the buyer is passive and can be moved to purchase by the use of the right stimulus words, pictures, terms, and actions. Thus an encyclopedia salesperson might describe the encyclopedia as "a once-in-a-lifetime buying opportunity" and show some beautiful four-color pages of pictures on sports, hoping that these will trigger an irresistible desire for the encyclopedia on the part of the prospect. Canned presentations are used primarily in door-to-door and telephone canvassing and have been pretty much abandoned by other companies in favor of more flexible approaches.

*The formulated approach* is also based on stimulus-response thinking, but attempts to identify early the prospect's needs and buying style and then use a formulated approach to this type of prospect. In this approach, the salesperson does some presenting at the beginning and attempts to draw the prospect into the discussion in a way which will indicate the prospect's needs and attitudes. As these are discovered, the salesperson moves into a formulated presentation that is appropriate to that prospect and shows how the transaction will satisfy that prospect's needs. It is not canned but follows a general plan.

The *need-satisfaction approach* does not start with a prepared presentation designed to sell the prospect, but with a search for the prospect's real needs. The prospect is encouraged to do most of the talking so that the salesperson can really grasp the prospect's real needs and respond accordingly. This approach calls for good listening and problem-solving skills.

Sales presentations can be improved considerably with various demonstration aids, such as booklets, flipcharts, slides, movies, and samples. To the extent that the prospect can participate by seeing or handling the offer, he or she will better remember its features and benefits.

**Handling objections.**     Prospects will almost always pose objections during the presentation or when asked to sign up. Their sales resistance could take a psychological or logical form. *Psychological resistance* includes:[9] (1) resistance to interference, (2) preference for established habits, (3) apathy, (4) reluctance to giving up something, (5) unpleasant associations with other person, (6) tendency to resist domination, (7) predetermined ideas, (8) dislike of making decisions, and (9) neurotic attitude toward money. *Logical resistance* might consist of objections to the terms or organization. To handle these objections, the salesperson uses such techniques as maintaining a positive approach, trying to have the prospect clarify and define the objections, questioning the prospect in such a way that the prospect has to answer his or her own objections, denying the validity of the objections, and turning the objection into a reason for buying. The salesperson needs training in the broader skills of negotiation, of which handling objections is a part.[10]

**Closing.**     In this stage, the salesperson attempts to close the sale. Some salespeople never get to this stage, or do not do it well. They lack confidence in themselves or their organization or product; or feel guilty about asking for the sale; or do not recognize the right psychological moment to close the sale. Salespersons have to be trained in recognizing specific closing signals from the prospect, including physical actions, statements or comments, and questions signaling a possible readiness to close. Salespersons can then use one of several closing techniques. They can ask the prospect for the sale; recapitulate the points of agreement; offer to help write up the agreement; ask whether the prospect wants A or B; get the prospect to make minor choices among possible variations; or indicate what the prospect will lose if the transaction is not completed now. The salesperson may offer the prospect specific inducements to close, such as a concession or gift item.

**Follow-up.**     This last stage is necessary if the salesperson wants to assure buyer satisfaction and repeat business. Immediately after closing, the salesperson should attempt to complete any necessary details. The salesperson should consider scheduling a follow-up call to make sure everything has gone smoothly. This call is designed to detect any problems, to assure the buyer of the salesperson's interest and service, and to reduce any cognitive dissonance that might have arisen.

## SUPERVISING SALES REPRESENTATIVES

The new sales representative is given more than an assignment, a compensation package, and training—he or she is given supervision. Supervision is the fate of everyone who works for someone else. It is the expression of the employers' natural and continuous interest in the activities of their agents. Through supervision, employers hope to direct and motivate the sales force to do a better job.

### DIRECTING SALES REPRESENTATIVES

Organizations undertake a number of activities to improve their sales representatives' performances:

**Developing customer and prospect call levels.**     Many organizations classify their customers into account types, such as A, B, and C, reflecting the sales and growth potential of the different accounts. For example, army recruiters may classify different high schools into these groups. They establish a certain desired call level per period that their recruiters should make to each account type. The call levels that are set depend upon competitive call norms and expected account responses.

Organizations also like to specify how much time to spend prospecting for new accounts. Organizations like to set a minimum requirement for the canvassing of new accounts because salespeople, if left alone, will spend most of their time with current customers. Current customers are better-known quantities. The sales representatives can depend upon them for some business, whereas a prospect may never deliver any business or deliver it only after many months of effort.

**Using sales time efficiently.**    The sales representatives should know how to schedule planned sales calls and use their time efficiently. One tool is the preparation of an *annual call schedule,* showing which customers and prospects to call on in which months and which ancillary activities to carry out. The other tool is *time-and-duty analysis* to determine how to use sales call time more efficiently. The sales representative's time is spent in the following ways:

1. *Travel.* Travel time is the time spent in travel between rising in the morning and arriving at lodgings in the evening. It can amount in some jobs to as much as 50 percent of total time. Travel time can be cut down by substituting faster for slower means of transportation, recognizing, however, that this will increase costs. More organizations are encouraging air travel for their sales force in order to increase their ratio of selling to total time.

2. *Food and breaks.* Some portion of the sales force's workday is spent in eating and breaks. If this involves dining with a prospect, it will be classified as selling time, otherwise, as food and breaks.

3. *Waiting.* Waiting consists of time spent in the outer office of the prospect. This is dead time unless the sales representative uses it to plan or fill out reports.

4. *Selling.* Selling is the time spent with the prospect in person or on the phone. It breaks down into "social talk," which is the time spent discussing other things and "selling talk" which is the time spent on the offer.

5. *Administration.* This is a miscellaneous category consisting of the time spent in report writing, attending sales meetings, and talking to other departments in the organization.

No wonder actual selling time may amount in some companies to as little as 15 percent of total working time! If it could be raised from 15 percent to 20 percent, this would be a 33 percent improvement. Organizations are constantly seeking ways to help their sales representatives to use their time more efficiently. This takes the form of training them in the effective use of the telephone ("phone power"), simplifying the record-keeping forms, using the computer to develop call and routing plans, and supplying them with marketing research information on the prospect or customer.

## MOTIVATING SALES REPRESENTATIVES

A small percentage of sales representatives in any sales force can be expected to do their best without any special prompting from management. To them, selling is the most fascinating job in the world. They are ambitious and self-starters. But the majority of sales representatives on nearly every sales force require personal encouragement and special incentives to work at their best level. This is especially true for creative field selling for the following reasons:

1. *The nature of the job.* The selling job is one of frequent frustration. Sales representatives usually work alone, the hours are irregular, and they are often away from home. They confront aggressive competing sales representatives; they have an inferior status relative to the buyer; they often do not have the authority to do what is necessary to win an account; they lose important sales that they have worked hard to obtain.

2. *Human nature.* Most people operate below capacity in the absence of special incentive. They won't "kill themselves" without some prospect of financial gain or social recognition.

3. *Personal problems.* The sales representative, like everyone else, is occasionally preoccupied with personal problems, such as sickness in the family, marital discord, or debt.

Management can affect the morale and performance of the sales force through its organizational climate, sales quotas, and positive incentives.

**Organizational climate.**      Organizational climate describes the feeling that the sales force gets from their organization regarding their opportunities, value, and rewards for a good performance. Some organizations treat their recruiters, fundraisers, and others as being of minor importance. Others treat them as highly critical to the organization's success. The company's attitude toward its sales representatives acts as a self-fulfilling prophecy. If they are held in low esteem, there is much turnover and poor performance; if they are held in high esteem, there is less turnover and high performance.

The quality of personal treatment from the sales representative's immediate superior is an important aspect of the organizational climate. An effective sales manager keeps in touch with the members of the sales force through regular correspondence and phone calls, personal visits in the field, and evaluation sessions at headquarters. At different times the sales manager is the sales representative's boss, companion, coach, and confessor.

**Sales quotas.**      Many organizations set sales quotas for their sales representatives specifying sales objectives for the period. Thus, a U.S. Navy recruiter is expected to produce five enlistees each month. Sales quotas are developed in the process of developing the annual marketing plan. The organization first decides on a sales forecast that is reasonably achievable. This becomes the basis of planning production, workforce size, and financial requirements. Then management establishes sales quotas for all of its regions and territories, which typically add up to more than the sales forecast. Sales quotas are set higher than the sales forecast in order to stretch the sales managers and salespeople to their best effort. If they fail to make their quotas, the organization nevertheless may make its sales forecast.

Each sales manager takes the assigned quota and divides it among the sales representatives. Actually, there are three schools of thought on quota setting. The *high-quota school* sets quotas that are above what most sales representatives will achieve but that are possible for all. They are of the opinion that high quotas spur extra effort. The *modest-quota school* sets quotas that a majority of the sales force can achieve. They feel that the sales force will accept the quotas as fair, attain them, and gain confidence from attaining them. Finally, the *variable-quota school* thinks that individual differences among sales representatives warrant high quotas for some, modest quotas for others.

**Positive incentives.**    Organizations use a number of positive motivators to stimulate sales force effort. Periodic *sales meetings* provide a social occasion, a break from routine, a chance to meet and talk with the organization's leaders, a chance to air feelings and to identify with a larger group. Organizations also sponsor *sales contests,* with the best sales performers winning a product or a trip somewhere. Other motivators include conferring *honors and awards* to the high sales performers.

---

## EVALUATING SALES REPRESENTATIVES

We have been describing the *feedforward* aspects of sales supervision—the efforts of management to communicate to the sales representatives what they should be doing and to motivate them to do it. But good feedforward requires good feedback. And good feedback means getting regular information from and about sales representatives to evaluate their performance.

### SOURCES OF INFORMATION

Management gains information about its sales representatives in a number of ways. Probably the most important source of information is the sales representative's periodic reports. Additional information comes through personal observation, through customers' letters and complaints, and through conversations with other sales representatives.

A distinction can be drawn between sales reports that represent *plans for future activities* and those that represent *writeups of completed activities.* The best example of the former is the *salesperson's work plan,* which most sales representatives are required to submit for a specified future period, usually a week or a month in advance. The plan describes the calls they will make and the routing they will use. This report serves the purposes of encouraging the sales force to plan and schedule their activities, informing management of their whereabouts, and providing a basis for comparing their plans with their accomplishments. Sales representatives can be evaluated on their ability to "plan their work and work their plan." Occasionally, management contacts individual sales representatives after receiving their plans to suggest improvements.

Organizations moving toward annual marketing planning in depth are beginning to require their sales representatives to draft an *annual marketing plan,* in which they outline their program for developing new accounts and increasing business from existing accounts. The plan formats vary considerable, some asking for general ideas on account development and others asking for detailed sales volume and cost estimates. This type of report reflects the conception of sales representatives as market managers and cost centers. The plans are studied by their sales managers and become the bases for rendering constructive suggestions to sales representatives and developing local sales quotas and estimates for higher level management.

Several reports are used by sales representatives to write up their completed activities and accomplishments. Perhaps the best known is the *call report,* on which the salesperson records pertinent aspects of his or her dealings with a customer, including customer needs and wants, customer perceptions, best time for calling, and account promise. Call reports serve the objectives of keeping sales management informed of the salesperson's activities, indicating the status of the customers' accounts, and providing information that might be useful in subsequent calls. Sales representatives also report *expenses* incurred in the performance of selling duties, for which they are partly or wholly reimbursed. The objective, from management's standpoint, is primarily to exercise control over the type and amount of expenses, and secondarily to have the requisite expense data for income tax purposes. It is also hoped that the sales representatives will exercise more care in incurring expenses when they must report them in some detail. Additional types of reports that some companies require from their sales representatives are: a report on *new business secured and potential new business;* a report on *lost business;* and a report on *local, economic, and social conditions.*

These various reports supply the raw data from which sales management can extract key indicators of sales performance. The key indicators they watch are: (1) average number of sales calls per salesperson per day, (2) average sales call time per contact, (3) average revenue per sales call, (4) average cost per sales call, (5) entertainment cost per sales call, (6) percentage of orders per hundred sales calls, (7) number of new customers per period, (8) number of lost customers per period, and (9) sales force cost as a percentage of total sales. An analysis of these statistics will raise useful questions, such as: Are sales representatives making too few calls per day? Are they spending too much time per call? Are they spending too much on entertainment? Are they achieving enough sales per hundred calls? Are they producing enough new customers and holding onto the old customers?

## FORMAL EVALUATION OF PERFORMANCE

The sales force's reports, along with other reports from the field and the manager's personal observations, supply the raw materials for formally evaluating members of the sales force. Formal evaluation procedures lead to at least three benefits. First, they lead management to develop specific and uniform standards for judging sales performance. Second, they lead management to draw together all its information and impressions about individual sales representatives and make more systematic, point-by-point evaluations. Third, they tend to have a constructive effect on the performance of sales representatives. The constructive effect comes about because the sales representatives know that they will have to sit down one morning with the sales manager and explain certain facets of their routing or sales call decisions or their failure to secure or maintain certain accounts.

**Salesperson-to-salesperson comparisons.**     One type of evaluation frequently made is to compare and rank the sales performance of the various sales representatives. Such comparisons, however, must be done with care. Relative sales performances are meaningful only if there are no variations among sales assignments in market potential, workload, degree of competition, promotional effort, and so forth. Furthermore, sales are not the only denominator of achievement. Management should be interested in how much each sales representative contributed to net surplus. And this cannot be known until the sales representatives' sales mix and sales expenses are examined. A possible ranking criterion would be the sales representative's *actual contribution to surplus as a ratio to his or her estimated potential surplus.* A ratio of 1.00 would mean that the sales representative delivered the potential sales in his or her market segment. The lower a sales representative's ratio, the more supervision and counseling he or she needs.

**Current-to-past-sales comparisons.**     A second common type of evaluation is to compare a sales representative's current performance with past performance. Each salesperson is expected to improve along certain lines, such as producing more sales, bringing down costs, opening new accounts, and so on. His or her progress can be measured and a judgment made about whether there is enough improvement, and if not, what the problem is.

**Qualitative evaluation of sales representatives.**     The evaluation usually extends to the salesperson's knowledge of the organization, products, customers, competitors, territory, and responsibilities. Personality characteristics can be rated, such as general manner, appearance, speech, and temperament. The sales manager can also consider any problems in motivation or compliance. Since an almost endless number of qualitative factors might be included, each company must decide what would be most useful to know. It should also communicate these criteria to the sales representatives so that they are aware of how their performance is judged and can make an effort to improve.

---

# SUMMARY

Many organizations utilize sales representatives and assign them a pivotal role in the creation of sales. The high cost of the sales resource calls for effective sales management, consisting of six steps: (1) establishing sales force objectives, (2) designing sales force strategy, structure, size, and compensation, (3) recruiting and selecting, (4) training, (5) supervising, and (6) evaluating.

As an element of the marketing mix, the sales force is capable of achieving certain marketing objectives effectively. The organization has to decide on the proper mix of the following sales activities: prospecting, communicating, selling and servicing, information gathering, and allocating.

Given the sales force objectives, the sales force is then designed to answer the question of what sales force strategy would be most effective (individual selling, team selling, etc.), what type of sales force structure would work best (territorial, product, or customer structured), how large a sales force is needed, and how the sales force should be compensated.

Sales representatives must be recruited and selected carefully to avoid the high costs of hiring the wrong persons. Their training should familiarize them with the organization's history, products and policies, and customer and competitor characteristics, and the art of selling. The art of selling itself calls for training in a seven-step sales process: prospecting and qualifying, preapproach, approach, presentation and demonstration, handling objections, closing, and follow-up. The salesperson needs supervision and continuous encouragement because he or she must make a large number of decisions and is subject to many frustrations. Periodically, the person's performance must be formally evaluated to help him or her do a better job.

## QUESTIONS

**1.** What sales force structure would you recommend to a major opera for (a) subscription ticket sales, (b) block ticket sales to organizations, (c) benefit performance sales, (d) raising funds from corporations and foundations?

**2.** A small college is planning to send representatives to high schools to talk to students to interest them in the college. The Admissions Office is trying to decide whether to send (a) Admissions Office staff, (b) college alumni who live near each high school, (c) current students at the college, (d) professors, or (e) professional recruiters. Which group(s) would you recommend? Explain your choice.

**3.** What type and level of compensation would you recommend for each of the groups in question 2?

**4.** Describe a customer need-satisfaction approach for encouraging a wealthy industrialist to endow a scholarship fund.

**5.** The National Organization for Women encourages members to come to Washington, D.C., to talk with their senators and congressional representatives and encourage their support for the Equal Rights Amendment. What principles of salesmanship would be useful?

**6.** Suppose NOW asked those who lobbied (see question 5) to provide the Central Office with call reports. What information should be included in the reports to make them useful?

## NOTES

**1.** See Sidney J. Levy, *Promotional Behavior* (Glenview, Ill.: Scott, Foresman, 1971), pp. 65–69.

**2.** John Steinbrink, *Compensation of Salesmen: Dartnell's 19th Biennial Survey* (Chicago: Dartnell, 1978).

**3.** Walter J. Talley, "How to Design Sales Territories," *Journal of Marketing,* January 1961, pp. 7–13.

**4.** The survey was conducted by the Sales Executives Club of New York and was reported in *Business Week,* February 1, 1964, p. 52.

**5.** Robert N. McMurry, "The Mystique of Super-Salesmanship," *Harvard Business Review,* March-April 1961, p. 117.

**6.** *Ibid.,* p. 118.

**7.** David Mayer and Herbert M. Greenberg, "What Makes a Good Salesman?", *Harvard Business Review,* July–August 1964, pp. 119–25.

**8.** The following discussion draws in part from W. J. E. Crissy, William H. Cunningham, and Isabella C. M. Cunningham, *Selling: The Personal Force in Marketing* (New York: Wiley, 1977), pp. 119–29.

**9.** *Ibid.,* pp. 289–94.

**10.** See Gerald I. Nierenberg, *The Art of Negotiation* (New York: Hawthorn Books, 1968); and Chester L. Karrass, *The Negotiating Game* (Cleveland: World, 1970).

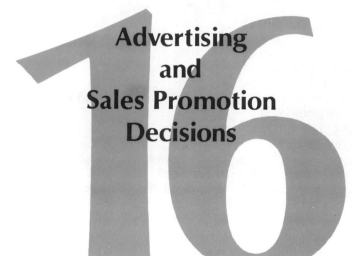

# Advertising and Sales Promotion Decisions

Large-scale commercial marketing techniques are being used to promote the performing arts in New York, and the results thus far have been highly successful.

With the help of the Ford Foundation, the Robert Sterling Clark Foundation, and the New York Community Trust, five dance companies have developed a unique cooperative approach to ticket pricing, subscription offers, promotional planning, and budgeting for performances at the City Center.

The program, called "Masters of American Dance," is being conducted by Rapp & Collins Inc., New York, a direct marketing agency.

"Several distinct direct-mail subscription offers have been tested to determine the popularity of different ticket combinations and the prices different groups of people will pay for them," said Russell L. Lapso, vice president of Rapp & Collins. "This will enable the dance companies to target their subscription offers more effectively.

"Multiple-offer testing lowers the risk associated with traditional ticket-selling techniques by allowing the public to indicate its purchase preference.

"This test-marketing method increases subscription mailing cost effectiveness and accurately projects anticipated expenses and revenue."

The companies involved in the Masters of American Dance program are Alvin Ailey American Dance Theater, Merce Cunningham Dance Co., Jose Limon Dance Co., Murray Louis Dance Co., and Nikolais Dance Theatre.

In forming the cooperative, the five dance companies feel they can still "preserve artistic individuality," while affording themselves an opportunity to use techniques traditionally associated with large-scale commercial marketing efforts, Lapso said.

The first step in the program was taken in June when Rapp & Collins mailed thousands of subscription offers, attempting to gather quantifiable information about the types of dance series, prices, and product positionings which would appeal to the public.

The final direct-mail brochures offer the consumer 15 possibilities in terms of seat location, number of performances, types of companies, ticket discounts, etc. Test objectives were to increase subscriber base, sell more seats in advance, and maximize advance subscription revenue for the five dance companies, Lapso said.

"Masters of American Dance will drastically alter the income/time curve for the companies' New York season," Lapso explains. "The average net revenue of companies surveyed for their last New York season was $25,000 after subtracting promotional expenses.

"An average of only $6,000 was realized prior to opening night. If test results are duplicated in the rollout, each company will realize approximately $45,000 net prior to box office opening and single ticket advertising."

The success of the program, Lapso said, is due to "enthusiastic receptiveness to the dance offer from outside the traditional dance market. The concept tapped a totally new market, a market not necessarily sophisticated with respect to modern dance, that is interested in sampling the companies at an attractive price."

One of the most popular options, according to Lapso, was the "$99 Subscription For Two." This provided two top-dollar seats to five dance performances for $99, a $50 savings off regular box office tickets.

Murray Louis, artistic director of the Murray Louis Dance Co., said that "this utilization by the arts of modern business marketing techniques is long overdue."

SOURCE: Quoted from "New Marketing System Increases Revenue for Modern Dance Group," *Marketing News,* October 5, 1979, p. 11.

Today's organizations have to do more than develop attractive services and make them available to target consumers. They have to communicate to and motivate their various markets and publics. They cannot avoid this task. Everything about an organization—its products, employees, facilities, and actions—communicates something. Each organization should examine its communication style, needs, and opportunities—and develop a communication program that is impactful and cost-effective.

Communications must be directed to target consumers to keep them informed and to promote market exchanges—selling a good or service, attracting members, raising money, or gaining support for a cause. Thus, each year the

New York Philharmonic undertakes to sell at least 8,000 subscriptions to its concert season. The U.S. Navy seeks to attract 112,000 new recruits into the navy.

The organization's communications responsibilities go beyond communicating to target consumers. The organization must communicate effectively with other publics in its external environment, such as the press, government agencies, and the financial community. It must communicate effectively with its internal publics, particularly its board members, middle management, and professional and clerical employees. The organization must know how to market itself to various groups in order to gain their support and goodwill.

## PROMOTIONAL TOOLS AND THE COMMUNICATION PROCESS

In a broad sense, all of the four P tools of the marketing mix—product, price, place, and promotion—are communication tools. Thus messages are carried to the market by the product's styling and features, its price, and the places where it is available. However, we will confine our attention to the subset of marketing tools that are primarily "promotional"—that are classified under promotion, one of the four Ps. The other three Ps perform other functions besides promotion.

Promotional tools are extremely numerous and varied. Examples include:

- Space and time advertising
- Loudspeaker advertising
- Mailings
- Speeches
- Sales presentations
- Demonstrations
- Trading stamps
- Contests
- Premiums

- Free samples
- Price specials
- Coupons
- Posters and show cards
- Point-of-sale displays
- Sales literature
- Catalogs
- Films
- Trade exhibits
- Sales conference

- Packaging
- House-organ publications
- Product publicity
- Corporate publicity
- Corporate identification programs
- Endorsements
- Atmospheres

In specific institutional settings, distinct promotional tools may evolve to serve the needs of that institution. Fundraising organizations make heavy use of benefit dinners and dances, auctions, bazaars, concerts, telethons, walkathons, door-to-door campaigns, plate passing, and direct mail to raise money. Summer camps make heavy use of camp brochures, get-acquainted parties, T-shirts with camp name, camp movies, and direct mail.

A classification of the various promotional tools is desirable to facilitate analysis and planning. The tools fall into four groups.[1]

- *Advertising:* Any paid form of nonpersonal presentation and promotion of ideas, goods, or services by an identified sponsor.
- *Sales promotion:* Short-term incentives to encourage purchase or sales of a product or service.
- *Personal selling:* Oral presentation in a conversation with one or more prospective purchasers for the purpose of making sales or building goodwill.
- *Publicity:* Nonpersonal stimulation of demand for a product, service, or business unit by planting commercially significant news about it in a published medium or obtaining favorable presentation of it upon radio, television, or stage that is not paid for by the sponsor.

To use these tools effectively, they should be viewed in a *communication framework.* Figure 16–1 shows the eight elements involved in every communication. There are two parties—a *sender* and *receiver.* One or both send a *message* through *media.* They also engage in four communication functions—*encoding, decoding, response,* and *feedback.* These elements are defined as follows:

**Sender:** the party sending the message to another party (also called the *source* or *communicator*)

**Encoding:** the process of putting thought into symbolic form

**Message:** the set of symbols that the sender transmits

**Media:** the paths through which the message moves from sender to receiver

**Decoding:** the process by which the receiver assigns meaning to the symbols transmitted by the sender

**Receiver:** the party receiving the message sent by another party (also called the *audience* or *destination*)

**Response:** the set of reactions that the receiver has after being exposed to the message

**Feedback:** the part of the receiver's response that the receiver communicates back to the sender

**FIGURE 16–1**

Elements in the Communication Process

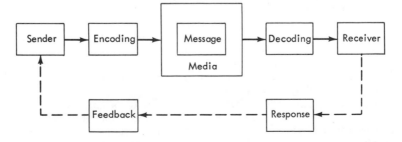

The model underscores the key factors in effective communication. Senders must know what audiences they want to reach and what responses they want. They must be skillful in encoding messages that take into account how the target audience tends to decode messages. They must transmit the message over efficient media that reach the target audience. They must develop feedback channels so that they can know the audience's response to the message.

We will discuss advertising and sales promotion in this chapter and publicity in the next chapter.

## ADVERTISING

Advertising consists of *nonpersonal forms of communication conducted through paid media under clear sponsorship.* It involves such varied media as *magazines* and *newspapers; radio* and *television; outdoor* (such as posters, signs, skywriting); *novelties* (matchboxes, calendars); *cards* (car, bus); *catalogs; directories* and *references; programs* and *menus; circulars;* and *direct mail.* It can be carried out for such diverse purposes as long-term buildup of the organization's name (institutional advertising), long-term buildup of a particular product (product advertising) or brand (brand advertising), information dissemination about a sale, service, or event (classified advertising), announcement of a special sale (sales advertising), and so on.

Total advertising in the United States amounted to over $49 billion in 1979. Advertising is coming into increasing use by nonprofit organizations—public and private—and may amount to as much as $4 billion. The major categories of nonprofit organization advertising are as follows:

1. *Political advertising.* Political advertising has skyrocketed in recent elections. The 1976 presidential candidates alone spent $22 million in political advertising.[2] Various state and local candidates spent many millions more.
2. *Social cause advertising.* For many years, the Advertising Council, Inc., a nonprofit organization financed by American industry, has used advertising to promote social causes such as brotherhood, safe driving, aid to education, religious faith, forest fire prevention, and so on. It accepts a number of causes each year and arranges for the donated services of advertising agencies and media to prepare and broadcast this advertising (estimated value of these services in 1979: $563 million). It tends to avoid more controversial causes. Social cause organizations such as ecology groups, family planners, and women's liberation organizations have also stepped up their advertising budgets to get their messages out to the public.[3]
3. *Charitable advertising.* Charitable advertising is distinguished from social cause advertising in being specifically directed to raising donations, on a regular or emergency basis, where the money will be used to help the needy, unfortunate, or sick. Examples include the paid or donated advertising done by the Red Cross, United Way, Easter Seal Society, and so on.
4. *Government advertising.* Various government units are frequent advertisers. Municipalities and states spend considerable sums to attract new residents, tourists, and industrial developers. Park and recreation departments advertise outdoor recreational facilities. Police departments issue messages to the general public on

safety issues. The federal government has used paid advertising to sell products (U.S. postage stamps), services (Amtrak train travel), and ideas (energy conservation). Its largest advertising expenditures are on military recruitment, where it requested a budget of $106 million in 1978. And it arranged for $38 million of donated advertising (courtesy of the Advertising Council) to encourage people, especially blacks and Hispanics, to cooperate with the census takers in the 1980 census.

5. *Private nonprofit advertising.* Universities, museums, symphonies, hospitals, and religious organizations all have strong communication programs and develop annual reports, direct mailings, classified ads, broadcast messages, and other forms of advertising. Various professionals whose ethical codes formerly banned advertising —social workers, psychologists, etc.—are now free to advertise ever since the Federal Trade Commission ruled that the American Medical Association could not prevent physician members from advertising.

6. *Association advertising.* Professional and trade associations have substantially increased their use of paid advertising. The American Bankers Association, the American Dental Association, and the National Association of Realtors spend several million dollars annually on television and print advertising. Their objective is to improve their public image and also the public's knowledge of their services. Public service advertising programs have recently been undertaken by associations representing lawyers, accountants, engineers, and nurses.

In developing an advertising program, marketing management must make five major decisions. These decisions are shown in Figure 16–2 and discussed in the following sections.

### ADVERTISING OBJECTIVES SETTING

Before an advertising program and budget can be developed, advertising objectives must be set. These objectives must flow from prior decision making on the target market, market positioning, and marketing mix. The marketing strategy defines advertising's job in the total marketing mix.

## FIGURE 16–2

Major Decisions in Advertising Management

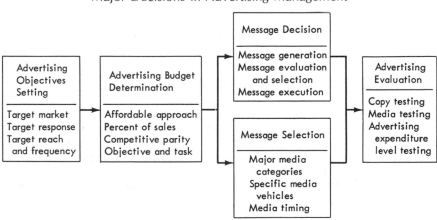

Developing advertising objectives calls for defining the target market, target response, and target reach and frequency.

**Target market.**    A marketing communicator must start with a clear target audience in mind. The audience may be potential buyers of the organization's services, current users, deciders, or influencers. The audience may consist of individuals, groups, particular publics, or the general public. The target audience will critically influence the communicator's decisions on *what* is to be said, *how* it is to be said, *when* it is to be said, *where* it is to be said, and *who* is to say it.

Consider this in terms of a small private college in Iowa called Pottsville. Suppose it is seeking applicants from Nebraska, and it estimates that there are 30,000 graduating high school seniors in Nebraska who might be interested in Pottsville College. The college must decide whether to aim its communications primarily at high school counselors in Nebraska high schools or at the high school students themselves. Beyond this, it may want to develop communications to reach the parents and other influentials in the college decision process. Each target market would warrant a different advertising campaign.

**Target response.**    Once the target audience is identified, the marketing communicator must define the target response that is sought. The ultimate response, of course, is purchase behavior. But purchase behavior is the end result of a long process of consumer decision making. The marketing communicator needs to know in which state the target audience stands at the present time and to which state it should be moved.

Any member of the target audience may be in one of six *buyer readiness states* with respect to the service or organization. These states—*awareness, knowledge, liking, preference, conviction,* and *action*—are described below:[4]

1. *Awareness.* The first thing to establish is how aware the target audience is of the service or organization. The audience may be completely unaware of the entity, know only its name, or know one or two things about it. If most of the target audience is unaware, the communicator's task is to build awareness, perhaps even just name recognition. This calls for simple messages repeating the name. Even then, building awareness takes time. Pottsville College has no name recognition among high school seniors in Nebraska. The college might set the objective of making 70 percent of these students aware of Pottsville's name within one year.

2. *Knowledge.* The target audience may be aware of the entity but may not know much about it. In this case the communicator's goal will be to transmit some key information about the entity. Thus Pottsville College may want its target audience to know that it is a private four-year college in Eastern Iowa that has distinguished programs in ornithology and thanatology. After waging a campaign, it can sample the target audience members to measure whether they have little, some, or much knowledge of Pottsville College, and the content of their knowledge. The particular set of beliefs that makes up the audience's picture of an entity is called the *image*. Organizations must periodically assess their public images as a basis for developing communication objectives.

3. *Liking.* If the target audience members know the entity, the next question is, How do they feel about it? We can imagine a scale covering *dislike very much, dislike*

*somewhat, indifferent, like somewhat, like very much.* If the audience holds an unfavorable view of Pottsville College the communicator has to find out why and then develop a communications program to build up favorable feeling. If the unfavorable view is rooted in real inadequacies of the college, then a communications campaign would not do the job. The task would require first improving the college and then communicating its quality. Good public relations call for "good deeds followed by good words."

4. *Preference.* The target audience may like the entity but may not prefer it over others. It is one of several acceptable entities. In this case the communicator's job is to build the consumers' preference for the entity. The communicator will have to tout its quality, value, performance, and other attributes. The communicator can check on the success of the campaign by subsequently surveying the members of the audience to see if their preference for the entity is stronger.

5. *Conviction.* A target audience may prefer a particular entity but may not develop a conviction about buying it. Thus, some high school seniors may prefer Pottsville to other colleges but may not be sure they want to go to college. The communicator's job is to build conviction that going to college is the right thing to do. Building conviction that one should buy a particular entity is a challenging communications task.

6. *Action.* A member of the target audience may have conviction but may not quite get around to making the purchase. He or she may be waiting for additional information, may plan to act later, and so on. A communicator in this situation must lead the consumer to take the final step, which is called "closing the sale." Among action-producing devices are offering the entity at a low price if bought now, offering a premium, offering an opportunity to try it on a limited basis, or indicating that the entity will soon be unavailable.

The six states simplify to three stages known as the *cognitive* (awareness, knowledge), *affective* (liking, preference, conviction), and *behavioral* (purchase). The communicator normally assumes that buyers pass through these stages in succession on the way to purchase. In this case, the communicator's task is to identify the stage that most of the target audience is in and develop a communication message or campaign that will move them to the next stage. It would be nice if one message could move the audience through all three stages, but this rarely happens. Most communicators try to find a cost-effective communication approach to moving the target audience one stage at a time. The critical thing is to know where the audience is and what the next feasible stage is.

Some marketing scholars have challenged the idea that a consumer passes through *cognition* to *affect* to *behavior* in this order. Ray has suggested that some consumers pass from *cognition* to *behavior* to *affect*.[5] An example would be a student who has heard of Pottsville, enrolls there without much feeling, and afterward develops a strong liking for (or dislike of) the place. Ray has also suggested that sometimes consumers pass from *behavior* to *affect* to *cognition.* Thus, a student may sign up for a course that he or she knows nothing about except that friends are taking it, develop a favorable feeling, and finally begin to understand the subject. Each version of the sequence has different implications for the role and influence of communications on behavior.

Clearly, this analysis can lead to many specific communication objectives for advertising. Colley has distinguished 52 possible advertising objectives in his Defining Advertising Goals for Measured Advertising Results (DAGMAR).[6] The various possible advertising objectives can be sorted into whether their aim is to inform, persuade, or remind. The *inform* category includes such advertising objectives as telling the market about a new service, suggesting new uses for a product, informing the market of a price change, explaining how the service works, describing various available services, correcting false impressions, reducing consumers' fears, and building an organizational image. The *persuade* category includes such advertising objectives as building brand preference, encouraging switching to the advertiser's brand, trying to change the customer's perception of the importance of different product attributes, persuading the customer to purchase now, and persuading the customer to receive a sales call. The *remind* category includes such advertising objectives as reminding consumers that the service might be needed in the future, reminding them where to obtain it, and keeping it in their minds during off seasons.

**Target reach and frequency.**     The third decision is to determine the optimal *target reach and frequency* of the advertising. Funds for advertising are rarely so abundant that everyone in the target audience can be reached, and reached with sufficient frequency. Marketing management must decide what percentage of the audience to reach with what exposure frequency per period. For example, Pottsville College could decide that it would use direct mail and would buy 20,000 advertising exposures. This leaves many choices as between target reach and frequency. It could send one letter to 20,000 different students. Or it could send two different letters a week apart to 10,000 students, and so on. The issue is how many exposures are needed to create the desired response, given the market's state of readiness. One exposure could be enough to convert students from being unaware to being aware. It would not be enough to convert students from awareness to preference.

### ADVERTISING BUDGET DETERMINATION

In Chapter 11, we reviewed the major ways organizations set their marketing budgets: affordable method, percentage-of-sales method, competitive basis method, and objective-and-task method. We prefer the last method. Suppose Pottsville College wants to send two letters to each of 10,000 students. This is a gross number of exposures of 20,000. Suppose the average mailing piece will cost $2 to design and mail. Then Pottsville College will need a rough advertising budget of $40,000 to accomplish its objectives.

In addition to estimating the total size of the required advertising budget, a determination must be made of how the budget should be allocated over different market segments, geographical areas, and time periods. In practice, advertising budgets are allocated to segments of demand according to their respective populations, sales levels, or some other indicator of market potential. It is common to spend twice as much advertising money in segment B over segment A if segment B has twice as much of some indicator of market potential. In fact, however, the budget should be allocated to different segments according to their expected marginal response to advertising. A budget is well allocated when it is not possible to shift dollars from one segment to another and increase total market response.

Many nonprofit organizations, especially charities, have avoided *paid advertising,* even though they acknowledge its potential value. They are the beneficiaries of *donated advertising,* which they fear will be withdrawn if they started to do paid advertising. For example, the American Red Cross has its advertising copy produced by a volunteering advertising agency (through the Advertising Council of America) and public service time and space are donated by the media. Unfortunately, the Red Cross has no control over the time when their ads are aired, and it is rarely prime time. Yet the Red Cross fears that if it started to buy media time, it would lose all the free media time it now gets.

## MESSAGE DECISION

Given the advertising objectives and budget, management has to develop a creative message. An ideal message is one that would manage to get *attention,* hold *interest,* arouse *desire,* and obtain *action* (known as the AIDA model). In practice, few messages will take the consumer all the way from awareness through purchase, but nevertheless the AIDA framework suggests some desirable qualities.

Advertisers and their agencies go through three steps: message generation, message evaluation and selection, and message execution.

**Message generation.**     Message generation involves the developing of a number of alternative messages (appeals, themes, motifs, ideas) that will hopefully elicit the desired response in the target market.

Messages can be generated in a number of ways. One approach is to talk with members of the target market and other influentials to determine the way they see the service, talk about it, and express their desires about it. A second approach is to hold a brainstorming meeting with key personnel in the organization to generate advertising ideas. A third method is to use some formal deductive framework for teasing out possible advertising messages.

One framework calls for generating three types of messages: rational, emotional, and moral.

> 1. *Rational messages* aim at passing on information and/or serving the audience's self-interest. They attempt to show that the service will yield the expected functional benefits. Examples would be messages discussing a service's quality, economy, value, or performance (see Figure 16–3).
> 2. *Emotional messages* are designed to stir up some negative or positive emotion that will motivate purchase. Communicators have worked with fear, guilt, and

**FIGURE 16–3**

A Rational Appeal Ad

If you've ever giggled yourself silly watching the monkeys, or leaned over the rail to watch the graceful seals swim by, or seen the delight on children's faces as they played with the animals in their own zoo, you know what a very special place a zoo is.

But what a lot of people don't know is how much it costs to buy and house and feed those animals.

That's why there's a Zoological Society of Houston, and that's why we need more members. Right now the zoo is working toward a large exhibit called the Island World. It is to be a highly informative and entertaining exhibit about all the animals living on the islands of the earth.

And we'd like to build similar exhibits to be known as the Arctic World, Tropical World and Desert World. And an aquarium big enough to display the world of fishes.

That takes money, and that's how you can help. For just $10.00, you can join the society. Membership entitles you to free admission to over 40 of the nation's zoos, a subscription to the society's "Hou-Zoo" magazine, and admission to society activities.

Best of all, you'll get an official certificate and a lapel button that tells the world you're a monkey's uncle. (Even monkey's aunts can have them.)

Considering the good your $10.00 membership can do for you, your family, and all the people of Houston, wouldn't it be nice to be a monkey's uncle?

# Be a monkey's uncle

## JOIN
## THE ZOO

Zoological Society of Houston, 1616 West Loop South, Houston, 77027.

I'd like to help build our zoo. And I'd like to receive all the benefits of membership in the Zoological Society.

1.  One-year membership in the Society
2.  Subscription to the "Hou-Zoo" magazine
3.  Free admission to over 40 of the nation's zoos
4.  Monthly newsletter
5.  Button and certificate declaring me a monkey's uncle

Enclosed is my check for:
___Family Membership–$10
___Sustaining Membership–$50
___Patron Membership–$100 - $500
___Life Membership–$500
All gifts tax deductible
Member's Name_____
Address_____
City_____State_____Zip_____

Published as a Public Service by The Houston Post

shame appeals, especially in connection with getting people to start doing things they should (e.g., brushing their teeth, having an annual health checkup) or stop doing things they shouldn't (e.g., smoking, overimbibing, abusing drugs, overeating). Advertisers have found that fear appeals work up to a point, but if there is too much fear the audience will ignore the message.[7] Communicators have also used positive emotional appeals such as love, humor, pride, and joy. Evidence has not established that a humorous message, for example, is necessarily more effective than a straight version of the same message.[8]

3. *Moral messages* are directed to the audience's sense of what is right and proper. They are often used in messages exhorting people to support such social causes as a cleaner environment, better race relations, equal rights for women, and aiding the disadvantaged. An example is the March of Dimes appeal: "God made you whole. Give to help those He didn't." Moral appeals are less often used in connection with everyday products.

Maloney proposed another deductive framework.[9] He suggested that buyers may be expecting any of four types of reward from a product: *rational, sensory, social,* or *ego satisfaction.* And they may visualize these rewards from *results-of-use experience, product-in-use experience,* or *incidental-to-use experience.* Crossing the four types of rewards with the three types of experience generates twelve types of advertising messages.

A third approach is to examine the product's actual and desired position in the product space and look for the themes that would shift the market's view of the product in the desired direction. The advertisement may try to change the belief about the product's level on some attribute, change the perceived relative importance of different attributes, or introduce new attributes not generally considered by the market.

**Message evaluation and selection.**    The task of selecting the best message out of a large number of possibilities calls for evaluation criteria. Twedt has suggested that contending messages be rated on three scales: *desirability, exclusiveness,* and *believability.*[10] He believes that the communication potency of a message is the product of the three factors because if any of the three has a low rating, the message's communication potency will be greatly reduced.

The message must first say something desirable or interesting about the product. This is not enough, however, since many brands will be making the same claim. Therefore the message must also say something exclusive or distinctive that does not apply to every brand in the product category. Finally, the message must be believable or provable. By asking consumers to rate different messages on desirability, exclusiveness, and believability, these messages can be evaluated for their communication potency.

For example, the March of Dimes was searching for an advertising theme to raise money for its fight against birth defects.[11] A brainstorming session led to over twenty possible messages. A group of young parents were asked to rate each message for interest, distinctiveness, and believability, assigning up to 100 points for each. For example, the message "Seven hundred children are born each day with a birth defect" scored 70, 60, and 80 on interest, distinctiveness, and believability, while "Your next baby could be born with a birth defect" scored 58, 50, and 70 (see Figure 16–4). The first message outperforms the second and would be preferred for advertising purposes. The best overall message was "The March of Dimes has given you: polio vaccine, German measles vaccine, 110 birth defects' counseling centers" (70, 80, 90).

**Message execution.** The impact of a message depends not only upon what is said but also upon how it is said. In fact, message execution can be decisive for those products that are essentially the same. The advertiser has to put the message across in a way that will win the target audience's attention and interest. It is the task of the creative people to find a *style,* a *tone, words,* an *order,* and *format* that make for effective message execution.

## FIGURE 16–4

### Advertising Message Evaluation

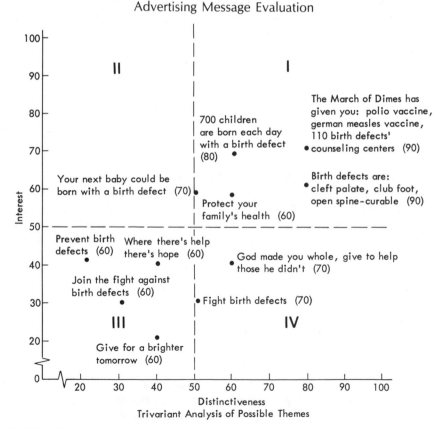

Trivariant Analysis of Possible Themes

SOURCE: William A. Mindak and H. Malcolm Bybee, "Marketing's Application to Fund Raising," *Journal of Marketing,* July 1971, pp. 13–18.

Any message can be put across in different *execution styles*. Suppose the YMCAs around the country are planning to launch an early morning jogging program (6:30 A.M.) and want to develop a 30-second television commercial to motivate people to sign up for this program. Here are some major advertising execution styles they can consider:

1. *Slice-of-life*. A wife says to her tired husband that he might enjoy jogging at the Y in the early morning. He agrees, and the next frame shows him coming home at 7:45 A.M. feeling refreshed and invigorated.
2. *Life style*. A 30-year-old man pops out of bed when his alarm rings at 6:00 A.M., races to the bathroom, races to the closet, races to his car, races to the Y, and then starts racing with his companions with a "big kid" look on his face.
3. *Fantasy*. A jogger runs along a path and suddenly imagines seeing his friends on the sidelines cheering him on.
4. *Mood*. A jogger runs in a residential neighborhood on a beautiful spring day, passing nice homes, noticing flowers beginning to bloom, and neighbors waving to him. This ad creates a mood of beauty and harmony between the jogger and his world.
5. *Musical*. Four joggers run side by side wearing YMCA T-shirts and singing a song in barbershop quartet style about the joy of running.
6. *Personality symbol*. A well-known sports hero is shown jogging at the Y with a smile on his face.
7. *Technical expertise*. Several Y athletic directors are shown discussing the best time, place, and running style that will give the greatest benefit to joggers.
8. *Scientific evidence*. A physician tells about a study of two matched groups of men, one following a jogging program and the other not, and the greater health and energy felt by the jogging group after a few weeks.
9. *Testimonial evidence*. The ad shows three members of a Y jogging group telling how beneficial the program has been.

The communicator must also choose a *tone* for the ad. The ad could be deadly serious (as in an antismoking ad), chatty (as in an ad on weight control), humorous (as in a zoo ad), and so on. The tone must be appropriate to the target audience and target response desired.

*Words* that are memorable and attention-getting must be found. This is nowhere more apparent than in the development of headlines and slogans to lead the reader into an ad. There are six basic types of headlines: *news* ("New Boom and More Inflation Ahead . . . and What You Can Do about It"); *question* ("Have You Had It Lately?"); *narrative* ("They Laughed When I Sat Down at the Piano, But When I Started to Play!"); *command* ("Save water—shower with a friend); *1-2-3 ways* ("12 Ways to Save on Your Income Tax"); and *how-what-why* ("Why They Can't Stop Buying"). Look at the care that airlines have lavished on finding the right way to describe their airline as safe without explicitly mentioning safety as an issue: "The Friendly Skies of United" (United); "The Wings of Man" (Eastern); and "The World's Most Experienced Airline" (Pan American).

The *ordering* of ideas in an ad can be important. Three issues arise.

1. The first is the question of *conclusion drawing,* the extent to which the ad should draw a definite conclusion for the audience or leave it to them. Experimental research seems to indicate that explicit conclusion-drawing is more persuasive than leaving it to the audience to draw their own conclusions. There are exceptions, however, such as when the communicator is seen as untrustworthy or the audience is highly intelligent and annoyed at the attempt to influence them.

2. The second is the question of *one- vs. two-sided arguments*—that is, whether the message will be more effective if one or both sides of the argument are presented. Intuitively, it would appear that the best effect is gained by a one-sided presentation —this is the predominant approach in sales presentations, political contests, and child rearing. Yet the answer is not so clear-cut. The major conclusions are that (a) one-sided messages tend to work best with audiences who are favorably disposed to the communicator's position, whereas two-sided arguments tend to work best with audiences who are opposed; (b) two-sided messages tend to be more effective with better-educated audiences; and (c) two-sided messages tend to be more effective with audiences who are likely to be exposed to counter-propaganda.

3. The third is the question of *order of presentation*—whether communicators should present their strongest arguments first or last. Presenting the strongest arguments first has the advantage of establishing attention and interest. This may be especially important in newspapers and other media where the audience does not attend to all of the message. In a two-sided message, the issue is whether to present the positive argument first (primacy effect) or last (recency effect). If the audience is initially opposed, it would appear that the communicator would be smarter to start with the other side's argument. This will tend to disarm the audience and allow the speaker to conclude with the strongest argument.[12]

*Format elements* can make a difference in an ad's impact, as well as in its cost. If the message is to be carried in a print ad, the communicator has to develop the elements of headline, copy, illustration, and color. Advertisers are adept at using such attention-getting devices as *novelty and contrast, arresting pictures and headlines, distinctive formats, message size and position, and color, shape, and movement.* For example, large ads gain more attention, and so do four-color ads, and this must be weighed against the higher costs. If the message is to be carried over the radio, the communicator has to carefully choose words, voice qualities (speech rate, rhythm, pitch, articulation), and vocalizations (pauses, sighs, yawns). If the message is to be carried on television or given in person, then all of these elements plus body language (nonverbal clues) have to be planned. Presenters have to pay attention to their facial expressions, gestures, dress, posture, and hair style.

## MEDIA SELECTION

Media selection is another major step in advertising planning. Some media thinking should take place before the message development stage and even before the advertising budget stage. For it is essential to determine which media are used by the target audience and which are most efficient costwise in reaching them. This information affects the advertising budget size and even the type of appeal to use.

There are three basic steps in the media selection process: choosing among major media categories, among specific media vehicles, and timing.

**Choosing among major media categories.**     The first step is to determine how the advertising budget will be allocated to the major *media categories.* The media planner has to examine the major media categories for their capacity to deliver reach, frequency, and impact. Table 16–1 presents profiles of the major advertising media. In order of their advertising volume, they are *newspapers, television, direct mail, radio, magazines,* and *outdoor.* Media planners make their choice among these major media types by considering the following variables:

1. *Target audience media habits.* For example, radio and television are the most effective media for reaching teenagers.
2. *Product.* Media types have different potentialities for demonstration, visualization, explanation, believability, and color. For example, television is the most effective medium for demonstrating a complex product or service.
3. *Message.* A message announcing an emergency blood drive tomorrow will require radio or newspapers. A message containing a great deal of technical data might require specialized magazines or mailings.
4. *Cost.* Television is very expensive, and newspaper advertising is inexpensive. What counts, of course, is the cost-per-thousand exposures rather than the total cost.

On the basis of these characteristics, the media planner has to decide on how to allocate the given budget to the major media categories. For example, the U.S. Army Recruiting Command might decide to allocate $14 million to evening television spots, $4 million to male-oriented magazines, and $2 million to daily newspapers.

**Selecting specific media vehicles.**     The next step is to choose the specific media vehicles within each media type that would produce the desired response in the most cost-effective way. Consider the category of male-oriented magazines, which includes *Playboy, Penthouse, Home Mechanics, Esquire, Motorcycle,* and so on. The media planner turns to several volumes put out by Standard Rate and Data that provide circulation and cost data for different ad sizes, color options, ad positions, and quantities of insertions. Beyond this, the media planner evaluates the different magazines on qualitative characteristics such as credibility, prestige, geographical editioning, occupational editioning, reproduction quality, editorial climate, lead time, and psychological impact. The media planner makes a final judgment as to which specific vehicles will deliver the best reach, frequency, and impact for the money. Media planners normally calculate the *cost per thousand persons* reached by a particular vehicle. If a full-page, four-color advertisement in *Newsweek* costs $30,000 and *Newsweek*'s estimated readership is 6 million persons, then the cost of reaching each one thousand persons is $5. The same advertisement in *Business Week* may cost $18,000 but reach only 2 million persons, at a cost per thousand of $9. The media planner would rank the various

**Table 16–1**

PROFILES OF MAJOR MEDIA CATEGORIES

| Medium | Volume in Billions (1978) | Example of Cost (1977) | Advantages | Limitations |
|---|---|---|---|---|
| Newspapers | $11.1 | $9,975 one page, weekday *Chicago Tribune* | Flexibility; timeliness; good local market coverage; broad acceptance; high believability | Short life; poor reproduction quality; small "pass-along" audience |
| Television | 7.6 | $2,700 for 30 seconds of prime time in Chicago | Combines sight, sound, and motion; appealing to the senses; high attention; high reach | High absolute cost; high clutter; fleeting exposure; less audience selectivity |
| Direct mail | 5.3 | $950 for the names and addresses of 19,000 veterinarians | Audience selectivity; flexibility; no ad competition within the same medium; personalization | Relatively high cost; "junk mail" image |
| Radio | 2.6 | $179 for one minute of prime time in Chicago | Mass use; high geographical, and demographic selectivity; low cost | Audio presentation only; lower attention than television; nonstandardized rate structures; fleeting exposure |
| Magazines | 2.2 | $30,915 one page, four color in *Newsweek* | High geographical and demographic selectivity; credibility and prestige; high-quality reproduction; long life; good pass-along readership | Long ad purchase lead time; some waste circulation; no guarantee of position |
| Outdoor | 0.4 | $824 prime billboard cost per month in Chicago | Flexibility; high repeat exposure; low cost; low competition | No audience selectivity; creative limitations |

Note: The volume in billions in column 2 is from *Advertising Age*, January 8, 1979, p. S-8. Miscellaneous media add another $9 billion, making the total $38.2 billion.

magazines according to cost per thousand and favor those magazines with the lowest cost per thousand.

**Deciding on media timing.**    The third step in media selection is *timing*. It breaks down into a macroproblem and a microproblem. The macroproblem is that of *seasonal timing*. For most products, there is a natural variation in the intensity of interest at different times of the year. There is not much interest in Senator X until his reelection; or much interest in university affairs during the summer. Most marketers do not attempt to time their advertising when there is little or no natural interest. This would take much more money and its effects would be dubious. Most marketers prefer to spend the bulk of the advertising budget just as natural interest is beginning to ripen in the product class and during the height of interest. Counterseasonal advertising is still rare in practice.

The other problem is more of a microproblem, that of *short-run timing* of advertising. How should advertising be spaced during a short period, say a week? Consider three possible patterns. The first is called *burst advertising,* and consists of concentrating all the exposures in a very short space of time, say all in one day. Presumably, this will attract maximum attention and interest and if recall is good, the effect will last for a while. The second pattern is *continuous advertising,* in which the exposures appear evenly throughout the period. This may be most effective when the audience buys or uses the product frequently and needs to be continuously reminded. The third pattern is *intermittent advertising,* in which intermittent small bursts of advertising appear in succession with no advertising in between. This pattern presumably is able to create a little more attention than continuous advertising, and yet has some of the reminder advantages of continuous advertising.

### ADVERTISING EVALUATION

The final step in the effective use of advertising is that of *advertising evaluation.* The most important components are copy testing, media testing, and expenditure level testing.

*Copy testing* can occur both before an ad is put into actual media (copy pretesting) and after it has been printed or broadcast (copy posttesting). The purpose of *ad pretesting* is to make improvements in the advertising copy to the fullest extent prior to its release.[13] There are three major methods of ad pretesting:

1. *Direct ratings.* Here a panel of target consumers or of advertising experts examine alternative ads and fill out rating questionnaires. Sometimes a single question is raised, such as "Which of these ads do you think would influence you most to buy the service?" Or a more elaborate form consisting of several rating scales may be used, such as the one shown in Figure 16–5. Here the person evaluates the ad's attention strength, read-through strength, cognitive strength, affective strength, and behavioral strength, assigning a number of points (up to a maximum) in each case. The underlying theory is that an effective ad must score high on all these properties if it is ultimately to stimulate buying action. Too often ads are evaluated only on

FIGURE 16–5

Rating Sheet for Ads

Attention: How well does the ad catch the reader's attention? ____(20)

Read-through strength: How well does the ad lead the reader to read further? ____(20)

Cognitive strength: How clear is the central message or benefit? ____(20)

Affective strength: How effective is the particular appeal? ____(20)

Behavioral strength: How well does the ad suggest follow-through action? ____(20)

```
|_____|_____|_____|_____|_____|   ____ Total
0          20         40         60         80        100
    Poor ad   Mediocre ad  Average ad   Good ad    Great ad
```

their attention- or comprehension-creating abilities. At the same time, it must be appreciated that direct rating methods are judgmental and less reliable than harder evidence of an ad's actual impact on a target consumer. Direct rating scales help primarily to screen out poor ads rather than identify great ads.

2. *Portfolio tests.* Here respondents are given a dummy portfolio of ads and asked to take as much time as they want to read them. After putting them down, the respondents are asked to recall the ads they saw—unaided or aided by the interviewer—and to play back as much as they can about each ad. The results are taken to indicate an ad's ability to stand out and its intended message to be understood.

3. *Laboratory tests.* Some researchers assess the potential effect of an ad by measuring physiological reactions—heartbeat, blood pressure, pupil dilation, perspiration—using such equipment as galvanometers, tachistoscopes, size-distance tunnels, and pupil dilation measuring equipment. These physiological tests at best measure the attention-getting and arousing power of an ad rather than any higher state of consciousness that the ad might produce.

There are two popular *ad posttesting methods,* the purpose of which is to assess whether the desired impact is being achieved or what the possible ad weaknesses are.

1. *Recall tests.* These involve finding persons who are regular users of the media vehicle and asking them to recall advertisers and products contained in the issue under study. They are asked to recall or play back everything they can remember. The administrator may or may not aid them in their recall. Recall scores are prepared on the basis of their responses and used to indicate the power of the ad to be noticed and retained.

2. *Recognition tests.* Recognition tests call for sampling the readers of a given issue of the vehicle, say a magazine, asking them to point out what they recognize as having seen and/or read. For each ad, three different Starch readership scores (named after Daniel Starch, who provides the leading service) are prepared from the recognition data:

- *Noted.* The percent of readers of the magazine who say they had previously seen the advertisement in the particular magazine.
- *Seen/associated.* The percent of readers who say they have seen or read any part

of the ad that clearly indicates the names of the product (or service) of the advertiser.

- *Read most.* The percent of readers who not only looked at the advertisement, but who say that they read more than half of the total written material in the ad.

The Starch organization also furnishes Adnorms—that is, average scores for each product class for the year, and separately for men and women for each magazine, to enable advertisers to evaluate their ads in relation to competitors' ads.

It must be stressed that all these efforts rate the communication effectiveness of the ad and not necessarily its impact on attitude or behavior. The latter are much harder to measure. Most advertisers appear satisfied in knowing that their ad has been seen and comprehended, and appear unwilling to spend additional funds to determine the ad's sales effectiveness.

Another advertising element that is normally tested is media. *Media testing* seeks to determine whether a given media vehicle is cost-effective in reaching and influencing the target audience. A common way to test a media vehicle is to place a coupon ad and see how many coupons are returned. Another media testing device is to compare the ad readership scores in different media vehicles as a sign of media effectiveness.

Finally, the advertising expenditure level itself can be tested. *Expenditure-level testing* involves arranging experiments in which advertising expenditure levels are varied over similar markets to see the variation in response. A "high spending" test would consist of spending twice as much money in a similar territory as another to see how much more sales response (orders, inquiries, etc.) this produces. If the sales response is only slightly greater in the high spending territory, it may be concluded, other things being equal, that the lower budget is adequate.

## SALES PROMOTION

Sales promotion comprises a wide variety of tactical promotional tools of a short-term incentive nature designed to stimulate earlier and/or stronger target market response. These tools can be subclassified into tools for *consumer promotion* (e.g., samples, coupons, money refund offers, prices off, gifts, contests, trading stamps, demonstrations), *dealer promotion* (e.g., free goods, merchandise allowances, cooperative advertising, push money, dealer sales contests), and *sales force promotion* (e.g., bonuses, contests, sales rallies).

Although sales promotion tools are a motley collection, they have two distinctive qualities:

1. *Insistent presence.* Many sales promotion tools have an attention-getting, sometimes urgent, quality that can break through habits of buyer inertia toward a particular service. They tell the buyers of a chance that they won't have again to get something special. This appeals to a broad spectrum of buyers, although particu-

larly to the economy-minded, with the disadvantage that this type of buyer tends to be less loyal to any particular brand in the long run.

2. *Product demotion.* Some of these tools suggest that the seller is anxious for the sale. If they are used too frequently or carelessly, they may lead buyers to wonder whether the brand is desirable or reasonably priced.

Sales promotion tools are used by a large variety of nonprofit organizations. Some colleges in recent years have passed out frisbees with their names on them on the beaches of Fort Lauderdale; sent up scholarship balloons; offered finder's fees; sponsored all-expense-paid college weekends for high school counselors and prospective students; and so on. Some hospitals have sponsored filet mignon candlelight dinners for new mothers; televised bingo games for patients; and provided country club memberships for new doctors joining their staff. And family planners in many parts of the world have offered incentives—transistor radios, cookware, costume jewelry, free bank accounts, and so on—to potential adopters of birth control measures.

Sales promotion expenditures have grown faster in recent years than advertising expenditures. Various factors have contributed to the rapid growth of sales promotion.[14] Internal factors include the following: (1) promotion has become more acceptable to management as an effective means to stimulate sales, (2) more managers are qualified to use sales promotion tools, and (3) managers are under greater pressure to obtain a quick sales response. External factors include the following: (1) the number of brands has increased, (2) competitors have become more promotion-minded, (3) inflation and recession have made consumers more incentive oriented, and (4) there is a belief that advertising efficiency has declined due to costs, media clutter, and government control.

No single purpose can be advanced for sales promotion tools, since they are so varied in form. Overall, sales promotion techniques make three contributions: (1) *communication*—they gain attention and usually provide information that will, it is hoped, lead to trying the product; (2) *incentive*—they incorporate some concession, inducement, or contribution that is designed to represent value to the receiver; and (3) *invitation*—they include a distinct invitation to engage in the transaction now.

We will define *incentives* as *something of financial or symbolic value added to an offer to encourage some overt behavioral response.*[15] The decision by an organization to use incentives as part of its promotional plan calls for seven distinct steps.

The first step is to specify *the objective* for which it is deemed necessary or desirable to undertake the use of incentives. Three objectives can be distinguished. Sometimes incentives are offered to create an immediate behavioral response because the organization has excess capacity or inventory. For example, inventories tend to build up for mature products, and organizations resort to price specials or dealer allowances to stimulate early purchase. Incentives may also be offered to promote trial of a product or service by groups which normally would not venture to try the product. Finally, incentives may be offered to win goodwill toward the organization, as when an organization offers to match its employees' contributions to a particular charity.

The second step is to determine the *inclusiveness of the incentive*—that is, whether it will be offered to individuals or to the groups to which the target individuals belong. Most incentives are offered to individuals for their direct benefit. A case of an incentive that is offered to a group is exemplified in communities which offer to provide free blood to all persons in the community if 4 percent or more of the community's residents make blood donations.

The third step is to specify the *recipient* of the incentive—that is, whether incentives should go to consumers, suppliers, or sales agents. For example, incentives to promote vasectomies may be offered to the consumer, to the doctor, or to the canvasser who recruits prospects. At one time, canvassers in India were so incentivized to find prospects that they brought in men who were too young to know better and men who were too old for it to matter.

The fourth step is to determine the *direction of the incentives*—that is, whether they should be positive (rewarding) or negative (punishing). Commercial organizations normally work with incentives rather than disincentives in promoting their offer. Governments work with both with equal facility: They offer subsidies and special advantages to encourage certain types of behavior and impose taxes or costs on other types of behavior. In any particular problem area, either option may be available. Nations wishing to expand the birthrate offer family allowances as an incentive. Nations wishing to contract the birthrate reduce family allowances or disproportionately tax large families.

The fifth step is to determine the *form of the incentive*—that is, whether it should consist of monetary or nonmonetary value. Monetary incentives include price-off, cash, bonds, and savings accounts. Nonmonetary incentives include a whole variety of things such as food, free education, health care, lottery tickets, or old age security. The form of the incentive must be carefully researched because its nuances may offend the target group. For example, although cash is a very tangible incentive, it may be viewed as a corrupt consideration if it is used to influence the decision on how many children to have. An offer of better housing may be received more favorably.

The sixth step is to determine the *amount of incentive.* An overly small incentive is ineffective and an overly large one is wasteful. If the incentive is nongraduated, the amount may seem too small for those in higher income brackets and too much for those in lower income brackets. This has led to interest in graduated incentives whereby the amount offered varies with the consumer's economic circumstances.

The seventh step is the *time of payment of the incentive.* Most incentives are paid immediately upon the adoption of the target behavior. Thus in the family planning area, the adoption of sterilization is usually immediately followed by payment. But the agreement to use birth controls pills may not be rewarded except on the basis of results each year.

In summary, incentives are an important means of promotion but they require several steps of analysis and research. Commercial companies tend to learn over time what incentives work best and their optimal amounts and timing. In the area of family planning, several propositions are emerging about incentives and their effective use.[16] Similar knowledge is accumulating on the use of incentives in other health-related areas, such as nutrition, immunization, and self-medication practices. The outlook is one of increasing use of incentives in social and organizational marketing.

## SUMMARY

All organizations engage in communication and promotion activity. This activity can be considered as the fourth major component in the marketing mix. Promotion is defined as the development of persuasive communications. The main tools of promotion fall into four categories: advertising, sales promotion, personal selling, and publicity. This chapter discusses the first two tools.

Advertising is an extremely important tool in the commercial world and is coming into increased use in the nonprofit sector. It is used to promote political candidates, social causes, philanthropic causes, military recruitment, and the services of hospitals, universities, churches, and other nonprofit organizations. It is a sophisticated and expensive tool that calls for skill in setting advertising objectives and budgets; in developing effective messages, media, and timing; and in evaluating advertising results.

Sales promotion consists of incentive tools designed to stimulate early product trial or win customer goodwill. The organization has to decide on such issues as the incentive's inclusiveness (individual or group), the recipient (dealer or final consumer), the direction (negative or positive), the form (monetary or nonmonetary), the amount (large or small), and the timing of payment (immediate or deferred).

## QUESTIONS

**1.** A downtown San Francisco hospital wants to attract as "walk-in" patients workers who commute to the city and who have colds, infections, or other ailments that can be treated in the hospital's clinic. What advertising objectives would be appropriate? What media and execution style(s) would you recommend?

**2.** The U.S. Postal Service wants to increase sales of commemorative stamps and first-day covers to stamp collectors. What media would you recommend? Explain your selection.

**3.** The National Safety Council has used advertising to promote seatbelt use. Suppose they planned a campaign directed at getting parents to be sure their infants and small children are safely restrained when they ride in automobiles. Describe a rational message, an emotional message, and a moral message that might be considered for this campaign.

**4.** Suppose the National Safety Council (question 3) found that many parents were unaware that infants were safer in special car seats than in the arms of an adult, while other parents were aware but had not purchased car seats. Still other parents had purchased and installed car seats but didn't always use them. What is the marketing communicator's task in dealing with these three different buyer readiness states?

**5.** Pottsville College is considering three types of media: billboard display space near the Omaha Airport, prime time radio spots, and display ads in local newspapers throughout Nebraska. Assuming that each of the three approaches has approximately the same annual cost, evaluate the limitations and advantages of each in relation to Pottsville's objective.

**6.** What incentives might a college offer to encourage its current students to attend summer session there?

## NOTES

**1.** These definitions, with the exceptions of the one for sales promotion, came from *Marketing Definitions: A Glossary of Marketing Terms* (Chicago: American Marketing Association, 1960).

**2.** H. E. Alexander, *Financing the 1976 Election* (Washington, D.C.: Congressional Quarterly Press, 1979).

**3.** See John A. Zeigler, "Social Change Through Issue Advertising," *Sociological Inquiry,* Winter 1970, pp. 159–65.

**4.** There are several models of buyer readiness states. See, for example, Robert J. Lavidge and Gary A. Steiner, "A Model for Predictive Measurements of Advertising Effectiveness," *Journal of Marketing,* October 1961, pp. 59–62.

**5.** Michael L. Ray, *Marketing Communication and the Hierarchy of Effects* (Cambridge, Mass.: Marketing Science Institute, November 1973).

**6.** See Russell H. Colley, *Defining Advertising Goals for Measured Advertising Results* (New York: Association of National Advertisers, 1961).

**7.** See Michael L. Ray and William L. Wilkie, "Fear: The Potential of an Appeal Neglected by Marketing," *Journal of Marketing,* January 1970, pp. 55–56; and Brian Sternthal and C. Samuel Craig, "Fear Appeals: Revisited and Revised," *Journal of Consumer Research,* December 1974, pp. 22–34.

**8.** See Brian Sternthal and C. Samuel Craig, "Humor in Advertising," *Journal of Marketing,* October 1973, pp. 12–18.

**9.** See John C. Maloney, "Marketing Decisions and Attitude Research," in George L. Baker, Jr., ed., *Effective Marketing Coordination* (Chicago: American Marketing Association, 1961).

**10.** Dik Warren Twedt, "How to Plan New Products, Improve Old Ones, and Create Better Advertising," *Journal of Marketing,* January 1969, pp. 53–57.

**11.** See William A. Mindak and H. Malcolm Bybee, "Marketing's Application to Fund Raising," *Journal of Marketing,* July 1971, pp. 13–18.

**12.** See C. I. Hovland, A. A. Lumsdaine, and F. D. Sheffield, *Experiments on*

*Mass Communication,* Vol. 3 (Princeton, N.J.: Princeton University Press, 1948).

**13.** Novelli reports that many public service announcements are dull and ineffective. New ads should first be pretested. He has devised a Health Message Testing Service that has been used to test and analyze messages on high blood pressure, breast self-examination, childhood immunization, smoking cessation, drug abuse prevention, physical fitness, and offers for telephone assistance and printed materials on cancer. See William D. Novelli, "Copy Testing Messages on Health," a presentation to the Advertising Research Conference of the American Marketing Association, New York chapter, May 16, 1978.

**14.** See Roger A. Strang, "Sales Promotion—Fast Growth, Faulty Management," *Harvard Business Review,* July–August 1976, pp. 115–24.

**15.** This definition, and the following discussion, relies largely on two sources: Edward Pohlman, *Incentives and Compensations in Birth Planning* (Chapel Hill: Carolina Population Center, University of North Carolina, 1971); and Everett M. Rogers, "Effects of Incentives on the Discussion of Innovations: The Case of Family Planning in Asia," a chapter in Gerald Zaltman, ed., *Processes and Phenomena of Social Change* (New York: Wiley, 1973).

**16.** *Ibid.*

# Public Relations Decisions

Suzanne Edwards has been Director of Public Relations for Chicago's 265-bed Children's Memorial Hospital for more than seven years. We asked her what her job involves.

"Our function includes a wide variety of activities to keep our diverse publics informed, interested, and supportive of the goals of Children's Memorial Hospital.

"We produce several kinds of publications during the year to reach different publics. Among them is the hospital's *Annual Report,* which we produce and distribute by mail to approximately 18,000 people, representing all of our publics. The *Children's Voice* is our feature-news magazine, issued six times a year and sent to the same 18,000 mailing list. Our 1,600 employees receive a copy of *Newsbreak,* a weekly one-page newsletter, devoted to news of hospital activities and personnel, and to community events of interest. Our medical and dental staff and Board of Directors and Woman's Board receive *Administrative Highlights,* a monthly newsletter. We mail a *Directory of Professional Staff and Services* to all referring physicians in the Midwest for a convenient reference to our professional staff and services.

"Our department also produces brochures for hospital-wide use, including: an informational booklet in Spanish and English for parents, to inform them about hospital procedures and services; a booklet for children, also in Spanish and English, to explain what will happen to them in the hospital and to alleviate their fears; a general fact book on hospital services; nurse and general employee recruiting booklets. We also develop a mailing for our Woman's Board for their annual fundraising campaign, and major brochures for the hospital fundraising staff. We assist individual hospital departments to produce printed materials, and distribute some health education pamphlets, designed to help parents learn how to deal with various children's problems.

"We also plan and promote hospital *special events.* There are Recognition Days to honor long-term employees and volunteers, groundbreaking and building dedications, and anniversary celebrations. We hold such events as Children's Art Fairs, Community Festivals, and Employee Arts, Crafts, and Hobby Shows. We also plan and implement the hospital's annual meeting of the corporation.

"One of our major responsibilities is *community relations.* Our neighbors are ambivalent about the hospital. They respect what we do for children, but don't like parking and traffic problems, or the sound of ambulances at 2:00 A.M. We needed community approval to build a new garage, and it took four years of dialog with our community to get our plans approved. We have tried to preserve the residential look of the area with landscaping and to be a good neighbor. Often, our job as public relations people is to turn lemons into lemonade. Some positive community relations efforts have been holding open houses for new facilities and hospital tours to bring members of the community into the hospital to see what we do for children.

"A hospital, like any other organization, benefits from positive external *publicity,* and it is the responsibility of our public relations office to coordinate all dealings with the media, either responding to media inquiries or initiating stories or features.

"There are always projects waiting on the backburner. We would like to produce a sound/slide film about Children's for hospital speakers to take out to schools, local groups, and organizations. We need an improved *corporate identification program* to bring a more uniform look to our printed materials. In 1982, Children's will be celebrating its 100th anniversary, a major milestone for which we have already started planning a year-long program of activities.

"A public relations person must be a jack-of-all trades. We must be competent communicators, have good interpersonal skills, good judgment, and be adept problem solvers. The challenges and opportunities are infinite."

SOURCE: Talk given by Suzanne Edwards, Director of Public Relations, Children's Memorial Hospital, to students at the J.L. Kellogg Graduate School of Management, Northwestern University, February 7, 1978.

Today, public relations (PR) is a well-established function in profit and nonprofit organizations that fulfills a number of needed functions for the organization. In the course of performing its basic tasks, an organization will seek the attention of certain publics and unavoidably attract the attention of other publics. The local community, news media, bankers, local politicians, government officials, social action groups—all may take an active or reactive interest in the organization's activities. The organization's managers can handle these publics in the course of carrying on their other duties. But sooner or later the organization recognizes the advantages of consolidating or coordinating these activities in the hands of a public relations manager. In employing a public relations manager, the organization can gain several advantages: (1) better anticipation of potential problems, (2) better handling of these problems, (3) consistent public-oriented policies and strategies, and (4) more professional written and oral communications.

The public relations function will be of high or low influence in the organization, depending on the board and chief officer's attitude toward the function. In some organizations, the public relations manager is a vice president and sits in on all meetings involving public-sensitive information and actions. He or she not only puts out fires but also counsels management on actions that will avoid starting fires. In other organizations, public relations is a middle-management function charged with getting out publications and handling news and special events. The public relations people are not involved in policy or strategy formulation, only tactics.

The recent emergence of marketing as a "hot topic" in nonprofit circles has raised a major question in the minds of chief administrators and public relations managers as to the relation between marketing and public relations in a nonprofit organization. Clearly, the two functions work well together in business firms, with marketing focusing on the development of plans to market the company's products to consumers, while public relations takes care of relations with the other publics. In nonprofit organizations, the relationship is less clear. Both are boundary functions concerned with achieving certain results with various internal and external publics. Are the two functions redundant? Is one more important or comprehensive than the other? Do they play equal but different roles?

This chapter advances the thesis that public relations is most effective when viewed and conducted as part of the marketing mix being used by the organization to pursue its marketing objectives. We will look at the following questions:

1. How did the public relations function evolve?
2. What is the relation between public relations and marketing in nonprofit organizations?
3. What are the main tools of the public relations practitioner?

## THE HISTORICAL EVOLUTION OF PUBLIC RELATIONS

Public relations, like marketing, is a relatively new corporate function although its roots go back into ancient history.[1] Edward L. Bernays, one of the fathers of modern public relations, posited that the three main elements of public relations are as old as society: informing people, persuading people, and integrating people with people.[2] Bernays traced public relations from primitive society—in which leaders controlled by force, intimidation, and persuasion—to Babylonia —where kings commissioned historians to paint favorable images of them. The Renaissance and Reformation freed men's minds from established dogmas, thus leading institutions to develop more subtle means to influence people. In America, historical milestones for "public relations" include:

- Samuel Adams' use of the press to unite the colonists against the British.
- The abolitionist movement's use of public relations as a political tool to rally support for blacks in the North, including the publication of *Uncle Tom's Cabin.*
- P. T. Barnum's use of public relations to generate newsworthiness about an event —the arrival of his circus—by placing articles in newspapers.

Corporate public relations first emerged in the late nineteenth century and passed through the five stages shown in Figure 17–1. In the first stage, corporations established a *contact* function to influence legislators and newspapers to support positions favorable to business. The legislative contact function became known as *lobbying,* and the newspaper contact function became known as *press agentry.* George Westinghouse is credited with the formal establishment of public relations when he hired two men in 1889 to fight the advocates of direct current electricity and to promote instead alternating current.[3]

The next stage occurred when companies began to recognize the positive value of planned *publicity* to create customer interest in the company and its products. Publicity entailed finding or creating events, preparing company- or product-slanted news stories, and trying to interest the press in using them. Companies recognized that special skills are needed to develop publicity and began to add publicists to their ranks.

Somewhat later, public relations practitioners began to recognize the value of conducting *research* into public opinion prior to developing and launching public relations campaigns. The emerging sciences of public opinion measurement and mass communication theory permitted more sophistication in the conduct of public relations. Forward-looking firms added specialists who could research public opinion.

These functions—contact, publicity, and research—were uncoordinated in the typical firm. The organization's lobbyists had little to do with the organiza-

## FIGURE 17–1

Historical Evolution of Public Relations

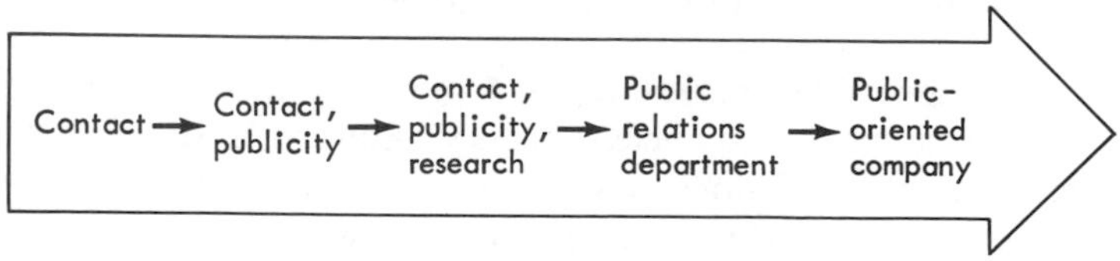

| Contact → | Contact, publicity → | Contact, publicity, research → | Public relations department → | Public-oriented company |

tion's publicists; the publicists had little to do with the researchers. This led finally to the concept of a *public relations department*, which integrated all the work going on to cultivate the goodwill of different publics of the company. In larger organizations, public relations departments grew to encompass subspecialties to deal with each public—stockholders, neighbors, employees, customers, government agencies—and each tool—publications, press relations, research, and so on.

The establishment of a public relations department did not ensure that the organization as a whole acted like a *public company*. The vice president of public relations had limited influence over other departments and needed the backing of top management to press for public-oriented actions by all departments. Organizations were facing growing challenges in the form of consumerism, environmentalism, energy conservation, inflation, shortages, employment discrimination, and safety. Public relations people wanted a more active role in counseling the organization and its departments on how to act as public citizens. PR practitioners emphasize that their job is not just to produce "good words" but to produce "good deeds followed by good words." Unless they can get the organization to act like a good citizen, good words alone will not be enough.

## THE RELATION BETWEEN PUBLIC RELATIONS AND MARKETING

Public relations is often confused with one of its subfunctions, such as press agentry, company publications, lobbying, fire fighting, and so forth. Yet it is a more inclusive concept. The most frequently quoted definition of PR is the following:

> **Public relations** is the management function which evaluates public attitudes, identifies the policies and procedures of an individual or an organization with the public interest, and executes a program of action to earn public understanding and acceptance.[4]

Sometimes the following short definition is given, which says that PR stands for *performance* (P) plus *recognition* (R).

Most of today's public relations people have come out of English departments and journalism schools. Management thinks of PR as essentially a communication tool. Journalism training adds the advantage that the PR person will know how the press thinks and will probably know a lot of press people, thus assuring greater access to the media.

When marketing has been proposed as a useful function to install in nonprofit organizations, public relations people have reacted in different ways. Some PR people feel that they are doing the organization's marketing work and that there is no need to hire a marketing person. Other PR people feel that they could learn quickly whatever is involved in marketing and that there is no need to add a marketer. Still other PR people see marketing and PR as separate but equal functions and do not feel threatened. Finally, other PR people see marketing as the dominant function to which they will one day have to report.

For our purpose, we shall view public relations as primarily a communication tool to advance the marketing objectives of the organization. We see the following differences between public relations and marketing:

1. Public relations is primarily a communication tool, whereas marketing also includes need assessment, product development, pricing, and distribution.

2. Public relations seeks to influence attitudes, whereas marketing tries to elicit specific behaviors, such as purchase, joining, voting, and so on.

3. Public relations does not define the goals of the organization, whereas marketing is intimately involved in defining the business' mission, customers, and services.

## THE PUBLIC RELATIONS PROCESS

PR practitioners view themselves as the caretakers and enhancers of the organization's image. At various times they are assigned the task of forming, maintaining, or changing attitudes. In this connection, they carry out the five-step process shown in Figure 17–2. We will examine each step below.

### IDENTIFYING THE ORGANIZATION'S RELEVANT PUBLICS

An organization would like to have the goodwill of every public that it affects or is affected by. This is usually not possible without an active program to communicate with and relate to each public. Given limited public relations

### FIGURE 17–2

The Public Relations Process

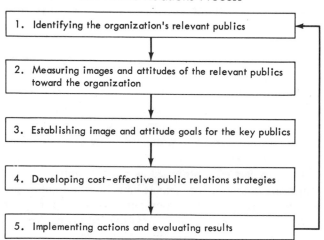

1. Identifying the organization's relevant publics

2. Measuring images and attitudes of the relevant publics toward the organization

3. Establishing image and attitude goals for the key publics

4. Developing cost-effective public relations strategies

5. Implementing actions and evaluating results

resources, the organization has to concentrate its attention on certain publics more than others. Most organizations will distinguish between its primary, secondary, and tertiary publics.

An organization's primary publics are those that it relates to on an active and continuous basis. The primary publics of an organization are its clients, employees, directors, and the community. The clients receive the services of the organization. The employees provide the services. The directors govern the organization. And the community provides the setting and location where the organization carries on its activities. If the goodwill of any of these groups disappears —clients stop coming, employees start quitting, directors lose their interest, or the community becomes hostile—the organization is in deep trouble.

An organization also faces four secondary publics that it must monitor and relate to on a fairly continuous basis, namely, suppliers, dealers, government groups, and competitors. Suppliers provide the organization with its equipment, office materials, fuel, and other inputs needed to carry on the organization's daily operations. Dealers carry the organization's goods and services to the final clients who may be scattered widely. Government groups are legislators, jurists, and agency heads who provide services, define and enforce the law, and collect taxes. Competitors are those direct and indirect groups representing alternative sources for the same goods, services, or satisfactions provided by the organization.

Finally, an organization will have to deal with various tertiary publics from time to time. General purpose groups are those that seek to advance the interests of their members, such as labor unions, churches, clubs, and associations. Special purpose groups are those that exist to carry out some purpose outside of themselves, such as charitable organizations and social action groups. The organization will contribute time or money to a number of these groups because their cause is worthwhile in itself (e.g., charitable groups) or it will benefit the organization directly (e.g., trade association). Other tertiary groups may take on a confrontation role toward the organization (e.g., a hostile labor union or social action group) and the organization must choose between appeasement and counterattack.

The publics are related not only to the organization, but also to each other in many important ways. A particular public may have a great deal of influence on the attitudes and behavior of other publics toward the organization. Consider a college whose students are highly satisfied. Their enthusiasm will be transmitted to their parents and to friends back home who might be potential students. Their enthusiasm will have a reinforcing effect on the faculty who will feel that their teaching is effective. Their enthusiasm will affect the future level of support they will give to the school as alumni. Thus, the satisfaction felt by students will influence the attitudes and behavior of other university publics.

Likewise, the dissatisfaction of a particular public will affect the attitudes of other publics. Suppose current students are highly dissatisfied with the college over some policy. If the students choose to act, they have several recourses. These recourses are suggested in Figure 17–3. First, they may go directly to the

**FIGURE 17–3**

Dynamic Relations between a University and Its Publics

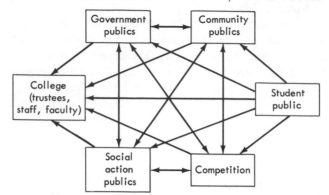

college (administration, trustees, faculty) and try to negotiate a better policy. Second, they may attempt to win the sympathy of the community as an effective pressure to bring on the college. Third, they may attempt to get the government to intervene. Fourth, they may solicit the support of various social action publics. Fifth, they might give up, leave the college, and go over to competitors. Thus, publics that are passive in one period might suddenly be spurred into action in another period because of sympathy with the grievance of a particular public.

From the organization's point of view, it is important to set up relations with its valued publics that produce satisfaction. The organization's task is to consider what benefits to offer each of its valued publics in exchange for their valued resources and support. Once an organization begins to think about cultivating the support of a public, it is beginning to think of that public as a *market,* a group to whom it will attempt to offer benefits in exchange for valued resources.

### MEASURING IMAGES AND ATTITUDES OF THE RELEVANT PUBLICS

Once the organization has identified its various publics, it needs to find out how each public thinks and feels about the organization. Management will have some idea of each public's attitude simply through its regular contacts with members of that public. But impressions based on casual contact cannot necessarily be trusted. Recently, a college wanted to rent its stadium facilities to a professional football team for five Sundays as a way to acquire more revenue. The college's administrators thought that most local residents and city council members would be agreeable. However, when it started to make the move, a group of local citizens organized themselves and attacked the college, calling it insensitive and arrogant. They complained that the football crowd would use up parking spaces, leave litter, walk on lawns, and be rowdy. A large number of citizens, including city council members, revealed deep-seated negative attitudes toward the college that only needed an issue in order to be brought to the surface. Even here, the college's administration dismissed the community spokesmen as a minority and unrepresentative of the real feeling of the majority. Needless to say, the vote went against the college, to its surprise.

To really know the attitudes of a public, the organization needs to undertake some formal marketing research. A good start is to organize a focus group consisting of six to ten members of that public and lead a discussion to probe their knowledge and feelings about the organization. While the observations of the focus group are not necessarily representative, they normally contribute interesting perspectives and raise interesting questions which the organization will want to explore more systematically. Eventually, the organization may find it worthwhile to conduct formal field research in the form of a public opinion survey. The public opinion survey measures such variables as awareness, knowledge, interest, and attitude toward the organization. Exhibit 17–1 describes the highlights of a public opinion survey for the American Red Cross.

### ESTABLISHING IMAGE AND ATTITUDE GOALS FOR THE KEY PUBLICS

Through periodically researching its key publics, the organization will have some hard data on how these publics view the organization (see Chapter 2, pp. 56–62). The findings can be assembled in the form of a scorecard such as the one illustrated for a college in Table 17–1. The scorecard becomes the basis for developing a *public relations plan* for the coming period. The college's scorecard shows that high school counselors have a medium amount of knowledge about the college and a negative attitude. Since high school counselors are important in influencing the college choice decision, the organization needs to develop a communication program that will improve high school counselors' knowledge and attitudes toward the college. The goals should be made even more specific and measurable, such as "80 percent of the high school counselors should know at least four key things about the college and at least 60 percent should report having a positive opinion about the college, within two years." Making the goals concrete means that the necessary activities can be planned at the right scale, the necessary budget can be estimated to finance these activities, and the results can be measured later to evaluate the success of the plan.

Looking at the next item on the scorecard, we see that communication also has to be directed at high school seniors to increase their knowledge and improve their attitude toward the college. As for alumni, their knowledge and attitude are ideal, and the college's job is simply to maintain their enthusiasm. As for the general public, the college may decide to do nothing. The general public's knowledge and attitude are not that important in attracting students, and the cost of improving the situation would be too high in relation to the value.

**EXHIBIT 17–1.** Public opinion research for the American Red Cross

The public opinion polling firm of Louis Harris conducts periodic surveys of public opinion toward the American Red Cross. Here is a sample of the questions asked in the 1976 survey.

### WHAT DOES THE PUBLIC KNOW ABOUT RED CROSS SERVICES?

1. What comes to mind first when you hear the words "American Red Cross"?
2. What other kinds of activities is the Red Cross engaged in?
3. For each activity, please say which statement on the list describes how important you feel that activity is (extremely important, very important, quite important, rather important, not too important, not at all important).
4. For each activity, please mention which one or more organizations provide that service.
5. Which one of these activities do you think the American Red Cross spends the most money on?

### HOW IMPORTANT IS THE WORK OF THE RED CROSS AND HOW WELL DOES IT DO ITS JOB?

1. These organizations serve the American community. Which one do you personally feel does the *most* important work? Which does the *next* most important work? Which does the *third* most important work?
2. For each organization, would you say its performance is extremely good, very good, good, just fair, or poor?
3. Is there anything you don't especially like about the American Red Cross?

### WHERE DOES THE RED CROSS GET ITS FUNDS?

1. Do any of the United Way contributions get distributed to the American Red Cross or not?
2. If yes, about what percent of the money raised by the United Way would you guess *is* distributed by it to the American Red Cross?
3. Which one of these statements best describes your feeling about the amount of money the Red Cross has available? It has more than it really needs. It has enough money to do the job. It doesn't have quite enough money to do its job. It has a serious lack of funds. Not sure.

The 1976 poll yielded a number of important findings: (1) The Red Cross is perceived almost exclusively as a disaster relief organization, its other services being less well known. (2) There is a vague antipathy toward the Red Cross. (3) Red Cross performance is perceived to be not as good as that of other organizations. (4) Perception of Red Cross need for funds is relatively low.

SOURCE: 1976 National Public Opinion Research Concerning the American National Red Cross.

## Table 17-1
### SCORECARD ON A COLLEGE'S PUBLICS

| Public | Knowledge | Attitude | Public's Importance |
|---|---|---|---|
| High school counselors | Medium | Negative | High |
| High school seniors | Low | Neutral | High |
| Alumni | High | Positive | High |
| General public | Low | Neutral | Low |

### DEVELOPING COST-EFFECTIVE PR STRATEGIES

An organization usually has many options in trying to improve the attitudes of a particular public. Its first task is to understand why the attitudes have come about so that the causal factors can be addressed by an appropriate strategy. Let us return to the college that found that it had weak community support when it wanted to rent its stadium to a professional football team. In digging deeper into the negative citizen attitudes, the college discovered that many local citizens harbored a history of resentments against the college, including that (1) the college never consults citizens or citizen groups before taking actions, (2) the college discriminates against local high school students, preferring to draw students from other parts of the country, (3) the college does not actively inform the local community about campus events and programs, and (4) the college owns local property which goes tax-free and raises the taxes of the citizens. Essentially, the community feels neglected and exploited by the college.

The diagnosis suggests that the college needs to change its ways and establish stronger contacts with the community. It needs to develop a *community relations program*. Here are some of the steps it might take:

1. Identify the local opinion leaders—prominent business people, news editors, city council people, heads of civic organizations, school officials—and build better relationships through inviting them to campus events, consulting with them on college–community issues, and sponsoring luncheons and dinners.
2. Encourage the college's faculty and staff to join local organizations and participate more strongly in community campaigns such as the United Way and American Red Cross Blood Bank program.
3. Develop a speakers' bureau to speak to local groups such as the Kiwanis, Rotary, and so on.
4. Make the college's facilities and programs more available to the community. Classrooms and halls can be offered to local organizations for meetings.
5. Arrange open houses and tours of the campus for the local community.
6. Participate in community special events such as parades, holiday observances, and so on.
7. Establish a community advisory board of community leaders to act as a sounding board for issues facing the college and the community.

Each project involves money and time. The organization will need to estimate the amount of expected attitude improvement with each project in order to
arrive at the best mix of cost-effective actions.

## Implementing Actions and Evaluating Results

The actions to be taken have to be assigned to responsible individuals within
the organization along with concrete objectives, time frames, and budgets. The
public relations department should oversee the results. Evaluating the results of
public relations activities, however, is not easy, since it occurs in conjunction with
other marketing activities and its contribution is hard to separate.

Consider the problem of measuring the value of the organization's publicity
efforts. Publicity is designed with certain audience-response objectives in mind,
and these objectives form the basis of what is measured. The major response
measures are exposures, awareness/comprehension/attitude change, and sales.

The easiest and most common measure of publicity effectiveness is the
number of *exposures* created in the media. Most publicists supply the client with
a "clippings book" showing all the media that carried news about the organization and a summary statement such as the following:

> Media coverage included 3,500 column inches of news and photographs in
> 350 publications with a combined circulation of 79.4 million; 2,500 minutes of air
> time on 290 radio stations and an estimated audience of 65 million; and 660 minutes
> of air time on 160 television stations with an estimated audience of 91 million. If
> this time and space had been purchased at advertising rates, it would have amounted
> to $1,047,000.[5]

The purpose of citing the equivalent advertising cost is to make a case for
publicity's cost-effectiveness, since the total publicity effort must have cost less
than $1,047,000. Furthermore, publicity usually creates more reading and believ-
ing than ads.

Still, this exposure measure is not very satisfying. There is no indication of
how many people actually read, saw, or heard the message, and what they
thought afterward. Furthermore, there is no information on the net audience
reached, since publications have overlapping readership.

A better measure calls for finding out what change in public *awareness/
comprehension/attitude* occurred as a result of the publicity campaign (after
allowing for the impact of other promotional tools). This requires the use of
survey methodology to measure the before-after levels of these variables. The best
measure is sales and profit impact.

Certain PR activities will be found to be too costly in relation to their
impact and might be dropped. Or the PR goals might be recognized as too
ambitious and require modification. Furthermore, new problems will arise with
certain publics and require redirection of the public relations resources. As the
public relations department implements these actions and measures the results,

it will be in a position to return to the earlier steps and take a new reading of where the organization stands in the mind of specific publics and what improvements in public attitudes it needs to pursue. Thus the public relations process is continually recycling, as shown in Figure 17–3.

## PUBLIC RELATIONS TOOLS

Here we want to examine the major public relations media and tools in more detail. They are: (1) written material, (2) audio-visual material, (3) corporate identity media, (4) news, (5) events, (6) speeches, and (7) telephone information service.

### WRITTEN MATERIAL

Organizations rely extensively on written material to communicate with their target publics. For example, a college will use such written material as an annual report, catalogs, employee newsletter, alumni magazine, posters and flyers, and so on.

In preparing each publication, the public relations department must consider *function, aesthetics,* and *cost.* For example, the function of an annual report is to inform interested publics about the organization's accomplishments during the year as well as about its financial status, with the ultimate purpose of generating confidence in the organization and its leaders. Aesthetics enter in that the annual report should be readable, interesting, and professional. If the annual report is published in mimeograph form, it suggests a poor and amateur-type organization. If the annual report is extremely fancy, the public may raise questions as to why a nonprofit organization is spending so much money on graphics instead of on needed services. Cost acts as a constraint in that the organization will allocate a limited amount of money to each publication. The public relations department has to reconcile considerations of function, aesthetics, and cost in developing each publication.

### AUDIO-VISUAL MATERIAL

Audio-visual material—such as films, slides-and-sound, and audio cassettes —are coming into increasing use as communication tools. In the old days, college recruiters, would visit different campuses and present a talk, answer questions, and pass out some written materials to the high school seniors gathered to hear about that college. The students had to concentrate hard on the recruiter's words and some would fall asleep. Today's recruiter, in contrast, comes prepared to deliver a high impact audio-visual presentation about the college. A recruiter from the University of Richmond, for example, shows a 16-mm full-color 12-minute film dramatizing life on the University of Richmond's campus. The film costs $13,000 to produce and has apparently paid for itself many times in improved recruitment effectiveness. Other colleges use a combination of slides and recorded campus sounds that can be very effective and cost much less to produce. Or slides by themselves with recruiter narration can be effective. In all cases, the visual materials should be put together with some care. The author witnessed a college recruiter make a presentation involving 100 slides showing mostly campus buildings, in no particular order, with several slides upside down. The whole presentation bored the high school seniors and, needless to say, few applications came in.

### CORPORATE IDENTITY MEDIA

Normally, each of the organization's separate materials takes on its own look, which not only creates confusion but also misses an opportunity to create and reinforce a *corporate identity.* In an overcommunicated society, organizations have to compete for attention. They should at least try to create a visual identity which the public immediately recognizes. The visual identity is carried through the organization's permanent media such as logos, stationery, brochures, signs, business forms, call cards, buildings, uniforms, and rolling stock.

The corporate identity media become a marketing tool when they are attractive, memorable, and distinctive. The task of creating a coordinated visual identity is not easy. The organization should select a good graphic design consultant. A good consultant will try to get management to identify the essence of the organization, and then will try to turn it into a big idea backed by strong visual symbols. The symbols are adapted to the various organizational media so that they create immediate brand recognition in the minds of various publics.

### NEWS

One of the major tasks of the public relations department is to find or create favorable news about the organization and market it to the appropriate media. The appeal of publicity to many organizations is that it is "free advertising"— that is, it represents exposures at no cost. As someone said: "Publicity is sent to a medium and prayed for while advertising is sent to a medium and paid for." However, publicity is far from free because special skills are required to write good publicity and to "reach" the press. Good publicists cost money.

Publicity has three qualities that make it a worthwhile investment. First, it may have *higher veracity* than advertising because it appears as normal news and not sponsored information. Second, it tends to catch people *off guard* who might otherwise actively avoid sponsored messages. Third, it has high potential for *dramatization* in that it arouses attention coming in the guise of a noteworthy event.

Consider a college suffering from low visibility that adopts the objective of achieving more public recognition through news management. The public relations director will review the college's various components to see whether any natural stories exist. Do any faculty members have unusual backgrounds or are any working on unusual projects? Are any new and unusual courses being taught? Are any exceptional students with unusual backgrounds enrolled? Are any interesting events taking place on campus? Is there a story about the architecture, history, or aspirations of the college? Usually a search along these lines will uncover hundreds of stories that can be fed to the press with the effect of creating much more public recognition of the college. Ideally, the stories chosen should symbolize the kind of college this college wants to be. The stories should support its desired market position.

Getting media organizations to accept press releases and press conferences calls for marketing skill. A good media relations director understands the needs of the press for stories that are interesting and timely. Press releases should be well written and eye-catching. The director will make a point of knowing as many news editors and reporters as possible and helping them interview the organization's leaders when news breaks out. The more the organization welcomes the press, the more likely it is to receive fair and favorable coverage.

### EVENTS

The organization can increase its newsworthiness by creating events that attract the attention of target publics. Thus a college seeking more public attention can host major academic conventions, feature well-known speakers and celebrities, celebrate anniversaries of important events in the history of the college, and hold news conferences. Each well-run event not only impresses the immediate participants, but also serves as an opportunity to develop a multitude of stories directed to relevant media vehicles and audiences.

*Event creation and management* is a particularly important skill in running fundraising drives for nonprofit organizations. Fundraisers have developed a large repertoire of special events, including *anniversary celebrations, art exhibits, auctions, benefit evenings, bingo games, book sales, cake sales, contests, dances, dinners, fairs, fashion shows, parties in unusual places, phonothons, rummage sales, tours,* and *walkathons.* For example, the American Cancer Society distributes a brochure to local units in which they outline the following ideas for special events:

> Dramatic special events attract attention to the American Cancer Society. They bring color, excitement, and glamor to the program. Well planned, they will get excellent coverage in newspapers, on radio and TV, and in newsreels. . . . A Lights-On-Drive, a one-afternoon or one-night House-to-House program have such dramatic appeal that they stir excitement and enthusiasm . . . keep in mind the value of burst of sound such as fire sirens sounding, loud-speaker trucks, fife and drum corps. . . . A most useful special event is the ringing of church bells to add a solemn, dedicated note to the launching of a drive or education project. This should be organized on a division or community basis, and the church bell ringing may be the signal to begin a House-to-House canvass. Rehearsals of bell ringing, community leaders tugging at ropes, offer good picture possibilities.[6]

Exhibit 17–2 provides examples of how churches have created events to attract and hold members.

**EXHIBIT 17–2.** Churches go into high event creation to attract and hold members

Many denominations whose churches used to be a primary center of town or village social life appear to be resorting to desperate measures to recover that sense of community.

In London, for instance, the dean of St. Paul's Cathedral leaped off the pinnacle of his temple and descended by parachute, in an attempt to relate to the young people.

In San Francisco's Grace Cathedral four months later, a capacity crowd of 3,000 attended what had been advertised as a "sensorium." The occasion featured a mixture of the cathedral organ and ear-splitting electric guitars, punctuated with recorded wolf howls and bird shrieks.

The Grace Cathedral "happening" took place almost concurrently with another vivid rite—held in Manhattan's St. Clement's Church near Broadway. Worshippers were blindfolded, told to remove their shoes and led to the basement, where they walked about in their bare feet reciting the general confession. One by one, they subsequently were led to an adjoining lavatory where, in the glare of a brilliant light, their blindfolds were removed. A smiling attendant, whose neck was wrapped in toilet paper, then ceremoniously flushed the toilet—in order to symbolize the absolution of sins.

That bizarre ceremony did not surprise some churchmen, who have seen some of the wildest extremes of group dynamics utilized in attempts to re-establish a sense of community in churches.*

Temple Solael is the domain of Rabbi Bernard Cohen, who has made a name for himself in the last two decades for his avant garde multimedia approach to his work and for his association with celebrities like Suzanne Somers and Henry Winkler.

"Organized religion has been made boring," asserts the 47-year-old clergyman. "In general, it denies full participation and refuses to discuss current issues. The Haggadah [Passover prayer book] is magnificent," he says, "but can we realistically relate to the 10 plagues? On the other hand, we can relate to the oil crisis, the peace negotiations and the PLO."

With the help of his wife, Doris, an art critic, he developed services that included art, drama, music, illusion and coloring prayer books for children.

Since he took over as spiritual leader of the Canoga Park congregation, attendance at services had quadrupled. Most popular are those featuring a talented young illusionist, David Avadon, who adds mime to the rabbi's readings and sermons. Recently, while Rabbi Cohen related the dramatic story of David and Goliath, Avadon faced an earthenware replica of the Philistine giant and, whirling an imaginary sling, shattered it. Other nights, his hands suddenly burst into flames or a bushel of fresh-picked corn turns to ashes—without visible props.

**EXHIBIT 17–2.** Churches go into high event creation to attract and hold members (continued)

> The popular coloring prayer book was inspired by Doris' observation that people doodle when they want to express something they can't put into words. "We noticed that a lot of kids at the service seemed totally uninvolved. So we designed something as an extension of the doodling idea." The result, fondly dubbed "Color Me In Prayer," is a 10-page booklet containing the traditional service and an assortment of pictures to color. There are also blank spaces for children to express their thoughts.
>
> The rabbi is gaining notoriety for spectacular marriage ceremonies. They feature a slide presentation depicting love between couples of all ages and an *a cappella* group called "Songs of the Earth," which sings about the unity of God, man and woman—in 40 languages.**

*SOURCE: Excerpted with permission from "Gimmicks Used to Aid Church Involvement," *Chicago Sun-Times,* May 10, 1969, p. 32. © *Chicago Sun-Times,* 1969.
**SOURCE: Quoted from "Religion Is Fun and Games with the Multimedia Rabbi," *US,* April 4, 1978, p. 20.

SPEECHES

Speeches are another tool through which the organization can communicate with target publics. The public relations director will look for effective spokespersons for the organization and will try to arrange speaking engagements. If a college's president is articulate and attractive, the public relations director will try to line up appearances on national and local talk shows, and at major convention meetings. The president's impact will be further enhanced by engaging a good speech writer and coach. Articulate faculty can also be lined up for speaking engagements and news conferences. The public relations director can set up a speakers' bureau to deliver appropriate talks to community organizations.

TELEPHONE INFORMATION SERVICE

A relatively new public relations tool is a telephone number through which members of the public can get information about the organization. Triton Community College, for example, set up a telephone number which gives prerecorded information about the college, registration times, and costs. Various health organizations have set up telephone numbers that provide health messages about specific symptoms and diseases. The American Cancer Society has set up a national network of offices, called Cancer Information Services Offices, to take calls. Going further, drug abuse centers have set up "hot lines" to take emergency calls. These telephone services suggest that the organization cares about the public and is ready to serve them.

## SUMMARY

Public relations is a well-established function in profit and nonprofit organizations. The recent introduction of marketing into nonprofit organizations has raised the question of marketing's relation to public relations.

There are five views on the subject. Public relations and marketing are seen by various people as separate but equal functions; or equal and overlapping functions; or marketing as the dominant function; or public relations as the dominant function; or public relations and marketing as the same function. This book assumes that public relations is a tool used to advance the marketing purposes of the organization.

The task of public relations is to form, maintain, or change public attitudes toward the organization and/or its products. The process of public relations consists of five steps: (1) identifying the organization's relevant publics, (2) measuring the images and attitudes held by these publics, (3) establishing image and attitude goals for the key publics, (4) developing cost-effective public relations strategies, and (5) implementing actions and evaluating results.

Public relations practitioners have to be skilled communicators and adept at developing written material, audio-visual material, corporate identity media, news, events, speeches, and telephone information service.

## QUESTIONS

**1.** The city of Evanston, Illinois, and the Evanston Chamber of Commerce hired a Chicago public relations firm to develop favorable news stories and press releases about Evanston and to get them published in newspapers and trade journals. One city alderwoman voted against the contract, saying "I don't think the city should be in the public relations business." How would you respond to her statement?

**2.** Draw a diagram showing the publics of (a) a public botanical garden, or (b) a zoo, indicating primary, secondary, and tertiary publics.

**3.** List an appropriate image or attitude goal for each public you identified in question 2.

**4.** A criticism of publicity is that it is difficult to measure its effectiveness. What approaches are available to assess effectiveness, and what are the advantages and disadvantages of each?

**5.** The logo of the American Red Cross is one of the most widely recognized organizational symbols in the United States. What are the advantages to the Red Cross having such a logo?

**6.** A county hospital association would like to build its reputation among county residents for being concerned about their health needs. Devise a telephone information service that would meet this objective.

## NOTES

**1.** Some of the material in this chapter is adapted from Philip Kotler and William Mindak, "Marketing and Public Relations," *Journal of Marketing,* October 1978, pp. 13–20.

**2.** Edward L. Bernays, *Public Relations* (Norman: University of Oklahoma Press, 1952).

**3.** Scott M. Cutlip, "The Beginning of PR Counseling," *Editor and Publisher,* November 26, 1960, p. 16.

**4.** *Public Relations News,* October 27, 1947.

**5.** Arthur M. Merims, "Marketing's Stepchild: Product Publicity," *Harvard Business Review,* November–December 1972, pp. 111–12.

**6.** *Public Information Guide* (New York: American Cancer Society, 1965), p. 19.

# V

## ATTRACTING
## RESOURCES

# Recruitment Marketing: Attracting People

The Dallas Police Department has been criticized in recent years for not having a sufficient number of minority police officers. The police department chief said that this was not due to discrimination, but to the difficulty of attracting members of minority groups who are interested in police work. The department used a variety of "shotgun" measures to attract minorities, with only limited success. A major problem is that police applicants must meet certain qualifications, the major one being the requirement of at least 1¼ years of higher education. The Dallas Police Department decided to solicit the assistance of marketing professors at Southern Methodist University to help them develop a minority recruitment plan.

The professorial team first proceeded to identify the potentially high yield segments of the market. They concluded that the highest yield segment was junior colleges because (1) the graduates have the necessary 45 hours of college credit; (2) there was less competition for these graduates than for senior college graduates; (3) the income prospects for these graduates were similar to police department starting salaries; and (4) junior colleges had a higher concentration of minority members, making it easy to be effective in personal contact and promotion. Senior colleges were chosen as a secondary target segment. The "at-large" market was considered the third, and least attractive, target segment.

The next step consisted of running focus groups and field surveys with minority members to ascertain their attitudes toward the police, police careers for minorities, their personal interest in police work, and their attitudes toward the Dallas community. This research yielded a number of findings. Minority members recognized the importance of police work but were critical of certain practices such as putting white police in black areas. They thought the pay was low and the advancement opportunities limited in relation to the hazards involved in police work. They saw some advantages in police work, although they regarded the Dallas community to be relatively unattractive for blacks.

These findings permitted the police department to develop a market plan for each market segment, consisting of personal recruitment calls, brochures, advertising, and so on. In addition, the plan called for heavy use of radio commercials in the Dallas area on black stations with black police officers describing the employment opportunities in the police force.

SOURCE: Based on information found in Richard W. Hansen, A. Benton Cocanougher, and Michael G. Harvey, "Marketing in the Public Sector: A Case Study," in Ron Curhan, ed., *New Marketing for Social and Economic Progress and Marketing's Contribution to the Firm and to the Society* (Chicago: American Marketing Association, 1974), pp. 248–52.

Every organization faces a *resource attraction* problem. Organizations need to attract people, funds, and so on. In this chapter we will examine the problem of attracting people, and in the next chapter, the problem of attracting funds.

Organizations may seek to attract up to four different types of people: *audiences, members, volunteers,* and *employees.* A performing arts group, for example, gets involved in audience building, membership enrollment, volunteer attraction, and employee recruitment. At the other extreme, a city license bureau is only involved in employee recruitment.

For many organizations, the various people-attraction tasks are interrelated. The possible interrelationships are shown in Figure 18–1 for a performing arts organization. The organization's first task is to convert nonattenders into attenders, namely, to build an audience for its performances. It also hopes to encourage many attenders to become members and donors, for which they receive such benefits as lower ticket prices, better seats, and a monthly magazine. The organization also hopes that some members will become volunteers and help in the hundreds of tasks required to run an arts organization. Finally, some of the volunteers may seek employment positions with the organization.

In the following paragraphs, we will study each of the four people-attraction tasks from a marketing point of view.

## FIGURE 18–1

People-Attraction Flows for a Performing Arts Organization

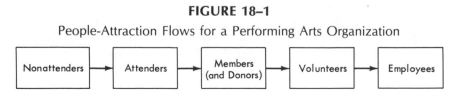

## AUDIENCE ATTRACTION

All organizations are engaged in producing a product or service for a set of consumers. When the offering is a presentation or exhibition, the target consumers are called an *audience*. Actually, the word "audience" suggests a group of people who come to "hear" something, such as a play, opera, sermon, or lecture. The word "spectator" suggests a group of people who come to "see" something, such as a sports event or exhibition. "Audience" and "spectators" can be called "attenders" or "visitors" at the event. We will use the word "audience" as the general term.

Audiences are the lifeblood of performing arts groups, museums, zoos, and sports organizations. Many of these organizations measure their success in terms of the size of the audience attracted. The Lyric Opera Company of Chicago considers itself successful because it has a "sellout" every season. The Metropolitan Museum of Art in New York City would like to increase its attendance each year.

We can distinguish two types of audience building problems facing organizations. Some organizations have to build an audience for a *single event*. Thus a university may want to attract a large audience to hear a well-known speaker, or a city may want to attract a large crowd to watch the Fourth of July parade. Here audience attraction is primarily accomplished by giving extensive advertising and publicity to the event. We will not say much about building an audience for a single event in this chapter.

Other organizations—performing arts groups, museums, and so on—want to build a long-term audience for their performances or exhibitions. For example, Wisdom Bridge Theatre in Chicago stages six new plays a year. It does not want to build a new audience for each new play. It would like to build a loyal group that subscribes to the whole series each season. This requires choosing plays that please the target audience and motivating them to resubscribe each season. The problem of long-term audience development consists of (1) researching the audience, (2) developing the product, (3) pricing the product, and (4) promoting the product.

### RESEARCHING THE AUDIENCE

Building a long-term audience involves attracting nonattenders and moving them through the following stages: infrequent attenders, frequent attenders, new subscribers, continual subscribers, and member/donors. Michaelis suggested that most subscribers start as single ticket buyers, then purchase tickets to several performances in a season, later become season ticket buyers, and finally become donors.[1] However, Ryans and Weinberg found that only 31 percent of current subscribers moved through this gradual process, another 21 percent were sudden subscribers (going from nonattenders to full subscribers), and the remainder showed other patterns of entry.[2] One implication is that theatres can often create

sudden subscribers by mailing attractive promotional brochures to high theatregoing groups.

Theatre management can use the preceding stages to research the characteristics of the different groups. Typically, continual subscribers have a higher
income, are older, and live in certain residential neighborhoods; whereas infrequent attenders have a lower income, are younger, and are less concentrated in
certain neighborhoods. This information helps management direct its promotion
to people with characteristics similar to its continual subscribers.

### DEVELOPING THE PRODUCT

In commercial marketing, the company tries to develop a product that will
satisfy a target market. In artistic marketing, the organization typically decides
on a product which appeals to its own sense of aesthetics and then hopes to attract
people to sample it. Thus, the conductor of a symphony assembles a program
containing works he thinks the audience ought to hear along with some popular
works to meet the audience's immediate tastes. Or a modern art museum director
may put on a show of seemingly meaningless art that will bore most visitors but
which he feels should be featured, even if only for the benefit of the few who will
appreciate it.

If the product is too esoteric, the art organization will never gain or hold
a sufficient size audience. On the other hand, if the product is too popular, the
arts organization will appear compromising and failing to advance the audience's
tastes. The normal solution is to "give something to everyone." A theatre director
told the author:

> In selecting six plays for this season, we select three popular ones so that
> subscribers can feel at least three of the six plays will be satisfying; two representing
> heavy drama that will probably depress the audience; and one that is so avant garde
> and experimental that it will lose most of the audience, but intensely satisfy the
> performers. We present the three popular plays at the beginning, middle, and end.
> By starting with a very popular play, we hope that some nonsubscribers will decide
> to buy a season ticket and also tell their friends to attend. The popular play in the
> middle of the season reestablishes their faith in the theatre. And the popular play
> at the end leaves the audience in a mood to buy a season ticket for the next year.

Although this is a reasonable solution, it results in satisfying everyone a little
rather than satisfying any group a lot.

A solution that creates more audience satisfaction calls for segmenting the
market and developing a separate product for each segment. As an example,
Stanford University presents 30 artistic performances each year divided into
several series (chamber music, dance, guitar, jazz). Each series appeals to a
different audience and delivers the appropriate satisfaction.

The arts organization that is intent about developing a satisfying product
for its audience can take a number of additional steps from a marketing point of
view:

1. *Research the audience's tastes and preferences.* The arts organization can run focus groups and surveys with members of the target audience to learn what they like and don't like. For example, the prospective audience can be asked to describe the type of music it prefers and even specific pieces that it would enjoy hearing.

2. *Research the audience's feelings about the location, physical facilities, services, and prices as part of the product.* The audience experiences not only a performance but an "augmented product" consisting of all the attributes it experiences in going to the performance. Management should learn what the audience thinks, feels, and wants with respect to these other attributes because this can lead to improving the audience's experience.

3. *Research the audience's reactions to each of the performances as a way of learning how to improve product selection and performance in the future.* By monitoring audience satisfaction in real time, the organization could take corrective actions on the spot as well as learn how to perform better in the future.[3]

## PRICING THE PRODUCT

Arts organizations can price their offer in a variety of ways. Performing arts groups, for example, will set a single ticket price, often accompanied by discounts to senior citizens, students, and veterans. The single ticket price will be based on considerations of demand, competition, and cost. Thus, Broadway theatres charge high prices for their shows because of the high level of demand and high costs of production. Off-Broadway ticket prices are lower because of the lower demand and cost. All of these theatres also develop a price for their subscription series, which usually represents a saving over buying single tickets for all the performances. The saving is often communicated as "six plays for the price of five" so the audience recognizes the advantage of becoming subscribers. Yet no one has definitely proven that season ticket buyers are motivated by the savings; many of them simply want to see all the plays, support the theatre, and/or get better seats. Ryans and Weinberg found that the subscription price discount of 15 percent was checked by less than 25 percent of the respondents as one of the two main benefits for becoming a subscriber.[4] In this case, the theatre might realize more total revenue by not offering a price discount to subscribers.

Museums, zoos, and other exhibition organizations also price attendance in a number of ways. Many of these institutions set aside one or more free days to make it possible for lower income persons to attend without cost. They also allow unlimited free admission to those who take out membership. Otherwise, they post a price schedule showing the adult price, as well as discounted prices for senior citizens and children. Some museums post only suggested prices, leaving it to the visitors to decide how much they will pay. In seeking a pricing policy, museums are torn between wanting as low a price as possible to attract a maximum number of visitors and charging an adequate price that will help them meet their rapidly rising expenses.

Pricing becomes especially complicated when one considers its joint impact on attendance, membership, and contributing behavior. Weinberg has argued that arts organizations might realize more revenue in the long run by setting low prices on attendance because this will encourage more "triers" which will lead to more "members" and eventually to more "donors."[5] If there is a strong flow from one audience stage into the next, then his argument for low prices is worth serious consideration.

### PROMOTING THE PRODUCT

Promotion plays a critical role in building and maintaining audiences. The arts organization must know how to promote its offer in a cost-effective manner to its target audience. This means it must know how to develop effective direct mail pieces, newspaper and other ads, and publicity. It must know how much to spend and how to mix the different promotional media for maximum impact.

The three tasks of promotion are to (1) attract new attenders to the theatre, (2) upgrade the attenders into subscribers, and (3) get subscribers to renew their membership.

Attracting new attenders requires directing appropriate forms of promotion to new groups of high potential triers. For example, North Light Repertory Theatre of Evanston, Illinois, determined that it was underattracting potential theatregoers from the neighboring town of Skokie, Illinois. To reach this target market, North Light used a combination of promotions, including sending direct mail pieces to certain zip code areas in Skokie, giving speeches about the theatre to major organizations in the community, and running teas in homes of Skokie friends of the theatre.

Encouraging the attenders to become season subscribers is the most important challenge facing a performing arts organization, according to Newman.[6] Newman sees the single ticket buyer as the nemesis of the theatre business. Single ticket buyers are fickle. They often decide at the last minute if they will attend a performance. If it rains or there are bad reviews, or something else comes up, they will decide against going and the theatre ends up with empty seats. Subscribers, on the other hand, have prepaid for their tickets. They have made a commitment to support the theatre whether the reviews are good or bad. They will show up. The key task, therefore, is to try to fill the theatre seats with subscribers. The ideal situation is where every seat has been sold to subscribers and those who want to see the plays have no choice but to wait for a time when they can buy a subscription. Even if the arts organization sold only 70 percent of its seats to subscribers, it would have to attract only 30 percent of single ticket buyers to its performances rather than 100 percent. To induce single ticket buyers to become subscribers, the organization should consider offering a discount to the series, or an extra play, or some other incentive which Newman describes in his *Subscribe Now!*

The third promotion task is to gain renewals from current subscribers. If there is high subscriber attrition, the arts organization has to work that much harder to attract new subscribers. Subscription renewal marketing calls for mailing attractive brochures describing the next season's offering to current subscribers, sending a second mailing to those who failed to respond, and even phoning nonrenewers to help bring about renewal or to learn the reasons for resistance.

The variety of promotional techniques available for audience building are vividly illustrated in the sample campaign plan (see Figure 18–2) prepared by Newman for a resident theatre located in a city of 2 million people, which has 8,000 current subscribers and a capacity of 15,000 seats for the run of each play. The plan calls for direct mailings, telephone selling, party selling, corporate sales visits, and so on. It aims for an overkill of 1,495 subscriptions in case some of the components fail to deliver their quotas. As elaborate as this plan is, it leaves out other forms of promotion such as radio and television promotion; newspaper advertising; door-to-door direct selling; brochure inserts into newspapers and other publications; and so on. The main question is whether it would be better to use fewer tools more intensely than many tools superficially.

## MEMBERSHIP DEVELOPMENT

Many nonprofit organizations have *membership* as either a core or ancillary component of their operation. *Members are people who join an organization and support it with dues and other forms of energy.* Members have a more permanent relation with an organization than its audience or consumers, who come and go. Yet they are not paid employees who work under contract. They may volunteer to do unpaid work, although this is not typically a condition for membership.

Membership is a core feature of such organizations as churches, unions, and trade associations. These organizations exist to serve their members, who are also in fact their major consumers. In other organizations, such as museums, performing arts groups, and charitable organizations, membership is an ancillary feature designed primarily to raise money and volunteered services in order to serve a separate group of consumers. We should be aware that some organizations use the term "membership" broadly, such as where a college believes it is made of many membership groups, such as students, professors, and alumni. Technically speaking, however, students are consumers, professors are employees, and only alumni (if they pay their dues) are members.

Membership organizations typically face a number of problems such as (1) too few members, (2) poor mix of members, (3) too many inactive members, and (4) too many nonrenewing members. *Membership development* is the general name given to the task of creating a healthy membership situation. Here we will examine, from a marketing point of view, the four major problems of a membership organization: *membership definition, membership attraction, membership motivation,* and *membership retention.*

### MEMBERSHIP DEFINITION

Every membership organization needs to define membership qualifications, membership classes, and membership benefits. These decisions will critically affect the ability of the organization to attract and retain members.

Organizations vary in the qualifications they place on membership. At one

## FIGURE 18–2
### Sample Plan for Selling 15,000 Tickets

SAMPLE CAMPAIGN OUTLINE
*Total Subscriptions Available: 15,000*

| *Component* | | *Goal* |
|---|---|---|
| Renewal | Re-enrollment of 70% of current list of 8,000 subscribers. | 5,600 |
| Conversion of single-ticket buyers | Sale of 2 subscriptions each to 5% of list of 2,500 single-ticket buyers. | 250 |
| Restoration of dropouts | Sale of 2 subscriptions each to 10% of list of 1,250 dropouts. | 250 |
| Current subscriber participation | Recruitment of 200 current subscribers to sell 2 pairs of subscriptions each. | 800 |
| Parties | Sale of 4 pairs of subscriptions at each of 50 coffee parties | 400 |
| Bloc sales | Sale of 5 pairs of subscriptions each to 50 corporations. | 500 |
| Sale on commission | Recruitment of outside philanthropic, civic, religious, and fraternal organizations to sell subscriptions on commission. | 1,000 |
| Xmas card list | Recruitment of 50 board members, guild members, or subscribers to write 100 personal letters each to friends, with anticipated return of 7% ordering 2 subscriptions each. | 700 |
| Telephone campaign | Sale of 2 subscriptions each to 4% of 7,000 people called by phone. | 560 |
| Student discounts | On-campus sale of specially priced subscriptions to students who can afford to buy them. | 500 |
| Senior citizen discounts | Sale of specially priced subscriptions to senior citizens who can afford to buy them. | 500 |
| Scholarships | Sale of 5 subscriptions each to 50 individuals, corporations, or service clubs, sponsoring scholarship subscriptions for students. | 250 |
| Donated subscriptions | Sale of 5 subscriptions each to 50 donors, earmarked as contributions for senior citizens. | 250 |
| Special letter to subscribers | Letter to renewing and new subscribers asking them to find additional subscribers among their family and friends. | 275 |
| Direct mail phase I | Sale of 2 subscriptions each to ⅓ of 1% of 350,000-name brochure mailing list during the spring and early summer. | 2,330 |
| Direct mail phase II | Sale of 2 subscriptions each to ⅓ of 1% of second 350,000-name brochure mailing list during the late summer and early fall. | 2,330 |
| | Total Campaign Goal: | 16,495 |

SOURCE: Danny Newman, *Subscribe Now!* (New York: Theatre Communications Group, Inc., 1977), pp. 36–37.

extreme are the professional associations who will only accept licensed or "schooled" practitioners into their ranks. Thus, the American Medical Association (AMA) will only accept licensed physicians as members while excluding osteopaths, chiropractors, and others who claim medical knowledge and status. Furthermore, they will drop members who violate the professional code of ethics. At the other extreme are museums and charitable organizations who will accept anyone as a member who is willing to pay the annual dues, without any attention to the moral character or other aspects of the person.

Membership qualifications can often become a divisive issue within the current membership ranks. During the sixties and seventies, many Protestant churches were torn between the conservatives who wanted to admit only people of their own kind to membership and the liberals who wanted churches to be run along open admission lines. The rate of membership growth of a church is certainly affected by this decision. Jews have remained a minority religious group because of their disinclination to proselytize, whereas Southern Baptists have shown spectacular growth because of their evangelical fervor.

Various membership organizations also define classes of membership. In fraternal organizations such as the Shriners, Lions, and so on, new members start at the lowest level of membership and rise through merit or seniority to higher levels of membership and "secret knowledge." In organizations that use membership primarily as a fundraising device, new members can "buy" into any membership class through the size of their gift or dues. For example, people can join the new Terra Museum of American Art (Evanston, Ill.) at any of eight membership levels: founder, $5,000; benefactor, $2,500; guarantor, $1,000; patron, $500; sustaining fellow, $250; sponsor, $100; annual member, $50; associate and student member, $25.

All members are entitled to a core set of benefits. Members of the Terra Museum receive advance notice of programs and events, invitations to exhibition previews, admission to all exhibitions without charge, calendars of events, and discounts on purchases at the Museum Shop. Higher classes of members receive some additional benefits, such as invitations to special programs and previews. Clearly, a major task of a membership organization is to formulate the benefit mix that will achieve the desired mix of members. The more generous the benefits, the greater the organization's ability to attract members.

## MEMBERSHIP ATTRACTION

An organization can view itself as having too few, enough, or too many members. Here we shall deal with the former problem, which is the most common. For example, AMA membership dropped from 62 percent of the nation's physicians in 1968 to 47 percent in 1980. The AMA is quite disturbed about this, since it hurts its revenue and its power in Washington as a spokesman for the medical profession. Many churches also suffer from too few members.

Attracting new members calls for carrying out the normal marketing steps of (1) defining and locating prospects, (2) determining their attitudes toward the organization, and (3) developing a plan to sell them on membership.[7]

**Defining and locating prospects.**    Organizations with a strict membership definition, such as unions and trade associations, usually have little or no trouble defining and locating prospects. Thus, the AMA knows the name and address of every U.S. physician since they are listed in a registry. Those physicians who are not AMA members constitute the prospect pool, and it is relatively easy to reach them with direct mail, phone calls, and personal visits to try to sell them on the benefits of membership.

Open membership organizations have a tougher problem defining their prospect pool. For a major art museum, the prospect pool, in principle, includes every adult living in or near the city. In practice, most city dwellers would not be interested or willing to pay membership dues. The museum must therefore classify its prospects, from those who would show the most interest and have the most financial ability to those with much less interest and/or ability to pay. The museum could "buy" the names and addresses of people who have joined other museums or supported arts organizations in general. Depending on the quality of its prospect list, the museum could direct appropriate and cost-effective communications.

**Determining prospects' attitudes toward the organization.**    The organization should interview some prospects to learn their reasons for not joining the organization. Each reason becomes something that the organization will want to handle. These reasons usually lead to a segmentation of prospects into three groups: resisters, indifferents, and uninforms.

*Resisters* are persons who dislike the organization. Among the reasons they give are: "I disagree with the organization's principles," "The organization doesn't do any good," "The membership is self-serving and hypocritical." If these beliefs are unfounded, the organization can offer evidence that refutes these views and attract some resisters. But where these views are well founded, the organization will gain little by pursuing this group.

*Indifferents* are prospects who don't see much net benefit to joining the organization. They will give as reasons for not joining: "The dues are high relative to the benefits" or "I don't like to join organizations." Included in this group are "free riders," people who feel they can get the benefits without being members. The best approach to indifferents is to try to demonstrate that the organization's value is high in relation to the cost.

*Uninforms* are prospects who have little information on which to base a judgment about the value of belonging to the organization. They say: "I guess I don't know what it really does" or "I have no idea of the dues but I think they are high." The best approach to the uninformed is to send information to them to increase their knowledge of the organization.

**Developing a plan to sell membership.**    An organization can pursue membership building along three lines. The first is *normal membership recruitment,* in which printed pieces are developed and sent through the mail, distributed at meetings, and handed out personally on appropriate occasions. The second is *person-to-person solicitation* by members or field staff, often directed at very desirable prospects. The third is the *major membership drive* waged at conventions and other meetings, through the use of speakers, visual aids, testimonials, and sign-up booths. Each approach is discussed below.

For a professional organization, normal membership recruitment boils down to developing printed material that communicates an effective case for the value of membership in relation to the cost. The organization must first take stock of the real benefits it offers members and whether they are sufficient in number and quality. For example, the AMA offers the following benefits to its physician members:

1. various journals and newsletters
2. insurance programs
3. seminars on medical, social, and political topics
4. placement services
5. services of one of the nation's most up-to-date medical libraries
6. a 32 percent discount on Hertz car rentals
7. lobbying for physician interests

The AMA should research prospects with respect to how important they regard each benefit. The results can be used to identify a set of *benefit segments.* Some prospects will be primarily motivated by personal nonmedical benefits such as insurance, Hertz discounts, chance for better placement, and collegial–social relations. Others will be motivated by the opportunity to improve their medical competence through seminars, journals, and library services. Still others will be motivated by seeing the AMA as a political instrument to protect and advance the interests of the medical profession. By identifying these different segments, different brochures could be developed and mailed that would maximize the appeal to each benefit segment. In addition, prospects should be asked for ideas of new benefits that would motivate them to join the AMA.

The professional association should also research prospects' (and members') opinions about the appropriateness of the dues level and structure. Hit with two successive dues increases (in which annual dues rose from $110 to $250), AMA membership continued its downward decline. Physicians, who have to pay another $200 for membership in their state and county medical associations, in many cases thought that another $250 for AMA membership was too much. Clearly, the AMA must either do a better job of selling the benefits of membership or think twice about raising membership dues.

Among the prospects that an organization seeks to attract are usually some VIPs who would make especially valuable members. For example, the AMA might consider it a real coup to attract a well-known physician to membership who had previously been publicly critical of the AMA. Obviously, this "conversion sale" would not be accomplished by simply mailing an attractive brochure to the physician describing the benefits of AMA membership. This physician requires a tailored marketing approach that relies heavily on a personal selling process.

The process consists of taking the VIP prospect through the following four stages designed to bring about growing commitment to the organization:

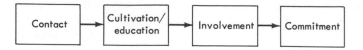

The first stage is *contact* in which the organization's representative makes an appointment to see the physician and describes the strong interest the organization has in his or her membership. The purpose of the meeting is simply to get acquainted and to offer information. The second stage is *cultivation/education,* in which the organization mails interesting things about its activities in the hope of increasing the physician's interest. The representative will take the physician to lunch or dinner from time to time. The third stage is called *involvement.* The representative asks the physician to join the organization and get involved. A specific high-minded type of involvement is usually proposed that the physician cannot easily refuse. The fourth stage is *commitment,* in which the physician, having joined, begins to meet new people and serve on committees and begins to feel a commitment to the organization.

From time to time, an organization will undertake a major *membership drive.* It will set a high membership goal, substantially increase its membership building budget, engage the services of advertising and marketing experts, and blitz the prospects with literature and appeals. The major membership drive derives part of its effectiveness through "turning on" the staff and current members to becoming more active recruiters, and it derives another part of its effectiveness through the offering of "special incentives" for joining at that time, such as "half-price memberships," "premiums," "public recognition of new members," and so on. One of the most dramatic major membership drives was undertaken by the Southern Baptists in Texas a few years ago:[8]

> The Baptist General Convention in Texas is about to launch a media blitz designed to share the good news of God's love with every man, woman, and child in the state an average of forty times apiece during a four-week campaign in February and March. The $1.5 million campaign, to be called Good News Texas, will feature commercials for Christ on television and radio, ads in newspapers and other print media, booster spots on billboards, pins on lapels, and an extensive personal visitation program to be run by the local churches.
>
> Baptists, of course, have always been aggressive. They sought "A Million More in Fifty-Four" and they have sponsored Billy Graham Crusades and hold "Win Clinics" to instruct people in the techniques of personal evangelism. But this is bigger, better, grander than anything they have ever done before.

Good News Texas would have three major targets: (1) the 4.7 million Texans —one-third of the state's population—who do not belong to any Christian group, persons "who are completely uninvolved in the things of Christ," (2) inactive and apathetic church members, including 700,000 Baptists, and (3) the active membership of local Baptist churches.

## MEMBERSHIP MOTIVATION

Ideally, an organization would like every member to be active, proud, and ready to serve the organization whenever called upon. In practice, only a small percent of the membership of any organization shows enthusiasm and takes a real interest in its affairs. A pastor reported to the author that about one-third of the members of his church are *inactives* (i.e., nominal Christians) who attend services only a few times a year on the major holidays; a third are *moderate actives* who attend fairly frequently but who don't get highly involved; and a third are *high actives* who contribute most of the time, money, and other things that make it possible to run the church. In other words, a small fraction of the membership of any organization will do most of the work involved in running it.

The first step for an organization is to determine the proportions of inactives, moderate actives, and high actives. A high or growing number of inactives is a sign that the organization is not creating value for these members, and this could eventually spell the demise of the organization. The organization should then proceed to survey the three groups to find out what aspects of the organization are satisfying and dissatisfying to them. Table 18–1 shows two key questions

### Table 18–1

SURVEY INSTRUMENT MEASURING MEMBERS' DISSATISFACTION

**1. HOW OFTEN DO YOU FIND ANY OF THE FOLLOWING PROBLEMS OR ANNOYANCES OCCURRING WHEN DEALING WITH THE SOCIETY?**

|  | *Often* | *Sometimes* | *Seldom* | *Never* |
|---|---|---|---|---|
| Lack of experienced staff |  |  |  |  |
| Return calls late |  |  |  |  |
| Impersonal service |  |  |  |  |
| No advisory assistance |  |  |  |  |
| Poor meetings |  |  |  |  |

**2. HOW MUCH DOES THE PROBLEM BOTHER YOU?**

|  | *Extremely Bothered* | *Very Bothered* | *Just a Little Bothered* | *Not at All Bothered* |
|---|---|---|---|---|
| Lack of experienced staff |  |  |  |  |
| Return calls late |  |  |  |  |
| Impersonal service |  |  |  |  |
| No advisory assistance |  |  |  |  |
| Poor meetings |  |  |  |  |

that can reveal areas of member dissatisfaction and their relative importance. By monitoring the feelings of members, the organization can learn what steps would improve members' satisfaction.

The organization should supplement its surveys with focus group discussions in which a sample of members are invited to consider new ways to create members' involvement and excitement. Its members want to feel that they are worthwhile members of a worthwhile organization. They need evidence that they are personally highly regarded in the organization (need for response and recognition), an expectation of new experiences (need for variety), and a sense that the organization is accomplishing important things for the members and the society. Too often organizations are run without change from year to year, and members' interest begins to flag as a sameness is felt.

### MEMBERSHIP RETENTION

The ultimate indicator of a failure to satisfy members is a high or growing nonrenewal rate. This is the annual "market test," where each member votes on whether the "product" is worth the cost. This is why membership organizations put a lot of effort into the task of membership renewal. Instead of sending a plain renewal notice as in the past, they send printed material (letter and/or brochure) listing all the benefits and accomplishments of the organization, along with "won't you please renew your membership, John Jones." If no renewal is forthcoming in the first few weeks, another membership renewal letter is sent, and eventually a phone call might be made to encourage the member's renewal.

The central need is to determine various reasons why members don't renew. A YMCA unit found 4 reasons accounting for 80 percent of its membership dropout:

1. move to a new community (10 percent)
2. switch of membership to a modern health club or tennis club (20 percent)
3. reported dissatisfaction with conditions of the facility (30 percent)
4. reported light use or nonuse of the facilities (20 percent)

The YMCA cannot do anything to stop members from moving out of the community, but clearly it can do something about the condition of its own facilities. In the short run, the YMCA may have to sell members on other benefits of membership; in the long run, it will have to improve its product to compete more successfully with other recreational facilities.

---

## VOLUNTEER RECRUITMENT

One of the common features of many nonprofit organizations is their use of volunteers—both to keep down expenses and to provide a channel for high-minded people to contribute time to a cause they believe in. Among organizations that make heavy use of volunteers are hospitals, arts organizations, charitable institutions, churches, and reform organizations; also, smaller volunteer units are found in schools and social service organizations.

The core concept of voluntarism is that individuals participate in spontaneous, private, and freely chosen activities that "promote or advance some aspect of the common good, as it is perceived by the persons participating in it."[9] These activities are not coerced by any institution in society and the behavior "is engaged in not primarily for financial gain."[10] Between 50 and 70 million Americans act as volunteers each year. In 1974, the economic value of volunteer time exceeded $34 billion. In recent years, however, the number of volunteers has been declining due to the rise in the proportion of working women. Organizations have to give increased attention now to the problem of volunteer attraction and satisfaction.[11]

Volunteers may seem to be a free "good" to the organization but this is not entirely true. Some cost is incurred in recruiting, training, and motivating volunteers. Further cost is incurred when volunteers fail to show up when needed, or show up tardily, or work at a slow pace. Some managements believe that competent paid staff members are ultimately better for the organization than unpaid volunteers. Each organization has to determine the optimal ratio of volunteers to staff to get its work done.

The proper way to attract and motivate volunteers is to recognize them as a distinct market segment with certain needs and expectations with whom the organization exchanges benefits. These needs and expectations have been changing over time. Years ago, volunteers talked about the gratification they derived from helping others. In addition, their sense of self-worth was enhanced. In some cases, volunteering allowed them to repay obligations. Volunteering also provides stimulation and socialization. Investigation in the 1950s began to reveal more self-serving gratifications: Volunteering conveyed and validated a higher social status.[12] The 1970s have brought other motives to light. Training and work experience is a major motivation for many types of volunteers, especially students and women volunteers who have been homemakers but intend to reenter the work force. Also volunteering provides social ties in a world where mobility, an increasingly nuclear family, and social conflict are rising.

### VOLUNTEER ATTRACTION

Volunteer organizations return these benefits to those who volunteer. New volunteers must be constantly attracted as others leave. Organizations need a systematic procedure to attract volunteers. The normal method is to ask current volunteers to recruit additional volunteers among their friends and acquaintances. If this method fails to produce enough qualified volunteers, a notice or advertisement would be distributed to members of the organization inviting them to volunteer. Beyond this, the organization can place ads in other media announcing the strong need for volunteers and the benefits that volunteers enjoy.

Not all volunteers can be accepted or assigned to the tasks they want to perform. People with undesirable characteristics and/or who won't mix well with others may be turned down on some excuse. Volunteers who want to handle specialized tasks such as publicity or fundraising must show the necessary qualifications. If Mr. Tedious volunteers to call on important donors, he may have to be told that this job is being well handled and that the organization really needs volunteers for other tasks, such as letter writing and envelope stuffing.

### Volunteer Motivation

Volunteers need recognition and occasional challenge. Since they are giving their time freely, they are especially sensitive to slights from management, such as being ordered to do something, like working extra long hours, and so on. Managing a volunteer force, therefore, calls for a supervisor who is sensitive to the needs and feelings of volunteers. The supervisor must be friendly and appreciative of their services and open to suggestions and complaints. Competent volunteer managers will normally arrange special benefits and recognitions for the contributions of volunteers. Thus, a hospital may do the following things: give special pins and ranks to recognize 10, 15, and 25 years of service; sponsor an annual dinner for its volunteers in which one or more staff physicians speak on a subject of interest; give free passes to plays to its volunteers; and so on.

---

## EMPLOYEE RECRUITMENT

All organizations face the task of recruiting employees—managers, clerical staff, operations and maintenance people. Employees can be defined as paid personnel who work under contract for the organization. Organizations can find themselves in one of three recruitment states regarding any class of employees. The class of employees may be in *oversupply,* in which case the organization's problem is not recruitment so much as selection. It may even decide to engage in demarketing in order to reduce the number of applicants it must handle. The second state is that of *normal supply,* in which case the organization carries out normal recruitment activity such as placing ads and phoning possible prospects or referral sources. The third state is that of *undersupply,* in which case the organization must undertake special effort to identify, locate, and attract that class of employee. The organization must find a way to stand out from its competitors as an attractive place to work. We shall be mainly concerned with employee marketing in the face of labor undersupply.

A further distinction needs to be drawn between *mass recruitment, normal recruitment,* and *star recruitment.* Large-scale recruitment is illustrated by the U.S. Navy, which must attract over 100,000 new enlistees each year. Normal recruitment is illustrated by a hospital that needs five to ten additional nurses, or a police force that needs few new recruits. Star recruitment is illustrated by a large foundation that is trying to recruit a new president. Each of these recruitment problems will be examined from a marketing point of view.

## MASS RECRUITMENT

Large organizations whose personnel serve for only a short time must recruit large number of new employees each year. This is true of large military organizations, such as the U.S. Army and the U.S. Navy.

Consider the task faced by the U.S. Navy. Each year the navy calculates the number of new enlistees it must attract in the coming year. This is based on calculating the target size of the navy, less the expected size given the number of enlisted personnel who will leave for one reason or another. If the navy could convince a larger number of its current enlistees to sign up for another six years, then its recruitment target would be lower. But reenlistments are a function of how well navy life satisfies the current enlistees and many of them see more pay, opportunity, and freedom in civilian life than in staying in the navy. This is not to deny that improved marketing to the current enlistees would boost the reenlistment rate.

Suppose the navy estimates that it needs 118,000 recruits in the coming year. This becomes the responsibility of the U.S. Navy Recruiting Command, which employs 4,000 people to recruit for the navy. This department is organized into several navy recruitment areas, each area is organized into many districts, and each district into many local recruitment stations. The target quota is broken into recruitment quotas for the separate areas, districts, and stations based on a formula which takes into consideration the geographical unit's past recruit yield, number of potential recruits, and other factors.

At the base of the recruiting system stands the individual recruiting station, staffed by one or more navy people who have been assigned to the recruitment function. Its job is to advertise locally, locate prospects in high schools and other places, make a sales presentation on the benefits of navy life, and move the prospects to signing up. Each recruiting officer has a quota and is judged by how well he fills the quota. High performers receive special citations that enter their military record and influence their rate of advancement.

The allocation of recruitment quotas is guided by a careful analysis of the high school graduating market. First, an estimate is made of the total number of male high school graduates expected in the coming year—say, 10 million. This number is then reduced by the percentage that would not qualify for navy life because of mental or physical disabilities; the remaining number (say, 5 million) constitute the *qualified military available* (QMA). This number is then further reduced because a certain percentage is not interested in, or actually is antagonistic to, military service; the remaining number (say, 750,000) constitutes the *potential military market*. The U.S. Navy competes for this market with the U.S. Army and the U.S. Marines. Since the navy in recent years has attracted a 30 percent share of this market, it appears that the navy faces a potential of 220,000 recruits, and should be able to attract the 118,000 recruits that it needs.

This analysis is repeated for each geographical area and modified by recruitment performance levels and other factors, in order to set the actual geographical quotas. For example, the navy has much more success recruiting high school graduates from the Midwest than from either coast; it appears that those who do not live near the oceans are more eager to see the world. Interest in the navy is also influenced by job opportunities in the area, parents' attitudes toward military service, and value placed on a college education. Thus the navy is in competition with companies and colleges, as well as with the other military services, for manpower.

The navy's marketing mix for identifying, reaching, and motivating prospects appears, on the surface, to be reasonably well designed. It consists of the following elements:

1. *Marketing research* to determine various characteristics of the target population; level of knowledge about the navy; attitudes toward the navy; consumer choice processes in deciding what to do after high school.
2. *Product development* to improve navy life so that it would produce better word-of-mouth from current enlistees.
3. *Retailing analysis* to improve the location, attractiveness, and operation of recruitment offices.
4. *Advertising and public relations analysis* to determine the strongest themes to promote about the navy (travel? education? adventure?) and the most cost-effective media for reaching the target population.
5. *Sales force training and analysis* to improve the ability of the recruiters to locate prospects and close sales.

The reason for expressing some reservations has to do with a lack of sophistication in the navy's managing some of these tools. To cite the major offending example, consider the sales force, which should be the key tool in that it is responsible for closing the sale. Although the recruiters constitute a sales force, they operate under conditions that no commercial sales force would exhibit. Consider the following:

1. Recruiters do not join the navy to be recruiters, and normally have no background or interest in sales. The command selects them and they have no choice.
2. Recruiters receive only a month of training in recruitment before serving as recruiters.
3. Recruiters do not receive any commission or bonus for the number of people they enlist. As long as they meet the minimum quota requirement, they are safe.
4. Recruiters serve only for two years and then move on to another duty, which is equivalent to having to rehire a whole sales force every few years.

One can speculate that if the navy would use recruiters who wanted to be recruiters, who were given adequate training and financial incentives, and who would remain recruiters for several years, they would be much more successful in attracting enlistees.

As it stands, the navy reviews its results each year by examining significant ratios that make up the recruitment yield pyramid shown in Figure 18–3. In the illustration, the navy found 2 million leads and ended up inviting 400,000 students for interviews. Approximately 300,000 showed up for interviews, and the navy made offers to 200,000 students. Half, or 100,000 of the students, made the decision to join the navy. Clearly, the navy could increase its yield by improving the ratios, and this requires studying what happens at each stage of the recruiting process to see what improvements could be made.

This extended example provides a good illustration of the problems and procedures involved in mass recruiting. The principles can also be applied to the recruitment problem facing colleges or the U.S. Peace Corps.

### NORMAL RECRUITMENT

Normal recruitment is the problem of adding or replacing employees in the normal course of the organization's operations. Hospitals have to attract nurses, police departments have to attract police personnel, and social agencies have to attract social workers. Normal recruitment is a little more difficult for nonprofit organizations than for commercial firms because the pay is typically lower and the amenities fewer. These organizations have to rely on finding people interested in making a contribution to others at some sacrifice of personal income.

When the nonprofit organization faces a labor undersupply situation, it must be especially adept at applying marketing concepts to locate and attract prospects. Consider the following example:

**Nurse recruiting.**    Johnson Hospital (name disguised) in Chicago is one of many hospitals in the nation currently facing a shortage of registered nurses. Johnson's problem is compounded because of its inner-city location, in an area of high crime, unattractive housing, and other negatives. The hospital's neighbor-

**FIGURE 18–3**

Recruitment Yield Pyramid

hood lacks a wide variety of services and other amenities which middle-class nurses have come to expect.

The hospital has searched for nurses everywhere, including the neighborhood, other neighborhoods, other cities, and even other countries, with poor results. The hospital called in a marketing consultant who recommended that primary effort be devoted to finding nurses who already live in the area. These people know the community and would not face serious relocation or transportation problems. Nurses in other parts of Chicago would be a good secondary market, while other cities and nations should not be seriously considered.

The consultant then recommended research into the following issues:

- What is the process by which a nurse typically decides to join any given nursing staff?
- What attributes of the job are most valued?
- How well do local hospitals fit these attributes and, specifically, what does Johnson offer relative to its competition?
- How do local nursing schools help their graduates, recent and earlier, find jobs? How can they be encouraged to pay more attention to Johnson's needs?
- What can Johnson do to differentiate its opportunities for nurses from those offered its competitors?

This information would provide Johnson Hospital with a better foundation on which to formulate its promotion and communication strategy in facing this challenging recruitment problem.[13]

### "STAR" RECRUITMENT

"Star" recruitment is the problem facing organizations when they have to recruit a highly qualified individual for an important position. This happens when a college searches for a new president or distinguished professor, when a hospital searches for a new chief administrator or leading specialist, and when a church searches for a new spiritual leader. Star recruitment is very expensive and time consuming. The organization may spend tens of thousands of dollars and many months compiling a list of candidates, interviewing them, narrowing the list, making a final choice, and negotiating the final terms.

Star recruitment is usually carried out by a committee that relies primarily on word-of-mouth referral. The committee does not generally place an ad, but contacts well-known persons in the field for their recommendations. When the committee believes it has identified a reasonable number of good candidates, it contacts them to assess their potential interest in the opportunity. Biographical information is requested as well as references, who are then contacted and invited to submit confidential letters about the candidate to the committee. The information allows the committee to rank the candidates. Then the committee invites the top three or four candidates to the organization's headquarters for interviews. Spending a day with each candidate gives the committee further information, often enough to know its first choice. At this point, its needs to know its prime candidate's needs and interests because it may be necessary to sell him or her on the opportunity. In turning to negotiation, the committee will want to use the concepts described under exchange analysis in connection with recruiting a leading physician (see Chapter 2, pp. 39–43).

Thus, we see that recruiting employees, especially in circumstances of labor undersupply, involves the organization in defining the best segments, learning their needs and attitudes, and developing an effective marketing program involving product, price, place, and promotion variables.

## SUMMARY

Organizations seek to attract up to four different types of people: audiences, members, volunteers, and employees. These tasks are interrelated in that some audience members move into becoming members, volunteers, and in some cases employees.

Audience attraction is a problem for performing art groups, museums, and other organizations seeking an audience for a single event or set of events. Audience development calls for four steps: researching the audience, developing the product, pricing the product, and promoting it. Audiences are developed over a long period and move through states of being infrequent attenders, frequent attenders, new subscribers, continued subscribers, and members/donors.

Membership development is a function of such organizations as churches, unions, trade associations, museums, charitable organizations, and so on. Membership organizations face a number of problems such as too few members, a poor mix of members, too many inactive members, and too many nonrenewing members. Membership development calls for defining the characteristics of desirable members, and preparing programs to attract members, motivate them, and ensure their renewal. To attract important new members, the process consists of contact, cultivation/education, involvement, and commitment.

Volunteer attraction and development is a problem for organizations that depend upon volunteers to do much of the work. Volunteers pose certain problems in that, being unpaid, they tend to be less reliable and more sensitive to slights or neglect. As the pool of volunteers diminishes because of the working women phenomena, organizations have to improve their approaches to attracting, motivating, and rewarding volunteers.

Employee recruitment is a problem of all organizations. Some organizations, such as the U.S. military services and various colleges, are in the business of mass recruitment which calls for generating a large number of leads, some of which turn into invites, interviews, offers, and hopefully hires. Normal recruitment is the problem of adding or replacing employees in the normal course of the organization's operations. Star recruitment is the problem facing organizations that have to recruit a highly qualified individual for an important position.

## QUESTIONS

**1.** How does long-term audience attraction differ from the process of attracting an audience for a single event?

**2.** What are the special problems associated with attracting new attenders to performing arts events? What marketing research can assist in the marketing task?

**3.** The National Council for the Social Studies (described in Chapter 9, question 4) would like to increase its membership. Suppose the council decided to encourage nonteachers to join. What types of people would be potential members? What membership benefits could be offered?

**4.** Common Cause has state liaisons, volunteers who live near its Washington, D.C., headquarters who come one or more days each week. Each liaison uses a WATS telephone line to call Common Cause leaders in a selected state to share information on Common Cause issues and activities. What are the benefits to the volunteer of serving in this capacity?

**5.** What are some benefits which Johnson Hospital might offer to attract more registered nurses to join its staff?

---

## NOTES

**1.** Donald Michaelis, untitled paper, *Association of College, University, and Community Arts Administrators Bulletin,* 1976.

**2.** Adrian B. Ryans and Charles B. Weinberg, "Consumer Dynamics in Nonprofit Organizations," *Journal of Consumer Research,* September 1978, pp. 89–95.

**3.** Weinberg and Shachmut describe a multiple regression program in which data on past attendance at various performing groups is used to select the following year's performing groups in a way that will maximize the size of the audience attracted. See Charles B. Weinberg and Kenneth M. Shachmut, "Arts Plan: A Model Based System for Use in Planning Performing Arts Series," *Management Science,* February 1974, pp. 654–64.

**4.** Ryans and Weinberg, "Consumer Dynamics."

**5.** See Charles Weinberg, "Marketing Mix Decision Rules for Nonprofit Organizations," in Jagdish Sheth, ed. *Research in Marketing,* Vol. 3 (Greenwich, Conn.: JAI Press, 1980), pp. 191–234.

**6.** See Danny Newman, *Subscribe Now!* (New York: Publishing Center for Cultural Resources, 1977), pp. 36–37.

**7.** Readers interested in membership attraction and development should contact the American Society of Association Executives, 1101 16th Street, N.W., Washington, D.C., which publishes useful materials and runs seminars.

**8.** Excerpts from William Martin, "The Baptists Want You!", *Texas Monthly,* February 1977, pp. 83–87, 149–57.

**9.** Gordon Manser and Rosemary H. Cass, *Voluntarism at the Crossroads* (New York: Family Service Association of America, 1976), p. 14.

**10.** Jon Van Til, "In Search of Voluntarism," *Volunteer Administration,* Vol. 12, No. 2 (Summer 1979), p. 9.

**11.** The interested reader should contact the National Center for Voluntary

Action, 1214 16th Street, N.W., Washington, D.C. 20036, for extensive publications and information on voluntarism.

**12.** David L. Sills, *The Volunteers—Means and Ends in a National Organization* (Glencoe, Ill.: Free Press, 1957).

**13.** Based on a report by Alan Minoff, Vice President of Management Analysis Center, 1980, with permission.

# Donor Marketing: Attracting Funds

The Chicago Lung Association (CLA) is a voluntary organization dedicated to the prevention and control of all lung diseases in Cook County. Originally founded in 1906 as the Tuberculosis Institute of Chicago and Cook County, the organization worked hard for years on problems of prevention and cure of tuberculosis, which was the main "killer" disease in the Western world at that time. This organization, along with other tuberculosis organizations, was affiliated with the American Lung Association. Its main fundraising tool was its annual Christmas Seal mailing campaign, which consisted of sending a sheet of Christmas Seals, a letter, a return envelope, and an information request form. This annual campaign produced 80 percent of CLA's annual revenue.

As the dreaded disease of tuberculosis came under control, tuberculosis associations started paying more attention to other lung diseases. The Tuberculosis Institute of Chicago and Cook County was renamed the Chicago Lung Association in 1972 in recognition of the fact that tuberculosis was no longer a leading cause of morbidity and mortality in the United States. CLA dedicated itself to helping people achieve and enjoy healthy lungs. Toward this end, it carried on myriad activities such as antismoking campaigns, air conservation programs, occupational health interventions, aid to people with respiratory diseases, research into respiratory diseases, and professional and community education.

During the past eight years the American Lung Association and its affiliates such as CLA slipped substantially in the amount of money raised compared with other leading health cause organizations. The declining revenue in an inflationary period has forced CLA to reduce its staff and trim its programs. The CLA decided to call in a marketing consultant to study the deteriorating situation and make recommendations. The consultant came up with a number of findings, such as:

1. Although CLA has moved away from being a single-disease organization, the public is largely ignorant of its many other activities. In particular, the public does not know about CLA's work in emphysema and asthma.
2. CLA needs to focus on a few activities and develop more recognition for its work in these areas.
3. CLA needs to develop new sources of funds since Christmas Seals were yielding diminishing net revenue with the rapid increase in mailing and postage costs.

The consultant made several specific recommendations:

1. CLA should increase its work in the prevention and treatment of emphysema. This disease causes hard breathing and a slow deterioration of health. People die from emphysema and associated conditions such as cancer or heart attack. CLA should provide more services to the victims of emphysema and their families as a basis for building up a bequest/memorial program. A well-run bequest/memorial program can be a major source of new revenue to CLA.
2. CLA should increase its work in the prevention and treatment of childhood lung disease and asthma. It should develop an appropriate fundraising approach appealing to people to help the unfortunate children who are victims of lung disease.
3. CLA should aggressively tap the corporate donor market, since it raises little money from this source at the present time. One stumbling-block is that CLA's social activism in calling for more industry pollution control has alienated a lot of corporations that see their costs going up.
4. CLA should consider creating a membership plan whereby people who contribute to the CLA become members, with different classes of members, different types of services available, and different benefits for each class of membership.

The board of directors is currently reviewing these recommendations to determine which, if any, should be implemented.

SOURCE: Adapted from David Burek, "The Chicago Lung Association," a paper written at Northwestern University, 1978.

The major resource attraction problem of nonprofit organizations is attracting money to carry on their activities. For-profit organizations get their funds primarily through issuing equities and debentures. They cover the costs of these "borrowed" funds by charging prices for their goods and services that exceed their costs. Nonprofit organizations, on the other hand, must rely on other sources of funds to support their activities in the absence of owners and profit-oriented price setting. Private nonprofit organizations rely mainly on gifts from generous donors. Public organizations receive their funds primarily from the public treasury through the mechanism of taxation. Fundraising strategy is, therefore, an essential component of all nonprofit organizations.

The total amount of charitable money raised by all organizations in 1979 was $43.3 billion. Over 84 percent of all contributions came from *individuals* ($36.54 billion), with the remainder coming from *bequests* ($2.23 billion), *foundations* ($2.30 billion), and *corporations* ($2.24 billion). Almost 50 percent of the money was raised by religious organizations ($20.14 billion) and the rest by education ($5.99 billion), health and hospitals ($5.95 billion), social welfare ($4.35 billion), arts and humanities ($2.70 billion), civic and public ($1.24 billion), and other ($2.94 billion). About one out of every three dollars was raised by mail or mail-assisted campaigns, and the rest by personal contact campaigns.[1]

The art of fundraising has passed through various stages of evolution. Its earliest form was *begging,* where needy people and groups would implore more fortunate people for money and goods. Beggars perfected many techniques to gain the attention and sympathy of their target audience, such as simulating pain or blindness, or showing their children with bloated stomachs. The next stage consisted of *collection,* where churches, clubs, and other organizations would regularly collect contributions from a willing and defined group of supporters. In recent times, *campaigning* emerged as a concept and involved organizations appointing a specific person or group to be responsible for soliciting money from every possible source in a systematic fundraising campaign. Most recently, fundraising has been reinterpreted as *development,* whereby the organization systematically builds up different classes of loyal donors who give consistently and receive benefits in the process of giving. Today's organizations vary considerably in their concept of raising money, some seeing it as begging, others as collection, others as campaigning, and still others as development.

Organizations that raise money tend to pass through three stages in their thinking about how to carry on fundraising effectively.

- *Product stage.* Here the prevailing attitude is "we have a good cause; people ought to support us." Many churches and colleges operate on this concept. Money is raised primarily by the top officers through an "old boy network." The organization relies on volunteers to help raise additional funds. A few loyal donors supply most of the funds.
- *Sales stage.* Here the prevailing attitude is "There's a lot of people out there who might give money, and we must go out and find them." The institution appoints a development director who eventually hires a staff. This staff raises money from all

possible sources, using typically a "hard sell" approach. The fundraisers have little influence on the institution's policies or personality since their job is to raise money, not improve the organization. A majority of large nonprofit organizations are in this stage.

- *Marketing stage.* Here the prevailing attitude is "We must analyze our position in the marketplace, concentrate on those donor sources whose interests are best matched to ours, and design our solicitation programs to supply needed satisfactions to each donor group." This approach involves carefully segmenting the donor markets; measuring the giving potential of each donor market; assigning executive responsibility for developing each market through using research and communication approaches; and developing a plan and budget for each market based on its potentials. A minority of large nonprofit organizations have moved into this stage, but it is attracting increased attention as fundraisers become aware of the differences between a sales approach and a marketing approach.

This chapter will analyze fundraising from a marketing perspective. The first section will examine four major donor markets: individual givers, foundations, corporations, and government. Section two will examine how organizations organize their fundraising effort internally. Section three will consider the important task of setting fundraising objectives and strategies, while section four will take a look at the multiplicity of fundraising tactics. The fifth section will consider how organizations can evaluate and improve their fundraising effectiveness.

## ANALYZING DONOR MARKETS

An organization can tap into a variety of sources for financial support. The four major donor markets are: *individuals, foundations, corporations,* and *government.* Small nonprofit organizations often solicit funds primarily from one source —often wealthy individuals—to meet their financial needs. Larger organizations tend to solicit all sources and, in fact, make specific executives responsible for each market. Ultimately, they seek to allocate the fundraising budget in proportion to the giving potential of each donor market. Here we will examine the institutional and behavioral characteristics of each donor market.

### INDIVIDUAL GIVERS

Individuals are the major source of all charitable giving, accounting for some 83 percent of the total. Almost everyone in the nation contributes money to one or more organizations each year, the total amount varying with such factors as the giver's income, age, education, sex, ethnic background, and other characteristics. Thus relatively more money is contributed by high-income people, people in their middle years, and people of high education. At the same time, giving levels vary substantially within each group. There are some wealthy individuals who give little and some lower income individuals who give a lot. Among wealthy people, for example, physicians tend to give less than lawyers.

Charitable causes vary in their appeal to individuals. In a study sponsored by Save the Children Foundation, the public was asked: "Which of the five (categories of charity) would rate as the most worthwhile?" The ranking turned out to be: (1) needy children, (2) disaster victims, (3) medical research, (4) aid to handicapped, and (5) religious organizations.[2] That is, Americans would be most ready to give to a cause involving needy children, followed by disaster victims, and so on. Paradoxically, they give relatively small amounts to these causes in relation to the amounts they give to their church.

Within each category of charity, the appeal levels also vary greatly. For example, within medical charities people give most readily to the American Red Cross ($381.5 million), American Cancer Society ($139.7 million), Easter Seals ($99 million), American Heart Association ($87 million), March of Dimes ($68.5 million), Muscular Dystrophy Association ($68.5 million), and Mental Health Association ($20.9 million) (figures as of 1978). Some of the difference in the amount raised is due to the fact that these organizations have different life spans and different degrees of effectiveness at fundraising. A larger part of the difference in giving levels is due to the opinions people hold about specific diseases, particularly about the disease's *severity, prevalence,* and *remediability.* Thus, heart disease and cancer are severe diseases—they kill—whereas arthritis and birth defects are considered less serious since they do not kill. Cancer has a higher prevalence than muscular dystrophy and therefore attracts more support. Finally, people believe that cures or preventions are possible for heart disease and less so for birth defects and this leads to more giving. Figure 19–1 shows the hypothetical positions of three diseases on the three variables. If the March of Dimes wants to attract more funds for its cause—birth defects—it must try to increase the perceived severity, prevalence, and remediability of birth defects.

## FIGURE 19–1

Public's Perception of Different Medical Causes (Hypothetical)

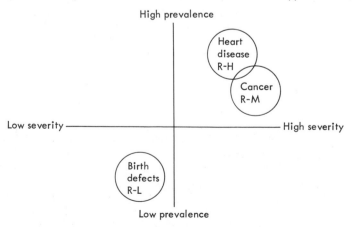

Note: The third variable, remediability (R), is shown next to each
disease with an indication of low (L), medium (M), and high (H).

Why do individuals give to charity? Nonprofit organizations need a good understanding of giving motives in order to be effective at fundraising. The answer called "altruism" tends to mask the complex motives that underlie giving or helping behavior. The best working hypothesis is that the individuals "give" in order to "get" something back. In other words, donations should not be viewed as a *transfer* but as a *transaction.* The question is: What does the donor get? Table 19–1 lists several motives underlying giving behavior. People give to get response or recognition, reduce fear, meet social pressure, or feel "altruistic."

Is there such a thing as giving without "getting"? Some people give and say that they expect nothing back. But, actually, they have "expectations." They expect the organization to use the money efficiently; they expect the fundraiser to show gratitude; and so on. Even the anonymous giver, while wanting no acknowledgment, may privately enjoy the self-esteem of being "big enough" to give money without requiring recognition.

The various motives for giving provide clues to marketing strategy for

### Table 19–1

#### INDIVIDUAL GIVING MOTIVES

1. *Need for self-esteem.* Person attempts to build his self-esteem through self-image, playing "God," or feeling good from giving. Opposite of this would be shame or guilt.

2. *Need for recognition from others.* Person attempts to build his social status or enhance his prestige in the eyes of others. There is a strong need to belong.

3. *Fear of contracting disease.* This need centers around an insecurity in people that they will contract the disease or that a member of their family will. They hope in some sense for immortality.

4. *The habit giver.* This person gives out of habit for no real reason other than a desire not to be embarrassed by not contributing to the cause. These people are very indifferent to contributions, but feel that they must give to someone because everyone else does.

5. *Nuisance giver.* This person only gives to get rid of the caller. He feels contributing to a cause of no real significance, but would rather donate a few dollars than be troubled by others.

6. *Required to give.* These people are required to give at work; they are under pressure from superiors to donate part of their checks to a fund. They therefore demand efficiency, credibility from the organization that they contribute to.

7. *Captive givers.* These people feel real sorrow for someone they know who might have contracted the disease. They are other-centered in that they earnestly would like to aid the victim in some way. Givers in this category may contribute at the death of a friend, rather than sending flowers, etc.

8. *People-to-people givers.* These people have a real feeling of the "commonness of man," a solidarity with other people. This group of people has internalized the idea of helping others because they want to.

9. *Concern for humanity.* This segment of givers are concerned about others for religious reasons and because they are "God's children." They feel a moral obligation to contribute to a charity. They have accepted the love-for-humanity idea because it is a requirement of their faith.

SOURCE: Unknown.

fundraisers. Harold Seymour has suggested that in many mass donor markets, one-third of the people are *responsible* (they donate without being solicited), one-third are *responsive* (they donate when they are asked), and one-third react to *compulsion* (they donate because of pressure).[3] Each market can be investigated further to discover the specific motive segments that exist. One group of givers to a university might respond to "pride," another to "let's catch up to the competition."

Too many organizations ask people to give to them as a needy organization rather than to give to them to support promising programs. The latter is more effective. People respond to what they sense as the relevance, importance, and urgency of a giving opportunity. Seymour suggests that the case for giving must be bigger than the institution. And it must be presented in a way that catches the eye, warms the heart, and stirs the mind.

Another important principle for segmentation is the donor's "giving potential." Fundraisers distinguish between small, medium, and large donors. Many fundraisers prefer to concentrate all or most of their energy on large potential donors, feeling that attracting a few large gifts would produce more funds than attracting many small gifts. If a college fundraiser spends thirty hours with a wealthy alumnus who ends up giving $1 million, the fundraiser's productivity is much greater than trying to raise $100 from each of 10,000 alumni. For this reason many college fundraisers in the past neglected building up the number of alumni givers and concentrated instead on increasing the size of the average gift received. This is now changing, as more colleges are seeking to involve all alumni in school support and giving.

Seeking the "large gift" is still the most important part of fundraising for many organizations. Fundraisers use a five-step approach: *identification, introduction, cultivation, solicitation,* and *appreciation.* They first identify wealthy individuals who could conceivably have a strong interest in the organization. They identify others who might supply information and arrange an introduction. They cultivate the person's interest without asking for any money. By asking too early, they may get less than is possible. Eventually they do ask for money and, upon receiving it, they express their appreciation.

Large individual gift fundraising is most effective when the organization has developed a "wish list" of exciting projects which it shows to the prospective donor. Large hospitals classify their wished-for gifts in several financial sizes, ranging from the purchase of small pieces of medical equipment for under $10,000 to the building of an entire wing for over $3 million. One of the most powerful appeals is offers to donors to have their names (or the names of loved ones) attached to physical facilities, research funds, distinguished chairs, and the like. In addition, fundraisers can offer these individuals all kinds of ways to make their gifts, including direct cash payment, gifts of stock and other property, and bequests where they will assign part or all of their estate to the organization upon their death. Organizations have worked up a variety of gift plans that can be tailored to the needs of individual wealthy donors.

Currently there are over 26,000 foundations in the United States, all set up to give money to worthwhile causes. They fall into the following groups:

1. *Family foundations,* set up by wealthy individuals to support a limited number of activities of interest to the founders. Family foundations typically do not have permanent offices or full-time staff members. Decisions tend to be made by family members and/or counsel.
2. *General foundations,* set up to support a wide range of activities and usually run by a professional staff. General foundations range from extremely large organizations such as the Ford Foundation and the Rockefeller Foundation, which support a wide range of causes and which give most of their money to large well-established organizations, to more specialized general foundations that give money to a particular cause, such as health (Johnson Foundation) or education (Carnegie Foundation).
3. *Corporate foundations,* set up by corporations and allowed to give away up to 5 percent of the corporation's adjusted gross income.
4. *Community trusts,* set up in cities or regions and made up of smaller foundations whose funds are pooled for greater impact.

With 26,000 foundations, it is important for the fundraiser to know how to locate the few that would be the most likely to support a given project or cause. Fortunately, there are many resources available for researching foundations. The best single resource is known as the Foundation Center, a nonprofit organization with research centers in New York, Washington, and Chicago which collects and distributes information on foundations. In addition, many libraries around the country also carry important materials describing foundations. The most important materials are:

1. *The Foundation Grants Index,* which lists the grants that have been given in the past year by foundation, subject, state, and other groupings. The fundraiser, for example, could look up visual arts and find out all the grants made to support the visual arts and identify the most active foundations in this area of giving.
2. *The Foundation Directory,* which lists over 2,500 foundations that either have assets of over $1 million or award grants of more than $500,000 annually. The directory describes the general characteristics of each foundation, such as type of foundation, types of grants, annual giving level, officers and directors, location, particular fields of interest, contact person, and so on. The directory also contains an index of fields of interest, listing the foundations that have a stated interest in each field and whether or not they gave money to this field last year.
3. *The Foundation News,* which is published six times a year by the Council on Foundations and describes new foundations, new funding programs, and changes in existing foundations.
4. *Fund Raising Management,* which is a periodical publishing articles on fundraising management.

The key concept in identifying foundations is that of *matching.* The nonprofit organization should search for foundations matched to its *interests* and *scale* of operation. Too often a small nonprofit organization will send a proposal to the Ford Foundation because it would like to get the support of this well-known foundation. But the Ford Foundation accepts about one out of every 100 proposals and may be less disposed toward helping small nonprofit organizations than more regional or specialized foundations would be.

After identifying a few foundations that might have high interest in its project, the organization should try to qualify their level of interest before investing a lot of time in grant preparation. Most foundations are willing to respond to a letter of inquiry, phone call, or personal visit regarding how interested they are likely to be in the project. The foundation officer may be very encouraging or discouraging. If the former, the fundseeking organization can then make the investment of preparing an elaborate proposal for this foundation.

Writing successful grant proposals is becoming a fine art, with many guides currently available to help the grant-seeker.[4] Each proposal should contain at least the following elements:

1. a *cover letter* describing the history of the proposal, and who has been contacted, if anyone, in the foundation
2. the *proposal,* describing the project, its uniqueness, and its importance
3. the *budget* for the project
4. the *personnel* working on the project with their resumes

The proposal itself should be compact, individualized, organized, and readable. In writing the proposal, the organization should be guided by knowledge of the "buying criteria" that the particular foundation uses to choose among the many proposals that it receives. Many foundations describe their criteria in their annual reports or other memos; or their criteria can be inferred by looking at the characteristics of the recent proposals they have supported, or by talking to knowledgeable individuals. Among the most common guiding criteria used by foundations are:

1. the importance and quality of the project
2. the neediness and worthwhileness of the organization
3. the organization's ability to use the funds effectively and efficiently
4. the importance of satisfying the persons who are doing the proposing
5. the degree of benefit that the foundation will derive in supporting the proposal

If the proposing organization knows the relative importance of the respective criteria, it can do a better job of selecting the features of the proposal to emphasize. For example, if the particular foundation is influenced by who presents the proposal, the organization should send its highest ranking officials to the foundation. On the other hand, if the foundation attaches the most importance to the quality of the proposal, the organization should put a lot of effort in fine-tuning the writing of the proposal.

Nonprofit organizations should not contact foundations only on the occasion of a specific proposal. Each organization should cultivate a handful of appropriate foundations in advance of specific proposals. This is called "building bridges" or "relationship marketing." One major university sees the Ford Foundation as a "key customer account." The development officer arranges for various people within the university to get to know people at their corresponding levels within the foundation. One or more members of the university's board arrange to see corresponding board members of the foundation each year. The university president visits the foundation's president each year for a luncheon or dinner. One or more members of the university's development staff cultivate relations with foundation staff members at their levels. When the university has a proposal, it knows exactly who should present it to the foundation and whom to see in the foundation. Furthermore, the foundation is more favorably disposed toward the organization because of the long relationship and special understanding they enjoy. Finally, the organization is able to do a better job of tracking the proposal as it is being reviewed by the foundation.

## CORPORATIONS

Business organizations represent another distinct source of funds for non-profit organizations. Corporations have been especially supportive of such causes as higher education, United Way, and health, civic, cultural, and social services. In 1979 American business contributed $2.3 billion of the $43.3 billion received in total charity. This amounts to slightly less than 1 percent of business's pretax income. Since business organizations are allowed by law to give up to 5 percent of their pretax income to charity, considerable potential for more corporate giving exists.

Corporate giving differs from foundation giving in a number of important ways. In the first place, corporations regard gift giving as a minor activity, in contrast to foundations where it is the major activity. Corporations will vary their giving level with the level of current and expected income. They have to be sensitive to the feelings of their stockholders, to whom they have the first obligation both in terms of how much to give to charity and what particular charities to support. Corporations are more likely to avoid supporting controversial causes than are foundations. Corporations typically handle the many requests for support they receive by setting up a foundation so that corporate officers are not personally drawn into gift decision making.

In the second place, corporations pay more attention than foundations to the personal benefit that any grant might return to them. If they can show that a particular grant will increase community goodwill (as a grant by a cigarette company to the cancer research foundation) or train more manpower that they need (as a grant by an engineering company to an engineering school), these grants will be more acceptable to their board of directors and stockholders.

In the third place, corporations can make more types of gifts than foundations can. The nonprofit organization can approach the business firm for *money, securities, goods* (asking a furniture company for some furniture), *services* (asking a printing company for some free printing or printing at cost), and *space* (asking a company for the use of its auditorium for a program). In the extreme, the nonprofit organization should be able to get office equipment, marketing research, advertising, and so on, free or at cost if it can identify the right corporate prospects to approach.

Effective corporate fundraising requires the nonprofit organization to know how to identify good corporate prospects efficiently. Of the millions of business enterprises that might be approached, relatively few are appropriate to any specific nonprofit organization. Furthermore, the nonprofit organization ordinarily does not have the resources to cultivate more than a handful of corporate givers. The best prospects for corporate fundraising have the following characteristics:

1. *Local corporations.* Corporations located in the same area as the nonprofit organization are excellent prospects. A hospital, for example, can base its appeal on the health care it offers to the corporation's employees and a performing arts group can base its appeal on its cultural offerings. Corporations find it hard to refuse to support worthwhile organizations in their area.

2. *Kindred activities.* Corporations located in a kindred field to the nonprofit organization's are excellent prospects. Hospitals can effectively solicit funds from pharmaceutical companies and colleges can attract funds from companies that hire many of their graduates.

3. *Declared areas of support.* Nonprofit organizations should target corporations that have a declared interest in supporting that type of nonprofit organization. Thus, a "support-the-arts" organization might approach the Borg-Warner Corporation because of the latter's active purchase of contemporary art.

4. *Large givers.* Large corporations and those with generous giving levels are excellent prospects. Yet fundraisers must realize that these corporations receive numerous requests and favor those nonprofit organizations in the local area or kindred field. Regional offices of major corporations are often not in a position to make a donation without the approval of the home office.

5. *Personal relationships or contacts.* Nonprofit organizations should review their personal contacts as a clue to corporations that they might solicit. A university's board of trustees consists of influential individuals who can open many doors for corporate solicitations. Corporations tend to respond to peer influence in their giving.

6. *Specific capability.* The fundraiser may identify a corporation as a prospect because it has a unique resource needed by the nonprofit organization. Thus, a charity hospital might solicit a paint manufacturer for a donation of paint to repaint the rooms in an old wing of a hospital.

The preceding criteria will help the nonprofit organization identify a number of corporations that are worth approaching for contributions. Corporations in the organization's geographical area or field are worth cultivating on a continuous basis ("relationship marketing") aside from specific grant requests. However, when the organization is seeking to fund a specific project, it needs to identify the best prospects and develop a marketing plan from scratch. We will illustrate the planning procedure in connection with the following example:

A well-known private university was seeking to raise $5 million to build a new engineering library. Its existing library was wholly inadequate and a handicap to attracting better students to the engineering school. The university was willing to name the new library after a major corporate donor who would supply at least 60 percent ($3 million) of the money being sought. This donor would be the "bell cow" that would attract additional corporate donors to supply the rest.

The first step called for the university to *identify one or more major corporations* to approach. The fundraisers recognized that major prospects would have two characteristics: they would be wealthy corporations and they would have a high interest in this project. The fundraisers developed the matrix shown in Figure 19–2 and proceeded to classify corporations by their giving potential and their interest potential. In classifying corporations, they realized that oil companies fell in the upper left cell. Oil companies have high profits ("giving potential") and a high interest in engineering schools ("interest potential"). They also want to give money to good causes to win public goodwill. The university decided that approaching an oil company would make sense.

Which oil company? Here the university applied additional criteria. An oil company located in the same geographical area had already given a major donation to this university for another project; it was ruled out. The university considered whether it had any good contacts with some of the other oil companies. The university identified one oil corporation in the East in which several of its graduates held important management positions. In addition, a member of the university's board of trustees—a major bank president—knew the president of the oil company. It was decided on the basis of this and other factors to approach this oil company for support.

The next step called for preparing a *prospect solicitation plan.* As a start, the university fundraisers researched the oil company's sales, profits, major officers, recent giving record, and other characteristics. This information was useful in deciding whom to approach at the corporation, how much to ask for, what benefits to offer, and so on. A decision was made to approach the corporation's

## FIGURE 19–2

Classifying Prospective Corporate Donors
by Level of Interest and Giving Potential

Giving Potential

|  | High | Medium | Low |
|---|---|---|---|
| High |  |  |  |
| Interest Potential  Medium |  |  |  |
| Low |  |  |  |

president, ask for $3 million for the new engineering library, and offer to name the library after the corporation.

The final step called for *plan implementation*. The bank president arranged an appointment to visit the oil corporation's chairman, who was an old friend. He was accompanied by the university's president, and also the vice president of development. When they arrived, they met the chairman and the oil company's foundation director. They made their presentation, and the chairman said the proposal would be given careful consideration. A subsequent meeting was held on the university's campus, and ultimately the oil corporation granted the money to the university.

The oil company responded positively to this solicitation because the proposal stood high on its major criteria. The oil company foundation rated each proposal on four criteria:

1. The proposal had to be worthwhile from a societal point of view. In this case, an engineering library would contribute toward better trained engineers in the United States.

2. The corporation had to feel that the soliciting institution was worthwhile and would handle the grant well. Here, the oil company had full confidence in the particular university.

3. The proposal should create some direct benefit, if possible, for the oil company. In this case, the oil company recognized a number of benefits: It would have an "in" on the best new graduates; it would memorialize its name on the campus; and it would get good publicity for supporting this private university.

4. The oil company foundation placed value on the personal relationships involved. The fact that an important bank president had taken the time to present personally the proposal to the oil company chairman was an important factor in carefully considering the proposal.

In general, corporations pay attention to these criteria in considering whether to "buy" a particular proposal, and therefore the seller ("fundraiser") should weave them into its planning and presentation.

### GOVERNMENT

Another major source of funds are government agencies at the federal, state, and local levels that are able to make grants to worthwhile causes. As an example, the federal government set up the National Endowment for the Arts (NEA) to grant over $100 million annually to support museums, ballet companies, art groups, and other art organizations, large and small. Art organizations, as well as individual artists, regularly subscribe to NEA's *Guide to Programs* and *The Cultural Post* to review the types of grants recently made by NEA as a basis for preparing their own proposals.

Other government agencies also make grants to support health care, university teaching and research, social services, and other worthwhile causes. Large nonprofit organizations will appoint a staff member as director of government grants to concentrate on cultivating opportunities in this sector. The director will monitor announcements of government grant opportunities that might have potential for his or her organization, as well as spend time in Washington and elsewhere getting to know officers at these various agencies.

Government agencies normally require the most detailed paperwork in preparing proposals. On the other hand, the agencies are very willing to review proposals, placing the main weight on the proposal's probable contribution to the public interest. Certain topics become "hot," such as "cancer research," "environmental health," and so on, and the granting agencies look for the best proposals they can find on these topics. They pay less attention to agency benefit or to personal relations with the requesting organizations.

## ORGANIZING FOR FUNDRAISING

Nonprofit organizations must develop an organized approach to fundraising. They cannot simply rely on money coming over the transom; this would make funding too erratic. Small organizations normally rely on one person who is chiefly responsible for fundraising. This person may be the organization's head or a director of development. He or she will be responsible for identifying fundraising opportunities and activating others—officers, employees, volunteers—to assist when possible.

Large nonprofit organizations—such as the American Red Cross and American Heart Association—will have entire departments of development, consisting of dozens of staff members plus volunteers numbering into the thousands. In these large organizations, development staff members take responsibility for either specific *donor markets, services, marketing tools,* or *geographical areas.* We shall illustrate this by showing how a large private college typically organizes its fundraising.

A model organization for university fundraising is shown in Figure 19–3. The board of directors has the ultimate responsibility for overseeing the financial health of the university and does this by making personal and company contributions, arranging donor contacts, and suggesting new fundraising ideas. The college president is the chief fundraiser when it comes to meeting important people and asking for money. The vice president of development is the chief planner of the fundraising strategy for the institution and also personally asks for money from potential donors. Day-to-day administration is often handled by a director of development, to free the vice president of development for strategic planning and outside travel. The remaining development staff carry out specialized activities. Some staff are specialized to donor markets—thus there are directors of alumni affairs, foundations, corporate giving, and so on. Other staff members manage marketing functions, such as public relations, research, and volunteers.

**FIGURE 19–3**

A Large University Fundraising Organization

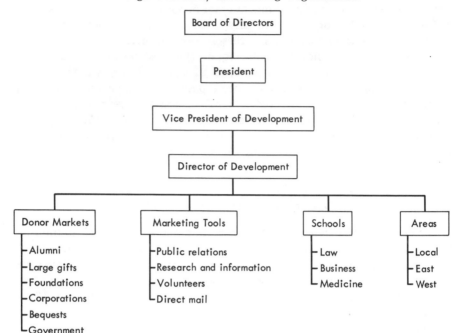

Others handle various schools, where they get to know the faculty and fundraising needs and opportunities. Finally, some staff members may manage regions of the country. For example, Cornell runs offices in eight cities which handle fundraising, alumni relations, and public relations.

The staff's effectiveness is amplified by managing a large number of volunteers—such as alumni, wealthy friends of the institution, deans, faculty, students, and so on. For example, Stanford runs a special program called the Inner Quad program for those who give (or may give) over $1,000 annually to Stanford. This program is run by eight professional staff members working through 250 volunteers operating in 16 regions of the country.[5] In this case, the staff really functions to activate the volunteers who are the main fundraising arm of the university.

The university's effectiveness in fundraising is also impacted by the quality of its information system. The development office needs to maintain up-to-date and easily accessible files on donors and prospects (individuals, foundations, corporations, etc.) so that past and/or potential giving can be identified and previous solicitations can be reviewed. To the extent that these files are computerized and data can be retrieved by year, school, giving level, and other key variables, the fundraiser is in a much better position to allocate his or her time effectively.

## FUNDRAISING GOALS AND STRATEGY

Organizations must set annual and long-range goals for fundraising. As an example, the March of Dimes set the following goals:

- to become the leading charitable organization in the area of birth defects
- to increase annual contributions received each year by an average of 10 percent
- to keep the expenses-to-contributions ratio below 20 percent
- to increase the median size contribution by 10 percent
- to increase grants from the government by 15 percent

Presumably, these goals would have to be checked for consistency and prioritized in terms of importance.

Every organization tends to set an annual goal for contributions because this allows the organization to (1) know how much to budget for fundraising, (2) motivate the staff and volunteers to high exertion, and (3) measure fundraising effectiveness. Organizations arrive at their fundraising goal in different ways, such as:

1. *Incremental approach.* Here the organization takes last year's revenue and increases it to cover inflation and then modifies it up or down depending on the expected economic climate. Thus, the American Heart Association may decide to raise about 15 percent more than it did in the preceding year.

2. *Need approach.* Here the organization forecasts its financial needs and sets a goal based on its needs. Thus a university's administration will estimate the future building needs and costs, faculty salaries, energy costs, and so on, and set the portion that has to be covered by fundraising as its target.

3. *Opportunity approach.* Here the organization makes a fresh estimate of how much money it could raise from each donor group with different levels of fundraising expenditure. It sets the goal of maximizing the net surplus. This approach can be illustrated with Figure 11–2, p. 278, in Chapter 11. The sales response function shows the gross revenue that would be raised with different levels of fundraising expenditure. Nonmarketing expenditures can be subtracted to reveal the gross surplus before marketing expenditures. The 45° line shows the marketing expenditures on fundraising. The vertical distance between the last two curves shows the net surplus associated with various fundraising expenditures. The highest point on the surplus curve shows the marketing expenditure level that will maximize net surplus.

The opportunity approach is the most sound. The vice president of development would be responsible for preparing this analysis by analyzing the potential of each donor group. If this goal is accepted, the vice president of development knows how much staff effort to allocate to each donor group.

After setting its fundraising goal, the organization has to develop an overall strategy. It must decide on how to present its case to the donors. For example, the American Heart Association has to decide whether to base its case on "hope," "fear," or some other major motive for giving. It has to decide how to allocate scarce staff time to different donor groups and geographical areas.

The role of the vice president of development in influencing the organization's objectives and strategies varies greatly among organizations. Most organizations treat the development officer as a technician rather than a policy maker. The president and/or board decides how much money is needed, selects the broad fundraising strategy, and then assigns its implementation to the development officer. This, unfortunately, robs the organization of a valuable contribution that the development officer can make. Some organizations grant more scope to the development officer. This officer participates with the other officers in developing the organization's institutional positioning and personality. By helping the organization develop a better position in the market, the development officer can raise money more easily.

## FUNDRAISING TACTICS

Fundraising strategy sets the overall parameters for the fundraising effort which the development officer must fill in with specific actions. The organization's job is to send messages to the potential donors through the most effective message channels and allow the donors to return money through the most efficient collection channels. This view of the channel options is shown in Figure 19–4.

The various channel opportunities give rise to a whole set of specific, well-known fundraising tactics. Table 19–2 lists the major tactics that are effective in four markets: mass anonymous small gift market, members and their friends market, affluent citizens market, and wealthy donors market.

### FIGURE 19–4
Communication and Collection Channels for Fundraising

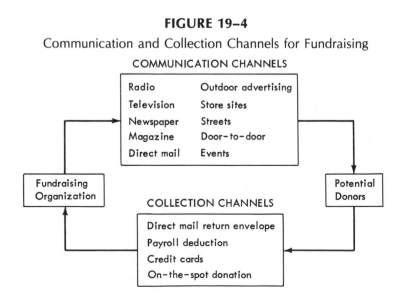

**Table 19–2**

FUNDRAISING METHODS

*Mass Anonymous Small Gift Market*

| | |
|---|---|
| Charity cans in stores | Raffles |
| Direct mail | Rummage sales |
| Door-to-door solicitation | Sporting events |
| Street and sidewalk solicitation | Tours |
| TV and radio marathons | Walkathons, readathons, bikeathons, |
| Thrift shops | danceathons, jogathons, swimathons |
| Plate passing | Yearbooks |

*Members and Their Friends Market*

| | |
|---|---|
| Anniversary celebrations | Dances |
| Art shows | Dinners, suppers, lunches, breakfasts |
| Auctions | Fairs |
| Benefits (theatre, movies, sports events) | Fashion shows |
| Bingo games | Parties in unusual places |
| Book sales | Phonothons (also called telethons) |
| Cake sales | |

*Affluent Citizens Market*

| | |
|---|---|
| Convocations | Parlor meetings |
| Dinners (invitational and/or testimonial) | Telephone calls from high-status |
| Letters from high-status individuals | individuals |

*Wealthy Donors Market*

| | |
|---|---|
| Bequests | Testimonial dinner for wealthy |
| Celebrity grooming | individuals |
| Committee visit to person's home, | Wealthy person invited to another's |
| office | home or club |
| Memorials | |

The *mass anonymous small gift market* consists of all citizens who might be induced to contribute a small sum (say, under $50) to a cause. The key idea is to use low-cost methods of fundraising, since the contributions from noninvolved individuals are expected to be low. One of the oldest forms of mass fundraising is the use of volunteers for street and sidewalk solicitation. The volunteers stand in high traffic areas holding out a can (Crippled Children), offering tags (Veterans' Day), ringing bells (Salvation Army), or distributing religious materials (Hare Krishna). Somewhat more costly is door-to-door solicitation because more time is involved and many people won't be home. Yet door-to-door canvassing is the preferred method of the American Heart Association (AHA), which has a massive army of volunteers organized by city, neighborhood, and block, who ring doorbells once a year for the AHA. Block volunteers are typically homemakers who solicit their neighbors for money and make a substantial contribution themselves. Some charities enlist retailers to keep donation cans in their establishments near the cash register where people might deposit their spare change. In recent years, direct mail has become one of the major fundraising tools. Organizations buy mailing lists of people who are likely to contribute and send attractive letters asking for support. They can calculate in advance the response rate required to break even on the mailing cost and usually do substantially better than this rate.

The *members and their friends market* consists of the people who belong to the organization and their friends, who have a personal interest in supporting the organization. This market can be tapped for donations in a number of ways. For example, art museums favor raising money through selling memberships and running theatre benefits, dinners, and tours. Churches, on the other hand, typically raise money by sponsoring bingo games, rummage sales, cake sales, plate passing, and raffles. Each of these fundraising methods requires careful planning in order to maximize its potential revenue. Fashion shows, for example, have to be planned and promoted far in advance of the day of their occurrence; the same can be said of dances and fairs. Fundraising consultants can be found who specialize in each method and know how to stage it for maximal effectiveness. These consultants can recommend the most effective and appropriate fundraising methods to an organization. Furthermore, they continue to invent new approaches each year.[6] No sooner had walkathons become popular than other organizations created "readathons," "bikeathons," and "jogathons." Each organization seeks to give a special or distinctive twist to its events. For example, the Boys Clubs of Chicago looked for an unusual place to hold a dinner for its members and decided on a black-tie dinner dance to be held in the Lion House of Lincoln Park Zoo, with the lions stalking around as the dinner guests dined and danced.

The *affluent citizens market* consists of persons whose income and interest in the organization or cause could lead them to give anywhere from $50 to several hundred dollars as a donation. The affluent citizens market is worth pursuing with more than direct mail. A highly effective technique is to issue invitations for special dinners or events. Political parties, for example, run $100 or $500 plate dinners to raise money for aspiring political candidates. Or the dinner might be free, with donations solicited after a round of enthusiastic speech making and drinking, both calculated to loosen the purse strings. Another popular method is letter writing and/or phone calling from supporters of the organization to their affluent friends asking for donations.

The *wealthy donors market* consists of persons whose wealth and potential interest is such that they might be induced to contribute anywhere from $1,000 to several million dollars to a cause or organization. These wealthy donors are usually well known in their community, and they are solicited by many organizations for financial support. Many of them set up foundations to handle these solicitations so that they do not have to be personally bothered. Yet some

**EXHIBIT 19–1.** Stanford tailors its fundraising tactics to each alumni segment

To raise money from its alumni, Stanford University's development office distinguishes different categories of alumni—according to the school they attended while at Stanford and also the year of their graduation. The development office then applies the most cost-effective method of fundraising to each category. For this purpose, Stanford further divides its alumni into groups according to their estimated giving potential: those who are believed able to give $1,000 or more; $100–$999; and less than $100. Personal solicitation has proven most effective with the two groups that give over $100. Phonathons have proved especially effective for getting nondonors to start giving and small donors to increase their gifts. A phone call from a classmate asking the alumnus to give a little more is often successful. On the other hand, mail appeals are more cost-effective in reaching alumni who have given under $50 in the past and who are not located in a geographical area where there is a large concentration of Stanford alumni (which is necessary to achieve economies of scale in a phonathon). Even here, the development office divides the under-$50 group into several segments: (1) gave last year, first time, over $25; (2) gave last year, first time, under $25; (3) gave last year, regular donors, over $25; (4) gave last year, regular donors, under $25; (5) gave only in the previous year; (6) gave only two or more years ago; and (7) never gave. Each of these groups receives a different pattern of mail. Those who gave last year, first time, over $25, receive up to five solicitation letters before the school gives up. For example, the first mail appeal comes from the school that the alumnus attended and describes its recent activities and accomplishments as a way of building pride. If this doesn't work, a second letter comes from a former classmate. If this doesn't work, a third letter comes from a school faculty member reporting on recent research. This is followed, if necessary, by the school's dean sending a letter. The final effort might be a letter from the university president or the chairman of the fund drive. Such an extensive mailing plan would be too expensive to use on those alumni who give small amounts less frequently, so this latter group would only receive up to four solicitation letters; meantime, those who have never given only receive up to two letters. Although these different mailing treatments seem arbitrary, they are based on experimenting with different approaches to each group and determining the most cost-effective approach by examining response rates and average gifts against mailing costs.

SOURCE: Adapted from "Stanford University: The Annual Fund," in Christopher H. Lovelock and Charles B. Weinberg, eds., *Cases in Public and Nonprofit Marketing* (Palo Alto, Calif.: Scientific Press, 1977), pp. 73–88.

fundraisers will spend inordinate amounts of time with these individuals in the hope of attracting a major grant to their institutions. One fundraiser from a major private eastern university has already spent seven years cultivating the friendship of a wealthy Chicago widow without yet receiving a major grant; yet he is not giving up. Some universities are skillful in putting on weekend retreats for wealthy donors in order to attract substantial money. One well-known private university invited fifty of its wealthiest alumni to an all-expense weekend on the campus, flying them in on private planes from their homes in various parts of the country. These alumni were put up in the best hotel, treated to some fine lectures, led in a religious service by the university president, and treated to a football game won brilliantly by the school's team. Their spirits were so high that the average alumnus attending that weekend gave a check to the university for over $100,000.

All of these fundraising tactics can be organized under the umbrella concept of a campaign. We define a campaign as follows:

> A **campaign** is an organized and time-sequenced set of activities and events for raising a given sum of money within a particular time period.

We can distinguish between an *annual campaign* and a *capital campaign.* Colleges, hospitals, churches, and charitable organizations will plan an annual campaign to raise a target amount of money each year. The campaign plan will spell out the "case," goals, events, and so on. A well-known person may be invited to be the campaign chairman to energize and symbolize that year's campaign.

Organizations will also run a capital campaign from time to time, to raise a large amount of money for major undertakings or expansions. In the year 1972, Stanford launched a five-year, $300 million capital campaign, and in 1974 Yale launched a three-and-a-half-year, $370 million capital campaign. These campaigns require the most careful planning. Here are some of the major considerations:

1. An organization cannot run a capital campaign too often. After Stanford ended its five-year capital campaign, it would not launch another capital campaign for at least three to five years. This "spacing" is necessary if the capital campaigns are to retain their specialness in the minds of donors.
2. The organization has to make decisions on the capital campaign's goal and duration. The goal should be achievable, for there is nothing more embarrassing than failing to reach the goal. And the campaign should not last too long because it will eventually lose its momentum.
3. The organization should try to add a matching gift feature to the campaign, where some wealthy donors or organizations promise to match, say, $1 for $1, the money raised. Early in the planning, the organization has to find and cultivate challenge grants.
4. The organization should prepare an attractive booklet showing the main items that the money will buy (called a *wish list*). Thus, MIT prepared a booklet showing what different amounts of money would buy, including buildings, endowed chairs, and so on.
5. The campaign strategy calls for approaching various potential donor groups in a planned sequence. First, board members should be asked for large gifts to be in

hand even before the campaign begins. Next, large potential donors should be approached. These steps will create the impression that the campaign is generating much support and enthusiasm and others will want to join the bandwagon.

An issue in designing a campaign is to decide whether potential donors should be "coached" in how much to give or whether this should be left to their judgment. In fact, there are three possibilities:

1. Don't specify any amount.
2. Suggest a specific dollar amount on the low side.
3. Suggest a specific dollar amount on the high side.

The first approach is the most common. People differ in what they can give, and it is felt that this is best left to their individual judgments.

Suggesting a specific amount on the low side is seen as accomplishing two things. It helps prospects know what is considered a minimum proper amount to give. And the "low-amount feature" allows people to get into the habit of giving ("foot-in-the-door").[7] The problem is that many people who might have given more will take this as an adequate amount to give.

Suggesting a high amount to give works on the theory of "door-in-the-face."[8] It stretches people's idea of what they should give and, hopefully, they would give this much or something close to it. Thus, the United Fund might suggest that citizens give 1 percent of their income, or a church might suggest that members give 5 percent of their income. Most people regard this as too high, but end up giving more than they normally would (see Exhibit 19–2).

---

## EVALUATING FUNDRAISING EFFECTIVENESS

Each organization must make a continuous effort to improve its effectiveness through evaluating its recent results, especially in the face of increasingly sophisticated competition and scarce funds. The organization can evaluate its results on a macro- and a micro-level.

### MACROEVALUATION

Organizations use several methods to evaluate their overall fundraising effectiveness. They are described below.

**Percentage of goal reached.** For organizations that set an annual goal, the first thing to look at is how close they came to achieving the goal. Every organization wants to achieve at least its goal or better. This creates a temptation to set the goal low enough to be achieved. Often, the development officer favors a low goal so that he or she could look good. The organization's president, however, is tempted to set a high goal to induce the development office to work hard.

**EXHIBIT 19–2.** How not to ask for money in a face-to-face situation

A successful young lawyer had a recent experience which graphically illustrates several subtle points about personal solicitation. He received a phone call from a person who said that he was from the lawyer's alma mater and would like to make an appointment to talk to the lawyer. At the appointed time the visitor appeared, a tall good-looking man with gray hair who looked like a college president. The visitor started to talk about the university's plan for the eighties and showed pictures of new buildings that the university needed. The lawyer now knew that the visitor was a development officer seeking a donation. After describing the university in glowing terms for fifteen minutes, the development officer came to the point: "In view of our needs and your affection for the university, I would like you to consider making a donation of $10,000 to your university." The lawyer at this point felt stunned by this request ("door-in-the-face"). He had never been asked for such a large contribution by any organization. He felt flattered that someone could think he could make such a large contribution; this meant that he had "arrived." On the other hand, he felt somewhat miffed to be asked without warning for such a large amount of money by a relative stranger. He told the development officer that he appreciated learning about his university's needs and would think it over, and hopefully would give, if not that amount, something substantial in any event. The officer looked a little disappointed, but thanked him for his time and left. At the time of this writing, the lawyer still had not made any donation to his university.

This episode illustrates several mistakes in the development officer's approach to the particular prospect. (Try to imagine these mistakes before reading on.) The development officer should have said over the phone who he was and his purpose for visiting. He should have sent an advance mailing describing the university's campaign, needs, and accomplishments. He should have considered bringing along an eminent lawyer who had also graduated from the same university. He should have done less talking and more listening, asking the lawyer how he felt about the university and what memories he had. The development officer should have asked for a more reasonable gift—say, $5,000. When the lawyer balked, the officer should have continued to try to "close the sale." He might have said that the lawyer could make a contribution of $5,000 over a five-year period in $1,000 annual amounts; this would ease the financial burden. Or he could have suggested a tangible benefit that would flow from this gift, such as a scholarship named after the lawyer to support a worthwhile student. Or he could have said that this would be a leadership gift, and the lawyer's name would be listed along with other leading contributors. Or he could have said that he would phone in two weeks to see how much the lawyer might be able to give. The development officer did not do any of these things, and his approach showed poor planning of this sales call.

**Composition of gifts.**    The organization should examine the composition of the money raised, looking at trends in the two major components:

Gifts = number of donors $\times$ average gift size

NUMBER OF DONORS.    Each organization hopes to increase the number of donors each year. The organization should pay attention to the number of donors in relation to the potential number of donors. Many organizations have a disappointing "reach" or "penetration." For example, 29 percent of Stanford's alumni has given each year. The question raised is not why Stanford has 29 percent penetration but why 71 percent of its alumni do not give. The development officer should interview a sample of alumni nongivers and identify the importance of such reasons as: "did not enjoy Stanford as a student," "do not like the way Stanford is evolving," "disagree with policies of the school in which I graduated," "couldn't care less," "was never asked," and so on. Each of these reasons suggests a possible plan of action.

AVERAGE GIFT SIZE.    A major objective of the fundraising organization is to increase the size of the average gift. The development office should review the size distribution of gifts. It should estimate the potential number of gifts that might be obtained in each size class against the current number to determine the size classes of gifts that deserve targeted effort in the next period.

**Market share.**    For some organizations, its share or rank in fundraising among comparable organizations can be a revealing statistic about whether the institution is doing a competent job. For example, a private midwestern university compared its results to the results of five comparable universities and found it was trailing in the number of alumni givers, and in the amount raised through government grants. This led to more effort being put in these two donor directions. As another example, the Chicago Lung Association found that, while it managed to raise more dollars each year, its rank among charitable causes had slipped from third place to eighth place. It was losing its "share of heart" in the giving community and needed to find ways to reverse this relative decline.

**Expense/contributions ratio.**    The fundraising organization is ultimately interested in its net revenue, not gross revenue. At one time the American Kidney Fund spent $740,000 to raise $779,434 and created a scandal. It is more normal for expense-to-contributions to run 10 and 20 percent, and the public generally accepts this. The American Red Cross runs its expenses at 5 percent of its contributions. Many large donors look at this key ratio before they decide whether to support an organization.

MICROEVALUATION

The organization should also rate its individual staff members on their fundraising effectiveness. This is not always done. One university vice president of development said he had a general idea of the funds brought in by each staff member but not specific numbers. Many gifts were the result of several staff people working together: one identifying the prospect, another grooming him, and still another getting the check. Still, it would be worthwhile evaluating each individual to help train them better or dismiss them if they are not tapping the existing potential. As an example, one university rates its staff that works with foundations by using the following indicators (the numbers are illustrative):

| | |
|---|---|
| Number of leads developed | 30 |
| Number of proposals written | 20 |
| Average value of proposal | $40,000 |
| Number of proposals closed | 10 |
| Percentage of proposals closed | 50% |
| Average value closed | $39,000 |
| Average cost per proposal closed | $6,000 |
| Cost per dollar raised | .20 |

## SUMMARY

One of the major problems of nonprofit organizations is fundraising. Organizations are gradually shifting from a product orientation to a sales orientation to a marketing orientation. A marketing orientation calls for carefully segmenting donor markets, measuring their giving potential, and assigning executive responsibility and resources to cultivate each market. Marketers assume that the act of giving is really an exchange process in which the giver also gets something that the organization can offer.

The first step in the fundraising process is to study the characteristics of each of the four major donor markets: individuals, foundations, corporations, and government. Each donor market has its own giving motives and giving criteria.

The second step is to organize the fundraising operation in a way that covers the different donor markets, organization's services, marketing tools, and geographical areas.

The third step is to develop sound goals and strategies to guide the fundraising effort. Goals are set on either an incremental basis, need basis, or opportunity basis.

The fourth step is to develop a mix of fundraising tactics for the various donor groups. Different tactics are effective with the mass anonymous small gift market, the members and their friends market, the affluent citizens market, and the wealthy donors market.

The fifth step is to conduct regular evaluations of fundraising results. A macroevaluation consists of analyzing the percentage of the goal reached, the composition of the gifts, the average gift size, the market share, and the expense/contributions ratio. Microevaluation consists of evaluating the performance of each individual fundraiser.

## QUESTIONS

**1.** Prepare a "wish list" that could be used in fundraising by a nonprofit organization with which you are familiar.

**2.** In what ways does successful grant proposal preparation involve marketing concepts and tools?

**3.** Diagram the exchange relationship between the oil company and the university described in the chapter.

**4.** Why is the opportunity approach considered the most sound basis for setting fundraising goals?

**5.** A small college plans to launch a capital campaign a year from now. The largest item on its "wish list" is a $5 million continuing education center, which is badly needed. The college is considering beginning construction in six months. What would you recommend, and why?

**6.** Large gifts are often obtained at a lower percentage cost than are small gifts. Would you recommend that nonprofit organizations put all their fundraising resources into attracting large gifts from major donors? Explain.

---

## NOTES

**1.** For additional information see *Giving USA—1979 Annual Report: A Compilation of Facts and Trends on American Philanthropy for the Year 1979* (New York: American Association of Fundraising Council, 1980).

**2.** "How Do We Choose the Charities We Support?", *Chicago Tribune,* July 30, 1972, Section 5, p. 9.

**3.** Harold J. Seymour, *Designs for Fund-Raising* (New York: McGraw-Hill, 1966).

**4.** Here are some useful books on grantsmanship. Virginia P. White, *Grants: How to Find Out About Them and What to Do Next* (New York and London: Plenum Press, 1975); Lois DeBakey and Selma DeBakey, "The Art of Persuasion: Logic and Language in Proposal Writing," *Grants Magazine,* Vol. 1, No. 1 (March 1978), pp. 43–60; F. Lee Jacquette and Barbara J. Jacquette, *What Makes a Good Proposal* (New York: Foundation Center, 1973); and Robert A. Mayer, *What Will a Foundation Look For When You Submit a Grant Proposal?* (New York: Foundation Center, 1972).

**5.** See "Stanford University: The Annual Fund," in Christopher Lovelock and Charles B. Weinberg, eds., *Cases in Public and Nonprofit Marketing* (Palo Alto, Calif.: Scientific Press, 1977), pp. 73–88.

**6.** For several examples see Suzanne Seixas, "Getting More from Givers," *Money,* September 1976, pp. 79–82.

**7.** In a study by Freedman and Fraser, the experimenters asked subjects to comply with a small initial request. Two weeks later, they were contacted and asked to comply with a large request. It was found that 76% of the experimental participants *agreed* to comply with the large request compared to a 17% compliance rate by those subjects approached with *only* the large request. See J. L. Freedman and S. Fraser, "Compliance Without Pressure: The Foot-in-the-Door Technique," *Journal of Personality and Social Psychology,* Vol. 4 (1966), pp. 195–202.

**8.** See R. B. Cialdini et al., "Reciprocal Concessions Procedure for Inducing Compliance: The Door-in-the-Face Technique," *Journal of Personality and Social Psychology,* Vol. 31 (1975), pp. 206–15.

# Voter Marketing: Attracting Votes

In 1966 Betty Friedan, author of *The Feminine Mystique,* joined with three hundred middle-class women and a few sympathetic men, and organized the National Organization for Women (NOW). NOW was organized to lobby for "women's interests" in much the same way that the National Association for the Advancement of Colored People (NAACP) lobbied for "black interests." NOW would work within the system and seek legal changes in the status of women, using lobbying, publicity, education, and membership recruiting. The NOW Bill of Rights in 1969 called for seven major improvements in the status of women:

    I. Equal Rights Constitutional Amendment
    II. Enforce Law Banning Sex Discrimination in Employment
    III. Maternity Leave Rights in Employment and in Social Security Benefits
    IV. Tax Deduction for Home and Child Care Expenses for Working Parents
    V. Child Care Day Centers
    VI. Equal and Unsegregated Education
    VII. The Right of Women to Control Their Reproductive Lives

By 1970 NOW reached a membership of 3,000, organized in 62 chapters.
    NOW placed much of its hope for women's rights in the passage of the Equal Rights Amendment (ERA) to the Constitution. Introduced into Congress every session since 1923 and defeated, the amendment called for the ending of all discrimination on the basis of sex. The amendment languished in the Senate Judiciary Committee and had a vague commitment from the

House Judiciary Committee. NOW officers undertook a massive effort and called upon every possible congressman to present their case. They issued a call to women throughout the country to write letters to their congressmen and to visit them in delegations. Members of NOW spoke on talk shows and gave news interviews to raise consciousness about women's inequality and the need to pass the ERA. They did not hesitate to use the carrot and the stick, offering to raise money and manpower to support the reelection of sympathetic legislators and to defeat their opponents at the polls.

NOW's lobbying efforts for the passage of ERA finally paid off. In early 1972, Congress passed the amendment. It was then sent for ratification to the states. Hawaii ratified it within hours and, by April 1974, 33 states had ratified it, with five more to go. The legislatures of Illinois and a few other states, however, held back although the votes were close. Unless these states ratified the amendment soon, it was going to expire. NOW lobbyists had to step up their lobbying activities in these states and needed to find new lobbying strategies that would work.

SOURCE: This case draws upon June Sochen's *Movers and Shakers: American Women Thinkers and Activists, 1900–1970* (New York: Quadrangle, 1973) and other sources.

Nonprofit organizations often need to obtain the votes of some group to support something they believe in or want. The target voter group might be legislators, citizens, government bureaucrats, or boards of directors. Here are some examples:

1. The Friends of the Earth (FOE) is lobbying Congress to pass more stringent industry pollution control laws.
2. The St. Louis Zoo wants to get the St. Louis City Council to vote a larger budget for next year's zoo operations.
3. The American Psychological Association wants to get Blue Cross and Blue Shield to include counseling by psychologists in their insurance coverage.
4. St. Joseph Hospital is petitioning the regional Health Systems Area board for permission to open a cancer treatment center.
5. The Bloomfield Michigan School District wants citizens to support a new bond issue and certain referenda in a forthcoming election.
6. The Republican Party wants to develop a vote-getting strategy for its candidate who is running for the state legislature in a heavily Democratic district.

All of these examples involve an *organization* that is trying to win the *votes* of some group in favor of some *proposition.* We can distinguish between seeking the votes through a selling approach versus a marketing approach. Consider the public school district that needs more tax money from the citizens to run the schools. A *selling approach* would involve the school board deciding, without any research, how much campaign money to spend and the arguments to present to the citizens for voting in favor of the referendum. The school board would broadcast these arguments to all citizens. In contrast, a *marketing approach* would involve the school board researching citizen concerns and their attitudes toward the public school system. The interests and attitudes of different groups would be observed, and the board would decide which groups needed to be reached most and what arguments needed to be stressed with each group. The school board might even test and fine-tune its case with different groups before opening the campaign.

This chapter will examine how an organization can market a proposition to a group of voters. The first part of the chapter discusses *legislative marketing* (i.e., lobbying), where the objective is to influence legislators to vote for or against a proposition. The second part deals with *citizen marketing* (i.e., political campaigning), where the objective is to influence a group of citizens to vote for a candidate or proposition.

## LEGISLATIVE MARKETING—LOBBYING

A legislature can be looked upon as a political marketplace whose members have a scarce currency called votes which they use to accept or reject various bills that come before them. Each bill excites the interest of certain outside groups—called interest groups or pressure groups—who try to influence the legislators' votes. An interest group will work through its lobbyists to gain these votes. The second edition of the Merriam-Webster dictionary defines "to lobby" as "to address or solicit members of a legislative body in the lobby or elsewhere with intent to influence legislation." Lobbying also includes efforts to solicit the support of legislators in nonlegislative matters such as appropriations, political appointments, and investigations. The Lobbying Act distinguishes the professional lobbyist from the ordinary citizen by defining a lobbyist as "a person or organization whose principal purpose is to influence the passage or defeat of legislation and who received money for that purpose."[1]

The stereotyped image of a lobbyist shows him calling on a legislator and presenting various arguments as to why a particular bill should be favored and the benefit that would accrue to the nation and/or the legislator in voting for it. The lobbyist would try to "make a sale," to get a vote commitment. In truth, most lobbyists take a much more market-oriented view of their task. A lobbyist would have made the acquaintance of various legislators before any particular bills were at issue. The lobbyist would take these legislators out to lunch, send them useful information from time to time, remember their hobbies, interests, family, and so on. When a bill would be at issue, the lobbyist would feed reliable information to the legislators. The lobbyist's main objective is to gain and maintain credibility with the legislators. Once lobbyists get a reputation for being unreliable, they lose their access to legislators.

Lobbying is the application of marketing principles to the target market known as legislators. Lobbyists need three understandings to be effective. First, they must have a good understanding of the way bills are passed in a legislature (i.e., *organizational buying behavior*). Second, they must know how legislators think, feel, and act (i.e., *consumer buying behavior*). Third, they must know how to select their target legislators and use the most cost-effective marketing tools (i.e., *marketing strategy development*). To these issues we now turn.

### MAPPING THE LEGISLATIVE PROCESS

An organization seeking to advance its interests through the successful passage of a bill must understand the legislative process. Enacting a bill into law is a long, tortuous process, whatever type of legislature is involved. The essential steps in this process are shown in Figure 20–1 and examined below.

**Drafting a bill.**    The organization's first task is to get a reasonable bill drafted that has a chance of accomplishing the objectives and getting sufficient votes for passage. For example, the Friends of the Earth (FOE) might want the government to establish a new agency to monitor noise levels and impose high penalties on violators. The organization needs to develop the broad outlines of a bill that would satisfy the objectives. It also needs to identify some key legislator(s) who might be willing to sponsor the bill. These needs interact. The proposed bill cannot be written before identifying potential sponsors because these sponsors will have their own ideas for the bill. They would want their staff to work with the organization to develop a bill that would accomplish the objectives and have a reasonable chance of passage. The final draft is often prepared by an Office of Legislative Counsel which assists Congressmen in turning rough proposals into legal language bills.

**Committee votes favorably on bill.**    It is relatively easy to get a bill drafted. It is much harder to avoid its "dying in committee." Every new bill is sent to an appropriate legislative committee for review. The committee it ends up in will make a big difference in its chance of becoming a law. It has the best chance if

**FIGURE 20–1**

A Model of an Effective Legislative Process

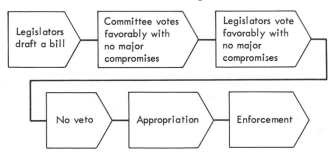

the bill's sponsor is a member of the committee. In any event, the lobbyist needs to identify the key committee members. Contact must be made with them and their staffs to offer additional facts and arguments in favor of the bill. The committee chairman has the most power, and if he or she is negatively disposed, the bill can be "shelved" for months. The lobbyist must also watch that the committee does not modify the bill such that it loses "its teeth." For example, the Truth in Packaging law was so modified in committee that the final law bore little resemblance to the original bill. The hope is that the committee will leave the bill largely intact and favor it strongly enough to become advocates and word-of-mouth influencers to the other legislators.

**Legislators vote favorably on bill.**     Bills that are favorably reported out of committee are put on a calendar to come up for floor discussion and a vote. Lobbyists have to put their campaign in high gear. They will call on key legislators and their staffs and engage in media publicity, mail campaigns, and grass-roots organizing. The overall purpose is to rally enough legislative support so that the bill is not amended or weakened during floor discussion and so that it is enacted into law.

**No veto.**     In most political systems, the executive head of government has the right to veto bills which he or she deems not to be in the public interest. The veto is rarely exercised because it implies that the executive head has more wisdom or is in better touch with the public interest than are the lawmakers. The sponsoring organization wants to make sure that the chief executive is not leaning toward veto; otherwise, it would have to plan a public campaign to discourage the veto or defeat it. The legislative body can overturn a veto with a two-thirds vote.

**Appropriation.**     Bills must not only be passed but also funded. The funding is in the hands of the appropriation committee, and this committee may decide to delay funding or reduce the expected funding substantially. The lobbyist's job is not over, and the appropriation committee may have to be lobbied if it delays or resists making a full appropriation.

**Enforcement.**     Not all new laws are enforced at the expected level. Various enforcement agencies have their own interpretation of what is important and may not allocate sufficient time and resources to enforcement. Some enforcement bodies may not be sympathetic with the new law and exercise minimal enforcement. For example, several state education systems have not enforced school busing because they lack sympathy for this law. The upshot is that the organization's representatives must collect evidence of poor enforcement and bring cases to the courts.

Thus, getting a bill enacted into law involves managing a total process, not just a one-time vote. The organization's lobbyists must plan a total strategy and be ready to redirect resources on a moment's notice as new problems and opportunities arise.

Lobbyists must understand not only the legislative process but also how legislators think, feel, and act. They need to understand legislators in general and know how to research the motivations, perceptions, and attitudes of particular legislators who must be reached.

What motivates the legislator? After all, the legislator had to go through a difficult and expensive electoral campaign to achieve this position and is never certain of reelection. Is the legislator acting out of civic consciousness, or are there other motives that operate? We have to assume that self-interest lies at the core of the legislator's behavior. The question is what do legislators seek? Over 2,000 years ago, Aristotle observed in *Politics* that legislators are motivated by three things. Some legislators want *fame,* that is, to be well known and highly regarded for serving their country. Other legislators are chiefly motivated by *power,* that is, they enjoy the influence they have over many people and society. Still other legislators are primarily motivated by *fortune,* that is, they want to improve their material welfare, either through favors received or afterward as a highly paid consultant.

Each type of legislator requires a different approach. Fame-oriented legislators respond best to suggestions that their support of a bill will increase the public's esteem for the legislator's humanitarianism and highmindedness. Power-oriented legislators respond best to innuendoes that their support will increase their voting strength and power within the legislature. Fortune-oriented legislators respond best to offers of material support such as campaign contributions, speech honoraria, and the like.

When it comes to influencing a particular legislator, much more needs to be known. Each legislator has a history, personality, political ties and obligations, voting record, and so on, and these must be researched by looking at the appropriate reference book.[2] Additional information can be gleaned by talking to political reporters, opposition candidates, and others who might know the legislator. The grapevine is so good that one can discover the legislator's favorite restaurants, hobbies, charities, and vices. The aim is to discover the most influential factors shaping his or her voting behavior.

Studies of legislator voting behavior indicate that legislators might pay attention to up to 12 different influence centers in determining how to vote on issues.[3] These are shown in Figure 20–2 and discussed below.

**Constituents.**     Legislators will pay major attention to the wishes and interests of their constituents. First, the legislators' overriding interest is to get reelected, and the key is to satisfy the voters in their district. Second, legislators are supposed to represent their constituents' interests. This calls for listening to them closely. Legislators might try to persuade their constituents that some bill is not in their interests, but in the end legislators will heed their constituents. Legislators stay in touch with constituent sentiment by reading the local newspapers, con-

## FIGURE 20–2

### Influence Centers Surrounding a Legislator

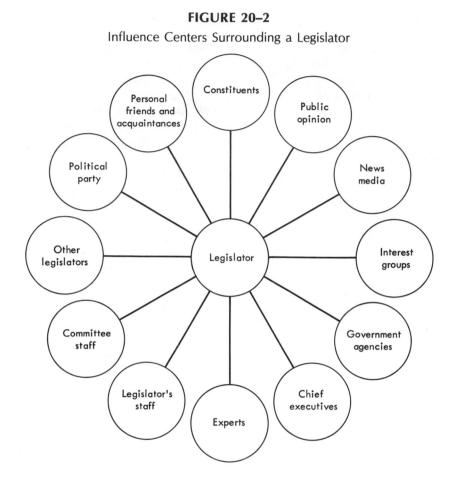

ducting public opinion surveys, appearing at local events, and welcoming visiting delegations.

This suggests for the lobbyist that an effective influence strategy is to activate grassroots support and get it expressed through letter writing campaigns, visiting delegations, and so on. The lobbyist must show that supporting the particular bill will win votes back home.

**Public opinion.**   Legislators pay attention to studies of public opinion, not only as it applies to their home district but to the nation as a whole. Most legislators want to take the majority position on an issue, especially if it is a strong majority. On the other hand, when public opinion is sharply split, it has less influence than other factors on how they will cast their vote.

The lobbyist can make use of public opinion surveys in two ways. When public opinion strongly supports the lobbying organization's position, the lobbyist can present this data to the legislator. If public opinion is weak, the lobbying organization might campaign to create stronger public opinion.

**News media.**     Public opinion is heavily influenced by the news, features, and editorials of leading news media. Influential media, such as *The New York Times,* the *Washington Post,* and major television and radio news programs, can have a major influence on public opinion through their selection of issues and presentation of positions. Furthermore, the amount of press coverage the media give to specific legislators can be a major asset or liability to these legislators. Therefore, legislators pay close attention to what the major news media are saying and not saying.

Lobbyists can augment their influence on legislators by developing good media connections. This will enable them to market more stories to the press that will influence public opinion. They may also offer to get favorable publicity for legislators through their media contacts.

**Interest groups.**     Legislators get elected with the support of various interest groups—business groups, trade unions, public interest groups—who see the legislators as a help in advancing their interests. These interest groups make financial and manpower contributions to political candidates, who in turn feel under some obligation to represent their interests or listen closely to their views.

The lobbyist has to identify the interest groups to whom a particular legislator pays attention. Some of these groups may be potentially strong supporters or sympathizers of the lobbying organization's cause. The lobbyist can try to interest these groups to use their influence and resources on the legislator in return for future support of their causes. Thus a public interest group like Friends of the Earth will try to enlist the support of other environmental groups, trade unions, religious organizations, fraternal organizations, and consumer groups to join in sponsoring the cause and reaching legislators. There is increasing use of "coalitions" and "united fronts" in trying to influence legislators.

**Government agencies.**     Government agencies have to lobby legislators for support of their agencies. They supply legislators and their staffs with needed information and evaluations of various issues. Legislators may be quite willing to go along with the views of certain respected government agency heads on certain issues.

Lobbyists will often try to market their position to sympathetic government agencies which in turn may influence key legislators.

**Chief executive.**     Legislators are influenced by the views and positions of the chief executive, whether it is the President of the United States, the state's governor, or the city's mayor. The chief executive can make a difference in legislators' careers, and they normally want to remain on good terms with the chief executive. If the President of the United States asks legislators for their votes, they have to think twice about refusing.

The lobbyist therefore includes in the influence strategy an effort to influence the chief executive to lend support to a cause. If successful, this can have a strong influence on the votes of the legislators.

**Experts.** Legislators put some credence in the views of acknowledged experts, especially when trying to decide complex issues, such as whether nuclear power is safe, or whether many jobs will be lost if a military base is closed. If the experts are in close agreement, this will have a strong influence on the legislators. If the experts disagree, their influence will be weak.

Lobbyists will want to put together evidence of high agreement among experts when making presentations to legislators, or at least try to line up the most credible experts in the hope that they can have some influence on the legislator.

**Legislator's staff.** Most legislators do not have the time or interest to study most of the bills they will have to vote on. They rely heavily on their staff to gather information about the bills and recommend a position.

A lobbyist needs to know the people on a legislator's staff, their relative influence on the legislator, and their own biases. The lobbyist may decide to spend most of the time trying to influence a key staff member rather than the legislator directly.

**Committee staffs.** Legislators pay attention to the views of staff members of committees that are reviewing a particular bill. These staff members can provide legislators with useful information and evaluations.

The lobbyist will want to know committee staff members and the opinions they are forming about a proposed piece of legislation. By presenting facts and arguments to committee staff members, the lobbyist may influence these staff members to have a positive influence on legislators.

**Other legislators.** Every legislator is ready to listen to the advice and opinions of other legislators, especially certain legislators who command high seniority, prestige, or power. There will be a lot of "logrolling" and "horsetrading," meaning that a legislator will support other legislators to whom the issue is important so that he or she can "collect" their votes in return.

Lobbyists try to figure out who the key legislators are, and which legislators have built up "credits or debts" with other legislators. By directing their energy to influencing the most influential legislators, lobbyists can gain a multiplier effect on the rest of the legislators.

**Political party.** The legislator's political party usually adopts a position on each bill, which the party's "whip" tries to enforce. Normally, legislators will vote with their party in order to continue to have their support.

Lobbyists consider whether they are able to influence the political parties to support their cause. If so, they will identify party leaders and figure out the best way to reach them.

**Personal friends and acquaintances.** Legislators have a life outside of their work consisting of friends, family, and acquaintances. In addition, they like to meet other "very important people" and enjoy the good life.

Lobbyists will research the legislator's social network to see if any natural allies exist. If they can win the support of the legislator's friends or acquaintances, the latter may carry the cause to the legislator.

### Developing the Lobbying Strategy

Given the legislative process and the influence centers impinging on legislators, the lobbying organization must decide how best to accomplish its legislative goals. It has to figure out how to allocate its limited time and scarce resources to an almost unlimited number of possible actions. Basically, it must decide on a target market strategy and a marketing mix strategy.

**Target market strategy.**      The lobbying organization must figure out which target markets are the most important to influence. How much time should be spent calling on legislators, their staffs, news editors, government agency heads, political party chiefs, and so on? Should the organization deal primarily with the legislators or work with influence centers that may have more ultimate influence on the legislators?

To the extent that the lobbying organization will contact legislators, there may not be time to see all of them. The lobbyists have to figure out which legislators are the most important to contact. Dexter puts the question this way:

> The problem is, granted a limited number of possible people to influence, should lobbyists take the standpoint of the salesmen who follow through on the good prospects but quickly abandon any effort to influence the unpromising ones—or should they imitate missionaries, eager to convert the unrighteous and hard of heart, as well as the malleable and persuadable?[4]

To describe the alternatives more carefully, we can identify five segments of legislators according to their probable degree of support for a cause or bill. The five segments are listed below, along with the appropriate marketing action that can be directed to each segment.

1. *Highly favorable.* Legislators who are highly favorable will not only give their votes but may also volunteer time to try to influence their colleagues. The lobbyist should meet with the highly favorables to supply facts and arguments, and express appreciation for their efforts to contact other legislators.
2. *Slightly favorable.* Legislators who are slightly favorable could easily change their mind. Therefore, this is an important group for the lobbyist to reach. Their vote is almost in hand and a little effort can go a long way.
3. *Neutral.* Many legislators will be neutral because of a lack of knowledge or interest in the particular bill. They might take their voting cue from their political party, or public opinion, or other legislators asking for their vote. This group is very important to call on because each effective presentation might win a vote.
4. *Slightly opposed.* Legislators who are slightly opposed should be approached if there is time left after working with the other segments and if their opposition is based on wrong information or belief. The lobbyist might help the legislator see the

bill in a different light. Also, the lobbyist will benefit by learning the key arguments of the opposition.

5. *Highly opposed.* Legislators who are highly opposed should not normally be contacted since arguments will do little good. A lobbyist may threaten to use his organization's power to defeat the legislator at the polls, but this generally does little good and deepens the legislator's hostility.

The amount of power and influence a legislator possesses can be another basis for segmenting the market. The effective lobbyist will direct energy to those legislators who have the greatest influence. They include members of the committee or subcommittee assigned to review the particular bill. Legislators who consider themselves experts on the issue are also good targets. So are the "grand old men" of the legislature.[5]

**Marketing mix strategy.**    The lobbying organization has a large number of tools available for reaching legislators and other influence centers. Fifteen of these tools are listed in Table 20–1. We will discuss the four major categories.

PERSONAL VISITATIONS.    Personal selling is generally regarded as more effective than any other communication approach to a target audience. The communicator can strike up a friendly note, get the total attention of the legisla-

**Table 20–1**

MAJOR TOOLS IN THE LOBBYING MARKETING MIX

*Personal visitations*

1. Lobbyist
2. Lobbying organization's leaders
3. Constituents
4. Interest groups
5. Friends, other legislators, government agency personnel, etc.

*Directed messages*

6. Letter, postcard, and telegram campaigns
7. Telephone campaigns

*Public opinion campaigns*

8. Public opinion studies
9. Media publicity
10. Advocacy advertising

*Incentive offers*

11. Campaign contributions of money/manpower
12. Speaking engagements
13. Business patronage
14. Entertaining and giving parties
15. Bribery

tor, listen and sense his mood, answer objections, and personalize the message. This is why lobbyists try to arrange personal calls on the legislator or his staff. The lobbyist may appear himself, bring his organization's president, or arrange visits by the legislator's constituents, friends, other legislators, allied interest groups, party leaders, government agency personnel, and so on. Bauer, Pool, and Dexter were surprised to find that lobbyists spent less of their time as personal callers on legislators and more of their time arranging for others to make calls on legislators.[6] Locating constituents and friends who would be effective and would be willing to call on their legislator takes a great deal of time. Milbrath reports that legislators regard calls from constituents to be somewhat more influential on them than calls of friends.[7]

Lobbyists and other callers have three resources to bring to the meeting: *facts, arguments,* and *power.* The legislator expects the caller to come armed with facts. The caller must avoid presenting anything but accurate facts, and the lobbyist spends a lot of time trying to gather relevant and reliable information. Milbrath notes:

> The harried decision-maker frequently utilizes information provided by lobbyists, sometimes without double-checking, in speeches or other public communications. If the information should later prove to be false or biased to the point of serious distortion, the decision-maker is publicly embarrassed and is likely to retaliate by cutting off further access sought by the delinquent lobbyist.[8]

The development of a trusting relationship involves demonstrating such characteristics as honesty, dependability, sincerity, respect for one's sources, and a willingness to provide information and services when called upon.[9]

The caller will also present arguments to the legislator. One of the major jobs of the lobbyist is to select and refine these arguments. The organization should initially imagine every conceivable argument that might be put forth to support the position.[10] Its argument inventory will contain logical, emotional, and moral arguments. The logical arguments are the most meaningful to legislators, although somewhat less to the public. Legislators think of themselves as being objective and logical. They respond to two major types of logical argument. The first is a *public interest argument,* namely, that the proposed legislation will improve society and enhance people's lives. The second is an *economics argument,* namely, that the proposal will make or save money, stimulate business, or create jobs. These arguments must be backed by as many facts as possible. Three kinds of evidence can be used, namely, uncontestable facts, contestable facts, and opinions. The opposition can be expected to challenge contestable facts and opinions, and the lobbyist must anticipate these objections and be prepared to counterargue.

Emotional arguments can play a role but should never be presented as the main case. Thus, the lobbyist may ask the legislator to support the bill because it helps "the poor." Finally, moral arguments tend to have little effect on the legislator's decision, although they will be used in expounding his stand to his constituents.

The various arguments should be sifted and weighed in terms of whom they can influence. The objective is not to use all of the arguments but those that would have the greatest influence.

Callers have one more resource—namely, power. Organizations with large national membership, a good name, and plenty of financial resources can imply their readiness to use power to support or hurt the legislator. The lobbyist must be subtle in how he communicates power. The hinted offer of campaign contributions and manpower support in a forthcoming election will have a positive effect on some legislators. On the other hand, hinting that power will be used to defeat nay-saying legislators at the polls is likely to get the lobbyist thrown out of the office. Even if the lobbyist could carry out his threats, use of these tactics could be detrimental in the long run. Most lobbyists strive to build supportive relationships with legislators. Milbrath has summarized what legislators see as the ideal presentation:

> Most people in Congress report that they prefer that personal presentations be informative, unbiased, clear, short, and unaccompanied by pressure. Many lobbyists follow the practice of leaving a short written summary behind for future reference and thus save the decision-maker, or his staff, the trouble of taking notes.[11]

DIRECTED MESSAGES.    Legislators are also influenced by mail, postcards, telegrams, and telephone calls they may get from voters in their district and other people urging them to favor or oppose a particular piece of legislation. Lobbyists often organize grassroots campaigns to urge members and voters to communicate their views to their legislators. These campaigns require considerable organizational efforts and the results are uncertain. Legislators tend to place more weight on letters that appear to come from concerned citizens who are not part of an organized letter writing campaign. The primary benefit of launching letter writing campaigns may not be influencing decisions of legislators, but stimulating political interest among the group's members.

PUBLIC OPINION CAMPAIGNS.    Another tool is to budget a major public relations campaign to influence public opinion. The organization might hold news conferences, sponsor speakers, draft news releases, compose feature articles, run advocacy ads, create dramatic events, and in other ways bring publicity and favorable attention to their cause. They may invite similar-minded groups to share the heavy cost of carrying out the public relations campaign. They might run the campaign openly or conceal their sponsorship. Overall, public opinion campaigns are highly expensive and work slowly, and often are less cost-effective than other techniques to influence legislators.

INCENTIVE OFFERS.    Legislators are human and respond to particular material incentives in deciding whom to give time to and possibly what positions to espouse. The lobbyist, for example, can imply that high contributions would be forthcoming to the legislator's campaign chest from organizational members who are pleased with his support. In 1976, members of interest groups contributed $23 million to congressional candidates' campaign funds.[12] Furthermore, the lobbyist organization can invite the legislator to give a high-paid talk at its annual meeting with the hope that meeting members will increase his interest and gain sympathetic support. Many legislators have a law practice or side business, and some organizations will direct some of their work to these firms as an incentive or reward. Lobbyists may also entertain the legislator at restaurants, in homes, or on trips, but many legislators report that instead of welcoming an invitation "to do the town" with a lobbyist, they would prefer to stay home. The most extreme material incentive is bribery. There is high consensus among legislators, legislative staffs, and lobbyists that bribery is ineffective, inappropriate, and risky. With rare exceptions, congressmen are not bribable, and may often choose to report publicly an offer of a bribe. Offering a bribe is usually a sign of a desperate organization that has not had the imagination to use the other lobbying tools effectively.

---

## CITIZEN VOTES MARKETING—
## POLITICAL CAMPAIGNING

Now we turn to another voter marketing problem, that of a political candidate or public agency seeking to win the votes of ordinary citizens. Campaigning to the public involves many of the marketing principles discussed earlier. We will use political candidate marketing as an illustration of these principles.

Political candidate marketing has become a major industry and area of specialization. Every few years the public is treated to an endless number of campaigns attempting to put various candidates for local, state, and national offices in the best light. In recent elections, the various candidates for all offices managed to spend nearly a billion dollars in the short space of their campaigns. The money was spent on media advertising, direct mail and telephone, and in other ways.

Interest in the marketing aspects of elections has been stimulated to a large extent by the spectacular growth in *political advertising*. There has also been a substantial growth of *scientific opinion polling* (i.e., marketing research), *computer analysis of voting patterns* (i.e., sales analysis), and *professional campaign management firms* (i.e., marketing organizations). The subtleties of the marketing approach go beyond the rising expenditure levels and the use of certain information and planning approaches. They are delineated in a series of popular books, such as White's *The Making of the President 1960*[13] and McGinness' *The Selling of the President 1968.*[14] In a quieter way, several scholarly works have also noted the marketing character of political elections.[15]

It would be a gross mistake to think that election campaigns have taken on a marketing character only in recent years. *Campaigning has always had a mar-*

*keting character.* Prior to the new methodology, candidates sought office through the handshake, baby-kissing, teas, and speech making. They still use these methods. *The "new methodology" is not the introduction of marketing methods into politics, but an increased sophistication and acceleration of their use.* According to Glick:

> The personal handshake, the local fund-raising dinner, the neighborhood tea, the rally, the precinct captain, and the car pool to the polls are still very much with us . . . the new campaign has provided a carefully coordinated strategic framework within which the traditional activities are carried out in keeping with a Master Plan. It centers on a shift from the candidate-controlled, loosely knit, often haphazard "play-it-by-ear" approach to that of a precise, centralized "team" strategy for winning or keeping office. Its hallmarks include the formal strategic blueprint, the coordinated use of specialized propaganda skills, and a more subtle approach to opinion measurement and manipulation. And, though there is a world of difference between selling a candidate and merchandising soap or razor blades, some of the attributes of commercial advertising have been grafted onto the political process.[16]

Nimmo takes a cynical view of this development:

> In screening potential candidates the mercenaries have given a new definition to the notion of "availability"; the marketable candidate is selected on the basis of his brand name, his capacity to trigger an emotional response from the electorate, his skill in using mass media, and his ability to "project." Analysis of social problems and issues yields to parroting of themes; televised debates between contenders produce meaningless confrontations rather than rational discussion. Negotiations with party politicians assume the form of "out-of-town tryouts"; primary elections are approached as "presale" campaigns; and general elections emerge as the "Giant Sweepstakes." In the end one candidate owes his election not to party but to his personal organization of paid and voluntary workers; once elected he responds not to party programs, but to the interests also represented by the professionals.[17]

The major fault with Nimmo's observation is that it takes on a moral, judgmental tone. It implies that something is happening to political contests that is called marketing and it is bad. It fails to recognize that the marketing problem exists no matter what means or style of marketing is used. In fact, marketing styles vary from product to product and time to time; but the marketing problem is always present.

We are now ready to analyze in marketing terms the vote-seeking process of a candidate. We will assume a male candidate who has decided to enter politics and his ultimate goal is to achieve an elective office. At the beginning, he is an unknown product. The office seeker must put himself on a market, the voters' market. He has to go through many of the steps that occur in product marketing: develop a personality (brand image), get the approval of an organization (company image), enter a primary election (market test), carry out a vigorous campaign (advertising and distribution), get elected (market share), and stay in office (repeat sales).

Looking ahead, he must solve four successive problems to reach his goal.

First, he must join a political organization and become known. He will want to develop a political style that will earn respect and leadership in his party. He knows that this means finding out what the members of the political organization appear to want from the political process and the extent that he can appear to be instrumental in their desires.

Second, he must eventually exhibit an interest in becoming his party's candidate in an upcoming election. He must fraternize with the leaders and attempt to get their backing. He must enter a primary election and win the support of the party's voters.

Third, if he wins the primary, he will have to go before the voters in the general election. He will have to make important decisions on campaign strategy, including issues, advertising, appearances, and funding. He will face a problem in voter analysis, choosing targets, allocating resources, and timing them for maximum impact.

Fourth, if he is elected, he must do the kind of job in office that will get him reelected. This will be a function of the organization he builds, the positions he takes, and the rhetoric he uses.

We shall concentrate on what the candidate can do to get nominated and elected by the voters. We will not discuss his need to also market himself to party politicians, interest groups, and miscellaneous contributors.

The candidate typically has to enter a primary election and run against others seeking the party's nomination. The primary is an election by the members of his political party in which they choose among alternative candidates. It is at this stage that he starts undertaking marketing activities designed to introduce him to a wider audience beyond the local actives of his party. The primary is a *test market*, a trial run. If he wins, he must place himself before the larger citizen voter market, using all the marketing activities at full scale.

The marketing activities that he must engage in to win the primary contest and the subsequent election are virtually the same. The marketing activities are: (1) marketing research, (2) candidate concept and strategy, and (3) communication and distribution strategy.

## MARKETING RESEARCH

The first rule of effective campaigning is that the campaign must be addressed to the interests of the voters. The voters' interests can only be ignored by politicians who are in the contest for reasons of personal vanity, or to educate voters, or to shock them. The typical office seeker must research the voters' needs, interests, and values and represent himself as the best perceived instrument for the voters to achieve their desires.

Some politicians may feel that they know the voters' opinions and interests so well that they need little formal marketing research. Dollars invested in marketing research are a subtraction from dollars that could be spent in advertising.

But the politician is usually mistaken in thinking that he knows what is on the electorate's mind. Even if he could guess at the major issues, he is not likely to know their relative importance in the minds of various groups of voters. He is even less likely to guess how the voters feel about different issue positions he might take.

Manufacturers of mass products no longer develop them and launch them on a hunch. They carefully research the major market segments and their needs, desires, product involvement, and loyalties. Politicians are increasingly doing this, too, in the form of elaborate precinct analysis. They research the demographics, past voting patterns, and involvement levels of voters in each precinct. They conduct opinion polls to learn the major issues and voters' stands on these issues.

The nagging question still remains: How much marketing research expenditure is feasible for the candidate in view of its alternative productivity in direct promotion? Business firms spend money on marketing research to the extent that this will contribute to creating a better product and more effective messages. They recognize that nothing is gained in spending advertising money on the wrong message or the right message reaching the wrong audience. The politician likewise must carry out enough marketing research to feel confident that he is able to formulate the best message and identify the best media for reaching the intended target audiences.

## CANDIDATE CONCEPT AND STRATEGY

Voters rarely know or meet the candidates; they only have mediated images of them. They vote on the basis of their images.

Candidates attempt to transmit a particular concept of themselves to voters. But the transmitted concept is not always the perceived image. Voters start with different cognitive maps and predispositions and this causes them to see different things in candidates. Furthermore, they are exposed to stimuli that come from sources other than the candidate himself that modify the candidate-intended image.

*The politician who wishes to succeed cannot leave his image-making to chance.* His clothes, manner, statements, and actions become news and shape the impression people have of him. The politician who wants to win must treat himself very much like a new product. He must formulate a look and behavior that match the target voters' perceptions and needs.

The term used to guide the image planning of the candidate is the candidate *concept.* The candidate concept is the *major orienting theme around which voter interest will be built.* It is the "unique selling proposition," the "promised benefit" of the candidate. The political candidate must choose the concept on which to attract votes. Does he want to come across as "the hard-hitting reformer," "the mature statesman," or "the experienced legislator"?[18] It would be wrong to think of the candidate concept as only a slogan. *The candidate concept is the basis for planning and organizing the entire campaign.* It shapes the coalitions that are formed, the issue positions that are embraced, the statements that are made, the public appearances, the allocation of effort to voter segments, and many other decisions. Choosing the candidate concept is the most important single decision made by the candidate.

How does the vote-seeking candidate choose his concept from the multitude of attributes he could feature? He must first determine the major issues in the election as seen and felt by the voters. At any point in time, the voters are seeking something from the candidates, some promise or answer to the problems they face. This varies from election to election and district to district. It might be "honesty in government" in one place, "law and order" in another, and "progressive legislation" in a third. The politician must listen for this voters' message with a third ear. It provides the major clue as to the type of symbolic reassurances that the voters want. It suggests major concepts or themes that might guide the campaign.

Given several possible concepts, the candidate must eschew any that is unnatural or unbelievable as a role for him to play, no matter how much it may match the voters' needs and feelings. The candidate will be placed in too many performance situations that could strain or destroy voter credibility in the candidate's concept. The candidate must choose a concept that is reasonably congruent with his personality, background, qualifications, and political philosophy. This still leaves a lot of possibilities.

Given some possible concepts, there is a need for precampaign *concept testing*. The possible themes are shown to a sample of target voters who are asked to rank or rate them in terms of interest or preference. Voters indicate how strongly they feel about "an honest candidate" versus "an experienced candidate" versus "a conservative candidate." The assumption is that the voters are in need of a certain political character at a given time who will champion their hopes and assuage their fears. The relative appeal strength of different concepts would be measured in the survey.

The final choice of a concept is influenced by this research and also by the expected concepts of the opposition candidates. The voter chooses from a field of possible candidates. Each candidate is presumably carrying out the same research on the best concept. It is quite possible for them to arrive at the same ideal concept and all build their campaign on it. This happens in many commercial product campaigns and the audience gets the feeling that the brands are all the same. All the detergents promise whiteness and all the razor blades promise a better shave.

Thus the candidate must not adopt the ideally best concept, but the one that best *positions* him with respect to the concepts adopted by the other candidates. This is called *candidate positioning*. If his opponent is a "law and order man," would he be more effective as a "civil rights candidate" or as a "fiscal watchdog candidate"? He must recognize that the voter market is made up of many segments and each concept will win him a certain market share in each segment, given his opponents' concepts.

Two additional points should be made. First, the candidate must decide how much emphasis to place on the chosen concept. He can project that concept in all his talk and action. This is the policy of *concept specificity*. Or he can use it more loosely so as not to become totally bound up with that concept. This is the policy of *concept diffuseness*. This is similar to a product that can be advertised strongly as offering one major benefit or weakly as offering a variety of benefits. The choice is a difficult one. By pursuing concept diffuseness, the candidate may just fail to come across with any specific identity in the voters' minds. On the other hand, the candidate who practices concept specificity will win the strong support of certain groups and alienate others. He is taking the risk of locking himself into an image from which he cannot escape if last-minute changes in issues or voters' moods should call for a change.

The second point is that the candidate can assume a secondary concept as well as a primary one. He could wear two concepts as long as they are not boldly inconsistent and as long as they do not confuse the best use of scarce resources. Thus, a candidate might decide on being primarily a "law and order man" and secondarily a "fiscally responsible candidate." He may project the first concept at meetings of ordinary citizens and the second at meetings of bankers and business groups. It is important, however, that he avoid trying to be all things to all people.

The concept he chooses and attempts to transmit is not necessarily the image voters will get of him. He controls only certain stimuli reaching them. The voters are also influenced by their peers, media commentators, opposition candidates, and fortuitous events which make his concept input, while quite important, less than perfectly determinant of the image that comes across.

## COMMUNICATION AND DISTRIBUTION STRATEGY

The candidate's concept becomes the basis for planning the communication and distribution program. His concept must be packaged into statements and actions that are matched and distributed to target voters. The candidate's ability to talk from prepared remarks versus extemporaneously, on television versus radio, in large mass rallies versus small home gatherings, are all factors to consider in the tactical development of his campaign. Everything the candidate does communicates something to the voters. He must rely on professional communication consultants to help him present the best possible image to the voters.

He and his campaign managers and specialists must lay plans for three important communication–distribution programs; namely, (1) advertising program, (2) personal appearance program, and (3) volunteer workers program.

**Advertising program.**    Political advertising has come a long way from the days when the major media were billboards and posters. Today, all the media are used, including newspapers, radio, and television; and television in particular has transformed the nature of political campaigning. Copy can no longer be left to amateurs; the task of advertising the political candidate must be turned over to advertising agencies that handle them like any other product. The advertising agency participates with the other campaign managers in developing some basic principles for the advertising campaign, covering such matters as:

1. the basic message
2. the way the candidate will be photographed
3. the ad sizes that will be made for print and broadcast media
4. the allocation of the budget over the various media categories
5. the percentage of the budget that will be spent in each week up to election day

The candidate must rely on their professional knowledge about the effectiveness of different messages and media. He is in the same position as Nixon, who had to say in the 1968 campaign: "We're going to build this whole campaign around television . . . you fellows just tell me what you want me to do and I'll do it."[19]

The candidate should not, however, give up all his judgment. He must be comfortable with the advertising messages. He must avoid a too-slick campaign where voters get the feeling that he is being sold like soap-flakes or is spending too much on advertising. Advertising can turn people off as well as on. A bad ad can hurt his chances as much as a good ad can help his chances. He must exercise the final decision on matters of conscience.

**Personal appearance program.**    If a candidate is at all attractive, he would normally gain by achieving a personal exposure to every voter. Meeting a candidate personalizes and intensifies the voter's interest in the election and normally wins a vote. The exceptions are candidates who do not make a good impression —who bore, confuse, or disappoint voters. Such candidates would do better to minimize their appearances or agree to them only under highly controlled and favorable circumstances.

The candidate who seeks voter exposure is rarely able to reach all the voters. His personal channels for reaching the voters consist of rallies, club meetings, coffees, and appearances at busy street corners. The *rally* gives him a chance to present his full case to the people who choose to come out to listen to him; and he can add *atmospherics* to the affair by featuring music and personalities from the entertainment and political world. The *club meeting* allows him to meet special groups of businessmen, church members, workers, and so on who might not have normally gone to see him at a rally. *Coffees* permit him the opportunity to meet friendly and curious neighbors in the intimate surroundings of a home where he can project a more personal quality. *Street corners* allow him to move into a crowd of strangers, many of whom might never have met him, and to communicate briefly but effectively with a smile or a handshake.

The candidate's time is severely limited and he, with his consultants, must carefully choose among all the possible functions he might attend. He must give some time to motivating his own party workers and committed voters. He must consider other opportunities in the light of their vote potential. He must estimate the number of uncommitted voters who might be there, the number of opinion leaders, and the chance that his appearance will be leveraged in the mass media. He must adjust his schedule as new trends and problems appear in the race. There are many factors to consider, and generally the task of scheduling the candidate's appearances is still a developing art.[20] It is not yet handled with the same analytical rigor as the analogous "sales call problem" in commercial marketing.

The candidate's organization must also think of specific promotional ideas to draw attention to the candidate. For he is competing not only against specific opponents but also against candidates for other contests, against detergent and soft drink commercials, against the soap operas, against the news reporting of thousands of other things happening in the world. The job calls for *event management*—that is, the staging of events designed to draw attention to the candidate. Examples include the announced plan to walk from one end of the city to the other meeting the voters, the calling of a special news conference to make an important announcement, and the appearance at a major sports event. At the same time, it is important not to create too many events and not to seem to be headline grabbing for its own sake.

**Volunteer workers program.** Although the candidate cannot distribute himself to reach every voter, he can achieve some of the effect by using agents, particularly speakers and volunteer workers. A speakers' bureau consists of various supporters who are articulate and individually effective with different types of groups. There should be every attempt to match the speaker to the audience: An older man should speak to the senior citizens, a woman to women's organizations, and a college student to college audiences. Studies of personal selling effectiveness indicate that effectiveness correlates with the degree of match between speaker and audience.[21] In addition, the candidate needs various volunteers who would carry out the multitude of tasks involved in an electoral campaign, including preparing mailings, canvassing and registering voters, providing transportation, and policing elections.

Managing the volunteers effectively has many similarities to the problem of managing a sales force effectively. The workers must be kept enthusiastic, work quotas must be set, accomplishments monitored. The organization must train these volunteers in what to say, when to call, how long to stay, and what to report back. Because the volunteers are a scarce resource, they must be managed as carefully as the money that the candidate commands.

Through the use of marketing research, candidate concept development, and communication and distribution planning, the candidate will wage a good fight for votes. These techniques do not guarantee victory because increasingly all candidates are resorting to modern marketing planning, and their efforts are somewhat self-canceling. Conscious marketing planning only promises to maximize the candidate's potential. It cannot ordinarily sell a bad candidate; and lack of careful marketing planning will not necessarily harm a good candidate. It provides a form of insurance that the candidate's campaign planning is systematic, efficient, and voter oriented.

The candidate who wins the office does not leave behind all of his promises, unless he is not interested in reelection. Most candidates will seek reelection and must fulfill the product expectations they generated during the campaign. They must live up to the concept they sold. The personality that the candidate sold early in his career tends, because of many forces, to stay with him afterward.

The reelection problem is analogous in marketing to the repeat sales problem. Business marketers who launch a new product are interested not only in first-time sales but also in repeat sales. It is only through repeat sales that the returns more than cover the investment. The key to repeat sales, in the marketer's mind, is the delivery of real satisfaction to the buyer. It is real satisfaction that will lead the buyer to pick the same product again in spite of new and possibly more colorful products vying for his or her attention.

But the delivery of customer satisfaction can mean a number of things. In the realm of commercial products, there are three types of satisfaction that can be offered to the buyers of a particular product, such as a particular brand of car. The first is to make sure that the car offers *good performance*—that is, that it yields the functional benefits that were promised and expected. In the political realm, this is analogous to the elected official actually carrying out his campaign promises and doing the things he said he would. The second is to make the car and its service very accessible to the buyers, which is a problem in *good organization*. In the political realm, good organization means that the elected official builds an organization that carries out various services in the community, organizes the voters, and so on. The third is to keep the product salient and interesting to the public, the problem of *good rhetoric*. In the political realm, this means that the official must fashion symbols during his administration that constantly and favorably remind the voters of him. All of the three strategies for getting reelected can be pursued simultaneously, although many elected officials often emphasize one more than the others.

---

## SUMMARY

Nonprofit organizations often need to obtain the votes of some group, such as legislators, citizens, government administrators, or boards of directors. This chapter examined legislative marketing and citizen votes marketing.

Legislative marketing, that is, lobbying, involves the application of marketing principles to attracting the votes of legislators for some proposal. Lobbyists need to understand the way bills are passed in a legislature, the steps being: drafting a bill, committee votes favorably on bill, legislators vote favorably on bill, no veto, appropriation, and enforcement. Lobbyists must work hard at each stage to make sure the bill is passed in a form that meets the original purposes. Lobbyists also need to understand how legislators are influenced by fame, power, and fortune considerations. The most important influences on legislators are their constituents, public opinion, news media, private groups, government agencies, the chief executive, experts, committee staffs, the legislator's staff, other legislators, the political party, and personal friends and acquaintances. Lobbyists must allocate their energy to the most critical legislators, using a marketing mix consisting of personal visits, directed messages, public opinion campaigns, and incentive offers.

Political campaigning for office has always had a marketing character, although in recent years much sophistication has been added in the form of scientific polling, computer analysis of voting patterns, mass advertising, and professional campaign management. The office seeker who wishes to maximize his votes would do well to analyze the problem in marketing terms. He has to join a party, be nominated for office, win a primary, and win the election. He is essentially a new product looking for a successful launch in a voters' market. He must research the makeup and motivations of his market; develop an appropriate and effective candidate concept; and lay careful plans for the communication and distribution of his concept. Once he achieves office, he must produce voter satisfaction through some blend of effective performance, organization, and rhetoric.

---

## QUESTIONS

**1.** What personal characteristics, education, and experience would be useful for a professional lobbyist?

**2.** Suppose a lobbyist represented an organization interested in increasing federal support for the performing arts. Outline an appropriate lobbying strategy based on marketing principles.

**3.** Diagram the exchange relationship between the performing arts organization in question 2 and an individual legislator.

**4.** Why is a candidate advised *not* to adopt "the ideally best concept" as a basis for positioning himself or herself in a campaign?

**5.** "Political advertising blackens advertising's other eye." Discuss.

**6.** Many political campaigns involve volunteers going door-to-door to hand out campaign literature and request votes. Based on your knowledge of marketing, prepare a handout that could be used to brief volunteers on how to carry out this task more effectively.

---

## NOTES

**1.** See James Deakin, *The Lobbyists* (Washington, D.C.: Public Affairs Press, 1966).

**2.** *The Almanac of American Politics* contains an account of each legislator's record, his votes on key issues, and how he is rated by citizen groups. *The Congressional Quarterly Almanac,* issued annually, provides an analysis of the legislator's voting record on each major issue.

**3.** See Raymond A. Bauer, Ithiel de Sola Pool, and Lewis Anthony Dexter,

*American Business and Public Policy: The Politics of Foreign Trade* (New York: Atherton Press, 1963).

4. Lewis Anthony Dexter, *How Organizations Are Represented in Washington* (Indianapolis: Bobbs-Merrill, 1969), p. 69.

5. See Ann Roosevelt, *The Art of Lobbying: How to Write and Influence Legislation, Not Man Apart* (magazine of Friends of the Earth—FOE), Mid-October 1976, pp. 1–3.

6. Bauer, Pool, and Dexter, *American Business and Public Policy.*

7. See Lester W. Milbrath, "Lobbying as a Communication Process," *Public Opinion Quarterly,* Spring 1960, pp. 32–53. This article presents excellent research findings on lobbying behavior and techniques.

8. *Ibid.*

9. Abraham Holtzman, *Interest Groups and Lobbying* (London: Macmillan, 1966), p. 77.

10. See George Alderson and Everett Sentman, *How You Can Influence Congress: The Complete Handbook for the Citizen Lobbyist* (New York: Dutton, 1979).

11. Milbrath, "Lobbying as a Communication Process."

12. Norman J. Ornstern and Shirley Elder, *Interest Groups, Lobbying and Policymaking* (Washington, D.C.: Congressional Quarterly Press, 1978), p. 70.

13. Theodore White, *The Making of the President 1960* (New York: Atheneum, 1961).

14. Joe McGinness, *The Selling of the President 1968* (New York: Trident Press, 1969).

15. See Stanley Kelly, *Professional Public Relations and Political Power* (Baltimore: Johns Hopkins Press, 1956); E. Glick, *The New Methodology* (Washington, D.C.: American Institute for Political Communication, 1967); and Dan Nimmo, *The Political Persuaders* (Englewood Cliffs, N.J.: Prentice-Hall, 1970).

16. Glick, *The New Methodology,* p. 1.

17. Nimmo, *The Political Persuaders,* pp. 67–68.

18. Gold has identified a number of classic images available to political candidates, including: (1) embattled underdog image; (2) chastised or reborn incumbent image; (3) front-runner image; (4) dark-horse image; (5) outsider image. See Victor Gold, "Image Stratagems: Pick One for the '80's," *Campaigns & Elections,* Summer 1980, pp. 43–48.

19. McGinness, *The Selling of the President 1968.*

20. See "How a 'Scheduler' Plans His Candidate's Time for Most Efficiency," *Wall Street Journal,* March 1, 1972.

21. Franklin B. Evans, "Selling as a Dyadic Relationship—a New Approach," *American Behavioral Scientist,* May 1963, pp. 76–79.

# VI

## ADAPTING
## MARKETING

# Marketing of Services, Persons, and Places

Until recently, Finland was a neglected area in the European travel market. It seemed too far away from the major tourist centers. Its climate was cold, its language unfamiliar. As a result, Finland attracted only a few thousand foreign tourists a year.

In recent years, tourism preferences began to change. Many travelers had already visited traditional tourist countries such as England, France, Spain, Italy, and Greece. These areas were overcrowded in the summer months. Their prices were constantly rising. Tourists showed a growing interest in exploring other countries in search of new experiences.

These factors led to the discovery of Finland by tourists. Perhaps the most important factor was the intensive information and marketing activity of the Finnish Bureau of Tourism. The bureau directed very heavy advertising campaigns in several countries; and it has made loans to hotel chains and other enterprises in the tourist business.

Its responsibilities covered the promotion of foreign tourism in Finland as well as domestic tourism, tourist enterprises and their financing, tourist information, vocational training for tourism, and the surveillance of government tourist property. The bureau has to work effectively with several different publics: airlines, hotel and motel chains, all media, foreign travel agencies, branch offices of Finnish travel organizations abroad, and foreign governments.

Having "discovered" Finland, the tourist market grew at 30 to 40 percent annually, while in most other European countries it has been only about 20 percent. Tourism became the third largest industry in Finland and turned the Finnish balance of trade from a deficit of $31.3 million in 1963 to a surplus of $34 million in 1970.

Who were the tourists? Of the 2.3 million foreign tourists, about half come from the other Scandinavian countries and the other half are non-Scandinavian. Of the non-Scandinavians, about 40 percent come from West Germany and the remainder are Americans, Englishmen, Dutchmen, Frenchmen, Swiss, Italian, and so forth.

It would seem that the Finnish people would feel pleased with the country's success in attracting foreign tourists. The people, on the contrary, have very mixed feelings. The rapid growth of tourism has been accompanied by several problems.

First, the tourist influx is highly seasonal. Nearly 50 percent of the tourists come in the three months of June, July, and August.

Second, most of the tourists come from lower- or middle-income classes with small travel budgets; they lived in tents or trailers; they brought their own food; they spent very little money in Finland. They crowded the Finnish vacation spots at a time when the Finnish people were also on vacation and seeking rest and recreation. This led to many complaints.

Third, Finnish environmental groups protested that their scenic land, particularly the lake area and Lapland, was being threatened with ruin. The Lapps complained about the litter and about tentfuls of tourists who camped next to their previously peaceful summer cottages.

The Finnish Bureau of Tourism recognized that it had a new problem to solve. The earlier problem was to attract people to Finland. They succeeded but now were forced to adopt new objectives. Their main objective was to reshape the composition and seasonal characteristics of the tourists. They adopted the following marketing objectives:

1. Attract fewer but wealthier tourists.
2. Attract fewer tourists in the summer and more in the other seasons.
3. Attract more tourists who were motivated by wanderlust rather than sunlust. The sunlusting tourists wanted facilities like they had at home, and this would call for much Finnish investment in new facilities. The wanderlust tourists, on the other hand, came to enjoy a different culture and live as people did in that culture.
4. Attract tourists to areas in Finland that would not overtax or threaten Finland's best sites with pollution and ruin.

SOURCE: Story prepared by the author from notes provided by Heikki Paronen.

In this chapter, we will look at the nature and challenges of marketing three types of entities: services, persons, and places. Most of this book has been about services marketing since most of what nonprofit organizations offer are services. Yet we want to look here in a systematic way at the marketing of services, which an increasing number of people regard as posing some distinct issues that do not arise in normal product marketing. As for person marketing, we have already examined how political candidates market themselves to voters in Chapter 20. Here we want to look at additional issues involved in the marketing of persons, particularly celebrities. Places, too, are marketed by business firms, such as tourist agencies and real estate operators, as well as by private and public nonprofit organizations such as chambers of commerce and government tourist bureaus.

## SERVICES MARKETING

One of the major developments in post–World War II America has been the phenomenal growth of service industries. From constituting then about 35 percent of the GNP, services now account for almost half of GNP. Furthermore, two-thirds of the nongovernment labor force is engaged in service industries, and the percentage is expected to increase as the United States moves more into a postindustrial society. As a result of rising affluence, increasing leisure, and the growing complexity of products that require increased servicing, the United States has become the world's first service economy.

Service industries are quite numerous and varied. The whole government sector, with its courts, employment services, hospitals, loan agencies, military services, police and fire departments, post office, regulatory agencies, and schools is in the service business. The private nonprofit sector, with its art groups and museums, charities, churches, colleges, foundations, and hospitals, is in the service business. A good part of the business sector, with its airlines, banks, computer service bureaus, hotels, insurance companies, law firms, management consulting firms, medical practices, motion picture companies, plumbing repair companies, and real estate firms, is in the service business.

### NATURE AND CHARACTERISTICS OF A SERVICE

A service can be defined as follows:

A **service** is any activity or benefit that one party can offer to another that is essentially intangible and does not result in the ownership of anything. Its production may or may not be tied to a physical product.

Thus, attending a play, calling the police for assistance, traveling on public transportation, seeing a mental health counselor, and attending church all involve receiving a service.

Services have four distinctive characteristics that must be given special consideration when designing service marketing programs.

**Intangibility.**      Services are intangible, that is, they cannot be seen, tasted, felt, heard, or smelled before they are bought. Thus, a patient getting plastic surgery cannot see the result before the purchase; and the patient walking into a psychiatrist's office cannot know the content or value of the service in advance. Under the circumstances, purchase requires having confidence in the service provider.

Service providers can do certain things to improve the client's confidence. First, they can try to increase the service's tangibility by a number of devices. A plastic surgeon can make a drawing or clay model showing the patient's expected appearance after the surgery. Second, service providers can place more emphasis on the benefits of the service rather than just describing its features. Thus, a college admissions officer can talk to prospective students about the great jobs its alumni have found instead of only describing life on the campus. Third, service providers can put brand names on their service to increase confidence, such as American Red Cross, Salvation Army, and Friends of the Earth. Fourth, service providers can use a highly regarded personality to add tangibility to the service, just as muscular dystrophy has done with its Jerry Lewis telethons.

**Inseparability.**    A service is inseparable from the source that provides it. Its very act of being created requires the source, whether a person or machine, to be present. In other words, production and consumption occur simultaneously with services. This is in contrast to a product which exists whether or not its source is present. Consider going to a Billy Graham religious happening. The spiritual impact is inseparable from the performer. It is not the same service if an announcer tells the audience that Billy Graham is indisposed and they will play his record instead, or that John Smith will substitute. What this means is that the number of people who can experience this particular service is limited to the amount of time that Billy Graham can perform.

Several strategies exist for getting around this limitation. The service provider can learn to work with larger groups. We have seen Billy Graham's organization rent larger and larger facilities so that more people could be accommodated. Or the service provider can learn to provide the same service in less time, so that more groups can be accommodated. Or the service organization can train additional service providers and build up client confidence in them: For example, the Billy Graham organization can train other evangelists to run local meetings.

**Variability.**    A service can be highly variable, depending on *who* is providing it, and even *when* it is being provided. A heart transplant operation by Dr. Christiaan Barnard is likely to be of higher quality than the same operation performed by a recently graduated M.D. And Dr. Barnard's quality can vary depending on his energy and mental state at the time of the operation. Purchasers of services are aware of their high variability and engage in normal risk-reducing behavior by talking to others and trying to learn who is the best provider.

Service firms should make an effort to deliver high and consistent quality in their service offers. The major step is to develop a good personnel selection and training program. For example, airlines, banks, and hotels spend substantial sums of money to train their personnel to provide uniform and friendly service. Another step is for the service providers to develop adequate customer satisfaction monitoring systems. The main tools for this are suggestion and complaint systems, customer surveys, and comparison shopping.[1]

**Perishability.**     Services cannot be stored. While a car can be kept in inventory until it is sold, the revenue on an unoccupied theatre seat is lost forever. The reason many doctors charge patients for missed appointments is that the service value only existed at that point when the patient did not show up. The perishability of services is not a problem when demand is steady, because it is easy to staff the services in advance. When demand fluctuates heavily, service firms have difficult problems. For example, public transportation companies have to use much more equipment because of peak demand during rush hours than if public transportation needs were smooth during the day.

Service organizations have several means available to try to produce a better match between demand and service capacity. Sasser has described several strategies for managing demand and supply.[2] On the demand side:

1. *Differential pricing* can be used to shift some demand from peak to off-peak periods. An example would be lower fares for riding buses in off-peak hours.
2. *Nonpeak demand can be developed* through marketing campaigns. For example, the Miami Beach Chamber of Commerce has attempted to convince people to vacation in Miami Beach during the summer months.
3. *Complementary services* can be developed during peak time to provide diversions or alternatives to waiting customers. For example, physicians' offices will provide magazines for patients to read while waiting.
4. *Reservation systems* are a way to presell service, know how much service is needed, and reduce consumer waiting. For example, hospitals assign patient beds by requiring physicians to make reservations.

On the supply side:

1. *Part-time* employees can be used to serve peak demand. For example, colleges will add part-time teachers when enrollment goes up.
2. *Peak-time efficiency* routines can be introduced. For example, hospitals will add paramedics to help physicians during peak periods.
3. *Increased consumer participation* in the tasks can be used. For example, new patients may be asked to fill out their own medical histories before seeing a physician.
4. *Shared services* can be developed. For example, several hospitals can agree to share medical equipment purchases.
5. *Facilities with built-in expansion possibilities* can be developed. For example, a zoo can buy up surrounding land that might be needed for future expansion.

## CLASSIFICATION OF SERVICES

Services are of many types, making it difficult to generalize about them. First, we can ask to what extent the service is *people based or equipment based.* Thus a psychoanalyst can serve patients with little equipment—namely, a couch

—whereas a pilot needs an expensive piece of equipment called an airplane. In people-based services, we can distinguish between those involving professionals (professors, physicians, curators), skilled labor (typists, key punch operators), and unskilled labor (museum guards, janitors). In equipment-based services, we can distinguish services involving automated equipment (blood analyzers, vending machines), equipment operated by relatively unskilled labor (buses, motion picture theatres), and equipment operated by skilled labor (airplanes, computers).[3] Even within a specific service industry, different service providers vary in the amount of equipment they use; contrast James Taylor with his single guitar and the Rolling Stones with their tons of audio equipment. Sometimes the accompanying equipment adds value to the service (stereo amplification) and sometimes it exists to reduce the amount of labor needed (automatic elevators).

Second, we can ask the degree to which the *client's presence* is necessary to the service. Thus, brain surgery involves the client's presence but a church organ repair does not. To the extent that the client must be present, the service provider has to be considerate of his or her needs. Thus, modern hospital rooms need to be nicely decorated and comfortable because they are part of the service.

Third, we can ask about the client's *purchase motive*, whether the service meets a personal need (personal services) or a business need (business services). For example, hospital physicians will price physical examinations differently depending upon whether they are serving personal patients or providing a prepaid service to the employees of a particular organization. Service providers can develop different service offers and marketing programs for personal service versus business service target markets.

## THE EXTENT AND IMPORTANCE OF MARKETING IN THE SERVICE SECTOR

Service-based organizations typically lag behind manufacturing firms in their development and use of marketing. George and Barksdale surveyed four hundred service and manufacturing firms and concluded:

> In comparison to manufacturing firms, service firms appear to be: (1) generally less likely to have marketing mix activities carried out in the marketing department, (2) less likely to perform analysis in the offering area, (3) more likely to handle their advertising internally rather than go to outside agencies, (4) less likely to have an overall sales plan, (5) less likely to develop sales training programs, (6) less likely to use marketing research firms and marketing consultants, and (7) less likely to spend as much on marketing when expressed as a percentage of gross sales.[4]

Why have service firms neglected marketing? Several reasons can be given. Many service organizations are small and do not use management techniques such as marketing which they think would be expensive. Many professional and nonprofit service organizations are antagonistic to the idea of marketing, believing that it is unprofessional to apply any marketing planning to their services and even prohibiting it in their codes of ethics. Other service organizations such as colleges and hospitals had so much demand for years that they had no need for marketing until recently.

Today, as competition intensifies, as costs rise, as productivity stagnates, and as service quality goes down, an increasing number of service organizations are taking an interest in marketing for the first time. They can profit by studying the few service industries that had moved into marketing earlier. Airlines were one of the first service industries to study formally their customers and competition and take positive steps to make the travelers' trips easier and more pleasant. They first had to build people's confidence in air travel and then compete in preflight, inflight, and postflight services to win customer loyalty. Banks represent a service industry that moved from hostility to marketing toward aggressive marketing in a relatively short period of time. At first they saw marketing mainly as promotion and friendliness, but over time they have moved toward setting up marketing organization, information, planning, and control systems.[5] Many banks have redesigned their atmospheres so they look more like living rooms than mausoleums; expanded their service hours; increased the number of service products; and so on. As far as other service industries, such as stock brokerages, insurance, lodging, law, and accounting, the marketing concept has come in unevenly, with some leaders taking major marketing steps (Merrill, Lynch, Hyatt Regency) and most other firms lagging behind.[6]

One of the main needs in services marketing is to find ways to increase productivity. Since the service business is highly labor-intensive, costs have been rising very fast, as exemplified in the soaring costs of hospital services. Many people assume that little can be done to increase productivity in service businesses but this view is mistaken. Here are five broad approaches to improving service organization productivity:

1. Service providers may be encouraged to work harder or more skillfully for the same pay. Working harder is not a likely solution, but working more skillfully can occur through better selection and training procedures.

2. The quantity of service can be increased by tolerating a small decline in quality. Thus, it is possible for doctors to give less time to each patient and for hospitals to increase the patients-to-nurse ratio.

3. The service organization can add capital-intensive equipment to increase its service delivery capabilities. Levitt has recommended that management adopt a "manufacturing attitude" toward the production of services as represented by the assembly-line principles that McDonald's applied to fast food retailing, culminating in the "technological hamburger."[7] Commercial dishwashing, jumbo jets, and multiple-unit motion picture theatres all represent technological solutions to expanded service.

4. The need for a service may be reduced or eliminated by inventing a product solution. Consider how birth control pills reduced the need for abortions, and how streptomycin reduced the need for tuberculosis sanitariums.

5. It may be possible to design a more effective service that eliminates or reduces the need for a less effective service. Thus, promoting nonsmoking clinics and physical exercise may reduce the need for more expensive curative medical services later on.

## PERSON MARKETING

In addition to services, persons are also marketed. *Person marketing* consists of activities undertaken to create, maintain, or alter knowledge, attitudes, and/or behavior toward particular persons. The two most common types of person marketing are political candidate marketing and celebrity marketing. We discussed political candidate marketing in Chapter 20; here we will take a brief look at celebrity marketing.

Celebrity marketing has a long history, going back to the Caesars and other great empire builders who had their retinue of publicists to build up awe and respect for their leaders. In recent times, celebrity marketing has been most closely associated with the building up of Hollywood stars, entertainers, and sports heroes. Aspiring celebrities hire press agents to get their names and pictures in the mass media as often as possible and to schedule appearances at highly visible events. One of the great promoters was the late Brian Epstein, who managed the Beatles' rise to stardom, and in the process received a larger share of the money than any Beatle. Many of today's celebrities are promoted not by single press agents but by whole organizations. Bucky Dent of the Yankees phoned the William Morris Agency one day and asked them to manage his public life.[8] They lined him up with visits to children's hospitals, little leagues, and conventions; to co-host *A.M. New York* and appear on the *Merv Griffin Show;* to have posters made and marketed; to make a commercial for a car manufacturer; and to get spreads in *Playboy* and other magazines.

Nonprofit organizations are not less immune from engaging in celebrity building. The world's major religions continuously cultivate and disseminate the image of their historical founder, whether Jesus Christ, Gautama Buddha, or Mohammed, as well as their current leaders, such as Billy Graham, Robert Schuller, and others. Ballet stars such as Nureyev and currently Baryshnikov have press agents building up legends for them. Most organizations engage in activities to create or maintain a favorable image of their founder and current leaders.

Celebrities, like other marketable entities, are subject to life cycles. Various patterns can be observed. Some celebrities rise fast and decline fast; others rise slowly and remain popular for a long time; still others decline and then make a comeback.

## PLACE MARKETING

Place marketing involves activities undertaken to create, maintain, or alter knowledge, attitudes, and/or behavior toward particular places. Place marketers are interested in attracting new residents, tourists, and/or investors to the particular city, state, or nation. Four types of place marketing are of particular interest to nonprofit marketers.

Various cities, states, and nations have an interest in attracting new residents. Here are some examples:

- Skokie, Illinois, a Chicago suburb, has been losing some of its white population to suburbs further north of Chicago. Several factors are at work: a growing neighboring black population; attractive housing available in the newer suburbs; some political tensions in Skokie. Skokie is undertaking a marketing effort to attract young white families by publicizing its many attractions, such as good retailing, nice homes, a fine public library, and good public transportation.
- The Woodlands, Texas, is one of several "new towns" that want to attract a young skilled population. The new town developers have prepared a marketing plan to promote The Woodlands as the city of the future.[9]
- Countries such as Australia and Canada are relatively underpopulated in relation to their land mass and resources. Both countries have mounted major efforts over the years to attract immigrants. The best Australia could do in its early days to attract settlers was to open their doors to the criminal and lower classes of England.

A city, state, or nation seeking to attract new settlers needs to make a number of decisions. It must decide, first, on how many settlers it wants to attract in a given time period. Otherwise, it might overshoot the mark, causing crowding and runaway real estate prices. Second, it must decide on the types of settlers in terms of age and ethnic, occupational, and educational characteristics. Third, it must decide on the best sources of these settlers so that it can focus its promotion and recruiting efforts.

Other cities, states, and nations, rather than wanting to attract settlers, are eager to discourage all of them or certain classes from coming. For example:

> The State of Oregon became very popular in the 1960s as a place where one could lead a simpler life amidst natural beauty. The number of new settlers pouring into Oregon disturbed the older inhabitants and the governor's office undertook a campaign to demarket the state. Negative publicity was developed such as "You can tell when it is summer in Oregon . . . the rain is warmer." This negative publicity succeeded only in increasing the level of interest in moving to Oregon.

## TOURIST MARKETING

Tourist marketing involves the effort to attract vacationers to spas, resorts, cities, states, and even whole nations. The effort is carried on by travel agents, airlines, motor clubs, oil companies, hotels, motels, and various government units. Tourism is one of the largest industries in the world, with total spending in 1978 of over $450 billion.[10]

Today most cities, states, and nations have an active tourist bureau attempting to attract tourists and their dollars. Tourist bureaus carry on a number of marketing activities: (1) they identify the area's tourist attractions,[11] (2) they propose new types of tourist attractions, (3) they encourage the building of more and better hotel facilities and retail businesses, (4) they analyze the most likely types and sources of tourists to attract, (5) they develop tourist marketing communications in the form of ads, brochures, direct mail, and publicity, and (6) they identify trade associations and try to persuade them to hold conventions in their locations.

Many studies have been undertaken to identify tourist segments and their needs, perceptions, and attitudes. Tourists are commonly segmented into age groups, income groups, life style groups, and benefit-seeking groups.[12] In the last case, a distinction is drawn between sunlust tourists seeking sun and fun and wanderlust tourists seeking historical sites and local culture. The most popular tourist destinations are those—such as Greece and Israel—that can appeal to both groups because they offer both sun and history.

The place marketer has to decide which tourist segments to attract. For example, the island of Bali for years fought having a jet port because it preferred to attract a small number of high-income, high-spending, long-staying tourists to a large number of mass tourists. The place marketer has to go further and research the knowledge, perception, and attitudes that the target market carries of the particular place. If the target market knows little or holds negative attitudes, a communication program must be developed to improve the perceptions.

Some places are upset about attracting too many tourists, and prefer to demarket themselves. Palm Beach, Florida, is letting its beach erode to discourage tourists. Yosemite National Park is considering prohibiting snowmobiling, conventions, and private car usage. And several European countries, such as Finland and France, prefer to discourage tourists from vacationing in certain areas where they feel the ravages of mass tourism exceed the benefits.

### Investor Marketing

Investor marketing involves efforts on the part of cities, states, and nations to attract investment capital that would go into real estate development, new manufacturing plants, and so on. Most states in the United States have established *economic development departments,* with staffs averaging 40 to 50 people and budgets of around $1 million. The less aggressive state departments develop brochures, supply information, and refer inquiries to other officials. The more market-oriented departments actively search and develop opportunities. They advertise the attractive industrial opportunities in their state in business periodicals read by business decision makers, and they also make heavy use of direct mail. They develop continuous publicity (news items and features) about opportunities in their state. They contact the chief executives of major companies to learn of any expansion plans. They run conferences for companies in which they describe the benefits of relocating in their state. They visit companies and make presentations demonstrating the money these companies would make or save by relocating.

Attempts to attract foreign capital are carried on by various nations such as Ireland, Turkey, Puerto Rico, and so on. For years, Ireland has conducted intense campaigns pointing out Ireland's major manufacturing advantages: abundant, skilled, and low-cost labor; ready-built factories; subsidies; fifteen years of tax freedom. Their economic development department carries out elaborate marketing programs involving media advertising and publicity, direct mail, personal sales calls, trade fairs, and holiday junkets to Ireland, all geared to stimulate the interest of targeted prospects in investing in Ireland.

NATION MARKETING

Nations undertake various activities to project a certain image of themselves in the eyes of the people of other nations. For example, the Netherlands hired the advertising agency of Ogilvy and Mathers to convey the image of the "friendly Dutch" so that more tourists would include the Netherlands in their European travel plans and even fly KLM airlines to Amsterdam as their first European stop. Years earlier, the Belgian government hired the public relations firm of Communications Counsellors Inc. (CCI) to put "Belgium on the map" so that it could attract more tourists and investments and sell more of its products abroad. Research showed that American citizens and businessmen knew little about Belgium and cared less.

CCI proceeded to identify the main assets of Belgium that would interest Americans. These turned out to be a royal family, Belgian lace, diamonds and crystal, and a few quaint cities. On this slim basis, CCI developed a publicity barrage. "Among the results were 704 stories in newspapers with a combined circulation of 75,000,000; 145 articles in the technical and trade press; use of canned scripts—largely of a women's interest character—on 1,251 television and 6,906 radio stations." In addition, CCI commissioned a skilled writer to write a major book about Belgium and a film producer to produce a travelogue. All of these efforts paid off and Belgium succeeded in attracting more tourists and investment dollars.[13]

---

## SUMMARY

Marketing, which was first developed in connection with products, has been broadened in recent years to cover other "marketable" entities, namely, services, persons, places, and ideas (the last is treated in Chapter 22).

Nonprofit organizations—both public and private—are primarily in the service business. Services can be defined as activities or benefits that one party can offer to another that are essentially intangible and do not result in the ownership of anything. Services are intangible, inseparable, variable, and perishable. Services can be classified according to whether they are people or equipment based, whether the client's presence is necessary, and whether the client is a consumer or a business. Service industries have lagged behind manufacturing firms in adopting and using marketing concepts. Yet rising costs and increased competition have forced service industries to search for new ways to increase their productivity and responsiveness.

Person marketing consists of activities undertaken to create, maintain, or alter knowledge, attitudes, and/or behavior toward particular persons. The two most common types are celebrity marketing and political candidate marketing. Aspiring celebrities often hire press agents or talent organizations to promote their name to the public, and sometimes to create a legend. Celebrities, like products, tend to exhibit one of several standard life cycles.

Place marketing involves activities undertaken to create, maintain, or alter knowledge, attitudes, and/or behavior toward particular places. Nonprofit organizations are primarily interested in four types of place marketing, namely, residential marketing, tourist marketing, investment marketing, and nation marketing.

## QUESTIONS

**1.** Producers of services have historically been more marketing oriented than have producers of products. Why do you think this has been the case?

**2.** A community mental health center is experiencing a very heavy demand for counseling services, and is considering putting more emphasis on group therapy so it can help more people with its limited professional staff. Evaluate this plan in light of the inseparability and perishability of the service involved.

**3.** In some medical clinics a patient is seen by whichever physician is available at the time. Using the four characteristics of a service, discuss (a) the advantages to the medical clinic of this practice, and (b) the possible disadvantages to the patient.

**4.** What factors account for variations in celebrity career life cycles? What role might marketing play in reducing the fluctuations?

**5.** Real estate salespeople often tell prospective home buyers that the three most important things to consider in selecting a home are "location, location, and location." What are the marketing implications of this for a city interested in attracting new residents?

**6.** Successful tourist and investor marketing efforts can be affected positively and negatively by macroenvironmental trends. For example, tourism declines in areas of political unrest. List some other examples of macroenvironmental trends that a tourist or economic development office should monitor as part of its marketing activities.

## NOTES

**1.** For a good discussion of quality control systems at the Marriott Hotel Chain, see G. M. Hostage, "Quality Control in a Service Business," *Harvard Business Review,* July–August 1975, pp. 98–106.

**2.** See W. Earl Sasser, "Match Supply and Demand in Service Industries," *Harvard Business Review,* November–December 1976, pp. 133–40.

**3.** See Dan R. E. Thomas, "Strategy Is Different in Service Businesses," *Harvard Business Review,* July–August 1978, p. 161.

**4.** William R. George and Hiram C. Barksdale, "Marketing Activities in the Service Industries," *Journal of Marketing,* October 1974, p. 65.

**5.** See Daniel T. Carroll, "Ten Commandments for Bank Marketing," *Bankers Magazine,* Autumn 1970, pp. 74–80.

**6.** Theodore Levitt, "Product-Line Approach to Service," *Harvard Business Review,* September–October 1972, pp. 41–52; see also his "The Industrialization of Service," *Harvard Business Review,* September–October 1976, pp. 63–74.

**7.** For marketing the services of a professional services firm, see Philip Kotler and Richard A. Connor, Jr., "Marketing Professional Services," *Journal of Marketing,* January 1977, pp. 71–76.

**8.** "Bucky Dent: The Selling of a Sudden Superstar," *Chicago Tribune,* December 16, 1978, Section 2, p. 1.

**9.** For a description of the marketing of a "new town" called The Woodlands, Texas, see Betsy D. Gelb and Ben M. Enis, "Marketing a City of the Future," in *Marketing is Everybody's Business* (Santa Monica, Calif.: Goodyear 1977).

**10.** See Stephen Papson, "Tourism: World's Biggest Industry in the Twenty-First Century?", *The Futurist,* August 1979, pp. 249–57.

**11.** The tourist attractiveness of a city or country is made up of five factors: (1) natural factors (natural beauty, climate), (2) social factors (artistic and architectural factors, fairs, and festivals), (3) historical factors (ancient ruins, religious significance), (4) recreational and shopping facilities (sports facilities, educational facilities, night-time recreation), and (5) infrastructure and food and shelter (health services, highways, hotels, restaurants). See Charles E. Gearing, et al., "Determining the Optimal Investment Policy for the Tourist Sector of a Developing Country," *Management Science,* Part I (December 1973), pp. 487–97

**12.** One study classified tourists into budget travelers, adventurers, homebodies, vacationers, and moderates. See William D. Perreault, Donna K. Darden, and William R. Darden, "A Psychographic Classification of Vacation Life Styles," *Journal of Leisure Research,* Vol. 9, No. 3 (1977), pp. 208–24.

**13.** The full story is told in Irwin Ross, *Image Merchants* (Garden City, N.Y.: Doubleday, 1959), pp. 196–202.

# Marketing of Ideas and Causes: Social Marketing

Northern California experienced a severe drought starting in 1977. The lack of water threatened to destroy much fruit and vegetables which California supplied to the nation; cause power shortages; increase fire hazards; destroy green lawns; and limit opportunities for fishing and boating. Long run solutions such as weather modification, water desalinization, and better irrigation would not be ready to help in the current crisis. Each community had to adopt strong measures to encourage major user segments—homes, industry, agriculture, and government—to cut down on their water consumption. For example, the community of Palo Alto initially sought a 10 percent reduction in water consumption in its area. To accomplish this, the community undertook a large number of actions, including:

1. Water consumption quotas were established for households and other types of users. For example, households were required to reduce their consumption by a certain percentage of their consumption in the previous year.
2. The price of water was raised but not expected to deter much usage by itself.
3. Citizens were sent water flow restrictors to use on their faucets.
4. Extraordinary media coverage was given to the water crisis on newspapers, radio, and television. Brochures were mailed to all home owners.
5. Citizens were asked to reexamine each water use and to bring it down. This meant fewer showers ("Save Water—Shower with a Friend"); fewer toilet flushes; less washing of clothes and dishes; less watering of lawns; less car washing; and so on.

The many campaigns were so effective in producing citizen awareness, interest, desire, and action that water consumption dropped by 17 percent in Palo Alto. Palo Alto residents, it appeared, competed in conspicuous nonconsumption, trying to outdo each other with stories of how they found ways to cut down on water. Some claimed, with civic pride, not to have taken a bath for a month. Other sectors, including business firms and government agencies, also managed to effect substantial reductions in their water consumption.

SOURCE: Adapted from Peter T. Hutchinson, Don E. Parkinson, and Charles B. Weinberg, "Water Conservation in Palo Alto," in Christopher H. Lovelock and Charles B. Weinberg, eds., *Cases in Public and Nonprofit Marketing*, (Palo Alto, Calif.: Scientific Press, 1977), pp. 183–96.

We are coming to recognize that there is a "marketplace of ideas" just as there is a "marketplace of goods." Examples abound of organizations striving to motivate some public to adopt a new idea or practice.

The National Safety Council wants people to wear their safety belts when driving. The American Cancer Society wants people to stop smoking. The American Medical Association wants people to take an annual physical checkup. The Federal Energy Office wants people to conserve on fuel and energy. The New York Police Department wants people to lock their car doors. The National Organization for Women wants men to view women as equals. The National Federation of Churches wants people to give greater support to religion in American life.

These efforts to alter the beliefs, attitudes, values, or behavior of target publics go under different names. They are called propaganda efforts by their critics and educational efforts by their supporters. They are perfectly normal activities and are found in all societies. Every group has its cause and actively attempts to market its viewpoint to others. In a totalitarian society, only one group is allowed to propagate openly for official causes. In a free society, all groups propagate their viewpoints in "the marketplace of ideas."

Idea marketers are known by many names—propagandists, agitators, charismatic leaders, publicists, lobbyists, change agents, and so on. Many of them see their task in narrow terms, as that of developing and disseminating persuasive messages. We shall argue, however, that effective communication is only one part of the total task required to successfully market an idea. The adoption of an idea, like the adoption of any product, requires a deep understanding of the needs, perceptions, preferences, reference groups, and behavioral patterns of the target audience, and the tailoring of messages, media, costs, and facilities to maximize the ease of adopting the idea. We use the term *social marketing* to cover these tasks. We believe that social marketing provides an effective conceptual system for thinking through the problems of bringing about changes in the ideas or practices of a target public.

Before proceeding, however, it is desirable to answer the objection that social marketing provides Machiavellian guidance on how to get people to do what they do not want to do—that is, provides a means of social manipulation and control. In the first place, it is a very difficult task to change people for good or bad.[1] Those who work in face-to-face relations with individual clients and have their trust, such as psychiatrists, social workers, physicians, or relatives, know how difficult it is to change another person. It is even more difficult to change a whole group of people when the means are mass media that appear infrequently and not from a necessarily disinterested source. Although social marketing attempts to harness the insights of behavioral science and exchange theory to the task of social change, its power to bring about actual change, or bring it about in a reasonable amount of time, is highly limited. The greater the target group's investment in a value or behavioral pattern, the more resistant it is to change. Social marketing works best where the type of change counts for least.

Second, social marketing goes on in society whether or not its methods are openly described. Some groups will be better at it than others. Rather than keep social marketing methodology a deep secret and thus leave certain groups at a disadvantage, this methodology should be openly discussed and examined. This will allow both sides of an issue to formulate improved plans as well as alert the public to how groups market a social cause. Hopefully this will cancel the advantage of any single side and lead more often to the resolution of public issues on their merits.

This chapter is divided into four parts. The first part examines the concept of social marketing more closely. The second part describes the various conditions that determine the effectiveness of a social marketing campaign. The third part distinguishes four types of social causes, each more challenging than the preceding one. The final part describes the seven major steps in the social marketing process.

## CONCEPT OF SOCIAL MARKETING

The term "social marketing" was first introduced in 1971 to describe the use of marketing principles and techniques to advance a social cause, idea, or behavior.[2] More specifically:

**Social marketing** is the design, implementation, and control of programs seeking to increase the acceptability of a social idea or cause in a target group(s). It utilizes concepts of market segmentation, consumer research, concept development, communication, facilitation, incentives, and exchange theory to maximize target group response.

Synonymous terms might be "social cause marketing," "idea marketing," or "public issue marketing."[3]

### Four Basic Approaches to Social Change

One can best understand social marketing by seeing it in relationship to the major approaches to producing social change—the legal, technological, economic, and informational approaches. Consider how these approaches apply in inducing people to reduce their cigarette consumption. The *legal* approach is to pass laws that make cigarette smoking either illegal, costly, or difficult (e.g., prohibiting smoking in public places). The *technological* approach is to develop an innovation that will help people reduce their smoking or the harm thereof (e.g., an antismoking pill, a harmless cigarette). The *economic* approach is to raise the price or cost of smoking (e.g., higher cigarette taxes, higher insurance rates for smokers). Finally, the *informational* approach is to direct persuasive information at smokers about the risks of smoking and the advantages of not smoking (e.g., "Warning: The Surgeon General Has Determined That Smoking Is Dangerous to Your Health").

### The Emergence and Evolution of Social Marketing

The roots of social marketing lie in the informational approach, in the form known as *social advertising*. Many cause groups, struck by the apparent effectiveness of commercial advertising, began to consider its potential for changing public attitudes and behavior. Family planning organizations in India, Sri Lanka, Mexico, and several other countries have sponsored major advertising campaigns attempting to sell people on the idea of having fewer children. Messages on billboards and over radio tell the public that they can have a higher standard of living with fewer children (India) or be happier (Sri Lanka). Nutrition groups have also used advertising extensively to encourage people to adopt better eating habits. The U.S. Department of Energy has plans for a multimillion-dollar advertising campaign to promote energy conservation to the American people.

Properly designed, these campaigns can influence attitudes and behavior. The problem is that all too often these campaigns are the only step taken to motivate new behavior and, by themselves, are usually inadequate. First, the message may be inadequately researched. For example, media campaigns to encourage people in developing countries to improve their diets miss the point that many people lack knowledge of which foods are more healthful; they may lack the money to buy these goods; and in remote areas, they may not find certain foods available. Second, many people screen out the message through selective perception, distortion, and forgetting. Mass communications have much less direct influence on behavior than has been thought, and much of their influence is mediated through the opinion leadership of other people. Third, many people do not know what to do after their exposure to the message. The message "Stop smoking—it might kill you" does not help the smoker know how to handle the urge to smoke or where to go for help.

As these limitations were recognized, social advertising evolved into a broader approach known as *social communication*. Much of current social marketing has moved from a narrow advertising approach to a broad social communication/promotion approach to accomplish its objectives. Social communicators make greater use of personal selling and editorial support in addition to mass advertising. Thus, the family planning campaign in India utilizes a network of agents, including doctors, dentists, and barbers, to "talk up" family planning to people with whom they come in contact. Events such as "Family Planning Day" and family planning fairs, together with buttons, signs, and other media, get across the message.

Only recently has *social marketing* begun to replace social communication as a larger paradigm for effecting social change. Social marketing adds at least four elements that are missing from a pure social communication approach.

One element is sophisticated *marketing research* to learn about the market and the probable effectiveness of alternative marketing approaches. Social advertising amounts to "a shot in the dark" unless it is preceded by careful marketing research. Thus social marketers concerned with smoking would examine the size of the smoking market, the major market segments and the behavioral characteristics of each, and the benefit-cost impact of targeting different segments and designing appropriate campaigns for each.

The second element added by social marketing is *product development.* Faced with the problem of getting people to lower their thermostats in winter, a social advertiser or communicator will see the problem largely as one of exhorting people to lower the thermostat, using patriotic appeals, fuel-cost-saving appeals, or whatever seems appropriate. The social marketer, in addition, will consider existing or potential products that will make it easier for people to adopt the desired behavior, such as devices that automatically lower home heat during the middle of the night or that compute fuel cost savings at various temperature settings. In other words, whenever possible the social marketer does not stick with the existing product and try to sell it—a sales approach—but searches for the best product to meet the need—a marketing approach.

The third element added by social marketing is *the use of incentives.* Social communicators concentrate on composing messages dramatizing the benefits or disbenefits of different kinds of behaviors. Social marketers go further and design specific incentives to increase the level of motivation. For example, social marketers have advised public health officials who are running immunization campaigns in remote villages to offer small gifts to people who show up for vaccinations. Some hospitals in South America run "price specials" on certain days whereby people who come in for health checkups pay less than the normal charge. The sales promotion area is rich with tools that the marketer can use to promote social causes.

The fourth element added by social marketing is *facilitation.* The marketer realizes that people wishing to change their behavior must invest time and effort, and considers ways to make it easier for them to adopt the new behavior. For example, smoking cessation classes must be conveniently located and conducted in a professional manner. Marketers are keenly aware of the need to develop convenient and attractive response channels to complement the communication channels. Thus they are concerned not only with getting people to adopt a new behavior, but also with finding ways to facilitate maintenance of the behavior.

Social marketing goes beyond social advertising and social communication in that it involves all "four Ps," not just one. Social communicators usually come into the planning process after the objectives, policies, and products have been determined. They have little or no influence on product design, pricing, or distribution. Their job is to promote the organization's objectives and products, using communication media. Social marketers, on the other hand, participate actively in the organization's planning. They advise what products will be acceptable to the target publics; what incentives will work best; what distribution systems will be optimal; and what communication program will be effective. They think in exchange terms rather than solely in persuasion terms. They have as much of an interest in improving the offer of the organization as in modifying the target market's attitude of the offer. Whereas propagandists take the product, price, and channels as given, social marketers treat them as variables.

## WHO DOES SOCIAL MARKETING?

All organizations can do social marketing. Many social causes would be accepted unambiguously as falling under social marketing—for example, civil rights, better nutrition, better health care, and environmental protection. Other causes are more ambiguous. The marketing of family planning is an example of social marketing, but so would be the antimarketing of family planning by religious groups who think it is not in society's interest. The protagonists and antagonists of abortion both regard their position to be in the interest of society and can plan the marketing of their idea in a social marketing framework. Any social cause, in fact, can be marketed; we cannot assume that everyone will agree that it is in the public interest.[4]

Furthermore, social marketing can be carried on by business firms as well as by nonprofit organizations. Consider the following examples:

- Seat belt manufacturers are major supporters of auto safety legislation, partly because they stand to gain.
- Bottled water manufacturers in France have backed efforts to influence French citizens to reduce their alcohol consumption.
- Condom manufacturers have lent support to campaigns against VD because they stand to gain through greater use of condoms.
- Life insurance companies are encouraging people to jog, cut down on fats and sugar, install smoke alarms, and in other ways reduce illness, accidents, and premature deaths, thus cutting insurance claims and raising company profits.

Clearly, business firms sponsor social marketing programs where they derive a benefit along with the public.

## THE REQUISITE CONDITIONS
## FOR EFFECTIVE SOCIAL MARKETING

A number of scholars have attempted to delineate the major conditions that determine the effectiveness of social communication and social marketing campaigns. Here we will review the analysis of Lazarsfeld/Merton, Wiebe, Rothschild, and Smelser/Kotler.

### LAZARSFELD/MERTON ANALYSIS

Lazarsfeld and Merton believe that mass media have limited effectiveness in social cause marketing because one or more of three conditions is usually lacking.[5]

The first condition is real or psychological *monopolization* by the media; that is, a condition marked by the absence of counterpropaganda. Most campaigns in a free society compete with so many other causes that the monopoly condition is lacking, and this condition reduces the effectiveness of such campaigns.

The second condition required for effective mass propaganda is *canalization,* the presence of an existing attitudinal base for the feelings that the social communicators are striving to shape. Typical commercial advertising is effective because the task is not one of instilling basic new attitudes or creating significantly new behavior patterns, but rather canalizing existing attitudes and behavior in one direction or another. Thus, the seller of toothpaste does not have to socialize persons into new dental care habits, but into which brand of a familiar and desired product to purchase. If the preexisting attitudes are present, then promotional campaigns are more effective, because canalization is always an easier task than social reconditioning.

The third condition is *supplementation*—that is, the effort to follow up mass communication campaigns with programs of face-to-face contacts. In trying to explain the success of the rightist Father Coughlin movement in the thirties, Lazarsfeld and Merton observe:

> This combination of a central supply of propaganda [Coughlin's addresses on a nationwide network], the coordinated distribution of newspapers and pamphlets and locally organized face-to-face discussions among relatively small groups—this complex of reciprocal reinforcement by mass media and personal relations proved spectacularly successful.[6]

This approach is standard in many closed societies and organizations and suggests a key difference between social advertising and social marketing. Whereas a social advertising approach contrives only the event of mass media communication and leaves the response to natural social processes, social marketing arranges for a stepdown communication process. The message is passed on and discussed in more familiar surroundings to increase its memorability, penetration, and action consequences. Thus supplementation, monopolization, and canalization are critical factors influencing the effectiveness of any social marketing campaign.

## WIEBE'S ANALYSIS

In 1952, G. D. Wiebe raised the question, "Why can't you sell brotherhood like you sell soap?"[7] This statement implies that sellers of commodities such as soap are generally effective, while "sellers" of social causes are generally ineffective. Wiebe examined four social campaigns to determine what conditions or characteristics accounted for their relative success or lack of success. He found that the more the conditions of the social campaign resembled those of a product campaign, the more successful the social campaign. However, because many social campaigns are conducted under quite unmarketlike circumstances, Wiebe also noted clear limitations in the practice of social marketing.

Wiebe explained the relative effectiveness of these campaigns in terms of the audience member's experience with regard to five factors:

1. *The force.* The intensity of the person's motivation toward the goal as a combination of his predisposition prior to the message and the stimulation of the message.
2. *The direction.* Knowledge of how or where the person might go to consummate his motivation.
3. *The mechanism.* The existence of an agency that enables the person to translate his motivation into action.
4. *Adequacy and compatibility.* The ability and effectiveness of the agency in performing its task.
5. *Distance.* The audience member's estimate of the energy and cost required to consummate the motivation in relation to the reward.

To show how these factors operate, Wiebe first analyzed the Kate Smith campaign to sell bonds during World War II. This campaign was eminently successful, according to Wiebe, because of the presence of force (patriotism), direction (buy bonds), mechanism (banks, post offices, telephone orders), adequacy and compatibility (so many centers to purchase the bonds), and distance (ease of purchase). In fact, extra telephone lines were installed on the night of the campaign at 134 CBS stations to take orders during her appeal. The effort to buy bonds

was literally reduced to the distance between the listener and his telephone. Psychological distance was also minimized. The listener remained in his own home. There were no new people to meet, no unfamiliar procedures, no forms to fill out, no explanation, no waiting.[8]

In the case of a campaign to recruit Civil Defense volunteers, many of the same factors were present except that the social mechanism was not prepared to handle the large volume of response, and this reduced the campaign's success. Teachers, manuals, equipment, and registration and administration procedures were *inadequate,* and many responding citizens were turned away and disappointed after they were led to believe that their services were urgently needed.

The third campaign, a documentary on juvenile delinquency, did not meet with maximum success because of the *absence of a mechanism.* People were urged to form neighborhood councils themselves. This certainly takes far more effort than picking up the phone to buy a war bond, or "stopping in" to register at the nearest Civil Defense unit.

The fourth campaign revolved around the goal of the Kefauver committee hearings to arouse citizens to "set their house in order." This campaign met with a notable lack of success, however, because citizens were not *directed* to an appropriate mechanism.

### ROTHSCHILD'S ANALYSIS

Rothschild sought to understand why social causes are generally harder to sell than commercial products; and, within social causes, why some are much harder to sell than others.[9] For example, many American cities have waged periodic antilitter campaigns without much success. These campaigns have taken mainly a social advertising approach, exhorting people not to litter and exhorting them to remove litter if they see it. Some of these campaigns have had a slight positive short-run impact but rarely a long-run impact. Here are the factors identified by Rothschild that affect the impact of an antilitter campaign, or any social cause campaign.

> 1. *Situation involvement.* The issue of littering has low current situation involvement for most people; that is, littering has very low salience compared to other issues people face.
> 2. *Enduring involvement.* People generally have not had much involvement in their own past with the issue of litter.
> 3. *Benefits/reinforcers.* Antilittering behavior produces only slight personal satisfaction and the person's actions do not seem to make a difference in the amount of litter in the society.
> 4. *Costs.* Antilittering behavior may involve a personal cost and inconvenience.
> 5. *Benefit/cost.* The benefit/cost ratio to the individual who does not litter or who picks up litter is low. (This is derived by putting together the previous two variables.)
> 6. *Preexisting demand.* There is some latent demand for a clean environment but it is not very strong or universal.
> 7. *Segmentation.* Antilittering must be sold to everyone, or else it will fail to produce a clean environment. If the environment is somewhat unclean, then most people will accept this as the norm and not engage in strong antilittering behavior.

For these reasons, Rothschild holds that antilittering communication campaigns tend to have a slight short-run impact and hardly any long-run impact. However, the impact can be strengthened by using the three other Ps. Cities should put more public garbage cans (product) in crowded locations (place) which have a high litter problem. Penalties (price) can be imposed on people who are caught littering.

Rothschild applied this set of variables to other idea marketing campaigns, such as selling people to cooperate with the 55 mph speed limit, selling high school graduates on the idea of a military career, and so on. Generally speaking, the lower the public's involvement in the issue and the lower the benefit/cost ratio, the lower the impact of the marketing communications campaign.

### SMELSER / KOTLER ANALYSIS

Success in marketing a social cause depends on the society's readiness for that cause, which varies at different times. Ralph Nader could not have made much headway with consumerism if he campaigned for it in the late 1950s. Consumerism was successfully launched in the mid-1960s because all of the conditions were ripe. These conditions, according to Smelser, are structural conduciveness, structural strain, growth of a generalized belief, precipitating factors, mobilization for action, and social control.[10] These six conditions have been applied by Kotler to explain why consumerism could be successfully launched in the mid-1960s (see Figure 22–1).[11]

*Structural conduciveness* refers to basic developments in the society that eventually create potent contradictions. Three developments are particularly noteworthy:

1. U.S. incomes and educational levels advanced continuously. This portended that many citizens would eventually become concerned with the quality of their lives, not just their material well-being.
2. U.S. technology and marketing were becoming increasingly complex and this would inevitably create consumer problems.
3. The environment was progressively exploited in the interests of abundance. Observers began to see that an abundance of cars and conveniences would produce a shortage of clean air and water. The Malthusian specter of man running out of sufficient resources became a growing concern.

These developments produced major *structural strains* in the society. The 1960s were a time of great public discontent and frustration. Economic discontent was created by steady inflation which left consumers feeling that their real incomes were deteriorating. Social discontent centered on the sorrowful conditions of the poor, the race issue, and the tremendous costs of the Vietnam war. Ecological discontent arose out of new awarenesses of the world population explosion and the pollution fallout associated with technological progress. Marketing system discontent centered on safety hazards, product breakdowns, commercial noise, and gimmickry. Political discontent reflected the widespread feelings that politicians and government institutions were not serving the people.

Discontent is not enough to bring about change. There must grow a *general-*

## FIGURE 22–1

Factors Contributing to the Rise of Consumerism in the 1960s

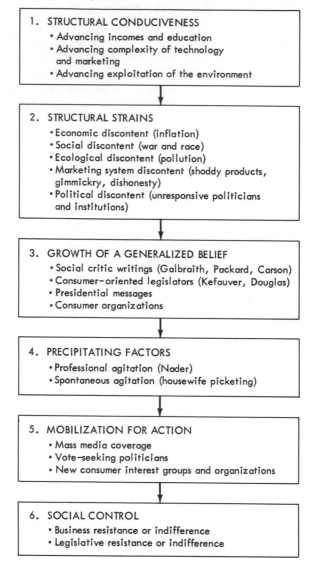

1. STRUCTURAL CONDUCIVENESS
   - Advancing incomes and education
   - Advancing complexity of technology and marketing
   - Advancing exploitation of the environment

2. STRUCTURAL STRAINS
   - Economic discontent (inflation)
   - Social discontent (war and race)
   - Ecological discontent (pollution)
   - Marketing system discontent (shoddy products, gimmickry, dishonesty)
   - Political discontent (unresponsive politicians and institutions)

3. GROWTH OF A GENERALIZED BELIEF
   - Social critic writings (Galbraith, Packard, Carson)
   - Consumer–oriented legislators (Kefauver, Douglas)
   - Presidential messages
   - Consumer organizations

4. PRECIPITATING FACTORS
   - Professional agitation (Nader)
   - Spontaneous agitation (housewife picketing)

5. MOBILIZATION FOR ACTION
   - Mass media coverage
   - Vote–seeking politicians
   - New consumer interest groups and organizations

6. SOCIAL CONTROL
   - Business resistance or indifference
   - Legislative resistance or indifference

*ized belief* about both the main causes of the social malaise and the potent effectiveness of collective social action. Here, again, certain factors contributed importantly to the growth of a generalized belief.

1. The writings of social critics such as John Kenneth Galbraith, Vance Packard, and Rachel Carson provided a popular interpretation of the problem and of actionable solutions.

2. The hearings and proposals of a handful of congressmen such as Senator Estes Kefauver held out some hope of legislative remedy.

3. The presidential "consumer" messages of President Kennedy in 1962 and President Johnson in 1966 helped to legitimate belief and interest in this area of social action.

4. Old-line consumer testing and educational organizations continued to call public attention to the consumers' interests.

Given the growing collective belief, consumerism only awaited some *precipitating factors* to ignite the highly combustible social material. Two sparks specifically exploded the consumer movement. The one was General Motors' unwitting creation of a hero in Ralph Nader through its attempt to investigate him; Nader's successful attack against General Motors encouraged other organizers to undertake bold acts against the business system. The other was the occurrence of widespread and spontaneous store boycotts by housewives in search of a better deal from supermarkets.

These chance combustions would have vanished without a lasting effect if additional resources were not *mobilized for action.* As it turned out, three factors fueled the consumer movement.

1. The mass media gave front-page coverage and editorial support to the activities of consumer advocates. They found the issues safe, dramatic, and newsworthy. The media's attention was further amplified through word-of-mouth processes into grassroots expressions and feelings.

2. A large number of politicians at the federal, state, and local levels picked up consumerism as a safe, high-potential vote-getting social issue.

3. A number of existing and new organizations arose in defense of the consumer, including labor unions, consumer cooperatives, credit unions, product testing organizations, consumer education organizations, senior citizen groups, public interest law firms, and government agencies.

Of course, the progress and course of an incipient social movement depends on the reception it receives by those in *social control,* in this case, the industrial-political complex. A proper response by the agents of social control can drain the early movement of its force. But this did not happen. Many members of the business community attacked, resisted, or ignored the consumer advocates in a way that only strengthened the consumerist cause. Most legislative bodies were slow to respond with positive programs, thus feeding charges that the political system was unresponsive to consumer needs and that more direct action was required.

Thus, all the requisite conditions were met in the 1960s. Even without some of the structural strains, the cause of consumerism would have eventually emerged because of the increasing complexity of technology and the environmental issue.

After a cause successfully takes hold, it goes through a life cycle. Cameron does not believe there is any one pattern:

There is no characteristic life cycle of social movements. . . . If we quantify the development of a movement by counting members, amounts of income and expenditures, number of outside persons needed, number of pieces of literature, and so on, we find great variations. . . . Some movements grow very slowly . . . others seem blessed with the vitality and reproductiveness of a mushroom and accumulate personnel and property with great rapidity . . . some skyrocket into prominence and then almost as quickly decline.[12]

Although there is great variation in the rates of growth and decline of social movements, many of them pass through certain well-defined stages. Each stage is characterized by a particular set of problems, strategic options, and leadership styles. One of the more typical patterns consists of four stages—the crusading stage, the popular cause stage, the managerial stage, and the bureaucratic stage.[13]

A great number of causes start out as a crusade led by a few zealous individuals who have a knack of dramatizing a social ill. To the extent their message is effective, new supporters are attracted and the cause may reach the stage of a popular movement. As a popular movement, it is still led by the original leaders, whose primary quality is total absorption in the cause and personal charisma. But as the ranks of this movement swell, new problems must be coped with, such as developing clearer definitions of roles and responsibilities, and attracting adequate resources to keep the organization going. New types of leaders start being favored—those who have organizational skills—and the cause passes into the managerial stage. The reins are tightened and more specific goal-setting, planning, and coordination take place. Nevertheless, with luck, the new leaders retain some of the original zeal. Finally, the movement passes into a bureaucratic phase in which the original zeal is lost, and the cause is in the hands of functionaries whose main concern is organizational survival. The cause is run like any other business with a product to sell, with a rigid hierarchy, established policies, much functional specialization, and so on. Even the job of maintaining a following and support is handled as a specialist function.

These four stages are not inevitable or irreversible. A new leader may appear who gives a flabby movement a new vitality. The political right was in a slump for years until people like Milton Friedman and Ronald Reagan gave it a new respectability. On the other hand, other cause organizations that once commanded power and public attention limp along, such as the Women's Christian Temperance Union, hoping, but not being able, to regain their former glory.

## DISTINCTIONS AMONG TYPES OF SOCIAL CAUSES

Social marketing aims to produce an optimal plan for bringing about a desired social change. The fact that the plan is optimal, however, does not guarantee that the target change will be achieved. It depends on how easy or difficult the targeted social change is. Without social marketing thinking, it may be that the desired social change has only a 10 percent chance of being achieved; the best social marketing plan may only increase this probability to 15 percent.

In other words, some social changes are relatively easy to bring about, even without social marketing; others are supremely difficult to bring about, even with social marketing.

We will distinguish among four types of social changes of increasing difficulty to bring about, namely, cognitive change, action change, behavioral change, and value change.

## COGNITIVE CHANGE

There are many social causes which have the limited objective of creating a cognitive change in the target audience. They are called public information or public education campaigns. Many examples can be cited:

- campaigns to explain the nutritional value of different foods
- campaigns to explain the work of the United Nations
- campaigns to expand awareness of Medicare and Medicaid benefits
- campaigns to bring attention to pressing social problems, such as poverty, bigotry, or pollution

Cognitive change causes would seem to be fairly easy to market effectively in that they do not seek to change any deep-rooted attitudes or behavior. Their aim is primarily to create awareness or knowledge. The optimal marketing approach would seem to be straightforward. Marketing research would be used to identify the groups that need the information the most. Their media habits are identified to serve as a guide for distributing and timing effective messages. The messages themselves are formulated on the basis of target audience analysis. They are carried to the audiences through advertising, publicity, personnel, displays, exhibitions, and other vehicles. The effectiveness of the campaign can be measured by postsampling members of the target groups to see how much increase in comprehension has taken place.

Although it would seem that information campaigns should easily succeed, the evidence is quite mixed. A massive campaign in Cincinnati to inform citizens about the United Nations produced no measured increase in the level of citizen knowledge.[14] A two-year campaign during World War II to inform people that war bonds were intended primarily to curb inflation rather than raise money produced no measurable increase in understanding whatever.[15] Other campaigns that failed to produce cognitive change are documented by Hyman and Sheatsley.[16] These authors give several reasons why information campaigns may fail:

1. There exists a hard core of "chronic know-nothings" who cannot be reached by information campaigns. In fact, "there is something about the uninformed that makes them harder to reach, no matter what the level or nature of the information."
2. The likelihood of being exposed to the information increases with interest in the issue. If few people are initially interested, few will be exposed.

3. The likelihood of being exposed to the information increases with the information's compatibility with prior attitudes. People will tend to avoid disagreeable information.

4. People will read different things into the information that they are exposed to, depending on their beliefs and values. The bigot, for example, often does not perceive antiprejudice literature as such. People emerge with a range of different reactions to the same material.

Thus, much thought has to be given to planning the simplest of campaigns —those designed to produce cognitive change. The message must be interesting, clear, and consonant with the intended audience values.[17]

### ACTION CHANGE

Another class of causes are those attempting to induce a maximum number of persons to take a specific action during a given period. Many examples can be cited:

- campaigns to attract people to show up for a mass immunization campaign
- campaigns to attract eligible people to sign up for Medicaid
- campaigns to influence the greatest number of voters to approve a school bond issue
- campaigns to attract women over 40 to take annual cancer detection tests
- campaigns to attract student dropouts back to school
- campaigns to attract blood donors

Action causes are somewhat harder to market than cognitive change causes. The target market has to comprehend something *and* take a specific action based on it. Action involves a cost to the actors. Even if their attitude toward the action is favorable, their carrying it out may be impeded by such factors as distance, time, expense, or plain inertia. For this reason, the marketer has to arrange factors that make it easy for target persons to carry out the action.

Consider mass immunization campaigns. Medical teams in Africa visit villages in the hope of inoculating everyone. Over the years, medical teams have evolved a procedure to increase the number of villagers they attract. A marketing team is sent to each village a few weeks before the appearance of the medical team. The marketers meet the village leaders to describe the importance and benefits of the program so that the leaders in turn will ask their people to cooperate. The marketers offer monetary or other incentives to the village leaders. They drive a sound truck around the village announcing the date and occasion. They promise rewards to those who show up. Posters are placed in various locations. The medical team arrives when scheduled and uses inoculation equipment that is relatively fast and painless. The whole effect is an orchestration of product, price, place, and promotion factors calculated to achieve the maximum possible turnout. (For another illustration of action marketing, see Exhibit 22–1.)

**EXHIBIT 22–1.** Getting people to sign up for Medicaid

In 1965, Medicare was enacted into law to provide medical benefits for the *elderly.* The following year, Medicaid was enacted into law to provide medical benefits for the *indigent and handicapped.* In the state of New York, persons and families earning under $6,000 were eligible for Medicaid. One year after Medicaid was enacted, only one million of the three million eligible persons in New York City were enrolled. A survey revealed three factors behind the low enrollment rate:

1. A widespread lack of knowledge of Medicaid and its benefits.
2. Confusion of Medicaid with Medicare by elderly indigents who failed to realize the additional benefits available from Medicaid.
3. A mistaken belief that one had to be literally on the welfare rolls to be eligible.

The city of New York decided to launch a one-month campaign in June 1967 to increase the number of eligible persons who signed up for Medicaid. The plan for social marketing Medicaid included the following elements:

1. The mayor declared the month of June as Medicaid Month.
2. Health educators in thirty health districts went into the community to organize public support. They enlisted the support of professional leaders, active lay leaders, informal leaders, volunteers from the police auxiliary, and persons from antipoverty programs.
3. Personnel and sound trucks appeared at busy locations on different days to answer questions.
4. Information tables were placed in three department stores in Brooklyn to reach shoppers who might be eligible for Medicaid.
5. Literature was distributed in the streets and through department stores, banks, post offices, supermarkets, and schools.
6. Publicity was placed in newspapers, radio, and television.
7. Car cards were placed in the city subway system.
8. Posters were distributed at hospital out-patient clinics, health centers, and antipoverty offices.

This campaign was so successful that it was extended into the month of July and for the two months, a total of 450,000 additional pesons were enrolled in Medicaid.

SOURCE: Raymond S. Alexander and Simon Podair, "Educating New York City Residents to Benefits of Medicaid," *Public Health Reports,* September 1969, pp. 767–72.

BEHAVIORAL CHANGE

Another class of social causes aims to induce or help people change some aspect of their behavior for the sake of their well-being. Behavioral change causes include:

- efforts to discourage cigarette smoking
- efforts to discourage excessive consumption of alcohol
- efforts to discourage the use of hard drugs
- efforts to help overweight people change their food habits

Behavioral change is harder to achieve than cognitive or one-shot action changes. People must unlearn old habits, learn new habits, and freeze the new pattern of behavior. For example, in the area of birth control, couples have to learn how to use new devices, such as a condom or diaphragm, and get into the habit of its regular use, without anyone being around to help them or to reinforce this behavior. In the area of safer driving, drivers who have a tendency to drink heavily at social gatherings must learn either to drink less or know when they are not fit to drive their own car. Various campaigns have been directed at problem drivers to condition them to be aware of the problem and the penalties. Exhibit 22–2 describes another behavior change campaign.

**EXHIBIT 22–2.** Getting all Swedish drivers to prepare for a switch to the right-hand side of the road

At five o'clock in the morning of September 3, 1967, Sweden changed her rule of the road from driving on the left to driving on the right. For the people of Sweden—almost 8,000,000 of them—this meant that an old and extremely well learned pattern of behavior would have to be changed. From that time, 2,000,000 motor vehicles and 1,000,000 other vehicles would have to be driven on the right instead of on the left, and people would have to pass each other on the left instead of on the right. In addition they would have to learn how to find their way about in the large towns, where traffic engineers were taking the opportunity to make a thorough reorganization of traffic and to introduce, for example, many new one-way streets.

The reorganization meant that the whole population—and of course those who happened to be visiting Sweden at the time—would have to be supplied with information telling them that traffic was to be reorganized, when and how the reorganization was to be effected, what traffic rules would be in force afterwards, and what local changes had been made for the regulation of traffic. For two weeks before September 3, therefore, and after that date until the end of the year, an information campaign of seldom-experienced dimensions was put into action. All conceivable media were used in the campaign—between three and four TV programs a day; an average of two daily radio programs and more than ten trailers; a 32-page brochure of which 7,900,000 copies were printed and which was distributed to every household in Sweden. The brochure was translated into nine languages and was directly distributed to aliens resident in Sweden. It was also issued in editions for the deaf, the blind, and other special groups.

Every pupil in Sweden's schools received study materials adapted to the various stages of education from kindergartens to higher secondary schools

**EXHIBIT 22–2.** Getting all Swedish drivers to prepare for a switch to the right-hand side of the road (continued)

and other advanced types of schools. Special printed matter was also produced for other public institutions such as pensioners' homes, hospitals, and prisons. For weeks after the changeover, practically every poster site in the country was used, and along the highways reminder signs were set up every three to five kilometers.

An advertising campaign was carried on in all the 130 daily newspapers and in weeklies and trade papers, from the last weeks in August until November. Even comics of the "Donald Duck" type carried advertising with traffic information adapted to their readers. In addition radio, TV, and newspapers gave information about the changeover in their news. On September 4, facts about right-hand traffic took up one-third of column space in the dailies.

Advertising films were shown before the main feature in movie houses and a sound track reminded audiences of right-hand traffic before they left at the end of the show. Spectators were given similar reminders at sports contests and other events. Traffic information and notices of various kinds were also given on, for example, milk cartons, soft drinks, plastic cups, coffee cans, and department stores' carrier-bags. Private enterprise produced right-hand traffic games, men's underpants suitably marked with admonitions, and warning devices of the most diversified kinds for car drivers.

During the autumn of 1967, detailed analyses of the accident statistics showed that bicycle and moped accidents were at a relatively high figure during the first two weeks after the changeover, and also that head-on collisions were two to three times more than "normal" during the period September–November. In both these cases, preventive measures were taken.

The conclusion that can be drawn from the course of developments after the changeover must reasonably be that it is possible to change the public's attitudes in traffic matters, that it is possible considerably to increase road users' traffic knowledge, and that it is possible to make a radical change in people's behavior in traffic.

SOURCE: Condensed and reprinted by permission of Unilever, Ltd., from *Progress* (the former Unilever Quarterly), Vol. 53, No. 279 (March 1968), pp. 26–32.

Change agents rely primarily on mass communication to influence changes in behavior. In some cases, mass communication can be counterproductive. In the late sixties, when many young people were experimenting with hard drugs, advertising agencies, social agencies, and legislators felt that advertising could be a powerful weapon for discouraging hard drug usage. Much money was funded privately and by the government, with donations of time by advertising agencies and media organizations. Fear appeals were first tried, followed by more informational advertising. Soon some people began to voice doubts about the good that this was doing. UN Secretary-General Kurt Waldheim, presenting a drug evaluation study to the UN, cautioned in 1972: "Special care must be exercised in this connection not to arouse undue curiosity and unwittingly encourage experimentation."[18] Antidrug messages, especially on television, reach a lot of young persons who may never have thought about drugs. These young persons do not necessarily perceive the message negatively and might in fact develop a strong curiosity about the subject. This is accompanied by the feeling that if the older generation is spending that much money to talk them out of something, there must be something good in it. They start discussing drugs with their friends and soon learn where to obtain illegal drugs, how to use them, and that they are not that dangerous if used carefully. Thus, mass advertising might provoke initial curiosity more than fear and lead the person into exploration and experimentation.[19] The main point is that nonprofit organizations often resort to advertising with insufficient knowledge of the audience or testing of the probable effects of their message upon the audience.[20] And they fail to create mechanisms that enable people to translate their motivation into appropriate actions.

### VALUE CHANGE

The final class of causes attempts to alter deeply felt beliefs or values that a target group holds toward some object or situation. Examples include:

- efforts to alter people's ideas about abortion
- efforts to alter people's ideas about the number of children they should have
- efforts to change the values of bigoted people
- efforts to socialize peasants into a factory work ethic

Efforts to change deeply held values are among the most difficult causes to market. People's sense of identity and well-being are rooted in their basic values. Their basic values orient their social, moral, and intellectual perceptions and choices. The intrusion of dissonance into their values creates heavy strain and stress. They will try to avoid dissonant information; or rationalize it away; or compartmentalize it so that it does not affect their values. The human psychological system resists information that is disorienting.

Any effort to change people from one basic value orientation to another requires a prolonged and intense program of indoctrination. Even then it is likely to succeed only to the smallest degree. Consider the classic case of the Chinese indoctrination program for American prisoners of war during the Korean War.[21] The circumstances were most propitious for attempting to change the values of a target group. The Chinese had complete control over the informational, physical, and social environment of their captives. Their aim was to alter the beliefs and values of the prisoners toward communism and toward who was to blame for the war. The Chinese suffused their captives with their newspapers and radio so that the prisoners saw and heard only the Chinese point of view. They divided the prisoners into small groups without their friends and without the normal leadership of officers. They planted spies in the midst of each group to create fear and a lack of trust of other Americans. They lectured endlessly on American war crimes and rewarded the prisoners who gave the slightest positive response. They started with trivial demands for intellectual concession and as Americans acceded, they escalated the responses required. They presented photographs, experts, and so on as evidence for their point of view. They tailored their techniques to the intelligence, race, and political views of each man. In the end, they succeeded in persuading only 21 prisoners out of tens of thousands to refuse repatriation after the armistice, although many more underwent some alteration of beliefs.

The major factor limiting the success of the Chinese, in spite of their total control over the environment, was that they were a negatively regarded source. Because the Chinese were the enemy, the prisoners discounted their credibility. At the same time this points out how effective a totalitarian state can be if it does have the trust of the people. Having control over all the instruments of information and reward, the totalitarian state can undertake to alter the value orientations of its people. Small-group experiments, conducted by Asch, Lewin, and others confirm the readiness of participants in a group to go along with the group's judgment in spite of their initially resistant opinions.[22]

The values that people hold often are pragmatic as well as ideological, making them even more difficult to change. For example, the preference of rural farmers in India for large families makes economic sense. The farmer sees his old age protection coming in the form of male heirs who will take care of him when he is old. Of six children that his wife might bear, only three or four may reach adulthood. Of these, only one or two may be male. So he thinks in terms of six children to produce a living male heir when he is 65. Furthermore, birth delivery in the rural area costs virtually nothing and he can feed his children with scraps of food. At age 6, his child starts running errands, helping in the field, or taking the mother's place, thus being productive. Consequently, when the rural farmer in India hears arguments that he should have fewer children because of overpopulation, it has no meaning for him in his life situation. Persuasive communication can have very little impact. In such cases, the state must resort to other measures if it is serious about bringing down the birthrate. Offering a positive economic incentive to have few children may not work because the value of the incentive is usually too small in relation to the value of having another child. The state may try negative economic incentives such as a tax on the number of children. Or it might make schooling compulsory at the age of 6, thus reducing the productivity of children in rural areas. Or it might require that all children be born in hospitals, which would increase the cost of children to the family. These are harsh measures, but they may become necessary as it becomes clear that the major target groups for family planning—rural families who have lots of children—are the least likely to change their minds because of persuasive communication. (See Exhibit 22–3).

When values are highly resistant to change, many social planners prefer to use the law to require new behaviors even if they are not accompanied by

**EXHIBIT 22–3.** Social marketing of family planning piles up some successes

Family planning has been a major focus of social marketing efforts. The majority of campaigns are government-sponsored, motivated by the availability of effective birth control products and by the growing awareness that economic and social gains can be wiped out by rapid population growth. Many of these social marketing campaigns have been successful, as the following cases show.

A successful social marketing campaign in Sri Lanka (formerly Ceylon) was based on principles of marketing research, brand packaging, distribution channel analysis, and marketing management and control. Consumer research prior to the campaign indicated widespread approval of the idea of family planning but little knowledge and use of contraception. The government, in cooperation with several agencies, centered its efforts on achieving widespread usage of condoms as a means of birth control. A brand was developed named "Preethi" (meaning happiness), and was sold in a three-pack for four cents (U.S.), one of the lowest costs in the world. Preethi achieved distribution in more than 3,600 pharmacies, teahouses, grocery and general stores, as well as by direct mail. Literature and order forms for condoms were distributed by agricultural extension workers on their regular visits to farm families. The sale of condoms was supported through a mass media campaign, including newspaper and radio ads, films, and a booklet entitled "How to Have Children by Plan and Not by Chance." Distributors also received large point-of-purchase displays. As a result of this orchestrated marketing approach, Preethi sales grew from 300,000 per month (in mid-1974) to an average of 500,000 per month in 1977. It was estimated that 60,000 unwanted pregnancies were averted by this social marketing project.

Similar campaigns have been successful in parts of India, Thailand, Bangladesh, and other countries. For example, in Bangladesh this type of campaign resulted in the monthly use of more than 1.5 million condoms and about 100,000 cycles of oral contraceptives, providing full contraceptive protection for approximately 400,000 couples at a yearly cost of about $4 per couple. In Thailand, the Community-Based Family Planning Services marketing program for promoting birth control includes some novel features. The agency stages contests with prizes to the person who inflates the biggest "balloon"—a condom—as a way to break down taboos about contraception. Contraceptives are accepted in rural villages, where villagers often ask local Buddhist monks to bless newly arrived shipments of contraceptives. The agency has recruited 5,000 rural distributors, including rice farmers, shopkeepers, village elders, and others who receive a one-day training course on selling condoms and keeping records, for which they receive a modest commission. The cost of all this effort is $3.50 per recipient per year, less than half of the cost of a similar government program in Thailand not using a marketing approach.

The effectiveness of social marketing of family planning can be assessed by looking at sales data, distribution systems, changes in knowledge, attitudes, and practices of consumers, cost-effectiveness, and, at the macro level, changes in fertility and birth rates. The Population Information Program reports micro-level measures indicating positive results. Positive results also can be claimed at the macro level. Bogue and Tsui, analyzing the effect of several different variables, found that family planning efforts explain much more of the birth rate reduction since 1968 than does any other factor, including changes in economic and social development which usually have been given most of the credit. According to their data, the recent decline in the world fertility rate has been primarily due to "the world-wide drive by Third World countries to introduce family planning as part of their national social-development services."

SOURCES: "Social Marketing: Does It Work?" *Population Reports,* Series J, No. 21 (Baltimore: Population Information Program, The Johns Hopkins University, January 1980); Donald J. Bogue and Amy Ong Tsui, "Zero World Population Growth?" *Public Interest,* Spring 1979, pp. 99–113; and Linda Mathews, "What Makes Meckai Run, or How to Curb the Birth of a Nation," *Wall Street Journal,* January 15, 1976, p. 1. For an excellent book on the social marketing of family planning, see Edwardo L. Roberto, *Strategic Decision Making in a Social Program: The Case of Family-Planning Diffusion* (Lexington, Mass.: Lexington Books, 1975).

attitudinal change. The theory is that as people have to comply with the new law, forces will be set into motion which will begin to produce the desired attitude change. Consider the hundred years of persuasive effort to get Southern schools in the United States to voluntarily desegregate. All attempts to change racially prejudiced attitudes failed. These attitudes were not only ideological but practical in supporting the system of white supremacy in the South. Unable to wait any longer for an attitude change, the Supreme Court in 1954 declared that all schools had to be desegregated. In the years that followed, school districts and citizens were forced to comply with a law that they did not like. Some resisted the court orders, so that their behavior would be congruent with their attitudes. Others who complied gradually found their attitudes softening somewhat to come more into line with their behavior. The passage of a widely disliked law sets several forces in motion that may accelerate the adoption of the targeted attitude change:

1. The new law helps the law's supporters gain new strength. They coalesce their forces and work harder for its implementation.
2. The new law stimulates more radical proposals, leading citizens to accept the original change in order to ward off the more radical proposals.
3. The new law creates sustained media attention and word-of-mouth discussion which leads people to examine their ideas and values more carefully.
4. The new law elicits conformity on the part of citizens who believe laws are to be obeyed. Conformity eventually leads from mere compliance to acceptance through processes of dissonance reduction.

Thus, when it comes to changing basic attitudes, the most effective means may be to pass laws requiring behavioral conformity, which set forces into motion that might accelerate the acceptance of new values. In this case, the social marketer's role is to build a climate favorable to the passage and acceptance of the new law.

---

## THE SOCIAL MARKETING PROCESS

In this final section, we shall describe the major steps in the planning of a social marketing campaign. The steps serve as a review of the marketing process itself. The steps are: (1) problem definition, (2) goal setting, (3) target market segmentation, (4) consumer analysis, (5) influence channels analysis, (6) marketing strategy and tactics, and (7) implementation and evaluation. We shall illustrate these steps in connection with the problem of encouraging people to give up or reduce their cigarette smoking.[23]

### PROBLEM DEFINITION

For a long time, antismoking groups such as the American Cancer Society, American Heart Association, and U.S. Surgeon General defined the antismoking problem as that of convincing smokers that cigarette smoking was harmful to their health. Most of the social marketing resources were put into disseminating rational and emotional messages about the harmful effects of smoking. Their success in creating public awareness is clear. A 1975 government-sponsored survey found that between 70 and 80 percent of current smokers agreed that smoking was harmful to their health.[24] However, it also became clear that the problem was deeper, in that nine out of ten smokers said they would like to quit but found it difficult; in fact, 57 percent expected to be smoking five years later.[25] Clearly, the problem is how to help smokers actually quit smoking, not simply convincing them to want to stop smoking. Social marketing cannot be effective unless it is addressed to the right problem.

Antismoking forces must begin by researching why smokers start to smoke, why they continue, and why they fail to be able to quit when they want to. A knowledge of the forces which encourage and discourage smoking helps to establish the nature of the problem as well as to suggest intervention strategies. The marketer should examine not only psychological forces but also economic, political, and cultural forces that support and reinforce the smoking habit.

### GOAL SETTING

The social marketers must set measurable goals that they can reasonably hope to accomplish. They might set an overall goal of "reducing the number of smokers by 20 million within a five-year period." They might establish separate goals for each segment of the market. These goals are needed for two reasons.

First, they enable the social marketers to develop a plan and budget. Second, they establish benchmarks for evaluating the success of the campaign.

## TARGET MARKET SEGMENTATION

The impact of social marketing efforts is enhanced by target market segmentation. The total population can be divided into nonsmokers, ex-smokers, light smokers, medium smokers, and heavy smokers, on the grounds that each group needs different marketing support. Each group can be subsegmented by demographic characteristics such as sex, age, socioeconomic status, and place of residence. A further subdivision is possible by such variables as length of use of cigarettes, motivations for smoking, readiness to discontinue smoking, and so on. Segmentation allows social marketers to do two things: (1) to select specific segments as the focus for their efforts, and (2) to study the behavior of each segment so as to identify the most cost-effective marketing strategies.

## CONSUMER ANALYSIS

Each target market segment needs to be researched in terms of how they think about smoking and what process would be necessary to help them move from their present attitudes and behavior to the desired attitudes and behavior. For example, an important target group is teenage girls; they have shown one of the highest increases of smoking in recent years. An analysis of why teenage girls smoke reveals such factors as a desire to be accepted, to feel grown up, and to reduce tension. Social marketers must try to discover and communicate other ways that teenage girls could satisfy these same needs.

## INFLUENCE CHANNEL ANALYSIS

Social marketers need the cooperation of a number of influence channels to carry out their program. They would like the mass media to donate more public service time to antismoking messages; public schools to put in more effective programs to educate students about the harmfulness of smoking; business establishments to set aside nonsmoking sections; social agencies to establish smokers' clinics; physicians to pass out "Helping Smokers Quit" kits; legislators to pass new laws; law enforcement officials to enforce these new laws; and so on. Each target channel must be analyzed with respect to its attitudes and likely response to various proposals and incentives. Not all channels are equally important, and the social marketers must choose which channels would be the most important to activate.

Social marketing campaigns have to be taken down to the grassroots level, namely, communities. It is often desirable to set up a staff in each community to implement the campaign plan. The workers should have skills in public speaking, preparing written communications, motivating volunteers, and identifying opinion leaders.

At times, the social marketing organization may need to bring pressure on certain groups. For example, business establishments such as restaurants may resist establishing separate sections for nonsmokers. They may refuse to talk to the change agents. In this case, a larger view of the influence channel problem is desirable. Figure 22–2 shows what might be done. The social marketing organization might turn the problem into one of convincing legislators to pass a "separate smoking section" law. To motivate legislators to pass these laws, the organization might first have to influence the general public to support nonsmoking areas in business establishments. To reach the general public, mass media would have to be used. To get mass media to publicize the cause, the marketing organization would visit editors to sell its cause. Thus, the problem of convincing business establishments to set up separate nonsmoking sections turns out to require an elaborate linking of influence channels.

### MARKETING STRATEGIES AND TACTICS

Change agents can now consider possible strategies and tactics for reducing cigarette smoking. They can review strategies used by other change agents and generate additional strategies by brainstorming and by reviewing the four Ps of the marketing mix. Table 22–1 shows an application of the four P framework to the problem of discouraging cigarette smoking. Each strategy can be further elaborated. For example, "create a substitute for cigarettes" has led to experiments with lettuce leaf as a tobacco substitute and most recently the development of a chewing gum that forestalls the person's need for a cigarette. Social marketers would then examine which strategies would be the most cost-effective with which target groups. Choices would be made and spelled out in a social marketing plan which would be the basis for developing the necessary budget to wage the campaign. For example, here is what Sweden recently decided to do:

> As illness and death caused by cigarette smoking continue to increase in countries throughout the developed world, Sweden has begun a program that aims

## FIGURE 22–2

### Influence Channel Analysis

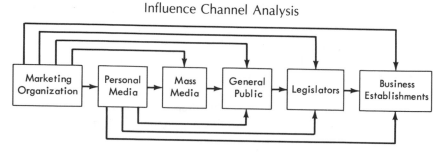

## Table 22–1

### POSSIBLE TACTICS FOR COUNTERMARKETING SMOKING

---

*Product*

- Require filters on all cigarettes
- Print line on each cigarette as "stop line"
- Make cigarettes shorter
- Sell separately or in individual packs only
- Market water filters or other technology to reduce harmful effects
- Create a substitute for cigarettes

*Price*

- Raise tax level on cigarettes
- Reduce insurance premiums for nonsmokers, raise for smokers
- Require cigarette companies to contribute to treatment of smoking-related diseases
- Reduce Medicare, Social Security, or other benefits to smokers

*Place*

- Limit places where cigarettes can be purchased, e.g., no sales in food or drugstores, vending machines, PX's, government hospitals
- Limit places where smoking is permitted
- Require registration to purchase cigarettes

*Promotion*

- Restrict cigarette advertising; e.g., no color ads; no pictures, text only; no targeting to "new recruits"
- Require half of cigarette ad space to present specific health warnings
- Ban all cigarette advertising
- Provide home self-help kits and "hot lines"
- Broadcast antismoking messages

---

to raise a nation of nonsmokers, starting with all Swedish children born this year. The program is expected to include intensive anti-smoking education in the schools and in all maternity clinics, progressive restrictions on cigarette advertising and promotion, regular price increases through higher taxation (cigarettes already cost about $1.50 a pack in Sweden), prohibitions on smoking in public places and greater efforts to help people who want to stop smoking.[26]

PROGRAM IMPLEMENTATION AND EVALUATION

The various actions have to be assigned to specific individuals to carry out according to a timetable, supported by a budget and the controls which would be used to monitor the implementation of the plan and evaluate its effectiveness. Most social marketing plans, unfortunately, are not developed with good evaluation design. Bloom points out that most program administrators are not interested in evaluation research.[27] The thinking of these administrators frequently runs like this:

> We have to spend money on marketing this cause or else Congress (or some other funding agency) won't believe that we're trying to fight the social problem they ordered us to fight. But that doesn't mean that we have to spend any money evaluating marketing. All an evaluation would do is cost us a lot of time, money, and energy without showing us very much. At most, marketing could be shown to have had a weak effect, and a result like this might only get our budget cut. We know our program is accomplishing something. Let's just keep trying our best and not get involved with the hassles and risks of an evaluation study.[28]

Evaluating the full effects of social marketing campaigns is not an easy task. A campaign, to be considered successful, would have to have the following attributes:

1. *High incidence of adoption.* A large number of people responded to the anti-smoking campaign by giving up or reducing their smoking.
2. *High speed of adoption.* Smokers responded to the campaign in a reasonable time.
3. *High continuance of adoption.* A high percentage of those who quit smoking remained nonsmokers for the rest of their lives.
4. *Low cost per unit of successful adoption.* The cost per converted ex-smoker was relatively low.
5. *No major counterproductive consequences.* Ex-smokers did not start suffering from other problems that were worse than smoking.

The last attribute raises an important issue, because social marketers often focus on the narrow problem and overlook its relation to a larger system of behaviors and consequences. For example, people who stop smoking have a tendency to eat more and gain weight. Overweight is estimated to shorten people's lives by approximately 14 years, whereas smoking is estimated to shorten people's lives by 7 years. Liquor, interestingly enough, is estimated to shorten consumers' lives by 4 years. This might suggest that the social marketer should have left the smoker alone or also figured out how to help him or her avoid becoming overweight.

## SUMMARY

Many nonprofit organizations are involved in marketing ideas and causes in order to change the behavior of certain groups. Behavior can be changed using legal, technological, economic, and information approaches. The information approach became refined into social advertising and later social communication. Social marketing is a more sophisticated approach that combines informational, economic, and technological approaches. Social marketing is the design, implementation, and control of programs seeking to increase the acceptability of a social idea or cause in a target group(s). It utilizes concepts of market segmentation, consumer research, concept development, communication, facilitation, incentives, and exchange theory to maximize target group response.

Scholars have attempted to describe the factors determining the effectiveness of a social marketing campaign. Lazarsfeld and Merton attributed the failure of many social campaigns to the frequent absence of conditions of monopolization, canalization, and supplementation in the social arena. Wiebe concluded that a campaign's effectiveness depended on the presence of adequate force, direction, an adequate and compatible social mechanism, and distance. Rothschild sees social marketing campaigns as most effective when the public has high involvement in the cause and the benefit/cost ratio is high. Smelser/Kotler see social marketing campaigns as being effective when the timing is right, namely, when conditions have reached a certain stage in the cause's life cycle.

The effectiveness of social marketing will vary with the type of social change being sought. Cognitive change is the most responsive to social marketing. Social marketing may also be effective in producing action change—that is, a particular act. Behavioral change, such as the modification of food, smoking, or drinking habits, is harder to achieve. So is value change, that is, efforts to modify the value orientation of a target market.

The social marketing process consists of the following seven steps: (1) problem definition, (2) goal setting, (3) target market segmentation, (4) consumer analysis, (5) influence channels analysis, (6) marketing strategy and tactics, and (7) implementation and evaluation.

A social marketing approach does not guarantee that the social objectives will be achieved, or that the costs will be acceptable. Yet social marketing appears to represent a bridging mechanism which links the behavioral scientist's knowledge of human behavior with the socially useful implementation of what the knowledge allows. It offers a useful framework for effective social planning at a time when social issues have become more relevant and critical.

---

## QUESTIONS

**1.** Describe how each of the four basic approaches to social change could be applied to getting people to use seat belts.

**2.** What are the differences between social advertising and social marketing?

**3.** What are some reasons why it is so difficult to get most Americans to exercise more? Then, based on the analyses by Rothschild, appraise the likely success of social marketing in encouraging regular exercising.

**4.** The American Heart Association's mission is to improve cardiovascular health. Analyze the influence channels from which it might want cooperation to carry out its mission.

**5.** Develop a social marketing program to influence teenagers not to drink alcoholic beverages. Include plans for segmentation, target market selection, and marketing mix (the 4 Ps).

**6.** How would you explain the fact that many social marketing efforts are not adequately evaluated?

## NOTES

**1.** There is an old story told by a religious leader. In growing up, he developed a great idealism and made up his mind that he would try to change the world. As he grew older and found how impossible this was, he decided that he would try to change his community. He found this too difficult, and so he lowered his sights to trying to change his own congregation. This too failed, but he would not give up. He began to concentrate his efforts on changing his friends. He finally realized that the human problem was in himself and began to focus his idealism on trying to change himself. Now he is an old man and still has not succeeded in even changing himself.

**2.** Philip Kotler and Gerald Zaltman, "Social Marketing: An Approach to Planned Social Change," *Journal of Marketing,* July 1971, pp. 3–12. This chapter is partly based on this article along with a new one, namely, Karen F. A. Fox and Philip Kotler, "The Marketing of Social Causes: The First Ten Years," *Journal of Marketing,* Fall 1980, pp. 24–33. The interested reader should also look at the first book to be published on the marketing of ideas, namely, Seymour Fine, *The Marketing of Ideas and Social Issues* (Columbus, Ohio: Grid, 1981).

**3.** The term "social marketing" unfortunately has taken on other usages since then. Some authors use it to describe the whole of "nonprofit organization marketing." Others use it to describe socially responsible business marketing, which is better called "societal marketing."

**4.** For a discussion of ethical issues posed by social marketing, see Gene R. Laczniak, Robert F. Lusch, and Patrick E. Murphy, "Social Marketing: Its Ethical Dimensions," *Journal of Marketing,* Spring 1979, pp. 29–36.

**5.** Paul F. Lazarsfeld and Robert K. Merton, "Mass Communication, Popular Taste, and Organized Social Action," in William Schramm, ed., *Mass Communications* (Urbana: University of Illinois Press, 1949), pp. 459–80.

**6.** *Ibid.*

**7.** G. D. Wiebe, "Merchandising Commodities and Citizenship on Television," *Public Opinion Quarterly* (Winter 1951–52), pp. 679–91, esp. p. 679.

**8.** *Ibid.,* p. 633.

**9.** Michael L. Rothschild, "Marketing Communications in Nonbusiness Situations or Why It's So Hard to Sell Brotherhood like Soap," *Journal of Marketing,* Spring 1979, pp. 11–20.

**10.** See Neil J. Smelser, *Theory of Collective Behavior* (New York: Free Press, 1963).

**11.** See Philip Kotler, "What Consumerism Means for Marketing," *Harvard Business Review,* May–June 1972, pp. 48–57.

**12.** W. B. Cameron, *Modern Social Movements* (New York: Random House, 1966).

**13.** See Philip Kotler, "The Elements of Social Action," *American Behavioral Scientist,* May–June 1971, pp. 691–717.

**14.** Shirley A. Star and Helen MacGill Hughes, "A Report on an Educational Campaign: The Cincinnati Plan for the United Nations," *American Journal of Sociology,* Vol. 55 (1950), pp. 389–400.

**15.** See Mason Haire, *Psychology in Management* (New York: McGraw-Hill, 1956).

**16.** See Herbert H. Hyman and Paul B. Sheatsley, "Some Reasons Why Information Campaigns Fail," *Public Opinion Quarterly,* Vol. 11 (1947), pp. 412–23.

**17.** For an information campaign that succeeded (on mental retardation), see Dorothy F. Douglas, Bruce H. Westley, and Steven H. Chaffee, "An Information Campaign That Changed Community Attitudes," *Journalism Quarterly,* Autumn 1970, pp. 479–92.

**18.** "Wrong Publicity May Push Drug Use: UN Chief," *Chicago Sun-Times,* May 8, 1972, p. 30.

**19.** See "Drug Ed a Bummer," *Behavior Today,* November 13, 1972, p. 2.

**20.** See Michael L. Ray, Scott Ward, and Gerald Lesser, *Experimentation to Improve Pretesting of Drug Abuse Education and Information Campaigns: A Summary* (Cambridge, Mass.: Marketing Science Institute, September 1973).

**21.** Edgar H. Schein, "The Chinese Indoctrination Program for Prisoners of War," *Psychiatry,* May 1956, pp. 149–72.

**22.** Solomon E. Asch, "Effects of Group Pressure upon the Modification and Distortion of Judgment," in Dorwin Cartwright and Alvin Zander, eds., *Group Dynamics* (New York: Harper & Row, 1953), pp. 151–62; and Kurt Lewin, "Group Decision and Social Change," in Theodore M. Newcomb and Eugene L. Hartley, eds., *Readings in Social Psychology* (New York: Holt, Rinehart and Winston, 1952).

**23.** This section is based on Karen Fox and Philip Kotler, "Reducing Cigarette Smoking: An Opportunity for Social Marketing," *Journal of Health Care Marketing,* January 1981.

**24.** *Adult Use of Tobacco 1975* (Washington, D.C.: Bureau of Health Education, Center for Disease Control, U.S. Public Health Service, June 1976).

**25.** *Ibid.*

**26.** "Sweden Aims to Forge a Nonsmoking Nation," *New York Times,* June 3, 1978.

**27.** Paul N. Bloom, "Evaluating Social Marketing Programs: Problems and Prospects," *1980 Educators Conference Proceedings* (Chicago: American Marketing Association).

**28.** *Ibid.*

# Indexes

# Topic Index

# Subject Index